Large-Scale Assessment Programs for All Students:

Validity, Technical Adequacy, and Implementation

Large-Scale Assessment Programs for All Students:

Validity, Technical Adequacy, and Implementation

Edited by

Gerald Tindal
University of Oregon

Thomas M. Haladyna
Arizona State University

 LAWRENCE ERLBAUM ASSOCIATES, PUBLISHERS
2002   Mahwah, New Jersey   London

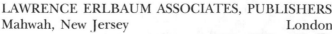

Lawrence Erlbaum Associates, Inc., Publishers
10 Industrial Avenue
Mahwah, New Jersey 07430

Cover design by Kathryn Houghtaling Lacey

Library of Congress Cataloging-in-Publication Data

Large-scale assessment programs for all students : validity, technical adequacy, and
implementation / edited by Gerald Tindal, Thomas M. Haladyna.
     p.   cm.
  Includes bibliographical references and index.
  ISBN 0-8058-3709-4
  1. Examinations—Validity.   2. Educational tests and measurements.   I. Tindal,
Gerald.   II. Haladyna, Thomas M.

LB3060.68 .L37   2002
371.26′01′3—dc21   2001033453
                                                                        CIP

Books published by Lawrence Erlbaum Associates are printed on acid-free paper,
and their bindings are chosen for strength and durability.

Printed in the United States of America
10 9 8 7 6 5 4 3 2 1

Contents

Preface

As our title suggests, this book deals with three issues we believe are critical to large-scale assessments of student achievement. Validity is the most important consideration in achievement testing. Technical adequacy continues to challenge us. We constantly face technical challenges in designing, administering, scoring, and reporting test results. Implementation of best practices and adherence to testing standards are much needed in all assessments of student achievement.

The emphasis on *all students* in our title addresses the need for large-scale assessments to be inclusive with regard to populations who are often underserved both in terms of their educational programs and assessment of their achievement. Specifically, we refer to students with disabilities and English-language learners.

This book includes five perspectives regarding large-scale assessments:

1. The *Standards for Educational and Psychological Testing* published by the American Educational Research Association, the American Psychological Association, and the National Council on Measurement in Education in 1999 provide a context for the many topics discussed in this volume. We believe these standards are very important in guiding us in the development of tests and the interpretation and use of test scores.

2. Validity has been cast as part of the decision-making process and not simply a function of the measures. This view is articulated clearly in all chapters throughout the book. The authors have used *validity* consistently

in relation to many of the issues addressed in this book. In some states, large-scale assessments are being used for instructional program evaluation. Increasingly, states also are using achievement tests to make promotion, certification, and graduation decisions. We think that validity is a paramount concern in large-scale assessment, but validation applies uniquely to one test score interpretation or use, not all test score interpretations and uses. Test sponsors and the public are increasingly finding new uses for tests. For each of these new uses, we need to address validation.

3. This book focuses on inclusion of *all* students in large-scale assessment programs. No longer can students with disabilities or non-English native language backgrounds be excluded from mainstream schools and large-scale assessments. To the degree that students participate in classroom instruction, they also must be included in our assessments. If we are to include all students in our assessments and if these outcomes are to be used in improving our programs, then the information must be accurate and unbiased. The measurement of student learning should not be influenced by student disability or language proficiency.

4. This book focuses on many complex technical issues associated with large-scale assessments. We have approached the validation process by suggesting research that helps inform educators about more effective ways to measure and evaluate student achievement. A number of different strategies are used to ensure that our measurement tools work well in helping us make decisions. Judgments need to be rendered in the sampling of content and scaling of items and problems, ensuring appropriate depth and breadth. On occasion, this technical rigor also is related to the actual items and the manner in which they are calibrated and included on multiple-choice tests. On other occasions, the focus needs to be on production responses in which students construct an answer and solve problems.

5. Implementation issues are addressed to ensure that the practices and principles supporting our assessments are indeed anchored to the context in which they are used. Testing should not be done just to students. Rather, tests should be conducted with teachers, students, and parents. They are implemented in classrooms and provide outcomes that are used by principals, superintendents, and directors of testing in making statements about the effects of our teaching and extent of student learning, the quality of our schools, and the directions that we need to move to improve student learning. By including the social applications of large-scale assessments, we believe students, teachers, and schools can be held accountable not just to the larger public, but also to effective practices. The real goal of all assessments is the improvement of student learning. This goal, however, requires a socially navigated process in which we all develop a common language to anchor the focus of our teaching, assessing, and reporting.

AUDIENCE FOR THIS BOOK

This book is designed for educators who are responsible for implementing large-scale assessment programs at the district or state level. Although the contents may have some bearing on classroom assessment, the book is not aimed for the classroom teacher, although clearly some chapters have great relevance for them. For example, opportunity to learn or delivery standards often are important issues in judging outcomes from any large-scale assessment program, and teachers need to be part of this process. Many classroom assessments may be relevant for students with disabilities or those who are English-language learners. Finally, with the stakes of large-scale assessment increasing, we have maintained a rigorous approach to the issues, again making the tone of the volume oriented to those with a minimum of technical training. We hope, however, that this book is useful in helping prepare educators to begin leadership roles and therefore would be useful for graduate students in many types of programs, including educational testing, special education, English-language learners, educational leadership, and policy.

FEATURES OF THIS BOOK

The book is divided into three sections to help organize its contents. As noted, however, we believe a strong relationship exists among validity issues, technical adequacy, and implementation. We use the first and last chapters to help frame these various sections and integrate them together. Each chapter is written independently by its author(s), but we think many chapters offer good complements to other chapters.

ACKNOWLEDGMENTS

This book would not be possible without the excellent work of many individuals who represent key professional organizations. Foremost is Dr. Wayne Neuburger, Assistant Superintendent for Assessment and Evaluation of the Oregon Department of Education. This book is the culmination of thoughtful discussions and research by many authors as part of an advisory panel to the Oregon Statewide Assessment organized by Dr. Neuburger. Many individuals at Behavioral Research and Teaching (BRT) in the College of Education at University of Oregon have been key participants in getting the book into a publishable format. Raina Megert began the process of keeping all the authors connected. Jodell Born finished this work during the last phase. Jerry Marr served as the initial editor, taking *wordsmithing* to a higher level. Students working at BRT helped organize the many pieces: Shane Mast, Kurstin Hollenbeck, and Heidi Langsholt. The indexing was completed by Sevrina Tindal and India Simon-Deglar.

Finally, the authors are to be commended for their commitment to this book. Despite the considerable diversity of contributors to this volume, a common theme throughout these chapters is a commitment to best practices in large-scale assessment and an empirical basis for each recommendation.

Chapter 1

Large-Scale Assessments for All Students: Issues and Options

Gerald Tindal
University of Oregon

Standardized, large-scale assessment clearly has proliferated in the past 10 to 20 years and is prominent in all 50 states. These testing programs are increasingly complex and include a number of subject areas and testing formats, including multiple-choice tests and various types of performance assessments. Although the public press may appear to be negative on testing, in fact, Phelps (1998) reported in an extensive summary of 70 surveys that have been conducted over the past 30 years that "the majorities in favor of more testing, more high stakes testing, or higher stakes in testing have been large, often very large, and fairly consistent over the years, across the polls and surveys and even across respondent groups" (p. 14). Nor only has assessment proliferated and been supported in the United States, but also throughout the world. A clear trend exists toward more, not less, large-scale testing programs. "Twenty-seven countries show a net increase in testing, while only three show a decrease. Fifty nine testing programs have been added while only four have been dropped" (Phelps, 2000). In summary, large-scale testing has been on the rise and is supported by the public.

Such support, however, begs the question: Have educational programs improved as a result of such proliferation of large-scale tests? It is not simply a question of the public having positive perceptions of schools that is important. Even improvement in test scores does not necessarily mean that schools have improved because of the need to make valid inferences on what that improvement means, which requires both a nomological net of variables and a logic for relating them together. Rather, the critical issue is that schools are effective institutions in teaching students the skill and knowledge needed to be successful in post-school environments. It is essential that students have declarative knowledge in the cultural electives and imperatives (Reynolds, Wang, & Walberg, 1987) to understand how the social (economic and political) and physical (geographic) worlds operate. Students also need to be skilled in using that declarative knowledge to solve problems. They need to know when and how to use information, reflecting conditional and procedural knowledge, respectively (Alexander, Schallert, & Hare, 1991).

This focus on declarative as well as conditional and procedural knowledge has been incorporated into the measurement field through the increasing use of both selected and constructed responses. Students continue to take multiple-choice tests—an example of a selected response format—as part of most large-scale assessment programs. However, they also are being asked to solve open-ended problems and construct a response in which both the process and product are evaluated. In summary, our measurement systems have become more complex, and our understanding of them has deepened to include validation in reference to inferences or interpretations as well as use.

This chapter provides a preview of these two major issues currently being addressed in educational measurement. First, with the most recent Standards for Educational and Psychological Testing (American Educational Research Association, American Psychogical Association, & National Council of Measurement in Education, 1999), the validation process is focused on constructs and decisions. Although content and criterion validity (predictive and concurrent) continue to be important components in understanding our measurement systems, the clear focus is on the inferences we make from the outcomes of our measurements. Second, with an emphasis on decision making, the validation process is more anchored to how we use measurement systems in educational practices. Changing practices, however, requires a different look at the role of measurement. Rather than being simply documentary and used in a static manner with program evaluations, the argument is made that more quasi-experimental designs be used to better understand our measurement systems and hence the decisions we make from them.

CONSTRUCT VALIDITY: EVIDENTIAL
AND CONSEQUENTIAL COMPONENTS

With Messick's (1988, 1994) work serving as an influential guide in the emerging conception of validity, we first need to consider our interpretations. Both the evidential and consequential basis of interpretations from large-scale testing programs must be considered (Messick, 1989). In some cases, the research on the evidential basis has addressed components of the testing program, letting us understand specific aspects of how large-scale tests should be constructed or implemented. For example, Haladyna, Hess, Osborn-Popp, and Dugan (1996) studied local versus external raters in a state writing assessment program, and Linn, Betebenner, and Wheeler (1998) studied student choice of problems in a state math testing program. The earlier study on writing reflected potential bias from raters, whereas the latter study highlighted bias from students' choice of problems to solve. Both studies reflect exemplary research on construct validity and a potential source of systematic error (bias) that can influence our interpretations.

In both studies, however, only one component of the state-testing program was being analyzed. The focus of validity was on the construct being assessed in relation to the bias involved in the assessment. In contrast to this attention to specific practices, other research has focused on an entire statewide assessment program and the impact of large-scale testing programs. This growing body of research has focused on consequential validity, particularly unintended consequences. For example, according to Strong and Saxton's (1996) evaluation of the Kentucky assessment program in reading, a substantial percentage of students performed relatively (and uniquely) low on the Kentucky Instructional Results Informational System (KIRIS) (novice or apprentice) but not on the American College Test (ACT). They concluded that "the KIRIS test fails to identify a significant percentage of students who read quite well according to the ACT. . . . Approximately 64% of students who score at the Apprentice level will achieve average and above on the ACT" (pp. 104–105). The question then moves to using the ACT as a measure of outcome success. In terms of validating large-scale testing programs in this manner, such an emphasis on concurrent validity results in an endless spiral with no eventual resolution.

A different problem emerged in a comprehensive review of the Maryland School Performance Assessment Program (MSPAP) by Yen and Ferrara (1997). Although they reported extensively on various design and psychometric components supporting MSPAP, they found a school-by-form interaction. With some schools and with certain forms, the results were uniquely different than other schools and forms. Therefore, they recommended the use of two to three forms for measuring school performance. They also noted that the "instructional validity is a weakness for MSPAP as evidenced by current low performance and resulting low teacher morale and by legal vulnerability when high-stakes consequences (described earlier) are enforced" (pp. 79–80). Yet with no attention to classroom variables, this line of research also becomes an endless documentation of problematic consequences of little help in understanding relationships to measure or change.

Such research on the impact of large-scale testing certainly has been a concern both in the measurement field and in practice (see *Educational Measurement: Issues and Practice*, Vol. 17, No. 2). This issue, however, is not new, but may have become more critical as large-scale assessments apply to more and different purposes and with higher stakes attached to them. Clearly, we have seen more negative impacts being reported. For example, Hass, Haladyna, and Nolen (1989) reported on the negative consequences of using the results from the Iowa Test of Basic Skills (ITBS) to evaluate teachers, administrators, and schools. Smith (1991) also documented the same kinds of negative effects from testing such as (a) generation of shame, embarrassment, and guilt; (b) questions of validity that lead to dissonance and alienation; (c) creation of emotional impact and anxiety by students; (d) reduction of time available for teaching; (e) resultant narrowing of the curriculum; and (f) provision of teaching that is deskilled from teaching in a testlike manner. In a similar survey on the effects of standardized tests on teaching, Herman and Golan (1993) found similar negative effects in that teachers felt pressure to improve student scores, administrators focused on test preparation, instructional planning was affected (in both content and format), and more student time was spent preparing for testing.

Yet Herman and Golan (1993) also noted some very positive results. Teachers continued giving attention to nontested instructional areas, schools gave attention to instructional renewal, and teachers were both positive about their work environment and felt responsible for student performance. They concluded that the findings depend on "whether or not one views the standards and skills embodied in mandated tests as educationally valid and significant" (p. 24). As mentioned earlier, there is growing evidence that much of the public does view them in this way.

Certainly, this kind of work on the components and impacts of large-scale assessment programs must continue. Specific construct validation studies need to be at all levels whether we are measuring specific skill areas to make inferences about students' proficiencies or entire systems to document accountability and perceptions of impact. This system-level focus on perceptions and impact concurrently needs to be documented for all stakeholders in our large-scale assessment programs. Parents and teachers are obviously critical participants. As we move to high-stakes accountability systems, administrators also are key individuals. With the increasing use of standards, critical stakeholders become more embedded in our economic and political systems as business leaders and state directors of testing. However, we also need to understand the relationship between that which we measure on the large-scale tests and that which we manipulate at the individual level, whether student or teacher. In this next section, the focus is on changing practices in the classroom. We need to use measurement systems more dynamically in our research and educational practices. This research on measurement needs to be technically adequate and the practice systemically related to classrooms.

Technical Issues in Using Measurement in the Classroom

To begin using our measurement systems in classrooms, we first need to operationalize performance tasks and then define the domain they represent. Although performance tasks are likely to be related to classroom instruction, they also are related to many other things. As Messick (1994) described them, performance assessments are purportedly both authentic and direct, a validity claim that needs evidence. For him, "authenticity and directness map, respectively, into two familiar tenets of construct validity, that is minimal construct under-representation and minimal construct-irrelevant variance" (p. 14). When constructs are underrepresented, testing is not sensitive enough to ascertain the full range of skill and knowledge exhibited in a performance. For example, writing tests that require students to edit grammar and syntax may be viewed as underrepresenting the construct of writing. In contrast, when constructs are overrepresented in a test, the opposite problem is occurring in which more is being measured than intended. Many problem-solving tasks in content areas (math, science, and social sciences) exemplify this problem because they require writing as an access skill.

These two features of validity represent trade-offs "between breadth and depth in coping with domain coverage and limits of generalizability" (p. 13), with coverage referring to both content and process and generalizability referring to all dimensions of the context as well as the domain. In these examples, selected response writing tests may suffer from a lack of depth and limit the generalizations that can be made when making inferences about a student's writing (composition) skills. Performance tasks in content areas may be providing more depth in problem solving, but at a cost of being too broad in response dimensions and too narrow in content coverage. This again limits the inferences that can be made of a student's skill and knowledge.

The measurement field has tended to focus primarily on construct-irrelevant variance of performance assessments through generalizability studies, with an emphasis on making inferences from a student's obtained score to the student's universe score (Cronbach, Gleser, Nanda, & Rajaratnam, 1972; Shavelson, Webb, & Rowley, 1989). That is, assuming the obtained score is only that which is attained at that time and under those specific circumstances (both of which contain error), what would a student's score be when considering all such possible attempts and circumstances? To answer this question, variance generally is partitioned into error and true score and can be attributable to the person (test taker), markers (judges), tasks, or scales in determining the reliability of a response: When performance assessments result in great variance, they can lead to erroneous generalizations. In the end, generalizations are made from a specific performance to a complex universe of performances, incorporating all possible combinations of these components in which unreliability arises from tasks, occasions, raters, or any combination.

Kane, Crooks, and Cohen (1999) put forth one of the most elegant strategies for addressing the validation process. They essentially proposed establishment of a sequence of propositions in the form of a bridge with three links that refer to scoring, generalization, and extrapolation:

1. A connection must be established between observations (of a performance) to observed scores (as part of administered tasks and as rated by judges). In this link, threats to validity must be countered that arise from the conditions of administration and contexts of assessments, as well as from the adequacy of the judgments that are rendered. This connection refers to scoring.

2. Assuming the first link can be made adequately, another connection needs to be made from the observed score to a universe of scores (as sampled by various representative tasks from which there are many). The most significant problem is the generalizability over tasks, which they noted "tends to be the weak link in performance assessments and therefore deserves extra attention" (p. 16). This connection refers to generalization.

3. Finally, assuming the prior link from sampled to possible tasks is adequate, a connection must be made from this range of tasks to a target score that reflects the broad construct for making inferences. This connection refers to extrapolation.

In their summary of the validation process, they argued that equal attention needs to be given to precision (generalization across tasks) and fidelity (extrapolation) for assessments to be useful in making decisions. "If any inference fails, the argument fails" (p. 16). For Kane et al. (1999), simulations and standardized tasks are suggested as a strategy for better controlling the task variance without fully compromising the (extrapolation) inferences made to the universe.

The Symbiotic Relationship Between Teaching and Learning

Although we may have the logic in validation of performance measures, we certainly do not yet have adequate information on how to integrate such information into the classroom. We have little empirical research to help us guide teachers or testers in the process of preparing students to

learn and perform. For example, Shepard, Flexer, Hiebert, Marion, Mayfield, and Weston (1996) reported that classroom performance assessments had little influence on achievement. Using a fairly elaborate research
design, two groups were compared: a participant group that focused on
performance assessments and a control group that had no such focus. At
the end of 1 year, however, they found that the participating teachers had
not really implemented the treatment until late in the year and into the
next year. Yet what was the treatment and how much of it was needed?

The central question is how to relate teaching to learning. This issue
implies a focus on teaching, not just making inferences from our measures
or ascertaining perceptions of impact. We must shift our focus to include
both teaching as well as improved student learning because in the absence
of well-defined instruction, the field is not better off: Replication and
scalability then become lost and disconnected from systemic reforms.

This focus on teaching and learning naturally drifts to the relationship
between learning and testing or measuring outcomes. How do we prepare
students to perform better on performance measures in a manner that can
be generalized beyond the immediate tasks and reflect a larger universe?
Rather than viewing test preparation as problematic, this issue could be
viewed as the nexus of teaching and learning, in which a critical distinction
is made "between teaching students how to respond to a specific task and
teaching students the critical attributes of the construct domain from which
the task was sampled" (p. 19) (see Mehrens, Popham, & Ryan, 1998, for a
careful review of this issue). This focus allows us to distinguish it from the
pollution noted by Haladyna, Nolen, and Haas (1991). Similar to the continuum of test preparation presented by Mehrens and Kaminski (1989),
such preparedness can be considered ethical (see Miller & Seraphine, 1993,
for an analysis of such preparedness with authentic tasks). With the introduction of performance assessment, a closer link with instruction may be
possible. "This linking of assessment to the curriculum is ... one of the
most positive aspects of the proposed test-based reforms" (Linn, 1993, p. 5).

If we take the purposes of large-scale educational assessments to be defined as Haertel (1999) has organized them, they can be reduced to: (a) accountability, (b) media attention, and (c) change in practice (of curriculum
and instruction). It is this last issue that appears to be missing in most of
the large-scale assessment literature. Within the past decade, debate has
waxed and waned about this issue, often focused as the "opportunity to
learn" and delivery standards that initially were present early in the standards reforms.

This focus on the classroom is not new. Frederiksen and Collins (1989)
long ago defined a form of validity that has been addressed seldom in the
field of measurement: "A systemically valid test is one that induces in the
educational system curricular and instructional changes that foster the de-

velopment of cognitive skills that the test is designed to measure" (p. 27). In the introduction to a special series of articles in the *Journal of Educational Research* (Vol. 89, No. 4), Baker (1996) described similar assumptions in the efforts of CRESST, the nation's leading assessment research center, to develop technically sound performance assessments with three tenets.

First, they focus on developing assessments that would be feasible at both the classroom and policy level "for a limited but essential set of cognitive demands: conceptual understanding, problem solving, teamwork, search strategies, and metacognition" (p. 195). The field can no longer only assess that which is easy to measure. Rather, measurement needs to reflect the complex environments of the classroom, which includes how students approach and resolve problems. Second, they address explicit scoring systems. Once open-ended problem solving is viewed as worth measuring, attention must be focused on scaling performance in defensible and replicable ways. Students and teachers must be familiar with them. Finally, they emphasize the need for assessments to be sensitive to instruction. The ultimate worth of any measurement system is its capacity to reflect change. In this sense, education can be considered as a large quasi-experimental, naturalistic study, with interventions being vindicated on the basis of measurement systems that are thoughtfully related and relevant to instruction.

Although the field of measurement has acknowledged classroom practice (e.g., curriculum, instruction, and assessment), rarely has it been effectively operationalized in any systematic program of research, particularly within large-scale assessment programs. Essentially, the argument centers on the consequences of test use and interpretation as a major component in the validation process. Obviously, we need evidence that assessments are measuring the intended constructs. However, "evidence is also needed that the interpretations are contributing to enhanced student achievement and, at the same time, not producing unintended negative outcomes" (Linn, 1994, p. 8). Increasingly, this focus needs to be present in the validation of large-scale assessments.

Porter (1993, 1995) has probably written the most on school delivery standards (formerly referred to as opportunity to learn), presenting three possible purposes: (a) for school-by-school accountability, (b) as indicators that describe the extent to which teachers implement instruction consistent with curriculum standards, and (c) for a clearer vision of challenging curriculum and pedagogy for all students. Formerly, accountability focused on inputs (e.g., number of teachers, equipment availability, size of library) rather than the quality of curriculum, instruction, and assessment of student performance. In contrast, delivery standards indicators describe the educational opportunities and are used to monitor progress toward school reform. They also provide explanations for lack of student achievement or perhaps the reasons for a particular level of achievement. Finally, a clearer vision of the enacted curriculum and pedagogy provides specific information on the changes that teachers make to promote a more challenging curriculum and guide school reform. Clear delivery standards would help a teacher to see what changes can be beneficial to students.

The actual monitoring of improvement in classroom practice, however, has been a significant problem. Quantitative variables have been used such as (a) time spent in school, (b) time allocated to instruction, (c) engaged time, (d) amount of funding and provision of resources, and (e) content coverage/instructional practices (Ysseldyke, Thurlow, & Shin, 1994). Qualitative variables also have been considered such as those described by Porter (1993), with teachers maintaining a daily log to document not only content coverage, but also general instructional strategies content and engagement of students in exposition, and other activities used to help deliver the content (e.g., seatwork, labs, discussions, working on novel problems, designing experiments, etc.). The problem, however, has been that "the measuring devices being developed and distributed by the large-scale assessment community are not designed to detect the differences of instruction-even first-rate instruction" (Popham, 1999, p. 14). In summary content coverage, whether of the adopted or enacted curriculum, misses important instructional events. Yet consideration of such instructional events has been difficult to quantify and is likely comprised of multiple scales.

The results of large-scale assessments may thus continue to focus on outcomes without contributing to a knowledge base on *how* to teach children what they need to know (Popham, 1999). He recommended that instructional enhancements be given equal attention to educational accountability. In part, this can be accomplished by increasing the "instructional acumen" of test developers. Yet the skills and knowledge that are tested of students also must be within reach of teachers, with full domain specification needed in test development. Finally, large-scale assessments need to cease purporting to evaluate educational quality. In the end, these recommendations may be appropriate, but are likely to fail in developing an empirical basis for changing assessments systems to promote achievement. Rather, "more direct evidence such as evidence obtained through an analysis of classroom instruction and assessment activities" is needed (Lane, Plake, & Stone, 1998, p. 25).

VALIDATING IMPROVEMENTS IN CLASSROOM PRACTICE

Large-scale testing programs should not be limited to only descriptive and correlational studies, but need to be evaluated using variables that we manipulate. Intervention studies are needed with independent variables anchored to curriculum and instruction. Using quasi-experimental research designs, large-scale assessment programs must be evaluated in which the curriculum and teaching is manipulated as an independent variable and the effects are ascertained using large-scale tests as the dependent variable.

In moving to this level, however, we must be cognizant of three types of variables:

> (a) variables that we manipulate (in the narrow sense of the word experimental); (b) variables that we do not manipulate but can hold constant or effectively exclude from influence by one or another means, isolating the system under study; and (c) variables that are quasi-random with respect to the phenomenon under study, so that they only contribute to measurement error or the standard deviation of a statistic. (Meehl, 1978, p. 810)

Quasi-Experimental Research in the Validation Process

"To validate an interpretive inference is to ascertain the degree to which multiple lines of evidence are consonant with the inference, while establishing that alternative inferences are less well supported" (Messick, 1989, p. 13). This represents the fundamental principle that both convergent and discriminant evidence are required in test validation. Using quasi-experimental research to validate large-scale assessment systems requires us to provide evidence that effective instructional programs result in improvements and that changes in test scores do not result when ineffective instructional programs are used. Obviously, the term *effective instructional programs* needs to be vindicated, requiring multiple lines of evidence. Furthermore, changes in tests scores should not serve as a rising tide that reflect changes in general that are not due to specific practices. When all the data are in, the findings should provide a consistent pattern that is both convergent and discriminant.

To validate an action inference requires validation not only of score meaning, but also of value implications and *action outcomes*, especially of the relevance and utility of the test scores for particular applied purposes and of the social consequences of using the scores for *applied decision making*. Thus, the key issues of test validity are the meaning, relevance, and utility of scores; the import or value implications of scores as a basis for action; and the functional worth of scores in terms of social consequences of their use (Messick, 1989, p. 13).

To illustrate this proposition for conducting quasi-experimental research in validating large-scale assessments, two studies are presented that cannot be explained without an intervention study. In the first study, the writing performance of students within a state has been tracked for 8 years with little substantial improvement. One inference drawn from such data is that the scales used to measure performance are not sensitive enough to measure meaningful improvement or progress. Another equally compelling inference, however, is that students' performance simply has not improved and better instructional programs are needed. Using Kane's (1992) argument-based approach to validation, systematic research would ascertain the sensitivity of the large-scale assessment program to instructional manipulations.

In the second study, student performance on multiple-choice reading and math tests is analyzed using cohorts of students over time (the same students in both testing periods). As in the writing study, it appears that either the assessment system is insensitive or that instruction is ineffective for a large group of students. Again, a quasi-experimental program of research is needed to ascertain the sensitivity of the large-scale assessment program to instructional manipulation.

Writing Assessment and Intervention.   In Oregon, scores on the state writing test have improved little over an 8-year period on six different traits: ideas and content (I&O), organization (Org), voice (Vc), word choice (WC), sentence fluency (SF), and convention (Cnv). Although the most recent reports reflect some improvement, these changes cannot be adequately interpreted because the reporting system has moved from an average performance to percent passing and the manner for aggregating data now includes conditional passing rather than the more stringent passing levels used earlier. See Tables 1.1 and 1.2.

TABLE 1.1
Fifth-Grade Student Writing Performance
Over Time on Oregon's Writing Test

Grade 5	IO	Org	Vc	WC	SF	Cnv
1991	3.5	3.6	3.9	3.6	3.6	3.9
1995	3.7	3.6	4	3.7	3.7	3.6
1997	3.7	3.6	3.9	3.8	3.7	3.6
1998	3.7	3.6	3.9	3.8	3.6	3.5

TABLE 1.2
Tenth-Grade Student Writing Performance
Over Time on Oregon's Writing Test

Grade 10	IO	Org	Vc	WC	SF	Cnv
1991	3.4	3.5	3.8	3.6	3.4	3.6
1995	4.1	4.0	4.3	4.0	4.0	3.9
1997	4.0	3.9	4.2	4.0	4.0	3.8
1998	4.0	3.9	4.2	4.0	3.9	3.8

Two primary inferences from these data are (a) the measurement system is not sensitive enough to pick up any improvements that may be appearing, or (b) students simply are not learning to write better. These data actually corroborate the reports from National Assessment of Educational Progress (NAEP), in which no significant growth has occurred in writing over 12 years. In the 1997 report from NAEP, the average writing score of 11th graders has shown an overall pattern of decrease. Eighth graders decreased for 3 years, bounced up, and then decreased to same original level (see Tables 1.3 and 1.4). Yet in Grades 8 to 11, students reported writing more essays, letters, poems, and reports. Clearly, the issue of measurement sensitivity is important, both at the state and national levels, because it appears on the surface students report they are writing more. Yet we know little about specific instructional strategies in either of these reports and therefore cannot attribute the lack of change to insensitive measures.

Nevertheless, measurement insensitivity cannot be totally ruled out because in either assessment system (Oregon or NAEP), two procedural aspects of the writing evaluation could explain the lack of improvement: During the evaluation process, raters render their judgments in the context of grade level samples. In essence, the criteria for judgment may be taking on a norm-referenced anchor. Furthermore, with each successive year of the assessment, a different sample of students is evaluated, with no earlier samples from previous assessments used to calibrate the judgments over time. In effect, improvement could be sneaking into the sample but is ignored as part of each successive normative sample from year to year. This inference would need to be tested by including samples from earlier assessments as anchors for later evaluations and rendering judgments without reference to grade levels.

TABLE 1.3
Percentage of Students With Effective
Coherent Writing by Year (1984–1996)

Grade	1984	1988	1990	1992	1994	1996
8	0	0	1	2	1	1
11	2	1	4	2	3	2

TABLE 1.4
Percentage of Students With Complete
Sufficient Writing by Year (1984–1996)

Grade	1984	1988	1990	1992	1994	1996
8	13	13	12	25	17	16
11	39	39	37	36	33	31

The other proposition, however, is that instruction simply is not effective, although we know little about it from either of these reports. At the very least, as Lane et al. (1998) noted, classroom activities could be documented that would help the public understand these outcomes. An even stronger test of the lack of growth, however, would be to directly and specifically intervene in writing and ascertain any differential effects. With the introduction of the writing process as part of the California Writing Project (Olson, 1987), the educational system has witnessed a tremendous increase in different instructional strategies that use the writing process. Further advances have been made in metacognitive strategies for supporting writing performance of students (see Scardamalia & Bereiter, 1986, for a summary of research on written composition; also see Gersten & Baker, 2001, in the recent *Elementary School Journal* for a meta-analysis of writing strategies).

In summary, we need to continue addressing issues of measurement sensitivity in which administration and scoring of performance is the focus. We also need to conduct smaller scale studies with highly defined treatments and use large-scale tests as outcomes measures.

Cohort Analysis of Change in Reading and Math Performance. Another example of measurement insensitivity or ineffective instruction can be cited using recent data from a cohort group of students within a school district participating in the Oregon statewide reading and math test. In math, the test includes five different domains for sampling problems: (a) number concepts, (b) measurement, (c) geometry, (d) algebraic relations, and (e) statistics and probability. The reading test includes six different domains: word meaning, literary interpretations, literal comprehension, inferential comprehension, evaluative comprehension, and literary forms.

Although improvements have been noted over the course of 5 years in the state, this outcome reflects cross-sectional data: Different students are participating in each of the successive years. Therefore, with different students being tested and compared each year, an unambiguous interpretation cannot be made about changes in performance because they could be attributable to population differences. In an analysis of a cohort group, however, in which a student's score is compared across two different time periods, it is possible to more clearly understand whether performance changes are real. With this analysis, another picture emerges. These data are taken from a large district in the state and at two different times: (a) 1998 when students were in one benchmark year, and (b) 2000 when the students were in another benchmark year. Furthermore, because the state classifies performance as *at or above mastery* or *below mastery level*, two types of analyses are possible with reference to both changes in score *and* change in status (mastery vs. nonmastery). The comparison of change in performance as a function of passing status provides a far more interesting analysis because the data set is richer and potentially more explainable. Four groups can be identified in this analysis: (a) failing in the earlier test and again in the later test, (b) failing in the earlier test and then passing in the later test, (c) passing in the earlier test and then failing in the later test, and (d) passing in both the earlier and later tests.

Clearly Groups (a) and (d) reflect stable performance with respect to the decision outcome. However, the other two groups reflect interesting anomalies. As a false negative, a student moves from failing to passing with the implication that an earlier prediction of failure was not borne out. As a false positive, a student moves from passing to failing: Although a prediction of success might be implied in the earlier performance levels, such an outcome does not bear out, and the later test performance is a failure. It is this last group that poses a serious problem and needs careful breakout analyses.

Across all grades, the largest percentage of students moved from passing in an earlier year to again passing in a later year. Another group of students remained consistently below passing across both successive years. As the grade levels of the cohorts increased, the percentage of students failing in the earlier test and again failing in the later test also increased. Finally, a significant percentage of students moved from passing to failing, far more than moved the other way in their passing status. In fact, the percentage of students in this group increased over the cohort grades, and in the last one (benchmark 4 at Grade 10) 1 in 7 students in math and 1 in 11 students in reading went from passing to failing. The smallest group to change in status involved students who moved from failing to passing. In summary, it is the group of false positives that represents a major concern for interpreting state performance (see Table 1.5).

To help explain these results, a transcript analysis for classes relevant to the last benchmark (Grade 10) was used to match opportunity to learn in terms of achievement (grade point average) and course/class scheduling. No patterns were found in the level of difficulty of the tests, the classes taken by students, the school they attended, or the grade point averages (GPAs) they achieved in the classes. This explanation, however, can never be fully explanatory without some reference to actual instruction. Simply analyzing transcripts and GPAs is unlikely to serve as an adequate proxy for teaching. Rather, a strong test of the premise would require a quasi-experimental intervention research study with the large-scale test serving as the dependent variable and other criterion measures utilized as well.

Summary of Measurement Issues

In summary, we have a measurement research agenda that appears to be only partially specified. We have begun focusing on important constructs, both as interpretations and inferences of large-scale assessment programs.

TABLE 1.5
Analysis of Passing–Failing for a Cohort
Across Two Benchmarks 1998–2000

Math	Cohort Grades	Fail–Fail	Fail–Pass	Pass–Fail	Pass–Pass	Total
1998–2000	3–5	127	109	53	805	1,094
1997–2000	5–8	94	52	54	424	624
1998–2000	8–10	245	33	136	611	1,025
1998–2000	3–5	12%	10%	5%	74%	100%
1997–2000	5–8	15%	8%	9%	68%	100%
1998–2000	8–10	24%	3%	13%	60%	100%

Reading	Cohort Grades	Fail–Fail	Fail–Pass	Pass–Fail	Pass–Pass	Total
1998–2000	3–5	83	56	69	889	1,097
1997–2000	5–8	68	28	50	487	633
1998–2000	8–10	193	87	93	655	1,028
1998–2000	3–5	9%	3%	9%	79%	100%
1997–2000	5–8	11%	4%	8%	77%	100%
1998–2000	8–10	19%	8%	9%	64%	100%

Certainly, given the high stakes of many of these programs, we have been
appropriately concerned with the impact they have had on major stakeholders. As a field, we also have begun addressing the technical characteristics of performance assessments. With performance assessments being
such an important component of classrooms, such attention is warranted.
However, as a field, we have not addressed specific (quasi) experimental
impacts of our measurement systems. It is hoped that this book provides
readers the range of issues and options that arise when we focus on the interpretations and inferences as well as the use of our measurement systems
in large scale testing programs. Much like this introductory chapter, we
have divided the contents into three equal sections.

A PREVIEW OF THE BOOK: LARGE-SCALE
ASSESSMENT ISSUES AND OPTIONS

First (Part I), we address issues of validity, including many important and
current features that have appeared with the latest 1999 revision of the
standards (AERA, APA, NCME). Second (Part II), we consider critical
technical issues in the development of tests and measures used in large-
scale assessment systems, many of which perforce must be addressed to
even entertain discussions of validity. Third (Part III), with inferences and
decision making being such an important component of validity, we present a range of issues on implementation of large-scale assessments with

special populations. Each section includes six chapters and addresses a broad array of issues. The chapters are to be read both independently and collectively, in that the voice of this book is on the integration of issues and options in the current practice of large-scale assessments so that all students may participate.

Part One: Validity Issues

We begin the first section on validity with a chapter by Linn (chap. 2), who provides not only a historical accounting of the emergence of standards, but also focuses on the latest 1999 standards published by the American Educational Research Association (AERA), American Psychological Association (APA), and the National Council on Measurement in Education (NCME). As he notes, these latest standards continue the trend toward unification of the terms: "Content, criterion, and construct considerations were retained, but as types of evidence supporting a validity argument rather than as types of validity." In his review of specific standards, Linn provides exceptional clarity in helping us understand such terms as *content standards*, *cognitive processes*, *test modifications*, *linguistic considerations*, *performance standards*, *criterion-referenced interpretations*, *diagnostic use*, *high-stakes decision making*, *opportunity to learn*, *intended and unintended consequences*, and *score reporting*.

Gersten and Baker (chap. 3) focus directly on Messick's view of validity, providing a far-ranging discussion of the interplay between the evidential and consequential basis of validity. They anchor their chapter in clear examples that create the context for making interpretations and inferences from tests and measures. As they note: "In many cases, state assessments lack studies of use." It is this aspect in which they are so lucid: how data are actually used to make decisions about students, programs, and the way we conduct our research with students and on programs. Their description of the issues on traditional concurrent and predictive validity studies that are needed is extremely compelling, only superceded by their subsequent presentation of the value implications: what test scores mean and how they should be interpreted.

In the chapter by Ryan and DeMark (chap. 4), issues of validity are addressed using meta-analytic techniques, comparing the performance of girls and boys on selected versus constructed responses. Their analysis of the data from many different primary studies done in different content areas provides an excellent model for not only documenting the differences but also understanding how to interpret them. Indeed, as they note, the difference between females and males is small, although "females generally perform better than males on language measures regardless of assessment format, and males generally perform better than females on mathematics measures also regardless of format." They then provide a model for examining the construct that the assessments are designed to measure, asking whether it is the actual construct or is integral, correlated, or uncorrelated to the construct.

Haladyna (chap. 5) addresses the documentation needed to link the practices of large-scale testing programs with the 1999 standards (AERA, APA, NMCE). He proceeds by providing a clear framework in which we can understand the kind of interpretations being made (criterion or norm referenced), the constructs being tested (knowledge, skills, or abilities), and the unit of analysis being reported (level of aggregation). The strength of his chapter is his acumen in considering the audience who receives documents, the parties who are responsible for collecting and reporting documents, and the actual contents of documents. "At the heart of this validation is supporting documentation, which is a coordinated activity that presents validity evidence to different audiences in different forms." Whether aligning testing programs to the latest standards, using results as part of accountability systems, or providing achievement data that are legally defensible, this chapter provides both a framework and a strategy.

A natural sequence to the discussion of documentation is its use. For Phillips (chap. 6), use is contextualized in the court of law. She begins her chapter by noting that, "in legal proceedings, the issue is what validity evidence is required . . . [though] presentation of the unified view of validity in legal proceedings may obscure rather than clarify the issues." Her legal arguments focus on precedence from Debra P. and the G.I. Forum as well as other rulings. She also tackles the issues of testing students with disabilities and English-language learners by addressing the logic of accommodations and modifications. Her analysis provides legal rationales as well as strategies and tactics for not only meeting the requirements of the law but also fulfilling the spirit of the law. Using specific examples, legal standards are integrated into a number of clear recommendations about test construction, management of educational programs, inclusion of students into testing programs, and documentation and reporting of outcomes.

In the last chapter of Part I, Mehrens (chap. 7) provides a thorough and rigorous review of the literature on the consequences of (large-scale) assessment programs. "In general, there is much more rhetoric than evidence about the consequences of assessment." He addresses such issues as curricular and instructional reform; motivation, morale, and stress of teachers and students; whether achievement truly improves or test scores simply increase; and the degree to which the public is adequately informed. His final conclusion is that the jury is still out, and these issues may be viewed positively or negatively. Educators and the public may disagree on curricular and instruction reform. Teachers may indeed be facing considerable stress. Students may need to be both more motivated and more realistic in their self-appraisals. Public awareness may need to be more carefully addressed. Nevertheless, impact is relative to a number of issues, and more research is needed before we can draw firm conclusions.

Part II: Technical Issues

Beginning with the assumption that test structures can be adequately explained using a unidimensional model, Tate (chap. 8) addresses sources of multidimensionality, empirical assessment of dimensionality, and the decisions that need to be addressed in the context of dimensionality, whether planned or unplanned. Certainly issues of dimensionality have bearing when large-scale tests are used to track students across years, when reporting subscores, and when examining different populations. He describes item factor analytic methods for examining dimensionality, whether exploratory or confirmatory, and considers conditional item associations after controlling ability. Finally, he addresses the consequences of dimensionality violations, particularly with the use of differential item functioning (DIF) and the discriminant validity of subscores. Acknowledging that all tests are likely to violate assumptions of unidimensionality, "to avoid serious problems, the design and development of the test must be informed by an awareness of possible sources of multidimensionality and the associated consequences."

Rodriguez (chap. 9) eventually highlights a critical question that all test developers and users must consider when planning large-scale assessment programs. "The primary question is: Do multiple-choice items and constructed-response items measure the same cognitive behavior? The quick answer is: They do if we write them to do so." While addressing both the historical development and the nuances in possibilities, the heart of the chapter is in the elegant manner in which he reports a meta-analysis of 61 empirical studies. He reports on 29 correlational studies (using stem, content, and noncontent equivalent items as well as essay type items) in which a mean weighted corrected correlation of .92 was found. He ends the chapter with advice from the measurement community addressing purpose and practice, extending the argument to include economic and political considerations.

In Taylor's chapter (chap. 10), both rationale and requisite steps are provided for including classroom-based assessments into large-scale testing programs. As she so eloquently notes, "collections of classroom work could give policymakers a window into the educational experiences of students and the educational practices of teachers." Furthermore, inferences can be more appropriately guided about students and tasks when based on direct classroom experiences. Yet she also acknowledges that (a) teachers need to be systematically trained in preservice programs, (b) the criteria used to select evidence needs to be considered (to reflect complex performances that are interdisciplinary), (c) the rating process needs to be calibrated, and, finally, (d) irrelevant variance must be minimized. Given an anchor to curriculum standards, she then provides a series of thoughtful strategies for addressing procedural questions so that classroom assessments can be effectively integrated in large-scale testing programs. The chapter ends by providing a necessary reflection on validation to complete the integration process.

Starting from the assumption that "raters bring a variety of potential response biases that may unfairly affect their judgments regarding the quality of examinee responses," Engelhard (chap. 11) describes a number of issues that need to be addressed in any rater-mediated assessment system. Based on the concept of invariance, he focuses specifically on indexes of rater errors and the detection of response biases. He considers rater severity, domain difficulty, task difficulty, and structure of the rating scale in his analysis, as well as writing ability, which is usually the target of measurement. For him, rater bias is method variance and therefore construct irrelevant. Using the Many Facet Rasch Measurement Model, he provides an analytic approach to fitting data to a model in achieving invariant measurement. He concludes by addressing rater errors (severity/leniency, halo error, central tendency, and restriction of range) to investigate all possible facets: raters, domain, task, and examinee.

Noting that the standards (AERA, APA, NCME) call for using multiple measures to make decisions, Ryan (chap. 12) describes three strategies for applying the standards and four procedures for collecting measures from different sources. He argues that more valid inferences may be possible with multiple measures, however, only with careful consideration of curriculum, using reliable (and valid) individual measures, applying criteria for combining measures, scaling and standardizing the scores, and finally weighting and combining data. He then describes three strategies for collating the information from multiple measures using disjunctive or conjunctive models (with standards set separately by students passing any one or each of multiple measures, respectively) or compensatory models (with composites averaged across multiple measures). Finally, he describes several specific strategies for making judgments when using multiple measures, ending the chapter with two procedures for combining data to classify students as mastered/nonmastered: discriminant function analysis and geometric distances. In the end, "the use of multiple measures does not perform magic."

Choi and McCall (chap. 13) use translated mathematics items (side-by-side items written in both English and Spanish) to extend a state testing program to English-language learners (ELLs) and create an equivalent test using a common scale. They critique common methods for linking tests through common items or examinees and then describe a study in which they assume comparable item difficulties in both languages. They first ask: "How much group difference remains when size and ability density differences are taken into account" and "then compare the results of using different types of anchor items in equating." They report that one or more items may function differently due to translation error and/or group membership, but otherwise the side-by-side version is not different from the English version. This lack of difference extends to the judgment of mastery decisions being made with the scores.

Part III: Implementation Issues

For Almond et al. (chap. 14), participation in large-scale testing is a topic appearing with the standard-based reforms that emerged in the late 1990s. Citing legislative mandates (Title 1, IDEA, and civil rights), she and her co-authors describe the cross-pressures faced by schools to deliver results that also satisfy multiple purposes: "To earn their keep, state assessment systems attempt to do it all, often by asking the same assessment to serve several of these purposes." They then review a wide array of research on participation, its current status, the use of accommodations and alternate assessment, and the way that data are reported and decisions are made. They conclude with a compendium of recommendations on the validation of large-scale tests—in particular, how results are used with diverse populations and for multiple purposes, as well as how nonstandard and alternate assessments are used to monitor progress not just performance.

Duran, Brown, and McCall (chap. 15) consider federal mandates in the context of equity and fairness as they address issues in the assessment of students classified as English-language learners or Limited English Proficiency (LEP). They emphasize consideration of student characteristics, decision-making models for inclusion/exclusion, the manner in which students participate, and how data are analyzed and reported. The elegance of their chapter comes from the specificity of direction they provide in reviewing the process for including ELL/LEP students in one state's testing program. In this example, they highlight state standards, options for participation and type of decisions needing to be made, development (and validation) of assessment protocols using side-by-side English/Spanish presentations, and reporting and analysis of outcomes. At the same time, they conclude by noting the need for more work in the development of plain English for items in both reading and writing, as well as implementing side-by-side English/Spanish in science tests.

Hollenbeck (chap. 16) provides a clear and explicit summary of the convoluted issues that arise when changes in tests are made. First, he distinguishes between accommodations and modifications, both of which are anchored to a very current literature base established since IDEA '97. He provides a succinct list of attributes for accommodations by noting four in particular: lack of changes in the construct, basis in individual need, generation of differential effects, and resultant sameness of inference. Furthermore, he notes that, "not only must all teachers function as classroom measurement experts, but they also must understand that their choices about the use or nonuse of accommodations affect the validity of decisions at all levels resulting from the students' score." To help guide decision making, he addresses the growing and considerable body of research on accommodations: (a) settings, (b) presentation, (c) response, and (d) statewide raters.

Helwig (chap. 17) extends test changes as accommodations to changes that result in modifications, in which different constructs are being measured. He describes a systematic process that states can deploy, in which student populations are targeted, domains for assessment sampling are identified, and results of the field testing are reported. The methodology that he describes explicates several aspects of validity, particularly the interconnectedness of content and criterion validity between state measures of standards and alternate assessment, "in which relatively strong congruence [exists] between the conceptual knowledge, skills, and proficiencies assessed by the two measures." The power of his argument is in the maintenance of similar (or related) cognitive processes between the standard and alternate assessments. He completes his chapter with an explicit descriptive example for actually developing an alternate assessment by reference to all aspects of validity: content, construct, and criterion.

The central question for Thurlow, Bielinski, Minnema, and Scott (chap. 18) is the possibility of using out-of-level tests to accurately document the achievement of a student. They first anchor the issue in a historical sketch of the eventual development of norms for published achievement tests that extend interpretations for students' performance above and below their grade level. Using precision as a proxy for reliability and accuracy for validity, they provide a persuasive argument that, "Having scores that are more precise, however, does not ensure that they are more accurate measures of the student's performance." They then reference psychometric issues needing to be resolved through item response theory (IRT) and vertical equating. In the end, they note the limited literature that is available on the use of out-of-level testing: in documenting achievement outcomes, in the psychometric and scaling properties, and finally with respect to the consequences for individuals and systems.

This section ends with Ysseldyke and Nelson's (chap. 19) focused description of reporting formats, what they should include, and how they should be formatted. They contrast what should be with the current state of affairs. "Clarity is the most important characteristic of good reports" in addressing audience, purpose, conceptual framework, and content (target) of the report. They also emphasize comprehensiveness by including information on inputs, processes, and results. Comparative analyses should be possible with any report, allowing interpretations to made and validated. Concision is to be valued in reports, with cautionary statements helping avoid misinterpretations and confidentiality addressed with disaggregation of data. Finally, the format of reports is addressed by providing several exemplary guidelines. They summarize their chapter by describing state reports as they currently exist, highlighting the long road yet needing to be traveled in attaining their standards.

Haladyna's epilogue summarizes the key issues presented by the authors in this book with a glimpse into the future as it must be for large-scale testing programs. He identifies three factors that are likely to hold sway: attending to systemic reform of educational programs, using cognitive theories of learning to measurement and testing, and advancing our conception of validity in measurement use and interpretation. The promising areas of research are encompassing as he reminds us of how little we really know.

"We should expect to continue to see the growth of validity as a central paradigm in achievement testing." Issues loom that the field needs to address such as understanding dimensionality, testing with computers (based, assisted, simulated, and scored), and choosing item formats.

Construct-irrelevant variance no doubt needs to be part of all research and development in large-scale testing. "We are just beginning to understand the scope of this threat to validity," including construct underrepresentation, vertical scaling to track growth, standard setting in reference to decision making, and including ALL students.

Finally, "systemic reform and high-stakes testing will have a profound effect on students and their parents, teachers, and the public." Theory and research needs to develop in coordination with public application and interpretation for measurement and testing to build effective and accountable educational programs.

REFERENCES

Alexander, P. A., Schallert, D. L., & Hare, V. C. (1991). Coming to terms: How researchers in learning and literary talk about knowledge. *Review of Educational Research, 61*(3), 315–343.

American Educational Research Association, American Psychological Association, and National Council of Measurement in Education. (1999). *Standards for educational and psychological testing*. Washington, DC: Author.

Baker, E. L. (1996). Introduction to theme issue on educational assessment. *The Journal of Educational Research, 89*(4), 194–196.

Cronbach, L. J., Gleser, G. C., Nanda, H., & Rajaratnam, N. (1972). *The dependability of behavioral measurement: Theory of generalizability of scores and profiles.* New York: Wiley.

Frederiksen, J. R., & Collins, A. (1989). A systems approach to educational testing. *Educational Researcher, 18*(9), 27–32.

Gersten, R., & Baker, S. (2001). Teaching expressive writing to students with learning disabilities. *Elementary School Journal, 101*(3), 251–272.

Haertel, E. (1999). Validity arguments for high-stakes testing: In search of evidence. *Educational Measurement: Issues and Practice, 18*(4), 5–9.

Haladyna, T. M., Nolan, S. B., & Haas, N. S. (1991). Raising standardized achievement test scores and the origins of test score pollution. *Educational Researcher, 20*(5), 2–7.

Haladyna, T., Hess, R., Osborn-Popp, & Dugan, J. (1996). *A comparison of locally and externally scored statewide writing assessments.* Salem, OR: Oregon Department of Education.

Hass, N. S., Haladyna, T. M., & Nolen, S. B. (1989). *Standardized testing in Arizona: Interveiws and written comments from teachers and administrators* (Technical Report No. 89-3). Phoenix, AZ.: Arizona State University West Campus.

Herman, J., & Golan, S. (1993). The effects of standardized testing on teaching and schools. *Educational Measurement: Issues and Practice, 12*(4), 20–25, 41–42.

Kane, M. (1992). An argument based approach to validity. *Psychological Bulletin, 112,* 527–535.

Kane, M., Crooks, T., & Cohen, A. (1999). Validating measures of performance. *Educational Measurement: Issues and Practice, 18*(2), 5–17.

Lane, S., Plake, C. L., & Stone, C. A. (1998). A framework for evaluating the consequences of assessment programs. *Educational Measurement: Issues and Practice, 17*(2), 24–28.

Linn, R. (1993). Educational assessment: Expanded expectations and challenges. *Educational Evaluation and Policy Analysis, 15*(1), 1–16.

Linn, R. L. (1994). Performance assessment: Policy promises and technical measurement standards. *Educational Researcher, 12*(9), 4–14.

Linn, R. L., Betebenner, D. W., & Wheeler, K. S. (1998). *Problem choice by test takers: Implications for comparability and construct validity.* University of Colorado at Boulder: Center for Research on Evaluation, Standards, and Student Testing.

Meehl, P. E. (1978). Theoretical risks and tabular asterisks: Sir Karl, Sir Ronald, and the slow progress of soft psychology. *Journal of Consulting and Clinical Psychology, 46*(4), 806–834.

Mehrens, W. A., & Kaminski, J. (1989). Methods for improving standardized test scores: Fruitful, fruitless, or fraudulent? *Educational Measurement: Issues and Practice, 8*(1), 14–22.

Mehrens, W. A., Popham, W. J., & Ryan, J. M. (1998). How to prepare for performance assessments. *Educational Measurement: Issues and Practice, 17*(1), 18–22.

Messick, S. (1988). The once and future issues of validity: Assessing the meaning and consequences of measurement. In H. Wainer & H. I. Braun (Eds.), *Test validity* (pp. 33–46). Hillsdale, NJ: Lawrence Erlbaum Associates.

Messick, S. (1989). Meaning and values in test validation: The science and ethics of assessment. *Educational Researcher, 18*(2), 5–11.

Messick, S. (1994). The interplay of evidence and consequences in the validation of performance assessments. *Educational Researcher, 23*(2), 13–23.

Miller, D., & Seraphine, A. (1993). Can test scores remain authentic when teaching to the test? *Educational Assessment, 1*(2), 119–129.

Olson, C. B. (1987). *Practical ideas for teaching writing as a process.* Sacramento, CA: California State Department of Education.

Phelps, R. P. (1998). The demand for standardized student testing. *Educational Measurement: Issues and Practice, 17*(3), 5–23.

Phelps, R. P. (2000). Trends in large-scale testing outside the United States. *Educational Measurement: Issues and Practice, 19*(1), 11–21.

Popham, W. J. (1999). Where large scale educational assessment is heading and why it shouldn't. *Educational Measurement: Issues and Practice, 18*(3), 13–17.

Porter, A. (1993). School delivery standards. *Educational Researcher, 22*(5), 24–30.

Porter, A. (1995). The uses and misuses of opportunity to learn standards. *Educational Researcher*, 21–27.

Reynolds, M. C., Wang, M. C., & Walberg, H. J. (1987). The necessary restructuring of special and regular education programs. *Exceptional Children, 53*(5), 391–398.

Scardamalia, M., & Bereiter, C. (1986). Research on written composition. In M. C. Wittrock (Ed.), *Handbook of research on teaching* (pp. 778–803). New York: Macmillan.

Shavelson, R. J., Webb, N. M., & Rowley, G. L. (1989). Generalizability theory. *American Psychologist, 44*(6), 922–932.

Shepard, L., Flexer, R., Hiebert, E., Marion, S., Mayfield, V., & Weston, T. (1996). Effects of introducing classroom performance assessments on student learning. *Educational Measurement: Issues and Practice, 15*(3), 7–18.

Smith, M. L. (1991). Put to the test: The effects of external testing on teachers. *Educational Researcher, 20*(5), 8–11.

Strong, S., & Saxton, L. C. (1996). Kentucky performance assessment of reading: Valid? *Contemporary Education, 67*(2), 102–106.

Yen, W. M., & Ferrara, S. (1997). The Maryland School Performance Assessment Program: Performance assessment with psychometric quality suitable for high stakes usage. *Educational and Psychological Measurement, 57*(1), 60–84.

Ysseldyke, J., Thurlow, M., & Shin, H. (1994). *Opportunity to learn standards* (Synthesis Report No. 14). Minneapolis, MN: University of Minnesota National Center on Educational Outcomes.

Part I

VALIDITY ISSUES

Validation of the Uses and Interpretations of Results of State Assessment and Accountability Systems

Robert L. Linn
University of Colorado–Boulder

The purpose of this chapter is to provide an overview of validity within the context of current assessment and accountability systems mandated and developed by states in recent years. Following usage in the *Standards for Educational and Psychological Testing* (American Educational Research Association, American Psychological Association, & National Council on Measurement in Education, 1999), hereafter referred to as the *Test Standards*, we use the term *test* in a broad sense to include any systematic evaluative device or assessment procedure. We make frequent reference to the *Test Standards*, using them as an organizing tool to discuss the types of evidence and logical arguments that those responsible for state assessment and accountability systems should develop to evaluate the validity of the uses and interpretations that are made of the results. We begin with a brief overview of the concept of validity and the way in which thinking about validity in the measurement profession has evolved over time. We then turn to a discussion of specific uses and interpretations of results of state assessment and accountability systems and the requirements of the *Test Standards* to evaluate the validity of those uses and interpretations.

VALIDITY

There is a broad professional consensus that validity is the most important consideration in evaluating the quality of the uses and interpretations of the results of tests and assessments. This consensus was reaffirmed in the most recent edition of the *Test Standards* (American Educational Research Association, American Psychological Association, National Council on Measurement in Education, 1999), which provides the most authoritative statement of consensus in the field. The *Test Standards* define *validity* as follows. "Validity refers to the degree to which evidence and theory support the interpretations of test scores entailed in the uses of tests" (p. 9). The *Test Standards* go on to say that "Validity is, therefore, the most fundamental consideration in developing and evaluating tests" (p. 9).

Evolution of the Concept of Validity

As is true of many fundamental concepts, the concept of validity has evolved over time. Early discussions of validity emphasized the relationship of test scores to external criterion measures or the degree to which a test measured what it was intended to measure. For example, Gulliksen (1950) argued that "the validity of a test is the correlation of that test with some criterion" (p. 88), whereas Lindquist (1942) stated that "the validity of a test may be defined as the accuracy with which it measures that which it is intended to measure" (p. 213; cited in Ebel, 1961, p. 640). These two views of validity came to be known as *criterion validity* and *content validity*.

According to the first view, a test was considered valid if it correlated with a criterion measure such as grades in school or ratings of performance on the job. Distinctions were made between correlations obtained from measures taken at approximately the same time (concurrent validity) and situations where the criterion measure was obtained at some point in time after test scores were obtained (predictive validity). Together these two types of evidence came to be known as *criterion validity* (American Educational Research Association, American Psychological Association, National Council on Measurement in Education, 1974). The criterion validity perspective was dominant in employment testing and tests used for college admissions, where the emphasis was more on predicting future performance than documenting past accomplishments.

Focus on Content

Educational achievement tests focus on content domains such as reading, mathematics, or science. Such tests are often intended to provide evidence of what a student knows and is able to do in a content domain without regard to an external criterion measure, such as subsequent performance in college on the workplace. Therefore, it is not surprising that validity arguments for educational achievement tests tended to emphasize the content of the test items and how well that content represented the content of the domain of achievement being assessed. Validity arguments relied on the use of tables of test specifications, which mapped the test items according to specific content (e.g., addition, subtraction, multiplication) and process (e.g., factual knowledge, conceptual understanding, problem solving) categories. Content validity was judged in terms of the definition of the content domain and the representativeness of the coverage of that domain by the test.

Emergence of Construct Validity

In the early 1950s, two separate efforts were undertaken to codify the thinking of the professional measurement community into technical recommendations for the field. The *Technical Recommendations for Psychological Tests and Diagnostic Techniques* (American Psychological Association, 1954) and the *Technical Recommendations for Achievement Tests* (American Educational Research Association, & National Council on Measurements Used in Education, 1955) included the content, predictive, and concurrent categories of validity, but added a fourth category—construct validity—because it was concluded that the other three categories were "insufficient to indicate the degree to which the test measures what it is intended to measure" (American Educational Research Association & National Council on Measurements Used in Education, 1955, p. 16; cited in Moss, 1992, p. 232).

Construct validity was explicated by Cronbach and Meehl (1955) in an article that had a lasting impact on subsequent thinking about and discussions of validity. Initially, however, the ideas of construct validation were seen as relevant when dealing with psychological constructs such as anxiety or hostility especially within theoretical research perspectives. Construct validity was embraced by psychologists working on theories of individual differences. For example, Loevinger (1957) wrote that ". . . construct validity is the whole of validity from a scientific point of view" (p. 636). Yet some leading educational measurement figures objected to the vagueness of construct validation (e.g., Ebel, 1961), preferring the traditions of operational definitions and notions of content validity and operational definitions when dealing with achievement tests. Objections were heard from industrial and organizational psychologists, who found construct validity to be too theoretical and of less practical value than criterion validity. Gradually, however, construct validity came to be widely accepted as relevant to educational achievement tests as well as to tests designed primarily as predictors of some criterion measure.

Several factors contributed to the wider acceptance of construct validity. Leading theorists such as Cronbach (1971) and Messick (1975) continued to promote the concept of construct validity. They made it appear less theorybound and more practical by illustrating how construct validity considerations necessarily enter into an evaluation of the uses and interpretations of any test. For example, Messick (1975) recognized the important role of both content considerations and relationships to criterion measures to the evaluation of a test's validity. However, he argued that neither type of evidence was sufficient for judging the validity of a use or interpretation of test scores.

Movement Toward an Integrated View of Validity

The 1974 edition of the *Test Standards* (American Educational Research Association, American Psychological Association, & National Council on Measurement in Education) continued the partition of validity into three parts: content, criterion (including predictive and current categories from the past), and construct. A step was taken, however, toward a more integrated view of validity, which was defined as "the appropriateness of inferences from test scores or other forms of assessment" (p. 25). Guion (1980), the lead author of the 1974 *Test Standards*, recognized not long after they were published that the *Standards* had not gone far enough in providing a unified view of validity. He argued against the three-part view, which he dubbed a *trinitarian doctrine*, in favor of a unified view of validity. He concluded that,

> Validity is . . . an evaluative judgment based on a variety of considerations including the structure of the measurement operations, the pattern of correlations with other variables, and the results of confirmatory and disconfirmatory investigations. (p. 385)

The 1985 edition of the *Test Standards* (American Eduactional Research Association, American Psychological Association, & National Council on Measurement in Education) continued this movement toward an integrated view of validity, which was described as the "most important consideration in test evaluation" (p. 9). Validity was treated as a "unitary concept" (p. 9), referring "to the appropriateness, meaningfulness, and usefulness of specific inferences made from test scores" (p. 9). Content, criterion, and construct considerations were retained, but they were retained as types of evidence supporting a validity argument rather than as types of validity. Thus, the *Test Standards* referred to content-related evidence, criterion-related evidence, and construct-related evidence rather than content validity, criterion validity, and construct validity.

Not long after the 1985 edition of *Test Standards* was published, Messick (1989) objected that the document still had not moved far enough toward a unified view. Content and criterion-related evidence were still not seen as aspects of an overall validity argument, and notions of construct validation were not yet considered preeminent. Messick's (1989) chapter, which Shepard (1993) described as the "most cited authoritative reference on the topic" (p. 423), began with the following definition:

> Validity is an integrated evaluative judgment of the degree to which empirical evidence and theoretical rationales support the *adequacy* and *appropriateness* of *inferences* and *actions* based on test scores or other modes of assessment. (Messick, 1989, p. 13; italics in original)

This definition, which opens Messick's influential chapter, is so packed with meaning that the author required 91 pages to explicate the concept. He presented a two-by-two table corresponding to the adequacy/appropriateness and inferences/actions distinctions of the definition. The two rows of the table distinguish two bases of support for validity claims—the *evidential* and *consequential* bases. These are used to support claims of adequacy and appropriateness. The two columns of the table distinguish between *interpretations* of assessment results (e.g., only 30% of the students are proficient in mathematics) and *uses* of those results (e.g., award or a high school diploma).

Although some professionals in the field disagree about the desirability of including consequences as part of validity (see, e.g., Green, 1990; Moss, 1994; Wiley, 1991), there is broad consensus about other parts of Messick's comprehensive formulation and about the importance of investigations of consequences as part of the overall evaluation of particular interpretations and uses of assessment results (Baker, O'Neil, & Linn, 1993; Cronbach, 1980, 1988; Linn, 1994; Linn & Baker, 1996; Linn, Baker, & Dunbar, 1991; Shepard, 1993). Mehrens (chap. 7, this volume) notes that, although he is not a fan of the term *consequential validity*, he does support the need to obtain evidence of the consequences of assessments—both those intended by the system designers and those unintended and possibly negative. Thus, there is general support for the broad framework that includes consequences regardless of whether consequences are seen as part of validation or part of a more general evaluation of interpretations and uses of assessment results. Of course, affirmation of primacy of validity based on a comprehensive framework is one thing. Validity practice is quite another. Validity practice is too often more in keeping with outmoded notions of validity that base validity claims on a demonstration that test items correspond to the cells of a matrix of test specifications or the demonstration that scores on a test are correlated with other relevant measures (e.g., teacher ratings or another test administered at a later time). Although both content- and criterion-related evidence are relevant to validity judgments, they do not provide a sufficient basis for the kind of integrated evaluative judgment that Messick encourages.

The 1999 *Test Standards* completed the trend that began with the 1974 edition and continued in the 1985 edition. Again, the trend is toward an integrated view of validity as a unitary concept that incorporates the use of a variety of types of evidence and logical analyses to make an evaluation of the degree to which a specific use or interpretation of assessment results is justified. Evidence would include a consideration of content relevance and representativeness as well as correlations of scores with other variables. This information might include judgments about the degree of alignment of the test content with content standards. Correlations with student characteristics and instructional experiences (e.g., measures of opportunity to learn the material assessed) as well as with potential criterion measures such as teacher grades would be considered relevant as well. In addition, the relevant evidence would be expected to include information that in the past would have been associated with construct validation, such as information about the internal structure of the test and the cognitive processes used by students responding to the test items.

The 1999 *Test Standards* not only calls for an array of evidence that in the past would have been characterized as content-related, criterion-related, or construct-related evidence, but they go beyond these traditional categories to include evidence based on the consequences of test use and interpretation. With regard to consequences, however, *Test Standards* distinguishes between "evidence that is directly relevant to validity and evidence that may inform decisions about social policy but falls outside the realm of validity" (American Educational Research Association, American Psychological Association, & National Council on Measurement in Education, 1999, p. 16).

An example of a consequence that would be relevant to informing social policy but that would be outside the realm of validity is differences in average scores or passing rates for identifiable groups of students (e.g., African Americans and Whites, or boys and girls) when those differences are not attributable to construct-irrelevant factors. Yet evidence of the educational benefits and potential negative consequences for students of a test used to place children in different educational tracks or determine promotion from grade to grade would be relevant in the evaluation of the validity of those uses of assessment results.

A single assessment may have a variety of uses (e.g., diagnostic feedback for teachers and students, global information for parents, requirement for promotion to the next grade, school accountability) and many different interpretations (e.g., the student is proficient in mathematics, the school is exemplary). Because validity is a property of the uses and interpretations rather than a property of a test per se, a test may have evidence to support a claim of adequate validity for one interpretation, good validity for a specific use, and poor validity for another use of the results. Thus, it is not appropriate to conclude that a test is valid. Instead validity claims should be made in reference to specific uses and interpretations.

PLANNING AND EVALUATING THE VALIDATION FOR STATE ASSESSMENT AND ACCOUNTABILITY SYSTEMS

Two chapters of the 1999 *Test Standards* are especially relevant for planning a program of validation or evaluating the validity of a state assessment system. Chapter 1 presents the general standards for validity that are intended to apply to a full array of types of tests and test uses in settings outside education as well as those in educational settings. Chapter 13 is directed explicitly toward the use and interpretation of tests and assessment in formal educational settings. Other chapters that are also relevant to validity considerations for state assessment systems (particularly chaps. 7, 9, and 10). Although we refer briefly to the latter chapters, the bulk of the following discussion centers on the standards presented in chapters 1 and 13 and their implications for state assessment and accountability systems.

SPECIFICATION OF PURPOSES AND SUMMARY OF SUPPORTING EVIDENCE

Because validity is specific to particular uses and interpretations of test results, the first two 1999 validity standards articulate expectations for those who mandate, develop, or use test results to be explicit about the intended uses and interpretations of test results. Standard 1.1 also makes demands that a comprehensive summary of the evidence on which recommended interpretations and uses are based:

> *Standard 1.1:* A rationale should be presented for each recommended interpretation and use of test scores, together with a comprehensive summary of the evidence and theory bearing on the intended use or interpretation. (p. 17)

> *Standard 1.2:* The test developer should clearly set forth how test scores are intended to be interpreted and used. The population(s) for which a test is appropriate should be clearly delimited, and the construct that the test is intended to assess should be clearly described. (p. 17)

State assessment and accountability systems introduced in recent years are intended to support a variety of interpretations and to be used for a variety of purposes. They are generally intended to assess how well students are meeting expectations specified by content standards (also called curriculum standards or guidelines) that have been developed and adopted by states during the 1990s. They may be expected to provide diagnostic information to teachers as well as general information to parents about how well their children are doing. Also, they may be used for making high-stakes decisions about students, such as determining grade-to-grade promotion or awarding high school diplomas. At the aggregate level, the test results may be used to rate school performance, monitor progress, and report results to the public and the media as well as to school administrators and school boards. The results may also have high-stakes accountability uses, such as school accreditation or the determination of rewards and sanctions for schools and teachers.

Consideration of Content

Each of these examples of uses and interpretations or assessment results raises validity questions that need to be answered by evaluating logical arguments and empirical evidence. Because content standards are often the starting point for developing assessments, they provide a natural initial focus of validation efforts. Content standards are expected to specify what should be taught and what students should learn. They identify important concepts and skills, but they do not mandate any particular curriculum, textbook, instructional approach, or series of lessons. Although content standards adopted by states vary greatly in their specificity and emphasis, they generally identify a range of knowledge and skills that students are expected to develop. Typically, content standards emphasize conceptual understanding and the ability to solve problems in addition to factual knowledge and routine skills.

Whatever the breadth and depth of coverage of content standards, it is generally intended that the associated assessment will be sufficiently aligned with them that student performance can serve as the basis for making inferences about the student's mastery of the content domain defined by the standards. Detailed analyses of the relationship between the content domain of the content standards and the specific content of the assessment are needed to support such inferences. Confirmation of alignment of assessment tasks and content standards by independent judges provides one type of support. This may be accomplished by having judges assign assessment tasks to content standards they believe the tasks measure and comparing those assignments with those of the developers of the assessment tasks. The 1999 *Test Standards* addresses this issue of basing validation on an analysis of content as follows:

> *Standard 1.6:* When the validation rests in part on the appropriateness of test content, the procedures followed in specifying and generating test content

should be described and justified in reference to the construct the test is intended to measure or the domain it is intended to represent. (p. 18)

Chapter 13 more explicitly states the need to align the content of the assessment to that of the content standards, which are referred to here as *curriculum standards*:

Standard 13.3: When a test is used as an indicator of achievement in an instructional domain or with respect to specified curriculum standards, evidence of the extent to which the test samples the range of knowledge and elicits the processes reflected in the target domain should be provided. Both tested and target domains should be described in sufficient detail so their relationship can be evaluated. The analyses should make explicit those aspects of the target domain that the test represents as well as those aspects that it fails to represent. (p. 145)

As noted in the last sentence, tests are unlikely to cover the full domain of content covered by content standards. Hence, it is important to clarify which aspects of the content standards are left uncovered by the test, which are covered only lightly, and which receive the greatest emphasis. Such an analysis provides a basis for judging the degree to which generalizations from the assessment to the broader domain of the content standards are defensible. Messick (1989) referred to the threat to validity of inadequate coverage of the domain as *construct underrepresentation*. Construct underrepresentation is a major concern in large-scale assessment because potential aspects of the domain that are relatively easy to measure will be assessed, and this in turn can lead to a narrowing and distortion of instructional priorities.

Cognitive Processes

Content standards adopted by states not only identify the content students are expected to learn, but more often than not specify the cognitive processes that students are expected to be able to use (e.g., reasoning, conceptual understanding, problem solving). For example, if a test to assess mathematical reasoning is intended to align with the content standards, then "it becomes important to determine whether examinees are, in fact, reasoning about the material given instead of following a standard algorithm" (American Educational Research Association, American Psychological Association, & National Council on Measurement in Education, 1999, p. 12). This validity expectation is codified in Standard 1.18:

Standard 1.18: If the rationale for a test use or score interpretation depends on premises about the psychological processes or cognitive operations used by examinees, then theoretical or empirical evidence in support of those premises should be provided. (p. 19)

Support for a claim about cognitive processes might include expert review and logical analyses of the test items and their relationships to instructional materials. More systematic evidence also might include analysis of student responses to open-ended problems, where they are asked to explain their reasoning, interviews of students about their test responses, or think-aloud protocols for a sample of students as they respond to test items.

Participation (With Accommodations, if Nessecary)

Fairness requires that efforts be made to include persons with disabilities in assessment and accountability systems. For individuals with disabilities, however, test demands that are not central to the intended construct being measured may undermine the validity of inferences about a student's content knowledge understanding of concepts or ability to solve problems. Considerations of both fairness and validity often require that accommodations be made to allow the test to measure the intended knowledge, skills, and abilities rather than the individual's disability. Accommodations may involve changes in test format (e.g., printing a single item per page), changes in response format (e.g., allowing student to point to preferred response), or modifications of testing conditions (e.g., allowing extended time or administration of the test on an individual basis).

The purpose of accommodations is to remove disadvantages due to disabilities that are irrelevant to the construct the test is intended to measure without giving unfair advantage to those being accommodated. Questions about the adequacy of achieving this purpose are fundamentally questions of validity of interpretations and uses of tests for individuals with disabilities. In keeping with this view, Standards 10.4 and 10.7 specifically address the need for validity evidence within the context of testing individuals with disabilities:

Standard 10.4: If modifications are made or recommended by test developers for test takers with specific disabilities, the modifications as well as the rationale for the modifications should be described in detail in the test manual, and evidence of validity should be provided whenever available. Unless evidence of validity for a given inference has been established, test developers should issue cautionary statements in manuals or supplementary materials regarding confidence in interpretations based on test scores. (p. 106)

Standard 10.7: When sample sizes permit, the validity of inferences made from test scores and the reliability of scores on tests administered to individuals with various disabilities should be investigated and reported by the agency or publisher that makes the modification. Such investigations should examine the effects of modifications made for people with various disabilities on resulting scores, as well as the effects of administering standard unmodified tests to them. (p. 107)

Language

As is noted in the *Test Standards*, ". . . any test that employs language is, in part, a measure of the language skills" (p. 91) of the test taker. Linguistic considerations become particularly important, however, when individuals with diverse linguistic backgrounds are tested. Students with a first language other than English may be faced with added difficulty when taking a test in English if they have not had sufficient opportunity to learn English. If the focus of the test is other than English-language skills, the language of the test may introduce construct irrelevant difficulty for such students and thereby undermine the validity of interpretations and uses of the test scores. The language of the test can be a critical factor in assessment and accountability systems because of the diverse linguistic backgrounds of U.S. students. Issues of translation, adaptation, and modifications of tests and test administration conditions require careful attention to the design and conduct of assessment and accountability systems, as well as to the evaluation of the validity of the interpretations and uses of the results they produce. These issues are addressed in chapter 9 of the *Test Standards*. Two of the standards in that chapter speak directly to evaluations of validity. Standard 9.2 applies to the full range of testing practices: administration of an unmodified test using standard procedures, administration of tests with accommodations or modifications, and administration of tests translated into another language.

> *Standard 9.2:* When credible research evidence reports that test scores differ in meaning across subgroups of linguistically diverse test takers, then to the extent feasible, test developers should collect for each linguistic subgroup studied the same form of validity evidence collected for the examinee population as a whole. (p. 97)

Standard 9.7 focuses only on situations where a test is translated into another language.

> *Standard 9.7:* When a test is translated from one language to another, the methods used in establishing the adequacy of the translation should be described, and empirical and logical evidence should be provided for score reliability and the validity of the translated test's score inferences for the uses intended in the linguistic groups tested. (p. 99)

Performance Standards

With encouragement from the Goals 2000 legislation of 1994, many states have not only adopted content standards, but also have adopted performance standards. Content standards specify the content that teachers are expected to teach and students are expected to learn, but they do not specify the level of performance that is expected. Performance standards are supposed to specify "how good is good enough." In some states, a single performance standard—meets the standard—is set. More commonly, several levels of performance are established that are given labels and elaborated on by descriptions of what students at various levels know and are able to do in a content area. One level, most commonly called *proficient* or *meets the standard*, is set as the target performance level for essentially all students. There is usually a higher level called *advanced* or *exceeds the standard*, and two or more levels of performance that fall short of the proficient category (e.g., *partially proficient* or *basic* and *unsatisfactory* or *below basic*).

The performance levels adopted by the National Assessment Governing Board (NAGB) for the National Assessment of Educational Progress (NAEP) are called *advanced, proficient, basic,* and *below basic*. These illustrate the use of multiple performance-level labels. For each performance level, NAGB provides a description of what students who attain that level are believed to know and be able to do. For example, the fourth-grade proficient level in mathematics is described as follows: "Fourth-grade students performing at the proficient level consistently apply integrated procedural knowledge and conceptual understanding to problem solving in each of the five NAEP content strands" (Reese, Miller, Mazzeo, & Dossey, 1997, p. 43). A more elaborated description is also provided, along with examples of assessment items that are pegged to the proficient level. The performance levels become operational, however, when they are translated into cut scores on a test or assessment. The cut scores are then used to divide the test score distribution into categories that are used to report student performance on the assessment. In the case of NAEP, which has no scores for individual students, the categories are used to report the percentage of students who fall in each performance level (e.g., the percentage of students in the proficient category or the percentage of students who score below the proficient category). For state assessments, percentages of students in a school, district, or state who score at various levels may be reported in an analogous manner. States also generally report the performance of individual students using the labels of the performance levels. Thus, a student may receive a scale score of, say, 235 on the test and be told that he or she is partially proficient. Performance standards result in the placement of students into categories for which criterion-referenced interpretations are provided by the performance-standard names and descriptions. According to the *Test Standards*, persons responsible for this type of score reporting need to give a rationale for it.

During the past decade, the setting of performance standards by the National Assessment Governing Board for NAEP and by states for their state assessments has occurred in the context of a desire for high standards—sometimes called *world-class standards*. In keeping with this desire, the standards that have been set have often been established at levels that are met by a relatively small fraction of students. For example, only 21% of fourth-grade students scored at the proficient level or higher on the 1996 NAEP mathematics assessment (Reese, Miller, Mazzeo, & Dossey, 1997). Also in fall 1999, slightly less than half (47%) of the fifth-grade students in Colorado scored at the proficient or advanced levels on the Colorado State Assessment Program assessment in mathematics (*http://www.cde.state. co.us/cdedepcom/as_latestcsap.htm*). Possibly this reflects, in part, the difference in the assessments and associated stakes attached to the results, but probably reflects more a difference between the stringency of the proficent level on NAEP and the proficient level on CSAP. The Colorado results on the 1996 NAEP mathematics assessment in fourth grade were similar to those of the nation, with 22% of the Colorado fourth-grade students scoring at the proficient level or higher.

There is nothing wrong with high standards per se, but there are questions that need to be addressed in evaluating the validity of interpretations associated with the performance standards. The headline of a front-page *Denver Post* article reporting that 47% of the students in Colorado scored at the proficient level or higher was: "More than half in test fall short. . . . Fewer than half of students pass test" (Bingham, 2000, pp. 1–18). The latter headline was consistent with the interpretation of the Colorado Commissioner of Education, William Moloney, who stated: "It's not good news when half the kids flunk" (Bingham, 2000, p. 18). The validity of interpretations such as these as well as interpretations derived directly from descriptions of performance standards and exemplar test items need to be evaluated.

Standard 4.9: When raw score or derived score scales are designed for criterion-referenced interpretations, including classification into categories, the rationale for recommended score interpretations should be explained. (p. 56)

Several validity issues are raised by the use of performance standards to report student results on a test. The rationale of these issues needs to be addressed and, to the extent feasible, supported by evidence. First, the names given to the levels invite interpretations. The student who is rated at the proficient level knows and is able to do what is expected in a content domain (e.g., is proficient in mathematics). Second, the descriptions associated with each performance standard specify what a student at that level knows and is able to do. Together the performance labels and associated descriptions provide an elaboration of the construct the test is intended to measure. Logical analysis and supporting evidence are required to ensure that interpretations entailed in the elaboration of the construct by the performance standards are justified. In other words, the labels and descriptions make validity claims, and evidence needs to be provided to support those claims. How likely are proficient students to correctly answer items that map directly into the description of the proficient level? Does the test include items that correspond to specific aspects or the description? If not, what evidence is there that performance on the test generalizes to the nontested parts of the description for the level?

The use of performance standards for reporting test results reduces the score scale of a test to a few categories. Although fewer classification errors are made with fewer categories, whenever errors are made, they are more substantial. Valid inferences about student proficiency are undermined by measurement errors that result in misclassification of students. Hence, it is critical that the probability of misclassification be evaluated and the information be provided to users of the performance standards results.

Standard 13.14: In educational settings, score reports should be accompanied by a clear statement of the degree of measurement error associated with each score or classification level and information on how to interpret the scores. (p. 148)

Diagnostic Uses of Test Results

The diagnostic use of test results by teachers usually depends on the reporting of results for subsets of items corresponding to specific aspects or subdomains of content standards, rather than the global level used for monitoring overall achievement or progress in a domain such as reading or mathematics. Reporting of results for small subsets of items with the intent that teachers use such information to make diagnostic instructional choices for students presumes that valid interpretations can be made on the basis of different patterns of performance in the subdomains. Validity evidence is needed to evaluate this underlying premise.

Standard 1.10: When interpretation of performance on specific items or small subsets of items is suggested, the rationale and relevant evidence in support of such interpretation should be provided. (p. 19)

High-Stakes Decisions About Students

Diagnostic uses of assessment results by teachers generally involve only low-stakes decisions that can be easily and rapidly reversed in the light of new information. Hence, the expectations for supporting validity evidence are less demanding than they are in settings where high-stakes decisions with lasting consequences for students are made on the basis of test results. This distinction is reflected in the 1999 *Test Standards*. For high-stakes uses, the *Test Standards* calls for evidence regarding the opportunity students have to learn the material for which they are being held responsible, the use of alternative sources of information about student achievement, and the availability of multiple opportunities to take the test. The *Test Standards* makes no similar demands for low-stakes uses of test scores by teachers.

> *Standard 13.5:* When test results substantially contribute to making decisions about student promotion or graduation, there should be evidence that the test adequately covers only specific or generalized content and skills the student has had an opportunity to learn. (p. 146)

Opportunity to learn emerged as an issue in justifying test use in the legal challenge to the Florida minimum competency test. The 5th Circuit Court of Appeals concluded in *Debra P. v. Turlington* (1981) that the state should not be allowed "to deprive its high school seniors of the economic and educational benefits of a high school diploma until it has demonstrated that the [test] is a fair test of that which is taught its classrooms" (1981). The expectation that validation of high-stakes uses for promotion of graduation should include evidence of opportunity to learn was introduced in the 1985 edition of *Test Standards* and repeated in the 1999 edition. In neither instance, however, did the *Test Standards* elaborate on the nature of evidence that was expected to support a claim of adequate opportunity to learn the material tested.

Opportunity to learn was a part of the Goals 2000 legislation enacted by Congress in 1994, where three types of standards—content, performance, and opportunity-to-learn standards—were distinguished. As used in the Goals 2000 legislation,

> The term opportunity to learn standards means the criteria for, and basis of, assessing the sufficiency or quality of the resources, practices, and conditions necessary at each level of the education system (schools local education agencies, and States) to provide all students with an opportunity to learn the material . . . in the State content standards. [*Goals 2000: Education America Act of 1994*, S. 3 (a,7)]

It is certainly reasonable to expect that students should be provided with an adequate opportunity to learn if they are held accountable for mastering a defined body of content. Unfortunately, it is far from simple to accumulate convincing evidence on this point. There are potentially useful leads on how to proceed from work on opportunity-to-learn measures (e.g., Burstein, 1994; Porter, 1994). As indicated by Porter (1994), however, teacher self-reporting procedures that work well in a descriptive research context do not function so well in a high-stakes accountability context, where teachers feel pressure to report that they have covered the material for which their students are being held accountable. Nonetheless, it is clearly incumbent on those responsible for instituting high-stakes uses of tests for promotion or graduation to give serious attention to Standard 13.5 and, at least, attend to such issues as the match of instructional materials to the test and the preparation of teachers to teach the tested content.

As stated in Standard 13.6, students should also be provided with a reasonable number of chances to take equivalent versions of the test before being retained in grade or denied a diploma and provided with additional opportunity to learn between test administrations.

> *Standard 13.6:* Students who must demonstrate mastery of certain skills or knowledge before being promoted or granted a diploma should have a reasonable number of opportunities to succeed on equivalent forms of the test or be provided with construct-equivalent testing opportunities of equal difficulty to demonstrate the skills or knowledge. In most circumstances, when students are provided with multiple opportunities to demonstrate mastery, the time interval between the opportunities should allow for students to have the opportunity to obtain the relevant instructional experiences. (p. 146)

Because no test can provide a perfectly accurate or valid assessment of a student's mastery of a content domain, the *Test Standards* cautions against overreliance on a single test score when making high-stakes decisions about students.

> *Standard 13.7:* In educational settings, a decision or characterization that will have a major impact on a student should not be made on the basis of a single test score. Other relevant information should be taken into account if it will enhance the overall validity of the decision. (p. 146)

This statement is consistent with conclusions reached in a National Academy of Sciences report prepared by a committee formed in response to a congressional mandate to review the use of tests for purposes of tracking, grade-to-grade promotion, and graduation (Heubert & Hauser, 1998). According to a recent decision by the U.S. District Court for the Western District of Texas (*G. Forum et al. v. Texas Education Agency*, 2000), inclusion of other information in a decision that may have a major impact on students need not be done in a compensatory manner. The Court ruled that Texas could require students to exceed a specified score on the TAAS test as well as pass certain required courses, thus allowing a conjunctive use of a test requirement together with other relevant information.

CONSEQUENCES

The *Test Standards* also requires that validation of test use for high-stakes decisions about students include attention to evidence about the intended and unintended consequences of those uses. As noted earlier, the focus of the *Test Standards* is limited to consequences that are directly relevant to the validity of uses and interpretations of test scores. Test requirements for promotion or graduation have the clear intent of ensuring that students have mastered specified content before they are allowed to move onto the next grade or graduate. There is also the implicit intent that students will learn more in the long run if they are held accountable for achieving at a specified level for the promotion or graduation decision. The *Test Standards* requires that evidence be provided to obtain a reasonable evaluation of the degree to which these intentions are realized by the promotion or graduation policy:

> *Standard 13.9:* When test scores are intended to be used as part of the process of making decisions for educational placement, promotion, or implementation of prescribed educational plans, empirical evidence documenting the relationship among particular test scores, the instructional programs, and desired student outcomes should be provided. When adequate empirical evidence is not available, users should be cautioned to weigh the test results accordingly in light of other relevant information about the student. (p. 147)

Desired student outcomes would include, for example, improved performance following retention in grade. Arguably, they would also include better performance in subsequent grades.

The *Test Standards* also suggests that evidence be provided that a student scoring below the cut score would be expected to benefit more from retention in grade than he or she would if promoted to the next grade. This follows directly from Standard 1.19.

> *Standard 1.19:* If a test is recommended for use in assigning persons to alternative treatments or is likely to be so used, and if outcomes from those treatments can reasonably be compared on a common criterion, then, whenever

feasible, supporting evidence of differential outcomes should be provided. (p. 22)

In grade-to-grade promotion decisions, the alternative treatments are repetition of a grade or promotion to the next grade, and the common outcomes are performance on subsequently administered achievement tests and possibly teacher-assigned grades.

Although the intended outcomes of high-stakes test uses are clearly positive, plausible unintended negative outcomes also need to be considered particularly if it is reasonable to expect that they are the result of inadequate representation of the construct or of construct-irrelevant influences on test scores.

> *Standard 1.24:* When unintended consequences result from test use, an attempt should be made to investigate whether such consequences arise from the test's sensitivity to characteristics other than those it is intended to assess or to the test's failure to fully represent the intended construct. (p. 233)

Reading difficulty or linguistic demands of a test, for example, could be sources of construct-irrelevant difficulty for some students on a test intended to measure mathematics. Such a possibility is recognized in the *Test Standards'* chapter on fairness in testing and test use.

> *Standard 7.7:* In testing applications where the level of linguistic reading ability is not part of the construct of interest, the linguistic or reading demands of the test should be kept to the minimum necessary for valid assessment of the intended construct. (p. 82)

Aggregate Results for Schools

In addition to the myriad ways that state assessment results are used to draw inferences and make decisions about individual students, they are also used to draw inferences and make decisions about schools, teachers, and districts. The average test scores or percentage of students meeting specified performance standards may be intended to provide educators with information potentially useful in making low-stakes diagnostic decisions. More often than not, such summaries are also provided to the media and, in recent years, posted on the Internet. The results are used by the media to rank schools according to current performance and/or changes in performance and have become part of the information realtors give to prospective home buyers. States are also incorporating the use of school assessment results in their school accreditation procedures and instituting school accountability systems that assign rewards and sanctions based on assessment results. Schools failing to show improvement in their test results, for example, may be subject to requirements to submit school improvement plans or even reconstituted, reassigning principals and teachers to other schools.

The distinction between low- and high-stakes uses of test results is relevant in planning validation and evaluating the validity of test use and interpretation of aggregate results. In general, the higher the stakes, the more demanding the validity requirements. Thus, validity information may be sparse or lacking for teachers' instructional planning. Yet when school-level results are used to make school accreditation decisions or determine rewards and sanctions for educators, the expectation is much higher that there be supporting validity evidence.

Although the *Test Standards* provides some guidance regarding validation of uses and interpretation of aggregate test results for schools, the focus is mainly on the use of scores for individuals. Some of the standards are equally applicable at both the individual and group levels. For example, standards requiring that those responsible for testing systems provide a statement of intended uses and interpretations, together with rationale and summary of supporting evidence, apply equally well to groups and individual students. Standards dealing with the alignment of the test and content standards and with the cognitive processes measured are clearly relevant whether the focus is on interpretations of individual students or on schools. That would also be true for standards such as the following one, which focuses on information about the accuracy of score reports.

Standard 13.14: In educational settings, score reports should be accompanied by a clear statement of the degree of measurement error associated with each score or classification level and information on how to interpret the scores. (p. 148)

Classification errors are just as relevant to the evaluation of the validity of test interpretation when schools are classified as when individual students are classified according to a set of performance standards.

Validity of an interpretation of test results for schools or individual students depends on premises about the comparability test administration conditions and test-specific preparation provided to students. Providing students with test preparation that is highly specific to the particular items that are on the test undermines the validity of interpretations that depend on generalizations to the broader domain that the test is intended to sample. If some schools provide students with such preparation while other schools do not, the fairness of school comparisons is also undermined.

Standard 13.11: In educational settings, test users should ensure that any test preparation activities and materials provided to students will not adversely affect the validity of test score inferences. (p. 148)

The rationale for holding schools accountable for test results generally includes an expectation that student achievement will thereby be improved in the content areas tested. The *Test Standards* asks that expected indirect benefits of this kind be made explicit and the logical and evidential basis for the expectations be provided.

> *Standard 1.23:* When a test use or score interpretation is recommended on the grounds that testing or the testing program per se will result in some indirect benefit in addition to the utility of the information from the test scores themselves, the rationale for anticipating the indirect benefit should be made explicit. Logical and empirical evidence for the indirect benefit should be provided. (p. 23)

CONCLUSION

Serious efforts to validate the uses and interpretations of results of state assessment and accountability systems requires considerable planning and a great deal of effort to accumulate the evidence needed to support each intended use and interpretation. There are no easy answers to the question of what evidence is essential or when there is an adequate basis for supporting a particular use or interpretation of results. However, the 1999 *Test Standards* provides an excellent framework for planning the needed effort. The comprehensiveness and high expectations of the *Test Standards* can be rather daunting, especially given the limited resources and other demands placed on state assessment systems. What is needed is a basis for setting priorities so that the most critical validity questions can be addressed.

Shepard (1993) called for "a coherent framework for prioritizing validity questions" (p. 444). She expanded on Cronbach's (1989) suggestions and Kane's (1992) discussion of validity arguments and asked, "What does the testing practice claim to do? . . . What are the arguments for and against the intended aims of the test?" and "What does the test do in the system other than what it claims?" (Shepard, 1993, p. 429). For such questions, it is helpful to consider the level of stakes that are involved in the use or interpretation of results and then give the highest priority to those areas with the highest stakes.

ACKNOWLEDGMENT

Preparation of this chapter was supported, in part, by the Educational Research and Development Center Program PR/Award number R305B60002 as administered by the Office of Educational Research and Improvement, U.S. Department of Education. The findings and opinions expressed in this publication do not reflect the position of the National Institute on Student Achievement, the Office of Educational Research and Improvement, or the U.S. Department of Education.

REFERENCES

American Educational Research Association, American Psychological Association, & National Council on Measurement in Education. (1971). *Standards for educational and psychological tests*. Washington, DC: American Psychological Association.

American Educational Research Association, American Psychological Association, and the National Council on Measurement in Education. (1985). *Standards for educational and psychological testing*. Washington, DC: American Psychological Association.

American Educational Research Association, American Psychological Association, & National Council on Measurement in Education. (1999). *Standards for educational and psychological testing*. Washington, DC: American Educational Research Association.

American Educational Research Association & National Council on Measurements Used in Education. (1955). *Technical recommendations for achievement tests*. Washington, DC: National Education Association.

American Psychological Association. (1954). *Technical recommendations for psychological tests and diagnostic techniques*. Washington, DC: Author.

Baker, E. L., O'Neil, H. F., Jr., & Linn, R. L. (1993). Policy and validity prospects for performance-based assessment. *American Psychologist, 48*, 1210–1218.

Bingham, J. (2000, March 3). The math challenge: More than half fall short. *The Denver Post*, pp. 1A, 18A.

Burstein, L. (1994). *Intertwining of assessment and learning opportunities: Grounding national performance standards in a cross-national perspective*. Unpublished manuscript, National Center for Research on Evaluation, Standards, and Student Testing, UCLA, Los Angeles.

Cronbach, L. J. (1971). Test validation. In R. L. Thorndike (Ed.), *Educational measurement* (2nd ed., pp. 443–507). Washington, DC, American Council on Education.

Cronbach, L. J. (1980). Validity on parole: How can we go straight? *New Directions for Testing and Measurement, 5*, 99–108.

Cronbach, L. J. (1988). Five perspectives on validation argument. In H. Wainer & H. Braun (Eds.), *Test validity* (pp. 3–17). Hillsdale, NJ: Lawrence Erlbaum Associates.

Cronbach, L. J. (1989). Construct validation after 30 years. In R. L. Linn (Ed.), *Intelligence: Measurement theory and public policy (Proceedings of a symposium in honor of Lloyd G. Humphreys)* (pp. 147–171). Urbana: University of Illinois Press.

Cronbach, L. J., & Meehl, P. E. (1955). Construct validity in psychological tests. *Psychological Bulletin, 52*, 281–302.

Debra P. v. Turlington, 644 F. 2d 408. (5th Cir. 1981).

Ebel, R. L. (1961). Must all test be valid? *American Psychologist, 16*, 640–647.

G. Forum et al. v. Texas Education Agency. U.S. District Court for the Western District of Texas (2000).

Goals 2000: Educate America Act of 1994, Public Law 103-227, Sec. 1 et seq. 108 Stat. 125 (1994).

Green, B. F. (1990). A comprehensive assessment of measurement. *Contemporary Psychology, 35*, 850–851.

Guion, R. M. (1980). On trinitarian doctrines of validity. *Professional Psychology, 17*(3), 385–398.

Gulliksen, H. (1950). *Theory of mental tests*. New York: Wiley.

Heubert, J. P., & Hauser, R. M. (Eds.). (1998). *High-stakes testing for tracking, promotion, and graduation*. Washington, DC: National Academy Press.

Kane, M. T. (1992). An argument-based approach to validity. *Psychological Bulletin, 112*, 527–535.

Lindquist, E. F. (1942). *A first course in statistics* (rev ed.). Boston: Houghton Mifflin.

Linn, R. L. (1994). Performance assessment: Policy promises and technical measurement standards. *Educational Researcher, 23*(9), 4–14.

Linn, R. L., & Baker, E. L. (1996). Can performance-based student assessments be psychometrically sound? In J. B. Baron & D. P. Wolf (Eds.), *Performance-based student assessment: Challenges and possibilities. Ninety-fifth yearbook of the National Society for the Study of Education, Part I* (pp. 84–103). Chicago: University of Chicago Press.

Linn, R. L., Baker, E. L., & Dunbar, S. B. (1991). Complex, performance-based assessment: Expectations and validation criteria. *Educational Researcher, 20*(8), 15–21.

Loevinger, J. (1957). Objective tests as instruments of psychological theory. *Psychological Reports, 3*, 635–694 (Monograph Supplement 9).

Messick, S. (1975). The standard problem: Meaning and value in measurement and evaluation. *American Psychologist, 30*, 955–966.

Messick, S. (1989). Validity. In R. L. Linn (Ed.), *Educational measurement* (3rd ed., pp. 13–103). New York: Macmillan.

Moss, P. A. (1992). Shifting conceptions of validity in educational measurement: Implications for performance assessment. *Review of Educational Research, 62*, 229–258.

Porter, A. (1994, May). *The uses and misuses of opportunity to learn standards*. Paper presented at a Brookings Institution Conference, Beyond Goals 2000: The Future of National Standards in American Education, Washington, DC.

Reese, C. M., Miller, K. E., Mazzeo, J., & Dossey, J. A. (1997). *NAEP mathematics report card for the nation and the states*. Washington, DC: National Center for Education Statistics.

Shepard, L. A. (1993). Evaluating test validity. *Review of Research in Education, 19*, 405–450.

Wiley, D. E. (1991). Test validity and invalidity reconsidered. In R. E. Snow & D. E. Wiley (Eds.), *Improving inquiry in social science: A volume in honor of Lee J. Cronbach* (pp. 75–107). Hillsdale, NJ: Lawrence Erlbaum Associates.

Chapter 3

The Relevance of Messick's
Four Faces for Understanding the
Validity of High-Stakes Assessments

Russell Gersten
Scott Baker
Eugene Research Institute/University of Oregon

In a quiet but profound way, the work of Samuel Messick (1988, 1989, 1994, 1995) has revolutionized how we think about valid assessment procedures. His early writings probed the meaning of test reliability and validity in terms of classic psychometric theory. His later writings challenged us to radically shift from classic notions of test psychometrics to an expanded view of valid assessments.

Messick's full conceptualization of validity—not just his concept of consequential validity—is critical for understanding the new set of high-stakes assessments administered by virtually every state in this country. His framework for discussing validity encompasses both classic technical issues first raised in the writings of Nunnally and Cronbach and the other psychometric giants of the 20th century. These issues relate to how well a test is constructed. More important, Messick's writings address the issue of test adequacy. It is in this area that many measurement experts believe Messick has most effectively shaped the thinking of the measurement community. He strongly advocates empirical study of the social and instructional ramifications of testing.

In his view, the traditional validity and reliability indexes provided by test developers, although essential, serve only as a point of departure—a necessary but not sufficient condition for understanding the ultimate validity of an assessment. In Messick's taxonomy of test validity, classic conceptualizations of test reliability and validity provide the underlying *evidential* base supporting possible interpretations about validity of the assessment procedure for one or more uses. They also help us understand if the theories underlying test construction are supported by the evidence. Before we can assert that a test is valid, it is necessary to document the consequences attributable to the actual use of the test. Thus, Messick's contribution is that validity entails the study of how tests are actually used.

Studying the consequences of test use is much trickier than studying tests from a classic psychometric perspective. For one thing, the consequences of test performance may not be immediately clear and/or may shift dramatically over time. This makes it necessary for users and other professionals to probe plausible meanings of the data and examine whether test misuse or unintended or inappropriate use of assessment data is taking place (Gersten, Keating, & Irvin, 1995). Such analysis might require collection of data over multiple administrations and over a certain period of time. It also requires awareness that any decision may be interpreted differently by various clients. For example, some parents may consider their children's placement in special education for a reading disability as stigmatizing and aversive. Others may view the identical decision as a blessing—as an opportunity for the school to finally respond seriously to their requests to provide intensive reading instruction to their son who has not been learning to read (Berninger, 2000; Gersten & Smith-Johnson, 2000). Similarly, having to repeat a grade because of performance on standardized tests can be interpreted by reasonable people positively or negatively. This means that an expanded view of test validity involves statistical and psychologically oriented research, requiring input from sociologists, policy researchers, and historians.

The implications of Messick's conceptual framework go far beyond decisions about placement, graduation, and grade-level retention (Gersten et al., 1995). Messick's framework is also useful in understanding validity as it initially applied to the placement of students into special education or remedial programs on the basis of intelligence or achievement test scores. This focus is clearly still relevant today. As researchers focus on disproportionate representation of certain ethnic minority groups in certain types of special programs, it is critical that the effects of these programs be determined. We believe his framework has great potential for helping us understand the extent to which a given assessment is used to improve the quality of instruction provided to students.

In this chapter, we begin to address issues that are relevant in the context of both statistical conceptions of test administration and use, and more consequential notions of test validity. In many cases, state assessments lack studies of use. Here, we begin to explain what such studies should entail, why they are important, and what are necessary subjects for systematic inquiry. We also address psychometric issues and dilemmas, relevant material from historians and policy researchers, and our own understanding of the research on how teachers use or fail to use assessment information (e.g., Fuchs, Fuchs, Hamlett, Phillips, & Bentz, 1994; Gersten, Carnine, Zoref, & Cronin, 1986; Gersten et al., 1995; Marks & Gersten, 1998).

APPLYING MESSICK'S FOUR FACES OF VALIDITY TO HIGH-STAKES STATE ASSESSMENTS

In Table 3.1, we present our adaptation and extension of Messick's (1988) four faces of validity. In particular, we stress the issue of how teachers use, or fail to use, assessment data to improve the quality of classroom instruction. Clearly, Messick's conception of test validity is relevant to the recent wave of high-stakes assessments that accompany the standards-based reform movement. Virtually every state in the United States now administers state-level tests, which have major implications for students, teachers, schools, and districts. Some states have decided to use tests developed by

TABLE 3.1
Examples of Applications of Messick's Faces
of Validity to Instructional Assessment

Variable	Interpretation of Assessment Data	Use of Assessment Data
Evidential Basis for Claims of Validity	• Correlations with other measures of achievement • Conventional indexes of reliability	• Data on how teachers use the assessment procedure to make ongoing changes in teaching practices; data on how states, districts, or schools use assessment data for curricula decisions • Data on ultimate impact of use on student performance
Consequential Basis	*Value Implications* • Do data lead to refined theories of teaching and learning? • Do teachers perceive assessment information as helpful in terms of providing directions for improving classroom instruction? • Do teachers find the test data useful in understanding which students are progressing or failing to progress?	*Social Consequences* • Does use of the assessment in fact refine the teaching and learning process (e.g., help identify students who require intensive services, help teachers refine curricula approaches or provide more instruction on topics that are difficult for their students)? • Are there unintended side effects of use for the new assessment (e.g., tracking)?

Note. Adapted from Gersten, Keating, and Irvin (1995).

major test publishers, such as the Stanford Achievement Test or the California Test of Basic Skills, as yardsticks for assessing student learning. Other states have decided to undertake, with considerable expense, the development of their own tests.

One clear implication of Messick's framework for this expanded, high-stakes role of assessment is that evaluating the validity of an assessment procedure will almost certainly transcend what any one constituency can do. Test validation will need to involve the work of a community of researchers, educators, and others who have expertise in areas affected by the interpretations and consequences of test data (Gersten et al., 1995). This line of research can and should help us grapple with how high-stakes assessments are used to determine whether, for example, a student receives a high school diploma or has to repeat a grade level in school.

THE FIRST FACE: EVIDENTIAL BASIS FOR CLAIMS OF VALIDITY

Messick's work consistently struggles with the notion that there is a unitary concept of validity, rather than the traditional categories of content, criterion-related, and construct validity. On the one hand, he embraces the notion that validity is best thought of as a unified concept, which he strongly supports in his early writings. On the other hand, he also has written that, "to speak of validity as a unified concept does not imply that validity can not be usefully differentiated into distinct aspects to underscore issues and nuances that might otherwise be downplayed or overlooked" (p. 5).

A cornerstone of traditional test validation procedures is demonstrating that the pattern of results on a new or innovative measure is similar to other measures of the same construct and dissimilar to measures of a different construct. It is surprising that many states in developing their own high-stakes tests have paid surprisingly little attention to this cell of Messick's framework. This aspect of validity is extremely important, and we believe test development should systematically collect and seriously utilize data on the traditional psychometric indexes of concurrent and predictive validity.

It may be that part of the reason states have expended so little effort on the traditional test-development and validation process is that states quickly bypassed these labor-intensive procedures to get at more cutting-edge test construction techniques, such as item-response theory (IRT). Using IRT to develop test items seriously addresses issues involved in both test reliability and validity. It is considered a central construction requirement in the development of any high-stakes test of educational achievement.

With respect to traditional reliability indexes, the recent wave of tests developed and used by states is strong. Improved methods of construction help ensure the attainment of high internal-consistency reliability coefficients in traditional subject areas such as mathematics and reading. Although many states describe the underlying assumptions behind their assessments, and often utilize elegant IRT models to select items and determine scores, we lack a sufficient database on several issues that fit in the classic areas of concurrent validity and construct validity.

To determine the construct validity of a test, one must know the purpose for which it is being used. Unfortunately, contemporary assessments are often asked to serve many different purposes, appropriate for some but ill suited for others. The information is supposed to address system accountability, determine whether students have learned enough to graduate from high school, and give information that teachers can access and use to improve teaching and learning in the classroom. Often the tests are reliable benchmarks of annual progress, but are not reliable enough to provide diagnostic information to teachers

Hoff (1999) recently pursued the issue of content and construct validity with a set of scholars in evaluation and assessment. He concluded, "even though states declare that their tests are aligned with curriculum standards they have developed" (p. 27), few experts agree. Baker (cited in Hoff, 1999) noted: "The present watchword of alignment is mostly a farce" (p. 27). Popham (cited in Hoff, 1999) noted that "So general are many of the standards that test writers need to do little more than revise off-the-shelf products. . . . More often than not, they look like warmed-over versions of standardized tests (of the past)" (p. 27).

The following provides several examples of how the first face of validity can be used to develop a research agenda around a state's assessment program. Several of these examples come from a series of discussions hosted by the Oregon Department of Education from 1997 to 1999 to explore the state's assessment system. The issues, however, are applicable to a wide range of assessments.

In terms of traditional psychometric indexes, there was consensus that the reading measure had high internal consistency (coefficient alpha) reliability. In part, this was because the test was developed using IRT. However, the panel noted that there were no data on the temporal stability of the measure (i.e., test–retest reliability) and suggested that a study with a small subsample of students be conducted.

Despite the negative view many reading educators have about multiple-choice items, this testing format remains the best way to reliably assess reading performance. This is part of the reason that states inevitably use this format when they develop their own measures of reading. Consequently, it remains unclear to the general public, teachers, and many measurement experts just how a state's own reading assessment is different from other standardized reading tests that have already been developed. For example, there is considerable confusion concerning the relationship between the National Assessment of Educational Progress (NAEP) and state assessments. It would be particularly valuable for state department-of-education agencies to identify the major differences, and show how their own reading assessments correlate with the high-quality reading tests now available.

Another issue was the extent to which the reading assessment or mathematics assessment was measuring abilities and skills that were truly different than the older, nationally normed achievement tests, such as the Stanford Achievement Test–9 (SAT–9). Unfortunately, Oregon, like many other states, has not explored this issue empirically. Concurrent validity studies such as these are essential.

Critical questions emerging from these validity studies include the following: Do rank orderings of students differ on the two measures of reading? If so, how? Are differential rankings more an issue for one type of student than another? Are there features of these students—or of how they were taught to read—that explain these differences? These questions and others like them are important in exploring the concurrent validity of a high-stakes measure.

States should be able to provide a priori hypotheses that might account for why student performance is different on their reading test versus another reading test, or how student rankings differ on the two tests. For example, are the newer assessments with longer passages more in line with teachers' sense of students' abilities to read with understanding?

The NAEP panel also questioned the use of a one-parameter model to measure reading when numerous developmental models of reading (e.g., Chall, 1989) indicate that the focus of reading shifts as children develop. Does it make sense to measure the ability to read accurately (i.e., decoding) as an identical construct to the ability to read with understanding (i.e., comprehension).

Understanding the construct underlying the reading assessment in depth may be particularly important as the state begins to test and validate accommodations and modifications for students with disabilities, who often read years below grade level. One issue in testing is that if there is large variability in student skill on the subject being assessed, and if all students are going to take the same assessment, then the test needs to be constructed to account for the range of skills of students taking the test. In other words, there must be enough relevant items at the lower end for students who have low skills and difficult items at the upper end for students who have high skills. If there are too few or too many items at either end, or too many items in the middle, then an accurate assessment of student skill is not possible.

Related to this is the fact that some students need changes in the test administration procedures to provide an accurate account of their real skill levels on the subject being assessed. For example, some students with disabilities need more time to complete a test than is normally allotted. Assuming that the dimension of time is not part of the construct being assessed (as it would be, e.g., in a speeded fluency test), the change in test format may or may not result in a score that can be compared to the scores of students who were not given extra time. One very important consideration is that, to obtain a valid score, it must be shown that giving more time to students who normally would not be eligible for more time under real test conditions (e.g., students without disabilities) does not change their score. In this case, the change may be considered an accommodation, resulting in a valid score that can be part of the analysis conducted with students who were not provided the accommodation. If this condition is not met (e.g., giving students without disabilities more time also changes their score), then the change in test procedure is usually termed a *test modification*. Scores resulting from tests in which administration procedures have been modified typically are not considered valid for including in analyses with scores from students on which tests were not modified.

A related issue involves a reexamination of the method used for test construction. For reading tests, Oregon, like many states, moved to longer passages and more questions per passage to more closely reflect the way individuals read complex information and tried to understand it. Some members of the task force suggested this might be a less valid assessment of reading comprehension, pointing out that prior research had demonstrated correlations among questions from the same passage were higher than correlations among questions from different passages. Simply stated, task force members felt that the test might penalize students more than earlier tests for the following reason: A given passage may cover a topic for which a student has extremely strong or extremely weak background knowledge, including the vocabulary used in the passage as well as the content of the passage. If that passage is heavily weighted (e.g., is one fifth of a student's score), certain students may have unfair advantage or disadvantage. The argument was made that earlier reading tests, with more frequent and shorter passages and fewer questions per passage, may be more valid indicators of reading performance because they sample more types of passages and more topics. This seemed a worthy subject for empirical research.

Another critical issue is the sensitivity of high-stakes assessments to instruction (Cronbach, 1971). Popham (cited in Hoff, 1999) stated the central point: "High-stakes tests have items in there that do a terrible job at measuring school quality. . . . What is being measured is what kids come to school with, not what they learn there" (p. 27). In other words, tests should reflect what teachers are teaching. Student performance on high-stakes tests should be high if they learn what they are being taught in school and low if they do not learn what they are being taught. Of course, some students may come to school knowing a great deal about what the teacher will be teaching that year. In that case, whether the student pays a great deal of attention in class may not reflect how well the student does on the test. It becomes obvious how critical instruction becomes for those students who do not know the content before it is taught.

FACE TWO: VALUE IMPLICATIONS AND MEANINGS OF ASSESSMENT DATA

The second face of validity is, in our view, the most intricate and subtle. It deals with the value implications test scores have, how they are interpreted, and what meanings are attached to them. This facet of validity encompasses traditional issues of construct validity so elegantly articulated by Cronbach (1971) and Kerlinger (1973) in the 1970s.

Messick (1995) raised several value-related issues that are salient to understanding the validity of state assessments. He argued, for example, that asserting test validity required an understanding of "the role of score meaning in applied use" (p. 5). It is not enough that constructs be grounded in theoretical issues—important as they are. They must also be grounded in pragmatic issues. Particularly, we should ask what test scores mean to a teacher, administrator, or student. We should ask what a high or low score in writing, math, or reading will mean for a student, in the practical sense of leading to something good for that student (e.g., taking a challenging course) or something unfortunate (e.g., dropping out of school, feeling ignorant).

It is in this pragmatic context that Linn (chap. 2, this volume) points out that most current state assessments and accountability systems are intended to support a variety of interpretations and are to be used for a variety of purposes. It is not at all clear that there is a high degree of alignment among these different interpretations, as there should be. So far, it seems easy for these varying uses and interpretations to become intermingled, confused, and sometimes openly contradictory.

Content/Construct Validity

First and foremost, the new state assessments are intended to assess how well students are meeting content standards set by the state. Some states have comprehensively linked their assessments to these standards, which is commendable. In other states, assessments have actually preceded the writing of state standards, which is problematic in terms of asserting that teachers had a reasonable opportunity to instruct students on what they would be tested. This cart-before-the-horse ordering also makes it more likely that content standards will be developed to correspond to what is on a multiple-choice test; this exposes the state to the potentially justifiable criticism that it focuses on superficial content. Reading with comprehension can become synonymous with filling in bubble sheets.

Messick would urge us to ask what exactly each assessment is measuring. For example, is an assessment of mathematics skills in Maryland similar to a mathematics test in Texas or California—states that seem to use more traditional means of assessment? To the best of our knowledge, answers to these questions are unclear, and public confusion abounds.

It is often legislators' goal that their state's high-stakes assessments will provide diagnostic information to teachers and parents as well as determine whether a student is performing at an acceptable level of competence in the area tested. From Messick's analytic framework, the diagnostic level information is of questionable reliability and validity. Yet states continue to present data on various subtests, such as Literal and Evaluate Comprehension in reading or Currency and Ratios in mathematics. We would urge states to clarify which scores are reliable and which scores are, at best, guesses as to relative competence.

In most states, student testing begins in second, third, or fourth grade. Students are tested every few years until they complete high school. Some states, such as Texas and California, test every year. Serious discussion of the pros and cons of each system had rarely been conducted until it became a major issue in the 2000 presidential campaign and a major legislative agenda item for President Bush (Olson, 2001). The importance of annual testing, especially in Grades 3 through 8, seemed to be widely accepted by the educational community and most certainly by the public at large.

Yet unfortunately little empirical research has been conducted to begin to unpack the nature of what is being measured in these tests. Notable exceptions are the work of Tindal and his colleagues in understanding the nature of the Oregon mathematics assessment and instructional variables that influence shifts in test scores. Other examples are the efforts of David Francis and colleagues to begin to understand the construct validity of measures of reading, writing, and oral language development for English-language learners by conducting longitudinal research on students subjected to very different types of educational experiences in the primary grades.

This type of renewed work on construct validity is essential. As Messick (1988) noted: "After all, constructs are the medium of exchange of ideas in scientific and social discourse" (p. 40). Serious examination of the underlying nature of, for example, reading assessments to explore whether they reflect Chall's (1996) stages of reading should be of paramount importance.

As indicated in Table 3.1, some questions that come to mind when studying state assessments are:

- Do data lead to refined theories of teaching and learning?
- Do teachers perceive assessment information as helpful in terms of providing directions for improving classroom instruction?
- Do teachers find test data useful in understanding which students are progressing or failing to progress?

FACE THREE: UNDERSTANDING THE IMPACT OF STATE ASSESSMENTS ON STUDENTS AND THOSE WHO TEACH THEM: EVIDENCE AND CONSEQUENCES

Messick (1988) stated, "if measurement is science, then research on the use of measurements is applied (political) science" (p. 43). As Mehrens noted in his excellent chapter (chap. 6, this volume) on consequential validity, despite widespread discussion of the consequences of high-stakes assessments, there is little serious evidence (Face 3). Because Mehrens covers most of the small body of empirical studies of consequential validity in his chapter, we focus on one very recent empirical study.

Case Study of Performance Assessments in Two States: An Analysis of an Empirical Study of Consequential Validity

The development and use of assessments for system, student, and teacher accountability have occurred at the state level, and in many cases states are expending considerable resources and energy doing exactly what their neighboring states are doing. In some cases, the outcomes look very different despite that many states have very similar goals. It is instructive to begin with examples from two states, both of which played leading roles in the development of performance-based assessments in mathematics.

These were two of the first states to use performance-based assessments to determine eighth graders' knowledge of mathematics. In both states, the intent of the tests was to probe knowledge of mathematics in more depth than a traditional standardized test. Firestone et al (1999) conducted in-depth case studies of the very different experiences of Maine and Maryland.

The mathematics assessments used in 1999 looked very different in the two states. According to Firestone, Fitz, and Broadfoot (1999), there is minimal evidence that either of these two states was assessing what they intended to assess: students' ability to apply mathematical concepts and principles to real-world situations. Their case study helps illuminate how such an unfortunate outcome could emerge.

Although both states use open-ended formats, items are shorter on Maine's test assessment than Maryland's. Maryland's test has much more of the look and feel of the assessments proposed in the older National Council of Teachers of Mathematics (1989) standards, which argued for *radical* reform of mathematics instruction. On Maryland's test, some of the mathematics problems combine mathematics with other school subjects such as science, permitting cross-subject applications.

The most important difference is that the predominant focus on Maine's test is calculating the one best answer to a problem; no credit is given for comparing different methods for calculating a problem or inventing strategies to solve the problem. On Maryland's test, each problem is introduced by a context described in a written introduction, and students must perform several tasks related to the initial information provided. For example, students might need to construct a figure, record data from an observation or experiment, or explain their solutions to a problem. Students are given repeated prompts to provide written justification for their solutions. They are given credit not just for calculating the correct answer, but also for the work they show in arriving at the solution. On Maine's test, this is not the case. All of the problems are strict mathematics problems. In the perspicuity of hindsight, one may conclude that Maine represents the thinking behind the current National Council of Teachers of Mathematics (2000) standards, which balance traditional notions of mathematics. Note how the Firestone et al. (1999) article described underlying theory and operationalization of theory, much as Messick would desire.

Consequences for performance on state tests are more severe for schools in Maryland than in Maine. The primary sanction is school reconstitution—a policy that enables the state to take over schools where performance indicators are low or declining. The state also requires schools to establish school improvement teams that must report annual school development plans with school strategies to improve scores.

Maryland provides more opportunities than Maine for teachers to learn from student performance on the performance-based assessments and improve their teaching. On the Maryland Assessment Consortium, teachers and experts worked together to develop teaching tasks similar to those on the state assessments. Also the state's mathematics academy focused more broadly on mathematics and provided opportunities for teachers to work on ways to align the curriculum with the state's tests. Still relatively few teachers took part in either the consortium or the academy. The heavy security surrounding state assessments limited teachers access to relevant items. This is exactly what Messick would note as an unintended consequence of the new assessment in his Four Faces of Validity. In other words, the high-stakes nature of the assessment precludes teachers' use of sample problems as instructional tools.

The consequences of student performance on Maine's assessments are much less severe. Test scores are published in the newspaper, but there is no parental choice of schools and there is no threat of reconstitution, so their sanction value is limited. The state education department has limited capacity either to devise policy or oversee implementation.

Opportunities for meaningful involvement in teacher professional development to use student performance on the state's mathematics test are few. There is no equivalent to Maryland's Assessment Consortium or mathematics academy. Test security is less stringent, however, so teachers have greater access to example problems from which students could learn. In the Firestone et al. (1999) investigation, only a small percentage of the teachers interviewed said they had ever seen any of the sample items.

Although opportunities for involvement and professional development were greater in Maryland than in Maine (Firestone et al., 1999; Hoff, 2000), the conclusion reached by Firestone and colleagues is discouraging for both states. Results of observations in the classroom and interviews with teachers and administrators suggest that "teachers' basic instructional strategies had not changed" (p. 779). Firestone et al. explained that, although influence of high-stakes testing can lead to "larger, easily documented changes, the amount of learning promoted by these policies has not been sufficient to modify instructional approaches" (p. 779). Examples of easily documented changes were the assessment consortium and mathematics academy in Maryland.

The specifics of mathematics performance assessments in Maryland and Maine illustrate the rather somber conclusion reached by Linn (2000) in his analysis of several waves of educational reforms since World War II involving test use. Linn concluded that each wave of educational reform has relied heavily on assessment and accountability changes as a major focus because (a) it is relatively easy to mandate testing and assessment practices, (b) testing and assessment changes can be rapidly implemented (within the term of an elected official), and (c) test results are visible. The final reason that testing and accountability are in the forefront of this educational reform movements as well, and previous educational reform movements, is that changes in testing and assessment practices are relatively inexpensive to implement. Compared with changes in instructional time, instructional quality, reducing class size, attracting more skilled people to teaching, or providing better professional development for teachers, "assessment is cheap" (Linn, 2000, p. 4).

FACE FOUR: REFLECTIONS ON THE PROCESS OF STUDYING CONSEQUENTIAL VALIDITY

Easily Won Victories

The most common type of evidence reported on state assessments is the extent to which scores in a given state rise after implementation of a comprehensive state assessment system. Unlike data on the previously discussed issues, these data are usually easily available as the state legislature and newspapers eagerly report on improvements due to the state's educational reform program.

Recently, researchers have begun to reflect on—if not study systematically—both the short- and long-term effects of high-stakes assessments. The views and understandings of researchers on this issue were summarized recently in an excellent article by Hoff (2000). Hoff began by noting that, in states such as Washington, which was in its third year of its assessment program, scores rose substantially. But in Maryland, one of the first states to embark on the wave of high-stakes assessment, scores have begun to decline, if only slightly. In pondering the seeming paradox, Hoff noted,

> Both announcements made headlines in their respective states. But the stories could have been written long ago by testing experts. Test scores follow a predictable cycle. . . . They start low, rise quickly for a couple of years, level off for a few more, and then gradually drop over time (p. 1)

To reach his conclusion, Hoff asked several assessment experts to comment about these phenomena and discuss implications. These brief, informal interviews provided some fascinating insights into the consequential validity of high-stakes tests, but also to some potential benefits that have yet to be tapped. They led to the following conclusion:

> Test researchers say scores stagnate or fall because schools do the easy things first and then don't address the other needs. The generous early gains in scores occur because students and teachers become familiar with the tests and their content. . . . Teachers start to tailor their instruction to the exams. (p. 12)

Hoff's conclusion is supported by the Firestone et al. (1999) in-depth case study. They concluded that "assessment policy is useful in promoting easily observable changes but not deep modifications in teaching practice" (p. 359).

Mary Kennedy (1980, 1982) found a similar phenomenon in her research in the early days of mandated Title One assessments. She found that teachers tended to alter the topics covered to be more closely aligned to test content. She noted the major impact of Title One testing was not necessarily improvement in the quality of reading and mathematics instruction, but a shift in the teaching of topics such as fractions or proportions to the grades when they were tested.

During his interview with Hoff, Linn noted that the leveling off occurs because schools fail to make the necessary and costly changes required, such as improvement of the quality of teaching. If, in fact, deep modifications in the nature of instructional practice are desired, then merely implementing a new state assessment system is unlikely to lead to this outcome.

What Are the Intended Consequences of the New Round of State Assessments?

These pessimistic views need to be tempered with the fact that this generation of school reform agents may have learned something from past failures. For example, a representative from one state noted, "The easy things have been done. Now people are really probing" (Hoff, 2000, p. 13). She went on to describe an extensive state initiative involving ongoing assessment of students. Students who seem to be experiencing difficulty will be provided with summer intervention. Large numbers of states are utilizing ongoing assessments to discern which students need additional help in reading in the early grades.

Other states have gone even farther. California and Texas have been leaders in launching major initiatives to improve performance in reading and language arts by providing a wide array of professional development activities for teachers in the early grades. More recently, Texas launched an initiative to improve the nature of math instruction in middle school. This initiative was guided, in large part, by the unacceptably low performance of students on the high school math assessment. All of these initiatives show a more concerted effort than in the past to utilize assessment data to improve the quality of classroom instruction and other educational services provided to students who appear to need help.

Valencia and Wixson (1999) concluded that state assessments seem to consistently influence practice. Yet they noted that the depth of this influence is shaped by local efforts. Spillane and Jennings (1997; cited in Valencia & Wixson, 1999) looked closely at nine teachers' reactions to a new state assessment system in reading. They noted that the state assessment and state standards only seriously influenced classroom practice when they were elaborated by the district. By elaboration, they mean professional development activities, serious analyses of curriculum, development of ongoing assessment of students learning, and other related activities.

One interesting feature worthy of future examination is the purpose of state assessments. Many attempted to use the new state assessment as a means to reshape the way reading, mathematics, and science were taught—toward a more constructivist, child-centered, progressive orientation (Shepard, 2000; Valencia & Wixson, 1999). The Firestone et al. (1999) case study is an example.

Currently we all see signals of a sea change. States such as Texas and California utilize tests that are in no way influenced by theories of contructivism. Their goal, in some cases, is to actively encourage use of research-based practices in beginning reading. In other cases, the goal is to ensure learning of core essential academic skills. In these states, one would—and should—examine consequences of these assessments. Do they in fact lead to greater use of research-based strategies in beginning reading? Do they encourage teachers to spend more time on building foundational academic skills? Most important—and of high national interest   do they help promote equity by translating the message that teachers should have high standards and expectations for all students, rather than lowering standards for students from low-income families or students who are ethnic minorities?

These are pivotal issues for future research. As state databases become more sophisticated and allow for longitudinal tracking of students, we believe such data can become available. Furthermore, we feel there is a need for more research on how teachers use these assessments. When teachers receive information from a screening measure such as those that Maryland is developing and Texas is using, what do they do with this information? Do the majority of teachers feel equipped to translate the ongoing assessment information into specific instructional techniques?

Research by Fuchs et al. (1994) suggests that often this is not the case. Many teachers are uncertain how to utilize this information to provide better instruction for their struggling students. Fuchs and colleagues have generated specific instructional suggestions that accompany the assessment data. By and large, they have found that the combination of ongoing ascent and specific suggestions can lead to enhanced performance. This is a hypothesis well worth studying on a larger scale.

We also believe that there should be serious empirical study of the effectiveness of these various state initiatives. How useful do teachers feel the various state institutes and trainings are? Do these efforts translate into improvements in actual classroom reading and math instruction?

TENSIONS BETWEEN IDEAL PRINCIPLES
AND REAL-WORLD PRACTICES

In Messick's view, it is incumbent on test developers to explain the under-lying theories and assumptions behind their assessment strategies and in-struments; explain how they intend for teachers, administrators, and stu-dents to use them; and document in some manner what are likely to be the benefits of such applications. Increasingly the test developers are state de-partments of education and state legislatures.

This explanation and documentation may be an impossible task. Mc-Donnell (1997; cited in Mehrens, chap. 7, this volume) insightfully ob-served: "The assessments often *embody unresolved value conflicts* about what content should be taught and tested, and who should define that content." It is possible that the perennial eclecticism of standardized assessments may be a benefit that veering too much toward the past and traditional practices or too much toward radical reform may lead to deeply flawed tests. Mc-Donnell's caveat needs to be heeded as we continue to study test validity.

The flood of topics that can and should be studied empirically in the wake of the current wave of state assessments appears to be quite over-whelming. Messick (1988) helped articulate the "tension between ideal principles and real world practices" (p. 34) as the key area for serious re-search and scholarship. In the past, these tensions often have been the source of complaints and disgruntlement for both test experts and practi-tioners. A crucial point that Mehrens makes in his chapter is that if teach-ers do not see any connection between the results on a state assessment and their teaching approach, the assessment system is unlikely to have an impact on instruction.

Currently, there is wide variability in the linkage of assessments to state standards, the comprehensibility of state standards, and the coherence of state standards. If this "fault line" persists, it is likely to become a serious impediment to student learning. The interviews conducted by Hoff (1999) with leading experts in the field (discussed earlier in this chapter) give the reader a sense of the deep cynicism in the field. Viewing these tensions as the source of cutting edge research is an elegant and essential conceptual leap. If tests continue to remain strong only in content validity (i.e., ap-proval by some board of experts and/or consumer panel) and internal consistency reliability, the current state of affairs, the potentials for mis-use, abuse, and disenchantment are high. Yet serious inquiry that looks at validity from all of the four facets that Messick proposed can build deeper understanding of strengths and weaknesses of current practice, and pro-vide detailed information on problems as they arise.

Messick was not clear as to the types of research designs and methodol-ogies that should be used. In his 1988 essay, he reminded us that "the justification and defense of measurement and its validity is and may always be a rhetorical art" (p. 43). He thus views validity as an intellectual pursuit involving (a) well-designed empirical research, (b) a solid grounding in the social and political issues that influence the measurement environment, and (c) relationships among variables and constructs that are elegantly and thoughtfully articulated. Like Messick, we feel that these discussions should be driven by data and research, however difficult and delicate, political and controversial, this line of inquiry is likely to be.

ACKNOWLEDGMENT

The authors wish to thank Larry Irvin for his invaluable feedback on an earlier version of this manuscript.

REFERENCES

Berninger, V. W. (2000). Dyslexia the invisible, treatable disorder: The story of Einstein's Ninja Turtles. *Learning Disabilities Quarterly, 23,* 175–195.

Chall, J. S. (1989). Learning to read: The great debate 20 years later—a response to "Debunking the great phonics myth." *Phi Delta Kappan, 70,* 521–538.

Chall, J. S. (1996). *Stages of reading development* (2nd ed.). Fort Worth, TX: Harcourt Brace.

Cronbach, L. J. (1971). Test validation. In R. L. Thorndike (Ed.), *Educational measurement* (2nd ed., pp. 443–507). Washington, DC: American Council on Education.

Firestone, W. A., Fitz, J., & Broadfoot, P. (1999). Power, learning, and legitimation: Assessment implementation across levels in the United States and the United Kingdom. *American Educational Research Journal, 36*(1), 759–793.

Fuchs, L. S., Fuchs, D., Hamlett, C. L., Phillips, N. B., & Bentz, J. (1994). Classwide curriculum-based measurement: Helping general educators meet the challenge of student diversity. *Exceptional Children, 60,* 518–537.

Gersten, R., Carnine, D., Zoref, L., & Cronin, D. (1986). A multifaceted study of change in seven inner city schools. *Elementary School Journal, 86*(3), 257–276.

Gersten, R., Keating T. J., & Irvin, L. K. (1995). The burden of proof: Validity as improvement of instructional practice. *Exceptional Children, 61,* 510–519.

Gersten, R., & Smith-Johnson, J. (2000). Song of experience: Commentary on "dyslexia the invisible" and "promoting strategic writing by postsecondary students with learning disabilities: A report of three case studies." *Learning Disabilities Quarterly, 23,* 171–174.

Hoff, D. J. (1999, June 16). Made to measure. *Education Week,* pp. 21–25, 26–27.

Hoff, D. J. (2000, January 26). Testing's ups and downs predictable. *Education Week,* pp. 1, 12–14.

Kennedy, M. M. (1980). *Longitudinal information systems in early childhood Title I programs.* Washington, DC: Department of Education.

Kennedy, M. M. (1982). *Working knowledge and other essays.* Cambridge, MA: Huron Institute.

Kerlinger, F. N. (1973). *Foundations of behavioral research* (2nd ed.). New York: Holt, Rinehart & Winston.

Linn, R. L. (2000). Assessments and accountability. *Educational Researcher, 29*(2), 4–16.

Marks, S. U., & Gersten, R. (1998). Understanding engagement and disengagement between special and general educators: An application of Miles and Huberman's cross-case analysis. *Learning Disabilities Quarterly, 21,* 34–56.

Messick, S. (1988). The once and future issues of validity: Assessing the meaning and consequences of measurement. In H. Wainer & H. I. Braun (Eds.), *Test validity* (pp. 33–46). Hillsdale, NJ: Lawrence Erlbaum Associates.

Messick, S. (1989). Validity. In R. L. Linn (Ed.), *Educational measurement* (3rd ed., pp. 13–103). New York: Macmillian.

Messick, S. (1994). The interplay of evidence and consequences in the validation of performance assessments. *Educational Researcher, 23*(2), 13–23.

Messick, S. (1995). Standards of validity and the validity of standards in performance assessment. *Educational Measurement: Issues and Practice, 14*(4), 5–8.

National Council of Teachers of Mathematics. (1989). *Curriculum and evaluation standards for school mathematics*. Reston, VA: Author.

National Council of Teachers of Mathematics. (2000). *Standards 2000 project*. Retrieved February 8, 2001, from the World Wide Web: *http://standards.nctm.org/document/index.htm*.

Olson, L. (2001, January 31). Few states are now in line with Bush testing plan. *Education Week*, pp. 1, 25.

Shepard, L. A. (2000). The role of assessment in a learning culture. *Educational Researcher, 29*(7), 4–14.

Valencia, S. W., & Wixson, K. K. (1999). *Policy-oriented research on literacy standards and assessment* (ERIC Document Reproduction Service No. ED 429 309). Ann Arbor, MI: Center for the Improvement of Early Reading Achievement.

Chapter 4

Variation in Achievement Scores Related to Gender, Item Format, and Content Area Tested

Joseph M. Ryan
Arizona State University West

Sarah DeMark
Arizona State University

Validity is the central issue in evaluating the appropriateness of all forms of assessment and must remain the critical criterion guiding assessment development, applications, and the use of assessment results. The analysis and evaluation of validity, however, has become increasingly complex because of changes in three major areas of educational activity. These major areas include curriculum reform efforts, greater emphasis on constructed-response assessment formats that support the curriculum reforms, and a reconceptualization of validity as a unitary characteristic of assessment organized under the superordinate concept of construct validity.

Among the most important factors and forces that have shaped the current reconsideration and debate of validity are curriculum and assessment reform efforts such as those initiated by the National Council of Teachers of English (NCTE, 1996) and the National Council of Teachers of Mathematics (NCTM, 1989) among others. Early on, NCTE challenged the validity of indirect measures of writing, such as tests of grammar, writing mechanics, and editing tests. NCTE insisted that the valid measurement of students' writing ability required the assessment of actual samples of students' writing performance evaluated against standards or rubrics defining critical characteristics of grade-level expectations for written work. In a similar vein, NCTM contributed the curriculum-broadening view that mathematical ability should refer to rich, comprehensive, and integrated forms of mathematical reasoning and communication and not merely to a set of discrete skills. This shift in the construct definition of mathematics has, of course, important implications for mathematics assessment. The mathematics curriculum shift has refocused mathematics assessment away from discrete and decontextualized computation skills that can easily and appropriately be assessed by selected-response items and toward more integrated and contextualized mathematics knowledge and skills that can most appropriately be assessed by constructed-response performance assessments.

Messick (1989, 1995), among others, has offered a new approach to defining validity and has helped expand the framework within which issues of validity are examined. The traditional measurement perspective generally views validity as an attribute of a test, and it refers to different types of validity, including content, criterion-related, and construct validity (Magnusson, 1966; Nunnally, 1967). The more recent measurement perspective views validity as an attribute of the inferences and conclusions drawn from an assessment and as a unitary feature of an assessment. Messick posited six aspects of validity, all of which he subsumed under the concept of construct validity. Messick's six aspects serve as the basis for collecting different types of evidence for making the overall validity argument. Examples of four of these are noted next. This view appears in most contemporary commentaries on validity and is substantially reflected in the recently published Standards for Educational and Psychological Testing (American Educational Research Association, American Psychology Association, National Council on Measurement in Education, 1999).

Efforts in curriculum reform, emphasis on constructed-response assessment formats, and new views of validity are strongly interconnected. Viewed from Messick's perspective on validity, the case for using constructed-response formats to assess complex, integrated cognitive skills and processes, is supported by pointing out that such assessments (a) are relevant and representative of the construct domain, (b) provide a reasonable basis for making inferences about the processes engaged in by students constructing their work, (c) employ scoring rubrics that embody and reflect the construct domain structures and processes, and (d) have consequences likely to shape instruction to reflect new curricular emphases.

Changes in curriculum, instruction, and assessment formats make it critical to reexamine whether educational tests fairly assess and accurately reflect what students know and are able to do. As Willingham and Cole (1997) pointed out, "Fair test design should provide examinees comparable opportunity, as far as possible, to demonstrate knowledge and skills they have acquired that are relevant to the purpose of the test" (p. 10).

Gender differences represent one of the most carefully scrutinized aspects of test fairness. The pioneering work of Maccoby and Jacklin (1974) reviewed over 1,600 studies and concluded that some gender differences were clear and well established. They concluded that girls tended to have higher levels of performance on tasks measuring verbal ability and boys tended to perform better on tasks measuring quantitative ability. Subsequent meta-analytic studies by Hyde and Linn (1986) and Hyde, Fennema, and Lamon (1990) also found gender differences, but they concluded that the differences were small and varied based on sample characteristics. More recently, Willingham and Cole (1997) also found small and variable gender differences in mathematics and language assessments.

RESEARCH QUESTION

Most of the earlier work examining gender differences occurred prior to the curriculum reform efforts of the late 1980s and 1990s and before the broader adoption of constructed-response assessments. The more extensive use of constructed-response formats in the context of newly defined curricula raises a variety of important validity questions: Do constructed-response formats operationally define curriculum domains that include construct-related or construct-irrelevant sources of variation? Do constructed-response formats reflect verbal comprehension and production abilities that influence all assessments using this format? Are students with superior verbal skills advantaged by the use of constructed-response formats regardless of the content area being assessed?

The research reported in this chapter examines a question related to these issues and to the interaction of several factors that influence conclusions that might be drawn about the validity of an assessment. Specifically, the chapter addresses this question:

> *Does existing research reveal performance differences in the assessment measures of males and females that are related to the assessment format used, the content area tested, or the interactions among students' sex, assessment format, and subject area tested?*

Chapter Overview

We address the question through two related meta-analytic studies of published and presented research. The initial study is broad in scope and is described in detail. It examines 178 effects from 14 studies and includes assessments in language, mathematics, science, and social studies. The second study is an extension of the first and focuses specifically on gender and format differences in language and mathematics assessments. The second study examines 330 effects including many from the first study as well as effects from 23 additional studies. The procedures used in the second study are not described in detail since they are identical to those employed in the initial study. The major results from the second study, presented in summary form, are very similar to those found in the initial study. The second study is described in detail by DeMark (2000).

The assessment formats examined in both studies included constructed-response and selected-response formats. Constructed-response formats included short answer, essay, as well other types of performance assessments; selected-responses included multiple-choice, matching, and true–false items.

STUDY ONE: THE INITIAL INVESTIGATION

Sample Characteristics: Studies and Effects

One hundred and seventy-eight effects found in 14 studies reflecting mean differences between the achievement of females and males were included in the meta-analysis. The selection process focused on studies in which both constructed-response and selected-response formats were used. Many studies reported data on several variables or on subscales of a more global measure, and these data were used to calculate several different effects for each study. Many of the effects from a particular study are based on the same students. Hence, the effects from within the same studies may not be independent. This dependency among the effects within studies could not be accounted for statistically because none of the studies reported the within-group covariance matrix reflecting the relationship among the measures within sex groups.

The individual effects were originally classified based on the assessment format, subject area assessed, country of study, grade level of students, ethnicity (when available), and sample size. Selected characteristics of the studies and their effects are provided here as an overview and framework.

Format and Subject Areas. The assessment formats have been grouped into two categories: constructed-response and selected-response. The effects from each study were originally classified into many different content areas. An initial analysis indicated considerable heterogeneity among the studies, and these findings led to classifying the content of the effects into four groups: language, mathematics, science, and social studies. The number and proportion of effects by format, content, and format-by-content are shown in Table 4.1.

Grade Level and Test Type. The classification of the 178 effects into grade levels is summarized in Table 4.2. The majority of the effects examined in this study were from the high school level and the fewest effect

TABLE 4.1
Study 1: Frequency (and Percentage) of Effects
by Assessment Format and Content Area

	Assessment Format		
Content Area	Constructed Response	Selected Response	Content Frequency
Language	31 (17%)	39 (22%)	70 (39%)
Mathematics	28 (16%)	46 (26%)	74 (42%)
Science	5 (3%)	10 (6%)	15 (9%)
Social studies	8 (4%)	11 (6%)	19 (10%)
Format frequency and percentage	72 (40%)	106 (60%)	178 (100%)

TABLE 4.2
Study 1: Frequency (and Percentage) of Effects by Grade Level

Grade Level	Effects Frequency (%)
Postsecondary	12 (7)
High school	107 (60)
Middle school	34 (19)
Elementary	25 (14)

sizes were from the post-secondary level. The elementary and middle school-level tests were generally administered as part of a statewide testing program. The high school tests included standardized tests such as the Advanced Placement (AP) tests, the Iowa Test of Educational Development (ITED; part of the Iowa testing programs reported in Etsey, 1996), and the General Certificate of Education (GCE) examinations of the Associated Examining Board (AEB; Murphy, 1982). The postsecondary test was the Graduate Management Admission Test (GMAT).

Other Characteristics of the Studies/Effects. The studies varied considerably in sample sizes, ranging from 44 to 50,280 students. The mean number of females in the studies was 4,106 and the standard deviation for the number of females used to calculate the effect sizes was 4,412. The mean number of males in the studies was 4,445 and the standard deviation for the number of males used to calculate the effect sizes was 5,102. Later this chapter addresses the implications of these very large sample sizes and the resulting applicability of various parametric statistical procedures.

Only 12 of the 178 effects were based on ethnic minority students. These were all in the study of Bridgeman and McHale (1997). The studies of Murphy (1982) and Wood (1978) were conducted in England, and the study of Bolger and Kellaghan (1990) was conducted in Ireland.

Statistical Procedures

The procedures described by Hedges and Olkin (1985) were used in conducting the meta-analysis. Effect size was estimated using the d statistic, an unbiased estimate weighted for sample size. The mean performance of females was subtracted from the mean performance of males (male–female). Consequently, positive effect sizes indicate higher performance by males and negative effect sizes indicate higher performance by females. Homogeneity of effects was examined via the Q statistic and also visually, as demonstrated by Hedges and Olkin. Studies were included if they reported sufficient information for calculating effect sizes for male–female mean differences. The information required included group means, standard deviations, and sample sizes.

The interpretation of the effect size magnitudes employed the commonly used criteria of Cohen (1988, 1992), who classified effect sizes of .20 as small, .40 as medium, and .70 as large. In addition, the effect size magnitudes were also interpreted in terms of impact and consequential validity.

Results

Results of the meta-analysis are presented in three sections. First, the homogeneity of the effect sizes is described. Second, the major findings related to the investigation of gender and format research questions are presented. Third, a brief discussion of effect sizes that appear to be outliers or are of special interest is presented.

Homogeneity of Effect Sizes. The first step in the analysis was to determine whether the effects in various content and format categories should be pooled. Pooling the effects assumes that they are reasonably homogeneous. The Q statistic testing the homogeneity of the 178 effects was 14,415. This exceeds the chi-square critical value (approximately 212), indicating that the effects are not homogeneous.

Next, the effects were grouped by format to determine if the effect sizes were homogeneous within format category. The Q statistics for the constructed-response and selected-response effect sizes are 5,212 (df = 71) and 7,001 (df = 105), respectively. These results indicate that the effect sizes are not homogeneous within format category.

The homogeneity of effect sizes for different content areas was examined by classifying the effects into one of the four broad content areas of language (70 effects), mathematics (74 effects), science (15 effects), and social studies (19 effects). For language, the Q statistic was 3,946; for mathematics, 1,726; for science, 386; and for social studies, 2,296. Each of these values exceeds the critical value for the null case, indicating that the effect sizes are not homogeneous.

The final analysis disaggregated the data into a 2 × 4 structure with two levels of format and four content areas. This design is shown in Table 4.3 along with the number of effects and the Q statistic for each cell. These results also show a relatively high degree of heterogeneity.

The Q statistics reported in Table 4.3 are still quite large compared with their respective critical values. Advice offered by Hedges and Olkin (1985) seems to apply to the interpretation of these statistics:

> When the sample size is *very* large, however, it is worth studying the variation in the values of d_i, since rather small differences may lead to large values of the test statistic. If the d_i do not differ much in the absolute sense, the investigator may elect to pool the estimates even though there is reason to believe that the underlying parameters are not identical. (p. 123)

Hedges and Olkin did not operationally define *very large*, but many of the sample sizes in this study would seem to qualify because they exceed 1,000, and several even exceed 10,000. The heterogeneity reflected in the Q statistics reflects the very large samples used in the various studies. The sample size is a denominator in the estimation of the Q statistic, and thus Q increases as a function of sample size. This situation is an instance of a typical problem with parametric statistics. They become overly powerful with large sample sizes and lead to conclusions of statistical significance, or, in this case, effect size heterogeneity, when the differences may not be critical when viewed from a practical perspective. Discussion of the major findings will proceed by focusing on the results when the effects are pooled in the format-by-content framework. Because of the heterogeneity of the effects, nonparametric indexes including the median and interquartile range were employed. The results are presented next.

Major Findings. The major findings of this initial study are presented first with a simplified view based on group statistics, followed by a more comprehensive view, looking at the data more broadly. The medians and

TABLE 4.3
Study 1: Number of Effects (k) and Q Statistic
for Each Format-by-Content Combination

Content Area	Constructed Response		Selected Response	
	k	Q	k	Q
Language	31	768.23	39	2252.27
Mathematics	28	860.99	46	674.87
Science	5	29.19	10	320.67
Social studies	8	394.39	11	1335.08

TABLE 4.4
Study 1: Effect Size Median and Interquartile
Range by Format and Content

Content Area	Constructed-Response		Selected-Response	
	Median	Interquartile Range	Median	Interquartile Range
Language	−0.25	0.18	−0.10	0.26
Mathematics	−0.02	0.15	0.08	0.15
Science	0.05	0.12	0.09	0.36
Social studies	−0.03	0.17	0.14	0.52

interquartile ranges for the effect sizes in the format-by-content framework are shown in Table 4.4. The results show relatively modest effect sizes
in all categories. Only the median effect size of −.25, found for constructed-
response assessments in language, would be considered as even reaching
the small criterion of .20 as defined by Cohen (1988, 1992). To be sure,
some variability in the distribution of the effect sizes exists, but the most obvious result in these data is that, in general, the effect sizes for the difference
between female and male students related to assessment format and content are quite small. These results can also be examined graphically in the
graph and box plot displayed in Figs. 4.1 and 4.2, respectively.

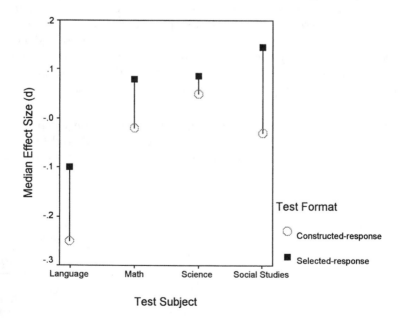

FIG. 4.1.   Median effect sizes for assessment formats within content area.

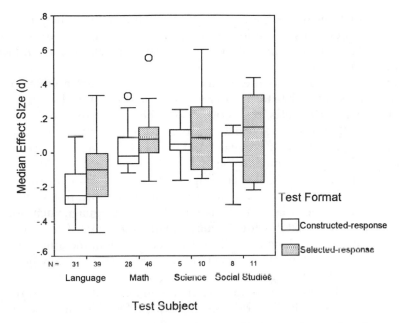

FIG. 4.2. Box plots for effect sizes for content areas and assessment formats.

As mentioned earlier, the effect sizes are all calculated as boys' performance minus girls' performance, therefore positive values indicate higher achievement by boys compared with girls and negative values reflect lower achievement by boys. Figure 4.1 shows that boys have lower achievement in language measures, especially on constructed-response assessments. Boys outperform girls on selected-response social studies assessments, and all other differences are relatively small. The data displayed in Fig. 4.2 reveal several important findings. The median effect size is shown by the solid line in each box. The median effect sizes are all around the value of 0, except for language constructed-response. The area of the box represents the interquartile range, and these ranges clearly overlap for the mathematics, science, and social studies effect size ranges for both formats. The variability of effect sizes in science selected-response and social studies selected-response effect sizes is relatively large as indicated by the broader interquartile ranges. The comparison of effects due to format within content area can also be seen in Fig. 4.2. In all cases, there is little difference in the effect sizes as a function of assessment format, and the interquartile ranges overlap considerably. The data in Table 4.4 and illustrated in Fig. 4.2 show that males score slightly higher than females using the selected-response format compared with the relative performance of males and females using the constructed-response format. Note carefully, however, that females outperform males in both language categories and in mathematics and social studies when constructed-response assessments are used. Most of the format effect size differences are about one tenth of a standard deviation.

A more detailed view of the results focuses on language and mathematics effect sizes only. The effect sizes for science and social studies are based on only 15 and 19 effects, respectively, and the effect sizes for these content areas reflect considerable heterogeneity within assessment format category. The effect sizes for language and mathematics can be represented visually in box plots shown in Fig. 4.3.

Several features of Fig. 4.3 are important to note. Many of the effect sizes, especially in mathematics, hover around zero, indicating very small male–female differences. The variability for the language measures is greater than the variability for the mathematics measures. The variability for selected-response language effect sizes is larger than the other categories of language and mathematics effect sizes. Females generally perform better than males on language measures regardless of assessment format; males generally perform better than females on mathematics measures regardless of format. All of the differences between females and males, however, are relatively small.

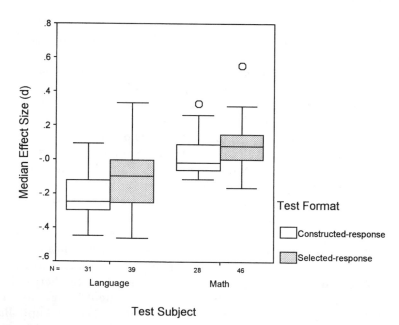

FIG. 4.3. Box plots for effect sizes for language and mathematics by assessment format.

Outliers and Special Cases. An examination of the two box plots for the mathematics effect sizes reveals two circles outside of the whiskers. These represent two outliers in mathematics with effect sizes well beyond the limits of the whiskers. Both of the outliers in mathematics are from the study performed in Ireland (Bolger & Kellaghan, 1990) and reflect males outperforming females at an unusually high level relative to all the other effect sizes.

The extreme cases were also examined in the box plots representing language effect sizes. There were no effect size outliers in the statistical sense. Both of the language box plots, however, appeared to be stretched at the whiskers in the positive direction. The direction of these results reflects a study in which males had higher achievement levels than females. Both of the extreme cases for constructed-response and selected-response formats in language were derived from the Asian/Asian-American samples from the only study reporting desegregated ethnic minority data (Bridgeman & McHale, 1997).

Several methodological issues need to be considered before discussing the substantive results of this study. First, it is important to recall the limitations of this study. The study reviews 178 effect sizes, but these come from 14 research investigations. As mentioned earlier, there may be a certain dependency between effect sizes within study because some of them are based on the same students. Additional effect sizes from other studies need to be added to the meta-analysis to increase the generalizability of the results. The study focused on research that included both constructed-response and selected-response measures. Other studies that report gender differences based on both types of measures need to be included, and studies reporting gender differences for either constructed-response or selected-response measures should be examined as well. It is also important to note that most of the effects come from studies of high school students. The results may be different if a proportionally larger sample of effects based on elementary school children is included.

Within categories that appeared relatively homogeneous based on the category definition (e.g., language or mathematics), the effect sizes had Q statistics indicating statistically significant heterogeneity. However, these results are due directly to the statistical power of large sample sizes. Statistical tests of relatively small differences in the mean performance of females and males also appear significant with sample sizes of thousands. This observation merely reminds us that caution must be exercised in focusing on statistical significance without examining the practical meaning in the magnitude of the differences.

A major value of meta-analysis is that it provides a broader description of the overall trends in a general body of research. That the effect sizes are heterogeneous within content and format categories is an important part of the description of the overall trends in the body of research results examined in this study.

STUDY TWO: LANGUAGE AND MATHEMATICS IN MORE DETAIL

The results of a second meta-analytic study are used in this chapter to extend the investigation of gender differences in language and mathematics assessments. The characteristics of the studies selected for inclusion in the second study are described, and a summary of the major results is presented.

Sample Characteristics: Studies and Effects

The second study focused on gender differences in language and mathematics. Studies were included if they: (a) employed assessments in verbal or quantitative knowledge, skills, and abilities; (b) were based on samples from the United States; (c) were published in English; (d) included students in kindergarten to grade 12 only; and (e) had been published after 1994 (even if the assessment was completed prior to that year).

A detailed search that applied these criteria to a wide range of databases led to the identification of 31 studies and 330 effects. Of these, 7 studies and 121 effects had been included in the initial meta-analysis reported in Study 1. Sample sizes varied considerably, ranging from 80 students to hundreds of thousands of students taking American College Testing (ACT) assessments and the Scholastic Assessment Test (SAT). Language assessments included reading, writing, literature, vocabulary, locating information, and general language. Mathematics assessments included arithmetic, algebra, geometry, measurement, data analysis, problem solving, and general mathematics.

Methodological Procedures

Like the first study, methodological procedures used in the second study are based on Hedges and Olkin (1985).

Results

The Q statistic testing for heterogeneity of effect sizes indicated considerable heterogeneity, as would be expected given the very large sample sizes. Following the rationale presented in the initial meta-analysis, the in-

TABLE 4.5
Study 2: Effect Size Median and Interquartile
Range by Format and Content

	Constructed Response		Selected Response	
Content Area	Median	Interquartile Range	Median	Interquartile Range
Language	−0.30	0.23	−0.02	0.17
Mathematics	−0.18	0.38	0.06	0.13

vestigation proceeded with the examination of the effects by gender and content area.

Major results of the study are shown in Table 4.5, with the effect size medians and interquartile ranges by assessment format for language and mathematics. These results are quite similar to those of the initial study (not surprising because more than 30% of the effects are from the first study). The results show that the typical effect size for selected-response formats in both language and mathematics is very close to zero.

The mathematics constructed-response median effect size is −.18. This shows that girls are typically outperforming boys in mathematics when students actually have to construct their responses on mathematics assessments. The effect size of −.18 almost reaches Cohen's small effect size category and approaches one fifth of a standard deviation. It is useful to note that the variability for the mathematics constructed-response effects, as reflected in the interquartile range, is quite large and clearly overlaps with zero.

The median effect size is −.30 for constructed-response assessments of language skills and abilities. This shows that girls are typically, by about one third of a standard deviation, outperforming boys on assessments related to language skills and abilities when the assessment format requires students to construct their responses. The effect size of −.30 is in the middle of Cohen's small effect size category. The variability for the language constructed-response effects as reflected in the interquartile range is .23, which does not quite overlap with zero.

DISCUSSION OF FINDINGS

The results of the two meta-analytic studies reported in this chapter show several important findings. First, the analyses reveal relatively little difference between the achievement of males and females across a very large number of studies and effects. The effect sizes in science, social studies, and mathematics do not reach the .20 criterion used to identify a small effect. In these content areas, the body of research results combined in the meta-analyses does not reveal any large or major differences in the achievement of boys and girls in general.

The analysis of students' achievement in language assessments presents a more complicated picture. The effect sizes of −.25 and −.30 in the initial and follow-up meta analyses, respectively, suggest that females are outperforming males on language assessments if the constructed-response format is employed. These results substantially reflect gender differences in scores of writing performance assessments. Females are outperforming males when samples of their writing are reviewed and rated, but not when students' language skills are scored based on their selecting responses from a set of options. Thus, the gender differences seem to be influenced by assessment format.

The difference of one quarter to one third of a standard deviation falls into the small category of Cohen's classification system. A difference of one quarter to one third of a standard deviation, however, could translate into one, two, or possibly even three score points. Even one or two score points could result in a noticeable difference in the percentage of boys who do not reach the cut score on a high-stakes test. For example, in a normal distribution of students' scores, approximately 10% of the students fall between the mean and one quarter of a standard deviation above or below the mean.

The possibility that gender differences vary based on assessment format is a problematic finding for two reasons. First, it raises the possibility of assessment bias related to assessment format. However, if the assessments are valid for males and females, the second problematic possibility is that boys and girls are not receiving equally effective writing instruction.

The critical factor to examine in this context is the construct that the assessments are designed to measure. Learning to write is a critical learning goal, and the construct domain *writing* refers to a complex, integrated body of knowledge and set of skills that are combined to produce written text. The evaluation of the written text is almost certainly an inherently valid way to look at the writing construct domain and to make inferences about the process students engaged in to produce written work. Selected-response formats simply may not measure all aspects of the construct domain. Additionally, selected-response formats may provide information about many aspects of the construct writing, but do so by evaluating them separately and therefore do not assess the writing process that integrates the various components.

If performance assessments of written work seem to be valid, then another explanation for the gender differences may be differential school experiences. It would be important to know if there are curriculum materials or instructional practices that somehow favor girls during the early years when they are developing the basic language skills of reading and writing. Any such materials and practices would result in differential opportunity to learn and would need to be corrected.

Finally, broader socialization dynamics must also be recognized as influencing gender differences in children's writing. There are certainly some reasons to believe that the activities and games that girls may be encouraged to pursue and come to prefer contrast to those of boys and could give them more writing practice and advice about writing quite apart from what is taught in school.

Format Effect and the Influence of Verbal Skills

The prior discussion focuses on the finding that females outperformed males on constructed-response language assessments with an effect size of $-.30$. This is in contrast to the effect size of $-.02$ on selected-response language assessments. A somewhat similar trend was observed in constructed-response mathematics assessments with an effect size of $-.18$. The effect size for selected-response mathematics was $+.06$. The differences between the effects for constructed- versus selected-response mathematics assessments again suggest the possibility of a format difference.

A number of the discussions offered by the authors of the studies used in the meta-analyses suggest that effects due to assessment format may reflect the influence of verbal skills required for constructed-responses. Constructed-response assessments require verbal ability to read, comprehend, process, and produce. Verbal ability is needed in all constructed-response assessments regardless of the content area being assessed. The influence of language ability on constructed-response assessments creates a validity problem when such assessments are used in science, mathematics, and other areas, where students' content-specific knowledge and abilities may be confounded by their verbal skills.

The review of this question has led to the development of a four-category framework for examining validity in the context of the influence that language ability might play in constructed-response assessments. This framework explores how the interaction of assessment format and the nature of the construct being measured can inform our understanding of validity and focuses specifically on the influence of verbal ability in constructed-response. The conceptual issues being investigated are whether the verbal abilities needed for constructed-response formats validly reflect the construct domain being measured or whether these verbal abilities reflect a construct-irrelevant source of variation. The four categories in this framework include assessments in which verbal knowledge, abilities, and processes are

1. the constructs being measured;
2. an integral part of the construct being measured;
3. correlated to the construct, but are not necessarily part of it; and
4. uncorrelated to the construct being measured.

The first category is most obviously exemplified by the assessment of writing ability using a constructed-response format. In such cases, the construct of interest is the students' ability to construct a written piece, and therefore the use of the constructed-response format seems inherently valid. Certain other performance measures might also be put in this category if the actual construction of the response is the process of interest (e.g., public speaking).

The second category reflects measurement situations in which verbal ability is an integral part of the construct of interest. Breland, Danos, Kahn, Kubota, and Bonner (1994) provided a useful example from the Advanced Placement (AP) history test. In one part of this test, students are required to read historical documents and write an analysis of what they mean when considered as a group. The task clearly requires verbal ability in reading and comprehending the material, in synthesizing their common meaning, and in writing a response. This is an example of a history test that requires verbal ability and also reflects a process in which historical researchers are frequently engaged. Verbal ability is an integral part of the construct being measured, and its influence on students' achievement reflects a valid source of variation. Other examples of measures in this category might include the ability to write a report of a scientific investigation or on the results of a meta-analysis.

The third category of measures includes situations in which verbal ability is correlated to the construct of interest but is not an integral part of it. This could include a wide range of measures related to knowledge of facts, concepts, principles, and procedures; the comprehensive understanding of concepts, principles, and procedures; and the ability to apply concepts to the analysis of problems and complex tasks. Assessments in this category can be designed to minimize or remove the variance introduced by students' verbal abilities. Also assessments can be designed to allow students' verbal abilities to play a role in the measurement process. The influence of verbal ability on the validity of the measurement depends on how the curriculum outcomes or targets are defined. A case can be made for articulating curriculum outcomes for students' knowledge and abilities in such subjects as mathematics, science, and social studies removing the role of verbal ability. In such situations, the influence of verbal ability would represent a source of construct-irrelevant assessment variation. At the same time, a case can be made for describing curriculum outcomes in these content areas in the context of grade level- or age level-appropriate verbal abilities. In this case, verbal ability is part of the intended outcome and targeted construct, and its influence does not diminish the validity of the measure. The National Council of Teachers of Mathematics, for example, views communicating mathematically as an important learning outcome. Quite clearly, verbal ability is an important component of this mathematics learning outcome.

The final category in this framework refers to measurement situations in which verbal abilities are uncorrelated to the construct being measured. This might include such abilities as mathematics computation, mathematics done in purely symbolic systems, certain aspects of chemistry and other sciences, and possibly musical and artistic performances. The validity of such assessments is diminished if verbal ability plays a role in their measures.

SUMMARY

In this chapter, we answered this question:

> *Does existing research reveal differences in the achievement measures of males and females that are related to the assessment format used, the content area tested, or the interactions among students' sex, assessment format, and subject area tested?*

The results of the analyses show little or no influence due exclusively to assessment format. They did show small but potentially important differences on language-related measures using constructed responses. Females outperform males on such assessments. An analysis of outliers and extreme cases suggests that effect sizes may be influenced by cultural and/or ethnic group differences. A four-category model for discussing the influence of verbal ability on assessment validity suggests two categories in which verbal ability is the construct or an integral part of the construct being measured, and a third category in which verbal ability might play a valid role. Verbal ability seems to be a possible source of construct-irrelevant variance only when the curriculum goal reflects an outcome inherently unrelated to verbal ability.

Females appear to have modestly higher levels of achievement compared with males on language-related measures. These differences are unlikely to be a reflection of format artifacts and are more likely to reflect influences related to instruction and socialization. These differences are not large, but the difference between females and males on constructed-response language assessments should be a matter of concern because they reveal a circumstance in which boys seem to be disadvantaged in the vitally important area of language.

IMPLICATIONS

The research reported in this chapter has important implications for those involved in test development, for educators and policymakers who interpret and use test results, and for curriculum leaders and classroom teachers responsible for helping students learn the essential life skill of writing. The critical issue for all those involved in the assessment process remains the central concern for validity.

In an effort to build validity into the assessment, test developers must carefully define the assessment purpose, the construct the assessment is designed to measure, and the role of language in the assessment. Messick (1995) spoke directly to these issues when he discussed the need to specify the boundaries and structures of the construct domain and the need to clearly describe the interrelationships among the elements in the domain. The design of validity studies and procedures for collecting validity evidence requires a clear understanding of the assessment intent and of the construct domain the assessment is designed to measure. The potential consequences of language ability on students' constructed-response assessment results must be taken into account during the assessment development process. The influence of language can enhance or diminish validity depending on the assessment intent and the construct to be measured. The classification system presented in this chapter suggests that language may be the focus of the measurement, an integral part of it, merely correlated to it, or unrelated to what is being measured. It is essential that the role that language ability plays in an assessment is intentional and valuable and not unanticipated or detrimental.

Practitioners, including parents, educators, and policymakers, must also clearly understand the role that language is intended to play and may play unintentionally in the assessment process. Educators must be very careful in determining whether the influence of language enhances or diminishes the validity of conclusions about what students know and are able to do. This is especially critical in bilingual settings and settings with a large number of English language learners. The use of language-influenced constructed-response formats in such settings needs to be reviewed carefully.

Finally, educators should be concerned about and respond to the weakness boys seem to have in written language. Writing is an essential part of school and also of life, and the data examined in this study suggest that boys seem to be disadvantaged in this critical academic and life skill area. Socialization factors may contribute to the differences in the writing skills of boys and girls. If so, schools must be all the more responsive to boys' needs for effective writing instruction that might have to compensate for socialization influences.

A wide range of issues has been raised about group differences in achievement, assessment formats, and assessment in various content areas. However, the single most important lesson of this chapter is that validity is the central criterion when evaluating the appropriateness of all forms of assessment, and it must remain so, guiding assessment development, applications, and the use of assessment results.

REFERENCES

* Indicates sources included in Study 1
** Indicates sources used in Study 2
*** Indicates sources used in Studies 1 and 2

American Educational Research Association, American Psychological Association, National Council on Measurement in Education. (1999). *Standards for educational and psychological testing*. Washington: DC: American Psychological Association.

***Bell, R. C., & Hay, J. A. (1987). Differences and biases in English language examination formats. *British Journal of Educational Psychology, 57*, 212–230.

*Benson, J., & Cocker, L. (1979). The effects of item format and reading ability on objective test performance: A question of validity. *Educational and Psychological Measurement, 39*, 381–387.

***Bielinski, J., & Davison, M. L. (1997, March). *Gender differences by item difficulty interactions in multiple-choice mathematics items*. Paper presented at the annual meeting of National Council of Measurement in Education, Chicago, IL.

*Bolger, N., & Kellaghan, T. (1990). Method of measurement and gender differences in scholastic achievement. *Journal of Educational Measurement, 27*, 165–174.

*Breland, H. M., Danos, D. O., Kahn, H. D., Kubota, M. Y., & Bonner, M. W. (1994). Performance versus objective testing and gender. An exploratory study of an advanced placement history examination. *Journal of Educational Measurement, 31*, 275–293.

*Bridgeman, B. (1988). *Comparative validity of multiple-choice and free response advanced placement biology items*. Princeton, NJ: Educational Testing Service.

***Bridgeman, B., & McHale, F. J. (1997, March). *Potential impact of the addition of a writing assessment on admissions decisions*. Paper presented at the annual meeting of the National Council on Measurement in Education, Chicago, IL.

**Campbell, J. R. (1996). *NAEP 1994 Reading Report Card for the nation and the states: Findings from the National Assessment of Educational Progress and Trial State Assessment* (ERIC Document Reproduction Service No. ED 402 356).

Cohen, J. (1988). *Statistical power analysis for the behavioral sciences* (2nd ed.). Hillsdale, NJ: Lawrence Erlbaum Associates.

Cohen, J. (1992). Statistical power analysis. *Current directions in psychological science, 1*(3), 98–101.

DeMark, S. F. (2000). *A meta-analytic review of gender differences in test subject and test format*. Unpublished master's thesis, Arizona State University, Tempe, AZ.

**DeMars, C. E. (1998). Gender differences in mathematics and science on a high school proficiency exam: The role of response format. *Applied Measurement in Education, 11*(3), 279–299.

**Du, Y. (1996). *Differential facet functioning detection in direct writing assessment* (ERIC Document Reproduction Service No. ED 400 293).

***Etsey, Y. K. (1996, April). *Gender differences in guessing tendencies on multiple-choice tests*. Paper presented at the annual meeting of the American Educational Research Association, New York, NY.

**Fan, X. T., Chen, M., & Matsumoto, A. R. (1997). Gender differences in mathematics achievement: Findings from the National Educational Longitudinal Study of 1988. *Journal of Experimental Education, 65*(3), 229–242.

***Garner, M. L., & Engelhard, G. (1996, April). *Gender differences in performance on multiple-choice and constructed response mathematics items*. Paper presented at the annual meeting of American Educational Research Association, New York, NY.

*Hanna, G. (1986). Sex differences in mathematics achievement of eighth graders in Ontario. *Journal of Research in Mathematics Education, 17*, 231–237.

*Harding, J. (1980). Sex differences in performance on science examinations. In R. Deem (Ed.), *Schooling for women's work* (pp. 87–97). London: Routledge & Kegan Paul.

**Hedges, L. V., & Nowell, A. (1995). Sex differences in mental test scores, variability, and numbers of high-scoring individuals. *Science, 269*, 41–45.

Hedges, L. V., & Olkin, I. (1985). *Statistical methods for meta-analysis*. Orlando, FL: Academic Press.

Hyde, J. S., Fennema, E., & Lamon, S. J. (1990). Gender differences in mathematics performance: A meta-analysis. *Psychological Bulletin, 107*, 139–155.

***Hyde, J. S., & Linn, M. C. (Eds.). (1986). *The psychology of gender: Advances through meta-analysis*. Baltimore: Johns Hopkins University Press.

**Knudson, R. E. (1995). Writing experiences, attitudes, and achievement of first to sixth graders. *Journal of Educational Research, 89*(2), 90–97.

**Langer, J. A. (1995). *Reading assessment redesigned: Authentic texts ans innovative instruments in NAEP's 1992 survey* (ERIC Document Reproduction Service No. 378 548).

Maccoby, E. E., & Jacklin, C. N. (1974). *The psychology of sex differences*. Stanford, CA: Stanford University Press.

Magnusson, D. (1966). *Test theory*. Reading, MA: Addison-Wesley.

**March, C. C. (1998). The effect of age at entrance to school on academic success in reading and mathematics. *Dissertation Abstracts International, 59*, 0123.

**Marsh, H. W., & Yeung, A. S. (1998). Longitudinal structural equation models of academic self-concept and achievement: Gender differences in the development of math and English constructs. *American Educational Research Journal, 35*(4), 705–738.

Messick, S. (1989). Validity. In R. L. Linn (Ed.), *Educational measurement* (3rd ed., pp. 13–104). New York: American Council on Education and Macmillan.

Messick, S. (1995). Validity of psychological assessments: Validation of inferences from person's responses and performance as scientific inquiry into score meaning. *American Psychologist, 50*, 741–749.

**Muller, C. (1998). Gender differences in parental involvement in adolescents' mathematics achievement. *Sociology of Education, 71*(4), 336–365.

*Murphy, R. J. L. (1982). Sex differences in objective test performance. *British Journal of Educational Psychology, 52*, 213–219.

***Myerberg, N. J. (1996, April). *Performance on different test types by racial/ethnic group and gender*. Paper presented at the annual meeting of the American Educational Research Association, New York, NY.

National Council of Teachers of English. (1996). *Standards for English language arts*. Urbana, IL: Author.

National Council of Teachers of Mathematics. (1989). *Curriculum and evaluation standards for school mathematics*. Reston, VA: Author.

Nunnally, J. C. (1967). *Psychometric theory*. New York: McGraw-Hill.

**Pajares, F., & Graham, L. (1999). Self-efficacy, motivation constructs, and mathematics performance of entering middle school students. *Contemporary Educational Psychology, 24*(2), 124–139.

**Pajares, F., & Johnson, M. J. (1996). Self-efficacy beliefs and the writing performance of entering high school students. *Psychology in the Schools, 33*(2), 163–175.

**Pajares, F., & Kranzler, J. (1995). Self-efficacy beliefs and general mental ability in mathematical problem-solving. *Contemporary Educational Psychology, 20*(4), 426–443.

**Pajares, F., & Miller, M. D. (1997). Mathematics self-efficacy and mathematical problem solving: Implications of using different forms of assessment. *Journal of Experimental Education, 65*(3), 213–228.

**Pajares, F., & Valante, G. (1996). *Predictive utility and causal influence of the writing self-efficacy beliefs of elementary students* (ERIC Document Reproduction Service No. ED 394 144).

**Park, H. S., Bauer, S. C., & Sullivan, L. M. (1998). Gender differences among top performing elementary school students in mathematical ability. *Journal of Research and Development in Education, 31*(3), 133–141.

***Pomplun, M., Sundbye, N., & Kelley, J. (1996). *Open-ended and objective assessment formats: Why are there gender score differences?* Center for Educational Testing and Evaluation University of Kansas by the Kansas State Board of Education.

**Pomplun, M., & Sundbye, N. (1999). Gender differences in constructed response reading items. *Applied Measurement in Education, 12*(1), 95–109.

***Power, D. E., Fowles, M. E., Farnum, M., & Ramsey, P. (1994). Will they think less of my handwritten essay if others word process theirs? Effects on essay scores of intermingling handwritten and word-processed essays. *Journal of Educational Measurement, 21*, 220–233.

*Pressly, M., & Ghatala, E. S. (1988). Delusions about performance on multiple-choice comprehension tests. *Reading Research Quarterly, 23*, 454–464.

**Robinson, N. M., Abbott, R. D., Berninger, V. W., & Busse, J. (1996). The structure of abilities in math-precocious young children: Gender similarities and differences. *Journal of Educational Measurement, 88*(2), 341–352.

***Rowley, G. L. (1974). Which examinees are most favored by the use of multiple-choice tests? *Journal of Educational Measurement, 11*, 15–23.

***Ryan, J., Franz, S., Haladyna, T., & Hammond, D. (1997, December). *Substantive and psychometric relationships among reading, writing, and mathematics achievement with analyses of gender and format by gender differences.* Technical report, Oregon Department of Education.

**Ryan, K. E., & Fan, M. (1996). Examining gender DIF on a multiple-choice test of mathematics: A confirmatory approach. *Educational Measurement: Issues and Practice, 15*(4), 15–20.

*Scheuneman, J. D., Clyman, S. G., & Fan, Y. V. (1997, March). *An evaluation of gender differences in computer-based case simulations.* Paper presented at the annual meeting of the National Council on Measurement in Education, Chicago, IL.

***Schmitt, S. E., Mazzeo, J., & Bleistein, C. (1991, April). *Are gender differences between Advances Placement multiple-choice and constructed response sections a function of multiple-choice DIF?* Paper presented at the annual meeting of the National Council on Measurement in Education, Chicago, IL.

***Smith, S. E., & Walker, W. J. (1988). Sex differences in New York Sate Regents examinations: Support for the differential course-taking hypothesis. *Journal for Research in Mathematics Education, 19*, 81–85.

**Strong, S., & Sexton, L. C. (1997). Kentucky performance assessment of mathematics: Do the numbers add up? *Journal of Instructional Psychology, 24*(3), 202–206.

**Stumpf, H., & Stanley, J. C. (1996). Gender-related differences on the College Board's Advanced Placement and Achievement Tests, 1982–1992. *Journal of Educational Psychology, 88*(2), 353–364.

**Tissot, S. L. (1997). An examination of ethnic variation in gender differences in mathematics attitudes and performance. *Dissertation Abstracts International, 58,* 2158.

**Trapp, C. M. (1995). *The effects of school entry age and gender on reading achievement scores of second grade students* (ERIC Document Reproduction Service No. ED 379 633).

**Willingham, W. W., & Cole, N. S. (1997). *Gender and fair assessment.* Mahwah, NJ: Lawrence Erlbaum Associates.

**Willingham, W. W., & Johnson L. (1997). *Supplement to gender and fair assessment* (ETS RR-97-1). Princeton, NJ: Educational Testing Service.

*Wood, R. (1976). Sex differences in mathematics attainment at GCE ordinary level. *Educational Studies, 2,* 141–160.

*Wood, R. (1978). Sex differences in answers to English language comprehension items. *Educational Studies, 4,* 157–165.

Chapter 5

Supporting Documentation: Assuring More Valid Test Score Interpretations and Uses

Thomas M. Haladyna
Arizona State University West

We develop large-scale assessment programs for various purposes. Some of these purposes involve high-stakes consequences for the test takers. Such tests influence promotion, graduation, certification, licensure, selection, or college admissions. Other uses of achievement test scores are more benign. Some examples are where test scores are used for curriculum evaluation or diagnosis of student learning of various aspects of a subject matter.

According to the *Standards for Educational and Psychological Testing* (AERA, APA, NCME, 1999), testing programs have an obligation to communicate with their constituency about the purpose of the test and the validity of test score interpretations and uses. This constituency may be the public, congressional or state legislators, school boards, professional certification and licensing board members, parents, students, and the public.

Supporting documentation plays an essential role in validating a test score interpretation or use. Supporting documentation is a continuous process of planning, collecting, organizing, and archiving information that satisfies this need to know about the validity of test score interpretation and use. Supporting documentation refers to specific documents, such as manuals, reports, press releases, plans, legislation, student or candidate study guides or handbooks, research studies, or web pages dedicated to sharing information about the testing program. Supporting documentation also can refer to processes, procedures, and policies that may exist in paper or electronic forms and housed in the archives of the test sponsor or its contracted provider of testing services. Thus, supporting documentation is a means toward an end, and that end is validity.

The purpose of this chapter is to expand the idea of supporting documentation, showing its vital link to validity and to the *Standards* (AERA, APA, NCME, 1999). By valuing technical documentation and providing it, we serve our constituencies in many important ways. Because validity and technical documentation are interwoven, the next two sections discuss two central aspects of validity: interpretation and use of tests scores as an introduction to the process of supporting documentation.

INTERPRETATIONS OF TEST SCORES

The focus of this book has been primarily measurement of student achievement from an implicit or explicit set of content standards or curriculum framework. We can also consider test scores used for licensing or certification in professions such as teaching. Three important ideas are presented here regarding test score interpretations.

Criterion-Referenced and Norm-Referenced Interpretations

A test score can yield absolute or relative interpretations (Kaplan, 1963). The absolute interpretation is usually referred to as *criterion referenced* (*CR*) because it tells us how much of an ability or knowledge a person has acquired. A score of 75% might suggest that a student has acquired 75% of the knowledge that the test sampled. Another kind of CR interpretation is comparing our score (75%) to a cut or passing score (80%), as we do with a certification or graduation test.

The relative interpretation is usually called *norm referenced* (*NR*) because this interpretation allows comparison of one score to other scores for a test-score scale. NR interpretations tell us how different scores are from one another. Some test-score scales that allow NR interpretations include percentile rank, stanine, normal-curve equivalent, grade equivalent, or standard score. Another type of NR interpretation uses categories or levels of performance, such as used in the National Assessment of Educational Progress (*http://nces.ed.gov/nationsreportcard/civics/civ_assess_achieve.asp*):

Basic	Partial mastery of prerequisite knowledge and skills that are fundamental for proficient work at each grade.
Proficient	Solid academic performance for each grade assessed. Students reaching this level have demonstrated competency over challenging subject matter, including subject-matter knowledge, application of such knowledge to real-world situations, and analytical skills appropriate to the subject matter.
Advanced	Superior performance.

These categories possess NR properties, but also provide descriptive information that educators increasingly find useful. We can count the number of students whose test scores fall into these categories and, over time, note how these frequencies change.

Because CR and NR are types of test-score interpretations, strictly speaking, we do not have CR or NR tests. However, the terms CR and NR are often associated with tests that lend themselves to such interpretations. For instance, classroom tests and tests built to carefully reflect a set of content standards, curriculum, or instructional objectives are often called CR because they conveniently tell us how much a student has learned. Published, standardized achievement tests have norms based on large representative samples, so they are often referred to as NR tests because they conveniently offer NR interpretations. Ironically, any test can give us NR interpretations, but CR interpretations come from tests designed to tell us how much a student has learned.

What Do Achievement Tests Measure? Knowledge, Skills, or Abilities?

The kinds of constructs for which we interpret scores can vary. Recently, performance testing and reform in teaching and testing have focused attention on the measurement of fluid, developing, or learned abilities (Lohman, 1993; Messick, 1984; Sternberg, 1998). These abilities are well known and include writing, reading, mathematical problem solving, creative thinking, and critical thinking. The kind of interpretation we make from tests of any school ability is said to be construct referenced (Messick, 1984) because the construct/ability is the object of measurement, not the antecedent knowledge or skill. A performance test item elicits complex behavior that we usually evaluate via a set of scoring guides (rubrics) leading to a test score that describes the student's ability. Although measurement of traits (characteristics) of the ability is possible, the focus of construct-referenced interpretation is the description of the ability. The meaning of the test score is not referenced to amount of knowledge or skill, but to the developmental level of the ability. We have many examples of people with highly developed abilities—Marion Jones' track ability and Ernest Hemingway's writing ability. Among the greatest problems with performance-based tests of complex abilities are the enormous technical issues threatening the validity of interpretation and using performance-based test scores. Supporting documentation is a greater need with these types of tests.

Some achievement tests concentrate on measuring knowledge or knowing (called *declarative knowledge* by educational psychologists) and doing or skills (called *procedural knowledge* by educational psychologists). These achievement tests of knowledge and skills often appear in multiple-choice formats. Published standardized achievement and CR tests are often thought of as measuring knowledge and skills.

Interpretations of reading and writing abilities based on performance tests are more difficult to make due to technical problems (see Linn, 1994; Linn, Baker, & Dunbar, 1991). Interpretations of knowledge and skills are generally easier to make because we have a long history of test theory, research, and technology supporting this kind of measurement and interpretation.

Unit of Analysis

We can report test scores for each individual student or groups of students such as we see in a class, school, school district, state, region, or even a nation. Sirotnik (1980) discussed the meanings of test-score interpretations when the unit of analysis varies. Not only are the reliabilities of individual and group scores different, but their meanings may vary. For instance, if we believe an ability or body of knowledge to be meaningful at the individual unit of analysis, it does not follow that the same measure will have the same meaning at the group level. If we believe an ability or body of knowledge to be systemic in nature, then it will have a pervasive effect on all students, and group means—as we see with classes, schools, and school districts—will have a specific meaning.

Because a primary goal of educators is to give tests that help teachers plan more effective instruction to increase student learning, individual score reports with diagnostic information are crucial. Group scores at the classroom level show strengths or weaknesses that may be teacher influenced, but few tests are designed to be instructionally sensitive to a single school year's teaching. School and school district group scores may also provide information useful for curriculum analysis and evaluation, and evaluation of an instructional program only if the test is designed to reflect the content standards that a state or school district adopts. State achievement scores have little value if we compare them state by state because the ability or body of knowledge we are measuring is not systematically influenced at the state level by a particular form of instruction or curricular emphasis. Thus, misinterpreting achievement test scores at a state level is easy. If achievement test scores are used over time, as Linn (2000) suggested, we might find value in studying state trends in important subject matters if and only if the measure of achievement is meaningfully related to a state's achievement goals or content standards.

Summary

The interpretation of test scores varies in several ways. We may want to make absolute or relative interpretations, which we commonly call CR and NR interpretations. We may want our test score to refer to an ability, knowledge, or skills that we use in performing a complex task exemplary of that ability. Finally, we may want to interpret a test score by various units of analysis ranging from individuals to many types of groups (e.g., class, school, nation).

USES OF TEST SCORES

Table 5.1 provides a list of the many uses of test scores and tests commonly associated with these uses. This table should give you a sense of the extensiveness of test-score use in large-scale testing in the United States. Considerable debate exists about the validity of test-score use in many situations, including for teacher or school evaluation, state-to-state or school district-to-school district comparisons, and merit pay. Also, we have many documented instances of test-score pollution (Haladyna, Nolen, & Haas, 1991). For instance, some educators may (a) narrow the curriculum to fit

TABLE 5.1
Uses of Test Scores and Tests Associated With These Uses

Test Score Use to Be Validated	Standardized Tests With Validity Evidence Relevant or Supporting That Use
College admissions	American College Test
Scholarship criteria	Scholastic Assessment Test
Graduate or professional school admissions	Graduate Record Examination
	Medical College Admissions Test
High school graduation or certification	Many states (e.g., Oregon, Ohio, Pennsyl-
Grade promotion	vania) and Chicago, Illinois.
Keeping public informed about student learning	Stanford Achievement Test (9th ed.)
	Iowa Test of Basic Skills
Curriculum evaluation	State-sponsored student testing program linked
Diagnosis of student learning	to state content standards
Feedback about student learning	
Merit pay for teachers, principals, others	
Evaluation of educational quality for states, school districts, schools, and classes	School district-sponsored testing program linked to state content standards or school district curriculum
School closure	
Accountability (Linn, 2000)	
Inform test sponsor for purposes of making policies and allocating resources	
Professional licensing and certification in teaching and other professions	Many national testing programs involving such professions as accountancy, architecture, dentistry, law, medicine, nursing, pharmacy, police work, social work, and teaching

the test better, (b) engage in unusual motivational tactics to get students to perform better than the other students who are less motivated, or (c) cheat in some way when administering or scoring the test.

Most scholars who study validity and the *Standards* (AERA, APA, NCME, 1999) submit that, for each interpretation or use for a set of test scores, we need separate validation. This need for separate validation is a very demanding requirement indeed.

VALIDITY: THE MOTIVATING FORCE BEHIND SUPPORTING DOCUMENTATION

Bob Linn's chapter in this volume, *Validation of the Uses and Interpretations of Results of State Assessment and Accountability Systems* (chap. 2) provides an excellent introduction to the present chapter. In turn, this chapter complements Linn in terms of this process of collecting and documenting validity evidence to support test-score interpretations and uses. In Linn, he discusses the history of validity that culminates in a consensus that the current approach to validity is unified under the term *construct validity*, and both content validity and criterion-related validity are aspects of construct validity. This integrated view of validity is well represented in the new *Standards* (AERA, APA, NCME, 1999), which Linn cites frequently in relation to critical aspects of a large-scale testing program. Other influential essays on the subject of validity include Haertel (1999), a chapter on validity by Messick (1989) or shorter essays on validity by Messick (1984, 1995a, 1995b), Kane (1992), Kaplan (1963), and Shepard (1993).

Validation is the process of evaluating the degree to which theory and evidence support a specific test-score interpretation or use. As Kane (1992) stated, validity involves the building of an interpretive argument that may start with a theoretical analysis and supporting information culled from procedures used to develop the testing program and also validity studies that include empirical evidence (reliability coefficients, descriptive statistics, correlations, factor analyses, and other forms of data). Validity evidence can also include the use of procedures that are often recommended or typical of high-quality testing programs. Thus, we augment or enhance the validity argument to the extent that validity evidence supports a specific test-score interpretation or use.

In a high-stakes testing environment, such as in a state where test scores are used to make pass–fail decisions as part of the high school graduation criteria, the test sponsor is obligated to make a validity argument and gather appropriate evidence in support of making valid pass–fail decisions. Linn (chap. 2, this volume) and Shepard (1993) pointed out that, as the stakes get higher, the demands for validity also increase.

SUPPORTING DOCUMENTATION

According to the *Standards* (AERA, NCME, APA, 1999), *supporting documentation* is defined as a collection of supporting documents used to inform test users and other audiences about the validity of interpreting or using test scores for some clearly stated, intended purpose.

Why Do We Need Supporting Documentation?

There are at least four good reasons for wanting supporting documentation for a testing program particularly if the stakes for test takers are high:

> **Validity evidence.** Documentation contains the validity evidence that supports the interpretation and use of test scores. Although supporting documentation is not as organized a body of evidence as we might like, supporting documentation provides the raw evidence that testing specialists, other educators, media, legislators and appointed officials, legal experts, or the public can use. Validity evidence provides a basis of support for a testing program's viability.
>
> **Accountability.** Since mass education sprang up in the middle of the 19th century in the United States, the public has been interested in knowing about its schools and the effectiveness of education. The establishment of standardized testing in the 20th century, in particular, the introduction of the *Stanford Achievement Test* in 1923, marked a revolutionary shift in education. Suddenly, the public could learn about its students in ways it could understand. Linn (2000) traced the history of accountability as he witnessed it emerging over his long career. We have seen test use go through waves of reform in 50 years, leaving in its wake criterion-referenced testing, minimum competency testing, content standards, performance testing, and the emerging accountability based on standardized achievement test results. By this version of accountability, we mean that teachers and administrators take increasing responsibility for student learning as operationally defined as test scores on standardized achievement tests. We know that these test scores can be corrupted in a number of ways and that test scores do not give us a complete picture of achievement, but noneducators have virtually mandated such accountability. At the heart of this accountability issue is validity. Accountability will never be of much value to educators or students unless the information we obtain about student learning and the conditions for learning are valid and help teachers plan better instruction. Although Linn concluded that the accountability movement has more negative than positive consequences, his final seven recommendations for large-scale, high-stakes testing programs are well

grounded in the new *Standards* (AERA, APA, NCME, 1999). Validity is the key to making an accountability system work, and supporting documentation is the tool for producing our validity evidence.

Standards for Educational and Psychological Testing. The current *Standards* (AERA, APA, NCME, 1999) cited 15 guidelines governing supporting documentation (chap. 6). The volume was published through the joint efforts of three professional organizations interested in improving the quality of testing programs: the American Educational Research Association, the American Psychological Association, and the National Council on Measurement in Education. These organizations have endorsed the idea of supporting documentation, making it a primary means of reporting to various audiences on the validity of interpreting and using test scores seen in Table 5.1.

Legal perspective. Many high-stakes testing programs have uses that are more likely to be legally challenged, particularly when pass–fail decisions are made on the basis of test scores. Sireci and Green (1999) reviewed the history of legal challenges to teacher certification, and by generalization their article affects other professional certification and licensing boards. Several important articles have appeared that capture the importance of legal threats to testing programs (Mehrens, 1995; Phillips, 1996; and the entire issue of *Educational Measurement: Issues and Practice*; Nitko, 1990).

As Phillips (1996) noted:

Clearly documented procedures which adhere to professional recommendations and are administered fairly will be the hallmark of defensible standards. Considering potential legal challenges in the formative stages of state and district standards will facilitate the collection and documentation of important evidence. While such activity may not prevent litigation, it will make a successful outcome more probable. (p. 13)

In situations where a use of a test score may be legally challenged, supporting documentation can provide evidence in a court of law. Testing programs that provide supporting documentation is more likely to withstand legal attack, whereas testing programs that do not have supporting documentation have little defense and a higher probability of losing in the courts.

Mehrens (1995) concurred that documentation can do much good for testing programs facing legal challenge. He supported the use of our testing *Standards* (AERA, APA, NCME, 1999). However, he pointed out that some controversy exists about which standards are most important or useful and how standards are to be used. To think of the current standards as the basis for a checklist for making a legally defensible test score interpretation or use would be a mistake. Validation is a subtle and more complex process than simply meeting or not satisfying these standards.

Summary

Supporting documentation is important for many reasons: validity and the process of validation, the need for accountability, our professional testing standards, and legal challenges to testing programs. It is easy to see such documentation is recognized in the *Standards* (AERA, APA, NCME, 1999) as a critical part of a testing program—it is essential to validity and these other important issues. With any high-stakes testing program—such as for graduation, certification, or licensure—supporting documentation takes on added value because of the potential for legal challenges to invalid test score use.

WHO ARE THE AUDIENCES FOR SUPPORTING DOCUMENTATION?

The audience for supporting documentation ranges from the very technically sophisticated to the highly uninformed. No matter the technical expertise of various audiences, each is very important because each plays an important role in the social dynamics of creating, using, and continuing (or terminating) any large-scale achievement testing program. Next we evaluate some of these audiences and their information needs.

The Public

Press releases are intended for public consumption and provide information that appears in daily newspapers, TV or radio, news magazines, and other periodicals. Essays written in these outlets inform the public about testing policies and procedures. One example of this is the *Fair Test Examiner*, a quarterly journal of The National Center for Fair and Open Testing. It regularly publishes articles about standardized testing. News magazines such as *Newsweek* and *Time* regularly publish articles on testing and its consequences. Newspapers regularly report to the public on state and national testing programs—in particular, the state's mandated test results. If a nationally used achievement test such as the *Stanford Achievement Test* or the *Iowa Test of Basic Skills* is used, we see stories in the local newspaper discussing some aspect of the testing program. Some states such as Oregon provide parents and members of the public with pamphlets or newspaper-style publications informing them about the state-mandated tests.

Virtually all states have web pages on the Internet often featuring the state's testing program and its content standards.

Such reporting to the public is seldom comprehensive and at times arguably inaccurate. Nonetheless, the public has a great thirst for test information. An obligation of any large-scale test sponsor, especially those involving educational achievement tests, is to keep the public informed about its tests and test-score interpretations and uses.

The Legislator or School Board Member

Because legislators and school board members make policies and allocate resources at the state and local school district levels, they are the most important lay consumers of information about testing. How much attention they receive is much higher than that which the public receives and includes all information available to the public. Additionally, it may include executive summaries, position or white papers, plans, proposals, and testimony for or against various positions regarding a testing program. Technical reports are less useful to these individuals, but well-written summaries of technical issues are key to helping them understand the mysteries of testing.

The Media

Newspapers, news magazines, and academic journals usually have sophisticated writers, data processing capabilities, and larger budgets to produce their stories. These publications are more likely to get supporting documentation, read articles and research, and even ask for data to analyze trends. They conduct interviews and synthesize results before their stories appear in print. They are active consumers of supporting documentation ranging from very simple material to very sophisticated technical reports. The *Education Writers' Association* includes in its membership more than 250 reporters who represent daily newspapers and regularly write education stories, many of which involve testing.

The Courts

Legal challenges on testing programs are increasing especially with high-stakes testing. Test sponsors want to document all aspects of their testing program as a means to ward off legal challenges to their interpretation and use of test scores. The best defense a testing sponsor has against legal attacks is a complete archive of supporting documentation correlated with the *Standards* (AERA, APA, NCME, 1999; Mehrens, 1995; Phillips, 1996, chap. 6, this volume).

The Testing Specialist

As Downing and Haladyna (1996) suggested, external review of testing programs by qualified specialists is one means to improve supporting documentation and organizing validity evidence. Such external technical reviews not only assemble, review, and evaluate supporting documentation, but these testing specialists can also find weaknesses in the testing program and make short- and long-term recommendations that will help the testing sponsor plan improvements to strengthen the validity evidence/ supporting documentation they need. These external reviews lend credibility to a testing program if the external review has a positive conclusion.

With larger testing programs, rather than have a single technical evaluator who studies the documentation, a team of testing specialists may be assembled to perform this task. For example, the states of Kansas, Michigan, Ohio, Oregon, and Washington have or have had technical committees of leading test specialists who regularly advise the state testing programs. Although the public and educators may not be aware of these committees' work, the wisdom of forming such a group is considerable. They provide valuable service in the quest for supporting documentation and validity evidence. These highly specialized groups of testing experts can also identify issues or problems that need to be researched or solved.

WHO DEVELOPS SUPPORTING DOCUMENTATION?

The responsible party for developing supporting documentation is the test sponsor, but a variety of people can provide supporting documentation. Any testing company, such as the American College Testing, Incorporated, Educational Testing Service, Riverside Publishing, the California Test Bureau of McGraw-Hill, Harcourt Brace and Jovanovich, or National Evaluation Systems may serve a test sponsor by providing testing services. As part of their annual work, they may produce the myriad documents described later in this chapter. A responsible testing company will aggressively develop a plan with the test sponsor for supporting documentation that meets the *Standards* (AERA, APA, NCME, 1999) and then supply as many documents as the testing sponsor is interested in or can afford. A responsible testing company should inform the test sponsor of the standards and uphold these standards. The test company should make validity and the establishment of validity evidence a key goal in the testing program because it serves many good purposes as previously described.

The process of supporting documentation may fall to personnel within a test sponsor's organization. For instance, if the test originates from a state, members of the state department of education's assessment staff may be responsible for supporting documentation. But the process of supporting documentation may be very time-consuming, and most testing sponsors are more likely to outsource this work, depending on an independent testing specialist to best accomplish the task of identifying, assembling, evaluating, and synthesizing this validity evidence.

Sometimes a testing specialist may be hired as an external evaluator or auditor. Although it is the primary duty of this person to evaluate validity evidence and judge the evidence against the standards, this evaluator/auditor may also develop or collect validity evidence as needed—perhaps through studies conducted for their client. Such studies may supplement the validity evidence brought from other sources.

In short, any of the previously mentioned organizations or individuals can participate in supporting documentation. The use of divergent sources of documentation may lend credibility to the process especially if the sources of evidence agree or confirm conclusions about the validity of test score interpretation and use.

WHAT STANDARDS SHOULD BE APPLIED TO SUPPORTING DOCUMENTATION?

According to Linn (chap. 1, this volume), The *Standards* (AERA, APA, NCME, 1999) reflect an evolutionary process dating from standards issued in 1954, 1955, 1974, and 1985. For those of you deeply invested in validation and supporting documentation, a reading of the current *Standards* is essential to the process of supporting documentation. Although this chapter focuses on the 15 standards found in chapter 6, *Supporting Documentation for Tests*, it is important to note that the entire *Standards* bears on *all* validity evidence that should be found in our supporting documentation for that testing program.

Part I of the *Standards* (AERA, APA, NCME, 1999) addressed test construction, evaluation, and documentation. Chapter 1 gives us a background on validity that is a consistent unified view of validity that test experts now support. Chapter 2 discusses a major type of validity evidence: reliability. Chapter 3 provides test development standards that are germane to the concerns in this chapter. Chapter 4 provides standards for the development and use of norms and scale, and the need for documenting equating. This chapter is also critical to supporting documentation. Chapter 5 discusses test administration, scoring, and reporting. As noted previously, chapter 6 addresses supporting documentation.

Part II deals with fairness, rights and responsibilities, the problems of testing persons from diverse linguistic backgrounds, and disabilities. Most of Part II addresses the problems encountered by English language learners and students with disabilities. As you might expect, Part II is very significant to supporting documentation and validity.

Part III is a potpourri of five chapters that differ greatly from one another. Chapter 13 is especially salient for educational uses of tests, as is discussed throughout this volume. Chapter 14 is relevant for teacher licensing testing and other forms of professional licensing and certification. Several standards in chapter 14 bear on the issue of high school graduation and promotion testing.

Table 5.2 supplies a brief discussion of each of the 15 guidelines for supporting documentation found in chapter 6 of the *Standards* (AERA, APA, NCME, 1999). Although these guidelines are fairly comprehensive and informative, they hardly exhaust the realm of possibilities achievable in supporting documentation. Therefore, one of the goals of this chapter is to increase the scope and specificity of meaning for supporting documentation to include important categories of validity evidence that can be used to support an interpretive argument about validity.

WHAT CAN SUPPORTING DOCUMENTATION INCLUDE?

We examine the kinds of information that reflect supporting documentation and the publications in which this documentation may appear. Although supporting documentation cannot appeal or be useful to all audi-

TABLE 5.2
Technical Standards on Documentation

Standard	Comment About Standard
6.1 Test documents should be available to those interested in this information.	This basic standard justifies supporting documentation.
6.2 Documents should be complete, accurate, and clearly written for their intended audiences.	This standard applies universally to all supporting documents.
6.3 The rationale for the test and the intended interpretations and uses should be clearly stated. Evidence should support these interpretations and uses. When misuse is possible, cautions should be stated.	This standard identifies the important idea that validation must occur for each intended interpretation and use, and those who identify new interpretations and uses to test scores are responsible for providing validity evidence supporting that new interpretation or use.

(Continued)

TABLE 5.2
(Continued)

Standard	Comment About Standard
6.4 Provide test specifications and a description of the population to be tested.	This shows the content of the test and identifies the population to be tested, so validity evidence applies to that content and that population.
6.5 Technical data including descriptive statistics should be provided in a technical report.	This standard identifies the value of the technical report, which is discussed in the last section of this chapter.
6.6 When a test reflects a course or specific training, a curriculum, textbook or packaged instructions, the supporting documentation should identify and describe these materials.	In most instances, this would be content standards for a state, but it might refer to a training curriculum, or a job analysis or specific reference materials for each test item in the item bank.
6.7 Test documents should specify qualifications for administering the test and interpreting the test scores.	In most instances cited in this chapter, this standard probably would not apply.
6.8 If the test taker scores and interprets results, the documents should help the test taker do this.	In most instances cited in this chapter, this standard probably would not apply.
6.9 Studies should be cited that provide validity evidence.	In many instances, research provides important guidelines and support for certain testing practices.
6.10 Materials should be presented that help interpret test results.	This standard addresses the importance of publications that explain test results, showing proper, validated interpretations and uses of test scores.
6.11 If administration methods vary, then evidence should be presented for the interchangeability of results.	This standard refers to paper-and-pencil and various forms of computerized administration.
6.12 Computer-generated scores and score interpretations should be clearly explained.	The transition to computer-generated scoring needs to be well supported to assure test takers and public as to its equivalence with traditional paper-and-pencil testing.
6.13 When substantial changes are made to a test, documentation should be supplemented or revised to keep information current.	Any significant test revision motivates another round of validation.
6.14 Every test form and supporting document should carry a copyright date or publication date.	No comment.
6.15 Test developers, publishers, and test distributors should provide general information.	This information appears in many public documents and on web pages generated by test sponsors.

ences, it fills information needs for many unique and diverse audiences. In this section, different documents are named and the contents of these documents are discussed. In as many instances as possible, reference to the *Standards* (AERA, APA, NCME, 1999) is provided.

The last section of this chapter features two important tables. Table 5.3 provides a partial listing of the kinds of documents that might be generated to satisfy the need for supporting documentation. Table 5.4 provides a model of one of the most important supporting documents—the technical report.

Documents Containing Validity Evidence

Table 5.3 presents a sample of the kinds of documents that contain validity evidence. Standards 6.1 and 6.2 apply to all documents. In Table 5.3, some attempt has been made to link each of these documents to the kinds of validity evidence we might see in each document and standards reported in chapter 6 of the *Standards*. Each document refers to at least one standard in the *Standards*, but in actuality most documents cover many more standards than we can possibly cite in this table. These documents probably appeal to a wide range of audiences because validity evidence is open for interpretation and evaluation from many perspectives, including lay persons.

The variety of documents and the linkages to standards may seem haphazard. Yet with concerted planning, the documentation can have the collective purpose of providing the needed validity evidence and keeping various constituencies informed about the quality of the testing program and the validity of test-score interpretations and uses.

The Technical Report

A main source of documentation that includes many categories of validity evidence is the technical report, which is usually written annually by the testing company serving the testing sponsor or its staff. This document may vary according to the interests of the testing sponsor or test company, but ideally it should address all the important categories of validity evidence. The *Standards* (AERA, APA, NCME, 1999) provide a useful outline of the categories of validity evidence. If validation is truly a process for gathering evidence supporting an argument about the validity of a specific test-score use or interpretation, then the technical report is the main source for displaying the assembled evidence in a readable format. However, the technical report is more than a repository of validity evidence. It can and should offer short- and long-term recommendations for improve-

TABLE 5.3

Samples of Types of Documents Comprising Supporting Documentation

Document	Standards or References
Archive: legislation, policies, procedures, correspondence, miscellaneous documents providing a paper trail of test development.	6.1
State content standards or practice/job analysis.	6.6, 6.7 Messick (1995a) *Oregon Content Standards* (1998)
Test specifications derived from the above activity.	6.4
Plan for the development of the assessment.	6.3, 6.4, 6.6
Technical reports, containing many specific details about test development, administration, scoring, and reporting.	6.5 *Technical Data Report-Stanford Achievement Test Series, Ninth Edition.* Harcourt Brace Publisher (1997)
External audit/evaluation reports, containing an evaluation against the *Standards*.	Downing & Haladyna (1996)
Student/candidate handbook	6.1, 6.4, 6.8
Student/candidate study guide	*NABPLEX 1990 Candidate's Review Guide* (The
Intertpretive guides.	National Association of Boards of Pharmacy)
Item-writing and item review guide.	Downing & Haladyna (1997)
Internal reports: Intended to document important activities, such as scaling, equating.	Many of an unspecified nature
Test administration manual.	6.7 *Oregon Statewide WritingAssessment Administration Manual* (1997)
Score reports and other reports to constituents.	6.7, 6.8, 6.10 *NAEP 1992 Writing Report Card* Applebee, Langer, Mullis, Latham, & Gentile (1992)
Empirical studies bearing on the standards, perhaps comprising a reference list. Studies like one cited number in the thousands, but contribute importantly to useful concepts, principles, and procedures for testing.	6.9 DeMars (2000) Test stakes and item format interactions. *Applied Measurement in Education, 13*, 55–78
Released examinations.	6.8, 6.10 *Uniform CPA Examination (May 1989) Questions and unofficial answers.* American Institute of Certified Public Accountants
Public relations/media/press releases and documentations, intended to inform the public.	6.1, 6.3, 6.10, 6.13, 6.15 *Education for the 21st century*, Oregon Department of Education (November 1995)
Technical notes (specific statements that document an usual or detailed activity of a technical nature that is important to the testing program).	Usually confidential. Not citable.
Special studies. Studies commissioned to address a perceived problem with the testing program.	Downing & Haladyna (1996)
Passing score study.	Usually confidential. Results of study are often publicly reported.
Test scoring/quality control.	Usually confidential.

TABLE 5.4

Model Technical Report for Any Large-Scale Student Achievement
Testing Programs or a Teacher Licensing Test

Table of Contents	Standards
Rationale for validity and validity evidence	1.1, 1.3, 1.4
Definition of the constructs to be measured	1.2, 3.11
Intended test score interpretations and uses	1.1, 1.3, 3.2, 3.4, 3.7, 3.26, 4.1, 4.3, 4.8, 4.9, 4.16, 5.12, 6.4, 7.9
	11.1–11.5, 11.19, 11.24, 13.1, 13.2, 13.4, 13.9, 13.12, 13.13
Basis for defining content (content standards or practice/job analysis)	1.6, 1.7, 3.5, 13.3, 14.6, 14.8, 14.10–11, 14.8 14.11, 14.14
Development of test specifications including topics covered and cognitive behaviors	1.8, 3.2, 3.3, 4.16
Test design	3.6, 3.11, 13.5, 13.6
Construct-irrelevant variance	1.9, 5.6, 5.14, 7.2, 7.10, 12.19, 13.18
Construct underrepresentation	7.10
Reliability	2.1–2.7, 2.10, 2.17, 14.15
Structure of data dimensionality	pages 13, 1.11, 1.14
Item quality	3.6–3.9, 7.3, 7.4, 7.7
Standard setting: Passing score study and report	1.7, 4.19–4.21, 13.7, 13.8, 14.15 14.17
Scaling/equating/comparability	4.2, 4.10–4.13, 4.15, 4.17, 11.6
Test administration	2.16, 2.17, 3.12, 3.18–3.20, 5.1–5.6, 7.12, 13.10, 13.12, 13.1
Testing policies for special populations	3.21, 5.3, 7.1, 7.2, 7.5, 7.10, 7.11, 10.1–10.12, 11.22, 11.23
Security policies and procedures	5.7, 8.6, 11.7
Scoring test results	1.12, 2.13, 3.14, 3.17, 3.22–3.24, 5.9, 9.1–9.11, 14.13, 14.16
Reporting results	1.10, 1.12, 4.8–5.1, 5.10, 5.12–5.16, 7.8, 7.12, 8.5, 8.6, 8.8–8.13, 11.6, 11.9, 11.12–11.14, 11.17, 11.18, 11.20, 11.21, 13.12–13.17, 13.19, 15.11
Consequences of testing	1.23, 1.24, 8.7, 11.15
Special studies	1.13, 3.25
Summative evaluation	Messick (1989)
Short- and long-term recommendations for improvement (vis-à-vis Standards, 1999)	7.9

ment of the testing program, recognizing that all successful testing programs are evolutionary in nature.

Table 5.4 provides an ideal table of contents; some references to key chapters, essays, articles, or books on the topic; and specific references to standards that seem to apply. In practice, however, we seldom achieve this level of inclusiveness in writing a technical report. Nonetheless, it seems beneficial to present an ideal table of contents from which to set our goals for supporting documentation of validity evidence.

Depending on resources and staff and the degree of high-stakes use of test scores, a technical report can range between *very comprehensive* and *bare bones*. In planning a technical report, one should keep in mind that not all sections can be included, and some decisions should be made about which sections to include and omit. However, validation is serious business, and to shorten or lessen the technical report may lead to undesirable consequences. Before one decides how much information or how many standards one will address in one's technical report, one should consider the four reasons that we produce supporting documentation: accountability, validity evidence, *Standards* (AERA, APA, NCME, 1999), and legality.

The author or authors of the technical report should go beyond simply providing a compilation of validity evidence, as suggested by the ideal table of contents. The last section of the report should contain a summative evaluation about the adequacy of evidence for supporting the clearly stated test-score interpretation and use. Messick (1989) and others argued that this summative judgment comes from a consideration of the mix of evidence in support of the interpretive argument. The report should end with recommendations for improvement of the testing program and improved validity evidence. These recommendations can lead to short- or long-term perspectives. The test sponsor then has the responsibility to read and understand the report and make wise decisions about future policies and resource allocations. Testing companies are well suited to provide this advice, but in many circumstances where the test sponsor is not served by a testing company an external, qualified evaluator can offer the same kind of service.

ADVICE TO THOSE RESPONSIBLE FOR AND THOSE WORKING IN TESTING PROGRAMS

Validation of test-score interpretations and uses is the most important concern of any testing program. At the heart of this validation is supporting documentation, which is the result of a coordinated activity that presents validity evidence to different audiences in different forms. In this chapter, it was suggested that any plan for validation include a process for supporting documentation. By creating a plan and executing it, the test sponsor is assured of a collection of validity evidence that will satisfy many constituencies, including legislative, legal, educators, media, and the public. Table 5.1 provides a list of potential uses of test scores for which validity evidence may be needed. Table 5.2 lists standards directly related to supporting documentation. Table 5.3 suggests a variety of documents that comprise supporting documentation. Table 5.4 presents a model technical report as a major repository of validity evidence. Again, Linn (chap. 2, this volume) and Shepard (1993) pointed out that as the stakes for test-score use increase the need for validity grows. Supporting documentation can be a critical process in validating your testing program's interpretation and uses of test scores. You might consider supporting documentation as a type of health insurance for your testing program.

REFERENCES

American Educational Research Association, American Psychological Association, National Council on Measurement in Education. (1999). *Standards for educational and psychological testing*. Washington, DC: American Educational Research Association.

Applebee, A. N., Langer, J. A., Mullis, I. V. S., Latham, A. S., & Gentile, C. A. (1992). *NAEP 1992 writing report card*. Washington, DC: Office of Educational Research and Improvement.

Downing, S. M., & Haladyna, T. M. (1996). Model for evaluating high-stakes testing programs: Why the fox should not guard the chicken coop. *Educational Measurement: Issues and Practice, 15*, 5–12.

Downing, S. M., & Haladyna, T. M. (1997). Test item development: Validity evidence from quality assurance procedures. *Applied Measurement in Education, 10*, 61–82.

Haladyna, T. M., Nolen, S. B., & Haas, N. S. (1991). Raising standardized achievement test scores and the origins of test score pollution. *Educational Researcher, 20*, 2–7.

Haertel, E. H. (1999). Validity arguments for high-stakes testing: In search of evidence. *Educational Measurement: Issue and Practice, 18*(4), 4–9.

Kane, M. T. (1992). An argument-based approach to validity. *Psychological Bulletin, 112*, 527–535.

Kaplan, A. (1963). *The conduct of inquiry: Methodology for behavioral science*. New York: Harper & Row.

Lohman, D. F. (1993). Teaching and testing to develop fluid abilities. *Educational Researcher, 22*, 12–23.

Linn, R. L. (1994). Performance assessment: Policy, promises and technical measurement standards. *Educational Researcher, 23*(9), 4–14.

Linn, R. L. (2000). Assessment and accountability. *Educational Researcher, 29*(2), 4–16.

Linn, R. L., Baker, E. L., & Dunbar, S. B. (1991). Complex performance assessment: Expectations and validation criteria. *Educational Researcher, 20*(8), 15–21.

Mehrens, W. A. (1995). Legal and professional bases for licensure testing. In J. C. Impara (Ed.), *Licensure testing: Purposes, procedures, and practices* (pp. 33–58). University of Nebraska-Lincoln: Buros Institute of Mental Measurements.

Messick, S. (1984). The psychology of educational measurement. *Journal of Educational Measurement, 21*, 215–237.

Messick, S. (1989). Validity. In R. L. Linn (Ed.), *Educational measurement* (3rd ed., pp. 13–104). New York: American Council on Education and Macmillan.

Messick, S. (1995a). Validity of psychological assessment: Validation of inferences from persons' responses and performances as scientific inquiry into score meaning. *American Psychologist, 50,* 741–749.

Messick, S. (1995b). Standards of validity and the validity of standards in performance assessment. *Educational Measurement: Issues and Practice, 14*(4), 5–8.

Nitko, A. J. (Ed.). (1990). *Educational Measurement: Issues and Practice, 9*(4), 3–32.

Phillips, S. E. (1996). Legal defensibility of standards: Issues and policy perspectives. *Educational Measurement: Issues and Practices, 15,* 5–14.

Shepard, L. A. (1993). Evaluating test validity. *Review of Research in Education, 19,* 405–450.

Sireci, S. G., & Green P. C. III (1999). Legal and psychometric criteria for evaluating teacher certification tests. *Educational Measurement: Issues and Practice, 18,* 22–32, 34.

Sirotnik, K. (1980). The unit-of-analysis in scale development. *Journal of Educational Measurement, 17*(4), 245–282.

Sternberg, R. J. (1998). Abilities are forms of developing expertise. *Educational Researcher, 27*(3), 11–20.

Chapter 6

Legal Issues Affecting Special Populations in Large-Scale Testing Programs

S. E. Phillips
Consultant

Legal challenges to state assessment programs have focused primarily on the issues of adverse impact, parental rights, and testing accommodations. However, once a case goes to trial, issues of test validity, reliability, passing standards, and adherence to other professional standards are typically raised. The *Debra P. v. Turlington* (1984) and *G.I. Forum et al. v. Texas Education Agency et al.* (2000) cases provide precedent for many of the testing standards reviewed briefly in subsequent sections. The major focus of this chapter is on the difficult area of testing accommodations when there are few legal precedents and tough policy questions.

PROFESSIONAL STANDARDS

Professional standards assume a central role in legal debates about the psychometric quality of state graduation tests. Specific standards from the 1985 American Educational Research Association, American Psychological Association, National Council on Measurement in Education (AERA/APA/NCME) *Test Standards*, applicable at the time many such tests were initially developed and implemented, have been cited by expert witnesses and their interpretation debated.[1] Introductory material reinforced the essential role of professional judgment in interpreting the standards:

---

[1]A revised version of the *Test Standards* was released in late 1999. The 1985 *Test Standards* should still be applicable to existing tests, whereas the revised version should apply to future test revisions and newly developed tests. The 1985 *Test Standards* are discussed in this chapter because cited cases to date have been based on those standards.

Evaluating the acceptability of a test or test application does not rest on the literal satisfaction of every primary standard in this document, and acceptability cannot be determined by using a checklist. Specific circumstances affect the importance of individual standards. Individual standards should not be considered in isolation. Therefore, evaluating acceptability involves the following: professional judgment that is based on a knowledge of behavioral science, psychometrics, and the professional field to which the tests apply; the degree to which the intent of this document has been satisfied by the test developer and user; the alternatives that are readily available; and research and experiential evidence regarding feasibility. (p. 2)

In the Preface to the 1985 *Test Standards*, the Development Committee also stated several guidelines that governed the work of the committee and remain good advice for test developers and users: "The Standards should . . . be a statement of technical standards for sound professional practice and *not a social action prescription*. . . . Make it possible to determine the technical adequacy of a test . . . and the reasonableness of inferences based on the test results" (p. v; italics added).

Debra P. & G.I. Forum Requirements

In the Debra P. case, the court instituted two additional due process requirements for graduation tests: notice and curricular validity. A property interest is a threshold requirement for a due process claim. The G.I. Forum court reaffirmed the Debra P. court's holding that a high school diploma is a property interest "created by the requirement of compulsory education, attendance requirements, and the statute detailing graduation requirements" (*G.I. Forum et al. v. Texas Education Agency et al.*, 1999). The court characterized the factual issue in dispute under the due process claim broadly as the validity of the graduation test (i.e., whether the implementation and use of the graduation test was a substantial departure from accepted professional standards).

Relationship of Debra P. & G.I. Forum Cases

The situation in Texas when its graduation test was implemented differed from that of Florida at the time of the Debra P. case. Texas had a state-mandated curriculum, whereas Florida did not. Unlike the Florida students in the Debra P. case, African-American and Hispanic minority students subject to the graduation test requirement in Texas had not been required by statute to attend segregated schools. Moreover, graduation testing was not a new concept in Texas as it was in Florida. At the time the G.I. Forum case was filed in 1997, high school graduation tests had been in existence for nearly two decades nationwide and over a decade in Texas, beginning with the challenged test's predecessor implemented in 1985.

Consistent with the ruling in the Debra P. case, the state in the G.I. Forum case asserted that even if there had been prior discriminatory conduct by some educators in Texas, the graduation test would help remedy any potential vestiges of past discrimination. In upholding the Florida graduation test once Florida high school students had all been educated in unitary schools and the state had demonstrated the curricular validity of its graduation test, the Debra P. (1984) appeals court stated:

> We affirm the district court's findings (1) that students were actually taught test skills, (2) that vestiges of past intentional segregation do not cause the [test's] disproportionate impact on blacks, and (3) that use of the [test] as a diploma sanction will help remedy the vestiges of past segregation. Therefore, the State of Florida may deny diplomas to students. . . . (pp. 1416–1417)

The G.I. Forum (2000) court agreed:

> Only one case cited by any party or this Court is both controlling and directly on point—Debra P. . . . In reviewing the diverse cases that underpin this decision, the Court has had to acknowledge what the Defendants have argued throughout trial—this case is, in some important ways, different from those cases relied upon by the Plaintiffs. . . . [T]his case asks the Court to consider a standardized test that measures knowledge rather than one that predicts performance. . . . [T]he TEA's evidence that the implementation of the [graduation test], together with school accountability and mandated remedial follow-up, helps address the effects of any prior discrimination and remaining inequities in the system is both credible and persuasive. (pp. 2–4, 14)

Notice

Notice requires the state to disseminate information about graduation test requirements to all affected students well in advance of implementation. Notice periods of less than 2 years have been found unacceptable by the courts; notice periods of 4 years in the Debra P. case and 5 years in the G.I. Forum case were found acceptable. The courts have not mandated a specific length for the notice period; with extensive dissemination efforts, solid curricular validity, and demonstrated achievement of prerequisite skills in earlier grades, 3 years may be adequate.

Curricular Validity

The curricular validity requirement, also referred to as *opportunity to learn* (OTL), was included as Standard 8.7 in the 1985 revision of the *Test Standards*. OTL means that students must be taught the skills tested on a graduation test. In practice, evidence of OTL is often gathered by examining the official curricular materials used in instruction and surveying teachers to determine whether they are teaching the tested content. In the G.I. Forum case, the court held, on all the facts and circumstances, that the state had satisfied the curricular validity requirement with a mandated state curriculum, teacher committee item reviews that considered adequacy of preparation, remediation for unsuccessful students mandated by statute, and continuity of the graduation test with its predecessor based on the same curriculum and for which an OTL survey of teachers had been completed.

Remediation. Remediation efforts were also persuasive in the Debra P. and G.I. Forum cases. The Debra P. (1984) appeals court stated: "[The state's] remedial efforts are extensive. . . . Students have five chances to pass the [graduation test] between 10th and 12th grades, and if they fail, they are offered remedial help. . . . All [of the state's experts] agreed that the [state's remediation] efforts were substantial and bolstered a finding of [adequate opportunity to learn]" (pp. 1410–1411). In the G.I. Forum case, the Texas Education Code provided: "Each school district shall offer an intensive program of instruction for students who did not [pass the graduation test]" (§ 39.024 (b)) and the court held that:

> [A]ll students in Texas have had a reasonable opportunity to learn the subject matters covered by the exam. The State's efforts at remediation and the fact that students are given eight opportunities to pass the [graduation test] before leaving school support this conclusion. (p. 29)

Validity

The unified view of validity (Linn, chap. 2) provides a comprehensive theoretical framework for measurement professionals. However, in legal proceedings, the issue is what validity evidence is required. The G.I. Forum court identified content and curricular validity evidence as meeting legal and professional standards for a high school graduation test. Thus, I have chosen to discuss validity according to traditional categories to clearly distinguish the types of evidence courts have and have not required for high-stakes achievement tests. Presentation of the unified view of validity in legal proceedings may obscure rather than clarify the issues and might, for example, lead a fact finder to erroneously conclude that predictive validity evidence is necessary for a high school graduation test.

Content Validity. For a graduation test, scores are used to decide whether students have attained sufficient academic skills in specific subject areas, such as reading, mathematics, and writing, for the award of a high school diploma. The most important evidence of validity in this situation is a measure of the degree to which the items on each subject test measure the knowledge and skills prescribed by the state curriculum and/or content standards. Documentation of the content validity for a state graduation test typically appears in its technical manual and includes descriptions of the development of the state objectives/curricula, test blueprint, item development, item review, field testing, item statistics, bias reviews, construction of final test forms, and equating.

Criterion and Construct Validity Evidence.   The construct being measured by a state graduation test is achievement of the stated objectives in a specified content area (e.g., achievement of state reading objectives). Thus, demonstration of the validity of a state graduation test does not require criterion or construct validity evidence; evidence of content and curricular validity is sufficient.

Nonetheless, states may choose to provide research data on the relationship between state test scores and other variables, such as courses taken, grades, norm-referenced tests, or college admissions tests. However, when such information is provided, low correlations should not be interpreted as demonstrating lack of validity because courses, grades, and other tests measure different attributes than the state graduation test. For example, grades may be based on nontested skills, attitude, effort, or improvement. Thus, grades cannot be viewed as alternative measures of the tested content.

The G.I. Forum court upheld the validity of the Texas graduation test based on extensive evidence of content validity. The Court stated:

> [The graduation test] measures what it purports to measure, and it does so with a sufficient degree of reliability . . . The Court also finds that the Plaintiffs have not demonstrated that the [graduation test] is a substantial departure from accepted academic norms or is based on a failure to exercise professional judgment. . . . Educators and test-designers testified that the design and the use of the test was within accepted norms. . . . In addition, the State need not equate its test on the basis of standards it rejects, such as subjective teacher evaluations. (pp. 29–30)

Reliability

Under the unified view of validity, reliability may be treated as one type of validity evidence. However, in cases such as G.I. Forum, plaintiffs have presented arguments of alleged reliability deficiencies as a separate violation of the *Test Standards*. In particular, in the G.I. Forum case, the plaintiffs specifically criticized the type of reliabilities reported (see Phillips, in press). Thus, evidence of test reliability may be most effectively presented separately from evidence of test validity. For high school graduation tests, where remediation is typically mandated for students who are unsuccessful, expected changes in students' knowledge and skills from one test administration to the next is an important consideration when calculating reliability estimates. The prefatory material in the chapter on reliability in the 1985 *Test Standards* stated: "Differences between scores from . . . one occasion to another . . . are not attributable to errors of measurement if maturation, intervention, or some other event has made these differences meaningful . . . (p. 19).

There are two major procedures for calculating test reliability: repeat testing and measures based on a single test administration. The 1985 *Test Standards* did not specify any particular type of reliability estimate as mandated or preferred. Rather, Primary Standard 2.1 states: "[E]stimates of relevant reliabilities and standard errors of measurement should be provided in adequate detail to enable the test user to judge whether scores are sufficiently accurate for the intended use of the test" (p. 20). Primary Standards 2.2 and 2.3 specified documentation of sample characteristics and methods used to calculate reported reliability estimates. Conditional Standard 2.9 recommended separate reliability estimates for subpopulations, and Secondary Standard 2.10 recommended reporting standard errors at the cut score. Typically, the standard error at the cut score is about the same as the overall standard error for the total test.

Passing Standards

The responsibility for setting passing standards on a graduation test typically resides with the State Board of Education by statute or administrative regulations. Such boards often consider recommendations from educator committees and state agency staff, the content and format of the test, and impact data. Primary Standard 6.9 required that the procedures used to establish the passing standard on a graduation test be documented and explained but did not require any specific method to be used. All passing standards are somewhat arbitrary and reflect human judgment of appropriate expectations for high school graduates.

Some professionals have advocated an adjusted passing standard that is a number of standard errors below the passing score set by a policymaking board. The rationale for this recommendation is to minimize false negatives (students incorrectly identified as not achieving the required standard). This argument might have some merit if passing decisions were being based on a single attempt because negative errors of measurement could cause a student with true achievement at or slightly above the passing score to fail a single administration of a graduation test. However, when states provide multiple opportunities for students to pass a graduation test, false negatives (denying a diploma to a student who has achieved the state objectives) is an extremely rare event. Conversely, multiple retakes significantly increase the probability that a student with true achievement below the cut score will pass due to random positive errors of measurement.

In summary, although false negatives are corrected via repeat testing, false positives are neither identified nor corrected. That is, a student who fails erroneously has additional opportunities to pass, whereas a student who passes erroneously is allowed to retain the benefits of an unearned passing score. Therefore, lowering the passing standard to adjust for possible errors of measurement has little effect on the negligible number of erroneous diploma denials, but substantially increases the already significant number of students who pass without having actually met the required standard. In the G.I. Forum case, the plaintiffs argued that the state's passing standards were invalid because a research-based methodology had not been employed. The Court discounted this argument finding.

Whether the use of a given cut score, or any cut score, is proper depends on whether the use of the score is justified. In *Cureton*, a case relied upon heavily by the Plaintiffs in the G.I. Forum case, the court found that the use of an SAT [Scholastic Aptitude Test] cut score *as a selection practice for* the NCAA [National Collegiate Athletic Association] must be justified by some independent basis for choosing the cut score. . . .

Here, the test use being challenged is the assessment of legislatively established minimum skills as a requisite for graduation. This is a conceptually different exercise from that of predicting graduation rates or success in employment or college. In addition, the Court finds that it is an exercise well within the State's power and authority. The State of Texas has determined that, to graduate, a senior must have mastered 70 percent of the tested minimal essentials. . . . The Court does not mean to suggest that a state could arrive at *any* cut score without running afoul of the law. However, Texas relied on field test data and input from educators to determine where to set its cut score. It set initial cut scores 10 percentage points lower, and phased in the 70-percent score. While field test results suggested that a large number of students would not pass at the 70-percent cut score, officials had reason to believe that those numbers were inflated. Officials contemplated the possible consequences and determined that the risk should be taken. The Court cannot say, based on the record, that the State's chosen cut score was arbitrary or unjustified. Moreover, the Court finds that the score bears a manifest relationship to the State's legitimate goals. (pp. 24–26; citations omitted; italics original)

Basis for Decision Making

Contrary to the assertions of many testing critics, state graduation tests are not used in isolation to make graduation decisions. In addition to passing the graduation test, students are also expected to successfully complete all required coursework, attendance requirements, and other graduation obligations imposed by their districts. A student who fails a single course may be unable to graduate on time just as a student who does not pass the graduation test may have to delay graduation. Students are required to meet both testing and course requirements because each represents a different kind of accomplishment that is valued in a high school graduate.

The inclusion of Standard 8.8 suggests that the drafters considered graduation tests separately from the educational placement tests referred to in Standard 8.12 and viewed graduation tests acceptable as long as students had multiple opportunities to pass. When denial of a high school diploma is based on the opportunity to obtain multiple scores from multiple forms of the test administered on several different occasions, it is virtually impossible for the true achievement of an unsuccessful student to be at or above the graduation test passing standard.[2] Thus, these students are not false negatives, and the decision to delay award of their high school diplomas until they have attained the essential skills and passed the graduation test benefits the student and is justified.

Title VI Challenges

Title VI (1964) prohibits intentional discrimination by entities receiving federal funding. Title VI Regulations, however, only require a showing of adverse impact on minorities. Under a Title VI Regulations challenge, the burden of proof alternates between plaintiffs and defendants. Plaintiffs establish a presumptive violation with adverse impact data. Defendants can counter this presumption with evidence of educational necessity. Plaintiffs may still prevail if they can demonstrate that an equally valid, less discriminatory alternative is available (G.I. Forum, 2000; cited in Wards & Cove, 1989; Watson, 1988).

Adverse Impact

Differential performance occurs when passing rates for African-American and Hispanic students (minority groups) are lower than the passing rates for White students (majority group). When the differential performance between minority and majority groups becomes too great, it is labeled *adverse impact*. An important issue in this context is determining when differential performance becomes large enough to qualify as adverse impact.

---

[2]P (pass graduation test in 8 attempts | true achievement at the passing standard) = .996; with true achievement .5 SEM above the passing standard, the probability of passing in 8 attempts increases to .9999.

Cumulative Passing Rates. In employment testing, two types of significant differences are commonly used to assess adverse impact: practical significance and statistical significance. A judgmental criterion for practical significance is contained in the EEOC Uniform Guidelines on Employee Selection Procedures (1978), which label differential performance as adverse impact when the passing rate for the minority group is less than 80% of the passing rate for the majority group. However, employment cases typically involve hiring or promotion decisions based on a single administration of a test instrument, whereas students required to pass state graduation tests have repeated testing opportunities with targeted remediation in between. Thus, when an adverse impact standard is applied to a graduation test, comparisons should be based on cumulative passing rates rather than initial passing rates. The G.I. Forum court supported this position:

> In considering how to handle the dilemma of choosing between cumulative and single-test administration, the Court has taken into account the immediate impact of initial and subsequent in-school failure of the exam—largely successful educational remediation. In addition, the Court has considered the evidence that minority scores have shown dramatic improvement. These facts would seem to support the TEA's position that cumulative pass rates are the relevant consideration here.
>
> In determining whether an adverse impact exists in this case, the Court has considered and applied the [EEOC's 80% Rule]. . . . Plaintiff's statistical analysis, while somewhat flawed, demonstrates a significant impact on first time administration of the [graduation test]. . . . However, cumulative pass rates do not demonstrate so severe an impact and, at least for the classes of 1996, 1997, and 1998, are not statistically significant under the [EEOC's 80% Rule]. (pp. 20–21)

Statistical Tests. Statistical significance is important when the group differences being used to evaluate potential adverse impact represent samples from their respective populations. In such cases, the relevant question is whether the sample differences are the result of random error or true population differences. Statistical tests can be used to evaluate whether the differential performance among the samples is large enough to justify the conclusion that there is differential performance among the respective minority and majority populations.

In the G.I. Forum case, the plaintiffs urged the court to consider statistical significance tests for evaluating adverse impact. In Texas, calculated passing rates were based on subpopulations of majority and minority students. Thus, no sampling had occurred, and inferential statistics were inappropriate. In fact, the use of statistical tests with large populations resulted in a conclusion of statistical significance even when the difference in passing rates between the two groups was less than .5%. Nonetheless, the

G.I. Forum Court credited inferential statistics in finding adverse impact for the graduation test:

> [T]he Court finds that, whether one looks at cumulative or single-administration results, the disparity between minority and majority pass rates on the [graduation test] must give pause to anyone looking at the numbers. . . . Disparate impact is suspected if the statistical significance test yields a result, or z-score, of more than two or three standard deviations. In all cases here, on single and cumulative administrations, there are significant statistical differences under this standard. Given the sobering differences in pass rates and their demonstrated statistical significance, the Court finds that the Plaintiffs have [met their burden of showing] significant adverse impact. (pp. 22–23)

The Court then considered whether TEA had met its burden of producing evidence of a manifest relationship between the graduation test and a legitimate educational goal and whether plaintiffs had demonstrated equally effective alternatives to the current use of the graduation test. The Court held that TEA had met its burden but that plaintiffs had not. The Court concluded:

> While the [graduation test] does adversely affect minority students in significant numbers, the TEA has demonstrated an educational necessity for the test, and the Plaintiffs have failed to identify equally effective alternatives. . . . The TEA [Texas Education Association] has provided adequate notice of the consequences of the exam and has ensured that the exam is strongly correlated to material actually taught in the classroom. In addition, the test is valid and in keeping with current educational norms. Finally, the test does not perpetuate prior educational discrimination. . . . Instead, the test seeks to identify inequities and to address them. (pp. 31–32)

Item Screening

When minority and majority students exhibit differential levels of performance on an achievement test, some observers want to believe that the test items are biased against members of the lower scoring minority group. However, an equally plausible explanation for the differential performance is a true difference in average achievement levels for the two groups. To address the issue of differential performance for a graduation test, states typically calculate differential performance statistics, which are then reviewed by panels of educators with proportional representation from relevant minority groups. Statistical indicators of differential performance do not necessarily indicate unfairness; it is up to the panels of educators to make a final determination of the fairness and appropriateness of each item. If an item is rejected, it may be revised and field tested again or discarded permanently.

In the G.I. Forum case, the plaintiffs argued that the graduation test was biased because differences between the percentages of majority and minority groups correctly answering each item were related to a measure of the degree to which each item distinguished between high- and low-scoring students. This led the plaintiffs to argue that test development procedures for the graduation test were flawed because the "methods employed by defendants are not designed to reduce racial/ethnic differences in either item performance or passing rates" (Shapiro, 1998, p. 2). Plaintiffs' experts opined that statistics measuring the degree to which an item distinguishes between high- and low-scoring students should not be used in the test development process or, alternatively, such statistics should be based on minority group members only. Contrary to any legal or professional standard, this argument implied that defendants had a duty to minimize majority/minority differences in correct answer rates, and was an attempt to institute the *Golden Rule* procedure previously renounced by the Educational Testing Service in an insurance licensure case and soundly discredited by measurement professionals.[3]

Accepted professional practice has established that comparisons designed to quantify bias must compare groups of equal knowledge and skills. To the extent that evidence of differential performance is based on groups of unequal knowledge and skills, the purported measure of *bias* is confounded by achievement differences in the two groups. Further, illustrative comparisons of items selected using total-group versus minority-group statistics relating item performance to total test performance indicated substantial overlap in the sets of selected items and content validity distortions for the unique items (Phillips, in press). The G.I. Forum Court declined to invalidate the graduation test based on evidence of unequal item performance for majority and minority students. The Court held:

> The Court also finds that the Plaintiffs have not demonstrated that the [graduation test] is a substantial departure from accepted academic norms or is based on a failure to exercise professional judgment. . . .
>
> The Court, in reaching this conclusion, has considered carefully the testimony of Plaintiffs' expert . . . demonstrating that the item-selection system chosen by TEA often results in the favoring of items on which minorities will perform poorly, while disfavoring items where discrepancies are less wide. The Court cannot quarrel with this evidence. However, the Court finds that the Plaintiffs have not been able to demonstrate that the test, as validated

---

[3]See Phillips (1990) for a discussion of the *Golden Rule* settlement and quotations from measurement professionals.

and equated, does not best serve the State's goals of identifying and re-
mediating educational problems. *Because one of the goals of the [graduation test]
is to identify and remedy problems in the State's educational system, no matter their
source, then it would be reasonable for the State to validate and equate test items on
some basis other than their disparate impact on certain groups.* (pp. 29–30; italics
added)

Test Security/Parental Rights

In Maxwell v. Pasadena I.S.D. (1994), Texas parents alleged that the statewide assessment violated first amendment guarantees of free exercise of
religion and freedom of speech by requiring their children to answer personal questions and respond to questions contrary to their religious beliefs. The parents demanded the right to review all assessments prior to
being administered to their children and asserted that the state's nondisclosure policy violated their fundamental constitutional right to direct
the upbringing and education of their children.

Although the Maxwell court held that the parents had sincerely held religious beliefs, the court found no violation of the First Amendment right
to free exercise of religion. The court did hold that the parents' fundamental right to direct the education of their children had been violated.
The violation of a fundamental right can be upheld only if the state has a
compelling interest and the means are narrowly tailored. Although the
Maxwell court found that the state had a compelling interest in ensuring
an adequate education for Texas children, the court ruled that the state's
nondisclosure policy was not narrowly tailored to serve that interest. The
final judgment of the court enjoined the state from administering tests to
Texas students unless parents of such students were provided an opportunity to view the test within 30 days after it had been administered.

While the Maxwell decision was on appeal by the state, the Texas legislature passed a law requiring annual release of all assessment items administered by the state to Texas students. Fortunately, pretest items were
exempted from release, and annual release of scored items allowed for re-
use of items within the year prior to release. Ohio, with a similar law, also
exempts items eliminated from scoring postadministration. Although
these disclosure procedures have defused claims of inappropriate item
content, they have also substantially increased the cost of administering
the statewide assessments in these states. This is due to the need to field
test a much larger number of items each year and the increased complexity of equating designs necessary to ensure a comparable standard across
administrations.

If parents and the public are allowed to review secure assessment materials used in statewide assessments, the state should develop a policy estab-

lishing procedures and delineating responsibilities. Important issues to be covered by such a policy include nondisclosure agreements, location of review, supervision, and timing and responsibilities of local staff. It is essential that any person allowed to view secure materials be required to sign a nondisclosure agreement. Staff that supervise the reviews should also sign a nondisclosure agreement to reinforce the expectation that all persons who view or handle secure materials will maintain strict confidentiality.

Review of secure materials at a central location is desirable to ensure an orderly process with maximum protection for secure materials. It is desirable to have at least two staff members supervise each review of secure materials. This policy protects both the staff supervisors and the state or district. Each supervisor is a witness to the actions of the other supervisor and to the actions of the person reviewing the secure materials. In the event of any questionable activity or diversion of the attention of one of the supervisors, the other supervisor can maintain the continued security of the room and materials.

Accommodations and Modifications[4]

State assessment staff face a variety of difficult policy decisions in crafting an accommodations/modifications policy for students with disabilities and limited English proficient (LEP) students. This section addresses a series of issues related to the decisions state assessment staff must make to create a test accommodations policy. These issues highlight the tradeoffs between competing policy goals advocated by different constituencies. State assessment staff will probably be unable to achieve all of the competing policy goals and will have to make some hard choices and set priorities related to the purpose of the statewide assessment.

ADA and IDEA Requirements

The Americans with Disabilities Act (ADA, 1990) states that:

> No *qualified individual with a disability* shall be excluded from participation in or be denied the benefits of the services, programs, or activities of [an educational institution]. (italics added)

---

[4]This portion of the chapter has been adapted from a report on testing accommodations for the Voluntary National Test prepared for the National Assessment Governing Board (NAGB) under contract with the American Institutes for Research (AIR). The content of the original report and this chapter are solely the responsibility of the author and do not necessarily reflect the views of NAGB or AIR.

The language of the ADA is similar to its predecessor, Section 504 of the Rehabilitation Act (1979), which provided that:

> No *otherwise qualified handicapped individual* . . . shall, solely by reason of his handicap, be excluded from the participation in, be denied the benefits of, or be subjected to discrimination under any program or activity receiving Federal financial assistance. . . . (italics added)

The Section 504 term *otherwise qualified* has been defined by the U.S. Supreme Court as "one who is able to meet all of a program's requirements in spite of [a disability]" (Southeastern Community College, 1979, p. 406). In a Georgia diploma testing case involving mentally retarded students, a federal district court added that:

> [I]f the [disability] is extraneous to the activity sought to be engaged in, the [person with a disability] is "otherwise qualified." . . . [But] if the [disability] *itself* prevents the individual from participation in an activity program, the individual is not "otherwise qualified." . . . To suggest that . . . any standard or requirement which has a disparate effect on [persons with disabilities] is presumed unlawful is farfetched. The repeated use of the word 'appropriate' in the regulations suggests that different standards for [persons with disabilities] are envisioned by the regulations. (Anderson, 1981; italics original)

In another diploma testing case involving disabled students, the Court listed Braille, large print, and testing in a separate room as accommodations mandated by Section 504. The Court also interpreted the earlier *Davis* case (Southeastern Community College v. Davis, 1979), which held that accommodations do not include "lowering or substantial modification of standards," as follows:

> Altering the content of the [test] to accommodate an individual's inability to learn the tested material because of his [disability] would be a "substantial modification" as well as a "perversion" of the diploma requirement. *A student who is unable to learn because of his [disability] is surely not an individual who is qualified in spite of his [disability].* (Brookhart, 1983; italics added)

Because the wording in the ADA, *qualified individual with a disability*, is similar to the wording of its predecessor, Section 504, *otherwise qualified handicapped individual*, the definitions provided in Section 504 cases should also apply to ADA cases. Based on these precedents, the legal requirement to provide accommodations appears to refer only to those alterations in standard testing conditions that are extraneous to the academic skills being assessed. The case law does not require testing alterations that substantially modify the assessed skills. A New York Supreme

Court justice summarizing the requirement stated, "The statute merely requires even-handed treatment of the [disabled and nondisabled], rather than extraordinary action to favor the [disabled]" (Board of Education of Northport, 1982).

The Individuals with Disabilities Education Act (IDEA, 1991) requires students with disabilities to be included in state assessment programs "with appropriate accommodations if necessary." This does *not* mean that:

- All requested testing condition alterations must be provided.
- Students receiving functional curricula must take an academic skills test.
- Students who receive substantial modifications (for purposes of maximizing inclusion) must have their scores interpreted identically to students tested under standard conditions.
- Scores from altered administrations must be aggregated with scores from standard administrations.
- All students must be assessed with exactly the same test. The alternative test given to these students can be developed by a different contractor using different test specifications.

The IDEA provision does mean that each student must be assessed with an appropriate instrument, but it does not mandate that the instrument be the on-grade-level state test.

ACCOMMODATIONS VERSUS MODIFICATIONS

The term *accommodation* has come to refer to any assistance given to a student with a disability during the administration of an assessment. This is unfortunate because some alterations in testing conditions that are being made for students with disabilities do not fit the legal or psychometric definition of an accommodation.

The 1985 *Test Standards* stated:

[U]nless it has been demonstrated that the psychometric properties of a test . . . are *not* altered significantly by some modification, the claims made for the test . . . cannot be generalized to the modified version. . . . When tests are administered to [persons with disabilities], particularly those [disabilities] that affect cognitive functioning, a relevant question is whether the modified test measures the same constructs. Do changes in the medium of expression affect cognitive functioning and the meaning of responses? (p. 78)

The Code of Fair Testing Practices (1988) is in agreement with the *Test Standards* in advising users that test scores obtained from nonstandard administrations should be interpreted with caution.

Policymakers at all levels (local, state, and national) should be encouraged to distinguish between nonstandard assessment administrations that alter the skill being measured and those that do not. Nonstandard testing conditions that change the skill being measured result in student scores that do not have the same interpretation as scores obtained under standard testing conditions. Such alterations can be distinguished from *accommodations* by referring to them as assessment *modifications*.

Conversely, assessment accommodations are designed to remove the effects of extraneous, unrelated factors while preserving the intended test score interpretation. A test user or test-information consumer should be indifferent to accommodations because they do not alter the validity of the test score interpretation. Yet one would expect users and consumers to view results from modified assessments differently than those from standard administrations.

The distinction between accommodations and modifications is important for appropriate test score interpretation and reporting. Scores from accommodated administrations can be aggregated with and use the same normative information as scores derived from standard administrations. However, scores from modified administrations must be reported separately and should not include normative information from standard administrations.[5]

The tendency of states to tie testing modifications to specific disabilities indicates that they implicitly recognize that test scores from modified administrations are not comparable to those obtained from standard test administrations. If a state allows scores from modified administrations to be interpreted the same as scores from standard administrations, it has conferred a benefit on those students who received the modifications. When benefits are conferred, the state must establish eligibility criteria and evaluate the qualifications of persons who seek the benefit. Effectively, the conferring of such benefits means that if a student can document a disability, the student is permitted to satisfy the state testing requirement by substituting an alternative skill or being exempted from the tested skill. Instead of awarding diplomas to students who have received the benefit of modifications on a graduation test, some states substitute a certificate of completion for these students.

Classifying Alterations in Testing Conditions

Not all persons with disabilities require an alteration in testing conditions. In some cases, a substantial alteration in standard testing conditions is required for a person with a disability to access the test. The following ques-

---

[5]See Phillips (1993, 1994) for an expanded discussion of these issues.

tions should be considered when classifying a testing condition alteration as an accommodation or a modification:

1. Will the test score obtained under altered testing conditions have a different interpretation than scores obtained under standard test administration conditions? Are the scores comparable?
2. Is the alteration in test format or administration conditions part of the skill or knowledge being tested?
3. Would allowing the alteration for *all* students help nondisabled students achieve higher scores and change the interpretation of their test scores?
4. Can valid and reliable procedures and appeals be established for determining which students will be allowed which alterations?
5. Do students with disabilities included in regular education classrooms have any responsibility for adapting to standard testing conditions when feasible?[6]

Alterations in testing conditions fall on a continuum from little or no relationship to the skill being measured (an accommodation) to being significantly intertwined with the skill being assessed (a modification). For example, for cognitive measures, a different height table for students in wheelchairs is highly unlikely to bear any relationship to the academic skills being assessed by an achievement test. Yet a read-aloud alteration will change a reading comprehension test into a listening comprehension test because the cognitive skills involved are substantially different. The former example would be labeled an *accommodation*, whereas the latter is a *modification*.

Unfortunately, there are alterations that fall in the center of the continuum—a gray area that is difficult to classify as an accommodation or a modification. The most straightforward way to evaluate these gray area alterations is to closely examine what the written literature about the test says it is intended to measure. This means that states should take great care when developing written descriptions of what the state tests are intended to measure.

Some observers have argued that any alteration that helps a disabled student achieve a higher score is a valid accommodation that should be treated the same as scores obtained by students with common accessories such as eyeglasses (Fraser et al., 1999). Unfortunately, this view fails to distinguish between alterations for extraneous factors and alterations that are closely related to the cognitive skill being measured. Eyeglasses are an

---

[6]Adapted from Phillips (1993, p. 27).

accommodation for a math computation test because vision is not part of the skill the test is intended to measure. Alternatively, although a calculator on the same math computation test might assist a learning disabled (LD) student in achieving a higher score, it would be a modification because its use changes the skill being measured from application of computational algorithms to pushing the correct buttons on the calculator.

Some observers have also questioned policy decisions that exclude modified test administrations from high-stakes decisions. Yet the lack of availability of such scores for use in making high-stakes decisions is appropriate when those scores have different interpretations than scores obtained from standard or accommodated administrations. For example, it would be misleading and unfair to other students to treat a modified test score obtained from a read-aloud administration of a reading comprehension test (a measure of listening comprehension) as having the same meaning as scores obtained from administrations where students read the test material silently by themselves. Alternatively, when accommodations are limited to only those alterations that maintain test score comparability, accommodated scores should be treated the same as scores obtained from standard administrations.

Extended Time.   Extended time is a particularly difficult alteration to judge. The decision depends on the degree of intentional and unintentional speediness of the test. For example, if the purpose of the test is to measure how quickly a student can copy a pattern of numbers and letters, speed is part of the skill being measured. In this situation, an extended time alteration would change the skill being measured from accuracy and speed to accuracy only. This change in the skill being measured would change the interpretation of the resulting test score, so the extended time alteration in this case should be classified as a *modification*.

Alternatively, an achievement test may intentionally be designed to be a power test with generous time limits. The purpose may be to measure pure academic knowledge irrespective of the time taken to demonstrate that knowledge. In this case, extended time may be judged to be an accommodation of a factor extraneous to the skill being measured. Even so, normative score information would be valid only for scores obtained under the same timing conditions as the norm group.

There is a tendency for some educators to argue that all achievement tests should be power tests with no speediness. There are two reasons that this position may be counterproductive. First, if given unlimited time, some students will continue working on the test well beyond the point of productivity. This behavior wastes instructional time and may unnecessarily tire and frustrate the student. Second, one of the goals of education is to help students automate skills so that they are readily available for use.

Thus, students who take 4 hours to complete a task that most students can complete in 1 hour may not have the same level of skill development. Assuming all other relevant factors equal, it is unlikely that an employer would be indifferent between these two potential applicants. Huesman et al. (2000) demonstrated that both LD and regular education students significantly improve their scores on a standardized, norm-referenced achievement test when given extended time.

An extended time alteration may be combined with other testing-condition alterations, such as administration of the test in several smaller sections interspersed with extended rest breaks. This combination of alterations in testing conditions can result in a 1-hour test, typically administered in a single sitting with one break between sections, being administered over a period of 6 hours spread across 1 to 2 weeks. Does this combination of alterations produce scores with the same interpretation as standard administrations?

To answer this question, the combined effects of taking four times as long in actual time and completing the task in much smaller increments, possibly with review or coaching in between, must be considered. Because most students find a final exam over all the material covered in a course much more difficult than a series of tests over individual units, it would seem that measurement of skills at a single point in time is different than measurement of a series of subskills at different points in time. Thus, if additional time is permitted to compensate for an extraneous factor such as reading Braille, the time extension should have reasonable limits within a single day (and preferably within a single block of time) to be classified as an accommodation. Extending test administration across multiple days in small segments appears more consistent with the characteristics of a modification.

Read Aloud for Nonreading Tests. Another difficult gray area on the accommodations/modifications continuum is a read-aloud alteration for a mathematics test. The classification of this alteration, again, depends on the purpose of the test and may involve competing educational goals. On the one hand, curriculum specialists may argue for more authentic tasks that require students to complete real-world exercises that require reading text and graphical information, applying mathematical reasoning, and writing a coherent explanation of the results. On the other hand, advocates for LD students may argue that assessing communication as part of a mathematics test penalizes these students for their reading/writing disabilities and does not allow them to demonstrate their knowledge of mathematics.

However, poor performance for low-achieving students without disabilities may also be the result of poor reading or writing skills. Whereas a read-aloud alteration is often available to a LD student, it usually is not provided to a nondisabled student with poor reading skills. One might wonder why nondisabled students who read slowly have limited vocabularies, have difficulty interpreting symbols, respond slowly, suffer test anxiety, or have difficulty staying on task are less deserving of the opportunity to demonstrate maximum performance than is a student who has been labeled *learning disabled*. Perhaps no one has yet discovered the disability that causes the nondisabled students to experience the listed difficulties.

Some evidence suggests that disabled students profit more from a read-aloud alteration than do low-achieving students (Tindal, 1999). This may be because instructional prescriptions for LD students often require all text to be read to the student, whereas low-achieving students continue to struggle to read text by themselves. Therefore, LD students may have received extended practice listening to text being read aloud and little practice reading the text themselves, whereas the experience of low achievers has been exactly the opposite. However, Meloy et al. (2000) found that both LD and non-LD students benefited from a read-aloud alteration on a standardized, norm-referenced achievement test. Generally, altered testing conditions are most effective when students have had practice using them, although that may not always be the case. A student given a calculator for a math computation test may benefit even when the student has not regularly used the calculator in the classroom.

The policy dilemma is whether to (a) penalize the low achiever while assisting the LD student, (b) classify a read-aloud alteration as a modification for all students, or (c) allow read aloud as an accommodation for all students. Choosing (a) creates the inconsistency of arguing that reading is part of the skill being measured for regular-education students but not for LD students. Yet choosing (c) means that the communication component of mathematics is being minimized. A more straightforward method for minimizing skills other than pure mathematics is to develop less complex items that use simplified text and pictorial representations. Choosing (b) would retain the intended skill, but would be unpopular with advocates for LD students because their reading/writing disabilities would be considered part of the intended skill being measured.

An important consideration in the formulation of a policy on read-aloud alterations is its unintended effects on student and teacher behavior. If read-aloud alterations are allowed for all students or if mathematics items are simplified to reduce reading/writing complexity, this may encourage teachers to engage in less integrated instruction in the classroom, or it may encourage a read-aloud instructional strategy for all students who are having difficulty reading text themselves. However, disallowing a read-aloud alteration for all students might discourage read-aloud instructional strategies for LD students and give greater emphasis to improving students' abilities to read text themselves. This latter unintended outcome might provide greater benefits to individual students than the former (see later section on "Students' Best Interests" for an argument supporting the benefits of independent reading).

Calculator Use. If a section of a math test has been constructed so that calculators are not allowed and students with dyscalculia (difficulty handling numerical information) use a calculator during testing, this may so alter the skill being assessed that it effectively exempts the disabled student from demonstrating the cognitive skills the test measures.

For example, consider the following estimation item:

About how many *feet* of rope would be required to enclose a 103" by 196" garden?

A. 25   *B. 50   C. 75   D. 100

Students without calculators might round 103 and 196 to 100 and 200, calculate the approximate perimeter as 2(100) + 2(200) = 600", and convert to feet by dividing by 12. Students with calculators would likely use the following keystrokes: "1 0 3 + 1 0 3 + 1 9 6 + 1 9 6 = ÷ 1 2 = ." The calculator would display "49.833 . . ." and the student would only need to choose the closest answer: 50. Clearly, use of the calculator would completely subvert the skill intended to be measured because the student would *not* have to do any estimation to select the correct answer. In this case, the student's disability is *not* an irrelevant factor to be eliminated, but an indication that the student does *not* have the cognitive skills measured by the mathematics test

In concluding that use of a calculator on a noncalculator section of a math test is a modification, one considers the test specifications as they are *currently* written. If advocates want students tested on different skills, they must first convince test developers to change the test specifications. Alternatively, this modification can be provided to LD students so long as the resulting scores are neither aggregated with scores from standard administrations nor compared to cut scores/norms obtained from standard administrations.

Qualifications

The policy question here requires a decision about the purpose of accommodations. If the purpose is to allow only alterations for extraneous factors—that is, to preserve the validity of the test score interpretation—it should not matter who receives the accommodation. In this situation, an accommodated score has the same interpretation as scores obtained under standard administration conditions. Yet if the purpose of accommodations is to confer a benefit on a specific subset of students, it becomes important to determine who qualifies for the benefit. In this case, relevant considerations may be: recent written documentation of the disability by a trained professional, routine provision of the accommodation in the student's educational program, an appropriate relationship between the disability and the desired accommodation, and the availability of facilities for providing the accommodation.

In the past, most testing programs have relied on the student's Individualized Education Plan (IEP) or 504 Plan to certify a disability. In many cases, achievement below expectations has been sufficient to label a student *disabled*. However, recent Supreme Court decisions suggest a narrower interpretation of the term *disability*. In two recent cases, the Court held that persons are disabled only if substantial life activities are affected *after correction or mitigation of an impairment* (Murphy, 1997; Sutton, 1997). The Court specifically stated that an employee with a corrected impairment was not disabled even if the person theoretically would have difficulties in the absence of medication or corrective apparatus (e.g., medication for high blood pressure or eyeglasses). This decision suggests a duty to take feasible corrective action for a disability and then be evaluated for the level of impairment. In an educational context, these decisions may mean that a student would qualify as having a reading disability and be eligible for a read-aloud alteration only if it is impossible for the student to learn to read, not merely because the student might have difficulty learning to read or because the student's current skill level might be inadequate for an adult. Nonetheless, a blind student, for whom reading printed text is impossible, would still qualify for a Braille administration. Such an interpretation would have the advantages of reserving alterations in standard testing administrations for those whose conditions cannot be modified or corrected and reducing the incentive to label a student *disabled* whenever the student has difficulty with academic tasks.

Leveling the Playing Field

Advocates for alterations in testing conditions for students with disabilities have argued that the purpose is to "level the playing field." There are two ways this statement could be interpreted: equalizing scores or removing extraneous factors.

Equalizing Scores. Some advocates appear to believe that *leveling the playing field* means providing a compensating advantage to offset the disability so that the student has an equal opportunity to obtain a high or qualifying score relative to the student's nondisabled peers. A model for this interpretation is a golf handicap tournament. Based on prior performance, golfers are given a handicap that is subtracted from the final score. In a handicap tournament, a poor golfer who plays well that day can win over a good golfer with a lower score who has not played as well as usual that day. Handicapping prevents the good golfers from always winning.

Similarly, using a handicapping model for interpreting *leveling the playing field* would create a testing scenario in which the highest achieving students would not always receive the highest scores. In such a scenario, the test would be viewed as a competition for which all participants, regardless of their level of knowledge and skills, should have an equal chance of obtaining a proficient score. Under this interpretation, each student with a disability would be given whatever assistance was necessary to neutralize the effects of the student's disability. For example, students who were not proficient at estimation would be given a calculator for those items; students who had difficulty processing complex textual material would be given multiple-choice items with only two choices rather than the usual five. Low-achieving students whose poor performance could not be linked to a specific disability would not receive any assistance; they would be required to compete on the same basis as the rest of the regular education students.

Removing Extraneous Factors.   The second interpretation of *leveling the playing field* is elimination of any extraneous factors that interfere with a disabled student's performance but that are unrelated to the skill being assessed. This interpretation would maximize the validity of the test score interpretation by requiring students with disabilities to demonstrate all relevant skills while not penalizing them for unrelated deficiencies. For example, on a multiple-choice reading comprehension test, a paraplegic student might be allowed to dictate answer choices into a tape recorder or have a scribe record the student's answer choices on the answer sheet. In either case, only the physical act of blackening an oval has been eliminated as an extraneous factor; the disabled student must still do all the cognitive work of reading the text and selecting a response. Case law supports this second interpretation (see, e.g., *Southeastern Community College v. Davis, 1979*).

Students' Best Interests

When selecting accommodations and modifications for students, test users must consider the purpose for testing. They should also consider what is best for the student in the long as well as the short run. Consider the following actual example from a statewide graduation testing program.

A first-grade student, let us call him Joey, was struggling in school relative to the earlier performance of his gifted older brother. The parents requested a special education referral, and Joey was tested. His performance in math was about 1 year below grade level, and his performance in reading was about half a year below grade level; there was a small discrepancy with ability in math and none in reading. The IEP developed for Joey, with significant parental input, labeled him learning disabled in math and required all written material to be read aloud to him. When Joey entered high school, an enterprising teacher chose to disregard the IEP and began intensive efforts to teach Joey to read. Within about 18 months, Joey went from reading at a second-grade level to reading at a sixth-grade level. Had this teacher not intervened, Joey would have graduated from high school dependent on others to read all textual material to him. Although his sixth-grade reading skills were not as high as expected of high school graduates, they provided some reading independence for Joey and allowed him to eventually pass the state's mathematics graduation test without a read-aloud modification.

The prior example illustrates an important trade-off in providing testing condition modifications. The parents in that scenario pushed for all instructional materials to be read aloud to Joey so he could avoid the frustration of struggling with a difficult subject. The downside was that Joey became totally dependent on the adults in his life to read everything to him. Yet when he finally was expected to learn reading skills, he was able to develop some functional independence. Although he still may require assistance with harder materials, there are many simpler texts that he can read on his own. The trade-off in learning to read was the shame of still being one of the worst readers among his peers.

The relevant question for policymakers is this: What are the relative costs of a set of proposed modifications to the recipients and to society? For the prior scenario, is it better to withhold the read-aloud modification and force the student to learn to read at whatever level is possible? Or is it better to do the reading for the student to avoid shame and low test scores? The former alternative may result in greater reading skill in the long run, but may cause frustration and low test scores in the short run. The latter alternative, while removing short-run frustration and increasing test scores, may result in long-term dependence on others.

Goals of Federal Legislation

One of the goals of federal legislation is access. A goal of access reflects an understanding that there is value in having students with disabilities participate in testing programs under any circumstances. One reason school districts value access may be that it results in greater accountability for school districts in providing instruction and demonstrating educational progress for special-needs students. If this is the case, any alteration that moves a student from an exclusionary status to one of being included in the test is desirable. However, in the case of statewide assessments, complying with this mandate may leave students and parents dissatisfied. This is because test scores obtained under modified conditions will receive little interpretive feedback. Any normative data will not be valid, including achievement classifications such as *proficien* or *basic*. In such cases, students and parents will receive only uninterpretable raw scores. Furthermore, modified scores should not be included in aggregate data, so the scores will probably be excluded from summary data. Thus, the question is whether the goal of access is worth having students take tests for which feedback is extremely limited.

There are always some students for whom a state test is not appropriate even with modifications. The state test is designed to measure academic skills taught in the regular education curriculum. For students with disabilities who are receiving instruction in functional skills rather than the regular education curriculum, or who are at an academic level significantly below grade level, the state test will be an inappropriate measure of instructional expectations. The IDEA mandate for inclusion in statewide assessment programs can be met for these students through the use of alternative assessments prescribed by the states. These alternative assessments may include academic assessments at a lower skill level or performance checklists/assessments of functional skills. As with other modified assessments, scores for these alternative assessments should be reported separately.

An alternative goal to access may be increased success (higher test scores) for students with disabilities. Those who support this view suggest that students should not be penalized for biological conditions outside their control. They believe that the intent of the legislation was to confer a benefit on students with disabilities that would change the skill being measured from skills the student cannot do to something the disabled student is able to do. In this case, any alterations in testing conditions would be permissible so long as the student has a documented disability. Score reports for such students would contain all the same normative and interpretive information as score reports for standard administrations. However, if this interpretation is adopted, some designation would need to be placed on the report to indicate that the score was obtained under nonstandard administration conditions. Such a designation should not identify the disability, but may identify the altered testing conditions. Identifying scores obtained under altered testing conditions is essential for appropriate interpretation because such scores do not have the same meaning as scores obtained under standard testing conditions.

Needs Versus Wants

There is a difference between truly needing something and wanting something. Humans need food and water to survive, but they do not need to eat apple pie and drink coffee to survive. Some people may want the latter and be unhappy if they do not get it, but they can meet their survival needs with other less appealing foods and plain water. Similarly, a blind student needs an alternative method to access written text or he or she will be unable to provide any response to the assessment. However, a LD student does not necessarily need to have a test read aloud. The LD student may be able to access the written test, but may want the test read aloud to achieve a higher score or because the student's parents and teachers have been doing so in the classroom.

The challenge for any testing program is to separate those students who truly cannot participate without an alteration in testing conditions from those who simply want the additional assistance to make the task easier. Nonetheless, even an alteration that is truly needed for a student to access the test may invalidate the intended score interpretation. In such a case, policymakers must determine whether the benefits of inclusion with a modification outweigh the costs of losing interpretive information and being excluded from aggregate results.

Purpose of the Test

One of the stated purposes of a state test may be the provision of relevant achievement data to students and parents. Given this purpose, an important consideration for an accommodations/LEP policy for the state test is what best supports the intended use of the test results. That is, will parents be better served by having their LD or LEP students tested with modifications but receiving little feedback, having them tested under standard conditions for which the score may be extremely low and frustration high, or having them excluded from testing altogether if their access to the test is limited or impossible under standard or true accommodation conditions? The answer may vary depending on the goals of the parents and the particular disability. There may be no overall consensus on this issue. If so, allowing a local decision with appropriate designation of scores from nonstandard administrations may be a reasonable compromise.

LEP Haves and Have Nots

There has been a lot of debate about whether a state test should be translated into languages other than English. Some districts have lobbied for native language versions, particularly in Spanish; others have objected to measuring skills in any language but English. As with accommodations, developing an appropriate policy for assessing LEP students on a state test depends on the articulated purpose(s) for the test (see Clark, 1999; Porter, in press).

On one side are those who believe the function of public education is to prepare students to live and work in an English-speaking country. They argue that students with good English skills are more likely to be accepted by postsecondary institutions and be hired by employers for the more desirable and better paying jobs. Furthermore, they cite research that indicates that students who learn a language at an early age tend to have greater fluency and less of an accent as adults—assets they believe are related to better life opportunities. Because languages take many years to learn, these reformers believe that the sooner students begin operating in English, the better their skills will be when they leave high school. Because many LEP students for whom no English is spoken in the home may enter elementary school already behind their peers, this view takes the position that all their time in school should be spent in intensive English instruction designed for non-native speakers.

On the other side of the argument are those who believe bilingual education is most desirable for LEP students. They argue that students should learn to read and write in their native language before learning English as a second language. They also believe that it is the duty of public schools to assist students' transition to learning English by first teaching and assessing students in their native language. Such programs move gradually from mostly native language instruction to instruction mostly in English over a period of 6 or more years. With respect to assessments, bilingual educators argue that tests in English are unfair to LEP students because such tests assess both English language skills and the content skills being measured. Bilingual educators want English language skills to be assessed separately from content knowledge/skills in a subject area such as mathematics or reading.

The first task in developing an LEP policy for a state testing program is to determine which view the purpose of the state test supports. Is the state test designed to assess reading and math skills in English? Or should the effects of limited English proficiency be removed from the assessment so that only the content knowledge/skills are being assessed? If the purpose of the state test is to provide a pure measure of student achievement not dependent on English-language skills, then policymakers may want to translate the state test into other languages. Yet if the purpose of the state test is to provide a measure of achievement of those skills that are necessary for future productivity in postsecondary education and the workplace, demonstration of the content skills in English may be designated as the skill intended to be measured. In that case, no translations would be provided.

Suppose policymakers decide to translate the state test into other languages. What languages should have translations? Large urban schools report 50 to 100 different languages in their LEP populations. With limited resources, it is clearly not feasible to develop translations in all these languages. So if the state test is translated, someone has to decide which one or maybe two languages can be supported with the existing resources. Many educators have argued that at least a Spanish translation should be provided because it represents the native language of the majority of LEP students. The argument seems to be that the Spanish-speaking LEP students should receive native language assessment because of their significant numbers in the public schools. Although the native language of a majority of LEP students in some states is Spanish, Chinese, Vietnamese, or Russian are the dominant native languages in other states and districts.

In whatever way the decision is made about which language(s) to translate, there will be an inherent inequity. Having native language assessment for some but not all LEP students creates two unequal groups: the *haves* and the *have nots*. The arguments for the haves are that (a) they should receive native language instruction and assessment as they learn English because it is the best way to teach, and (b) they deserve special treatment because they are the majority LEP group. However, for the have nots, it does not matter what the best instructional strategy is; their only options are to test in English or be excluded.

The equal protection clause of the 14th Amendment to the U.S. Constitution requires similarly situated students to be treated equally. Court cases based on this clause have invalidated educational programs that favored White students over African-American students (e.g., *Brown v. Board of Education*, 1954). In particular, any classification based on race or ethnicity has been considered suspect, and impossibly high standards must be met to justify such a program (Nowak et al., 1986). Therefore, it seems conceivable that the courts would take a dim view of a program that provides a benefit to Spanish-speaking LEP students but denies that same benefit to Vietnamese-speaking LEP students. In the context of the LEP classification, students of the majority ethnic group would be treated differently than students from minority ethnic groups. It is not clear that the court would accept numerical dominance as a compelling reason for doing this, particularly when there is disagreement about whether LEP students are better served in English immersion or bilingual programs. In fact, courts in the past have tended to side with a minority ethnic group receiving differential treatment.

Aside from the possible legal challenges to a Spanish version of a state test, there are psychometric difficulties as well. Creating an equivalent Spanish (or other language test) for which the scores have the same interpretations as the English version is a daunting task at best. Direct translation only works on some of the items, and adaptations made for other items may change the skill being measured (see Hambleton, 1996).

Equating translated tests is difficult because it requires a group of students who are equally proficient in both languages—a difficult condition to assess. One can also ask whether equivalent performance on, for example, a Vietnamese version really represents the same level of skill as its corresponding score on the English version. That is, if an employer could choose between two students who are equally proficient on all relevant variables, the only difference being that one is proficient in English and the other in Vietnamese, would the employer be indifferent about which student to hire? If not, the purported equivalence is illusory, and students may be misled about the level of their achievement. One possible compromise is to administer an English-language test to LEP students and use the results to augment the interpretation of scores on a state achievement test administered in English. Another possibility is to test LEP students in both English and their native language using the English version scores for accountability and the native language version scores for classroom diagnosis and instructional decisions. Further, all LEP students may not be proficient in their native language. Thus, testing in the native language may not remove the language barrier, but rather may create a new one.

The argument is often made that students should not be assessed in a language in which they are not proficient (Fraser et al., 1999). The intended reference is to non-native speakers of English. However, there are native speakers who perform poorly on tests given in English because they also are not proficient in English. Yet for the native speaker, one rarely worries about the effects of language proficiency on test performance, and typically these students do not have the effects of poor language skills removed from their scores. Thus, the argument seems to be that the effects of lack of English proficiency should be removed from test scores for non-native speakers but not native speakers, although both may need intensive additional instruction in English to achieve proficiency.

There have been suggestions that test items should be developed with LEP students in mind (Fraser et al., 1999). Items for large-scale assessments, including state tests, are carefully reviewed for potential cultural disadvantages or stereotypes by representative panels of educators. However, attempts to simplify language, include pictures, change vocabulary, or avoid idioms may create an inherent contradiction for a test designed to measure high standards in academic subjects. The suggested changes might significantly alter the difficulty of the test and the match of the test items to the content intended to be measured. If a simplified test is desired for LEP students, it should be developed as a separate test, perhaps linked to the same score scale, if feasible.

The dilemma for policymakers in developing an LEP test administration policy is similar to that faced in deciding how to test students with disabilities. There are competing policy goals and costs on opposite sides of each argument. Policymakers must determine which of the competing goals is most consistent with the purpose of the state test, is in the best interests of its students, and has the least detrimental costs. For example, policymakers who favor translated tests must consider the effects of ethnic-based differential treatment of LEP students, reporting only raw scores, justifying the equivalency of these modified tests to the corresponding English language versions, and arguing that students benefit more from taking translated tests than from taking the tests in English.

Whatever decision is made about providing translated tests, it is difficult to argue that translated tests measure the same skills as the English versions of the state test. For example, in terms of content, it may be difficult to argue that there is a pure reading skill that exists apart from the context of the language in which the text is written. The content argument may be more compelling in mathematics, but some policymakers might argue that by the time students reach high school they should be receiving instruction in English. The exception would be newly arrived students, who may also not be literate in their native languages if they have not received formal schooling in their home countries. Newly arrived students should expect to spend additional years in school if they want to earn a high school diploma.

Testing in another language with at least some different items appears to most closely resemble an alteration in testing conditions that changes the skill being measured and therefore is a modification. As with other modifications in testing conditions, such scores should not use normative interpretations or be aggregated with scores from nonstandard administrations. However, although such tests may provide access to students who might otherwise be excluded, they may also limit opportunities for inclusion in regular classrooms and practice with the content and types of test items included on graduation tests.

Nonetheless, state test literature should be careful not to claim that a translation is being made available to Spanish-speaking LEP students for pedagogical reasons because this argument collapses when LEP students with other native languages are considered. It is probably best advertised as a modification designed to include more students and/or as a transition to administration of the English version. Yet even this latter position leaves the issue of fairness to have not LEP students unresolved.

LEP Accommodations

Many states provide accommodations for LEP students. However, the term *accommodation* is probably inappropriate because LEP is not like other disabilities. Disabilities are generally thought to describe characteristics over which students have no control and generally are not reversible over time. LEP students can "lose their disability" by becoming proficient in English through instruction. It is not clear at this point whether it is in LEP students' best interests to label them as *disabled*.

To the extent that a test intends to measure content skills in English, any alteration that provides assistance with English is providing help with the skill being measured. Thus, the alteration is compensating for a relevant factor, not an extraneous factor. This is clearly contrary to the definition of an accommodation. Therefore, if special testing condition alterations (such as bilingual dictionaries or responses in the native language) are provided to give LEP students greater access to a state test, they should be labeled and treated as modifications.

Undue Burdens

Case law has established that an accommodation is not required if it imposes an undue burden. However, most interpretations have required extreme expense or disruption to qualify as an undue burden. Testing programs face issues of cost and scheduling burdens for some testing condition alterations. For example, more space and substantially increased numbers of administrators are required when significant numbers of students are tested individually. An individual administration may be required due to frequent breaks, attention problems, read aloud, use of specialized equipment, medical monitoring, and so on. Such administrations may pose a major challenge for schools when testing windows are narrow.

Another problem for schools can be the cost of providing an expensive alteration for a single student. In one statewide program, a student requested a 99-point large-print version. This size print allowed only one to two words per page and required special large-paper versions for diagrams. The cost of producing such a large-print version for a single test form was over $5,000. Because it was a graduation test, there was a potential issue of additional versions to be created if the student was unsuccessful on the initial attempt. In addition, due to fatigue, the student could only work for about 10 minutes at a time and for only a few hours each day, so testing was scheduled over several weeks.

The previous situation involved a visual impairment that could not be further corrected. Thus, it was impossible for the student to take the test without the requested alteration. However, the cost was significant for the state to pay for a single student. In such a case, the requested alteration might be judged an undue burden and a state not be required to provide it.[7]

---

[7]The stated reason for requesting the alteration in testing conditions was a parental desire for the student to attend a particular state university that required a high school diploma for admission. Due to the severity of the disability, some educators questioned the student's ability to handle college level course requirements even if the student passed the modified test.

Similarly, state test policymakers have to prioritize the use of available test alteration resources. It may not be possible to provide the test in all requested formats, even when such requests are consistent with the state Test Accommodations/LEP Policy. An alternative may be to allow local test administrators to decide which accommodations/modifications to provide. Such a policy would have the advantage of limiting the state cost, but would have the disadvantage of resulting in similarly situated students being treated differently depending on local policy in their geographic area. In addition, there would probably still be a duty for state test policymakers to provide guidance to local policymakers regarding accommodations/ modifications decisions, appropriate use and interpretation of the resulting test scores, and informed consent of parents/students.

Choice of Decision Makers

Many educators and policymakers have felt that accommodations/modifications decisions should be made by a student's IEP or 504 committee. Such committees make those decisions for instruction and some local district tests. However, without some guidance, it is likely that these committees would choose test condition alterations that invalidate the intended test score interpretation of a state test.

For example, IEPs exist that have mandated the following alterations for LD students included in regular education classes:

- all tests to be read to the student;
- provision of word lists for choosing answers to completion items;
- crossing out multiple-choice options so that only two remain for each item;
- individual test administration where the administrator explains the questions;
- home study of the test questions for several days prior to oral administration of the questions in exactly the same order as on the written version;
- calculators for estimation and computation questions;
- rewriting questions to decrease the reading level and complexity of the questions;
- assistance of the student's aide and tutor during testing;
- unlimited time and/or unlimited breaks with continuation of testing on subsequent days; and
- use of specified reference materials during testing.

In most of the cases described before, the mandated testing alteration would not be consistent with valid test score interpretation. Yet allowing the local IEP or 504 committee to make the decision would most likely result in the provision of such alterations for some students. Although such actions might further the goal of including all students, little, if any, useful interpretive or aggregate information could be provided. Alternatively, inappropriate normative information might be provided if the scoring entity was not apprised that a modified test had been given. Such a policy of broad acceptance of local decisions might also further encourage IEP and 504 committees to continue mandating alterations that substantially change the skill being measured in the regular education classroom as well as for the state test.

Another disadvantage of leaving such decisions in the hands of local committees is the inequity that may occur across jurisdictions. That is, a particular alteration may be labeled an accommodation in one district and a modification in another. This would defeat the purpose of providing comparable state testing results to all teachers, parents, and students. Such discrepancies would result in test score interpretations that varied depending on the district where the test was administered. It would also erode any state assertions that all students were being held to the same high standards or that recipients of a high school diploma had achieved a set of specified skills.

To have some control over test administration conditions, state policymakers should consider developing a policy that specifies which testing condition alterations will be treated as accommodations and which as modifications. Although prior provision of accommodations/modifications is a reasonable inquiry as one factor in the determination of the existence of a bona fide disability, it does not necessarily mean that that specific alteration should be permitted on the state test. State policymakers will not satisfy their duty to ensure appropriate test score interpretation and use, to the degree feasible, if they blindly accept committee mandates that may be inconsistent or may invalidate test scores. Although IDEA specifies that these committees will make instructional decisions for special education students, the law does not mandate that these committees be given sole discretion for testing policy.

For some statewide tests, a permissible list of accommodations is provided, and all other committee mandates are treated as modifications. If a committee feels that testing a student with the state test using allowable accommodations or losing interpretive information with the use of a modification is not in a student's best interests, the committee can choose to exclude the student from testing. If the parent disagrees, the parent can request a due process hearing under the IDEA.

REPORTING AND INTERPRETING SCORES

If policymakers believe that students will benefit from having access to the test in any form, the policy will probably encourage modified administrations. However, when test modifications invalidate the intended test score interpretation, policymakers must decide what results will be provided and what interpretive cautions will be stressed. That is, if modified administrations are permitted to achieve the goal of access, state test policymakers must be careful that the resulting scores are not misinterpreted. This is an important duty because some advocates want to interpret tests administered with modifications in the same way as tests administered under standard conditions. Such interpretations are invalid and, if permitted, will undermine the validity of the state test testing program.

What should policymakers do with test scores obtained under modified conditions? To maintain the validity of score interpretations, normative information (e.g., national percentile ranks or standard scores) obtained from groups tested under standard conditions should not be reported. This includes achievement levels that were determined using student performance data from standard administrations. For example, it would be misleading to report that an LD student with a read-aloud accommodation achieved at the proficient level when regular education students labeled proficient were required to read the test themselves, and their data were used in the determination of the cutoff scores for the reported achievement levels.

Role of Research

Research is useful in answering specific questions about the effects of certain administration conditions on identifiable groups of students. However, because the severity of a disability differs across students and a student may have multiple disabilities, it is difficult to obtain meaningful summary data for disability groups. It is also difficult to disentangle the effects of instructional practice and those of the specific testing condition alteration. That is, do LD students score higher than poor readers when given a read-aloud accommodation because they have had more instructional practice with listening comprehension or because such an alteration can only help disabled students, not low-achieving students?

Another issue with research is that it does not answer some important policy questions, such as: What is the purpose of the test? Is access a more important policy goal than valid score comparisons? Such policy questions are mostly political and require policymakers to decide based on logical argument, program goals, and interpretation of legislative intent. Postponing a decision to collect more research evidence begs the question. In the end, policymakers must choose between competing goals and trade-offs that will not go away no matter how many research studies are undertaken. Further, there is not enough time or resources to investigate all the questions that must be answered in formulating an accommodations/LEP policy for a state test.

State policymakers must consider the short- and long-term benefits of alternative policies to a variety of potential users and decide which policies are most consistent with the purpose and goals of the state testing program and state law. No matter what state test policymakers decide, some constituencies will disagree. Thus, policymakers must be prepared to clearly articulate the specific goals and arguments that inform their final decisions.

Some observers have argued for validation of the state test for students with disabilities by including them in sampling, pilot testing, field testing, and norming of the test. Students with disabilities who can take the test under standard test administration conditions or with true accommodations should be included, especially if they are receiving instruction in the regular education curriculum.

However, inclusion of students with disabilities tested with modifications would decrease the validity of the resulting data. Although policymakers may decide to include such students to achieve the goal of greater access, modified test scores should be reported separately. Because different modifications alter the validity of test score interpretation in different ways, aggregating all modified test scores into a single category may not be especially meaningful. It may be more informative to aggregate by type of modification.

MULTIPLE GOALS

Full inclusion will probably require the use of assessment modifications. Modified test scores have different interpretations and must be treated separately both at the individual and aggregate levels. Valid score interpretation is possible under a full inclusion model only if nonstandard administrations are identified and score reports are adjusted accordingly.

State policymakers must also work hard to educate users about appropriate interpretations and uses of modified test administrations. There will probably be extended debate about which testing alterations should be classified as modifications, and users who disagree with the final results may be tempted to report normative information for modified tests and aggregate those scores with scores from standard administrations. State policymakers must decide whether these potential misuses of the data outweigh the benefits of including more students via modified testing. State policymakers must also decide whether the limited, valid, score-inter-pretation information that will be available for modified administrations justifies the testing costs to students, parents, districts, and state testing programs.

RECOMMENDATIONS

The following recommendations are based on current legal requirements and psychometric principles. Specific implementation details may vary depending the configuration of a state testing program, its purposes, and its implementing state legislation and administrative regulations. These recommendations can be used as a starting point for development of a state testing accommodations/LEP policy.

1. For students with disabilities and LEP students, have IEP/504 committees and local LEP program directors select one of the following exhaustive, mutually exclusive categories. For nondisabled students, allow administrators to authorize category II accommodations.

I. **Standard administration conditions.**

II. **Accommodated administration** using one or more of the accommodations designated in the state test administration manual as acceptable for each subject matter test. The list should include only those testing condition alterations judged to retain the validity of the intended test score interpretation(s). Students tested with accommodations receive the same interpretive information as category I students, and their scores may be aggregated with category I scores.

III. **Modified administration** using testing condition alterations that are not on the state test accommodations list but are regularly provided in the student's instructional program. Students tested with modifications would receive only raw scores with no achievement levels, no pass/fail designations and no normative information. Category III scores may not be aggregated with category I and II scores.

IV. **Exclusion from testing** because the student cannot access the test with modifications or is being instructed with a functional curriculum that does not include the academic skills measured by the state test. The student is provided an alternative lower level academic test or alternative functional skills test. Category IV scores are reported separately.

2. Provide a list, such as the sample in Table 6.1, that classifies testing condition alterations for the state test as accommodations or modifications. If a school/parent wants a testing condition alteration not on the list,

TABLE 6.1
Sample Accommodations/Modifications Chart

Reading	*Mathematics*
Accommodations	
• Braille/large print/magnification • small group/separate room	• Braille/large print/magnification • small group/separate room • read aloud (if not measuring math communication)
• noise buffer/special lighting • markers/templates/colored overlay	• noise buffer/special lighting • markers/templates/colored overlay • abacus (calculator section)
• scribe/tape recorder (record answers) • record answers in test booklet • extended time* (if test not at all speeded) • extra breaks* • scheduling/time of day* • seating/table height • signing oral directions	• scribe/tape recorder (record answers) • record answers in test booklet • extended time* (if test not at all speeded) • extra breaks* • scheduling/time of day* • seating/table height • signing oral directions
Modifications	
• read aloud	• read aloud (if measuring math communication)
• translation into sign or other language • paraphrasing/simplifying text • computer use • extended time (if test speeded) • administer small segments over multiple days • individual, interactive administration • dictionary, word list, thesaurus • limiting number of answer choices • assistance of aide to read/answer items	• translation into sign or other language • abacus/calculator (noncalculator section) • computer use • extended time (if test speeded) • administer small segments over multiple days • individual, interactive administration • dictionary, word list, thesaurus • limiting number of answer choices • assistance of aide to read/answer items

*Within a single day for each test; no assistance given; no additional references available; no contact with students already tested.

provide a contact person to receive and act on written requests. The contact person may be aided by outside consultants in making a decision on each request. Add these decisions to the appropriate list for the next state test administration.

3. Permit the parent(s)/guardian(s) of any student (with or without a disability; LEP or non-LEP) to choose a category I, II, III, or IV state test administration by signing a written form that includes full disclosure of the options and their consequences. Require IEP/504 committees to include a form in the IEP, signed by school personnel and the parent(s), documenting consideration of testing options and the final decision of the committee.

4. Collect information about the specific disability or LEP status and specific accommodations or modifications on the student answer sheet. Conduct separate research studies as resources and funds become available.

5. Pay the costs of accommodated test administrations from state test program funds, and require local districts to pay the costs of modified test administrations. Provide additional written guidelines to aid local districts in making accommodations/modifications decisions.

6. Administer an English-language test to LEP students to augment the interpretation of the state test scores. This information will assist users in judging the effects of language proficiency on test scores and will provide useful information for assessing nonnative speakers' progress in achieving essential English-language skills.

7. If policymakers decide to allow scores from modified test administrations to be interpreted the same as standard administrations, acknowledge that a benefit is being conferred on eligible students, and adopt policies that require appropriate written documentation and evaluation to determine whether the students qualify for the benefit. Eligibility criteria for which written documentation should be required include: (a) certification of the disability by a trained professional, (b) confirmation of regular use of the modification by the student in the classroom, (c) rationale for and relationship of the requested modification to the specific disability, and (d) certification of the impossibility of the student accessing the test without the requested modification. School and/or department officials may be aided by outside consultants when evaluating written documentation and should follow a written policy. Consider transcript and/or diploma notations that identify scores obtained with modifications. Possibilities include general notations such as "tested under nonstandard conditions" or describing the modification (e.g., read aloud, calculator) but not the specific disability.

8. Establish an appeals procedure for persons desiring to challenge an accommodations decision. Such a procedure might begin at the local school level and be reviewable by state officials on request.

CONCLUSION

Graduation tests are visible and accessible targets for those who disagree with state educational policy decisions. Challenges can come from a variety of groups on an assortment of issues. To be prepared, state testing programs must follow legal and psychometric standards, comprehensively document program decisions and activities, and work closely with legislators, administrators, and educators. Maintaining a defensible testing program is a challenging task, but as the G.I. Forum case demonstrates, it is achievable.

REFERENCES

American Educational Research Association, American Psychological Association, National Council on Measurement in Education. (1985). *Standards for Educational and Psychological Testing* [hereinafter *Test Standards*]. Washington, DC: American Psychological Association.

Americans with Disabilities Act (ADA) Pub.L. No. 101-336, 42 U.S.C. §12101 et seq. (1990).

Anderson v. Banks, 520 F.Supp. 472, 510-11 (S.D. Ga. 1981).

Board of Educ. of Northport-E. Northport v. Ambach, 90 A.D.2d 227, 458 (1982).

Brookhart v. Illinois State Board. of Ed., 697 F.2d 179 (7th Cir. 1983).

Brown v. Board of Education, 347 U.S. 483 (1954).

Clark, K. (1999, June). *From primary language instruction to English immersion: How five California districts made the switch.* READ ABSTRACTS Research and Policy Brief, Washington, DC.

Debra P. v. Turlington, 644 F.2d 397 (5th Cir. 1981), 730 F.2d 1405 (11th Cir. 1984).

Shapiro, M. M. (1998, November 23). *Declaration of Martin M. Shapiro*, G.I. Forum v. TEA.

Fraser, K., & Fields, R. (1999, February). *NAGB Public Hearings and Written Testimony on Students with Disabilities and the Proposed Voluntary National Test October–November 1998, Synthesis Report.*

G.I. Forum et al. v. Texas Education Agency et al., __ F.Supp __ (W.D. Tex 1999).

Hambleton, R. K. (1996, April). *Guidelines for adapting educational and psychological tests.* Paper presented at the NCME annual meeting, New York.

Huesman, R. L., & Frisbie, D. A. (2000, April). *The validity of ITBS reading comprehension test scores for learning disabled and non learning disabled students under extended-time conditions.* Paper presented at the NCME annual meeting, New Orleans.

Individuals with Disabilities Education Act (IDEA), Pub. L. No. 102-119, 20 U.S.C. §1400 et seq. (1991).

Joint Committee on Testing Practices. (1988). *Code of fair testing practices in education.* Washington, DC: Author.

Maxwell v. Pasadena I.S.D., No. 92-017184, 295th District Court of Harris County,TX, Dec. 29, 1994.

Meloy, L. L., Deville, C., & Frisbie, D. (2000, April). *The effect of a reading accommodation on standardized test scores of learning disabled and non learning disabled students.* Paper presented at the NCME annual meeting, New Orleans.

Murphy v. United Parcel Service, No. 97-1992.

Nowak, J., Rotunda, R., & Young, J. (1986) *Constitutional Law* 3rd ed. §§ 14.1–14.3, 10.6, 11.4.

Phillips, S. E. (1990, Dec. 20). *The Golden Rule Remedy for Disparate Impact of Standardized Testing: Progress or Regress?* 63 Ed. Law Rep. 383.

Phillips, S. E. (1993, March 25). *Testing accommodations for disabled students*, 80 Ed. Law Rep. 9.

Phillips, S. E. (1994). High-stakes testing accommodations: Validity versus disabled rights. *Applied Measurement in Education, 93*(2).

Phillips, S. E. (in press). G.I. Forum v. TEA: Psychometric Evidence. *Applied Measurement in Education.*

Porter, R. (in press). Accountability is overdue: Testing the academic achievement of Limited-English Proficient (LEP) students. *Applied Measurement in Education.*

Section 504 of the Rehabilitation Act, 29 U.S.C. §701 et seq. (1973).

Southeastern Community College v. Davis, 442 U.S. 397, 406 (1979).

Sutton v. United Airlines, No. 97-1943.

Tindal, G. (1999, June). *Test accommodations: What are they and how do they affect student performance?* CCSO Large Scale Assessment Conference, Snowbird, UT.

Title VI of the Civil Rights Act of 1964, 42 U.S.C. §2000d.

Title VI Regulations, 34 C.F.R. §100.3 (1964).
Uniform Guidelines on Employee Selection Procedures. (1985). 29 C.F.R. § 1607.
Wards Cove Packing Co. v. Antonio, 490 U.S. 642 (1989).
Watson v. Fort Worth Bank and Trust, 487 U.S. 977 (1988).

Chapter 7

Consequences of Assessment: What Is the Evidence?

William A. Mehrens
Michigan State University

This chapter[1] addresses what I believe to be an important question: What evidence do we have regarding the consequences of assessment? As most readers probably know, I am not a fan of the term *consequential validity*. However, I am interested in the consequences of assessment. I have heard speeches and read articles on the topic and concluded that, although not enough evidence was available, it would be worthwhile to review the available evidence more thoroughly.

In addition to the fact that previous scholarly presentations left me unsatisfied with respect to the evidence on consequences, there are additional rationales for choosing this topic. Many, but certainly not all, political leaders at the national, state, and local levels have been touting the value of large-scale assessment. For example, former President Clinton and former Secretary of Education Richard Riley have argued that voluntary national tests of reading at Grade 4 and mathematics at Grade 8 would have positive consequences for education. Secretary Riley has said, "I believe these tests are absolutely essential for the future of American education" (Riley, 1997a; cited in Jones, 1997, p. 3).[2] President Clinton also asked each state to adopt tough standards for achievement. The argument seems to be that if tough standards are adopted, achievement will rise.

Educational reformers suggest that:

---

[1]This chapter is a slight revision of an article published in *Education Policy Analysis Archives*, 6(13), under the same title. It is printed here with permission.

[2]As Jones has wondered, "Can he really mean that?" (Jones, 1997, p. 3).

149

Assessments play a pivotal role in standards-led reform, by: communicating
the goals . . . providing targets . . . , and shaping the performance of educators and students. Coupled with appropriate incentives and/or sanctions—
external or self-directed—assessments can motivate students to learn better,
teachers to teach better, and schools to be more educationally effective.
(Linn & Herman, 1997, p. iii)

Note the word *can* in the previous quote. The question is, do they? Linn,
Baker, and Dunbar (1991) pointed out that we cannot just assume that a
more authentic assessment will result in better classroom activities. Linn
(1994) also correctly suggested that we need evidence that the uses and interpretations are contributing to enhanced student achievement while not
producing unintended negative outcomes.

There is no question that assessment is perceived by many as having a
potential for good in both evaluating and, if necessary, reforming schools.
But there are reasons to question whether that potential will be realized.
Goodling (1997) stated that: "If testing is the answer to our educational
problems, it would have solved them a long time ago. American students
are tested, tested, tested, and the Clinton administration is proposing to
test our children again" (p. A21).

Goodling suggested that thinking that new tests will lead to better students is "akin to claiming that better speedometers make for faster cars"
(Goodling, 1997; cited in Froomkin, 1997, p. 3).

There are both potential values and dangers in large-scale testing. Is
the potential value of assessment a vision or an illusion? Are the potential
dangers likely to be realized? What is the evidence?

For testing to be a good thing, the positive consequences must outweigh the negative consequences by some factor greater than the costs.
The costs of large-scale assessments are particularly high for alternative
forms of assessment, such as have been used in Kentucky. Are the consequences of assessment worth the cost? Are the consequences of alternative
assessments worth the much greater cost? What is the evidence?

GENERAL OVERVIEW

In this chapter, I wish to (a) spend a brief amount of time on the prevalence of large-scale assessments (focusing primarily on state assessments),
(b) discuss the purported purposes of these assessment programs, (c) enu-
merate some potential dangers and potential benefits of such assessments,
(d) investigate what the research says (and does not say) about assessment
consequences (including a discussion of the quality of the evidence), (e)
discuss how to evaluate whether the consequences are good or bad, (f)

present some ideas about what variables may influence the probabilities for good or bad consequences, and (g) present some tentative conclusions about the whole issue of the consequences of assessment and the amount of research available and needed.

Because the evidence is insufficient, my tentative conclusions about the consequences of assessment, at times, are obviously and necessarily based on less than adequate evidence. It may seem that drawing such conclusions runs counter to a general value of educational researchers—that inferences should be based on evidence. I firmly believe that more research is needed and inferences should be drawn from such research. I am firmly against passing off pure proselytizing as research based. I do not oppose drawing tentative conclusions from less than perfect data, but crossing the line from basing inferences on evidence to basing inferences on a will to believe should not be done surreptitiously. I try hard to avoid that in this chapter. For those of you who do not make it to the end of this chapter, the conclusion is that the evidence is reasonably scarce and equivocal.

POPULARITY, PREVALENCE, PURPOSES, AND FORMAT OF LARGE-SCALE ASSESSMENT PROGRAMS

Popularity

Large-scale assessment programs are, in the abstract, popular with politicians and the public. This is true for both proposed and actual state assessments and the proposed national voluntary assessments. One example of this popularity is obtained from a recent Gallup Poll, which showed that 57% of the public favored President Clinton's proposed voluntary national test (Rose, Gallup, & Elam, 1997). However, when proposals get more specific, there can be opposition—as witnessed by the opposition of many groups after the proposed testing plan got more specific (e.g., with respect to what languages the test would be administered in). It should be noted that frontline educators—those who might be most informed about the potential value of the proposed voluntary national test—are far less favorable toward large-scale assessments than the general public. Langdon (1997), reporting on the Phi Deltan Kappan poll of teachers, found that 69% opposed Clinton's proposal. Measurement specialists also might have a reasonable claim to being more informed than the politicians or the public. Earlier comments that appeared on the Division D listserve suggested that there were far more negative views among listserve authors about the value of such tests than there were positive views.

Prevalence

State assessment programs have been prevalent for at least 16 years. As early as 1984, Frank Womer stated that "clearly the action in testing and assessment is in state departments of education" (p. 3). In identifying reasons for this, Womer stated that: "Lay persons and legislators who control education see testing-assessment as a panacea for solving our concerns about excellence in education" (p. 3). Anderson and Pipho (1984) reported that, in 1984, 40 states were actively pursuing some form of minimum competence testing.

Of course, it turned out that these minimum competency tests were not a panacea for concerns about educational excellence, although there exists some debate about whether they were, in general, a positive or negative force in education. In general, a change has taken place from testing what were called *minimum competencies* to testing what we might now call *world-class standards*. There has also been a change in how we assess students—with a movement away from multiple-choice tests toward numerous alternative forms of assessment. A recent survey of trends in statewide student assessment programs (Olson, Bond, & Andrews, 1999) revealed that 48 of 50 states have some type of statewide assessment, and 1 of the remaining 2 had legislation mandating local assessment by the year 2000.

Purposes and Stakes of State Assessment Programs

The two most popular purposes for assessment according to respondents to a survey of state assessment practices, are (a) improvement of instruction, and (b) school accountability (Olson, Bond, & Andrews, 1999). However, measurement experts have suggested for some time that "tests used primarily for curriculum advancement will look very different from those used for accountability" (Anderson, 1985, p. 24), and they will have different intended and actual impacts. Likewise, tests used for high-stakes decisions (e.g., high school graduation and merit pay) are likely to have different impacts than those used for low-stakes decisions (e.g., planning specific classroom interventions for individual students).

It is not always possible to keep purpose and stakes issues separated when discussing consequences. However, when evidence (or conjecture) about consequences applies to only a specific purpose or level of stakes, I try to make that clear.

Format Questions

A fairly hot issue in recent years is whether the format of the assessment should vary depending on purposes and whether assessments using different formats have different consequences. In the Olson, Bond, and Andrews (1999) survey of states, multiple-choice items were used by almost all states, and extended response item types were used second most frequently.

Performance assessment advocates have claimed that the format is important, and positive consequences come from such a format and negative consequences come from multiple-choice formats. Others, like me, are less sure of either of these positions. As with purpose and stakes issues, it is not always possible to keep these format issues separated in this presentation, but attempts are made.

Because in recent years more positive claims have been made for performance assessments, many of the recent attempts to gather consequential evidence have been based on assessments that have used performance assessments. However, I tend to agree with Haney and Madaus (1989) when they suggested over a decade ago that ". . . what technology of assessment is used probably makes far less difference than how it is used" (p. 687).

RESEARCH ON THE CONSEQUENCES OF ASSESSMENT PROGRAMS

Lane (1997) developed a comprehensive framework for evaluating the consequences of assessment programs, concentrating primarily on performance-based assessments. She suggested that both negative and positive consequences need to be addressed, and that one needs to consider both intended and plausible unintended consequences.

For purposes of this chapter, I discuss the following issues surrounding assessment programs:

1. Curricular and/or instructional reform: Good, bad, or nonexistent?
2. Motivation/morale/stress/ethical behavior of teachers: Increase or decrease?
3. Motivation and self-concepts of students: Up or down?
4. True improvement in student learning or just higher test scores?
5. Restore public confidence or provide data for critics?

Research on consequences is somewhat sketchy, but the *Lansing State Journal* did report one result in big headlines: "Test Results Make School Chief Smile" (Mayes, 1997, p. 1). Many of you have seen such headlines in your own states. When scores go up, administrators are happy and act as if that means achievement has gone up. It may have, but note that the consequence I report here is that the superintendent smiled, not that achievement had improved!

In general, there is much more rhetoric than evidence about the consequences of assessment, and "too often policy debates emphasize only one side or the other of the testing effects coin" (Madaus, 1991, p. 228). Baker, O'Neil, and Linn (1993), in an article on policy and validity for performance-based assessment, reported that "less than 5% of the literature cited empirical data" (p. 1213). They also pointed out that:

> Most of the arguments in favor of performance-based assessment . . . are based on single instances, essentially hand-crafted exercises whose virtues are assumed because they have been developed by teachers or because they are thought to model good instructional practice. (Baker et al., 1993, p. 1211)

I agree with Baker and colleagues that "a better research base is needed to evaluate the degree to which newly developed assessments fulfill expectations" (p. 1216).

Koretz (1996) suggested that,

> Despite the long history of assessment-based accountability, hard evidence about its effects is surprisingly sparse, and the little evidence that is available is not encouraging. . . . The large positive effects assumed by advocates . . . are often not substantiated by hard evidence. . . . (p. 172)

Reckase (1997) pointed out one of the logical problems in obtaining evidence on the consequences of assessments. The definition of a *consequence* implies a cause and effect relationship, but most of the data have not been gathered in a manner that permits a scholar (or anyone else with common sense) to draw a causative inference.

Green (1997) mentioned many problems that arise when conducting research on the consequences of assessment. Among them are that (a) few school systems will welcome reports of unanticipated negative consequences, so cooperation may be difficult to obtain; (b) there will be disagreements about the appropriate criterion measures of the consequences; (c) cause–effect conclusions will be disputed, and (d) much of the research is likely to be undertaken by those trying to prove that what exists is inferior to their new and better idea.

Much of the research has been based on survey information from teachers and principals. As many authors have pointed out, classroom observations might provide more compelling information (see, e.g., Linn, 1993; Pomplun, 1997). Research by McDonnell and Choisser (1997) employed three data sources: face-to-face interviews, telephone interviews, and assignments collected from the teachers along with a one-page log for each day in a 2-week period. As the authors pointed out, using instructional artifacts is a relatively new strategy; it is not likely to be as good as classroom observations, but not as expensive either. Although evidence is sketchy, there is some. I discuss it next.

Curricular and Instructional Reform: Good, Bad, or Nonexistent?

Curricular and instructional reform typically means changing the content of the curriculum or the process of instruction. Not quite fitting either of those categories is changing the length of the school day or the school year. Pipho (1997) reported that one change between the first and second year of state assessments in Minnesota was the addition of summer school offerings, Saturday classes, and after-school remedial programs. That kind of reform is mentioned elsewhere in the literature and is, at least arguably, a valuable consequence.

With respect to the more traditional meanings of curricular and instructional reform, it has been commonly assumed that assessments (at least high-stakes assessments) will influence curriculum and instruction. One often hears the mantra "WHAT YOU TEST IS WHAT YOU GET." Taleporos (1997) stated flatly that "we all know that how you test is how it gets taught" (p. 1). Actually, the evidence for a test's influence on either curricular content or instructional process is not entirely clear. It varies by the stakes. Porter, Floden, Freeman, Schmidt, and Schwille (1986) reported more than 14 years ago that:

> Another myth exposed as being only a half truth is that teachers teach topics that are tested. Little evidence exists to support the supposition that national norm-referenced, standardized tests administered once a year have any important influence on teachers' content decisions. (p. 11)

Yet the myth persists. Is it a half truth, a full truth, or completely wrong? Logic suggests it may depend on stakes, rigor of the standards, and the content (Airasian, 1988). Some anecdotal evidence also supports the importance of stakes. For example, Floden (personal communication, 1998) stated that in the Content Determinants work (the Porter et al. study just cited), few teachers paid attention to the tests. However, he reported more recently that teachers paid a great deal of attention to districts where loss of accreditation was a real threat. He found that they were busy aligning curriculum to the Michigan Educational Assessment Program (MEAP) and setting aside time prior to testing for MEAP-specific work.

Impact of Multiple-Choice Minimum Competency Tests on Curriculum and Instruction. Minimum competency tests were not primarily designed to reform the curriculum. Rather, they were intended to measure what schools were already teaching and to find out whether students had learned that material. If students had not learned the material, the tests served as motivators for both students and educators. The intended curricular/instructional effect was to concentrate more on the instruction of what were considered to be very important educational goals.

Some earlier writings on the impact of multiple-choice tests suggests that the tests resulted in teachers narrowing the curriculum and corrupting teaching because teachers turned to simply passing out multiple-choice worksheets. The critics argued that education was harmed due to the narrowing of the curriculum and the teaching and testing for only low-level facts.

Aside from the confusion of test format with test content (true measurement experts realize that multiple-choice tests are not limited to testing facts), there is insufficient evidence to allow any firm conclusion that such tests had harmful effects on curriculum and instruction. In fact, there is some evidence to the contrary. Kuhs et al. (1985) reported that "the teachers' topic selection did not seem to be much influenced by the state minimum competencies test or the district-used standardized tests" (p. 151). There is no evidence of which I am aware showing that fewer high-level math courses are taught (or taught to fewer students) in states where students must pass a low-level math test to receive a high school diploma.

A few studies (quoted over and over again) presumably show that elementary teachers align instruction with the content of basic skills tests (e.g., Madaus, West, Harmon, Lomax, & Viator, 1992; Shepard, 1991). I believe those studies have some validity. It is hard to believe that tests with certain stakes attached to them will not somehow influence curriculum and instruction. For example, Smith and Rottenberg (1991) report that "The consequences of external testing were inferred from an analysis of the meanings held by participants and direct observation of testing activities . . ." (p. 7). They concluded, among other things, that (a) external testing reduces the time available for ordinary instruction; (b) testing affects what elementary schools teach—in high-stakes environments, schools neglect material that external tests exclude; (c) external testing encourages use of instructional methods that resemble tests; and (d) "as teachers take more time for test preparation and align instruction more closely with content and format, they diminish the range of instructional goals and activities" (p. 11).

Thus, there are studies suggesting that multiple-choice tests result in a narrowing of the curriculum and more drill work in teaching. The studies are few in number, however, and critics of traditional basic-skills testing accept the studies somewhat uncritically. In my opinion, the research is not as strong as the rhetoric of those reporting it would suggest, and there is some evidence that teachers do not choose topics based on test content (Kuhs et al., 1985).

Green (1997) discussed the evidence and questioned the conclusion that multiple-choice tests are harmful, stating that "I believe that the data just cited opens to question the assertions about the evils of multiple-choice tests" (p. 4).

Impact of Performance Assessments on Curriculum and Instruction. Much of the recent research and rhetoric has been concerned with the effects of performance assessments. Performance assessments are popular in part because of their supposed positive influence on curricular and instructional reform. Advocates of performance assessment treat as an established fact the position that teaching to traditional standardized tests has "resulted in a distortion of the curriculum for many students, narrowing it to basic, low-level skills" (Herman, Klein, Heath, & Wakai, 1994, p. 1). Further, professional educators have been pushing for curricular reform, suggesting that previous curricula were inadequate, generally focusing too much on the basics. The new assessments should be more rigorous, and schools should be held responsible for these more rigorous standards. As a Southeastern Regional Vision for Education (SERVE, 1994a) document entitled *A New Framework for State Accountability Systems* pointed out, some legislative initiatives ignored a basic reality: Those schools that had failed to meet older, less rigorous standards were no more able to meet higher standards when the accountability bar was raised. As a result, state after state has been confronted with previously failing schools failing the new systems (SERVE, 1994b).

What does the research tell us about the curricular and instructional effects of performance assessments? Khattri, Kane, and Reeve (1995) visited 16 U.S. schools that were developing and implementing performance assessments. They interviewed school personnel, students, parents, and school board members; collected student work, and conducted classroom observations. They concluded that, "In general, our findings show that the effect of assessments on the *curriculum* teachers use in their classrooms has been marginal, although the impact on *instruction* and on *teacher roles* in some cases has been substantial" (p. 80; italics original).

Chudowsky and Behuniak (1997) used teacher focus groups from seven schools representing a cross-section of schools in Connecticut. These focus groups discussed their perceptions of the impact of the Connecticut Academic Performance Test—an assessment that uses multiple-choice, grid-in, short answer, and extended response items. Teachers in all but one of the schools reported that preparing students and aligning their instruction to the test "resulted in a narrowing of the curriculum" (Chudowsky & Behuniak, 1997, p. 8). Regarding instructional changes, "teachers most frequently reported having students 'practice' for the test on Clearing-house for Applied Performance Testing sample items" (p. 6). However the schools also reported using strategies "to move beyond direct test preparation into instructional approaches" (p. 6). Teachers also "consistently reported that the most negative impact of the test is that it detracts significantly from instructional time. Teachers at all of the schools complained vehemently about the amount of instructional time lost to administer the test" (p. 7).

Koretz, Mitchell, Barron, and Keith (1996) surveyed teachers and principals in two of the three grades in which the Maryland School Performance Assessment Program (MSPAP) is administered. As they reported, the MSPAP program "is designed to induce fundamental changes in instruction" (p. vii). Although about three fourths of the principals and half of the teachers expressed general support for MSPAP, 15% of the principals and 35% of the teachers expressed opposition. One interesting finding was that about 40% of fifth-grade teachers "strongly agreed that MSPAP includes developmentally inappropriate tasks" (p. viii). One of the summary statements made by Koretz et al. (1996) is as follows:

> The results reported here suggest that the program has met one of its goals in increasing the amount of writing students do in school. At the same time, teachers' responses suggest the possibility that this change may have negative ramifications as well, in terms of both instructional impact and test validity. Many teachers maintain that the emphasis on writing is excessive and that instruction has suffered because of the amount of time required for writing. . . . [also,] emphasis on writing makes it difficult to judge math competence of some students. (p. xiii)

Rafferty (1993) surveyed urban teachers and staff regarding the MSPAP program. Individuals were asked to respond in Likert fashion to several statements. When the statement was "MSPAP will have little effect on classroom practices," 33% agreed or strongly agreed, 24% were uncertain, 42% disagreed or strongly disagreed, and 1% did not respond. To the statement "Classroom practices are better because of MSPAP," 21% were in agreement, 36% were uncertain, 41% disagreed, and 2% did not answer. To the statement "MSPAP is essentially worthwhile," 24% agreed or strongly agreed, 25% were uncertain, 48% disagreed or strongly disagreed, and 3% did not respond. Perhaps a reasonable interpretation of these data is that MSPAP will likely have an impact, but not necessarily a good one.

Koretz, Barron, Mitchell, and Stecher (1996) did a study for Kentucky similar to the one done by Koretz and colleagues in Maryland (note there is some difference in the set of authors). They surveyed the teachers and principals in Kentucky regarding the Kentucky Instructional Results Information System (KIRIS) and found much the same thing as had been found in Maryland. Among other findings were the following:[3]

- Ninety percent of the teachers agreed that portfolios made it difficult to cover the regular curriculum (p. 37).
- Most teachers agreed that imposing rewards and sanctions causes teachers to ignore important aspects of the curriculum (p. 42).
- Portfolios were cited as having negative effects on instruction almost as often as having positive effects (p. xi).
- Almost 90% of the teachers in the study agreed that KIRIS caused them to deemphasize or neglect untested material (p. xiii).
- Other aspects of instruction have suffered as a result of time spent on writing, and emphasis on writing makes it difficult to judge the mathematical competence of some students (p. xv).

McDonnell and Choisser (1997) studied the local implementation of new state assessments in Kentucky and North Carolina. They conclude that,

> Instruction by teachers in the study sample is reasonably consistent with the state assessment goals at the level of classroom activities, but not in terms of the conceptual understandings the assessments are measuring. Teachers have added new instructional strategies . . . but . . . they have not fundamentally changed the depth and sophistication of the content they are teaching. (p. iv)

Stecher and Mitchell (1995) reported on the effects of portfolio-driven reform in Vermont:

> The Vermont portfolio assessment program has had substantial positive effects on fourth-grade teachers' perceptions and practices in mathematics. Vermont teachers report that the program has taught them a great deal about mathematical problem solving and that they have changed their instructional practices in important ways. (Stecher & Mitchell, 1995, p. ix)

Smith et al. (1997) studied the consequences of the now discarded Arizona Student Assessment Program (ASAP). Although the program consisted of several parts, including some norm-referenced testing with the Iowa tests, the most visible portion of ASAP was the performance assess-

---

[3]Space does not permit me to do justice to this very thorough report. I urge readers to obtain the report and study it carefully.

ment. Teacher opinion of the direction of the effect of ASAP on the curriculum was divided:

> Some defined "ASAP" as representing an unfortunate and even dangerous de-emphasis of foundational skills, whereas others welcomed the change or saw the new emphasis as encompassing both skills and problem solving. (p. 40)

Some interesting quotes by teachers found in the Smith et al. (1997) report are as follows:

> Nobody cares about basics. . . . The young teachers coming out of college will just perpetuate the problem since they are learning whole language instruction and student-centered classroom. Certainly these concepts have their merits, but not at the expense of basics on which education is based. (p. 41)

> The ASAP . . . is designed to do away with "skills" because kids today don't relate to skills because they are boring. By pandering to this we are weakening our society, not strengthening it. *It is wrong*! I was told by a state official that teachers would be more like coaches under ASAP. Ask any coach if they teach skills in isolation before they integrate it into their game plan. They will all tell you yes. I rest my case. (p. 41)

As Smith et al. (1997) reported, about two thirds of the teachers in their study believed that "pupils at this school need to master basic skills before they can progress to higher-order thinking and problem solving" (p. 41). Forty-three percent of the teachers believed that "ASAP takes away from instructional time we should be spending on something more important" (p. 44). Despite many teachers being unhappy with the content of ASAP, "about 40% of the teachers reported that district scope and sequences had been aligned with ASAP" (p. 46). As the authors reported, "changes consequent to ASAP seemed to fall into a typology that we characterized as 'coherent action,' 'compliance only,' 'compromise,' and 'drag' " (p. 46).

Miller (1998) studied the effect of state-mandated performance-based assessments on teachers' attitudes and practices in six different contexts (grade level and content areas). Two questions were asked relevant to curricular and instructional impacts:

> "I have made specific efforts to align instruction with the state assessments." (Percent who agreed or strongly agreed ranged from 54.5 to 92.7% across the six contexts.)
>
> "I feel that state mandatory assessments have had a negative impact by excessively narrowing the curriculum covered in the classroom." (Per-

cent who agreed or strongly agreed ranged from 28.7 to 46.8%. Only teachers in five of the contexts responded to that question.)

The two questions provide interesting results. Although the majority made specific efforts to align instruction, the majority did not feel it resulted in excessively narrowing of the curriculum. However, as Miller (1998) pointed out, "the assessments were usually intended to give supplemental information. Consequently, they do not reflect everything that students learn, and only provide a small view of student performance . . ." (pp. 5–6). To align instruction to assessments that provide only a small view of student performance without excessively narrowing the curriculum would seem to be a difficult balancing act.

A reasonable summary of the literature reviewed is that if stakes are high enough and if content is deemed appropriate enough by teachers, there is likely to be a shift in the curriculum and instruction to the content sampled by the test (or the content on the test if the test is not secure). If stakes are low and/or if teachers believe an assessment is testing developmentally inappropriate materials and/or teaching to the assessment would reduce the amount of time teachers spend on content they consider important, the impact is not so obvious.

Motivation/Morale/Stress/Ethical Behavior of Teachers: Increase or Decrease?

Many would argue, quite reasonably, that if we are to improve education, we must look to the frontline educators—the teachers—to lead the charge. Do large-scale assessments tend to improve the efforts, attitudes, and ethical behavior of teachers?

Smith and Rottenberg (1991) suggested that external tests negatively affect teachers. As they stated, "the chagrin they felt comes from their well-justified belief that audiences external to the school lack interpretive context and attribute low scores to lazy teachers and weak programs" (Smith & Rottenberg, 1991, p. 10). Although they were primarily discussing the effects of traditional assessments, one should expect the same reaction from performance assessments. Audiences external to the school are no more able to infer correct causes of low scores on performance assessments than they are to infer correct causes of low scores on multiple-choice assessments. The inference of teachers and weak programs is equally likely no matter what the test format or test content.

Koretz et al. (1996) reported that for the MSPAP,

Few teachers reported that morale is high, and a majority reported that MSPAP has harmed it. . . . 57% of teachers responded that MSPAP has led to a decrease in teacher morale in their school, while only a few (4%) reported that MSPAP has produced an increase. (p. 24)

Koretz, Barron, Mitchell, and Stecher (1996) in the Kentucky study reported that "about 3/4 of teachers reported that teachers' morale has declined as a result of KIRIS" (p. x). Stecklow (1997) reported that there were conflicts in over 40% of Kentucky schools about how to divide up the reward money. So affect was not necessarily high even in the schools that got the rewards. Koretz et al. (1996) also found that principals reported that KIRIS had affected attrition, but the attrition was for both good and poor teachers.

With respect to effort, at least the teachers in Kentucky reported that their efforts to improve instruction and learning had increased (Koretz, Baron et al., 1996). Yet at some point, increased efforts lead to burnout and thus attrition increases.

It is commonly believed that some teachers engage in behaviors of questionable ethics when teaching toward, administering, and scoring high-stakes multiple-choice tests. What about performance assessments? Koretz, Baron et al. (1996) reported that in Kentucky,

Appreciable minorities of teachers reported questionable test-administration practices in their schools. About one-third reported that questions are at least occasionally rephrased during testing time, and roughly one in five reported that questions about content are answered during testing, that revisions are recommended during or after testing, or that hints are provided on correct answers. (p. xiii)

In summary, the evidence regarding the effects of large-scale assessments on teacher motivation, morale, stress, and ethical behavior is sketchy. What little there is, coupled with what seems logical, suggests that increasing the stakes for teachers will lead to increased efforts, more burnout, decreased morale, and increased probability of unethical behavior.

Motivation and Self-Concepts of Students: Up or Down?

With respect to the impact of assessment on students, we are again in a subarea where there is not a great deal of research. Logic suggests that the impact may be quite different for those tests where the stakes apply to students than for tests where the stakes apply to teachers.

Also the impact should depend on how high the standards are. It is reasonable to believe that the impact of minimal competency tests would be minimal for the large majority of students for whom such tests would not present a challenge. However, for those students who had trouble getting over such a minimal hurdle, the tests probably would increase both motivation and frustration and stress—the exact mix varying on the personality of the individual students.

Smith and Rottenberg (1991) found that for younger students teachers believed that standardized tests "cause stress, frustration, burnout, fatigue, physical illness, misbehavior and fighting, and psychological distress" (p. 10). That belief of teachers may be true, but certainly does not constitute hard evidence. I come closer to Ebel's (1976) view that,

> Of the many challenges to a child's peace of mind caused by such things as angry parents, playground bullies, bad dogs, shots from the doctor, and things that go bump in the night, standardized tests must surely be among the least fearsome for most children. (p. 6)

Lane and Parke (1996), reporting on the consequences of a math performance assessment, found that some students developed feelings of inadequacy and, as a result, were less motivated. Miller (1998) found that the percentage of teachers responding positively to the statement that performance assessments "increased student confidence" ranged from only 9.1% to 37.6% across five different contexts.

However, Kane, Khattri, Reeve, and Adamson (1997) employed a qualitative, case-study methodology, visited 16 schools ("not confirmed to be representative," p. xvi), developing and implementing performance assessments. They reported that "many interviewees reported that students exhibit a greater motivation to learn and a greater amount of engagement with performance tasks and portfolio assignments than with other types of assignments" (p. 201).

Koretz, Baron et al. (1996) report that in Kentucky one third of the teachers they interviewed indicated that students' morale had deteriorated as a result of assessment. Virtually no one reported an increase in student morale. They also reported that an emphasis on writing caused students to become tired of writing.

As mentioned earlier, one of the factors affecting student response to assessment is the level at which standards are set. Minimum standards are not likely to have a major impact. High standards might. Linn (1994) pointed out that "The dual goals of setting performance standards for student certification that are both 'world class' and apply to 'all' students are laudable, but it cannot simply be assumed that only positive effects will result from this press" (p. 8). Linn also quoted Coffman as follows: "Holding common standards for all pupils can only encourage a narrowing of educational experiences for most pupils, doom many to failure, and limit the development of many worthy talents" (Coffman, 1993, p. 8; as quoted in Linn, 1994).

We are simply putting students and teachers under too much pressure if we hold unrealistically high standards for all students. As Bracey (1995) stated in an article entitled "Variance Happens—Get Over It!",

> We are currently in a period that adheres rabidly to an all-children-can-learn philosophy. . . . The stance is a philosophical, moral—almost religious—posture taken by a wide spectrum of educators and psychologists who ought to know better. . . . By telling everyone that all children can learn, we set the stage for the next great round of educational failure when it is revealed that not everyone *has* learned, in spite of our sincere beliefs and improved practices. (Bracey, 1995, pp. 22, 26)

Of course, his point is not that some children cannot learn anything, but that not everyone can achieve high standards in academics anymore than everyone can become proficient enough in every sport to play on the varsity teams.

True Improvement in Student Learning or Just Higher Test Scores?

In mandating tests, policymakers have created the illusion that test performance is synonymous with the quality of education (Madaus, 1985).

All of us recognize that it is possible for test scores to go up without an increase in student learning in the domain the test supposedly samples. For example, this occurs when teachers teach the questions on nonsecure tests. Teaching too closely to the assessment results in inferences from the test scores being corrupted. One can no longer make inferences from the test to the domain. The Lake Wobegon effect results. Many of us have written about that (e.g., Mehrens & Kaminski, 1989).

If the assessment questions are secure and the domain the test samples is made public, corrupting reasonable inferences from the scores is more difficult. If the inference from rising test scores of secure tests is that students have learned more of the domain that the test samples, it is likely a correct inference. However, those making inferences may not realize how narrow the domain is or that a test sampling a similar sounding but somewhat differently defined domain might give different results. Of course, if the inference from rising scores is that educational quality has gone up, that may not be true.

Improvement on Traditional Tests.   Pipho (1997) reported that: "Ironically, every state that has initiated a high school graduation test in Grade 8 or 9 has reported an initial failure rate of approximately 30%. By 12th grade, using remediation and sometimes twice-a-year retests, this failure rate always gets down to well under 5%" (p. 673). Is this true improvement or is it a result of teaching to the test? Recall that these tests are supposedly secure, so one cannot teach the specific questions.[4] However, one could limit instruction to the general domain the tests sample. My interpretation is that the increase in scores represents a true improvement on the domain the test samples, but it does not necessarily follow that it is a true improvement in the students' education.

Improvement on Performance Assessments. What about performance assessments? Do increases in scores indicate necessary improvement in the domain or an increase in educational quality? Certainly no more so than for multiple-choice assessments and perhaps less so. Even if specific tasks are secure, performance assessments are generally thought to be even more memorable, and reusing such assessments can result in corrupted inferences. If the inference is only to the specific task, there may not be too much corruption. Yet any inferences to a domain the task represents or to the general quality of education are as likely to be incorrect for performance assessments as for multiple-choice assessments.

Shepard et al. (1996) conducted a study investigating the effects of classroom performance assessments on student learning. They reported that,

> Overall, the predominant finding is one of no-difference or no gains in student learning following from the year-long effort to introduce classroom performance assessments. Although we argue subsequently that the small year-to-year gain in mathematics is real and interpretable *based on qualitative analysis, honest discussion* of project effects must acknowledge that *any benefits are small and ephemeral.* (p. 12; italics added)

Others, doing less rigorously controlled studies based on teacher opinion surveys, have been equally cautious in their statements. Khattri, Kane, and Reeve (1995), in their study of 16 schools, stated that, "Only a few teachers said performance-based teaching and assessment helped students learn more and develop a fuller multi-disciplinary understanding" (p. 82).

Koretz et al. (1996) reported that, "Few teachers expressed confidence that their own schools' increases on KIRIS were largely the results of improved learning" (p. xiii). The authors went on to suggest that, "A variety of the findings reported here point to the possibility of inflated gains on KIRIS—that is, the possibility that scores have increased substantially more than mastery of the domains that the assessment is intended to represent" (p. xv). Kane et al. (1997) concluded from their study that, "In the

---

[4]Most of these state assessments equate through anchor items, and these items may not be totally secure.

final analysis, the success of assessment reform as a tool to enhance student achievement remains to be rigorously demonstrated" (p. 217).

Miller (1998) asked teachers whether they believed the state-mandated performance assessments "have had a positive effect on student learning." Percentages across five contexts ranged from 11.3% to 54.7%. When asked whether the tests results were "an accurate reflection of student performance," the percentages ranged from 13.1% to 28.7%.

Finally, for some types of portfolio assessments, one does not even know who did the work. As Gearhart, Herman, Baker, and Whittaker (1993) pointed out, "This study raises questions concerning validity of inferences about student competence based on portfolio work" (p. 1).

Conclusions About Increases. In conclusion, there is considerable evidence that students' pass rates increase on secure high-stakes (mostly multiple-choice) graduation tests. There is at least some reason to believe that students have increased their achievement levels on the specific domains the secure tests are measuring. There is less evidence about increases in scores for performance assessments. Although it is true that some states (e.g., Kentucky) have shown remarkable gains in scores, evidence points to the possibility that the gains are inflated, and there is generally less confidence that achievement in the represented domain has also increased. In neither case can we necessarily infer that quality of education has increased. That inference cannot flow directly from the data. Rather, it must be based on a philosophy of education that says an increase in the domain tested represents an increase in the quality of education. As Madaus stated, it is an illusion to believe at an abstract level that test performance is synonymous with quality of education. Nevertheless, test performance can inform us about the quality of education—at least about the quality of education on the domain being assessed.

Restore Public Confidence or Provide Data for Critics?

At an abstract level, it seems philosophically wrong and politically short-sighted for educators to argue against the gathering of student achievement data for accounting and accountability purposes. My own belief is that an earlier stance of the NEA against standardized tests left the public wondering just what it was the educators were trying to hide. I suspect the NEA stance contributed to the action in the state departments that Womer mentioned in 1984. Certainly the public has a right to know something about the quality of the schools they pay for and the level of achievement their children are reaching in those schools.

Some educators strongly believe—with some supporting evidence— that the press has incorrectly maligned the public schools (e.g., Berliner &

Biddle, 1995; Bracey, 1996). Although their views have not gone unchallenged (see Stedman, 1996), it does seem true that bad news about education travels faster than good news about education. Will the data from large-scale assessments change the public's views?

The answer to the previous question depends, in part, on whether the scores go up, go down, or stay the same. It also depends on whether the public thinks we are measuring anything worthwhile. Finally, it depends on how successful we are at communicating the data and communicating what reasonable inferences can be drawn from the data.

Scores have generally been going up in Kentucky, but it has not resulted in all the press highlighting the great job educators are doing there. For example Stecklow (1997), in writing about the Kentucky approach, suggested, "It has spawned lawsuits, infighting between teachers and staff, anger among parents, widespread grade inflation—and numerous instances of cheating by teachers to boost student scores" (p. 1).

A conclusion of the KIRIS evaluation done by The Evaluation Center of Western Michigan University stated that,

> . . . all the cited evidence suggests stakeholders have questions concerning the legitimacy, validity, reliability, and fairness of the KIRIS assessment. We have no evidence to suggest that parents think the assessment component of KIRIS is a fair, reliable, and valid system. (The Evaluation Center, 1995, p. 20).

The Stecklow quote is not a ringing endorsement of the program or the quality of education in Kentucky. The Evaluation Center quote is not a ringing endorsement of the quality of the data in the assessment. Yet in general, the public is happier with high scores than they are with low scores. Families often decide which district to live in based on published test scores. (The public may be making two quite different inferences from these scores. One, probably incorrect, is that the district with the higher scores has better teachers or a better curriculum. Second, probably correct, is that if their children attend the district with the higher scores they will be more likely to be in classes with a higher proportion of academically able fellow students.)

There is currently considerable concern about whether the newer reform assessments cover the correct content. Reform educators were not happy with minimum competency tests covering basics, but the public is not happy with what it perceives as a departure from teaching and testing the basics. Baker, Linn, and Herman (1996) talked about the crisis of credibility that performance assessments suffer based on a large gap between the views of educational reformers and segments of the public. McDonnell (1997) stated that,

... the political dimensions of assessment policy are typically overlooked. Yet because of their link to state curriculum standards, these assessments often embody unresolved value conflicts about what content should be taught and tested, and who should define that content. (p. v)

As McDonnell pointed out, fundamental differences exist between what educational reformers and large segments of the public believe should be in the curriculum. The available opinion data strongly suggest that the larger public is skeptical of new curricular approaches in reading, writing, and mathematics (McDonnell, 1997). The truth of this can be seen in the fight over mathematics standards in California.

The press and public seem either reasonably unimpressed by the data educators provide and/or make incorrect inferences from it. What can change that? We need to gather high-quality data over important content and communicate the data to the public in ways that encourage correct inferences about students' levels of achievement. We need to be especially careful to discourage the public from making causative inferences if they are not supported by the research data.

ARE THE CONSEQUENCES GOOD OR BAD?

It should be obvious by now that I do not believe we have a sufficient quantity of research on the consequences of assessment. Further, the evidence we do have is certainly not of the type from which we can draw causative inferences, which seems to be what the public wants to do. Given the evidence we do have, can we decide whether it suggests the consequences of assessment are positive or negative? If the evidence were better, could we decide whether the consequences are positive or negative? I maintain that each of us can decide, but we may well disagree. Interpreting the consequences as being good or bad is related to differences in convictions about the proper goals of education. Let us look at the evidence regarding each of the five potential benefits and/or dangers with respect to the quality of the consequences.

Curricular and/or Instructional Reform

Although there is no proved cause-and-effect relationship between assessment and the curriculum content or instructional strategies, there is some evidence and compelling rationale to suggest that high-stakes assessments can influence both curriculum and instruction. Is this good or bad? It is a matter of one's goals. Reform educators were dismayed to think that minimum competency tests using multiple-choice questions were influencing curriculum and instruction. They pushed for performance assessments not because they abhorred tests influencing curriculum and instruction, but because they wanted the tests to have a different influence.

The public was not dismayed that educators tested the basics—they rather approved. They believe (some evidence suggests incorrectly) that educators have moved away from basics and are dismayed. Obviously the narrowing and refocusing of the curriculum and instructional strategies are viewed as either negative or positive depending on whether the narrowing and refocusing are perceived to be toward important content. Educators and the public do not necessarily agree about this.

Increasing Teacher Motivation and Stress

Increasing teacher stress may be perceived as good or bad depending on whether one believes teachers are lazy and need to be slapped into shape or whether one believes (as I do) that teachers already suffer from too much job stress.

Changing Students' Motivation or Self-Concepts

We might all favor an increase in student motivation. I, for one, do not believe a major problem in U.S. education is that students are trying too hard to learn too much. Yet some educators do worry about the stress that tests cause in students (recall the quote from Smith & Rottenberg). There is such a thing as *test anxiety* (more accurately called *evaluation anxiety*), but many would argue that occasional state anxiety is a useful experience— perhaps helping individuals learn how to cope with anxiety and to treat stress as eustress rather than distress.

What if assessment lowers students' self-concepts? Again, this could be either good or bad depending on whether one believes students should have a realistic view of how inadequate their knowledge and skills are. (In Japan, where students outperform U.S. students, the students do not feel as confident in their math competencies as do U.S. students.) As one colleague has pointed out to me, we are not necessarily doing students a favor by allowing them to perceive themselves as competent in a subject matter if that, indeed, is not the truth (Ryan, personal communication, 1997).

Increased Scores on Assessments

Surely this is good, right? Again, it depends. It depends on whether the gains reflect improvement on the total domain being assessed or just increases in scores, whether we care about the tested domain, and whether, as a result of the more focused instruction, other important domains (not being tested) suffer.

Public Awareness of Student Achievement

Is public awareness of how students score on assessments good or bad? Obviously one answer is that it depends on whether valid inferences are drawn from the data. One part of the validity issue is whether the scores truly represent what students know and can do. Another part of the validity issue is whether the public draws causative inferences that are not supported by the data.

In addition to the question of whether the inferences are valid, there is the issue of how the public responds. Would negative news stimulate increased efforts by the public to assist educators, for example, by trying to ensure that children start school ready to learn by providing better facilities and insisting their children respect the teachers? Or would negative news result in more rhetoric regarding how bad public schools are, how bad the teachers are, and how we should give up on them and increase funding to private schools at the expense of funding public schools? Would positive news result in teachers receiving public accolades and more respect, or would the public then place public education on a back burner because the *crisis* was over?

Although I come down on the side of giving the public data about student achievement, communication with the public must be done with great care. I believe there is a propensity for the public (at least the press) to engage in inappropriate blaming of educators when student achievement is not as high as desired. I am reminded of Browder's (1971) suggestion that accountability boils down to who gets hanged when things go wrong and who does the hanging. Educators have good reason to believe that they are the ones who will get hanged and the public, abetted by the press, will do the hanging. Dorn (1998) stated that "test results have become the dominant way states, politicians, and newspapers describe the performance of schools" (p. 2). He was not suggesting that is a positive development.

WHAT VARIABLES CHANGE PROBABILITIES FOR GOOD OR BAD IMPACTS?

Because whether consequences are good or bad is partly a matter of one's educational values, it is difficult to answer this question. Nevertheless, I provide a few comments.

Impact Should Be (and Likely Is) Related to Purposes

As mentioned earlier, there are two major purposes of large-scale assessment: to drive reform and see if reform practices have had an impact on student learning. These are somewhat contradictory purposes because current reformers believe assessment should be authentic if it is to drive reform, and most authentic assessment is not very good measurement—at least by any conventional measurement criteria.

Impact (and Purposes) Are Likely Related to Test Content and the Public Involvement in Determining Content and Content Standards

Successful assessment reform needs to be an open and inclusive process, supported by a broad range of policymakers, educators, and the public and closely tied to standards in which parents and the community have confidence (Center for Research on Evaluation, Standards, and Student Testing, 1997). The impact is not likely to be positive in any general sense if the public has not bought into the content standards being assessed.

One can also expect some problems if the content and test standards are set too high. The politically correct rhetoric that "all children can learn to high levels" has yet to be demonstrated as correct. Recall the earlier quote by Coffman. Recall also Bracey's article entitled "Variance Happens—Get Over It." As a colleague once said, would we require the PE instructor to get all students up to a level where they are playing on the varsity team?

Impact May Be Related to Item or Test Format

If the issue is whether the overall impact is good or bad, there is not much evidence that item or test format matters. The notion that teaching to improve performance assessment results means educators will be teaching as they should be teaching, whereas the notion that teaching to improve multiple-choice test scores means teaching is of poor quality is just nonsense.

Impact May Be Related to the Quality of the Assessment (Perceived or Real) and the Assessment Procedures

If educators do not believe the assessments provide high-quality data, they may not pay much attention to them. Cunningham (1995) made this point very forcefully in discussing the Kentucky Instructional Results Information System (KIRIS) program:

> As teachers begin to realize that the test has no legitimacy and that it is too technically deficient to be influenced by how they teach, they will stop paying attention to it. . . . Measurement driven instruction does not work when teachers fail to see the connection between measurement and instruction. (p. 2)

Whatever one believes about the technical adequacy of KIRIS, Cunningham's general point would seem accurate: If teachers do not see any connection between the assessment results and their instructional approaches, the measurement is unlikely to impact instruction.

Another example comes from a technical report Smith et al. (1997) wrote on the consequences of the Arizona Student Assessment Program (ASAP). Some teachers believed that the ASAP skills were not developmentally appropriate, some objected to what they perceived as poor-quality rubrics and to the subjectivity of the scoring process, and some thought ASAP was just a fad. One teacher even referred to ASAP as Another Stupid Aggravating Program. Again, the point is not whether the teachers' perceptions are correct. Yet if they perceive the assessment quality to be poor, they are not likely to be very impacted by it.

Impact May Depend on Degree of Sanctions

Some limited evidence regarding this variable comes from a McDonnell and Choisser (1997) study. They investigated the local implementation of state assessments in North Carolina and Kentucky. As they suggested, Kentucky's program involved high stakes for schools and educators, with major consequences attached to the test results. The North Carolina assessment had no tangible consequences attached to it. However,

> teachers in the two state samples perceive the new assessments in much the same way and take them equally seriously. With few exceptions, their teaching reflects the assessment policy goals of their respective states to a similar degree. (p. ix)

Of course, the North Carolina assessments have some consequences. Results are presented in district *report cards* and in school-building improvement results. At the time the study was conducted, McDonnell and Choisser (1997) reported that,

> probably the most potent leverage the assessment system has over the behavior of teachers is the widespread perception that local newspapers plan to report test scores not just by individual school, which has been done traditionally, but also by specific grade level and even by classroom. (p. 16)

One can imagine why teachers in North Carolina might think the stakes were fairly high despite no state financial rewards or sanctions.

Thus, despite evidence that shows no distinctions between Kentucky, which used financial rewards, and North Carolina, which simply made scores available, the perceived stakes to the teachers may not have been much different. I continue to believe that as stakes increase, dissatisfaction, fear, cheating, and lawsuits all increase. However, efforts may also increase to improve scores. If the procedures are set up to make it difficult to improve scores without improving competence on the domain, student learning should increase also.

Impact May Relate to Level of Professional Development

Unfortunately, many current reform policies concentrate more on standards and assessments than they do on teachers' professional development. In the ASAP program, for example, only 19% of the teachers surveyed felt that adequate professional development had been provided (Smith et al., 1997). Combs, in his critique of top–down reform mandates, stated: "Things don't change people; people change things" (cited in Smith et al., 1997, p. 50). As Smith et al. pointed out in their review, Cohen (1995) noted the apparent anomaly in the systemic reform movement and accountability intentions. Motivated by perceptions that public schools are failing,

> advocates of systemic reform propose to radically change instruction, and for that they must rely on teachers and administrators. But these agents of change are the very professionals whose work reformers find so inadequate. (cited in Smith et al., 1997, p. 105)

CONCLUSIONS

What can we conclude about the consequences of assessment? Consider the following.

1. There are a variety of purposes for and expectations regarding the consequences of assessment. Some of these may be unrealistic. "Evaluation and testing have become the engine for implementing educational policy" (Petrie, 1987, p. 175).

2. Scholars seem to agree that it is unwise, illogical, and unscholarly to assume that assessments will have positive consequences. There is the potential for both positive and negative consequences.

3. It would profit us to have more research.

4. The evidence we do have is inadequate to draw any cause–effect conclusions about the consequences. If instruction changes concomitant with changes in both state curricular guidelines and state assessments, how much of the change is due to which variable?

5. Not everyone will view changes (e.g., reforming curriculum in a particular way) with the same affect. Some will think the changes represent positive consequences and others will think the changes constitute negative consequences.

6. High-stakes assessments probably impact both curriculum and instruction, but assessments alone are not likely as effective as they would be if there was more teacher professional development.

7. Attempts to reform curriculum in ways neither teachers nor the public support seems unwise.

8. High-stakes assessments increase teacher stress and lower teacher morale. This seems unfortunate to me, but may make others happy.

9. Assessments can assist both students and teachers in evaluating whether the students are achieving at a sufficiently high level. This seems like useful knowledge.

10. High-stakes assessments will result in higher test scores. Both test security and the opportunity to misadminister or miss-score tests must be considered in evaluating whether higher scores represent increased knowledge. If the test items are secure (and reused items are not memorable) and if tests are administered and scored correctly, it seems reasonable to infer that higher scores indicate increased achievement in the particular domain the assessment covers. That is good if the domain represents important content and if teaching to that domain does not result in ignoring other equally important domains. If tests are not secure or are incorrectly administered or scored, there is no reason to believe that higher scores represent increased learning.

11. The public and the press are more likely to use what they believe are *inadequate* assessment results to blame educators than to use *good* results to praise them. They will continue to make inappropriate causative inferences from the data. The public will not be impressed by assessments over reform curricula they consider irrelevant.

12. There has been a great deal of confounding of item format, test content, and the stakes. Which format is used probably makes far less difference than how it is used.

REFERENCES

Airasian, P. W. (1988). Measurement driven instruction: A closer look. *Educational Measurement: Issues and Practice*, 7(4), 6–11.

Anderson, B. L. (1985). State testing and the educational community: Friends or foes? *Educational Measurement: Issues and Practice, 4*(2), 22–25.

Anderson, B. L., & Pipho, C. (1984). State-mandated testing and the fate of local control. *Phi Delta Kappan, 66,* 209–212.

Baker, E. L., Linn, R. L., & Herman, J. L. (1996, Summer). CRESST: A continuing mission to improve educational assessment. *Evaluation Comment.*

Baker, E. L., O'Neil, H. F., & Linn, R. L. (1993). Policy and validity prospects for performance-based assessment. *American Psychologist, 48*(12), 1210–1218.

Berliner, D., & Biddle, B. (1995). *The manufactured crisis: Myths, fraud, and the attack on America's public schools.* New York: Addison Wesley.

Bracey, G. W. (1995, Fall). Variance happens—get over it! *Technos, 4*(3), 22–29.

Bracey, G. W. (1996). International comparisons and the condition of American education. *Educational Researcher, 25*(1), 5–11.

Browder, L. H., Jr. (1971). *Emerging patterns of administrative accountability.* Berkeley, CA: McCutchan.

Center for Research on Evaluation, Standards, and Student Testing. (1997, Spring). Analyzing statewide assessment reforms. *The CRESST Line.*

Cohen, D. K. (1995). What is the system in systemic reform? *Educational Researcher, 24*(9), 11–17.

Cunningham, G. K. (1995). *Response to the response to the OEA panel report.* University of Louisville.

Dorn, S. (1998). The political legacy of school accountability systems. *Education Policy Analysis Archives, 6*(1), 1–30.

Ebel, R. L. (1976). The paradox of educational testing. *Measurement in Education, 7*(4), 1–12.

The Evaluation Center. (1995). *An independent evaluation of the Kentucky Instructional Results Information System (KIRIS)* [Report conducted for The Kentucky Institute for Education Research], Western Michigan University.

Froomkin, D. (Sept. 29, 1997). National education tests: An introduction. *Back to the top* [online], Digital Ink Company.

Gearhart, M., Herman, J. L., Baker, E. L., & Whittaker, A. K. (1993, July). *Whose work is it? A question for the validity of large-scale portfolio assessments.* CSE Technical Report 363. Center for the study of evaluation, National Center for Research on Evaluation Standards, and Student Teaching, Graduate School of Education, University of California, Los Angeles.

Goodling, B. (1997, August 13). More testing is no solution. *The Washington Post,* p. A21.

Green, D. R. (1997, March). *Consequential aspects of achievement tests: A publisher's point of view.* Paper presented at the annual meeting of the American Educational Research Association and the National Council on Measurement in Education, Chicago, IL.

Haney, W., & Madaus, G. (1989). Searching for alternatives to standardized tests: Whys, whats, and whithers. *Phi Delta Kappan, 70*(9), 683–687.

Herman, J. L., Klein, D. C. D., Heath, T. M., & Wakai, S. T. (December, 1994). *A first look: Are claims for alternative assessment holding up?* CSE Technical Report 391. National Center for Research on Evaluation, Standards, and Student Testing, University of California, Los Angeles.

Jones, L. V. (1997). *National tests and education reform: Are they compatible?* William H. Angoff Memorial Lecture Series, Educational Testing Service.

Kane, M. B., Khattri, N., Reeve, A. L., & Adamson, R. J. (1997). *Assessment of student performance.* Washington, DC: Studies of Education Reform, Office of Educational Research and Improvement, U.S. Department of Education.

Khattri, N., Kane, M. B., & Reeve, A. L. (1995). *How performance assessments affect teaching and learning* [Research Report]. Educational Leadership.

Koretz, D. (1996). Using student assessments for educational accountability. In E. A. Hanushek & D. W. Jorgenson (Eds.), *Improving America's schools: The role of incentives* (pp. 171–195). Washington, DC: National Academy Press.

Koretz, D., Barron, S., Mitchell, K., & Stecher, B. (1996, May). *Perceived effects of the Kentucky Instructional Results Information System (KIRIS)*. Institute on Education and Training, RAND.

Koretz, D., Mitchell, K., Barron, S., & Keith, S. (1996). *Final report: Perceived effects of the Maryland school performance assessment program* [CSE Technical Report 409]. Los Angeles, CA: National Center for Research on Evaluation, Standards, and Student Testing.

Kuhs, T., Porter, A., Floden, R., Freeman, D., Schmidt, W., & Schwille, J. (1985). Differences among teachers in their use of curriculum-embedded tests. *The Elementary School Journal, 86*(2), 141–153.

Lane, S. (1997, March). *Framework for evaluating the consequences of an assessment program*. Paper presented at the annual meeting of the National Council of Measurement in Education, Chicago, IL.

Lane, S., & Parke, C. (1996, April). *Consequences of a mathematics performance assessment and the relationship between the consequences and student learning*. Paper presented at the annual meeting of the National Council on Measurement in Education, New York.

Langdon, C. A. (1997). The fourth Phi Delta Kappan poll of teachers' attitudes toward the public schools. *Phi Delta Kappan, 79*(3), 212–220.

Linn, R. L. (1993). Educational assessment: Expanded expectations and challenges. *Educational Evaluation and Policy Analysis, 15*(1), 1–16.

Linn, R. L. (1994). Performance assessment: Policy promises and technical measurement standards. *Educational Researcher, 23*(9), 4–14.

Linn, R. L., Baker, E. L., & Dunbar, S. B. (1991). Complex, performance-based assessment: Expectations and validation criteria. *Educational Researcher, 20*(8), 15–21.

Linn, R. L., & Herman, J. L. (1997, February). *Standards-led assessment: Technical and policy issues in measuring school and student progress* (CSE Technical Report 426). National Center for Research on Evaluation, Standards, and Student Testing (CRESST) Center for the Study of Evaluation, Graduate School of Education & Information Studies, University of California, Los Angeles.

Madaus, G. F. (1985). Test scores as administrative mechanisms in educational policy. *Phi Delta Kappan, 66*(9), 611–617.

Madaus, G. F. (1991). The effects of important tests on students: Implications for a National Examination System. *Phi Delta Kappan, 73*(3), 226–231.

Madaus, G. F., West, M. M., Harmon, M. C., Lomax, R. L., & Viator, K. A. (1992, October). *The influence of testing on teaching math and science in grades 4–12*. Executive Summary. National Science Foundation Study, Center for the Study of Testing, Evaluation, and Educational Policy, Boston College, Chestnut Hill, MA.

Mayes, M. (1997, August 30). Test results make school chief smile. *The Lansing State Journal*, pp. 1A, 5A.

McDonnell, L. M. (1997). *The politics of state testing: Implementing new student assessments* (CSE Technical Report 424). National Center for Research on Evaluation, Standards, and Student Testing, University of California, Los Angeles.

McDonnell, L. M., & Choisser, C. (1997, September). *Testing and teaching: Local implementation of new state assessments* (CSE Technical Report 442). National Center for Research on Evaluation, Standards, and Student Testing (CRESST) Center for the Study of Evaluation (CSE) Graduate School of Education & Information Studies, University of California, Los Angeles.

Mehrens, W. A., & Kaminski, J. (1989). Methods for improving standardized test scores: Fruitful, fruitless or fraudulent? *Educational Measurement: Issues and Practices, 8*(1), 14–22.

Miller, M. D. (1998, February). *Teacher uses and perceptions of the impact of statewide performance-based assessments*. Council on Chief State School Officers, State Education Assessment Center, Washington, DC.

Petrie, H. G. (1987). Introduction to "evaluation and testing." *Educational Policy, 1*, 175–180.

Pipho, C. (1997). Standards, assessment, accountability: The tangled triumvirate. *Phi Delta Kappan, 78*(9), 673–674.

Pomplun, M. (1997). State assessment and instructional change: A path model analysis. *Applied Measurement in Education, 10*(3), 217–234.

Porter, A. C., Floden, R. E., Freeman, D. J., Schmidt, W. H., & Schwille, J. P. (1986). *Content determinants* (Research Series No. 179). Michigan State University, East Lansing, MI: Institute for Research on Teaching.

Rafferty, E. A. (1993, April). *Urban teachers rate Maryland's new performance assessments*. Paper presented at the annual meeting of the American Educational Research Association, Atlanta, GA.

Reckase, M. D. (1997, March). *Consequential validity from the test developers' perspective*. Paper presented at the annual meeting of the National Council on Measurement in Education, Chicago, IL.

Rose, L. C., Gallup, A. M., & Elam, S. M. (1997). The 29th annual Phi Delta Kappa/Gallup poll of the public's attitudes toward the public schools. *Phi Delta Kappan, 79*(1), 41–58.

SERVE. (1994a). *A new framework for state accountability systems* [Special report of The Southeastern Regional Vision for Education].

SERVE. (1994b). *Overcoming barriers to school reform in the southeast* [Special report of The Southeastern Regional Vision for Education].

Shepard, L. A. (1991). Will national tests improve student learning? *Phi Delta Kappan, 72*, 232–238.

Smith, M. L., Noble, A., Heinecke, W., Seck, M., Parish, C., Cabay, M., Junker, S., Haag, S., Tayler, K., Safran, Y., Penley, Y., & Bradshaw, A. (1997). *Reforming schools by reforming assessment: Consequences of the Arizona student assessment program (ASAP): Equity and teacher capacity building* (CSE Technical Report 425). University of California, Los Angeles: National Center for Research on Evaluation, Standards, and Student Testing.

Smith, M. L., & Rottenberg, C. (1991). Unintended consequences of external testing in elementary schools. *Educational Measurement: Issues and Practice, 10*(4), 7–11.

Stecher, B. M., & Mitchell, K. J. (1995, April). *Portfolio driven reform: Vermont teachers' understanding of mathematical problem solving and related changes in classroom practice* (CSE Technical report 400). National Center for Research on Evaluation, Standards, and Student Testing (CRESST). Graduate School of Education and Information Studies, University of California, Los Angeles.

Stecklow, S. (1997, September 2). Kentucky's teachers get bonuses, but some are caught cheating. *The Wall Street Journal*, pp. A1 & A5.

Stedman, L. C. (1996, January 23). The achievement crisis is real: A review of "The manufactured crisis." *Educational Policy Analysis Archives, 4*(1), 1–11.

Taleporos, E. (1997, March). *Consequential validity*. Paper presented at the annual meeting of the American Educational Research Association, Chicago, IL.

Womer, F. B. (1984). Where's the action? *Educational Measurement: Issues and Practice, 3*(3), 3.

Part II

TECHNICAL ISSUES

Chapter 8

Test Dimensionality

Richard Tate
Florida State University

Test dimensionality, roughly defined as the minimum number of examinee abilities measured by the test items, is a unifying concept that underlies some of the most central issues in the development and use of large-scale tests. To illustrate, consider four practical concerns that are prominent in the Standards for Educational and Psychological Testing (AERA, APA, NCME, 1999). First, the content-related aspect of test validity requires consistency of the test dimensionality and the target test content structure, suggesting that the usual logical comparison of the test items with the test specification plan should be supplemented with an empirical analysis of test structure. In addition, dimensionality-related tools are also essential in the search for possible construct-irrelevant factors that may threaten the validity of the test. Second, the standard methods of computing the score reliability and precision assume that the test is unidimensional—an assumption that is almost always violated to some extent. Thus, the test developer must ask whether the estimated reliability accurately represents the actual reliability despite the violations of unidimensionality. When there is a serious lack of robustness to such violations, alternative methods of estimating reliability can be sought.

A third major concern is the fairness of a test—an issue of particular importance in the current volume devoted to testing for diverse student populations. One of the possible threats to test fairness is the presence of bias in individual items (also known as differential item functioning). Item bias can be best understood as the result of a multidimensional test structure,

181

including one or more factors that are construct-irrelevant abilities. Thus, an empirical assessment of test dimensionality can help understand why some items may be biased and to avoid such bias in future item construction. Finally, a fourth concern in the development of a large-scale test is the maintenance of score comparability over time. The near-universal assessment goal of accurately describing trends of school, district, and state achievement over time requires the equating of the test forms used in different years, an equating that must be guided by careful consideration of test dimensionality. For example, when the test is multidimensional, it is important that the anchor items chosen for equating studies accurately reflect the test structure. Also, continuing dimensionality assessments over time would help identify changes in the test structure that may threaten the validity of descriptions of achievement trends.

The goal of this chapter is to describe how dimensionality-related concepts and empirical methods can be useful in addressing issues of test validity, reliability, fairness, and score comparability. Given the wide scope of this topic and the current space constraints, it is only possible to provide a relatively broad survey of these issues. Although some of the recommendations herein have long been standard practice in test construction (e.g., the use of common factor analysis to support the use of test subscores), others reflect more recent ideas found in the current psychometric literature. Research on all aspects of this topic is quite active, with numerous continuing additions to an already extensive literature. Because of this, current views of test dimensionality and associated recommendations for practice are best viewed as somewhat tentative and evolving. Therefore, it is necessary for those responsible for dimensionality assessments to develop and maintain a familiarity with the associated technical literature. To aid in this, a relatively large (but still incomplete) sample of the literature has been provided.

In the first section, a definition of test dimensionality is provided, followed in the next section by a discussion of the sources and consequences of multidimensionality. Next, a review of some current methods for empirically assessing the dimensionality of a test is given. Finally, ways in which the design, development, and evaluation of a test should be influenced by dimensionality issues are considered, and some possible remedies for dimensionality-related problems are identified.

SOME TERMS, DEFINITIONS, AND DIMENSIONALITY-RELATED ASSUMPTIONS

An important part of the empirical evaluation of a test is concerned with the congruence of the statistical test structure and the planned test content structure. In this section, the terms used to describe the test content structure are given and then the dimensionality of a test is formally defined. Finally, the assumption of unidimensionality associated with classical test theory and item response theory (IRT) is briefly stated.

Test Content

It is assumed that a test content domain of interest has been specified to reflect the purpose of the test.[1] For example, this might be a mathematics ability domain for a particular student population of interest. The content structure of such a domain is often operationally defined by a test plan organized by content area and level of examinee processing required for a correct response. To illustrate, a test plan for a test of mathematics might include the content areas of number concepts, algebra, geometry, and probability, and process levels of factual knowledge, conceptual understanding, and problem solving. Each individual test item is often written to reflect a specific test plan cell or combination of content area and process level (e.g., to measure problem-solving ability in geometry). In the context of discussion of the content domain, the term *ability* (or sometimes *component ability*) is used hereafter as an all-purpose expression for what the student knows and is able to do at some level in the content domain. The defined structure of the content domain implies a corresponding structure of content-defined abilities at different levels. For example, the term *mathematics ability* would reflect the student ability in the entire mathematics domain, and *problem-solving ability in geometry* would represent one of the component abilities of the domain.

There are two common ways of envisioning the relationship between the overall domain ability and the component abilities at lower levels in the content domain. First, it may be assumed that the structure of the content domain conforms to a hierarchical model, in which the multiple component abilities at a first level, perhaps reflecting the cells of the test plan,

---

[1]This discussion assumes that the purpose of a test can be viewed as the estimation of one or more continuous traits that summarize what a student knows and can do. It has been recently recommended that current test theory, developed under the influence of the trait and behavioral psychological paradigms, be extended and revised to move beyond a focus only on the estimation of traits (e.g., Mislevy, 1996). The proposed extension would reflect recent developments in cognitive psychology, attempting to make inferences about the *nature* of student cognitive processing and development. In the current context, such testing might, for example, provide information on solution strategies used by students, information that would be of value in the formative evaluation of school curricula. Some examples are given by Beland and Mislevy (1996) and Mislevy and Verhelst (1990). The formal modeling used in this approach often combines latent class theory for representing the probabilities of membership in distinct classes (e.g., Macready & Dayton, 1980) with the currently dominant latent trait theory approach incorporated in factor analytic/MIRT approaches. See Gitomer and Yamamoto (1991) for an example of this combination in the context of performance assessment.

are all determined in large part by a general ability at a higher level measured by the total test score. Alternatively, the domain ability measured by the total test score may be viewed as an implicit composite or weighted average of the cell component abilities, with the weights of the composite defined in part by the number of items in the cells of the test plan. When the test provides subscores in addition to a total score, the subscores are assumed to represent abilities at a lower level in the test structure (e.g., subscores for number concepts, algebra, geometry, and probability).

Test Dimensionality

Formally defined, *test dimensionality* is the minimum number of dimensions resulting in a model that is both locally independent and monotone for the population of interest (e.g., Stout, 1990). A monotone model is one in which the probability of a correct item response monotonically increases with increasing values of the dimensions, and local (or conditional) independence is the condition that all item responses are independent after controlling for the test dimension(s).[2] Statistically, any model of the correct dimensionality is not unique; an infinite number of equivalent models (i.e., models fitting the data just as well) can be obtained with transformations of the dimensions in the initial model (using, e.g., rotations of an initial factor solution). Substantive considerations based on the content and purpose of the test must guide the choice of an appropriate final statistical model.

Stated more informally, the test dimensionality is the minimum number of dimensions or statistical abilities required to fully describe all test-related differences among the examinees in the population. In some cases, the abilities in a statistical model may conform to content-defined abilities at some level in the target content domain. For example, a test may have a dimensionality of one, and the associated statistical ability may be congruent with the target domain ability. In this case, the single total test score fully captures all test-related differences among the examinees, and no additional information is provided by subscores. A test may also be highly multidimensional, with a separate statistical ability corresponding

---

[2]This assumption of local independence, often called the strong or full assumption of local independence, is formally defined by the condition that the probability of any pattern of responses to all of the items, conditioned on the abilities, is equal to the product of the conditional probabilities of each of the responses. A distinction is often made between this assumption and a weaker version referred to as the weak or pairwise assumption of local independence. This weaker assumption states that the covariances of all pairs of item responses, conditioned on the abilities, are equal to zero (e.g., McDonald, 1999). In characterizing methods of assessing test dimensionality and identifying local item dependencies, a similar distinction is made.

to, for example, each of the abilities defined by the test plan cells. In this case, all of a set of subscores representing the individual cells would be required for a full description of test-related examinee differences—a description not completely captured by use of only the total test score. In other cases, it is possible that the statistical structure of the test may not completely reflect the content structure. For example, the statistical dimensions may represent only some of the test plan cells, combinations of some of the cells, or composites of planned abilities and construct-irrelevant abilities (a.k.a. *nuisance factors*) not included in the test plan. As mentioned before, the question of the congruence of the statistical structure of a test and the content-defined structure is one of the primary concerns addressed in this chapter.

It is important to note the reference to an *examinee population* in the prior definition of test dimensionality. The dimensionality of a test not only depends on the test items, but is the result of the interaction of the examinees in the population with the items (e.g., Ackerman, 1994). To illustrate the role of the examinee population in determining test dimensionality, consider a test comprised of multiple algebra story items, each item measuring a different composite of algebra ability and reading ability. If the target population is heterogeneous with respect to the required levels of both algebra ability and reading ability, the test will be two dimensional. In contrast, if the population is homogeneous with respect to the level of reading ability required by all of the items, the test would be unidimensional, allowing discrimination among examinees with respect to only mathematics ability. (Note that if the test were comprised of items that all measured exactly the same composite of algebra ability and reading ability, the number of content-related abilities would be two, but the test statistical dimensionality would be one [Reckase, Ackerman, & Carlson, 1988].) When test items are constructed response items requiring the scoring of examinee responses by raters, the concept of an "interaction of an examinee with an item" must be further extended to recognize the item score as resulting from the interaction among the examinee, item, and rater. This implies that for such items the test dimensionality will be determined in part by the scoring rubric adopted by the raters and by the training provided for the raters.

In contrast to the definition of *strict* dimensionality given before, it has long been common practice to focus only on the more important dimensions among those measured by a test, ignoring minor dimensions. More recently, this common-sense idea has been formalized with the definition of *essential dimensionality* of a test of dichotomous items as the minimum number of dominant dimensions required to satisfy the condition of essential local independence (Stout, 1987). This concept of essential local

independence and essential dimensionality has been extended to polytomous items by Junker (1991).

Dimensionality Assumptions

In considering the implications of test multidimensionality in the next section, one concern is the consequences of violating any dimensionality-
related assumptions associated with the test theory used to determine the
test psychometric properties. Starting with classical test theory, there is no
formal assumption about test dimensionality in considering the content-
related aspect of validity. It is only required that the test items appropriately
reflect the test plan, and the goal then is to estimate a specified composite of
the component abilities of the plan. In contrast, the determination of standard measures of score reliability from classical test theory is based on the
assumption of homogeneous items—an assumption that is equivalent to
the assumption of unidimensionality (McDonald, 1999). For IRT, the
standard formulation used in current practice assumes unidimensionality
or, equivalently, that all item responses are locally independent after controlling for one ability. As mentioned earlier, in practice, it is universally
recognized that the strict assumption of unidimensionality is always violated to some extent, and practitioners are usually willing to accept essentially unidimensional structure for an IRT-based test (Stout, 1987) or an
essentially homogeneous set of items for a test based on classical test theory (McDonald, 1999).

   Thus, when empirical analyses indicate that (a) the test is essentially
unidimensional, and (b) the single, dominant statistical ability accurately
reflects the target composite of content-defined component abilities, the
possible complications due to multidimensionality considered in this chapter are usually minimal. For example, this finding would represent empirical evidence for the content-related aspect of validity of the total test
score, and it would promote confidence in the accuracy of the estimated
score reliability or precision. In addition, in combination with a careful review of item content, this finding would be evidence for the absence of
strong construct-irrelevant factors that might lead to widespread item
bias. Finally, the design of the equating studies required to maintain score
comparability over time would not be complicated by issues of multidimensionality. If, however, there is empirical evidence of more than one
dominant factor in the test (or, equivalently, evidence of local item dependency after controlling for one ability), it is necessary to consider the
consequences of violating the assumption of unidimensionality associated
with classical test theory and IRT.

MULTIDIMENSIONALITY: SOURCES AND CONSEQUENCES

Of primary interest in this section is the common situation in which the test is essentially multidimensional. This can occur because of the planned test structure and/or because of unintended construct-irrelevant factors. This section identifies some of these sources of test multidimensionality and discusses the associated consequences for validity, reliability, test fairness, and score comparability. The total test score is considered throughout most of this discussion, but dimensionality considerations for subscores are also briefly noted.

Multidimensionality Due Only to the Planned Content Structure

The inclusion of various content areas and process levels in the target test plan implies possible test multidimensionality. Suppose that a particular test does in fact exhibit essential multidimensionality closely conforming to the planned content structure. What are the implications for various concerns in the development and use of the test?

Validity. On the positive side, empirical test multidimensionality that is consistent with the planned content structure would represent evidence for the internal structure aspect of validity of the total score (e.g., AERA, APA, NCME, 1999). Moreover, for a test based on classical test theory, the close congruence of the test items with the test plan would be sufficient content-related evidence for score validity. For IRT-based tests, however, the question of the content aspect of validity is more complex. As indicated earlier, given a multifaceted test plan, the goal is to implicitly estimate a composite of the various component abilities defined by the plan.[3] For example, in a mathematics test, the goal may be to measure an equally weighted composite of examinee abilities in number concepts, algebra, geometry, and probability. Statistically, the single IRT ability estimate resulting from a multidimensional test can also be viewed as a measure of a composite of the multiple abilities underlying the examinee item re-

---

[3] This discussion is based on the current dominant IRT practice of scaling all of the test items to obtain a total test score regardless of the possible presence of subscores. As indicated in the chapter, such a total score is then viewed as representing an implicit composite of the component abilities. An alternative approach is to scale separately each of a set of subscales and then to form an *explicit* composite of the subscores to represent the total score. The evaluation of the psychometric properties of such explicit composites can then be based on standard procedures for linear combinations of scores—procedures that are not considered here.

sponses. The content aspect of validity for an IRT-based test, then, would require that the weights of the estimated ability composite correspond approximately to those in the target test composite.

Fortunately, there is extensive evidence that under relatively common conditions the single IRT ability estimate will reflect the target composite of abilities when the test is multidimensional due to the test structure. The required condition for this desirable outcome is the presence of moderate or stronger correlations among the multiple abilities—a condition that would be expected to hold for many large-scale assessments. This assessment of robustness is supported by the analytical developments of Wang (1987, 1988) and by results from simulation studies of the consequences of fitting multidimensional item data with unidimensional three-parameter IRT models (e.g., Ansley & Forsyth, 1985; DeAyala, 1994, 1995; Drasgow & Parsons, 1983; Kim & Stout, 1993; Way, Ansley, & Forsyth, 1988). However, if the abilities spanned by a test are only weakly correlated, some of the same studies indicate that the total test score will represent only one of the component abilities, not the desired ability composite, representing a serious threat to the content-related validity of the total score.

Other problems for IRT-based tests resulting from multidimensionality can be less benign. Consider, for example, the parameter invariance properties associated with the IRT item models. These properties, often viewed as primary strengths of the IRT approach to test construction, can no longer be completely trusted when the assumption of unidimensionality is violated (e.g., Hambleton & Swaminathan, 1985). To illustrate, one aspect of the property of item parameter invariance is that the estimated parameters for a specific item will not depend on the other items included in the test calibration as long as all items are measuring the same dimension. In contrast, for a multidimensional test, the estimated discrimination parameter for an item will depend on the measured test composite, which in turn will depend on the other items selected for the calibration (e.g., Ackerman, 1994; Wang, 1987, 1988). Thus, for example, if the ability composite measured by the test form used in a field test is different from that for the operational test, the estimated parameters for a specific item would be different in the two calibrations. A practical consequence of this failure of item parameter invariance is that the use of banked item parameters from previous calibrations in the scoring of the current operational test would be dangerous. In other words, it must be acknowledged that estimated item parameters are often context bound (e.g., Mislevy, Johnson, & Muraki, 1992).

Item Format Considerations.   Attempts to measure higher levels of cognitive processing (e.g., the ability to solve problems in a content area) are often based on item formats other than the traditional selected response format. Thus, tests consisting of both constructed response items and traditional selected response items are expected, implicitly, to be multidimensional with respect to the level of cognitive processing. When this is the case, some care is required, especially for IRT-based tests, to ensure that the target test composite is actually measured by the estimated IRT ability. For example, in a simulation study of mixed format tests of writing ability (Tate, 1996), a test was assumed to consist of two types of items—a single writing prompt to directly measure writing ability and, for an indirect measure of writing ability, 30 multiple-choice items measuring vocabulary and grammatical knowledge. The assumed item parameters reflected values found in previous calibrations of the item types considered separately, and the underlying direct ability and indirect ability were assumed to have a correlation of 0.6. Given the approximately equal time that would be required for the direct and indirect portions of the test, a test developer might hope that the direct and indirect abilities would be weighted approximately equally in the resulting estimated test composite. However, the simulation results indicated that the actual composite was aligned much more closely with the indirect ability, invalidating any test description implying that direct writing ability is an important part of the resulting score.

Equating.   Multidimensionality also poses complications in ensuring score comparability. First, the measured target ability composite must be stable from year to year.[4] Any appreciable instability over time, due perhaps to lack of care in representing all aspects of the test plan while constructing new forms, would pose a threat to the validity of descriptions of trends over time. In addition, violations of test unidimensionality also represent a potential complication for the year-to-year equating of tests, an equating required to maintain a stable scale for the valid description of changes in the average achievement of schools over time (e.g., Peterson, Kolen, & Hoover, 1989). Thus far, conclusions from many of the studies of the consequences for test equating of violations of the assumption of unidimensionality are encouraging. When the anchor items required for typical equating studies (i.e., the items that are common to the current and previous test forms) are properly selected to reflect the same composite measured by the complete test, studies of IRT test equating in single

---

[4]The concerns about maintaining comparable scores over time are also relevant if a test is to be designed to provide a developmental scale over a range of grades. It would be assumed, of course, that the test form for each grade is measuring the same composite of abilities, with the only difference in forms being appropriate differences in test difficulty. Grade-to-grade changes in the empirical test structure could pose a threat to the content-related aspect of validity and result in a scale shrinkage or expansion in which decreases or increases of the within-grade score variability are an artifact of the multidimensionality (e.g., Yen, 1985).

populations have often found the equating results to be robust to violations of the unidimensionality assumption (e.g., Camilli, Wang, & Fesq,
1995; Dorans & Kingston, 1985; Yen, 1984). Possible equating biases due
to different test dimensionalities for different subgroups of a heterogeneous population have also been considered and studied (e.g., Camilli et
al., 1995; De Champlain, 1996; Goldstein & Wood, 1989; Peterson et al.,
1989; Skaggs & Lissitz, 1986). This situation might occur, for example,
when a test is unidimensional for native-born students, but multidimensional for children from immigrant families, perhaps including a reading
comprehension factor for the latter. Such variation of dimensionality
across subpopulations may result in an equating transformation that would
not be appropriate for some subpopulations. Results of the limited empirical studies of this possibility have been somewhat mixed, with some indicating consequences of practical importance (e.g., Cook, Eignor, & Taft,
1988) but others suggesting reasonable robustness (e.g., De Champlain,
1996).

Subscores. When a test is designed to provide multiple subscores in
addition to a total score for a subject area (e.g., subscores for the content
areas of number concepts, geometry, algebra, and probability), the intent
is to provide diagnostic information about relative strengths and weaknesses. Two aspects of validity are of concern when subscores are used.
Both the internal structure aspect of validity and the discriminant validity
of the subscores (e.g., AERA, APA, NCME, 1999) require that the test be
multidimensional with the statistical structure reflecting the planned subscores. If, instead, a test is essentially unidimensional, due perhaps to a
homogeneous population and a standardized statewide curriculum, all of
the subscores would be measuring the same general ability, and any apparent differences among subscores for the same examinee would be due
mostly to random measurement error. The resulting decisions based on
apparent relative strengths and weaknesses for an individual would often
not be valid.

Unintended Sources of Multidimensionality

There are numerous other possible reasons for test multidimensionality in
addition to the planned content structure of the test domain (e.g., Yen,
1993). For example, correct responses to test items often require one or
more unintended nuisance or construct-irrelevant abilities in addition to
the target abilities. To illustrate, if (a) a test intended to measure only
mathematical ability also requires a certain level of both examinee reading
ability and examinee persistence, and (b) there is variability in the
examinee population on all three abilities, the reading ability and persis-

tence variables would be viewed as construct-irrelevant factors. As the importance of such nuisance factors increases (i.e., as their weights in the estimated test composite become larger), the associated threat to the content-related aspect of validity becomes more serious.

Other nuisance factors can result from inappropriate design of the test administration conditions. For example, when the testing time is inadequate for significant segments of the examinee population, the ability of an examinee to work quickly in taking a test will emerge as a speededness construct-irrelevant factor. In a similar fashion, an attempt to administer a very long test in one session may produce an endurance nuisance factor. Even when the test administration procedure is appropriate for the operational test, there may be some doubts about data collected in the field tests commonly used to empirically evaluate tests. For example, there is often concern that examinee motivation in a field test situation, where students believe the results "don't count," is less than that for the operational test. Such a difference may produce invalid conclusions from the field test data about various empirical questions, including that of test dimensionality. To illustrate, a recently developed statewide assessment of reading ability was administered in two separate days (Tate, 2001). A dimensionality assessment of the data from the first field test of the exam clearly indicated a violation of the assumption of essential unidimensionality, with the resulting two dominant factors representing the two testing days. It was speculated that this structure was probably due to the change in student motivation from the first to the second day of a test that "didn't count," and it was expected that this feature would disappear in the operational test. The data from the first operational test confirmed this expectation, supporting a conclusion of essential unidimensionality.

Item Format Considerations. Certain item formats can also unintentionally introduce local item dependencies representing a violation of the assumption of unidimensionality. One possibility is a single performance assessment task that requests examinee responses to each of a group of logically interdependent items (e.g., Ferrara, Huynh, & Michaels, 1999). For example, one item may request an answer requiring a mathematical computation, whereas the next item asks for an explanation of how the previous answer was obtained. Other possible local item dependencies resulting from certain item formats may be less obvious. For example, tests of reading ability are often comprised of clusters of items, each cluster based on a different reading passage. Even when the item writers attempt to write individual items that are logically independent of one another, passage dependencies may still be present in the group of items if some also unintentionally measure knowledge of the subject of the passage. A potentially serious consequence of passage dependencies is that the actual precision of the test score may be appreciably lower than the apparent or nominal precision determined by classical or IRT theory (e.g., Sireci, Thissen, & Wainer, 1991). As a result, an apparently accurate decision about whether an individual student has attained a goal may in fact be in error because the actual measurement error is larger than recognized.

Fairness. The presence of nuisance or construct-irrelevant abilities can also produce biased items exhibiting differential item functioning (DIF)—a bias that represents one of the threats to the fairness of a test. DIF for an item is present when the probability of a correct item response is different for examinees from different subgroups having the same value of the target ability (e.g., Ackerman, 1992; Shealy & Stout, 1993a, 1993b). Such item bias occurs when the conditional distribution for a nuisance ability at each level of the true ability is different for different examinee groups. Characteristics of items exhibiting DIF have been discussed (e.g., O'Neill & McPeek, 1993). The concern about item bias, important for any large-scale test, would of course be central in the development of a test to be administered to diverse student populations. See chapter 10 for further discussion of item bias and test fairness.

In sum, test multidimensionality can result from the planned test structure and from various unintended sources. Under some conditions (e.g., when the multidimensionality is due almost entirely to the planned test structure and the associated component abilities are at least moderately correlated), typical uses of the test score are robust to the violation of the assumption of unidimensionality. Under other conditions (e.g., when the component abilities measured by the test are weakly correlated or when there are strong construct-irrelevant factors), the consequences of the violation may be serious for test validity, reliability, fairness, and score comparability.

METHODS FOR THE EMPIRICAL ASSESSMENT OF DIMENSIONALITY

Careful test design and development activities are essential but do not ensure that the actual test structure will conform to the expected. Once data are available from a large field test or the first operational test administration, it is important to empirically confirm the expected dimensionality and identify any unintended sources of multidimensionality. No standard set of recommended dimensionality assessment procedures for large-scale testing has yet emerged, and no attempt is made here to provide such a recommendation. There are, however, certain general considerations that should guide the selection of one or more methods for a specific situation. First, the choice of a dimensionality assessment method will be constrained by the number of responses in the item format(s) chosen for the test. At this time, many of the commonly used assessment methods assume dichotomous items in which there are only two possible item response outcomes (e.g., correct and incorrect for multiple-choice items). Less common are procedures that would be appropriate for the increasingly popular polytomous items. Such items are represented by, for example, multipoint ratings of responses constructed by examinees and testlet scores summing correct answers over a set of dichotomous items.

The nature of the expected dimensionality of the test is another important consideration in selecting a method. If the test is expected to be essentially unidimensional for the examinee population of interest, virtually all of the methods discussed later would be of possible value in various ways. Of particular interest would be formal or informal tests of the hypothesis of essential unidimensionality and results indicating the sources and degree of any departures from unidimensionality. However, if there is a strong prior expectation of multidimensionality due to either the planned content structure (e.g., when subscores are to be reported) or the item format (e.g., when groups of items are based on reading passages), a confirmatory assessment method would be appropriate. Finally, the search for unintended multidimensionality due to either relatively general structural features (e.g., nuisance factors, including speededness) or to more localized item interdependencies could best be accomplished with an exploratory assessment method.

Not surprisingly, the choice of the appropriate dimensionality assessment method based on the previous logical considerations is sometimes constrained by current limitations of theory and computer software. For example, one of the most popular confirmatory factor analysis methods currently presents demanding sample size requirements when dichotomous data are analyzed. Other computer programs have practical limitations on the number of factors or the number of test items—limitations that would be problematic for many tests. Some of these current limitations are noted next, but the reader should remember of course that such limits tend to relax over time as computational power continues to increase.

The dimensionality assessment methods/programs currently available are a dramatic improvement over the often ad hoc methods that were common 15 years ago (see e.g., Hattie, 1985). The limited space here does not allow a comprehensive consideration of all such current methods. Instead, the following discussion identifies only several common techniques to represent each of the different approaches to the assessment of dimensionality. First, selected methods for dichotomous items are consid-

ered. One family of such methods consists of the item factor analytic procedures that have extended classical linear factor analysis procedures to
the more difficult problem of modeling item responses. Because an item
factor analysis model is essentially equivalent to recently developed models for multidimensional item response theory (MIRT), the results from
this family of methods can be viewed from either a factor analytic perspective or a MIRT perspective. Considered next, a second family of methods
for dichotomous responses is based on the estimation of conditional associations for item pairs after conditioning on the total test score. Then
some of the relatively small number of methods available for the assessment of dimensionality in tests with polytomous items are noted. Finally,
this section finishes with a brief discussion of a task related to assessing test
dimensionality, the assessment of the *consequences* of violations of the assumption of unidimensionality for a particular test. Most of the dimensionality assessment methods and associated software discussed later have
been applied by the author to both real and simulated data (Tate, 2001).

Item Factor Analytic Methods

The goal of any attempt to model an examinee response to a dichotomous
test item is to adequately represent the inherently nonlinear relationship
between the probability of a correct examinee response and one or more
examinee latent factors or abilities. Recognizing that the fit provided by
classical linear factor analysis, originally developed for continuous variables, may be unsatisfactory (e.g., McDonald, 1967), various authors have
proposed extensions of linear factor analysis, called here *item factor analytic*
procedures, for the task of modeling dichotomous items responses (e.g.,
Mislevy, 1986). Conceptually, these procedures can be viewed as consisting of two components, the first being a nonlinear model expressing the
probability of a correct response to an item as a function of an associated
latent response variable for the item. The second component is a classical
linear factor model relating the latent response variable for each item to
the multiple factors or abilities. The results from such methods can be expressed in familiar classical factor analysis terms.

A second perspective on dimensionality is provided by the fact that
item factor analytic procedures are virtually equivalent to the multidimensional extension of the item response theoretic model (MIRT; e.g., Goldstein & Wood, 1989; McDonald, 1967, 1999; Muthen, 1978; Takane & de
Leeuw, 1987). Briefly, a MIRT model states the probability of a correct response by an examinee to a dichotomous item as a function of two sets of
parameters: the person parameters (i.e., the examinee's values on the multiple abilities measured by the item) and the item parameters (Reckase,
1985, 1997; Reckase & McKinley, 1991). The latter often consist of an

item discrimination parameter for each ability, reflecting the information provided by the item for that ability; a single parameter representing the difficulty of the item; and a pseudo-guessing parameter representing the lower asymptote of the probability of a correct response. Geometric representations associated with MIRT (and with the methods based on conditional item associations to be discussed later) facilitate the understanding of dimensionality-related issues (e.g., Ackerman, 1996; Stout, Habing, Douglas, Kim, Roussos, & Zhang, 1996).

The item factor analytic procedures include both exploratory and confirmatory methods. An exploratory approach would be appropriate when test developers have no strong prior beliefs about the test dimensionality or when they hope to confirm the belief that the test is unidimensional by failing in the search for any additional dimensions. A confirmatory procedure would be of value when there are strong expectations about the nature of the test dimensionality (e.g., when the test has been designed to provide subscores reflecting presumed different content-related abilities).

Exploratory Methods. The three methods/programs mentioned here share the following features, all of which are traditional in classical exploratory factor analysis (e.g., Harman, 1976). After the user specifies the desired number of factors, an initial orthogonal factor solution is obtained. Associated results include the initial factor matrix containing the loadings of each item on each factor and various model fit indexes and/or tests based on the matrix of differences between the observed correlations and those implied by the model—a matrix called the *correlation residual matrix.* To determine the appropriate final test dimensionality, the user can repeat the analysis for different assumed dimensionalities, comparing the indexes of model fit to make a decision about the appropriate balance of model parsimony and adequacy of fit. In the attempt to improve the interpretation of the derived factors, the initial solution can be transformed or rotated to obtain other models with identical fit but different factor interpretations. The usual criterion for such rotations is the attempt to obtain *simple structure*; one common recent usage of this term refers to a model in which each item is determined by only a single factor. Oblique rotations allow the rotated factors to be correlated, whereas orthogonal rotations constrain them to be uncorrelated.

A linear factor analysis of the matrix of tetrachoric correlations was one of the first proposed remedies for the problems encountered when applying a traditional factor analysis of Pearson product moment correlations to dichotomous item responses. A tetrachoric correlation is the estimated correlation of two bivariate normally distributed latent response variables assumed to underlie the observed dichotomous responses for two items. The combination of the nonlinear model implied by the computation of the tetrachoric correlation and the linear factor analysis of the tetrachoric correlations is, in principle, equivalent to the item factor analysis and MIRT models described earlier. Although many have noted various practical problems associated with the use of tetrachoric correlations (e.g., Mislevy, 1986; Wothke, 1993), this approach is still viewed by some as a viable and perhaps preferred method of assessing dimensionality (e.g., Knol & Berger, 1991). One variation of an exploratory factor analysis of tetrachoric correlations is offered by the Mplus program (Muthen & Muthen, 1998). Possible ways to determine test dimensionality with Mplus would include the visual inspection of the scree plot of the eigenvalues of the tetrachoric correlation matrix or the consideration of the root mean square residual (RMSR) of the matrix of correlation residuals for models of different dimensionalities.

Another exploratory method, full information item factor analysis, has been provided by Bock, Gibbons, and Muraki (1988) and implemented in the TESTFACT 3 program (Bock, Gibbons, Schilling, Muraki, Wilson, & Wood, 1999). The TESTFACT results include model parameter estimates for both the item factor analytic and the MIRT parameterizations. Test dimensionality can be determined by using a chi-square test of the improvement of model fit due to adding more factors to a model. Relatively large numbers of items are easily handled by this program, but computer run times increase rapidly as the number of factors increases. A third approach to modeling the required nonlinear relationship between the probability of a correct response and the examinee abilities is provided by the normal-ogive harmonic analysis robust method (NOHARM) implemented in the NOHARM program (McDonald, 1967, 1997; Fraser & McDonald, 1988). This method uses polynomial functions to represent the nonlinear MIRT relationship and provides estimated parameters from both the item factor analytic and MIRT perspectives. The decision about dimensionality can be based on consideration of the RMSR of the matrix of covariance residuals for models of varying dimensionality. Alternatively, an approximate chi-square test of the model fit attained by NOHARM (DeChamplain & Gessaroli, 1991; Gessarolli & DeChamplain, 1996) is provided by the CHIDIM program (DeChamplain & Tang, 1997).

Confirmatory Methods. The confirmatory methods/programs discussed here are appropriate when there are relatively strong prior expectations about the test structure and the nature of any anticipated multidimensionality. All address the question of whether a hypothesized model is consistent with the observed variances and covariances of the item responses—an assessment based on a formal test of the model fit and/or one or more fit indexes. When a hypothesized model does not fit the data, all methods provide guidance on where the model has failed.

One common approach is provided by confirmatory factor analysis (CFA), a technique often considered to be a special case of structural equation modeling (SEM; e.g., Bollen, 1989). Most of the development and elaboration of SEM has been based on the assumption that the observed variables are continuous. See West, Finch, and Curran (1995) for a discussion of the problems resulting from applying standard SEM methods to dichotomous and polytomous data. There are, however, several available SEM/CFA variations for modeling dichotomous and polytomous observed variables. For example, a weighted least squares (WLS) analysis of the matrix of polychoric (or tetrachoric) correlations has been proposed by Joreskog (1990) and implemented in PRELIS/LISREL (Joreskog & Sorbom, 1988, 1989, 1993). Unfortunately, this approach requires a very large sample size, with three to five subjects per correlation recommended for trustworthy WLS estimates and tests. For a test of 60 items, this rule would indicate the need for roughly 5,000 to 9,000 examinees—a sample size that is larger than those usually employed for calibrations in large-scale assessments.

More recently, Muthen (1993) proposed a robust WLS estimation procedure for dichotomous variables, extended the method to polytomous variables (Muthen, duToit, & Spisic, 1999), and implemented it as an option in the Mplus program (Muthen & Muthen, 1998). This approach is expected to perform better than the WLS method for the sample sizes of 1,000 to 2,000 often used in test calibrations. The decision about dimensionality is based on a formal test of the model fit with the robust chi-square statistic. The computer run times for CFA analyses with the robust WLS option of Mplus become very lengthy as the number of items increases. Another possible confirmatory method is the Rasch MIRT modeling approach proposed by Adams, Wilson, and Wang (1997) and implemented in the ConQuest program (Wu, Adams, & Wilson, 1998). This approach is appropriate for situations in which the discrimination parameter is constant and there is no guessing. The fit of a hypothesized multidimensional factor model can be assessed with ConQuest by testing a chi-square statistic reflecting the difference in the model fit for a one-factor model and the hypothesized model. This relatively new program requires long run times for tests of typical length and increasing numbers of factors.

Some important questions related to the dimensionality of a test can be addressed by standard features of the confirmatory methods/programs. First, they allow the testing of more complex hypothesized models that do not assume simple structure. Tests including, for example, items designed specifically to require multiple abilities, clusters of items associated with passages or tasks, or items structured to reflect a two-level factor model, can be easily modeled with confirmatory factor analysis. Second, a multisample variation of these methods allows the formal testing of structure differences over multiple populations. As indicated earlier, such differences would pose potential threats to test validity and test fairness. Finally, the standard output of these procedures includes estimates of the validity and reliability of the individual items as measures of the abilities.

Two of the methods/programs discussed previously as exploratory methods also provide confirmatory options. The NOHARM program allows the user to specify a hypothesized model and determine the corresponding correlation residuals matrix and RMSR. A test of the resulting NOHARM fit is provided by the CHIDIM program. Also, TESTFACT 3 provides an option for a confirmatory bifactor analysis that would be appropriate when there is a single common factor for all items and multiple orthogonal group factors representing, for example, content knowledge of the subject matter of different reading passages. In addition to the estimated factor loadings, this program option also produces estimates of the common factor, controlling for differences in the group factors.

Group-Level Assessment of Dimensionality. Earlier discussion of the use of subscore differences for diagnostic purposes emphasized the importance of confirming the expected multidimensionality at the individual examinee level. A similar concern exists when curricular strengths and weaknesses for individual schools or districts are evaluated on the basis of differences in test subscore averages. Discriminant validity of this use of the subscores would require the appropriate multidimensionality at the school and district levels. For example, if a classical exploratory factor analysis with schools as the unit of analysis and data consisting of the subscore school averages was to indicate that the data are fit well with a one-factor model, the diagnostic use of average subscore differences would not be supported. One possible factor analytic approach to confirm the required dimensionality at the group level would involve grouping items into parcels, each comprised of, say, four or five items, followed by a group-level confirmatory factor analysis with a hypothesized model having two or more parcels as observed indicators for each of several latent variables corresponding to the subscore abilities.

Some Limitations of Item Factor Analytic Methods. The item factor analytic methods discussed here share the strengths and weaknesses of all parametric modeling approaches. A mathematical model with a limited number of parameters provides a relatively parsimonious summary of data, but it also introduces the strong assumption that the phenomenon of interest is represented accurately by the assumed model. Even if the correct number of abilities has been specified for a model, the model may still be seriously misspecified if it does not represent correctly the functional form of the relationship. For example, the factor analytic methods considered here vary with respect to the extent to which they allow variation of all of the parameters in the classic three parameter IRT model (i.e., the difficulty, discrimination, and guessing parameters). Least restrictive are the TESTFACT and NOHARM methods, allowing all three parameters. The exploratory and confirmatory analyses provided by Mplus don't allow inclusion of the effect of a guessing parameter, and the most restrictive is the Rasch model implemented by ConQuest, which considers variation only of a difficulty parameter.

Moreover, all current factor analytic/MIRT methods explicitly or implicitly assume a compensatory functional relationship in which a high level of one ability can compensate for a low level of a second ability. For many types of items, it might be expected that the process is actually noncompensatory. To illustrate for a mathematics item requiring both mathematics and reading ability, an increase in reading ability would not be expected to compensate for an absence of mathematical ability (e.g., Ackerman, 1989; Sympson, 1978). Attempting to fit a noncompensatory function with a compensatory model is analogous to the ill-advised attempt to use an additive regression model to represent an interactive relationship. Little is known about the robustness of current parametric assessment methods to violations of the assumption of a compensatory relationship.

A limitation of the exploratory versions of factor analytic methods for assessing test dimensionality is the typical use of rotation methods that attempt to transform the initial factor solution to simple structure in which each item loads on only one factor. This implicit goal in the exploratory search for interpretable factors is not appropriate for tests that incorporate performance items intentionally requiring multiple abilities. Confirmatory procedures would be required for this type of planned nonsimple test structure. Finally, as mentioned earlier, some of the current versions of item factor analytic programs still have relatively strict limits with respect to the number of items and/or factors that can be considered. Presumably, continued advances in computational power will continue to relax these limits.

Methods Based on Conditional Item Associations

Recall that a unidimensional test is one in which the responses for all items are locally independent after conditioning on a single ability. Therefore, a natural way to test the assumption of unidimensionality is to consider the conditional item associations after controlling for one ability. Conditional item associations larger than those expected due to chance alone would represent evidence for a violation of the unidimensionality assumption. In one sense, this general approach is confirmatory, being roughly analogous to a confirmatory item factor analysis hypothesizing a one-factor model. However, as described later, the procedures can also be used in an exploratory fashion. Two categories of these procedures are described here: one based simply on the review of individual conditional item associations for all item pairs and the other providing more global methods based on these associations.

Five measures of the conditional association for a pair of items are provided by the IRTNEW software (Chen, 1993). All of these indexes are parametric in the sense that the conditioning is based on the unidimensional IRT model. One of these, the Q_3 index of local item dependency proposed and studied by Yen (1984), is the correlation over examinees of the residuals for an item pair, where the residual for each item and examinee is the difference between the item response and the expected probability of correct response to the item for the examinee. Although Yen (1984) has speculated on an associated test, in practice a constant cut point for Q_3 has often been used to identify item pairs having problematic local item dependence. IRTNEW also includes four other indexes of local item dependency that have been proposed and studied by Chen and Thissen (1997). These indexes offer the possibility of formal tests of the assumption of no association by adapting traditional tests and measures for two-by-two contingency tables. Although the problem of inflation of family-wise error rate would complicate any attempt to use the collection of tests for all item pairs to address the omnibus null hypothesis that all conditional associations are zero, results from the IRTNEW program are useful in at least two ways. A relatively small number of prior hypotheses of possible local item dependency for selected item pairs could be tested in the absence of serious inflation of family-wise error rate. Also an exploratory search for any problematic item pairs could be conducted by identifying outliers in the distribution of all conditional associations.

The three global methods and programs based on conditional item associations discussed here (DIMTEST, HCA/CCPROX, and DETECT) are all based on a nonparametric computation of conditional item covariances. For each item pair, the subjects are stratified with respect to their number correct score on the remaining test items, the covariance of the responses for the two items is computed for each stratification group, and the final conditional item covariance is computed as a weighted or unweighted average of the group values. Stout et al. (1996) discussed and illustrated how these programs can be used in an integrated fashion to assess the dimensionality of a test.

The DIMTEST program (Stout, Nandakumar, Junker, Zhang, & Steidinger, 1993) provides a test of the assumption of essential unidimensionality (Stout, 1987, 1990; Nandakumar & Stout, 1993). In addition to using this test to detect any evidence of multidimensionality, it is also useful for exploratory follow-up tests if the null hypothesis of essential unidimensionality is rejected (Stout et al., 1996). For example, possible test structure suggested by HCA/CCPROX may be tested. In addition, in a confirmatory approach, DIMTEST can test for the presence of hypothesized structure based on the test plan. Studies of the performance of DIMTEST have been reported in, for example, Hattie, Krakowski, and Swaminathan (1996) and Nandakumar (1991, 1993a, 1994).

When there is evidence of a violation of the assumption of essential unidimensionality based on DIMTEST, the HCA/CCPROX program (Roussos, 1995; Roussos, Stout, & Marden, 1998; Stout et al., 1996) provides a hierarchical cluster analysis of items using a proximity measure based on the conditional item covariances. The resulting cluster analysis progressively forms item clusters based on item/cluster proximity, starting with one cluster of two items and finishing with a single cluster of all the items. The clusters of items formed early in the analysis help to identify those items with the strongest local item dependencies. If the test items are clustered with approximate simple structure, this structure will be exhibited by an intermediate HCA/CCPROX solution. The identification of the intermediate solutions of most interest depends largely on prior expectations of possible test structure.

The goal of the DETECT index and program (Kim, 1994; Stout et al., 1996; Zhang & Stout, 1999), the third method in this set of related techniques, is to estimate the extent of multidimensional approximate simple structure. The method is based on a search of various partitions of the test items seeking the partition that maximizes the DETECT index, an index defined in terms of the average of all of the signed conditional item covariances. The resulting maximized index represents the amount of multidimensional approximate simple structure. The program also provides the item cluster partition that resulted in the maximization of the DETECT index, offering insight into the nature of the test structure, and an index reflecting the extent of approximate simple structure.

An inherent strength of the nonparametric DIMTEST, HCA/CCPROX, and DETECT methods compared to parametric factor analytic methods is freedom from the strong assumption that an assumed parametric model fits the data. However, these nonparametric methods will not provide mathematical models of multidimensional tests. In addition, there are always limitations associated with specific methods. For example, DIMTEST may not detect a real departure from essential unidimensionality if the program user makes an inappropriate choice in a required initial selection of a subset of items. Also the measure of multidimensionality provided by the maximum DETECT index reflects approximate simple structure. The ability of DETECT to detect nonsimple multidimensional structure, such as that associated with single performance items measuring multiple abilities, is not clear.

Methods for Polytomous Item Responses

The versions of theories and software discussed thus far have assumed dichotomous item responses. When some or all of the items result in polytomous responses (e.g., for constructed response items or testlet scores), there are a number of options for assessing test dimensionality. Fortunately, some of the dimensionality assessment methods discussed before for dichotomous items also offer polytomous extensions. For example, the exploratory factor analysis and confirmatory factor analysis options provided by Mplus can also be used to analyze mixtures of tetrachoric and polychoric correlations representing relationships among responses to dichotomous and polytomous items. Moreover, the multidimensional Rasch modeling implemented by ConQuest and a polytomous extension of DIMTEST (PolyDIMTEST; Nandakumar, Yu, Li, & Stout, 1998) also allow polytomous items. Finally, when a test consists almost entirely of polytomous items designed to provide approximately interval scales with large numbers of response categories, the polytomous responses would approximate a continuous interval scale. In this case, traditional exploratory and confirmatory factor analyses of Pearson product moment correlations would be expected to provide reasonably accurate results (e.g., Green, Akey, Fleming, Hershberger, & Marquis, 1997).

Assessing the Consequences of Dimensionality Violations

In the previous discussion of the analysis phase of test development, the emphasis has been on the empirical assessment of test dimensionality in the effort to identify violations of the assumed dimensionality. Because the uses of the test score may in some cases be robust to violations of the assumed dimensionality, it is also essential to attempt to directly assess the practical consequences of any such violations. For example, when test subscores are to be provided for diagnostic purposes, it is always important to determine and report measures of the precision of differences of the subscores. Unacceptable precision may result from several sources, including the concern of interest here, an empirical test structure that does not support the discriminant validity of the subscores.

Another example of such assessment of consequences is the now standard practice of conducting differential item functioning (DIF) analyses in the search for items that may be biased against selected ethnic- or gender-based subgroups (Angoff [1993] provides an overview of DIF methods; see chap. 10 for more details). In addition to providing a screening tool for identifying problematic items, insights from DIF results can also be used to inform the design of future tests and item writing (e.g., Linn, 1993). Because the total test score is of primary interest, there is also strong interest in the cumulative effect of any DIF exhibited by individual items (e.g., Nandakumar, 1993b). There would obviously be more concern if there is DIF amplification, in which effects accumulate (say with many items being biased against females) than when the effects tend to cancel. DIF assessment can also be conducted for any item bundles or testlets in the test (e.g., Douglas, Roussos, & Stout, 1996; Wainer, Sireci, & Thissen, 1991). Finally, in addition to the search for differential item functioning across examinee subgroups, there would also be similar interest in such differences for the same item or testlet in different forms over time or over grade levels in developmental tests (Mislevy et al., 1992).

Both parametric and nonparametric procedures are available for the assessment of DIF. For example, it has already been noted that the option of specifying multisample models in standard SEM software will permit a confirmatory factor analysis that tests differences in test structure over multiple populations. In addition, McDonald (1999) illustrated the possible use of classical ideas of factorial congruence in the search for DIF. To mention a popular nonparametric approach, DIF for individual items and for groups of items can be assessed with the approach of Shealy and Stout (1993a, 1993b) as implemented by the computer program SIBTEST (Stout & Roussos, 1996). In the absence of prior hypotheses about expected DIF, exploratory one-at-a-time analyses can be conducted on each item separately. More strongly recommended would be a confirmatory approach in which a limited number of DIF hypotheses based on substantive considerations are tested (e.g., Roussos & Stout, 1996). SIBTEST has also been adapted for tests containing polytomous items (Chang, Mazzeo, & Roussos, 1996). Further detail about DIF procedures is given in chapter 10.

Another possible direct assessment of the consequences of any multidimensionality would focus on the validity of test-equating functions derived to maintain score comparability over time. Recall that if the test dimensionality varies across subpopulations, the equating function derived from a sample of the total population may not be valid for some subpopulations. One approach to addressing this possibility would involve first conducting dimensionality assessments separately for each of several examinee subpopulations of interest. If there is evidence of different test structures over the subpopulations, equating functions could then be derived for each of the subpopulations and compared with that from the entire population. This possible analysis strategy is illustrated by a study for a large-scale standardized test reported by DeChamplain (1996).

When comparing the methods available for assessing test dimensionality with those for assessing the practical consequences of multidimensionality, it is clear that the latter are far less developed. In the long run, one desirable goal will be the development of more theories and associated software that simultaneously provide, for a particular test, indications of any violations of dimensionality related assumptions *and* the consequences of those violations. One example of such theory is provided by Junker's (1991) definition of *essential independence* for polytomous items. In this theory, a proposed measure of departure from essential unidimensionality can also be used to determine the extent to which estimated standard errors based on unidimensional theory would be incorrect.

GUIDELINES AND REMEDIES

Test dimensionality issues are relevant during all phases of a large-scale testing program, starting with the design of the test, continuing with the development and evaluation of the test, and finishing with the long-term maintenance of the test. In the design phase, when specifying the test content domain, the item format(s), and the item construction process, it is important to be aware of typical related sources of multidimensionality and to understand when associated violations of assumptions may have serious consequences. For example, in specifying the scope of the content domain for an IRT-based test, the test developer should remember that the total score content-related validity is only robust to violations of the assumption of unidimensionality when the correlations among the component abilities are moderate or stronger. The goal then is to specify a domain that is broad enough to provide an economical assessment of student performance but still homogeneous enough to allow the anticipation of substantial correlations among any component abilities. In the development and evaluation phases, the test developers, using data from a large field test, would then hope to confirm this expectation with the empirical assessment of test dimensionality. If the assessment detects strong multidimensionality reflecting the expected dimensionality but indicates that some dimensions are nearly statistically independent, a possible remedy would be to reconsider the definition of the test domain, splitting the one domain into two or more domains that are still relatively broad but more homogeneous. A test score could then be estimated for each new domain (e.g., Luecht & Miller, 1992).

The use of subscores for diagnostic purposes should be planned only when it is anticipated that the statistical structure of the test will be consistent with the planned subscores. For example, if test developers expect that the ability subscores will be very highly correlated, they should question the value of subscores in the reporting of test results. If subscores are planned but the empirical assessment indicates that the required statistical structure is only partially present, it may be possible to merge some of the more highly correlated subscores, producing a smaller number of renamed subscores. If the assessment indicates that the test is essentially unidimensional, subscores should not be reported. The assumed multidimensional structure should also be present at the school and district levels if differences among subscore means are to used for evaluating schools and districts. Finally, the standard use of error bands on the subscores at both the student and group levels would help to avoid the overinterpretation of subscore differences that may be due only to chance. Alternatively, Bayesian procedures (e.g., Gelman, Carlin, Stern, & Rubin, 1995) that exploit the shared information provided by the subtest scores may be used to suppress the random measurement error in reporting subscore profiles.

The design and construction of the individual test items must also be sensitive to dimensionality-related issues. The selection of the item format(s) to be used in the test should be informed by an awareness of format-related sources of violations of the assumption of local item independence. For example, special attention should be given to the planned inclusion of item clusters such as those commonly used with reading passages or performance assessment tasks. In addition to ensuring that the items in a cluster are logically independent, the reading passages or performance assessment tasks should be chosen so that examinee knowledge of the substance of the passage does not become an unintended nuisance factor. The empirical assessment of dimensionality should include a search for any passage dependencies that may remain. If strong passage dependencies are present, possible remedies include the scoring of an entire group of items as a single testlet (e.g., Sireci et al., 1991) or the use of software like TESTFACT to estimate the general ability, controlling for passage factors. Another approach to modeling passage dependencies, a Bayesian modification of a standard IRT model to include an additional random effect for items nested in passages, has been proposed by Bradlow, Wainer, and Wang (1999).

The construction of items of any format should also include the continual search for any unintended nuisance abilities that may be required. For example, if the item construction team determines that a draft item purporting to measure only mathematics requires a level of reading ability not present in a significant proportion of the population, they may revise the item to lower the required reading level. Alternatively, if relatively large numbers of mathematics items exhibit the same construct-irrelevant factor, the test developers may consider a revision of the test plan and score labels to reflect the desired presence of reading ability in the measured ability composite (i.e., they may redefine the nuisance ability as a target ability). Also specification of the length of the test and the allowed time should be based in part on consideration of the abilities and test-taking skills of all segments of the examinee population to avoid speededness or fatigue nuisance factors. After data are available, exploratory empirical analyses should be used to identify nuisance factors that may still exist despite the best efforts of the item writing team. Finally, DIF analyses should be conducted for all items in the search for item bias due to any existing nuisance factors. Items that are problematic may be revised or dropped from the test.

Although it is often recommended that most test plan requirements be met with logically independent items, test developers sometimes may believe that logical interdependencies among some items may be necessary to measure certain complex abilities. To ensure an accurate representation of test score precision with such interdependent items, it may be best to plan from the outset to score them as one combined item. If they are scored separately, empirical methods based on conditional item covariances should be used to determine whether they are really providing independent information or whether at least some of the items should be combined in the scoring. Finally, in maintaining over time a test that has been shown to be multidimensional, the anchor items needed for the test equating should be selected carefully to fully represent all dimensions of the test structure. In addition, the test developers may estimate separate equating functions for selected ethnic- or gender-based groups to ensure that the equating function derived for the entire population is valid for various subpopulations.

SUMMARY

A test will always be multidimensional to some extent, violating the assumption of unidimensionality in classical and IRT measurement theory. It is important to distinguish between inconsequential violations and those that are potentially serious. In the attempt to avoid serious problems, the design and development of the test should be informed by an awareness of possible sources of multidimensionality and the associated consequences. For example, a violation of the assumed unidimensionality due to the planned dimensionality of the test plan is often likely, implying that attention must be given to satisfying the conditions under which the content-related validity of the test score will be robust to the violation. In addition, there are various possible unintended sources of multidimensionality, some potentially serious, that must be considered in the test design and development. Once the first test form is developed and administered, it is essential to empirically confirm the expected test dimensionality. The methods of empirical assessment considered in this chapter included item factor analytic methods (noted to be equivalent to multidimensional IRT models) and methods based on conditional item associations after controlling for a single ability. In addition, it is essential to directly assess the consequences of any violations of the assumed dimensionality, including a search for differential item functioning for various subpopulations. If these analyses suggest that serious dimensionality problems exist, remedies must be sought and applied.

ACKNOWLEDGMENTS

The author gratefully acknowledges the assistance, guidance, and suggestions of Thomas Haladyna and Robert Mislevy. Remaining inadequacies are of course the responsibility of the author.

REFERENCES

Ackerman, T. A. (1989). Unidimensional IRT calibration of compensatory and noncompensatory multidimensional items. *Applied Psychological Measurement, 13,* 113–127.

Ackerman, T. A. (1992). A didactic explanation of item bias, item impact, and item validity from a multidimensional perspective. *Journal of Educational Measurement, 29,* 67–91.

Ackerman, T. A. (1994). Using multidimensional item response theory to understand what items are measuring. *Applied Measurement in Education, 7,* 255–278.

Ackerman, T. A. (1996). Graphical representation of multidimensional item response theory. *Applied Psychological Measurement, 20,* 311–329.

Adams, R. J., Wilson, M., & Wang, W. (1997). The multidimensional random coefficients multinomial logit model. *Applied Psychological Measurement, 21,* 1–23.

American Educational Research Association, American Psychological Association, the National Council on Measurement in Education. (1999). *Standards for educational and psychological testing.* Washington, DC: American Educational Research Association.

Angoff, W. H. (1993). Perspectives on differential item functioning methodology. In P. W. Holland & H. Wainer (Eds.), *Differential item functioning* (pp. 3–24). Hillsdale, NJ: Lawrence Erlbaum Associates.

Ansley, T. N., & Forsyth, R. A. (1985). An examination of the characteristics of unidimensional IRT parameter estimates derived from two-dimensional data. *Applied Psychological Measurement, 9,* 37–48.

Beland, A., & Mislevy, R. J. (1996). Probability-based inferences in a domain of proportional reasoning tasks. *Journal of Educational Measurement, 33,* 3–27.

Bock, R. D., Gibbons, R., & Muraki, E. (1988). Full information item factor analysis. *Applied Psychological Measurement, 12,* 261–280.

Bock, R. D., Gibbons, R., Schilling, S. G., Muraki, E., Wilson, D. T., & Wood, R. (1999). *TESTFACT 3: Test scoring, items statistics, and full-information item factor analysis.* Chicago: Scientific Software International.

Bollen, K. A. (1989). *Structural equations with latent variables.* New York: Wiley.

Bradlow, E. T., Wainer, H., & Wang, X. (1999). A Bayesian random effects model for testlets. *Psychometrika, 64,* 153–168.

Camilli, G., Wang, M. M., & Fesq, J. (1995). The effects of dimensionality on equating the Law School Admission Test. *Journal of Educational Measurement, 32,* 79–96.

Chang, H., Mazzeo, J, & Roussos, L. (1996). Detecting DIF for polytomously scored items: An adaption of the SIBTEST procedure. *Journal of Educational Measurement, 33*, 333–354.

Chen, W. H. (1993). IRT-LD: A computer program for the detection of pairwise local dependence between test items. (Research Memorandum 93-2). Chapel Hill. University of North Carolina at Chapel Hill, LL. Thurstone Psychometric Laboratory.

Chen, W. H., & Thissen, D. (1997). Local dependence indexes for item pairs using item response theory. *Journal of Educational and Behavioral Statistics, 22*, 265–289.

Cook, L. L., Eignor, D. R., & Taft, H. L. (1988). A comparative study of the effects of recency of instruction on the stability of IRT and conventional item parameter estimates. *Journal of Educational Measurement, 3*, 225–244.

DeAyala, R. J. (1994). The influence of multidimensionality on the graded response model. *Applied Psychological Measurement, 18*, 155–170.

DeAyala, R. J. (1995). The influence of dimensionality on estimation in the partial credit model. *Educational and Psychological Measurement, 55*, 407–422.

DeChamplain, A. F. (1996). The effect of multidimensionality on IRT true-score equating for subgroups of examinees. *Journal of Educational Measurement, 33*, 181–201.

DeChamplain, A. F., & Gessaroli, M. E. (1991, April). *Assessing test dimensionality using an index based on nonlinear factor analysis.* Paper presented at the annual meeting of the American Educational Research Association, Chicago.

DeChamplain, A. F. & Tang, K. L. (1997). CHIDIM: A FORTRAN program for asessing the dimensionality of binary item responses based on McDonald's nonlinear factor analytic model. *Educational and Psychological Measurement, 57*, 174–178.

Dorans, N. J., & Kingston, N. M. (1985). The effects of violations of unidimensionality on the estimation of item and ability parameters and on item response theory equating of the GRE Verbal scale. *Journal of Educational Measurement, 22*, 249–262.

Douglas, J. A., Roussos, L. A., & Stout, W. (1996). Item-bundle DIF hypothesis testing: Identifying suspect bundles and assessing their differential functioning. *Journal of Educational Measurement, 33*, 465–484.

Drasgow, F., & Parsons, C. K. (1983). Application of unidimensional item response theory models to multidimensional data. *Applied Psychological Measurement, 7*, 189–200.

Ferrara, S., Huynh, H., & Michaels, H. (1999). Contextual explanations of local dependence in item clusters in a large-scale hands-on science performance assessment. *Journal of Educational Measurement, 36*, 119–140.

Fraser, C., & McDonald, R. P. (1988). NOHARM: Least squares item factor analysis. *Multivariate Behavioral Research, 23*, 267–269.

Gelman, A., Carlin, J. B., Stern, H. S., & Rubin, D. B. (1995). *Bayesian data analysis.* New York: Chapman & Hall.

Gessaroli, M. E., & DeChamplain, A. (1996). Using an approximate χ^2 statistic to test the number of dimensions underlying the responses to a set of items. *Journal of Educational Measurement, 33*, 157–179.

Gitomer, D. H., & Yamamoto, K. (1991). Performance modeling that integrates latent trait and class theory. *Journal of Educational Measurement, 28*, 173–189.

Goldstein, H., & Wood, R. (1989). Five decades of item response modelling. *British Journal of Mathematical and Statistical Psychology, 42*, 139–167.

Green, S. B., Akey, T. M., Fleming, K. K., Hershberger, S. L., & Marquis, J. G. (1997). Effect of the number of scale points on chi-square fit indices in confirmatory factor analysis. *Structural Equation Modeling, 4*, 108–120.

Hambleton, R. K., & Swaminathan, H. (1985). *Item response theory: Principles and applications.* Boston, MA: Kluwer-Nijhoff.

Harman, H. H. (1976). *Modern factor analysis.* Chicago: University of Chicago Press.

Hattie, J. (1985). Methodology review: Assessing unidimensionality of tests and items. *Applied Psychological Measurement, 9*, 139–164.

Hattie, J., Krakowski, K., Rogers, H. J., & Swaminathan, H. (1996). An assessment of Stout's index of essential dimensionality. *Applied Psychological Measurement, 20,* 1–14.

Joreskog, K. G. (1990). New developments in LISREL: Analysis of ordinal variables using polychoric correlations and weighted least squares. *Quality & Quantity, 24,* 387–404.

Joreskog, K. G., & Sorbom, D. (1988). *PRELIS: A program for multivariate data screening and data summarization* [Computer program]. Chicago, IL: Scientific Software, Inc.

Joreskog, K. G., & Sorbom, D. (1989). *LISREL 7: User's reference guide* [Computer program]. Chicago, IL: Scientific Software, Inc.

Joreskog, K. G., & Sorbom, D. (1993). *LISREL 8: Structural equation modeling with the SIMPLIS command language* [Computer program]. Chicago, IL: Scientific Software, Inc.

Junker, B. W. (1991). Essential independence and likelihood-based ability estimation for polytomous items. *Psychometrika, 56,* 255–278.

Kim, H. R. (1994). New techniques for the dimensionality assessment of standardized test data (Doctoral dissertation. University of Illinois at Urbana-Champaign). Dissertation Abstracts International, 55-12B, 5598.

Kim, H. R., & Stout, W. (1993, April). *A robustness study of ability estimation in the presence of latent trait multidimensionality using the Junker/Stout ε index of dimensionality.* Paper presented at the annual meeting of the American Educational Research Association

Knol, D. L., & Berger, M. P. F. (1991). Empirical comparison between factor analysis and multidimensional item response models. *Multivariate Behavioral Research, 26,* 457–477.

Linn, R. L. (1993). The use of differential item functioning statistics: A discussion of current practice and future implications. In P. W. Holland & H. Wainer (Eds.), *Differential item functioning* (pp. 337–347). Hillsdale, NJ: Lawrence Erlbaum Associates

Luecht, R. M., & Miller, R. R. (1992). Unidimensional calibrations and interpretations of composite abilities for multidimensional tests. *Applied Psychological Measurement, 16,* 279–294.

Macready, G. B., & Dayton, C. M. (1980). The nature and use of state mastery models. *Applied Psychological Measurement, 4,* 493–516.

McDonald, R. P. (1967). Nonlinear factor analyis. *Psychometric Monographs,* No. 15.

McDonald, R. P. (1997). Normal-ogive multidimensional model. In W. J. van der Linden & R. K. Hambleton (Eds.), *Handbook of modern item response theory.* New York: Springer.

McDonald, R. P. (1999). *Test theory: A unified treatment.* Mahwah, NJ: Lawrence Erlbaum Associates.

Mislevy, R. J. (1986). Recent developments in the factor analysis of categorical variables. *Journal of Educational Statistics, 11,* 3–31.

Mislevy, R. J. (1996). Test theory reconceived. *Journal of Educational Measurement, 33,* 379–416.

Mislevy, R. J., Johnson, E. G., & Muraki, E. (1992). Scaling procedures in NAEP. *Journal of Educational Statistics, 17,* 131–154.

Mislevy, R. J., & Verhelst, N. (1990). Modeling item responses when different subjects employ different solution strategies. *Psychometrika, 55,* 195–216.

Muthen, B. (1978). Contributions to factor analysis of dichotomous variables. *Psychometrika, 43,* 551–560.

Muthen, B. (1993). Goodness of fit with categorical and other non-normal variables. In K. A. Bollen & J. S. Long (Eds.), *Testing structural equation models* (pp. 205–243). Newbury Park, CA: Sage.

Muthen, B. O., Du Toit, S. H. C., & Spisic, D. (undated). Robust inference using weighted least squares and quadratic estimating equations in latent variable modeling with categorical and continuous outcomes. *Psychometrika* (accepted for publication).

Muthen, L. K., & Muthen, B. (1998). *Mplus: The comprehensive modeling program for applied researchers. User's guide.* Los Angeles: Muthen & Muthen.

Nandakumar, R. (1991). Traditional dimensionality versus essential dimensionality. *Journal of Educational Measurement, 28,* 99–117.

Nandakumar, R. (1993a). Assessing essential unidimensionality of real data. *Applied Psychological Measurement, 17,* 29–38.

Nandakumar, R. (1993b). Simultaneous DIF amplification and cancellation: Shealy Stout's test for DIF. *Journal of Educational Measurement, 30,* 293–312.

Nandakumar, R. (1994). Assessing the dimensionality of a set of item responses—Comparison of different approaches. *Journal of Educational Measurement, 31,* 17–35.

Nandakumar, R., & Stout, W. (1993). Refinements of Stout's procedure for assessing latent trait unidimensionality. *Journal of Educational Statistics, 18,* 41–68.

Nandakumar, R., Yu, F., Li, H. H., & Stout, W. (1998). Assessing unidimensionality of polytomous data. *Applied Psychological Measurement, 22,* 99–115.

O'Neill, K. A., & McPeek, W. M. (1993). Item and test characteristics that are associated with differential item functioning. In P. W. Holland & H. Wainer (Eds.), *Differential item functioning* (pp. 255–276). Hillsdale, NJ: Lawrence Erlbaum Associates.

Peterson, N. S., Kolen, M. J., & Hoover, H. D. (1989). Scaling, norming, and equating. In R. L. Linn (Ed.), *Educational measurement* (pp. 221–262). New York: American Council of Education and Macmillian Publishing Company.

Reckase, M. D. (1985). The difficulty of test items that measure more than one ability. *Applied Psychological Measurement, 9,* 401–412.

Reckase, M. D. (1997). A linear logistic multidimensional model for dichotomous items response data. In W. J. van der Linden & R. K. Hambleton (Eds.), *Handbook of modern item response theory.* New York: Springer.

Reckase, M. D., Ackerman, T. A., & Carlson, J. E. (1988). Building a unidimensional test using multidimensional items. *Journal of Educational Measurement, 23,* 193–208.

Reckase, M. D., & McKinley, R. L. (1991). The discriminating power of items that measure more than one dimension. *Applied Psychological Measurement, 15,* 361–373.

Roussos, L. (1995). *Hierarchical agglomerative clustering computer program user's manual.* Urbana-Champaign: Statistical Laboratory for Educational and Psychological Measurement, Department of Statistics, University of Illinois.

Roussos, L., & Stout, W. (1996). A multidimensionality-based DIF analysis paradigm. *Applied Psychological Measurement, 20,* 355–371.

Roussos, L. A., Stout, W. F., & Marden, J. I. (1998). Using new proximity measures with hierarchical cluster analysis to detect multidimensionality. *Journal of Educational Measurement, 35,* 1–30.

Shealy, R., & Stout, W. F. (1993a). An item response theory model for test bias. In P. W. Holland & H. Wainer (Eds.), *Differential item functioning* (pp. 197–238). Hillsdale, NJ: Lawrence Erlbaum Associates.

Shealy, R., & Stout, W. (1993b). A model-based standardization approach that separates true bias/DIF from group ability differences and detects test bias/DIF as well as item bias/DIF. *Psychometrika, 58,* 159–194.

Sireci, S. G., Thissen, D., & Wainer, H. (1991). On the reliability of testlet-based tests. *Journal of Educational Measurement, 28,* 237–247.

Skaggs, G., & Lissitz, R. W. (1986). IRT test equating: Relevant issues and a review of recent research. *Review of Educational Research, 56,* 495–529.

Stout, W. (1987). A nonparametric approach for assessing latent trait unidimensionality. *Psychometrika, 52,* 589–617.

Stout, W. (1990). A new item response theory modeling approach with applications to unidimensionality assessment and ability estimation. *Psychometrika, 55,* 299–325.

Stout, W., Habing, B., Douglas, J., Kim, H. R., Roussos, L., & Zhang, J. (1996). Conditional covariance based nonparametric multidimensionality assessment. *Applied Psychological Measurement, 20,* 331–354.

Stout, W., Nandakumar, R., Junker, B., Chang, H., & Steidinger, D. (1993). DIMTEST: A Fortran program for assessing dimensionality of binary item responses. *Applied Psychological Measurement, 16,* 236.

Stout, W., & Roussos, L. (1996). SIBTEST manual [Computer program manual]. Urbana-Champaign, IL: University of Illinois, Department of Statistics.

Sympson, J. B. (1978). A model for testing multidimensional items. In D. J. Weiss (Ed.), *Proceedings of the 1977 Computerized Adaptive Testing Conference* (pp. 82–98). Minneapolis: University of Minnesota, Department of Psychology.

Takane, Y., & de Leeuw, J. (1987). On the relationship between item response theory and factor analysis of discretized variables. *Psychometrika, 52,* 393–408.

Tate, R. L. (1996). *A study of aspects of writing assessment based on one direct item and multiple indirect items.* Tallahassee, FL: Technical report for the Florida Department of Education.

Tate, R. L. (2001). *A comparison of selected methods for assessing test dimensionality.* Unpublished manuscript.

Wainer, H., Sireci, S. G., & Thissen, D. (1991). Differential testlet functioning: Definitions and detection. *Journal of Educational Measurement, 28,* 197–220.

Wang, M. (1987, April). *Estimation of ability parameters from response data to items that are precalibrated with a unidimensional model.* Paper presented at the annual meeting of the American Educational Research Association, Washington, DC.

Wang, M. (1988, April). *Measurement bias in the application of a unidimensional model to multidimensional item-response data.* Paper presented at the annual meeting of the American Educational Research Association, New Orleans.

Way, W. D., Ansley, T. N., & Forsyth, R. A. (1988). The comparative effects of compensatory and noncompensatory two-dimensional data on unidimensional IRT estimates. *Applied Psychological Measurement, 12,* 239–252.

West, S. G., Finch, J. F., & Curran, P. J. (1995). Structural equation models with non-normal variables: Problems and remedies. In R. H. Hoyle (Ed.), *Structural equation modeling: Concepts, issues, and applications* (pp. 56–75). Thousand Oaks, CA: Sage.

Wothke, W. (1993). Nonpositive definite matrices in structural modeling. In K. A. Bollen & J. S. Long (Eds.), *Testing structural equation models* (pp. 256–293). Newbury Park, CA: Sage Publications.

Wu, M. L., Adams, R. J., & Wilson, M. R. (1998). *ACER ConQuest: Generalized item response modelling software.* Melbourne, Australia: The Australian Council for Educational Research.

Yen, W. M. (1984). Effects of local item dependence on the fit and equating performance of the three parameter logistic model. *Applied Psychological Measurement, 8,* 125–145.

Yen, W. M. (1985). Increasing item complexity: A possible cause of scale shrinkage for unidimensional item response theory. *Psychometrika, 50,* 399–410.

Yen, W. M. (1993). Scaling performance assessments: Strategies for managing local item dependence. *Journal of Educational Measurement, 30,* 187–214.

Zhang, J., & Stout, W. (1999). The theoretical DETECT index of dimensionality and its application to approximate simple structure. *Psychometrika, 64,* 213–249.

Chapter 9

Choosing an Item Format

Michael C. Rodriguez
University of Minnesota

Test developers face two issues: (a) what to measure, and (b) how to measure it (Lindquist, 1936). For most large-scale testing programs, test blueprints are developed that specify content and cognitive demands in terms of "what to measure." Regarding "how to measure," one dilemma facing designers is the choice of item format. The issue is significant in a number of ways. First, interpretations vary according to item format. Second, for policymakers, the cost of scoring open-ended items can be enormous compared with multiple-choice items. Third, the consequences of using any given format may affect instruction in ways that foster or hinder the development of cognitive skills being measured by tests—an effect related to systemic validity (Frederiksen & Collins, 1989). Everyone involved in these discussions points to the centrality of validity concerns. Whether our attention is to systemic validity, a unitary construct validity orientation (Messick, 1989), or a focus on consequential validity (see Mehrens, chap. 7, this volume; Messick, 1994), meaning and inference are our concerns.

For mostly practical reasons, the choice of item format is reduced to one between multiple-choice and constructed-response formats or some combination of the two. Often constructed-response items are employed because of a belief that they may directly measure some cognitive processes more readily than one or more multiple-choice items or because of a belief that they may more readily tap a different aspect of the content domain specified by the test design blueprint. Although some argue that this results from careful item writing rather than the inherent characteristics of a given item format, popular notions of authentic and direct assessment have politicized the item-writing profession, particularly in large-scale assessment programs. The primary question is: Do multiple-choice (MC) items and constructed-response (CR) items measure the same cognitive behavior? The quick answer is: They do if we write them to do so.

This chapter begins with a brief discussion of the language of item formats. It presents parallel classification schemes used throughout the literature to describe various item formats. The historical origins of the MC item are recounted with a focus on its large-scale adoption. This is an important discussion because, in the early 1900s, MC tests were considered the "new type" of tests, replacing centuries of essay and oral exams (and other performance exams). The chapter also examines nearly 80 years of research on item-format equivalence with some interesting results. Finally, an overview of several practical issues is presented, including recommendations from measurement specialists regarding the selection of item format, cost considerations important in the item-format debate, and a brief look at the politics of item-format selection. The focus here, presented through a comprehensive meta-analysis, is on the choice between various formats included in the MC and CR classifications.

Why Consider the Issue of Item-Format Selection?

As becomes evident throughout this chapter (and other chapters as well), the issues surrounding item-format selection, and test design more generally, are critically tied to the nature of the construct being measured. We might assert that driving ability can (and should) be measured via a driving ability performance test and not an MC exam, but knowledge about driving (procedures, regulations, and local laws) certainly can be measured by an MC exam (T. M. Haladyna, personal communication, June 15, 2000).

In reviewing the literature on cognition and the question of item format, Martinez (1999) concluded that no single format is appropriate for all educational purposes. He concurred with Traub (1993), who argued for the primacy of validity considerations in the selection of tests. Linn (chap. 2, this volume) provides a concrete outline of the sources of evidence appropriate for high- to low-stakes decisions that support the validity of test score interpretations and uses under various conceptions of validity. Martinez reviewed arguments that various formats have various levels of strengths in different areas, including cognitive features, item and test characteristics, and economic considerations. In a conclusion reached by others, he recommended employing a combination of formats to accrue strengths and dilute weaknesses of each format.

The bulk of Martinez's (1999) work resulted in seven propositions regarding item format and cognition. The first proposition points to the fact that CR items vary significantly in form and cognitions evoked, as do MC items. The variety found within each distinction complicates simple comparisons. More on this issue is presented in the next section. Martinez also reviewed evidence suggesting that MC items are typically written to evoke lower level cognitive functions. Although it is possible to write MC items to measure higher order thinking, the range of cognitive functions addressed by CR items appears to be wider. When complex cognition is the target, MC and CR items appear to measure similar constructs, although the results are generally mixed in comparability studies of MC and CR items. Martinez recommended a meta-analytic evaluation based on item complexity; however, this information is rarely available in published studies on item-format effects.

Similarly, Haladyna (1998) made a case for selecting item formats according to the kind of interpretation anticipated from a measure, which, in turn, is based on the constructs of *fidelity* and *proximity*. Fidelity is a continuum regarding the distance (logical or judged relationship) between a criterion measure and an unobservable criterion. Fidelity can be assessed through cognitive process analysis, content analysis, or logical analysis. Proximity is the statistical relationship among measures of varying fidelity. This chapter examines on the proximity argument and reaches a similar conclusion to that of Haladyna: When two measures of a criterion have strong proximity, the more efficient choice (usually MC) is reasonable. In cases of low proximity, the measure with higher fidelity is justifiable—where fidelity is the primary concern, performance tasks (CR) are favorable.

A Framework for Format Differentiation

There are several books devoted to the development and use of test items (e.g., Haladyna, 1999; Haladyna, 1997, Osterlind, 1998) aside from the more comprehensive measurement texts. These books briefly discuss terminology, purposes and characteristics of items, and technical and ethical considerations. However, the books have a more practical focus overall, presenting issues related to construction and evaluation of items and item performance. Even with such similarity of focus, no single framework or lexicon describes the variety of items commonly used in assessment instruments. In the few books devoted to item construction and in the dozens of measurement texts currently in print, numerous classification schemes are used to present item formats. Although the specific language adopted may convey slight differences in meaning, each scheme can be presented in a parallel manner in the spirit of building consensus in meaning and understanding.

Objective Versus Subjective.   A commonly used classification scheme, and a potentially misleading one, refers to the scoring of items. Objective items can be scored with significant certainty and, thus, objectivity. That is, the correct or best answer is known, and the application of a key (scoring guide) is simply a matter of comparing students' responses to the correct answer. The efficiency of objective scoring has driven the development of machine-scoring devices because human review of responses is not necessary. These formats primarily include multiple-choice, alternate-choice, true–false, matching items, and a few short-answer items. When human review is required, largely due to the possibility of there being more than one correct answer (or unique, unanticipated correct answers) or because the response cannot be machine read, subjective human judgment enters. Items that require human judgment are referred to as *subjective* because of these considerations, including some short-answer, sentence-completion, computation, and restricted- and extended-response essay items. This distinction is not as clean as it may sound because, for example, some short-answer formats can be quite objectively scored. Computer algorithms have been developed to machine score items where the possible responses are limited and well defined.

Another level of classification could be added that includes performance tasks that are also subjective, such as science experiments, any genre of public speaking, demonstrations, studio art products, performing arts, work samples, and portfolios. Consideration of these formats is beyond the focus of this chapter, and they have been addressed by others, including Kane and Mitchell (1996); LeMahieu, Gitomer, and Eresh (1995); Linn (1995); Osterlind (1998); and Shavelson, Baxter, and Pine (1992). Although there are large-scale assessment programs currently employing performance tasks, critical problems including scoring difficulties (reliability issues), task development (validity issues), and the enormous costs remain unresolved. In some areas, their use has been quite successful including, for example, the Advanced Placement (AP) Programs and the National Board of Professional Teaching Standards (NBPTS) portfolio assessment system for teachers seeking National Board certification. The few states that have heavily invested in performance tasks for their statewide testing programs have reported mixed results and have led some to abandon administration of performance tasks.

Selection Versus Production.   Another classification scheme, somewhat parallel to the objective–subjective dichotomy, refers directly to the response mode. For objectively scored items, an individual generally selects the option or response from those given. For subjectively scored items, the individual has to produce or supply the correct response (thus requiring the subjective judgment of human scorers). This scheme is also referred to as choice (selection or selected-response items) versus construction (production-type, supply-type, or constructed-response items). Yet another way to divide items by the response mode is to divide between items requiring recognition of the answer (selection) or recall of the answer (production).

Fixed Response Versus Free Response. A third way to classify items is in reference to the nature of the items. This scheme refers to fixed-response versus free-response items. The first set (objective, selection) includes items that offer fixed responses; that is, the responses are fixed or given. The other set (subjective, production) includes items that require a response that is not provided in the item; the item is free of the response or the response is open (open-response items).

Worthen, Borg, and White (1993) reminded us that some of these terms are limiting in meaningful ways. For example, they argued that essay responses can be scored objectively and MC items can be written to require more than mere recognition of the correct answers. Stiggens (1997) promoted use of the term *selected response* rather than *objective* to avoid the illusion of objectivity in a broader sense beyond the objectivity of scoring—reaffirming the role of human judgment in other aspects of item and test design. In large part, the differences in terms are not critical, and the parallels are more important than not. The language adopted in this chapter includes a combination of references to response mode and item format directly, focusing primarily on MC and CR item formats.

The Origins and Dominance of the Multiple-Choice Item

Several scholars have presented the case for the dominance of the MC item in large scale assessment programs. Bock (1995) reviewed much of the early work, noting that the merits of the MC item were first debated in the educational literature shortly after the introduction of the Army Alpha test, the recruit-screening and classification device employed when the United States entered World War I in 1917. Those reviews should be consulted for a thorough treatment of this debate, including Coffman (1971), Hogan, (1981), and Traub and MacRury (1990).

Whether MC items were used in classroom settings prior to their introduction to large-scale testing is unknown. Questions submitted orally by instructors could have been phrased in MC format, where a series of options were offered and the student was to select the best. DuBois (1970) reviewed records of formal written exams that existed as far back as 1219 at the University of Bologna for the assessment of competence in law. However, written tests were not regularly used for student placement and evaluation until the late 1500s, when Jesuits (the Catholic order founded by St. Ignatius of Loyola) uniformly adopted such practices in their schools. During the 1800s, written examinations were commonly replacing oral exams because of questions of unfairness and subjectivity.

It was not until the development of intelligence tests that discussions regarding large-scale assessment programs were widely conceived. By the time Terman published the Stanford revision of the Binet and Simon intelligence scales in 1916, there was an increasing call for group-administered intelligence tests. Otis, a student of Terman, developed an experimental group-administered test, which became the prototype of the Army Alpha.

Soon thereafter, achievement tests were developed in most subject areas, publishers distributed tests throughout the country, and test manuals were introduced providing background on tests, instructions for administration and scoring, with norms and reliability information. DuBois (1970) attributed objective scoring and the MC item to Otis and his successful implementation of these innovations in the Army Alpha test.

The use of MC items in published tests quickly followed their introduction in the Army Alpha. In the 1920s, the College Board began investigating the uses of MC items in college entrance exams. In 1926, the first SAT (then called the Scholastic Aptitude Test) was administered. By 1937, MC tests replaced most of the College Board's essay tests (Frederiksen, 1984). Many other exams in use today originated during this period; for example, the Stanford Achievement Test (Stanford 1) was introduced in 1923 and is now in its ninth edition.

With the invention of the optical scanner by Lindquist in the 1950s at the University of Iowa, the MC item became the dominant item format of choice (Haladyna, 1999). Today, testing companies score hundreds of thousands of forms each week. This dominance of objective formats was not unchallenged. By the 1960s, civil rights leaders severely criticized objective measurement and testing as biased and unfair to minority children. The debates surrounding large-scale testing were fueled by the abuses charged by minority researchers (Williams, 1970) and contemporary theories of learning and cognition. The recent inclusion of CR formats in large-scale assessment programs is, in part, a compromise in these debates. Although some educational researchers argued that the inclusion of performance assessment tasks would reduce the minority achievement gap found in standardized tests, reductions have not been evident. Since the introduction of the MC item, researchers have studied the equivalence of MC and CR formats. This literature was recently synthesized.

A META-ANALYSIS OF FORMAT DIFFERENCES

A meta-analytic review of the construct equivalence of MC and CR items was recently reported at a symposium on the subject at the American Educational Research Association annual meeting (Rodriguez, 1998). This synthesis characterized CR items as extensions of the MC format. Given the actual format and design features of the CR items used in studies evaluating equivalence of the two formats, a classification scheme was developed based on the intended similarity between the MC and CR items studied. Each level of the classification scheme was primarily based on the method used to construct the items.

In an exhaustive search of the literature, 61 empirical and 6 theoretical studies investigating issues related to construct equivalence of MC and CR items were located between 1925 and 1998. Of those, 29 studies reported 56 correlations between the two formats (several studies reported multiple results based on different subsets of students and/or tests). The remaining 32 studies employed a variety of techniques to investigate the issue of equivalence. They are reviewed briefly in the next section.

Stem-Equivalent Items

The first set of correlations ($n = 21$) included MC and CR items that were stem equivalent. This was accomplished in one of two ways. MC items were developed first and then, by removing the options from the stem of the MC items, the CR items were developed. In some cases, the CR items were initially developed, and then the MC items were constructed by adding options. In either case, the items were stem equivalent because they employed the same stem. Unfortunately, there were not enough studies that employed either construction method to evaluate differences due to the specific construction method used.

Content-Equivalent Items

The second set of correlations ($n = 12$) included MC and CR items that were content equivalent. The CR and MC items were written to tap the same aspects of the content domain and cognitive skills. In these studies, the authors attempted to evaluate the relationship between MC and CR items that were not identical in the stem, but were identical in purpose. Some argued that constructing CR items by removing the options from MC items is an unnatural technique. However, many item-writing guidelines suggest that a good way to construct MC items is by using commonly produced errors obtained from items originally written in CR form.

Noncontent-Equivalent Items

The third set of correlations ($n = 8$) included MC and CR items that were written so that they were not content equivalent. These authors often argued that the point of including CR items in a test is because of the belief that they tap a different aspect of the content domain or cognitive skill than do MC items. The CR items in these studies were written to do just that.

Essay-Type Items

Finally, 15 correlations were obtained from studies that employed essay-type or extended-response items that were substantially longer than the short-answer CR items in the other studies. Essays often require a substantially different level of skill and cognitive demand and tend to vary significantly in the amount of the content domain that can be covered per item.

Within any given classification, the specific design characteristics differed greatly, but potentially less so than the differences that existed between classifications. The classifications were an attempt to explain the significant heterogeneity that was found among the 56 correlations as a whole. It was also an attempt to investigate the effects of CR items as extensions of the MC format—from one that is nearly an MC item (stem equivalent) to one that is potentially quite distant from the task present in any given MC item (essay type).

Results

The mean weighted correlation (weighted by a function of study sample size) was 0.67 with a 95% confidence interval of 0.66 to 0.68. There was, however, substantial heterogeneity in reported correlations across studies. This indicated that there was no one population of correlations of which this sample as a whole was characteristic.

Two additional analytic strategies were employed. First, to evaluate construct equivalence of the two formats, the correlations were corrected for attenuation under the classical test theory framework where "the true-score scales of the multiple-choice and constructed-response instruments must be equivalent for the comparison . . . to be meaningful" (Traub, 1993, p. 30). Second, a random effects analysis was completed, adjusting the results for the heterogeneity of correlations across studies (this essentially accounted for an additional source of variance due to the sampling of studies from a hypothetical universe of studies that differ in study design).

Under the random-effects model, the mean weighted corrected correlation was 0.902 with a 95% confidence interval of 0.868 to 0.928 (wider due to the additional random-effects variance component). The interesting results came when the analysis accounted for format design. The results for each design are reported in Table 9.1.

Although the resulting correlations and confidence intervals approach unity (1.0, the criterion for construct equivalence), they fall short. In part, this may be due to a mathematical artifact in the usual methods of analyzing correlations—employing Fisher's distribution-normalizing and vari-

TABLE 9.1
Summary of Mean Weighted Corrected Correlations

	Lower Limit	Mean	Upper Limit	n
Stem equivalent	0.907	0.948	0.971	21
Not stem equivalent	0.815	0.860	0.894	35
If not stem equivalent				
Content equivalent	0.837	0.915	0.956	12
Not content equivalent	0.661	0.839	0.927	8
Essay-type items	0.674	0.810	0.893	15

ance-stabilizing Z transformation. The sampling distributions for correlations is recognized for its dramatic skewness as the values approach the extremes (−1.0 or +1.0). This creates a statistical conundrum when attempting to estimate a population parameter that may very well be at unity. However, Fisher's Z is undefined at unity. Aside from this statistical problem, the correlations from studies employing stem-equivalent items certainly do approach unity, at least in the 95% confidence interval (0.907, 0.971).

These results provide evidence regarding the construct equivalence of MC and CR measures when they are written to be construct equivalent and less so when they are written to be different. When items are content equivalent (especially the stem-equivalent items), the correlations are higher than those that are not content equivalent and even greater than those due to the use of essay-type items (the overlap of some confidence intervals may be due to the small number of studies available for analysis). When CR items are written in ways that remove them further from the construct tapped by MC items, the resulting correlations are lower.

Messick (1993) argued, "trait equivalence is essentially an issue of construct validity of test interpretation and use" (p. 61). He suggested that this conceptualization of the trait equivalence or construct validity of item formats is less restrictive than the traditional psychometric framework based on testing the congenericity of formats (which requires true scores to be perfectly correlated even though their errors of measurement may be different). It is less restrictive because "a kind of pragmatic trait equivalence is tolerated to facilitate effective test design for some important testing purposes" (p. 62). This pragmatic tolerance provides for small construct-irrelevant format-specific factors to exist, but in the presence of a dominant construct-relevant factor common to each format employed. We may seek to provide greater sampling of the domain in the use of MC items and greater depth of processes in the use of CR items. To Messick, the question then becomes: "What combination of formats serves our particular purpose better?"

Messick is generally regarded as a preeminent validity theorist. His point on pragmatic trait equivalence is important and deserves considerable attention. Although the requirements of trait equivalence can be framed in very technical ways, Messick recognized the need to create tests that are functional while supporting the central role of validity. Purpose and inference may be more closely tied than most realize—the question may not be "Do we use multiple-choice or constructed-response?", but pragmatically, "What types of questions will meet our purpose and support our intended inference?"

ALTERNATIVE EVIDENCE OF CONSTRUCT EQUIVALENCE

Aside from the meta-analysis of correlations, 32 studies used a variety of other methods to study construct equivalence. These methods included factor analysis, analysis of variance, and the analysis of item statistics. The evidence from factor analytic studies suggests that there may be uniqueness associated with constructed-response items; however, CR items remain strongly related to MC items. The analysis of variance designs illustrate the complexity of issues in investigations of format equivalence. Issues such as content complexity, cognitive complexity, and prior exposure to particular formats or training effects may be important to consider in attempts to isolate the format effect or ascertain construct equivalence.

Analysis of item and test statistics generally suggests that reliability is greater among some short-answer CR scores (exceptions were noted that may have resulted from the quality of item writing). This is perhaps a result of the reduction of error due to guessing and the presence of clues in MC options (both of which may also be present in CR items, however manifested differently). Item-response theory (IRT) analyses have evaluated format differences via item information—an index of the relative contribution an item makes to measuring ability at each level. This analysis has suggested that the information provided by items may depend just as much on the quality of the item writing as it does on the item's format, and that differences in item-specific characteristics that are difficult to capture in IRT models may result in inconsistent format effects. The format apparently does not matter as much as other item-specific characteristics, such as content or cognitive demand (beyond format or item difficulty).

There is a rich quality to the empirical studies conducted on item-format equivalence. However, at this time, we have only begun to understand the complexity and factors that seem to impact the functioning of MC and CR items. Traub and MacRury (1990) suggested that where differences between the two formats have been reported in the literature, the nature of the differences are not well understood. They ultimately recommended that both formats be used to obtain comprehensive assessment of scholastic achievement. "Test developers should not assume that MC tests measure the same cognitive characteristics as FR (free-response) tests, whether the latter are of the essay or discrete-item variety" (p. 43).

CONSIDERATIONS IN CHOOSING AN ITEM FORMAT

Clearly, empirical study is important and has played a central role in the development of test theory and test design practice. At the same time, we have learned a great deal from practice. In some ways, the lessons learned have resulted in principles that go beyond empirical evidence or theoretical constructions. Measurement specialists have promoted principles of test design for decades, other investigators have evaluated design considerations given costs, and anyone involved in test design can attest to the significant role of politics. Psychometrics alone will not answer the designer's questions regarding item format.

Advice From the Measurement Community

Since 1990, over two dozen textbooks have been published on educational measurement. Although most of these texts focus on classroom measurement, they all present issues related to test design and item writing (see Haladyna, Downing, & Rodriguez, in press, for a review of MC item-writing recommendations made by the authors of these texts). Very few of the authors, however, present issues pertinent to the designers of large-scale assessment. Although the focus is usually on classroom assessment, there are relevant recommendations regarding format selection. Some of those recommendations are reviewed here.

Carey (1994) presented five criteria for writing items, at least two of which are appropriate considerations for large-scale assessment. First, there should be congruence between items and the behavior, content, and conditions described in the objectives; that is, the response format should match the behavior targeted in the objective (also recommended by Kubiszyn & Borich, 1996; Payne, 1997). Second, the accuracy of measures may be affected by the novelty of items, resource materials associated with the items, susceptibility to guessing or cheating, and familiarity with item and test format (also highlighted by Oosterhof, 1994). Both of these issues were also presented by Martinez (1999) in his review of the literature regarding evidence of cognitive demand differences between MC and CR items. He also argued that policy decisions regarding format choice can be informed, but not prescribed, by research—there are advantages and disadvantages to both formats.

Similarly, Nitko (2001) reminded us that when we have the choice between MC and CR formats, each task should be crafted to secure the most valid assessment per learning target. Validity, not convenience, should be the priority (also the primary concern for Traub, 1993).

Among the advice offered by these authors were suggestions regarding the advantages and disadvantages of MC and CR items. These are summarized in Table 9.2.

Many of these recent authors refer to the wise advice in Ebel's writings regarding test development and item writing (e.g., Ebel, 1951, 1962). Ebel (1972) argued that to secure useful measurement, the test developer should strive to make each measurement tool as objective as possible regardless of item format. He is a champion of the MC and true–false item formats and particularly the alternate-choice item format (Ebel, 1970, 1981). He suggested that every aspect of cognitive educational achievement is testable through the use of MC or true–false items; that is, the thing measured by these items is determined by their content far more so than by their form. This message is found in many of the preceding comments.

Aside from the more theoretical and psychometric considerations, there are also very practical considerations that need to be addressed, including issues related to scoring and cost.

Issues Related to Cost

One might think that cost considerations weigh heavily in the choices policymakers pursue. In most cases, this is true. As argued later, the considerations in choice among costs are not often apparent. Nevertheless, cost estimates have been reported to fuel the debate between MC and CR formats. Wainer and Thissen (1993) analyzed costs involved in scoring MC and CR items in the AP Chemistry program in what they called *reliabuck* and *reliamin* analyses. To secure a test with a reliability of 0.92, the reliamin graph (reliability by minutes of testing) demonstrated that it would require 75 minutes of MC items or just over 3 hours of CR items. The reliabuck graph (reliability by cost of scoring) illustrated that the cost to score such tests would be about 1 cent for the MC test and about $30 for the CR test. CR items in chemistry are less expensive to score than items in biology, but more expensive than computer science, physics, and mathematics. These subjects are all less expensive to test than the arts and humanities. Wainer and Thissen also used the reliabuck and reliamin analyses with the AP Music: Listening and Literature exam. With CR items, over 10 hours of testing would be required to achieve a reliability of 0.75 with a similar cost of about $30 (it would cost nearly $100 to score a CR

TABLE 9.2
Advantages and Disadvantages of MC and CR Items

Items	Advantages	Disadvantages
Multiple choice	• Can provide direct assessment of many skills, including ability to discriminate, understand concepts and principles, judge possible courses of action, infer, reason, complete statements, interpret data, and apply information • Efficiency in administration • Does not require students to write out or give elaborate responses • Distractor analysis can provide diagnostic information • Broader sampling of content domain • Can be objectively scored	• Limited indirect assessments of some skills, including ability to recall, explain oneself, provide examples, express ideas, organize ideas, or construct something • Fixed options limit expression of ideas or novel solutions • Tend to be based on artificially structured knowledge and closed to interpretation • Reading skills may interfere when reading is not the target objective • Susceptible to guessing
Constructed response	• Appropriate when the target objective requires a written response • Single-word items are relatively easy to construct and score objectively • Short-answer items (requiring more than a single word) can assess higher levels of knowledge and skills • Allows a range of responses and novel solutions, providing broader reflection of variations in learning • Extended responses can assess complex processes: synthesizing, organizing, and sequencing • Difficult to guess correctly, reducing random error in scores	• The possibility of multiple logical answers creates scoring problems and may reduce reliability; requiring much greater testing time to achieve moderate reliability • Single-word answer format are less able to assess higher cognitive skills • Difficult to write items to limit responses without confusing students • Fewer items can be administered, resulting in limiting content coverage given the same testing time • Writing skills may interfere when writing is not the target objective

test that achieved a reliability near 0.90). That form of the AP Music test has been discontinued.

Although there is agreement that the costs are high, there is disagreement about how much expenditures will increase with the inclusion of subjective forms of assessment. Also, there is disagreement about how to calculate total costs, particularly in programs involving performance assessments. Several analysts have estimated costs of including performance tasks in large-scale assessment programs and reported that costs could be anywhere between $35 and $90 per student tested. These figures are largely based on equipment and scoring demands of the assessment (Monk, 1993; Picus & Tralli, 1998). Furthermore, employing an opportunity-cost framework (including indirect costs related to personnel time), Picus and Tralli (1998) estimated the total cost of the Kentucky assessment program for 1995–1996 to be between $850 and $1800 per student tested.

There is an important consideration in the intersection of psychometrics, cost, and politics. Shavelson, Baxter, and Pine (1992) argued that as the correlation or equivalence of alternate formats increases, justification of the additional expense in employing costly formats becomes more difficult. The role of politics may not be so clear cut, however. As policy analysts have argued, cost is relative and often with respect to reform alternatives that are far more costly than assessment programs that include performance tasks.

The Politics of Item-Format Selection

Education is not a new venue for politics. Although it is likely that schools have forever been the target of public policy and political debate, the issues presented to educators via policymakers have become embroiled in the demands of special interest groups (Airasian, 1987). In the recent past, the number and variety of politically active and legislatively protected special interests groups has increased dramatically. Airasian (1987) suggested that tests began to assume important monitoring functions in schools during the 1960s and 1970s, when the role of education grew in state and national policy agendas, particularly with the launch of Sputnik and ensuing calls for program evaluation. This was also a time during which civil rights leaders were calling for a moratorium on the use of MC tests with minority children (Williams, 1970). The policy-monitoring function of testing nevertheless took hold and led to another use: state-mandated certification testing. Finally, Airasian developed a set of propositions or generalizations to understand the present political context of testing, four of which provide a strong background for the following brief discussion:

1. Testing takes place in a politicized environment, in which the agendas of different interest groups compete for attention.
2. The crucial issues of testing are not technical. Issues of testing today are social, economic, and value-laden, involving the distribution and redistribution of resources and prerogatives.
3. Most tests supply redundant information. What is important politically is that tests appear to supply it in an objective, standard manner.

4. New tests must be evaluated not only in terms of their technical adequacy but also in terms of the likely social and legal implications of their use. (1987, pp. 408–409)

There are two sides to the drive to include less objective formats in large-scale tests. Linn (1995) suggested that there is a push to reject MC formats because of presumed negative consequences and a pull for performance-oriented tasks because of recent conceptions of learning and instruction. Linn also argued that the push and pull are tied to "a belief that assessment needs to mirror instruction and high-quality learning activities" (p. 53). Instructional reform seems to motivate policy initiatives regarding testing and assessment programs.

McDonnell (1994) agreed with arguments made earlier by Airasian and Madaus (1983) that policymakers are unlikely to reform instruction directly, although this would be their preferred target of reform. Even if more successful modes of instruction were widely known, policymakers are unlikely to be able to mandate them. Instead, they have focused on testing, "an available, well developed, relatively cheap, and administratively simple technology" (Airasian & Madaus, 1983, p. 108). The focus is not just on testing, but a certain kind of testing—more direct assessment. In the eyes of policymakers, more direct assessment translates into more subjective formats that appear to have greater face validity. Less objective forms of assessment cost much more than the widely used MC formats, but are viewed by policymakers as less expensive and more accessible than most school reform alternatives.

Several of the difficulties in the design and implementation of large-scale assessment programs derive from the political process. One of the greatest sources of difficulty is in the ability of policymakers to pass policy and legislation without consensus of purpose. Policies are developed and passed as long as they are perceived to meet the needs (common or unique) of a majority of policymakers. Based on results of interviews with national and state policymakers, McDonnell (1994) reported the following purposes among the expectations addressed by assessment policy:

- providing information about the status of the educational system,
- aiding in instructional decisions about individual students,
- bringing greater curricular coherence to the system,
- motivating students to perform better and parents to demand higher performance,
- acting as a lever to change instructional content and strategies,
- holding schools and educators accountable for student performance, and

• certifying individual students as having attained specified levels of achievement or mastery.

Regarding cautions expressed by testing experts about less objective assessment tools, policymakers rejected them as reasons to slow the pursuit of large-scale implementation. They viewed these cautions and the experts as too cautious, and argued that they, as policymakers, needed to move ahead nonetheless. The cautions of testing experts regarding the large-scale implementation of performance-type tasks have been based on resulting weak reliability and generalizability and limitations in validity evidence.

> In the politics of assessment, validity means that what the test measures is important (and taught); reliability means that the test measures the same thing in all test-takers. The resultant score is an *objective* representation of the individual's accomplishment, capacity, and worth. (Robinson, 1993, p. 315)

Other reports describe the role of politics in the design and implementation of large-scale assessment programs through detailed case studies. McDonnell (1997) analyzed the experiences of California, Kentucky, and North Carolina with the design and implementation of new student assessments in the 1990s. Smith, Heinecke, and Noble (1997) provided a case study of policy and political process regarding the development of the Arizona Student Assessment Program between 1990 and 1995, when the program was dropped. These tales are thorough descriptions of political processes surrounding the design and implementation of tests. They demonstrate, among other things, the specific nature of local politics and its impact on test design decisions. Decision makers do not completely ignore empirical evidence or test design principles recommended by experts, but test design issues must be tied to teaching and learning outcomes to make their way into the decision maker's framework.

Final Considerations

The choice of item format is more complex than we might first think. We need to keep in mind the essential process we use in developing any test: (a) define what you want to measure and how test scores will be used, (b) design a test that contains test items that elicit the kinds of behavior reflected in your definition, and (c) collect evidence attesting to the validity of accurately interpreting and using the resulting test scores. This should be done in a way that maximizes the financial and human investment in the assessment program and avoids undue negative consequences for the students, faculty, or others. Clarification of the assessment's purpose should lead to purposeful selection of item formats, item formats selected should contribute to securing sound instruments, and reporting should capitalize on the value and quality of the information available in the formats employed. These broad principles should form the core considerations in an assessment program whose purpose is imbedded in the curriculum and whose results contribute to the achievement of all students, either through the mechanisms of accountability or informed instructional planning and educational programming.

From the results of the meta-analysis described earlier, we may have evidence of construct equivalence for some types of CR and MC items. A form of convergent and divergent construct validity may be at work—something akin to what Messick (1993) referred to as *convergence of construct indicators*. The more we fashion CR items to function similarly to MC items, the more similar they actually are empirically. We have learned a great deal about what is at stake in test design and a bit less about the utility of our options in test design given our specific design purposes. Through consideration of objective formats, extensions of those formats toward less objective tasks, their equivalence, cost, and political constraints, the decision making regarding format choice should be more appropriately informed—or at least better clarified.

Is there a bottom line? When MC and CR items are viable options, the MC item will generally be the optimal choice. Because of the strong equivalence in MC and CR items, the cost makes defending administration of CR items more difficult. As the cognitive demands required by MC and nonequivalent CR items begin to diverge, the need to provide alternative evidence may justify administration of relevant CR items. Even so, the combination of resulting responses into a single score may obscure any gain in information toward a broader range of inferences. Local politics will also play a role. To the extent that testing is tied to teaching and learning, decision makers will have a clearer view of their role in deciding on item format.

Validity and fidelity should be overriding factors; however, they depend on a minimal level of psychometric quality. In the review of psychometric results here, the item formats are probably more alike in terms of rank ordering abilities than not alike, particularly when written to be equivalent. Although cognitive psychologists have clarified and distinguished psychometric equivalence from psychological equivalence (see e.g., Snow, 1993), both aspects are important for obtaining appropriate meaning from test scores. The expected meaning to be inferred from test scores should drive the design of any test. The results of the prior analyses and discussions should inform this process as well as contribute guidelines for future research.

REFERENCES

Airasian, P. W. (1987). State mandated testing and educational reform: Context and consequences. *American Journal of Education, 95,* 393–412.

Airasian, P. W., & Madaus, G. F. (1983). Linking testing and instruction: Policy issues. *Journal of Educational Measurement, 20*(2), 103–118.

Bock, R. D. (1995). Open-ended exercises in large-scale educational assessment. In L. B. Resnick & J. G. Wirt (Eds.), *Linking school and work: Roles for standards and assessment* (pp. 305–338). San Francisco, CA: Jossey-Bass.

Carey, (1994). *Measuring and evaluating school learning.* Needham Heights, MA: Allyn & Bacon.

Coffman, W. E. (1971). Essay examinations. In R. L. Thorndike (Ed.), *Educational measurement* (2nd ed., pp. 271–302). Washington, DC: American Council on Education.

DuBois, P. H. (1970). *A history of psychological testing.* Boston, MA: Allyn & Bacon, Inc.

Ebel, R. L. (1951). Writing the test item. In E. F. Lindquist (Ed.), *Educational measurement* (1st ed., pp. 185–249). Washington, DC: American Council on Education.

Ebel, R. L. (1962). External testing: Response to challenge. *Teachers College Record, 64,* 190–198.

Ebel, R. L. (1970). The case for true–false items. *School Review, 78,* 373–389.

Ebel, R. L. (1972). *Essentials of educational measurement* (2nd ed.). Englewood Cliffs, NJ: Prentice-Hall.

Ebel, R. L. (1981, April). *Some advantages of alternate-choice test items.* Paper presented at the annual meeting of the National Council on Measurement in Education, Los Angeles.

Frederiksen, J, R., & Collins, A. (1989). A systems approach to educational testing. *Educational Researcher, 18*(9), 27–32.

Haladyna, T. M. (1997). *Writing test items to evaluate higher order thinking.* Needham Heights, MA: Allyn & Bacon.

Haladyna, T. M. (1998, April). *Fidelity and proximity to criterion: When should we use multiple-choice?* Paper presented at the annual meeting of the American Educational Research Association, San Diego, CA.

Haladyna, T. M. (1999). *Developing and validating multiple-choice test items* (2nd ed.). Mahwah, NJ: Lawrence Erlbaum Associates.

Haladyna, T. M., Downing, S. M, & Rodriguez, M. C. (in press). A review of multiple-choice item-writing guidelines. *Applied Measurement in Education.*

Hogan, T. P. (1981). *Relationship between free-response and choice-type tests of achievement: A review of the literature.* Washington, DC: National Institute of Education.

Kane, M. B., & Mitchell, R. (1996). *Implementing performance assessment: Promises, problems, and challenges.* Mahwah, NJ: Lawrence Erlbaum Associates.

Kubiszyn, T., & Borich, G. (1996). *Educational testing and measurement* (5th ed.). Glenview, IL: Scott, Foresman.

LeMahieu, P. G., Gitomer, D. H., & Eresh, J. T. (1995). *Portfolios beyond the classroom: Data quality and qualities.* Princeton, NJ: Educational Testing Service.

Lindquist, E. F. (1936). The theory of test construction. In H. E. Hawkes, E. F. Lindquist, & C. R. Mann (Eds.), *The construction and use of achievement examinations* (pp. 17–106). Boston, MA: Houghton Mifflin.

Linn, R. L. (1995). High-stakes uses of performance-based assessments: Rationale, examples, and problems of comparability. In T. Oakland & R. K. Hambleton (Eds.), *International perspectives on academic assessment* (pp. 49–74). Norwell, MA: Kluwer Academic Publishers.

Martinez, M. E. (1999). Cognition and the questions of test item format. *Educational Psychologist, 34*(4), 207–218.

McDonnell, L. M. (1994). *Policymakers' views of student assessment*. Santa Monica, CA: RAND.

McDonnell, L. M. (1997). *The politics of state testing: Implementing new student assessments* (CSE Technical Report 424). Los Angeles, CA: University of California, Center for Research on Evaluation, Standards, and Student Testing (CRESST).

Messick, S. (1989). Validity. In R. L. Linn (Ed.), *Educational measurement* (3rd ed., pp. 13–104). New York: American Council on Education and Macmillan.

Messick, S. (1993). Trait equivalence as construct validity of score interpretation across multiple methods of measurement. In R. E. Bennett & W. C. Ward (Eds.), *Construction versus choice in cognitive measurement* (pp. 61–74). Hillsdale, NJ: Lawrence Erlbaum Associates.

Messick, S. (1994). The interplay of evidence and consequences in the validity of performance assessments. *Educational Researcher, 23*, 13–24.

Monk. (1993). *The cost of systemic education reform: Conceptual issues and preliminary estimates*. Unpublished manuscript, Cornell University, New York.

Nitko, A. (2001). *Educational assessment of students* (3rd ed.). Upper Saddle River, NJ: Prentice-Hall.

Oosterhof, A. (1994). *Classroom applications of educational measurement* (2nd ed.). New York: Macmillan.

Osterlind, S. J. (1998). *Constructing test items: Multiple-choice, constructed-response, performance, and other formats* (2nd ed.). Norwell, MA: Kluwer Academic.

Payne, D. A. (1997). *Applied educational assessment*. Belmont, CA: Wadsworth.

Picus, L. O., & Tralli, A. (1998). *Alternative assessment programs: What are the true costs?* (CSE Technical Report 441). Los Angeles, CA: University of California, Center for Research on Evaluation, Standards, and Student Testing (CRESST).

Robinson, S. P. (1993). Politics of assessment. In R. E. Bennett & W. C. Ward (Eds.), *Construction versus choice in cognitive measurement* (pp. 313–323). Hillsdale, NJ: Lawrence Erlbaum Associates.

Rodriguez, M. C. (1998, April). *Construct equivalence of multiple-choice and constructed-response items: A random effects synthesis of correlations*. Paper presented at the annual meeting of the American Educational Research Association, San Diego, CA.

Shavelson, R. J., Baxter, G. P., & Pine, J. (1992). Performance assessment: Political rhetoric and measurement validity. *Educational Researcher, 22*(2), 22–27.

Smith, M. L., Heinecke, W., & Noble, A. J. (1997). *The politics of assessment: A case study of policy and political spectacle* (CSE Technical Report 468). Los Angeles, CA: University of California, Center for Research on Evaluation, Standards, and Student Testing (CRESST).

Snow, R. E. (1993). Construct validity and constructed response tests. In R. E. Bennett & W. C. Ward (Eds.), *Construction versus choice in cognitive measurement* (pp. 45–60). Hillsdale, NJ: Lawrence Erlbaum Associates.

Stiggins, R. (1997). *Student-centered classroom assessment* (2nd ed.). New York: Merrill.

Traub, R. E. (1993). On the equivalence of the traits assessed by multiple-choice and constructed-response tests. In R. E. Bennett & W. C. Ward (Eds.), *Construction versus choice in cognitive measurement* (pp. 29–44). Hillsdale, NJ: Lawrence Erlbaum Associates.

Traub, R. E., & MacRury, K. (1990). *Multiple-choice vs. free-response in testing of scholastic achievement*. Toronto, Canada: Ontario Institute for Studies in Education.

Wainer, H., & Thissen, D. (1993). Combining multiple-choice and constructed-response test scores: Toward a Marxist theory of test construction. *Applied Measurement in Education, 6*(2), 103–118.

Williams, R. I. (1970). Black pride, academic relevance & individual achievement. *The Counseling Psychologist, 2*(1), 18–22.

Worthen, B. R., Borg, W. R., & White, K. (1993). *Measurement and evaluation in the schools*. New York: Longman.

Chapter 10

Incorporating Classroom-Based Assessments Into Large-Scale Assessment Programs

Catherine S. Taylor
University of Washington

Rachel is in the 11th grade. Throughout Rachel's junior high and high school career, she has earned As and Bs. This year she won a scholarship for her essay on the Bill of Rights. She is careful and precise when she completes mathematics homework and science labs. Last spring, she took the state's standards-based test that she must pass for graduation. The tests in reading and mathematics included multiple-choice and short-answer items. For the writing test, students wrote to a single persuasive writing prompt. Rachel did not pass the mathematics or writing tests. The teachers in her school have all attended workshops on how to incorporate writing in their courses. The district has adopted curriculum materials that are aligned with the state curriculum standards. The teachers say that Rachel has had opportunities to do the kinds of tasks that are on the state test because students do similar tasks in their classrooms. They are baffled that she did not pass the tests and are confident that, if she takes it again this fall, she will definitely pass.

This vignette is common in these times of world-class standards and standards-based large-scale tests. Administrators of districts and schools believe that they are helping teachers align their curricula to state standards and are providing the kinds of in-service necessary so that teachers can help students do well on tests. Teachers think they are preparing students for the tests. Yet good students find that, although they do well in school, they do not meet performance standards on large-scale tests. Given that large-scale tests are "a single moment of potential failure" (Resnick & Resnick, 1991), Rachel must retake the test even if other evidence suggests the test scores do not reflect her knowledge, conceptual understanding, and skills.

The use of large-scale tests to make decisions about curriculum and students is not new. The notion of *measurement-driven instruction* (e.g., Popham, 1987) emerged during the 1980s to describe a process wherein tests are used as drivers for instructional change. The thinking was, "If we value something, we must assess it." Tests were used throughout the minimum-competency movement of the 1980s to drive instructional practices toward desired outcomes of education (the knowledge, conceptual understanding, and skills considered basic to success in school). To a certain extent, this movement was successful. Teachers did teach to the tests. In fact, they taught too closely to the tests because of the stakes associated with test scores (Haladyna, Nolen, & Hass, 1991; Smith, 1991). Typically, the tests were multiple-choice measures of discrete skills, and one significant consequence of teaching to these tests was that instruction was narrowed down to only the test content and presented to students in the same form that it was tested.

In part, because of the success of measurement-driven instruction, large-scale achievement tests came under widespread criticism during the late 1980s and early 1990s for their negative impacts on the classroom and for their lack of fidelity to valued performances (Darling-Hammond & Wise, 1985; Madaus, West, Harmon, Lomax, & Viator, 1992; Shepard & Dougherty, 1991). Although studies comparing indirect (e.g., multiple-choice and short-answer items) and direct measures of writing (Stiggins, 1982), mathematical problem solving (Baxter, Shavelson, Herman, Brown, & Valadez, 1993), and science inquiry (Shavelson, Baxter, & Gao, 1993) demonstrated that some of the knowledge and skills measured in each assessment format overlap, the moderate to low correlations between different assessment modes led to questions about the validity of inferences made from scores on multiple-choice achievement tests. In addition, studies by Haladyna, Nolen, and Haas (1991), Shepard and Dougherty (1991), and Smith (1991) suggested that pressure to raise scores on large-scale tests can lead to narrowing of the curriculum to the content assessed by the tests (at the expense of other important knowledge and skills) as well as substantial classroom time spent teaching to the test and item formats.

In response to these criticisms, assessment reformers pressed for different types of assessment (e.g., Shepard, 1989; Wiggins, 1989). The thinking of assessment reformers was: We should build assessments that measure students' achievement of new curriculum standards in formats that more closely approximate the ways in which the knowledge, concepts, and skills are used in the world beyond tests. This will lead teachers to teach higher order thinking, problem solving, and reasoning skills rather than rote skills and knowledge.

In response to these pressures, states, testing companies, and projects such as the New Standards Project began to explore ways to incorporate performance-based assessments into testing programs. What has been called *performance-based assessment* ranges from short-answer items that require students to supply brief responses (similar to those asked for in multiple-choice items), to carefully scaffolded, multistep problems with several short-answer items (e.g., Yen, 1993), to open-ended performance tasks that required examination of a problem or text and extended responses (California State Department of Education, 1990; State of Washington, Superintendent of Public Instruction, 1997). Still writers have criticized these efforts because they are considered contrived and artificial (see e.g., Wiggins, 1992), and teachers have continued to complain that external tests do not assess what is taught in the classroom. As Shepard (2000) indicated in her address at the annual meeting of the National Council on Measurement in Education, the promises of high-quality performance-based assessments have not been realized. In part, this failure has been because complex performances conducted as part of large-scale assessment programs are costly to implement, time-consuming, and difficulty to evaluate.

There are many who still hope performance-based assessments will be the solution to some of the problems associated with large-scale assessment programs. Proponents believe that "assessment, properly conceived and implemented, [can] work in tandem with instruction to produce a highly effective system leading to rich learning outcomes . . ." (Martinez, 1999, p. 207), and that when students demonstrate, through their performances, that they can read effectively and use what they read to complete valued tasks (e.g., literary criticism and policy analysis), write with skill (e.g., to tell stories, to inform, to persuade others), solve complex mathematical problems, plan and conduct scientific studies, and engage thoughtfully in debates over controversial issues, they have demonstrated command of knowledge and skills in more powerful ways than can be shown through traditional (multiple-choice and short-answer) formats. This has led several states to consider including classroom-based assessments as part of their state assessment programs.

In an effort to increase the link between the classroom and the validity of inferences made about examinees skill in implementing valued performances, three states have worked to incorporate portfolios into their assessment programs: California (Kirst & Mazzeo, 1996), Kentucky (Kentucky State Department of Education, 1996), and Vermont (Fontana, 1995; Forseth, 1992; Hewitt, 1993; Vermont State Department of Education, 1993, 1994a, 1994b). These initial efforts were fraught with problems such as: (a) inconsistency of raters when applying scoring criteria (Koretz, Stecher, & Deibert, 1992b; Koretz, Stecher, Klein, & McCaffrey, 1994a);

(b) lack of teacher preparation in high-quality assessment development (Gearhart & Wolf, 1996); (c) inconsistencies in the focus, number, and types of evidence included in portfolios (Gearhart & Wolf, 1996; Koretz et al., 1992b); and (d) costs and logistics associated with processing portfolios (Kirst & Mazzeo, 1996).

In addition to the measurement and cost issues associated with the use of portfolios, the research results have been mixed in terms of whether these assessment programs had positive effects on classroom practices. Some evidence suggests that teachers and administrators have generally positive attitudes about use of portfolios (Klein, Stecher, & Koretz, 1995; Koretz et al., 1992a; Koretz et al., 1994a), that there are positive effects on instruction (Stecher & Hamilton, 1994), and that teachers develop a better understanding of mathematical problem solving (Stecher & Mitchell, 1995). Negative effects have included time spent on the assessment process (Stecher & Hamilton, 1994; Koretz et al., 1994a) and pressures on teachers to ensure that portfolios "look good" (Callahan, 1997).

There are many lessons to be learned from these early efforts to include classroom-based assessments into large-scale assessment programs. In this chapter, I provide a rationale for including classroom assessments into large-scale testing programs and outline the steps necessary to effectively include classroom-based evidence in large-scale assessment programs.

INCLUSION OF EVIDENCE FROM THE CLASSROOM IN LARGE-SCALE ASSESSMENT PROGRAMS

There are a number of important advantages to including classroom-based evidence as part of a large-scale assessment program. Particular advantages include (a) evidence that teachers are preparing students to meet state curriculum and performance standards (opportunity to learn), (b) broader evidence about student achievement than that which can be obtained from examinations administered in a brief time period, (c) opportunities to assess knowledge and skills that are difficult to assess via standardized large-scale tests (e.g., speaking and presenting, report writing, scientific inquiry processes), and (d) opportunities to include work that more closely represents the real contexts in which knowledge and skill are applied (e.g., mock UN conventions). Each of these advantages is more fully explored in what follows.

Opportunity to Learn

Since the groundbreaking efforts of the National Council for Teachers of Mathematics (NCTM) in the development of curriculum standards (National Council of Teachers of Mathematics [NCTM], 1989), new conceptions of knowing and doing have dominated conversations throughout the world of education. We have changed our thinking about teaching from content coverage to student achievement. Our concept of what should be achieved has shifted away from memorization of discrete knowledge and simple applications of memorized principles to the application of knowledge and skills to (a) constructing solutions to problems (National Council of Teachers of Mathematics, 1989), (b) learning new ideas and concepts, (c) examining the ideas and claims of others (e.g., Wineburg, 1999), and (d) participating in the subject disciplines to develop new knowledge (Schwab, 1978). Along with these revised notions of what must be learned has come a demand that teachers know how to help students achieve these ends and use classroom assessments aligned with national standards.

Although those engaged in state or national conversations about curriculum standards may have a fairly sophisticated understanding of what the standards mean, most educators have not been included in these conversations. Teachers learn instructional and assessment strategies based on their teacher preparation programs and their apprenticeships in schools (Lortie, 1975). Teachers become accustomed to their own ways of teaching and assessing. If national standards reflect new thinking about what is important to know and be able to do in various disciplines, practicing teachers may be ill prepared to help their students achieve standards.

Despite shifts to new forms of assessment, little evidence is available regarding whether teachers actually shift their instruction toward practices aligned with the latest curriculum standards. Claims about the positive impacts of performance-based assessment on instructional practices have been largely anecdotal or based on teacher self-report (Stecher, Barron, Kaganoff, & Goodwin, 1998). Legal challenges to tests for graduation, placement, and promotion demand evidence that students had the opportunity to learn tested curriculum (Debra P. v. Turlington, 1979). Yet no efficient method has been established for ensuring that all students have adequate exposure and opportunity to practice the skills and learn the concepts that are included in new curriculum standards. Collections of classroom work could give policymakers a window into the educational experiences of students and the educational practices of teachers. Classroom assessments could be used as evidence for the effectiveness of inservice professional development programs designed to help teachers incorporate new instructional and assessment practices. These collections could be used to assess whether teachers are making progress in implementing state curriculum standards. Finally, should the need arise, classroom assessments could be used to examine students' educational opportunities in court cases if students have been denied diplomas or other rights.

Broader Evidence

It is a common lament that some students function well in the classroom but do not perform well on tests. Recent studies on the *stereotype threat* have shown that fear of being associated with a negative stereotype can lead minority students and girls to perform less well than they should on standardized tests (Aronson, Lustina, Good, Keough, Steele, & Brown, 1999; Steele, 1999; Steele & Aronson, 2000). Students for whom English is a second language may perform more poorly on timed standardized tests than they do in school due to language barriers. Stereotype threat and language barriers are examples of factors that threaten the validity of test scores. Because they may affect test scores in unknown ways, such factors can lead to inaccurate inferences about examinees. One way to minimize the negative impacts of these factors is to ensure that assessments from the classroom are also considered as part of the evidence about student knowledge and skills when making important decisions about students.

In addition to the potential threats to the validity of scores from standardized tests, several studies have shown that multiple performances are necessary to obtain reliable examinee scores (e.g., Quellmalz, Capell, & Chou, 1982; Baxter et al., 1993; Shavelson, Baxter, & Gao, 1993). Quallmalz et al. (1982) found that the quality of students' writing was affected by the purpose and mode of writing they were asked to do. Although many researchers have focused on rater agreement as the major source of evidence for the reliability of performance assessment scores, Baxter et al. (1993) found, through generalizability studies, that unreliability of scores due to task differences far outweighed unreliability of scores due to rater inconsistencies. Shavelson et al. (1993) also found that measurement error for mathematics tasks was largely due to task variability. In each of these studies, multiple performances were given to each examinee to assess the impact of task variability. A common recommendation that emerged from these and other studies is that examinees should complete at least 10 performances in each domain if we are to trust examinee scores on standardized, performance-based tests (Linn & Burton, 1994).

Yet testing programs typically include few extended performances due to the limits of testing time. In many state and district assessment programs, a single writing prompt is given to examinees. Usually the number of extended mathematics tasks is also limited. The problem of sufficiency of evidence arises from the need to balance content coverage with adequate opportunities for students to apply their knowledge, conceptual understanding, and skills. To adequately represent the entirety of a subject domain and to do so reliably, much longer large-scale tests would be needed than are generally acceptable in schools.

Hence, well-focused classroom-based assessments could be used to supplement the types of performances included in standardized assessment programs to increase the reliability of inferences made about individual students' achievement. Although a large-scale test might include one or two writing prompts, classroom written work in the form of reports, letters to editors, position papers, short stories, poems, and so on could supplement scores from external tests. Similarly, written literary analyses, book reports, and literary journals could supplement brief reading performances typical of external tests. Collections of performances that require applications of mathematics concepts and procedures to solve real-world problems could supplement briefer, open-ended tasks included on standardized tests. A potential outcome of asking for such classroom performances might be the regular inclusion of problem-solving tasks, writing opportunities, and text examination throughout the school year. Performances developed and collected over a school year could give students sufficient time to do a thorough job.

Inclusion of Difficult-to-Measure Curriculum Standards

Some of our desirable curriculum standards are too unwieldy to measure on large-scale tests (e.g., scientific inquiry, research reports, oral presentations). Historically, standardized tests have measured these curriculum areas by testing knowledge of how to conduct more complex work (e.g., where to locate sources for reports; how to use tables of contents, bibliographies, card catalogues, and indexes; identification of control or experimental variables in a science experiment; knowledge of appropriate strategies for oral presentation or use of visual aids). As critics have often noted, knowing what to do does not necessarily mean one is able to do.

It is possible to incorporate actual scientific investigations, oral presentations, and social science research into large-scale performance-assessment programs. Of necessity, these performances would be brief: An impromptu speaking assessment might allow brief preparation; a science experiment might require that the process be broken into smaller, self-contained parts (e.g., summarizing a set of data graphically and descriptively and then drawing a conclusion); a research performance would likely eliminate the process of gathering resources—rather examinees would probably do tasks similar to the document-based items from the Advanced Placement History exams. Such efforts would also be limited by the same constraint as described earlier: a limited number of tasks resulting in unreliable inferences made from examinee scores. In addition, generalizability would be limited if performances were limited to paper-and-pencil tasks (e.g., speech preparation rather than authentic performance, description of the steps in an experiment rather than the scientific inquiry process). Therefore, it would be advantageous to incorporate classroom-based evidence of these performances that are difficult to capture in large-scale assessment programs.

Authenticity

Frederiksen (1984) first raised the question of authenticity in assessment when he examined the potential bias in assessment due to misrepresentation of domains by multiple-choice tests. Wiggins (1989) claimed that in every discipline there are tasks that are authentic to the given discipline. Frederiksen (1998) added that authentic achievement is a "significant intellectual accomplishment" that results in the "construction of knowledge through disciplined inquiry to produce discourse, products, or performances that have meaning or value beyond success in school" (p. 19). In the social sciences, there are policy analysis, historiography, geographic analysis of human movement, and political debate; in the language arts, there are story writing, literary analysis, literary critique, and poetry writing; in mathematics, there are mathematical modeling, profit and loss analyses, and growth modeling; in science, there are scientific modeling, reports of investigations, and theory development. The list goes on and on. Although some may question the use of the terms *authentic* and *direct* measurement (from the perspective that all assessments are indirect measures from which we make inferences about other, related performances; Terwilliger, 1997), it remains a valid argument that the degree of inference necessary from scores on standardized multiple-choice and short-answer tests of language expression and mechanics to generalizations about writing skill is a much greater than that necessary from a collection of written pieces to generalizations about students' writing skill.

Although large-scale assessments generally do a good job of measuring basic skills or knowledge of basic principles, classrooms are locations wherein students can use basic knowledge and skills to do valued work. For example, fifth graders in an elementary school in the Pacific Northwest were recently given the opportunity to work with community leaders to examine a local issue—that of *daylighting* a local creek. At the time of the study, the creek was being diverted into the city's sewer system, and community members were interested in bringing the creek back to the surface and allowing it to flow into a nearby lake to restore salmon habitat. To do so would require routing it through a shopping center and through the campus of a nearby university. Students at the elementary school were given an opportunity to survey people in the park, shoppers at the shopping center, store owners, and administrators, faculty, and students at the university to determine their opinions about and the impacts of daylighting the creek. Students then summarized the results of their work into a collection of reports for the city council and mayor. The council members, mayor, and community leaders who asked the children to conduct the research interviewed the students as well. For this event to be a fair assessment of each student's social science research skills (interviewing, questionnaire development, sampling), their knowledge of how to organize and represent data, and their ability to summarize results and make recommendations, each student had to complete aspects of research preparation, data gathering, data representation, summarization, and reporting. Although the final report was a joint effort, the teacher obtained evidence of each student's knowledge and skill.

The benefits of this type of work are obvious. Students learn how to integrate their knowledge and skills in meaningful ways. They see the value of what they are learning in school. Students begin to construct an image of various disciplines and how the knowledge and skills they are learning apply to the world beyond school. The problems associated with these types of performances are also obvious. Teachers must understand how and where the concepts and skills they teach are applied. They must avail themselves of opportunities to engage students in work beyond the classroom. Teachers must know how to structure the work to include individual evidence of the targeted concepts and skills. They must know how to evaluate the work fairly.

PROBLEMS ASSOCIATED WITH INCLUSION OF CLASSROOM ASSESSMENTS

Several potential problems arise when using classroom-based evidence for large-scale assessment programs. The main problems that have emerged to date are level of teacher preparation in classroom-based assessment (which can limit the quality of classroom-based evidence), selections of evidence (which can limit comparisons across students), reliability of raters (which can limit the believability of scores given to student work), and construct-irrelevant variance (which can limit the validity of scores). Each of these problems has been examined and strategies have been identified that may address these problems.

Teacher Preparation

The classroom context is one of fairly constant formal and informal assessment (Airasian, 1993; Stiggins, Faires-Conklin, & Bridgeford, 1986). However, few teacher preparation programs provide adequate training for the wide array of assessment strategies used by teachers (Schafer & Lissitz, 1987; Stiggins & Bridgeford, 1988). Further, teachers do not perceive the information learned in traditional tests and measurement courses to be relevant to their tasks as classroom teachers (Gullickson, 1986; Schafer & Lissitz, 1987; Stiggins & Faires-Conklin, 1988). For example, Taylor and Nolen (1996) compared the transfer of assessment concepts and skills for two cohorts of preservice teachers. One cohort had a traditional tests and measurement course, and the second had a hands-on classroom-based assessment course, wherein students developed an instructional unit and the associated assessments for that unit. Their results show significant differences in transfer for the two cohorts. The teachers who had the hands-on classroom-based assessment course could correctly identify issues related to validity and reliability in their classrooms. They thought about assessment when planning instruction and developed technically sound tools for classroom-assessment purposes. Their assessment strategies ranged from traditional, multiple-choice items to extended performance assessments. In contrast, the teachers who had the tests and measurement course reported that they did not understand reliability or validity—that they had "memorized it for the test." These teachers focused little or no preparation time thinking about assessment. They could evaluate short-answer and multiple-choice items, but did not believe they were able to create performance-based assessments.

Given the limited preparation of teachers, the misfit between the types of training teachers receive, and the needs they have for constructing and evaluating classroom-based assessments, one of the potential limitations to using classroom-based evidence for large-scale assessment programs is the quality of the evidence. Teachers must be taught how to select, modify, and develop assessments, as well as score and write scoring rules for assessments before including classroom-based evidence in large-scale assessment programs. A significant professional development effort is essential. Even for teachers who have received adequate training in assessment methods, new thinking about the important knowledge and skills within each discipline, broader targets of assessment, and recent developments in our understanding of how to create effective performance-based assessments must be provided as part of teachers' ongoing professional development.

Selection of Evidence

One question that must be asked when using classroom-based assessments is, "For which knowledge, concepts, and skills do we need classroom-based evidence?" Koretz et al. (1992a, 1992b) suggested that, because teachers were free to select the pieces that went into the Vermont portfolios, there was too much diversity in tasks. This diversity may have caused low interjudge agreement among raters of the portfolios. Koretz and his colleagues recommended placing some restrictions on the types of tasks considered acceptable for portfolios. Therefore, if classroom-based evidence is a part of large-scale testing programs, teachers need guidance in terms of what constitutes appropriate types of evidence.

Standardized assessments are very useful for measuring knowledge, simple applications, comprehension, and slightly extended applications of knowledge and skills to solve problems, interpret text, or develop a short written work. Therefore, it may make little sense to ask teachers to submit tests similar to external tests as evidence of student achievement unless the classroom tests add to our information about students. However, because external tests are generally samples from broad domains, additional classroom-based evidence of student knowledge and conceptual understanding via classroom tests may be needed if large-scale tests do not measure the knowledge and concepts in the subject domain sufficiently well. If classroom tests are to be included as part of large-scale testing programs, teachers may need test blueprints to ensure that these tests are designed to assess students' knowledge and conceptual understanding not adequately assessed by the large-scale tests. Examples of blueprints can be found in many textbooks on classroom-based assessments (e.g., Airasian, 2000; Linn & Gronlund, 2000; Mehrens & Lehmann, 1991; Nitko, 2001).

For important concepts and skills that are best shown through performances such as writing; literary interpretation; natural and social science inquiry; political, historical, and social analysis; mathematical reasoning; problem solving; and communication, classroom performances will greatly strengthen the decisions made about student achievement. Given the number of possible performances in each discipline and given the need to improve the reliability of scores, states must narrow the possible types of evidence to those that significantly enhance our information about students. Therefore, a case could be made that, when selecting the evidence to derive from classroom assessments, the focus should be on complex performances rather than classroom tests. But which performances are worth including, and how can states ensure that performances are comparable across different classrooms, schools, and districts?

One strategy for identifying classroom performances to be included in large-scale testing programs is to define *benchmark performances* (Taylor, 1998). Benchmark performances are performances that have value in their own right, that are complex and interdisciplinary, and that students are expected to perform by the end of a set period of time (e.g., the end of middle school). For students to complete each performance may require application of knowledge, concepts, and skills across subject disciplines. However, the major focus may be on authentic performances in one subject discipline (e.g., scientific investigations that require science experimentation and reasoning skills, science knowledge and conceptual understanding, writing skills, reading skills, and mathematics knowledge and skills).

TABLE 10.1
Expository Writing Performance Benchmarks for the Elementary Level

Level	Benchmark
Primary	By the end of primary level, students will be able to write an organized informational paragraph composed of a group of sentences with one coherent thought. The paragraph will be written in complete sentences with accurate capitalization, basic punctuation, and spelling.
Intermediate	By the end of the intermediate level, students will be able to write multiparagraph reports. Each paragraph will have a central thought that is unified into a greater whole with factual information that supports the paragraph topic. Topic areas for the report may be supplied by the teacher. The writing will be in complete sentences and in the student's own words, using correct capitalization and spelling and including a range of punctuation marks.

Identifying benchmark performances is a strategy that has been used by school districts and educational organizations in the Pacific Northwest to guide classroom assessment development. Table 10.1 presents two benchmark performance descriptions for expository writing: one for the end of the primary level of elementary school and one for the end of the intermediate level of elementary school. These descriptions were written by elementary teachers from a large urban school district in Washington State to guide their teaching of writing. Until the teachers had developed these descriptions, they had no common targets for writing in their building. With these defined performance targets, the teachers claimed that they raised expectations for students at all grade levels and made sure that they were actually teaching students in ways that made it possible for them to accomplish their performances.

Tables 10.2, 10.3, and 10.4 present examples of mathematics, science, and art benchmark performances from the same urban district. In each case, what is described is a performance valued by many teachers and common to many classrooms in the district. Although the teachers who wrote these performance descriptions all agreed as to their value, the descriptions were their first efforts to articulate their visions of desired performances and to share their visions across buildings and grade levels in the district. From these performance descriptions, teachers detailed the steps that students would take to complete the performance. Table 10.5 shows the steps students would take to complete the inquiry performances described in Table 10.4. Solano-Flores and Shavelson (1997) described a similar process for development of science performance assessments, although their task shells are for briefer, standardized tasks.

Once the teachers developed benchmark performance descriptions, they identified each Washington State curriculum standard that could be

TABLE 10.2
Character Analysis Performance Benchmarks
for the Intermediate Through High School Levels

Level	Benchmark Performance
	Literary Analysis for Character Development
Intermediate	By the end of **intermediate** level, students will select and describe one important character from a novel, short story, or play. They will also describe the influence of that character on the overall plot, as well as how the character was affected by of the overall events in the story. The description will be supported by factual material (excerpts from the reading). They will use the writing process, and the final work will be in complete sentences, in the students' own words, using correct capitalization and spelling, and a basic use of punctuation.
Middle School	By the end of **middle school**, students will select one important character from a novel, short story, or play and write a multiparagraph essay describing a character; how the character's personality, actions, choices, and relationships influence the outcome of the story; and how the character was affected by the events in the story. Each paragraph will have a central thought that is unified into a greater whole supported by factual material (direct quotations and examples from the text) as well as commentary to explain the relationship between the factual material and the student's ideas. They will use the writing process, and the writing will be in complete sentences, in the students' own words, and using correct capitalization and spelling and a range of punctuation.
High School	By the end of **high school**, students will select one important character from a novel, short story, or play and write a multiparagraph essay describing a character and the relationship between the character and the plot. The essay will describe the overall plot as well as how the character's personality, actions, choices, and relationships influence the outcome of the story. It will also include an analysis of the techniques the author used in developing the character. The writing will include an introduction and conclusion. The thesis will have at least three supporting arguments. The arguments will be supported by a variety of detail, including direct quotations and as well as other references to the text and commentary to explain the relationship between the textual examples and the arguments. Each paragraph will have a central thought that is unified into a greater whole. Students will use effective transitions within and between paragraphs. They will use the writing process, and the writing will be in complete and varied sentences, in the students' own words, and using correct capitalization and spelling, and a range of punctuation.

TABLE 10.3
Statistical Problem-Solving Benchmarks
for the Intermediate Through High School Levels

Level	Benchmark Performance
	Statistical Problem Solving
Intermediate	By the end of **intermediate** level, students will collect data about a given research question (which may include survey development and use with a sample from a population, experimentation, or research from printed sources) and display the data in a pictograph, single bar graph, or pie graph (as appropriate). The students will describe the information in the graph, analyze the data, and communicate the significance of the data in the graph. Graphs will be clearly labeled (including name of data, units of measurement, and appropriate scale) and informatively titled. Sources will be documented.
Middle School	By the end of **middle school**, students will collect data for a given research question (which may include survey development and use with a sample from a population, experimentation, or research from printed sources). The data will be organized into a frequency table with appropriate intervals. The students will select the graphs that best represent the data. The organized data will be displayed in several graphs, including circle graphs, bar graphs, histograms, line graphs, stem, and/or leaf plots. Students will interpret the data in the graphs and predict future outcomes based on the data. Graphs will be clearly labeled (including name of data, units of measurement, and appropriate scale) and informatively titled. Sources will be documented.
High School	By the end of **high school**, students will investigate and report on a topic of personal interest by collecting data for a given research question (which may include survey development and use or experimentation), some of which is categorical and some of which is quantitative. Data will be sampled from a relevant population. In the report, students will communicate the data in a variety of appropriate forms (including pictographs, circle graphs, bar graphs, histograms, line graphs, and/or stem and leaf plots and incorporating the use of technology), analyze, and interpret the data using statistical measures (of central tendency, variability, and range) as appropriate. In the report, students will describe the results, make predictions, and discuss the limitations of their data-collection methods. Graphics will be clearly labeled (including name of data, units of measurement, and appropriate scale) and informatively titled. References to data in reports will include units of measurement. Sources will be documented.

demonstrated in the performance. Teachers in this district now use these performance benchmarks to guide their instruction and articulate instruction across grade levels. The benchmark performances described in Tables 10.2 through 10.4 are ways that students can demonstrate state curriculum standards. Therefore, student performances based on these descriptions would be good candidates for inclusion in state assessment programs.

TABLE 10.4
Scientific Inquiry Performance Benchmarks
for the Intermediate Through High School Levels

Level	*Benchmark Performance*
	Scientific Inquiry
Intermediate	By the end of **intermediate** level, students will generate a hypothesis related to the research question. S/he will conduct a study related to the hypothesis and describe the observations using sensory observations and metric measurement. Research questions and events will be related to a scientific concept under study. They will present their observations using graphs and charts. Graphs and charts will be clearly labeled (including data source, units of measurement, and scale) and informatively titled. Students will interpret the data from their observations and offer explanations of the results as they relate to the scientific concept.
Middle School	By the end of **middle school**, students will complete a scientific investigation to include: • formulating a hypothesis on a given problem or question • designing and setting up an experiment • conducting the experiment and collecting relevant data • displaying data in graphs, charts, and tables • analyzing data (computing relevant statistics) • formulating a conclusion • presenting findings to peers Graphs, tables, and charts will be clearly labeled (including data source, units of measurement, and scale) and informatively titled. Reports will summarize results and show their relationship to hypothesis and/or relevant scientific concepts.
High School	By the end of **high school**, students will complete a scientific investigation to include: • identifying a research problem or question • researching literature related to the problem or question using at least three sources • formulating a hypothesis for the problem or question based on the literature • designing and setting up an experiment • collecting relevant data • displaying data in graphs, charts, and tables • analyzing data (computing relevant statistics) • formulating a conclusion • reviewing the experimental procedures and making suggestions for improvement and/or future research • presenting findings in standard scientific report format Graphs, tables, and charts will be clearly labeled (including data source, units of measurement, and scale) and informatively titled. Reports will summarize results and show their relationship to hypothesis and/or relevant scientific concepts.

TABLE 10.5
Inquiry Task Model for Intermediate Through High School Levels

Step	Task
STEP 1	Student generates a research question relevant to an issue or concept important to the student.
STEP 2	Student collects background information using at least three sources.*
STEP 3	Student generates one or more hypotheses related to the research question using the background information to guide hypothesis development.
STEP 4	Student identifies and describes the natural science methods and tools needed to carry out an investigation of the problem/situation.*
STEP 5	Student designs* or reviews a scientific investigation to test the hypothesis, including instruments, procedures, record-keeping devices, and planned analyses.
STEP 6	Student conducts scientific research using appropriate procedures and instruments.
STEP 7	Student documents observations using appropriate documentation methods (charts, logs, journals, photos, recording strategies, etc.).
STEP 8	Student organizes results in appropriate tables, charts graphs, and so on.
STEP 9	Student identifies an appropriate audience for her or his findings.*
STEP 10	Student prepares a written report of her or his findings that includes: • The research question • Background information and its relationship to the hypothesis • A description of the research procedures and tools • A summary of the results and their relationship to the hypothesis and research question • A conclusion that includes implications for the concept, theory, or issue under study** • Evidence for the conclusion based on references to research data • Implications for future research** • Appropriate writing conventions • Appropriate language for purpose and audience

*Middle and high school level only.
**High school level only.

Even with these performance descriptions and task models or task shells, teachers need to see examples of the instructions for these tasks as well as examples of student performances so they can build on these examples as they write instructions for students.

Reliability of Raters

Recent research suggests that a critical problem when incorporating classroom-based evidence into large-scale test programs is the degree to which raters agree with one another when evaluating student work. Yen (1993) described a study conducted for the Maryland School Performance Assessment Program (MSPAP), in which correlations were examined between scores assigned to performance-based assessments by trained teachers and scores assigned by professional scorers. Interrater agreement between teachers and professional scorers for students' responses to language usage items ranged from .75 to .87, and correlations between scores for responses to writing prompts ranged from .63 to .73. Interrater agreement between trained teachers and trained professional scorers was much better in reading and mathematics. The range of correlations across mathematics items was from .95 to .99; across reading items, correlations ranged from .87 to .95. One reason that it may be difficult for raters to agree when scoring written performances is that students can interpret the writing prompts in different ways. This can lead to large differences in the difficulty and complexity of the task for different examinees (Charney, 1984), which could affect raters' application of scoring rules. In contrast, reading and mathematics performances have an element of correctness that allows raters to be in agreement more easily when applying scoring rules.

Koretz et al. (1994a) examined the agreement among raters for the Vermont portfolios. Portfolios were scored at the dimension level (e.g., mathematical problem solving, writing conventions) and at the overall performance level. The researchers found that agreement among raters in the second year was low to moderate at the dimension level (.42–.65 in mathematics and .39–.52 in writing). Agreement was fairly good at the overall performance level in mathematics (.79). However, agreement on the overall level in writing was only moderate (.63). This suggests that, although raters may not have agreed when applying rubrics for a given dimension of performance, when evaluating students' overall performance agreement was stronger. These researchers also noted that the low level of agreement among raters was unusual for large-scale programs. They suggested that disagreement among raters might be due to the variability of portfolio entries and, in writing, problems with the rubrics and training of the raters. For example, they noted that "there was considerable confusion among the writing raters about the interpretation and application of the rubrics . . ." (1994a, p. 12).

In other studies, interjudge agreement on portfolio scores has been fairly high. For example, Gentile (1992; cited in Koretz et al., 1994a) investigated interrater agreement for writing portfolios for the National Assessment of Educational Progress (NAEP) and found rater agreement as high as .89. Other studies of writing have suggested that rater agreement can be higher when students all write to a similar prompt (e.g., Moss, Cole, & Khampalikit, 1982; Washington State Office of the Superintendent of Public Instruction, 1999). This suggests that when common tools (Valencia & Place, 1994) are used, raters can be trained to apply scoring rules consistently across student work. Therefore, one possible way to address the potential for low rater agreement is to use task shells or task models to guide the development of classroom-based assessments.

Because Washington State has developed focused, holistic scoring rubrics related to the different curriculum standards, teachers can use these holistic rubrics to evaluate each dimension of performance. In addition to helping teachers clarify the levels of quality expected from student performances, generic scoring rubrics can help teachers construct appropriate scoring rules to evaluate students' work. Scores from classroom-based assessments would then be comparable across classrooms. On many large-scale tests, task- and item-specific scoring rules are developed to ensure that scoring is consistent across raters and students. These task- or item-specific scoring rules are not very useful for helping teachers frame their own scoring rules related to the curriculum standards. Hence, generic scoring rubrics can be used (see e.g., the six-trait writing rubrics developed by the Northwest Regional Educational Laboratory, [Spandell & Culham, 1991]) to guide teachers in scoring rule development for their own performance assessments. These generic rubrics serve the same purpose as task shells or task models, in that they outline what should be the focus of the scoring rules and, therefore, what is expected in the task. Table 10.6 is an example of a generic scoring rubric that can be modified to the specific purposes of students' plans for a scientific investigation. Alternatively, if teachers are carefully trained in the meaning of the dimensions of performance evaluated through the rubrics, generic rubrics can be applied without modification.

Construct-Irrelevant Variance

Construct-irrelevant variance in scores results from sources other than students' knowledge, conceptual understanding, and skill, or their ability to apply knowledge, concepts, and skills in some performance. Three major sources of construct-irrelevant variance can affect scores for classroom-based evidence: (a) the degree to which examinees received assistance from others such as teachers, peers, and parents; (b) the differences in the difficulty of classroom-based work; and (c) the degree to which the classroom-based work represents the domain of reference.

If teachers believe that scores from the classroom-based work are to be used to make pass–fail or graduation decisions for students, or the scores are to be used to evaluate teacher competency (for large-scale assessment programs, both pressures are often present), teachers may provide inappropriate types of support for students in preparing their work. For example, Koretz, Stecher, Klein, and McCaffrey (1994b) found that three out of four Vermont teachers provided revision help or allowed other students to provide revision help for portfolio entries. In addition, 25% of the fourth-grade teachers and 60% of the eighth-grade teachers allowed students to get parental assistance. These factors can lead to invalid inferences about

TABLE 10.6
Generic Scoring Rubric for Planning Scientific Investigations

Science Inquiry Scoring Criteria

Scientific Inquiry Performance Criteria for Designing Investigations:

- generates questions and hypotheses
- designs investigations to test hypotheses, answer questions, or test models
- determines appropriate data-collection methods
- shows understanding of characteristics of effective inquiry

SCORING

4 points   Meets all relevant criteria

- hypothesis or question is precise and focused, given context
- design is directly linked to hypothesis, question, model; is systematic, complete, logical
- data are to be carefully and systematically obtained
- shows a thorough understanding of the characteristics of scientific inquiry process

3 points   Meets most relevant criteria

- hypothesis or question is reasonable, given context
- design is linked to hypothesis, question, model; is systematic and mostly complete
- data are to be obtained using acceptable strategies; however, there may be minor technical problems
- shows a good understanding of the characteristics of scientific inquiry process

2 points   Meets some relevant criteria

- hypothesis or question is given but may not be testable
- design is partially complete in addressing question, hypothesis or model; but may have some logical flaws
- planned data collection strategies may be disorganized or incomplete OR there may be significant technical problems
- shows some understanding of the characteristics of scientific inquiry process

1 point   Meets few relevant criteria

- hypothesis or question is given but is too general to be testable
- design is sketchy or vague **OR** may be disconnected from hypothesis **OR** has *major* logical flaws
- there may be many significant technical errors in methods for data collection
- shows weak understanding of the characteristics of scientific inquiry process

0 points   Shows no understanding of the characteristics of scientific inquiry process, no attempt, off topic

what students know and are able to do on their own. Yet many real-world tasks require peer or supervisor input. This chapter, for example, was reviewed by other chapter authors and researchers in the field of large-scale assessment. Therefore, if assistance is allowed and expected, safeguards must be put in place to ensure that teacher, peer, or outside assistance is consistent with the feedback and assistance typical of real-world performances. Early drafts of work and peer, teacher, or parent comments could be retained so that the scorer can examine how students use the feedback in their revisions. A third party could interview a random selection of students from each class about their portfolio entries and ask them to discuss how they made choices about changes from earlier to later drafts of a work.

Task difficulty is another potential source of construct-irrelevant variance when using classroom-based evidence. Koretz et al. (1994a) found that scorers in Vermont were troubled by tasks that were "nominally the same but varied markedly in difficulty" (p. 12). These researchers suggested that "if teachers assign variants of the same problem that vary markedly in difficulty, comparisons among their students would be deceptive" (p.13). Yet good teachers will vary tasks to make them more accessible to students. A less able student might choose to do a report on elephants, whereas a more able student might choose to do a report on duck-bill platypus. All requirements for these reports could be the same, but the availability of resources might be greater for one student than for the other. Therefore, teachers need guidance in how to appropriately vary tasks according to individual student interests and abilities. It may be that modified task models or shells could be provided for students who need more or less challenge. If these modifications were described along with the classroom-based artifact, then scores could be adjusted systematically to account for variability in difficulty. In either case, helping teachers create comparable tasks could be a benefit to teaching and student learning.

Finally, another threat to validity is the degree to which the classroom-based evidence represents the subject domain. Again, Koretz et al. (1994a) examined this problem in Vermont. The researchers claimed that raters had to "stretch general purpose rubrics to cover a wide variety of tasks" and that the "unstandardized tasks . . . did not elicit attributes included in the scoring system . . ." (p. 12). This issue is relevant to two of the most compelling reasons for including classroom-based evidence: (a) to assess aspects of the domain best measured through classroom-based performance, or (b) increase the depth of measurement in areas that are inadequately assessed by the large-scale test. To ensure that classroom-based assessments actually serve these purposes and provide measurement of relevant and desirable targets, some guidance must be given to teachers about the curriculum standards that are to be addressed through classroom-based evidence and how those standards should be assessed. Simply listing types of assignments (e.g., tests, homework, essays, performances) is unlikely to ensure that teachers and students select relevant work for consideration in large-scale testing programs. Exemplary tasks or test blueprints, as well as generic task models or task shells, can serve a valuable purpose in guiding assessment development. In addition, teachers must have access to professional training in assessment development and how to develop and use scoring rubrics for performances. They also must be given opportunities to participate in substantive conversations about the meaning of curriculum standards.

STRATEGIES FOR INCLUSION OF CLASSROOM-BASED EVIDENCE IN LARGE-SCALE TESTING PROGRAMS

If the decision is made to include classroom-based evidence in large-scale assessment programs, a number of steps must be taken to ensure that the evidence will actually add to the inferences drawn and decisions made about examinees. First, the curriculum standards (e.g., knowledge, skills, concepts) that are to be assessed must be clearly mapped out. Next, designers must do a careful analysis of the match between the items and tasks on large-scale tests (if such a test exists) and the curriculum standards to find those areas that are underrepresented and those that are not represented. If there is no existing test, developers must ask themselves which standards are best measured through standardized, large-scale tests, and a test blueprint should be developed to ensure adequate assessment of curriculum standards. A broad array of item types (multiple-choice, short-answer, extended tasks, etc.) should be examined so that as many standards as possible are assessed.

Once this task is complete, several questions must be asked: For which standards would classroom-based assessments give us more confidence in the generalizability of inferences made about students? For which standards would classroom-based assessments provide the *only* evidence about student achievement? For which standards is classroom-based evidence superfluous? What types of performances are likely to provide the most useful evidence? How many classroom-based assessments would be needed to increase confidence in inferences made about students? What strategies will be used to guide teacher development, selection, and evaluation of classroom-based assessments? How will task difficulty be addressed? What limits will be placed on coaching and outside assistance? If coaching and outside assistance are accepted, what must be collected, along with the evidence, to ensure that the student still has central ownership of the work? What training will be provided to help teachers understand the curriculum standards, scoring rubrics, and standards for high-quality assessments? Each of these questions must be answered in a way that helps yield high-quality information about students.

In addition to planning decisions, research should be conducted to assess the validity and reliability of the score-based inferences. Studies such as those conducted by Koretz and his colleagues (1994a) to examine rater agreement would be critical. If teachers are to score student work in the classroom and send scores along with classroom-based evidence, studies are needed to compare the scores resulting from teacher raters with those that are given by trained professional scorers or peer teachers. Studies that examine scoring consistency over time would also be essential. Fitzpatrick, Ercikan, Yen, and Ferrara (1998) examined the degree to which raters agreed on scores for the same papers at two scoring times (1 year apart). These researchers found that raters became more severe over time even though they were trained to use the same scoring rules and some of the raters were the same people.

Construct validity studies would be necessary to examine whether evidence that comes from the classroom is consistent with similar performances from the large-scale test. For example, Herman, Gearhart, and Baker (1993) found no correlation between scores on portfolio collections of written work and scores on a standardized assessment of writing. Does this mean that the classroom work is not an accurate reflection of student writing? Does it mean that the standardized assessment is not an accurate reflection of student writing? These questions merit closer examination. It would also be important to investigate whether scores on classroom-based evidence show the same variability as has been seen in standardized assessments (e.g., Shavelson et al., 1993).

To examine the consequences of gathering classroom-based evidence for large-scale assessment programs, some direct inquiry into schools is needed. Are teachers receiving adequate training and support for implementation of the standards? Are teachers adjusting instruction to include important processes and thinking skills that are in the curriculum? If not, why not? Are teachers *teaching to the test* in inappropriate ways? Are teachers providing inappropriate coaching or assistance? Do teachers modify tasks to adjust for interest while maintaining some consistency in difficulty? Is the collection of evidence causing undue burden for teachers or do they perceive the collection of evidence as adding to their understanding of standards and student achievement? How do students and parents feel about the collection of evidence? Has incorporation of new forms of assessment into schools had any effects on students' beliefs about the subject disciplines, students' attitudes toward school, teachers' beliefs about the subject disciplines, school climate, or achievement as measured by external indicators (e.g., SAT scores, graduation rates, etc.)? In short, a careful research program addressing each of these critical questions must be implemented if classroom-based evidence is to be an appropriate and useful supplement to large-scale testing programs (whether at the district or state level).

CONCLUSION

There are very good reasons for incorporating classroom-based evidence into large-scale assessment programs. Classroom assessments can provide evidence about achievement in domains that are not easily assessed via large-scale, paper-and-pencil tests; they can increase the reliability of inferences made about examinees, schools, and districts; they can allow for more authentic applications of concepts and skills; and they can help us gather evidence of opportunity to learn, as well as the effectiveness of inservice training programs. To do these tasks well, however, we must attend to problems that have emerged when efforts have been made to implement such a system.

Each of these problems can be addressed in ways that do not overburden schools or students. Mainly, each problem arises out of a fundamental lack of teacher training in assessment development, a lack of teacher training in how to develop and apply scoring rules to evaluate student performances, a lack of agreement in visions about what constitutes valued and high-quality work, and inappropriate levels of standardization when incorporating classroom-based assessments into large-scale assessment programs.

Lack of teacher training in assessment has been addressed extensively in the literature, and it is clear that where teacher preparation programs fail, inservice professional development programs must succeed. Better trained teachers are likely to understand curriculum standards better and are likely to develop more appropriate and valid classroom assessments. Time must be allotted, as part of the ongoing professional experiences of teachers, for training in how to develop and use high quality assessments and for conversations about standards of quality in student work. Although less standardization allows for local relevance, better instructional connections, and attention to students' interests, a complete lack of standardization means that classroom-based evidence is unlikely to serve any meaningful purpose in evaluating schools or in adding to our knowledge about individual students. In this chapter, I have recommended that test blueprints be given to teachers if classroom-based tests are to be used to ensure adequate assessment of all knowledge and concepts defined in curriculum standards. I have also recommended task models or shells be used to guide teacher development of performance assessments that are appropriate for inclusion as classroom-based evidence of student achievement. In addition, I have recommended that teachers be taught how to apply generic scoring rubrics or how to create their own rubrics using externally developed generic rubrics as guides. Finally, I have recommended that teachers have guidelines for adapting tasks while still controlling levels of task difficulty. Each of these recommendations would require a considerable amount of conversation among educators and assessment designers.

One of the main limitations of the use of models or guidelines is that the range of assessments and performances admitted as evidence might be limited to those valued by the developers of the guidelines. It is important to have input from different professions that use the knowledge and skills included in the standards so that a reasonable range of targeted standards and valued performances is included. In addition, public input on generic rubrics would be needed to ensure that all valued dimensions of performance are assessed. A lack of public input can lead to a set of scoring criteria that satisfy the test makers, but do not satisfy experts at large (Charney, 1984). As Charney said,

> A given set of criteria devised by one set of experts is no more valid than a different set of standards, arrived at by a different group of experts. Why should one set of criteria be imposed rather than another? (p. 73)

This is a valid question and one that should be answered before test blueprints, benchmark performance descriptions, task models, and generic criteria are established and disseminated to the public. As Charney (1984) has noted, "Whatever criteria are chosen, raters must be trained to use . . . those standards rather than their own" (p. 73). These cautions apply just as much to the development of task models or shells. They must represent performances worth doing as judged by experts in various disciplines.

For classroom-based assessments to add to our knowledge about student achievement, they must reflect standards of quality for assessment. Teachers must be trained, and guidelines must help them structure assessments and apply scoring rules so that the evidence provided is useful. Thoughtful planning, public input, effective training procedures, and carefully developed guidelines can improve the quality of evidence so that future attempts to incorporate classroom-based evidence into large-scale assessment programs are more fruitful than ever before.

REFERENCES

Airasian, P. (1991). Perspectives on measurement instruction for pre-service teachers. *Educational Measurement: Issues and Practice, 10*(1), 13–16, 26.

Airasian, P. (2000). *Assessment in the classroom: A concise approach*. Boston: McGraw-Hill.

Airasian, P. W. (1994). *Classroom assessment, Second edition*. New York: McGraw-Hill, Inc., 5.

Aronson, J., Lustina, M. J., Good, C., Keough, K., Steele, C. M., & Brown, J. (1999). When White men can't do math: Necessary and sufficient factors in stereotype threat. *Journal-of-Experimental-Social-Psychology, 35*(1), 29–46.

Baxter, G. P., Shavelson, R. J., Herman, S. J., Brown, K. A., & Valadez, J. R. (1993). Mathematics performance assessment: Technical quality and diverse student impact. *Journal for Research in Mathematics Education, 24,* 190–216.

California State Department of Education. (1990). *California Assessment Program: A sampler of mathematics assessment.* Sacramento, CA: Author.

Callahan, S. (1997). Tests worth taking? Using portfolios for accountability in Kentucky. *Journal of Research in the Teaching of English, 31,* 295–336.

Charney, D. (1984). The validity of using holistic scoring to evaluate writing: A critical overview. *Research in the Teaching of English, 18*(1), 65–81.

Darling-Hammond, L., & Wise, A. E. (1985). Beyond standardization: State standards and school improvement. *The Elementary School Journal, 85,* 315–336.

Debra P. v Turlington, 474 F. Supp. 244 (M. D. Fla. 1979).

Frederiksen, N. (1984). The real test bias: Influences of testing on teaching and learning. *American Psychologist, 39,* 193–202.

Frederiksen, N. (1998). An exchange of view on "Semantics, psychometrics, and assessment reform: A close look at 'authentic' assessments." *Educational Researcher, 27*(6), 19–22.

Fitzpatrick, A. R., Ercikan, K., Yen, W. M., & Ferrara, S. (1998). The consistency between raters scoring in different test years. *Applied-Measurement-in-Education, 11*(2), 195–208.

Fontana, J. (1995). Portfolio assessment: Its beginnings in Vermont and Kentucky. *NASSP-Bulletin, 79*(573), 25–30.

Forseth, C. (1992). Portfolio assessment in the hands of teachers. *School Administrator, 49*(11), 24–28.

Gearhart, M., & Wolf, S. (1996). *Issues in portfolio assessment: Providing evidence of writing competency (Part I: The purposes and processes of writing).* Los Angeles: Center for Research on Evaluation, Standards, and Student Testing.

Gullickson, A. R. (1986). Teacher education and teacher-perceived needs in educational measurement and evaluation. *Journal of Educational Measurement, 23*(4), 347–354.

Haladyna, T. M., Nolen, S. B., & Haas, N. S. (1991). Raising standardized achievement test scores and the origins of test score pollution. *Educational Researcher, 20*(5), 2–7.

Hewitt, G. (1993). Vermont's portfolio based writing assessment program: A brief history. *Teachers and Writers, 24*(5), 1–6.

Herman, J. L., Gearhart, M., Baker, E. L. (1993). Assessing writing portfolios: Issues in the validity and meaning of scores. *Educational-Assessment, 3,* 201–224

Kentucky State Department of Education. (1996). *Core content for assessment: Version 1.0.* Frankfort, KY: Author.

Kirst, M. W., & Mazzeo, C. (1996). The rise, fall, and rise of state assessment in California, 1993–96. *Phi Delta Kappan, 78,* 319–323.

Klein, S. P., Stecher, B., & Koretz, D. (1995). The reliability of mathematics portfolio scores: Lessons from the Vermont experience. *Applied Measurement in Education, 8,* 243–260.

Koretz, D., Stecher, B., & Deibert, E. (1992a). *The Vermont Portfolio Assessment Program: Interim Report on Implementation and Impact, 1991–92 School Year, CSE Technical Report 350.* Los Angeles: Center for Research on Evaluation, Standards, and Student Testing.

Koretz, D., Stecher, B., & Deibert, E. (1992b). *The Reliability of Scores from the 1992 Vermont Portfolio Assessment Program. CSE Technical Report 355.* Los Angeles: Center for the Study of Evaluation.

Koretz, D., Stecher, B., Klein, S., & McCaffrey, D. (1994a). The Vermont portfolio assessment program: Findings and implications. *Educational Measurement: Issues and Practice, 13,* 5–16.

Koretz, D., Stecher, B., Klein, S., & McCaffrey, D. (1994b). *The evolution of a portfolio program: The impact and quality of the Vermont program in its second year. CSE Technical Report 385*. Los Angeles: Center for the Study of Evaluation.

Linn, R. L., & Burton, E. (1994). Performance-based assessments: Implications of task specificity. *Educational Measurement: Issues and Practice, 13*(1), 5–8.

Linn, R. L., & Gronlund, N. E. (2000). *Measurement and assessment in teaching*. Upper Saddle River, NJ: Merrill.

Lortie, D. (1975). *Schoolteacher: A sociological study*. Chicago: University of Chicago Press.

Madaus, G. F., West, M. M., Harmon, M. C., Lomax, R. G., & Viator, K. A. (1992). *The influence of testing on teaching math and science in grades 4–12* (Report No. SPA8954750). National Science Foundation.

Martinez, M. E. (1999). Cognition and the question of test item format. *Educational Psychologist, 34*(4), 207–218.

Mehrens, W. A., & Lehmann, I. J. (1991). *Measurement and evaluation in education and psychology*. Fort Worth, TX: Holt, Rinehart, & Winston.

Moss, P. H., Cole, N. S., & Khampalikit, C. (1982). Comparison of procedures to assess written language skills at grades 4, 7, and 10. *Journal of Educational Measurement, 19*, 37–47.

National Council of Teachers of Mathematics. (1989). *Curriculum and evaluation standards for school mathematics*. Reston, VA: Author.

Nitko, A. J. (2001). *Educational assessment of students*. Upper Saddle River, NJ: Prentice-Hall.

Popham, W. J. (1987). The merits of measurement-driven instruction. *Phi Delta Kappan, 68*, 679–682.

Quellmalz, E. S., Capell, F. J., & Chou, C. P. (1982). Effects of discourse and response mode on the measurement of writing competence. *Journal of Educational Measurement, 19*, 241–258.

Resnick, L. B., & Resnick, D. P. (1991). Assessing the thinking curriculum: New tools for educational reform. In B. R. Gifford & M. C. O'Connor (Eds.), *Changing assessments: Alternative views of aptitude, achievement, and instruction*. Boston: Kluwer.

Schafer, W. D., & Lissitz, R. W. (1987). Measurement training for school personnel: Recommendations and reality. *Journal of Teacher Education, 38*(3), 57–63.

Schwab, J. J. (1978). Education and the structure of the disciplines. In I. Westbury & N. J. Wilkof (Eds.), *Science, curriculum, and liberal education* (pp. 229–272). Chicago: University of Chicago Press.

Shavelson, R. J., Baxter, G. P., & Gao, X. (1993). Sampling variability of performance assessments. *Journal of Educational Measurement, 30*, 215–232.

Shepard, L. A. (1989). Why we need better tests. *Educational Leadership, 4*(7), 4–9.

Shepard, L. A., & Dougherty, K. C. (1991, April). *Effects of high stakes testing on instruction and achievement*. Paper presented at the annual meeting of the National Council on Measurement in Education, Chicago.

Shepard, L. A. (2000, April). *1998 Career award winner address: Conceptual compatibility between large-scale and classroom assessments*. Paper presented at the annual meeting of the National Council on Measurement in Education, New Orleans.

Smith, M. L. (1994). Meanings of test preparation. *American Educational Research Journal, 28*, 521–542.

Solano-Flores, G., & Shavelson, R. J. (1997). Development of performance assessments in science: Conceptual, practical, and logistical issues. *Educational Measurement: Issues and Practice, 16*(3), 16–25.

Spandel, V., & Culham, R. (1991). *Writing assessment*. Portland, OR: Northwest Regional Educational Laboratory.

State of Washington, Superintendent of Public Instruction. (1997). *Assessment sampler: Grade 4*. Olympia, WA: Author.

Stecher, B. M., & Hamilton, E. G. (1994, April). *Portfolio assessment in Vermont, 1992–93: The teachers' perspective on implementation and impact*. Paper presented at the annual meeting of the National Council on Measurement in Education, New Orleans, LA.

Stecher, B. M., & Mitchell, K. J. (1995). *Portfolio driven reform: Vermont teachers' understanding of mathematical problem-solving and related changes in classroom practice: CSE Technical Report 400*. Los Angeles: Center for Research on Evaluation, Standards, and Student Testing.

Stecher, B. M., Barron, S., Kaganoff, T., & Goodwin, J. (1998). *The effects of standards-based assessment on classroom practices: Results of the 1996–97 RAND survey of Kentucky teachers of mathematics and writing: CSE Technical Report 482*. Los Angeles: Center for Research on Evaluation, Standards, and Student Testing.

Steele, C. (1999). Thin ice. *Atlantic Monthly, 284*(2), 44–54.

Steele, C. M., & Aronson, J. (2000). Stereotype threat and the intellectual test performance of African Americans. In *Stereotypes and prejudice: Essential readings*, C. Stangor (Ed), 369–389, Philadelphia, PA: Psychology Press/Taylor & Francis.

Stiggins, R. J. (1982). A comparison of direct and indirect writing assessment methods. *Journal for Research in the Teaching of English, 16*(2), 101–114.

Stiggins, R. J., & Bridgeford, N. J. (1988). The ecology of classroom assessment. *Journal of Educational Measurement, 22*(4), 271–286.

Stiggins, R. J., & Faires-Conklin, N. (1988). *Teacher training in assessment*. Portland, OR: Northwest Regional Educational Laboratory.

Stiggins, R. J., & Faires-Conklin, N. (1992). *In teachers' hands: Investigating the practices of classroom assessment*. Albany, NY: SUNY Press.

Stiggins, R. J., Faires-Conklin, N., & Bridgeford, N. J. (1986). Classroom assessment: A key to effective education. *Educational Measurement: Issues and Practice, 5*(2), 5–17.

Taylor, C. S. (1998, November). *Benchmarking performances: A strategy for classroom assessment planning and development*. Paper presented at the annual meeting of the California Educational Research Association, Monterey, CA.

Taylor, C. S., & Nolen, S. B. (1996). What Does the Psychometrician's Classroom Look Like?: Reframing assessment concepts in the context of learning. *Educational Policy Analysis Archives, 4*(17). Available online at epaa.asu.edu/epaa/v4n17.html

Terwilliger, J. S. (1997). Semantics, psychometrics, and assessment reform: A close look at "authentic" assessments. *Educational Researcher, 26*(8), 24–27.

Valencia, S. W., & Place, N. (1994). Portfolios: A Process for Enhancing Teaching and Learning. *The Reading Teacher, 47*, 666–69.

Vermont State Department of Education. (1993). *A Green Mountain challenge: Very high skills for every student—No exceptions, no excuses, 1992–93*. Montpelier, VT: Author.

Vermont State Department of Education. (1994a). *4th grade writing benchmark pieces*. Montpelier, VT: Author.

Vermont State Department of Education. (1994b). *8th grade writing benchmark pieces*. Montpelier, VT: Author.

Office of the Superintendent of Public Instruction (1999). *Washington Assessment of Student Learning 1999 Grade 4 Technical Report*. Olympia, WA: Author.

Wiggins, G. (1989). Teaching to the (authentic) test. *Educational Leadership, 46*(7), 41–47.

Wiggins, G. (1992). Creating tests worth taking. *Educational Leadership, 49*(8), 26–33.

Wineburg, S. (1999). Historical thinking and other unnatural acts. *Phi Delta Kappan, 80*, 488–499.

Yen, W. (1993, June). *The Maryland School Performance Assessment Program: Performance assessment with psychometric quality suitable for high stakes usage*. Paper presented at the Large-Scale Assessment conference, Albuquerque, NM

Chapter 11

Monitoring Raters in Performance Assessments

George Engelhard, Jr.
Emory University

As the number and variety of performance assessments increase in educational settings, it is essential to monitor and evaluate the quality of ratings obtained. Any assessment system that goes beyond selected-response (multiple-choice) items and incorporates constructed-response items that require scoring by raters must have procedures for monitoring rating quality. The general structure of rater-mediated (RM) assessments includes raters judging the quality of an examinee's response to a task designed to represent the construct being measured using a rating scale. The key feature of RM assessments is that the examinee's responses (e.g., essays and portfolios) become the stimuli that raters must interpret and evaluate to produce ratings. Although it may seem like a trivial issue, it is very important that the measurement models used to evaluate RM assessments are indeed models of rater behavior, performance, and response. RM assessments do not provide direct information regarding examinee achievement because the examinee's responses must be mediated and interpreted through raters to obtain judgments about examinee achievement. One of the major concerns regarding RM assessments is that raters bring a variety of potential response biases that may unfairly affect their judgments regarding the quality of examinee responses. There may be a variety of construct-irrelevant components that may appear in RM assessment systems related to response biases on the part of raters that impact the overall validation of particular uses and interpretations of test score results within the context of state assessment and accountability systems (Linn, chap. 2, this volume).

Historically, the evaluation of the psychometric quality of rating data has included "(a) traditional psychometric criteria such as reliability, construct validity, and interrater agreement; (b) indices of rater errors that reflect response biases on the part of the rater; and (c) direct measures of the accuracy of ratings" (Murphy & Cleveland, 1995, p. 268). This chapter focuses specifically on indexes of rater errors and the detection of response biases that represent construct-irrelevant components in RM assessments. Over time, a hodgepodge of indexes have been proposed to detect rater errors (Saal, Downey, & Lahey, 1980). Most of these have been atheoretical, ad hoc, and based on classical test theory. Recent advances in item-response theory (IRT) in general, and Rasch measurement theory in particular, provide an opportunity to develop theoretically sound and model-based methods for evaluating the quality of ratings and detecting rater errors. These IRT and model-based methods provide a framework for attaining fundamental measurement (Wright, 1999) and yield what Embretson and her colleagues (Embretson, 1996; Embretson & Hershberger, 1999) called the *new rules of measurement*.

The model-based approach to monitoring raters in performance assessments described here is based on the concept of *invariance* (Engelhard, 1994a). The purpose of this chapter is to illustrate how the principles of sample-invariant item calibration (Engelhard, 1984), and item-invariant measurement of individuals (Engelhard, 1991) can be adapted and used to detect various rater errors with a many-facet Rasch measurement (MFRM) model (Linacre, 1989). The first section of this chapter discusses a model-based approach to assessment that meets the requirements of invariant measurement. Next, the MFRM model is described (Linacre, 1989). In the following section, a family of rater errors is described that reflects a potential lack of invariance in numerous aspects of rater-mediated assessment systems. This section also includes examples from large-scale writing assessments to illustrate these psychometric indexes of rater errors. Finally, the implications of this chapter for future research and practice involving rater-mediated assessments are discussed.

ITEM-RESPONSE THEORY, INVARIANT MEASUREMENT, AND MODEL-BASED ASSESSMENT

As pointed out by Hattie, Jaeger, and Bond (1999) in their chapter on persistent methodological questions in educational testing, "item-response theory (IRT) is an elegant and powerful model of test performance that obviates virtually all of the shortcomings of classical test theory" (p. 399).

They noted that a "major advantage of the item response model derives from the promise of invariance" (p. 402). IRT is an example of model-based assessment that can meet the requirements of invariant measurement. In model-based assessments, the theoretical requirements of a psychometrically sound assessment system are defined; if the observed measurements meet these criteria, then invariant measurement has been achieved. Invariant measurement can be viewed as a hypothesis that must be confirmed or disconfirmed by data. Wright (1997) has shown that invariant measurement is required to support fundamental measurement (Campbell, 1920). Campbell defined *fundamental measurement* as the numerical representation of physical additivity; Michell (1999) provided a detailed description and critique of Campbell's theory of measurement. Wright and his colleagues (Fisher & Wright, 1994; Perline, Wright, & Wainer, 1979; Wright, 1999) also made the case that MFRM models provide a framework for achieving fundamental measurement because the models are special cases of simultaneous conjoint measurement (Luce & Tukey, 1964). Luce and Tukey proposed simultaneous conjoint measurement as a new type of fundamental measurement. In their words,

> ... the essential character of simultaneous conjoint measurement is described by an axiomatization for the comparison of effects of (or responses to) pairs formed from two specified kinds of "quantities." ... A close relation exists between conjoint measurement and the establishment of response measures in a two-way table, or other analysis-of-variance situations, for which the "effects of columns" and the "effects of rows" are additive. Indeed, the discovery of such measures, which are well known to have important practical advantages, may be viewed as the discovery, via conjoint measurement, of fundamental measures of the row and column variables. From this point of view it is natural to regard conjoint measurement as factorial measurement. (Luce & Tukey, 1964, p. 1)

Linacre, Engelhard, Tatum, and Myford (1994) presented the Rasch model as many-faceted conjoint measurement.

The Danish mathematician Georg Rasch (1980) stated the requirements of invariant measurement that he called *specific objectivity*:

> The comparison between two stimuli should be independent of which particular individuals were instrumental for the comparison; and it should also be independent of which stimuli within the consider class were or might also have been compared. Symmetrically, a comparison between two individuals should be independent of which particular simuli within the class considered were instrumental for the comparison; and it should also be independent of which other individuals were also compared on the same or on some other occasion. (Rasch, 1961, pp. 331–332)

Wright (1968) stated these requirements as follows:

> First, the calibration of measuring instruments must be independent of those objects that happen to be used for the calibration. Second, the measurement of objects must be independent of the instrument that happens to be used for the measuring. (Wright, 1968, p. 87)

The requirements of invariant measurement can be generalized in terms of sample-invariant calibration of rater-mediated assessments and rater-invariant measurement of individuals. In the case of rater-mediated assessments, all of the facets are based on the interpretive and judgmental framework brought to the situation by the raters. Strictly speaking, each facet and the rater error indexes described later in the chapter provide various sources of information about whether the rating process is functioning as intended to yield invariant measurement. Although the language would be somewhat awkward, it would be accurate to speak of judged writing ability, judged domain difficulty, and judgmental category coefficients to stress this point.

Before describing the requirements for invariant measurement within rater-mediated assessment systems, it is useful to define a few terms. *Facets* are separate dimensions in the assessment system, such as raters, tasks, and domains. In the language of the analysis of variance (ANOVA), facets are comparable to factors or independent variables. Facets are comprised of individual elements that vary in difficulty or severity; the substantive interpretation of difficulty varies depending on the facet. For example, if raters are the elements within a rater facet, then it is customary to refer to the hard raters as severe and the easy raters as lenient. The difficulty of individual elements within a facet defines its location on the construct or latent variable that the assessment system is designed to measure. The location of individual elements within each facet can be represented graphically by a variable map. In this chapter, the latent variable is writing ability. When facets are crossed, the cells within the assessment design are called *assessment components*; each assessment component yields an assessment opportunity for the examinee to obtain an observed rating that depends on the difficulties of the elements from the facets that combine to define that cell. The assessment components obtained from crossing several facets combine to define an overall assessment system. Engelhard (1997) provided a detailed description of how these concepts can be used to guide the construction of rater and task banks for performance assessments.

The basic measurement problem underlying sample-invariant facet calibration is how to minimize the influence of arbitrary samples of individuals on the estimation of the difficulty of elements within each facet. In the case of an item facet, the goal is to estimate the item scale values that are comparable across examinees. Differential item functioning (DIF) represents a set of procedures for examining whether the item difficulties are invariant over identifiable subgroups (e.g., gender, race/ethnicity, disability) of examinees. The underlying principle of DIF analyses can be extended to differential facet functioning that includes adding interaction terms to the basic MFRM described later in this chapter. The overall goal of sample-invariant calibration of elements within facets is to estimate the locations of these elements on the latent variable so that these locations remain unchanged across both individuals and subgroups of examinees. The locations of elements within and across facets should also be invariant over subsets of elements or facets. In other words, the calibrations of elements and facets should not be affected by the inclusion or exclusion of other elements and facets.

Rater-invariant measurement of individuals involves the minimization of influences of particular elements or facets used to estimate the location of the individual on the latent variable for the assessment system. The particular elements and facets that are used to estimate an individual's ability should not have an undue influence. For example, if examinees respond to different writing prompts that differ in difficulty, then some examinees who respond to an easy prompt may have their writing ability overestimated while examinees reponding to the hard prompt may be unduly penalized because of task difficulty. The overall goal is to obtain comparable estimates of an examinee's ability regardless of which elements and facets are included in the rater-mediated assessments. This requirement relates to equating issues when examinees are measured with different elements and facets. For example, if examinees are rated by different raters, then the scores of the examinees should be invariant over the particular raters used to obtained these scores; examinee scores should not depend on the luck of the rater draw.

Figure 11.1 provides the conceptual model for a prototypical performance assessment of writing ability. The dependent variable in the model is the observed rating. The three major facets that define the intervening variables used to make the latent variable—writing ability—observable are rater severity, domain difficulty, and task difficulty. The fourth facet that represents the target or object of measurement is writing ability. The structure of the rating scale (e.g., number of rating categories) also plays a fundamental role in defining the observed ratings. Although the structure of the rating scale is not explicitly considered a facet in the model, it is an important intervening component. A similar conceptual model was used by Engelhard (1992) to examine the quality of ratings obtained with Georgia's eighth-grade writing test. This general model can be easily modified to handle the structure of other large-scale performance assessments. For example, Oregon (Hollenbeck, Tindal, & Almond, 1999; Oregon Depart-

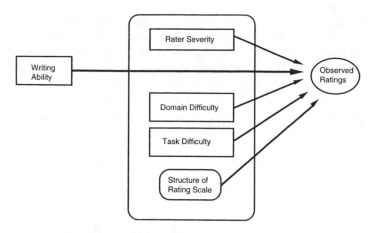

FIG. 11.1. Conceptual model for the assessment of writing ability.

ment of Education, 1998) uses six analytic traits (domains) called (1) ideas and content, (2) organization, (3) voice, (4) word choice, (5) sentence fluency, and (6) conventions with three prompts (tasks) and two judges (raters) to measure writing achievement in its statewide assessment program.

As pointed out in the *Standards for Educational and Psychological Testing* (American Educational Research Association, American Psychological Association, & National Council on Measurement in Education, 1999), "the validity of test score interpretations may be limited by construct-irrelevant components" (p. 23). In most cases, although not in all research (Cronbach, 1995), rater bias can be viewed as method variance and is construct irrelevant. According to Hoyt (2000), "for most users of ratings, rater bias is of no substantive interest and therefore contributes to error of measurement" (p. 65). Figure 11.2 presents a graphical display designed to convey some of the potential construct-irrelevant components that may have an impact on the estimation of writing ability within large-scale performance assessments. The first construct-irrelevant components represent potential interaction effects. Interaction effects (two-way and higher order interactions) indicate that the rater-mediated assessment system is not functioning as intended. When the model fits the data, the effects are additive. For example, if each rater interprets the domain differently, then domain difficulty would vary across raters; in this case, an examinee's ratings on the domains would not be invariant across raters—the domain ratings would depend on the idiosyncratic and biased views of a particular rater toward domains. Another example of an interaction effect that introduces rater bias is if each rater interprets the rating scale differently. For example, the developers of an assessment system might intend that the raters use the full rating scale (inadequate, minimal, good, and very good), but a

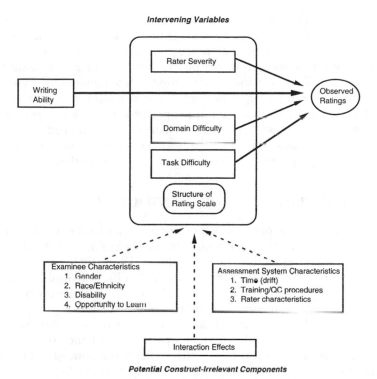

FIG. 11.2. Potential construct-irrelevant components in the assessment of writing ability.

rater might use only two implied categories (pass/fail); the rater has combined categories: inadequate with minimal = fail and good with very good = pass. This combining of categories would be empirically detectable because the rater might only use rating categories 2 and 3. In a meta-analysis of 79 generalizability studies, Hoyt and Kerns (1999) found that raters' differential interpretations of the rating scale were a major source of error variance.

In addition to examining interaction effects among the intervening variables, Fig. 11.2 also includes examinee and assessment system characteristics as potential construct-irrelevant components. For example, rater biases may appear if a rater assigns different ratings to males and females. In other words, rater severity may interact with examinee gender so that the rater's ratings are not invariant over gender groups (Gyagenda & Engelhard, 1999). As another example, rater severity may drift over time (Wilson & Case, 2000). Fatigue and other extraneous variables may affect the rater's performance so that the ratings are not invariant over time— the rater may start out a scoring session rating relatively leniently, but become progressively more severe as the day wears on. For all of these potential sources of rater bias and errors (interaction effects, examinee characteristics, and assessment system characteristics), an examinee's scores might be estimated incorrectly because of the particular rater assigned to do the scoring. To determine whether the requirements of invariant measurement are being met, potential construct-irrelevant components should be explicitly studied and appropriate actions taken to minimize the impact of rater biases on examinee scores. In the interest of detecting these response biases, the following sections of this chapter describe a family of rater-error indexes based on the MFRM model.

MANY-FACET RASCH MEASUREMENT MODEL

The MFRM model for ordered response categories is an extended version of the Rasch measurement model (Andrich, 1988; Rasch, 1980; Wright & Masters, 1982) developed by Linacre (1989). The MFRM model is essentially an additive linear model that is based on a logistic transformation of observed ratings to a logit or log-odds scale. The logistic transformation of ratios of successive category probabilities (log odds) can be viewed as the dependent variable with various facets, such as writing ability, rater, domain, and task conceptualized as independent variables that influence these log odds. The MFRM model that reflects the conceptual model of writing ability in Fig. 11.1 takes the following general form:

$$Ln[P_{nmijk} / P_{mnijk-1}] = \theta_n - \lambda_m - \delta_i - \alpha_j - \tau_k, \qquad (1)$$

where

P_{nmijk} = probability of examinee n being rated k on domain i for task j by rater m,

$P_{nmijk-1}$ = probability of examinee n being rated k-1 on domain i for task j by rater m,

θ_n = writing ability of examinee n,

λ_m = severity of rater m,

δ_i = severity of domain i,

α_j = difficulty of task j, and

τ_k = difficulty of rating category k relative to category k-1.

The rating category coefficient, τ_k, is not considered a facet in the model.

Based on the MFRM model presented in Eq. (1), the probability of examinee n being rated k on domain i for task j by rater m with a rating category coefficient of τ_k is given as

$$P_{nmijk} = exp[k(\theta_n - \lambda_m - \delta_i - \alpha_j - \tau_k) - \sum_{h=1}^{k} \tau_k] / \gamma, \qquad (2)$$

where τ_1 is defined to be zero and γ is a normalizing factor based on the sum of the numerators. As written in Eq. (1), the category coefficients, τ_k, represent a Rating Scale model (Andrich, 1978) with category coefficients fixed across exercises. Analyses using the Partial Credit model (Masters, 1982) with the category coefficients allowed to vary across facets can be designated by various subscripts on τ_k. For example, τ_{ik} would indicate that raters used a different rating scale structure for each domain i, whereas τ_{mk} would indicate that each rater m used his or her own version of the rating scale.

The MFRM is a unidimensional model with a single examinee parameter (writing ability in this example) that represents the target or object of measurement and a collection of other facets such as domains, tasks, and raters. Tate (chap. 8, this volume) provides an excellent discussion of methods for examining dimensionality in our measures and the importance of determining whether an essentially unidimensional construct has been defined. These other facets can be viewed as providing a series of assessment opportunities that yield multiple ratings for each student. For example, if each examinee is rated by two raters on five domains, then there are 10 assessment opportunities that define 10 ratings. As with other Rasch measurement models, the basic requirements of the model are "that the set of people to be measured, and the set of tasks (facets) used to measure them, can each be uniquely ordered in terms respectively of their competence and difficulty" (Choppin, 1987, p. 111). If the data fit the model and this unique ordering related to invariant measurement is realized, then a variety of desirable measurement characteristics can be attained. Some of these measurement characteristics are (a) separability of parameters with sufficient statistics for estimating these parameters; (b) invariant estimates of examinee writing ability, rater severity, domain difficulty, and task difficulty; and (c) equal-interval scales for the measures. Another way to think about the MFRM model is to view it as a type of equating model with raters and other facets viewed as analogous to test forms that may vary in difficulty. If different raters or facets are used to rate the performances of different examinees, then it may be necessary to equate or statistically adjust for differences in rater severity or the difficulty of the domains/tasks/prompts.

Once the parameters of the model are estimated using standard numerical methods, such as those implemented in the FACETS computer program (Linacre & Wright, 1992), model–data fit issues can be examined in a variety of ways. To attain invariant measurement, the model must fit the data; lack of model–data fit indicates that the requirements of invariant measurement have not been met. Useful indexes of rating quality can be obtained by a detailed examination of the standardized residuals calculated as

$$Z_{nmij} = (x_{nmij} - E_{nmij}) / [\sum_{k=1}^{m} (k - E_{nmijk})^2 P_{nmijk}]^{1/2}, \qquad (3)$$

where

$$E_{nmij} = \sum_{k=1}^{m} k P_{nmijk}. \qquad (4)$$

Thus, x_{nmij} is the observed rating for examinee n from rater m on task i for domain j. The standardized residuals, Z_{nmij}, can be summarized over different facets and different elements within a facet to provide indexes of model–data fit. These residuals are typically summarized as mean square error statistics called OUTFIT and INFIT statistics. The OUTFIT statistics are unweighted mean squared residual statistics that are particularly sensitive to outlying unexpected ratings. The INFIT statistics are based on weighted mean squared residual statistics and are less sensitive to outlying unexpected ratings. The expected value of both of these fit statistics is 1.0 when the model fits the data. Mean square error statistics with values less than 1.0 indicate less variability in the ratings than expected, whereas values greater than 1.0 indicate more variability than expected. Wright and Masters (1982) provided a lucid description and illustration of INFIT and OUTFIT statistics. The substantive interpretation of these mean square error statistics varies depending on the facet. The exact sampling distribution of these fit statistics is not known, and there are no exact tests of statistical significance. Various rules of thumb have been proposed for interpreting these values that are useful in practice. In my work on writing assessment, I have found that mean square error statistics with values greater than 1.50 typically yield statistically significant residuals for some individual ratings, whereas mean square error values less than .60 typically identify holisitic ratings of some sort (e.g., a rater uses only 2s and 3s on a 6-point rating scale) or a lack of local independence in the ratings.

Another useful statistic is the *reliability of separation* index. This index provides information about how well the elements within a facet are separated to reliably define the facet. For the examinee facet, this index is analogous to traditional indexes of reliability, such as Cronbach's coefficient alpha and KR20, in the sense that it reflects an estimate of the ratio of true score to observed score variance. It can be calculated as

$$R = (SD^2 - MSE) / SD^2, \qquad (5)$$

where SD^2 is the observed variance of element difficulties for a facet on the latent variable scale in logits and MSE is the mean square calibration error estimated as the mean of the calibration error variances (squares of the standard errors) for each element within a facet. Andrich (1982) provided a detailed derivation of this reliability of separation index. An approximate chi-square statistic for judging the statistical significance of the differences between elements within a facet can also be calculated. This statistic is analogous to the homogeneity test statistic Q described by Hedges and Olkin (1985).

RATER ERRORS IN PERFORMANCE ASSESSMENTS

The four most commonly identified rater errors are severity/leniency, halo error, central tendency, and restriction of range (Saal, Downey, & Lahey, 1980). Each of these rater errors is briefly described in Table 11.1. There is a hodgepodge of operational definitions and statistical indicators of these rater errors that have been proposed for evaluating and monitoring raters to detect these four categories of response bias. The ad hoc and atheoretical nature of the work on rater errors has led some researchers to conclude that "rater error measures should be abandoned" (Murphy & Cleveland, 1995, p. 285). Specifically, Murphy and Cleveland argued that current rater error measures are not useful criteria for evaluating performance ratings because (a) the unit of analysis is defined incorrectly, and (b) the distribution assumptions regarding examinees or ratees are frequently not met or are unreasonable. Both of these concerns are accurate and reflect the fact that current indexes of rater errors are based on classical test theory (CTT), and CTT typically defines the unit of analysis in terms of groups rather than individual raters. CTT also yields sample dependent results that are not invariant across examinees and depend on various distributional assumptions that may or may not be met with a particular group of examinees. These criticisms also apply to Generalizability Theory. Although Murphy and Cleveland (1995) are correct in their criticism of current rater error indexes, their call for the abandonment of rater error indexes in general is premature. The MFRM model provides a theoretically sound and conceptually clear way to define a family of rater errors (Engelhard, 1994b). It provides a focus on the individual rater as the unit of analysis, as well as issues of response biases across groups of raters. It also provides the opportunity to achieve invariant measurement that does not depend on the distributional vagaries of the particular sample of examinees used to calibrate the assessment system.

Table 11.1 defines the commonly examined rater errors: rater severity/leniency, halo error, response set/central tendency, and restriction of range. In addition to these, traditional concerns regarding rater bias, interaction effects, and differential facet functioning have been added to this

TABLE 11.1
Description of Rater Errors by Unit
of Analysis and Underlying Questions

	Unit of Analysis	
Definitions	Individual	Group
Rater Severity/Leniency: The tendency on the part of raters to consistently provide ratings that are higher or lower than warranted by examinee performances.	How severe is each rater? Where is the rater calibrated on the variable map?	Are the differences in rater severity significant? Can the raters be considered invariant and exchangeable?
Halo error: Rater fails to distinguish between conceptually distinct and independent aspects of examinee performances.	Is the rater distinguishing between conceptually distinct and independent domains?	Are the raters distinguishing between the domains?
Response sets (e.g., central tendency): Rater interprets and uses rating scale categories in an idiosyncratic fashion. Rater over uses middle categories of rating scale when not warranted by examinee performance.	Is the rater using the structure of the rating scale as intended?	Are the raters using the rating scales as intended?
Restriction of range: Ratings do not discriminate between examinees on the latent variable.	How well did each rater discriminate among the different examinees?	Did the assessment system lead to the identification of meaningful individual differences?
Interaction effects: Facets in the measurement model are not additive.	Is the rater interpreting and using the other facets in the model as designed?	Are the facets invariant across raters?
Differential facet functioning (DFF): Ratings are a function of construct-irrelevant components.	Are the ratings of each rater invariant over construct-irrelevant components?	Are the raters invariant over construct-irrelevant components for the overall assessment system?

list. The underlying questions for individual raters and the rater group are also presented in Table 11.1. Detailed descriptions that flow from the commonly examined rater errors to MFRM indexes are given in Engelhard (1994b). This chapter does not repeat those descriptions, but starts from the MFRM indexes and highlights the underlying questions addressed by each of these indexes. The MFRM indexes represent a model-based approach that subsumes the traditional concerns regarding rater bias, explores additional questions regarding response bias not traditionally considered, and adds to the methodological tool box of the researcher.

To provide a clear description of the MFRM indexes of rating quality that can be used to monitor raters in performance assessments, the statistical indexes and graphical displays used to evaluate model–data fit are described in detail in this section. Because the substantive interpretations of these indexes vary by facet (examinee, rater, domain, and task), separate tables highlighting the questions addressed are presented. Where appropriate, the rater errors as traditionally construed are highlighted. There are additional MFRM indexes that might be included (e.g., separation ratios for each facet). However, this chapter focuses on those indexes that have been primarily used in previous research and appear to hold the most promise for monitoring raters.

Rater Facet

Table 11.2 presents 10 indexes and displays that provide evidence regarding the quality of ratings for the rater facet. Rater severity error can be detected by calibrating the raters and estimating the precision (standard error) of these estimates. The location of the raters on the variable map can be used to graphically display the differences between the raters. Figure 11.3 presents the variable map for 15 raters using five domains (style, mechanics, content/organization, usage, sentence formation) from a statewide assessment of writing (Engelhard, 1994b); the scale on the left-hand side of the figure is in logits. Comparable information is presented in Table 11.3. VC stands for the validity committee (set of expert raters) that rates all of the essays and was used to anchor the assessment system. The raters range in severity from Rater 87, who is lenient (R87 = -1.22 logits), to Rater 118, who is severe (R118 = 1.12 logits). The overall differences among raters can also be summarized as a reliability of rater separation index and the chi-square statistic to estimate statistical significance. The overall differences between raters shown in Fig. 11.3 are statistically significant [$\chi^2(15) = 170.7$, $p < .01$], with a high reliability of separation index ($R = .87$). The reliability of separation index provides overall information regarding variability in raters and can be used as an omnibus descriptive index for rater effects at the group level. Using the standard errors (SE), an approximate t test can be calculated to compare the severities of two raters. For example, the differences between Raters 87 and 118 has a t value of 5.71. Values greater than $+2.00$ or less than -2.00 can be considered statistically significant. If multiple comparisons of raters are conducted, then a method (e.g., the Bonferroni method) should be used to control the Type I error rate.

TABLE 11.2
Statistical Indexes and Graphical Displays
of Rating Quality for Rater Facet

Indexes and Displays	Questions
Calibration of elements within facet	How severe is each rater?
Standard errors for each element	How precisely has each rater been calibrated?
Variable map (display of calibrated elements for each facet)	Where are the raters located on the latent variable or construct being measured?
Reliability of separation	How spread out are the rater severities? Can the raters be considered exchangeable?
Chi-square statistic	Are the differences between the raters statistically significant?
Mean square error (OUTFIT/INFIT)	How consistently has each rater interpreted the domains and categories across examinees?
Standardized residuals	How different is each observed rating from its expected value?
Quality control charts and tables (displays of standardized residuals)	Which individual ratings appear to be higher or lower than expected based on the model?
Interaction effects	Are there significant interaction effects between raters and other facets?
Differential facet functioning (bias analyses)	Are the rater severities invariant across subgroups?

Table 11.3 also includes a summary of the standardized residuals for each rater in terms of the mean square fit statistics (INFIT MS and OUT-FIT MS). There are two raters (R20 and R75) with OUTFIT values less than .6 and one rater (R59) with an OUTFIT value greater than 1.5. Raters with low mean square fit statistics have muted ratings that suggest a halo error. These raters tend to rate holistically rather than differentiating between the examinees on the domains. Rater 20 had rated 47.0% of the examinees with uniform rating patterns (e.g., 22222 or 33333), whereas Rater 75 had rated 66.7% with uniform ratings. Rater 59 had a noisy rating pattern with many unexpectedly high and low ratings based on the model.

Information regarding noisy rating patterns can be presented with quality control tables or charts. The observed ratings with standardized residuals less than −2.00 and greater than +2.00 should be flagged for further examination. Rater 59 rated 75 examinees. To save space, only six examinees are included in the quality control table and chart. The quality control table is presented in Table 11.4, and the quality control information is presented in Fig. 11.4. Table 11.4 provides a detailed summary of

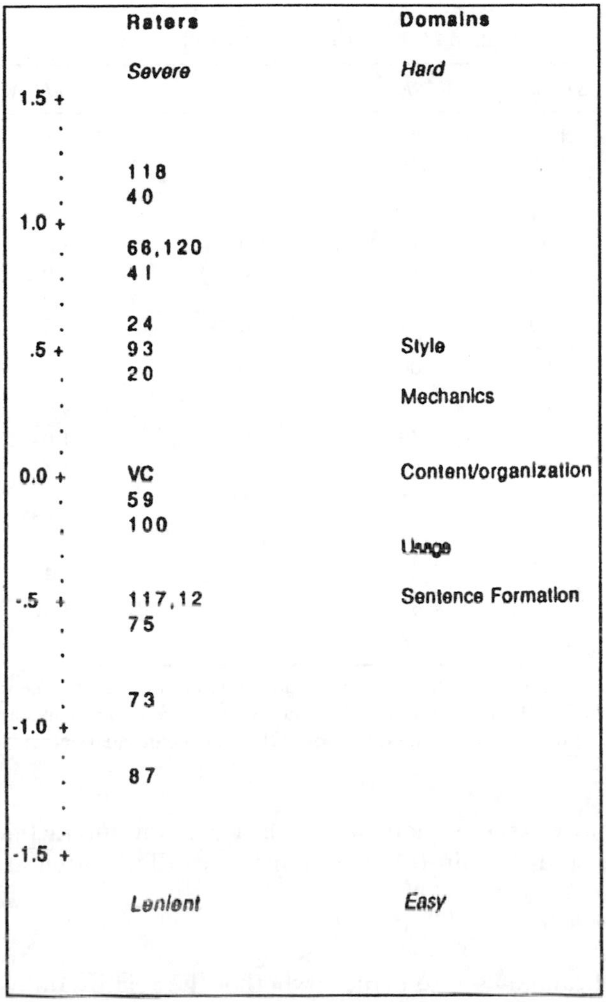

```
                 Raters              Domains

                 Severe              Hard
        1.5 +
            .
            .
            .       1 1 8
            .       4 0
        1.0 +
            .       66,120
            .       4 I
            .
            .       2 4
         .5 +       9 3                Style
            .       2 0
            .                          Mechanics
            .
            .
            .
        0.0 +       VC                 Content/organization
            .       5 9
            .       1 0 0
            .                          Usage
            .
        -.5 +       117,12             Sentence Formation
            .       7 5
            .
            .
            .
            .       7 3
       -1.0 +
            .
            .       8 7
            .
            .
       -1.5 +

                 Lenient             Easy
```

FIG. 11.3.   Variable map for calibration of raters and domains (Engelhard, 1994b, p. 103).

the ratings obtained from Rater 59 for six examinees. For example, index row 2 indicates that Rater 59 rated Examinee 170 lower than expected ($Z = -2.77$) on Domain 2; the expected rating was 2.38 while the observed rating was 1. This information regarding rating quality for Rater 59 is presented graphically in Fig. 11.4.

Although interaction effects can be detected by analyzing the standardized residuals, it is also useful for monitoring raters to consider interaction effects explicitly. For example, the model for a three-facet assessment sys-

TABLE 11.3
Calibration of Rater Facet (Engelhard, 1994b, p. 102)

Rater	Severity	SE	INFIT MS	OUTFIT MS	N
118	1.12	.33	.8	.8	8
40	1.06	.19	.9	.8	27
66	.91	.28	.9	.9	13
120	.91	.21	.9	.8	25
41	.83	.16	1.0	1.0	38
24	.60	.31	1.0	1.0	9
93	.53	.29	.9	1.0	11
20	.40	.24	.6	.5*	17
VC	.00	.06	1.0	1.0	254
59	−.06	.25	2.1	2.2*	15
100	−.15	.39	1.0	1.0	6
117	−.46	.34	1.2	1.2	8
12	−.53	.27	1.1	1.1	12
75	−.65	.22	.6	.5*	19
73	−.95	.19	1.2	1.3	28
87	−1.22	.24	1.4	1.4	18
M	.15	.25	1.0	1.0	
SD	.73	.08	.3	.4	

Note. N is the number of student compositions rated by each rater. The validity committee (VC) rated all of the compositions. Ten students had maximum scores and were not included. Asterisks indicate misfitting raters with OUTFIT mean square errors less than .6 and greater than 1.5.

tem (examinees, raters, domains) with a two-way interaction effect between rater and domain (rater × domain) can be written as:

$$Ln[P_{nijk} / P_{nijk-1}] = \theta_n - \lambda_m - \delta_i - \lambda_m \delta_i - \tau_k.$$

This model can be used to explore whether the relative difficulties of the domains are invariant over raters—in other words, are the raters using and interpreting the domains in a consistent and comparable fashion? The FACETS computer program (Linacre & Wright, 1992) can be used to calculate these interaction effects.

Differential facet functioning is numerically equivalent to looking at interaction effects, but is listed separately to highlight the fact that the interactions being explored are potential construct-irrelevant components related to examinee characteristics and assessment system characteristics. For example, the model for a two-facet assessment system (examinees, raters) with a third facet (e.g., gender) added to explore DFF can be written as:

$$Ln[P_{nijk} / P_{nijk-1}] = \theta_n - \lambda_m - \gamma_i - \lambda_m \gamma_i - \tau_k.$$

TABLE 11.4
Quality Control Table for Rater 59
(INFIT MS = 2.1, OUTFIT MS = 2.2)

Index	Examinee	Rater	Domain	Observed Rating	Expected Rating	Standardized Residual (Z)
1	170	59	1	2	2.59	−1.16
2	170	59	2	1	2.38	−2.77
3	170	59	3	4	2.64	2.69
4	170	59	4	4	2.49	2.92
5	170	59	5	3	2.43	1.12
6	577	59	1	2	2.38	−.75
7	577	59	2	2	2.20	−.47
8	577	59	3	2	2.43	−.84
9	577	59	4	2	2.29	−.62
10	577	59	5	3	2.24	1.70
11	619	59	1	2	1.95	.14
12	619	59	2	3	1.84	2.85
13	619	59	3	1	1.97	−2.86
14	619	59	4	2	1.90	.26
15	619	59	5	1	1.87	−2.22
16	920	59	1	3	1.86	2.89
17	920	59	2	3	1.72	2.75
18	920	59	3	2	1.89	.29
19	920	59	4	1	1.80	−1.88
20	920	59	5	1	1.75	−1.67
21	930	59	1	4	3.06	2.20
22	930	59	2	4	2.92	2.51
23	930	59	3	4	3.10	2.08
24	930	59	4	2	3.00	2.38
25	930	59	5	3	2.95	.11
26	975	59	1	3	3.06	−.15
27	975	59	2	4	2.92	2.51
28	975	59	3	2	3.10	−2.53
29	975	59	4	3	3.00	.01
30	975	59	5	4	2.95	2.47

1 = Content/organization, 2 = Style, 3 = Sentence formation, 4 = Usage, 5 = Mechanics.

In this case, the focus is on whether the gender facet, γ_i, interacts with the rater facet, λ_m. If there are significant interaction effects, $\lambda_m \gamma_i$, then this would serve as evidence that the severity of the raters was not invariant over gender groups. In other words, some raters are rating either girls or boys more harshly than justified by their performances. As another example, rater drift (potential construct irrelevant component related to characteristics of the assessment system) can be modeled similarly:

$$Ln[P_{nijk} / P_{nijk-1}] = \theta_n - \lambda_m - \varepsilon_i - \lambda_m \varepsilon_i - \tau_k,$$

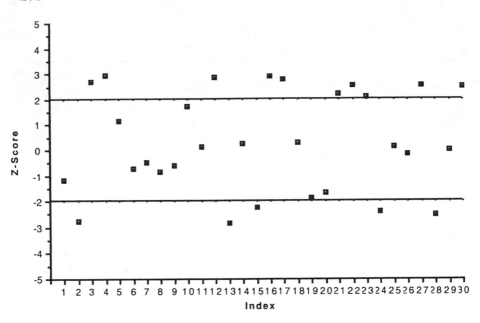

FIG. 11.4.   Quality Control Chart for Rater 59 (INFIT MS = 2.1, OUTFIT MS = 2.2).

where ε_i represents time and the interaction term, $\lambda_m\varepsilon_i$, examines the question of whether rater severity is invariant over time.

Domain Facet

Turning now to the domain facet, the same set of statistical indexes and graphical displays used to examine the rater facet can also be used to evaluate the functioning of the domains. Domains are referred to as analytic traits in some writing assessment programs (Oregon Department of Education, 1998). Table 11.5 presents the domain-specific interpretations and questions of the MFRM indexes. Similar information is provided by the MFRM indexes for both domains and raters, although the substantive questions being addressed by the indexes and displays vary somewhat for the domain facet. It should be stressed here that the domain difficulties and other domain-based indexes also provide information regarding how the raters are interpreting and using the rater-mediated assessment system. Domain difficulty is defined by the judgments and interpretations of the raters. The calibration of the domains is shown graphically in Fig. 11.3, and summary statistics are presented in Table 11.6 (Engelhard, 1994b). The difficulties of the domains range from –.51 logits (SE = .10) for sentence formation to .48 (SE = .10) for style. The overall differences

TABLE 11.5
Statistical Indexes and Graphical Displays
of Rating Quality for Domain Facet

Indexes and Displays	Questions
Calibration of elements within facet	How difficult is each domain?
Standard errors for each element	How precisely has each domain been calibrated?
Variable map (display of calibrated elements for each facet)	Where are the domains located on the latent variable or construct being measured?
Reliability of separation	How spread out are the domain difficulties?
	Are the raters distinguishing between domains?
Chi-square statistic	Are the differences between the domains statistically significant?
Mean square error (OUTFIT/INFIT)	How consistently has each domain been interpreted and used by the raters?
Standardized residuals	How different is each observed rating from its expected value?
Quality control charts and tables (displays of standardized residuals)	Which individual ratings appear to be higher or lower than expected based on the model?
Interaction effects	Are there significant interaction effects between domains and other facets?
Differential facet functioning (bias analyses)	Are the domain difficulties invariant across subgroups?

TABLE 11.6
Calibration of Domain Facet (Engelhard, 1994b, p. 105)

Domain	DIFF	SE	INFIT MS	OUTFIT MS	Domain Label
2	.48	.10	1.1	1.2	Style (S)
5	.30	.10	1.0	1.0	Mechanics (M)
4	.05	.10	.8	.8	Content/organization (C/O)
1	−.32	.10	1.1	1.2	Usage (U)
3	−.51	.10	.9	.9	Sentence formation (SF)
M	.00	.10	1.0	1.0	
SD	.37	.00	.1	.1	

Note. DIFF is the difficulty of the domain.

between the domains are statistically significant [$\chi^2(4) = 71.9$, $p < .01$], with a high reliability of separation index ($R = .93$). This provides support for the inference that the raters are adequately distinguishing between the domains as intended by the test developers. Based on the OUTFIT and INFIT mean square statistics, there is no evidence that the raters are using the domains in an inconsistent fashion; all of the mean square statistics are between .8 and 1.2.

Task Facet

The interpretation of task facet is comparable to that of the domain facet except that, in some contexts, task variability may be considered a construct-irrelevant component when the intent of the test developers is to create comparable tasks or forms of an assessment. This occurs frequently in writing assessment when test developers try to create equivalent prompts. The specific questions addressed for the task facet are presented in Table 11.7.

The calibration of a set of writing tasks from Engelhard (1992) is presented in Table 11.8. Writing Task 77, in which students are asked to write

TABLE 11.7
Statistical Indexes and Graphical Displays
of Rating Quality for Task Facet

Indexes and Displays	Questions
Calibration of elements within facet	How difficult is each task?
Standard errors for each element	How precisely has each task been calibrated?
Variable map (display of calibrated elements for each facet)	Where are the tasks located on the latent variable or construct being measured?
Reliability of separation	How spread out are the task difficulties? Are the raters distinguishing between tasks?
Chi-square statistic	Are the differences between the tasks statistically significant?
Mean square error (OUTFIT/INFIT)	How consistently has each task been interpreted and used by the raters?
Standardized residuals	How different is each observed rating from its expected value?
Quality control charts and tables (displays of standardized residuals)	Which individual ratings appear to be higher or lower than expected based on the model?
Interaction effects	Are there significant interaction effects between tasks and other facets?
Differential facet functioning (bias analyses)	Are the task difficulties invariant across subgroups?

TABLE 11.8
Calibration of Writing Task Facet (Engelhard, 1992, p. 183)

Writing Task	Difficulty	SE	INFIT MS	OUTFIT MS	Theme Statement
77	.12	.06	1.0	1.0	All-expense-paid trip
76	.06	.06	1.1	1.1	Your future
81	.05	.06	1.0	1.0	Your greatest hope for the future
80	.03	06	1.0	1.0	Discovery or invention that makes life better
79	−.01	.06	1.0	1.0	Settle another planet
74	−.04	.06	.9	.9	Favorite holiday
78	−.04	.06	1.0	.9	Hero or heroine
75	−.16	.06	1.0	1.0	Experience that turned out better
M	.00	.06	1.00	1.00	
SD	.08	.00	.05	.06	

about an "all-expense-paid trip," is the most difficult to write about for these students, with a difficulty of .12 logits (SE = .06). Writing Task 75 ("experience that turned out better") is the easiest to write about for these students, with a difficulty of −.16 logits (SE = .06). There is no evidence of misfit based on the INFIT or OUTFIT statistics, with all of the fit mean squares between .9 and 1.1. Although the reliability of separation is small ($R = .46$), the analysis suggests that the overall differences between the writing tasks are statistically significant [$\chi^2(7) = 15.2, p = .03$]. The writing tasks were designed by the developers of the writing assessment program to be equivalent, and the small differences between the difficulties of the writing tasks tend to reflect this intention. As long as the examinees respond to all of the writing tasks, then differences in task difficulty will not influence the estimates of writing ability. However, if students are assigned different writing tasks or allowed to choose the task, then adjustments for variability in writing task difficulty are needed to produce task-invariant estimates of student writing ability.

Examinee Facet

The object of measurement is the examinee. The MFRM statistical indexes, displays, and questions for the examinee facet are presented in Table 11.9. Using data from Engelhard (1994b), the estimates of writing ability ($N = 254$) ranged from −7.12 to 7.60 logits ($M = 1.19$, $SD = 2.75$). The overall differences between the students were statistically significant [$\chi^2(252) = 3537.6, p < .01$], with a high reliability of separation index ($R = .93$). Thirty-five (13.8%) of the students had noisy rating patterns, whereas 31 (12.2%) students had muted rating patterns. Noisy rating patterns have

TABLE 11.9
Statistical Indexes and Graphical Displays of Rating Quality
for Examinee Facet (Object of Measurement)

Indexes and Displays	Questions
Calibration of elements within facet	How good is the examinee's performance?
Standard errors for each element	How precisely has each examinee been calibrated?
Variable map (display of calibrated elements for each facet)	Where are the examinees located on the latent variable or construct being measured?
Reliability of separation	How spread out are the examinee abilities?
Chi-square statistic	Are the differences between the examinees statistically significant?
Mean square error (OUTFIT/INFIT)	How consistently has examinee performance been interpreted by the raters?
Standardized residuals	How different is each observed rating from its expected value?
Quality control charts and tables (displays of standardized residuals)	Which individual ratings appear to be higher or lower than expected based on the model?
Interaction effects	Are there significant interaction effects between examinees and other facets?
Differential facet functioning (bias analyses)	Are the examinee abilities invariant across raters?

a high number of unexpected ratings, whereas muted rating patterns tend to exhibit uniform ratings. Both of these patterns may reflect idiosyncratic ratings or response sets, such as central tendency. Table 11.10 provides quality control tables for two students (Examinees 700 and 56). Examinee 700 has a noisy rating pattern (INFIT = 2.5, OUTFIT = 2.6). This student received unexpectedly low ratings in mechanics from both Rater 87 and the validity committee (VC); this student also received an unexpectedly high rating on style from the validity committee. Examinee 56 has a muted rating pattern (INFIT = .1, OUTFIT = .1). Examinee 56 receive ratings of 3 on all of the domains from Rater 118 and the validity committee. The essays of both these students should be flagged and examined to determine whether there are any reasons to rescore these essays. Quality control charts can be created for examinees that mirror Fig. 11.4.

To illustrate the impact of rater errors on examinee scores, the biasing effects of not adjusting for rater severity are illustrated in Table 11.11. Examinees 613 and 459 have equal raw scores of 33. Examinee 613 was rated by a hard rater (R118 = 1.12 logits), whereas Examinee 459 was rated by an easy rater (R87 = -1.22). Although the examinees have the same raw score, if the differences in rater severity are taken into account, then the writing ability of Examinee 613 is underestimated by 1.17 logits

TABLE 11.10
Ratings for Select Students With Unexpected Rating Patterns

Index	Examinee	Rater	Domain	Observed Rating	Expected Rating	Standardized Residual (Z)
1	700	VC	1	4	3.22	1.65
2	700	VC	2	4	3.06	2.20
3	700	VC	3	3	3.27	−.55
4	700	VC	4	3	3.14	−.32
5	700	VC	5	2	3.10	−2.53
6	700	87	1	4	3.53	.93
7	700	87	2	4	3.32	1.37
8	700	87	3	4	3.57	.85
9	700	87	4	3	3.43	−.84
10	700	87	5	2	3.37	2.71

Raw Score: 33
INFIT MS: 2.5
OUTFIT MS: 2.6
Writing Ability: 3.41

11	56	VC	1	3	3.16	−.36
12	56	VC	2	3	3.01	−.03
13	56	VC	3	3	3.20	−.44
14	56	VC	4	3	3.09	.21
15	56	VC	5	3	3.05	−.11
16	56	118	1	3	2.96	.10
17	56	118	2	3	2.80	.43
18	56	118	3	3	2.99	.02
19	56	118	4	3	2.89	.26
20	56	118	5	3	2.84	.36

Raw Score: 30
INFIT MS: .1
OUTFIT MS: .1
Writing Ability: 3.13

1 = Content/organization, 2 = Style, 3 = Sentence formation, 4 = Usage, 5 = Mechanics.

as compared with Examinee 459. In other words, these examinees would be estimated to have the same writing ability on the raw score scale, but the MFRM scale (logits) provides a correction and statistical adjustment for rater severity that suggests that Examinee 613 is a significantly better writer than Examinee 459. It should be stressed here that these rater adjustments are only justified when there is good model–data fit. If the raters are rating inconsistently, then the estimates of examinee ability are not invariant over raters and adjustments for rater severity are inappropriate.

One of the persistent problems in evaluating ratings is deciding what criteria to use for examining the structure and functioning of the rating scale. It is beyond the scope of this chapter to address these issues, however. For readers wishing to further explore rating-scale category calibra-

TABLE 11.11
Ratings for Two Students With the Same Raw Score
and Consistent Rating Patterns

Index	Examinee	Rater	Domain	Observed Rating	Expected Rating	Standardized Residual (Z)
1	613	VC	1	3	3.52	−1.01
2	613	VC	2	3	3.31	−.63
3	613	VC	3	3	3.56	−1.12
4	613	VC	4	4	3.42	1.14
5	613	VC	5	3	3.35	−.70
6	613	118	1	3	3.23	−.49
7	613	118	2	3	3.07	−.17
8	613	118	3	4	3.28	1.49
9	613	118	4	4	3.15	1.88
10	613	118	5	3	3.10	−.24

Raw Score: 33
INFIT MS: 1.1
OUTFIT MS: 1.1
Writing Ability: 4.58

Index	Examinee	Rater	Domain	Observed Rating	Expected Rating	Standardized Residual (Z)
11	459	VC	1	4	3.22	1.65
12	459	VC	2	3	3.06	−.15
13	459	VC	3	3	3.27	−.55
14	459	VC	4	3	3.14	−.32
15	459	VC	5	3	3.10	−.22
16	459	87	1	4	3.53	.93
17	459	87	2	3	3.32	−.64
18	459	87	3	3	3.57	−1.15
19	459	87	4	4	3.43	1.12
20	459	87	5	3	3.37	−.72

Raw Score: 33
INFIT MS: .8
OUTFIT MS: .8
Writing Ability: 3.41

1 = Content/organization, 2 = Style, 3 = Sentence formation, 4 = Usage, 5 = Mechanics.

tions, two excellent sources are available: Linacre (1999) and Andrich (1996).

SUMMARY

This chapter describes a set of procedures based on the MFRM model (Linacre, 1989) that can be used to evaluate and monitor raters within the context of large-scale performance assessments. The MFRM model represents a model-based approach to assessment that meets the requirements of invariant measurement (Engelhard, 1994a) and reflects the new rules of measurement (Embretson, 1996; Embretson & Hershberger, 1999). It is essential that rater-mediated assessments move from ad hoc procedures to model-based indexes of rating quality. The indexes of rater errors described in this chapter are based on the theoretical requirements of invariant measurement and the application of Rasch measurement theory to detect whether invariant measurement has been realized.

Some of the major advantages of MFRM model described in this chapter are as follows:

- The MFRM model is a scaling model that employs a logistic transformation to convert qualitative ratings into linear measures. The observed ratings are on an ordinal scale, whereas the estimates of examinee ability on the construct are on a linear scale. If the degree of model–data fit is high, then the ability measures have equal-interval properties.

- The MFRM model provides an explicit and model-based approach for examining multiple facets encountered in performance assessment systems. A sound theoretical framework is provided for adjusting for differences in rater severity. If the degree of model–data fit is high, then invariant estimates of examinee ability can be obtained across different subsets of raters. Statistical adjustments for rater severity can only be justified when model–data fit is good. These invariant estimates improve the objectivity and fairness of the overall assessment system.

- When model–data fit is good, then invariant calibration of the rater-mediated assessment and rater-invariant measurement is possible. Various statistical indexes and graphical displays are available based on the MFRM to explore sources of misfit and identify potential problems.

The MFRM model offers a viable means to address a host of rater biases that may be encountered in rater-mediated performance assessments. To develop clear and unambiguous measures of variables, such as writing ability, based on rater-mediated assessments, it is essential that the various facets of the model be invariant across raters and other construct-irrelevant components. Of course, it is important to remember that there will be limitations to our efforts: "Raters are human and they are therefore subject to all the errors to which humankind must plead guilty" (Guilford, 1936, p. 272). The approach for identifying, evaluating, and monitoring rater errors based on the MFRM model can decrease some response biases, but it is unlikely that any assessment system can completely eliminate response biases simply because raters are human.

REFERENCES

American Educational Research Association, American Psychological Association, & National Council on Measurement in Education. (1999). *Standards for educational and psychological testing*. Washington, DC: American Educational Research Association.

Andrich, D. (1978). A rating formulation for ordered response categories. *Psychometrika, 43*, 561–573.

Andrich, D. (1982). An index of person separation in latent trait theory, the traditional KR. 20 indes and the Guttman scale response pattern. *Education Research and Perspectives, 9*, 95–104.

Andrich, D. (1988). *Rasch models for measurement*. Newbury Park, CA: Sage.

Andrich, D. (1996). Measurement criteria for choosing among models with graded responses. In A. von Eye & C. C. Clogg (Eds.), *Categorical variables in developmental research: Methods of analysis* (pp. 3–35). San Diego: Academic Press.

Campbell, N. R. (1920). *Physics: The elements*. London: Cambridge University Press.

Choppin, B. (1987). The Rasch model for item analysis. In D. I. McArthur (Ed.), *Alternative approaches to the assessment of achievement* (pp. 99–127). Norwell, MA: Kluwer.

Cronbach, L. J. (1995). Giving method variance its due. In P. E. Shrout & S. T. Fiske (Eds.), *Personality research, methods, and theory: A Festschrift in honor of Donald Fiske* (pp. 145–157). Hillsdale, NJ: Lawrence Erlbaum Associates.

Embretson, S. E. (1996). The new rules of measurement. *Psychological Assessment, 8*(4), 341–349.

Embretson, S. E., & Hershberger, S. L. (Eds.). (1999). *The new rules of measurement: What every psychologist and educator should know*. Mahwah, NJ: Lawrence Erlbaum Associates.

Engelhard, G. (1984). Thorndike, Thurstone, and Rasch: A comparison of their methods of scaling psychological tests. *Applied Psychological Measurement, 8*, 21–38.

Engelhard, G. (1991). Thorndike, Thurstone, and Rasch: A comparison of their approaches to item-invariant measurement. *Journal of Research and Development in Education, 24*(2), 45–60.

Engelhard, G. (1992). The measurement of writing competence with a many-faceted Rasch model. *Applied Measurement in Education, 5*(3), 171–191.

Engelhard, G. (1994a). Historical views of the concept of invariance in measurement theory. In M. Wilson (Ed.), *Objective measurement: Theory into practice* (Vol. 2, pp. 73–99). Norwood, NJ: Ablex.

Engelhard, G. (1994b). Examining rater errors in the assessment of written composition with a many-faceted Rasch model. *Journal of Educational Measurement, 31*(2), 93–112.

Engelhard, G. (1997). Constructing rater and task banks for performance assessments. *Journal of Outcome Measurement, 1*(1), 19–33.

Fisher, W. P., & Wright, B. D. (Eds.). (1994). Applications of probabilistic conjoint measurement [Special Issue]. *International Journal of Educational Research, 21*, 557–664.

Guilford, J. P. (1936). *Psychometric methods*. New York: McGraw-Hill.

Gyagenda, I. S., & Engelhard, G. (1999, April). *Using classical and modern measurement theories to explore rater, domain, and gender influences on student writing ability*. Paper presented at the annual meeting of the American Educational Research Association, Montreal, Canada.

Hattie, J., Jaeger, R. M., & Bond, L. (1999). Persistent methodological questions in educational testing. *Review of Research in Education, 24*, 393–446.

Hedges, L. V., & Olkin, I. (1985). *Statistical methods for meta-analysis*. San Diego, CA: Academic Press.

Hollenbeck, K., Tindal, G., & Almond, P. (1999). Reliability and decision consistency: An analysis of writing mode at two times on a statewide test. *Educational Assessment, 6*(1), 23–40.

Hoyt, W. T. (2000). Rater bias in psychological research: When is it a problem and what can we do about it? *Psychological Methods, 5*(1), 64–86.

Hoyt, W. T., & Kerns, M. D. (1999). Magnitude and moderators of bias in observer ratings: A meta-analysis. *Psychological Methods, 4*(4), 403–424.

Linacre, J. M. (1989). *Many-facet Rasch measurement.* Chicago: MESA Press.

Linacre, J. M (1999). Investigating rating scale category utility. *Journal of Outcome Measurement, 3*(2), 103–122.

Linacre, J. M., & Wright, B. D. (1992). *A user's guide to FACETS: Rasch measurement computer program.* Chicago: MESA Press.

Linacre, J. M , Engelhard, G., Tatum, D. S., & Myford, C. M. (1994). Measurement with judges: Many-faceted conjoint measurement. *International Journal of Educational Research, 21*(6), 569–577.

Luce, R. D., & Tukey, J. W. (1964). Simultaneous conjoint measurement: A new type of fundamental measurement. *Journal of Mathematical Psychology, 1*, 1–27.

Masters, G. N. (1982). A Rasch model for partial credit scoring. *Psychometrika, 47*, 149–174.

Michell, J. (1999). *Measurement in psychology: Critical history of a methodological concept.* Cambridge: Cambridge University Press.

Murphy, K. R., & Cleveland, J. N. (1995). *Understanding performance appraisal: Social, organizational, and goal-based perspectives.* Thousands Oaks, CA: Sage.

Oregon Department of Education. (1998). *Oregon statewide writing assessment: Results, analysis, sample student writings, 1993–1997, Grades 8, 10, 11.* Salem, Oregon: Author.

Perline, R., Wright, B. D., & Wainer, H. (1979). The Rasch model as additive conjoint measurement. *Applied Psychological Measurement, 3*, 237–255.

Rasch, G. (1980). *Probabilistic models for some intelligence and attainment tests.* Chicago: University of Chicago Press.

Saal, F. E., Downey, R. G., & Lahey, M. A. (1980). Rating the ratings: Assessing the psychometric quality rating data. *Psychological Bulletin, 88*(2), 413–428.

Wilson, M., & Case, H. (2000). An examination of variation in rater severity over time: A study in rater drift. In M. Wilson & G. Engelhard (Eds.), *Objective measurement: Theory into practice* (Vol. 5, pp. 113–133). Stamford, CT: Ablex.

Wright, B. D. (1999). Fundamental measurement for psychology. In S. E. Embretson & S. L. Hershberger (Eds.), *The new rules of measurements: What every psychologist and educator should know* (pp. 65–104). Mahwah, NJ: Lawrence Erlbaum Associates.

Wright, B. D. (1968). Sample-free test calibration and person measurement. *Proceedings of the 1967 invitational conference on testing problems.* Princeton, NJ: Educational Testing Service.

Wright, B D (1997). A history of social science measurement. *Educational Measurement: Issues and Practice, 16*(4), 33–45, 52.

Wright, B. D., & Masters, G. N. (1982). *Rating scale analysis: Rasch measurement.* Chicago: MESA Press.

Chapter 12

Issues, Strategies, and Procedures for Applying Standards When Multiple Measures Are Employed

Joseph M. Ryan
Arizona State University West

The evaluation of student knowledge and ability employing a variety of assessment procedures has been advocated in measurement theory and ignored in measurement practice for decades. Traditional belief about the value of using multiple measurements is reflected in a chapter by Mehrens (1990) on combining evaluation data from multiple sources when making decisions about teachers. Mehrens wrote, "In general, the more data that are gathered, the better the decision is likely to be. Certainly it is conventional psychometric wisdom that one should use more than one piece of data as the basis for important decisions" (p. 332).

Current interest in the use of multiple measures derives from several sources, including a continuing commitment to the conventional wisdom that multiple measures will be superior to any single measure. Current technology has also been an important force in raising interest. Collecting, processing, and merging large volumes of data from multiple sources have become much more manageable tasks with the availability of high-speed and high-capacity computers and user-friendly and efficient computer programs.

Many policy initiatives have also placed emphasis on the use of multiple measures. Title I of the Improving America's School Act of 1994 generated considerable interest in this topic when regulations mandated the use of multiple measures and multiple approaches to assessment. Although it is beyond the scope of this chapter to review the entire array of Title I requirements, a listing of key elements germane to the broader discussion of multiple measures is provided next. These include the following:

- Challenging content standards for all students
- Challenging performance standards for all students
- Multiple high-quality assessment procedures
- Demonstrated adequate yearly progress toward proficiency
- Accountability for improvement in student learning

The Title I call for challenging content and performance standards has encouraged and supported the standards-based reform effort. The requirement of challenging content standards has encouraged many educators to broaden and elevate their expectations for what students should be expected to know and be able to do. These content and performance demands have shaped the scope and depth of the construct domain with which assessment systems should be carefully aligned.

The validity chapter of the *Standards for Educational and Psychological Testing* from the American Educational Research Association, American Psychological Association, and the National Council on Measurement in Education (1999) repeatedly emphasized that important decisions about people should be based on broader sources of information than test scores alone. In Part III, on Educational Testing and Assessment, Standard 13.7 states the following:

> In educational settings, a decision or characterization that will have a major impact on a student should not be made on the basis of a single test score. Other relevant information should be taken into account if it will enhance the overall validity of the decision. (p. 146)

The American Educational Research Association (1999) underscored this message in its *AERA Position Statement Concerning High-Stakes Testing in PreK–12 Education*. The very first assertion in this document read as follows:

> *Protection Against High-Stakes Decisions Based on a Single Test*
> Decisions that affect individual students' life chances or educational opportunities should not be made on the basis of test scores alone. Other relevant information should be taken into account to enhance the overall validity of such decisions.

PURPOSE OF THIS CHAPTER

The purpose of this chapter is to provide a resource for educational practitioners and researchers interested in using multiple measures in the application of content and performance standards. We first examine a set of validity issues related to the use of multiple measures as well as a set of technical issues that must be addressed when multiple measures are employed. This is followed by a description of three general strategies for applying standards with multiple measures and four procedures for combining multiple measures. Then two procedures for classifying students based on multiple measures are presented: discriminant analysis and the use of geometric distances. These procedures have been used in other contexts, but have not yet been explored extensively in the context of classifying students based on multiple achievement measures. They are well-established statistical approaches based on a strategy of identifying criterion groups, developing achievement profiles for those groups, and then matching students to the most similar criterion group.

The application of standards when multiple measures are employed often involves the use of cut scores that are separately set on individual assessment instruments or measures. Procedures for setting cut scores on individual tests are not described in this chapter. A comprehensive and valuable description of procedures for setting cut scores and many related issues is provided in Cizek (2001).

VALIDITY ISSUES RELATED TO THE USE OF MULTIPLE MEASURES

The use of multiple measures to assess students' status and learning progress leads to the consideration of a wide range of validity issues. These issues concern the increased validity multiple measures may afford, criteria for selecting individual measures, and criteria for evaluating procedures used to combine multiple measures.

Increased Validity With Multiple Measures

A major value of using multiple indicators to measure or classify students lies in the increased validity that multiple indicators might provide in making inferences about what students know and are able to do. The case for increased validity can be framed within the six aspects of validity described by Messick (1995a, 1995b). First, the use of multiple indicators increases the likelihood that the assessments will more fully and completely reflect the construct domain simply because more measures can cover more content. This occurs even in the most limited case, when multiple assessments employ the same format (e.g., selected response) to measure the same type of knowledge (e.g., declarative knowledge). Second, assessment formats can vary when multiple assessments are used, and the types of assessments employed can more fully reflect different aspects of the construct domain. Such assessments might include selected response, constructed response, works samples, and performance assessments. The use of different types of formats enables students to demonstrate their full range of ability—a demonstration that could be constrained if only a single assessment format is used. Different assessment formats provide an opportunity to assess relevant and representative aspects of the construct domain, not just the portion that might be revealed through a single type of assessment. Third, the use of constructed response assessments involves the use of appropriate scoring rubrics. According to Messick (1995a, 1995b), these rubrics improve validity when they are developed to reflect the task, domain structure, and structural relationships among components of the domain. Last, educators may have greater opportunities to broaden and shape the consequences of an assessment program when multiple measures are employed. For example, educators may be able to influence instructional methods by using constructed and performance assessments.

Criteria for Selecting Individual Measures

Anyone designing a program to employ multiple measures can choose from a wide assortment of measurement instruments and procedures and use them in various combinations. The choice of which measurement instruments or procedures to use is the single most important step in any assessment program. Three considerations can help guide the choice of instruments: (a) curricular breadth or scope, (b) curricular importance, and (c) reliability or generalizability of the assessment data obtained from the instruments.

Curricular breadth refers to the extent to which an instrument covers the construct domain. In general, a single instrument that assesses a broad range of the curriculum, including many content standards, may be more useful than an assessment that captures only a narrow portion of the curriculum. However, the importance of the content being assessed by a given instrument must also be considered. In language arts, for example, assessing students' writing ability based on a single sample of their work would give a limited view of only one aspect of language arts ability. However, a student's ability to write is so vital a part of the language arts curriculum that no language arts assessment would be complete without a writing assessment. Conversely, a lengthy multiple-choice test might cover a broad range of knowledge, but the type of knowledge covered might not be as important as knowledge assessed by a direct writing task.

Concerns about how well the curriculum is reflected in the assessments must be balanced by concerns about the reliability of the data collected with the instruments. Data from the assessment instruments are the basis for making inferences about students, such as whether they belong in an advanced, proficient, or novice group. Some of these inferences may have an important impact on the lives of individual students or identifiable groups of students. Therefore, it is essential that educators have evidence that assessments of students' abilities do not fluctuate as a function of the particular test form or writing prompt used. It seems difficult to justify the use of measurement instruments that yield inconsistent information about students' knowledge and skills even if the knowledge and skills involved are highly valued.

One approach to using multiple measures is to combine them in a composite score or measure. Combining multiple measures has a particular impact on the reliability of the combined assessment. If a composite is constructed from several measures, the reliability of the composite may be constrained by the least reliable assessment used to construct it. Nunnally (1967) described a procedure for estimating the reliability of a composite that should be applied and evaluated in any setting where a composite is to be used.

The selection of assessment instruments for use in multiple-measurement applications must be based on an evaluation of the individual measures. The evaluation must consider the validity and reliability of the individual assessments and any composite formed from them. Combining data from multiple measures of dubious validity and low reliability may mask their deficiencies, but will not improve the quality of the assessment.

Criteria to Evaluate Procedures Used to Combine Multiple Measures

Discussions of standard-setting procedures and studies that compare various procedures for setting standards (see Cizek, 2001, for a definitive review) acknowledge that such procedures cannot be evaluated in terms of their being more or less accurate in identifying the correct cut score. All standards are a matter of judgment, and there are no true or correct standards out there waiting to be discovered. In response to the absence of clear-cut criteria to assess decision rules, Plake (1995) provided a set of criteria to evaluate standard-setting methods studied in the context of the National Board of Professional Teaching Standards. These criteria are:

> . . . (a) ease of administration, (b) comfort in the final decision rule for determining pass/fail decisions by the panel of judges, (c) confidence in the final decision rule for determining pass/fail decisions by the panel of judges, (d) potential for replicability of the cutscore decision rule. . . . (p. 8)

There are no correct procedures for combining and using multiple measures. Procedures must be judged according to the degree of validity they possess for supporting the inferences that are based on their use. The following criteria are suggested for evaluating procedures used to combine multiple measures. Several of these criteria are similar to those suggested by Plake (1995) and are used both implicitly and explicitly in the following discussion of procedures used to combine data from multiple measures.

Validity—What evidence is there for content, correlational, impact, and consequential aspects of validity? (Messick, 1995a, 1995b)

Classification Reliability—Are students classified consistently with the same procedure and when different procedures are compared?

Feasibility—Can practitioners organize the data and apply the procedure(s)?

Interpretability—Can the procedure and its results be meaningfully explained to the various groups that need to use the information?

TECHNICAL ISSUES RELATED TO THE USE OF MULTIPLE MEASURES

Researchers and practitioners must address a common set of technical issues when combining data from multiple measures for the purpose of applying standards. Three such issues are discussed here. How each issue is best handled varies according to educational context, assessment purposes, and intended consequences.

Scaling and Standardizing Data

All assessment data begin as raw scores of some sort. These may be the number of items answered correctly on a multiple-choice test or the score point assigned to a position on a scoring rubric. Several decisions about scaling and standardizing these raw data occur in the process of combining data from multiple measures. Data from multiple-choice tests must be scaled and may be standardized according to some common derived scale if multiple forms of the test are to be employed. This is common practice with published standardized achievement tests and is also routine when item response theory (IRT) procedures are employed. Data must also be scaled and standardized if a compensatory procedure for combining it across different measures is used. The compensatory procedure is described shortly, but it is sufficient to recognize that compensatory procedures generally involve combining scores across assessment instruments.

Such combined scores or composites can be seriously distorted if the scales for the different measures are not comparable.

Scaling and standardizing data from constructed-response assessments raises an interesting dilemma. It may serve a useful and important technical purpose. However, scaling and standardizing rubric score points may make it difficult to see the connection between the assessment results and the content standard being assessed. Rubric score points are extremely useful because they represent assessment data that simultaneously reflect performance and content standards. A rubric score point of 1, for example, is both a score and a statement of what students should know and be able to do. The link between the assessment result and content and performance standards can be obscured or even lost if the assessment results are rescaled and standardized. This happens because the assessment results will then employ a number system (e.g., a scale score or IRT logit value) different from the numbers used to define the content-referenced rubric score points.

The restricted range of many constructed-response assessments may also create problems in scaling and standardization. The relatively small number of score points on many rubrics may result in score distributions that are severely skewed, rectangular, or multimodal. Such data can be scaled and standardized. The transformed data, however, are not necessarily altered into a form that makes it wise to combine them with other data, nor are they necessarily appropriate for the application of certain statistical procedures.

Weighting and Combining Data

Educators are often interested in differentially weighting data from various measures to reflect beliefs about curricular importance or instructional emphasis. After data are weighted, they are generally combined to form an index or composite score that reflects the data from the weighted measure more heavily. There are several issues related to the use of weighted composites (Nunnally, 1967). First, the reliability of the composite of any set of measures is a function of the reliabilities and variances of each measure and the relationships among them. If the measures are not well correlated, the reliability of the composite approaches the average reliability of the individual measures. This average reliability would be lower than that of the relatively more reliable measures. Yet if the measures are highly correlated, the reliability of the composite will generally be higher than the reliability of the most reliable individual measure. If the measures are correlated so highly that their composite is more reliable than any single measure, then they may be supplying redundant information obtained at the expense of time and resources.

Wang (1998) provided a different approach with an algorithm that assigns weights to each measure that maximizes the composite's reliability. This approach reflects attention to an important psychometric criterion, but it may not be responsive to curriculum considerations and issues of validity.

A second issue involved in the use of weighting and composites of multiple measures concerns the relationship between curriculum and assessment. The connection between content standards and student performance (scores) is often transparent when scoring rubrics are employed. In such instances, a score of 4, for example, has a definition carefully crafted in the language of the curriculum. With multiple-choice tests, items and students can be placed on the same scale with some IRT procedures, and students' performance can be described in terms of the probability of their correctly answering certain questions or types of questions. The connection between content standards and students' performance is much more difficult to discern when scores are expressed in terms of weighted composites. Students can obtain an identical composite score in many different ways, with different scores on each of the measures. It is extremely difficult to say what a weighted index score means in terms of what students know and are able to do. There are advantages to using composite scores or weighted composite scores, but these advantages need to be evaluated against the decrease or loss of standards-referenced interpretation of students' performance.

Relevant to procedures presented in this chapter, it is important to note that weighting various measures does not change the results of any procedure that is based on the correlation among the measures. This would include factor analysis, regression, and discriminant function analyses.

Setting Standards for Individual Assessment
Instruments or Composite Indexes

Many of the procedures used for combining data from multiple measures are applied to measures for which performance standards have already been set. Among the commonly used standard setting procedures are those of Angoff (1971), Jaeger (1982), and Nedelsky (1954), each of which has been applied with a large number of modifications. Plake (1998) provided a useful analysis of these procedures and others in the context of standard-setting methods used in licensure and certification of teachers. Plake's discussion of the issues is general and broadly applicable to a wide number of assessment settings. As previously mentioned, the edited book by Cizek (2001) provided a valuable comprehensive description of standard-setting procedures and many other important issues related to standard setting.

Performance standards can be set on individual assessments or composite indexes formed by combining individual assessments. Many procedures for setting standards on individual assessments cannot be applied to composite measures. Any standard-setting procedure that involves a review or judgment related to test questions or stimulus materials is inapplicable to composite scores. Thus, neither the Angoff (1971) nor Nedelsky (1954) methods can be applied to composite scores. These standard-setting methods are especially useful in connecting content standards to performance standards. The value of using composite scores must be evaluated against the prospect of minimizing the applicability of standard-setting procedures that enhance curricular interpretation.

A recurring theme raised in the preceding discussion of technical issues deals with the value of preserving the connection between content and performance standards. The general guideline suggested here sees considerable value in working with data that are as close to being in raw data form as possible. Data in this form can be more closely tied to test questions and rubric score points than scaled and standardized data. In general, the fewer transformations or reexpressions of the data, the clearer the connection between content and performance standards. The value of staying close to the raw data or a one-to-one rescaling of it assumes that test questions and rubrics appropriately reflect content standards.

STRATEGIES FOR COMBINING DATA FROM MULTIPLE MEASURES

There are three general strategies for applying standards when multiple measures are employed: disjunctive, conjunctive, and compensatory (Gulliksen, 1950; Haladyna & Hess, 1000; Mehrens, 1990). In the disjunctive and conjunctive approaches, performance standards are set separately on the individual assessments. In the compensatory procedure, performance standards are set on a composite or index that reflects a combination of measures.

Disjunctive Strategy

With a disjunctive strategy, students are classified as an overall *pass* if they pass any one of the measures by which they are assessed. This approach seems most appropriate when the measures involved are parallel forms or in some other way are believed to measure the same trait. The disjunctive approach is seldom used during a single testing period. Haladyna and Hess (1999) pointed out that the disjunctive approach is employed in assessment programs that allow students to retake a failed test or different form of it on subsequent occasions until they earn a pass. The application of a disjunctive strategy to multiple measures in settings where multiple classifications are used (e.g., novice, proficient, and advanced) results in students being classified into the highest category attained on any one of the measures employed.

Conjunctive Strategy

With conjunctive strategy, students are classified as a pass only if they pass each of the measures by which they are assessed. The use of the conjunctive approach seems most appropriate when the measures assess different constructs or aspects of the same construct, and each aspect of the construct is highly valued. Failing any one assessment yields an overall *fail* because the content standards measured by each assessment are considered essential to earning an overall pass. The application of a conjunctive strategy to settings in which multiple classification levels are used results in students being classified into the lowest category attained on any one measure employed.

Compensatory Strategy

With compensatory approach, students are classified as a *pass* or *fail* based on performance standards set in a combination of the separate measures employed. Data are combined in a compensatory approach by means of an additive algorithm that allows high scores on some measures to compensate for low scores on others. The use of the compensatory strategy seems appropriate when the composite of the separate measures has important substantive meaning not represented by measures taken separately.

A useful combination of the compensatory and conjunctive models can be employed. Such an approach sets minimal standards on each measure that are applied in a conjunctive fashion; they must yield a pass before a compensatory approach is applied and a final rating is determined. This combined conjunctive-compensatory approach sets minimum standards that are necessary on each measure but not sufficient for the measures taken together. This approach prevents very low levels of performance on one measure to be balanced by exceptional performance on other measures (Mehrens, 1990).

PROCEDURES FOR APPLYING STANDARDS WITH DATA FROM MULTIPLE MEASURES

Numerous procedures have been described for setting and applying standards when data from multiple measures are employed. These all involve judgments about the adequacy of performance for the set of measures taken collectively rather than separately.

Mapping Scores From Multiple Measures
Into Performance Levels

Carlson (1996) described a procedure that examines scores on two measures and maps student performance on the two measures collapsed into a
single overall performance level. In Carlson's example, students are assessed on a direct-writing assessment, scored 1 through 6, and a standardized multiple-choice test, with scores ranging from 0 to 65. Scores on the
multiple-choice test are arbitrarily broken into nine score groups. The
data are presented to judges in a two-way table that crosses the six levels
(score points) on the direct-writing assessment with the nine levels (score
groups) of the multiple-choice test. Judges examine each of the 54 cells in
the table and decide how to classify the performance of students in that
cell. Carlson uses the classification categories *Below Partially Proficient*,
Partially Proficient, Proficient, and *Advanced.* This approach allows judges to
decide how to balance performance on the two measures and is clearly
compensatory. Carlson points out that additional assessment components
would require more complex mapping strategies.

Carlson (1996) offered a variation on the approach just described by
suggesting a two-step process. First, performance levels are used to define
classification categories for each assessment instrument separately (e.g.,
Below Partially Proficient, Partially Proficient, Proficient, and *Advanced*). In
Carlson's example, a 4 × 4 table is constructed by crossing the performance levels of the two measures. In the second step, judges examine each
of the 16 cells in the table and decide which combinations of categorical
performance levels from the two measures should be mapped onto each of
the four overall performance categories.

Judgmental Policy Procedure

The study of standard-setting procedures conducted by the National
Board of Professional Teaching Standards (NBPTS) is carefully described
in a special issue of *Applied Measurement in Education* (Impara & Plake,
1995). This issue is informative throughout, but the work of Jaeger (1995)
may have particular application to the general problem of combining data
from multiple sources for the purpose of classifying students.

Jaeger (1995) described a judgmental policy-capturing procedure that
is applied in two stages in the NBPTS standard-setting process. In both
stages, judges were asked to give a single overall rating to a set of profiles
that reflect different levels of achievement on different indicators. In
Stage 1, judges rated five exercises and gave an overall rating of 1 through
5 (*poor* to *excellent*) on profiles that have ratings of 1 through 4 on each of
three dimensions of an exercise. The overall ratings were regressed onto

the dimension point values to generate the best overall prediction of a total score. In Stage 2, judges rated a profile of performance across five different exercises. The dependent variable was the 4-point scale ranging from *Novice* to *Highly Accomplished*. Each judge responded to 200 profiles of five exercises which they were asked to rate independently. Again, the overall or summative rating served as the dependent variable, and the score points on the five exercises that defined the profile served as the five independent variables. The resulting regression equation gave a predicted total score that reflects a combination of the five different exercises via their regression coefficients. It is important to note that the criterion measure in this approach is the global judgment assigned to each profile by the panelist, and that correlations or collinearity among the measures would be detected in the regression analyses.

An IRT Scaling Procedure

Engelhard and Gordon (2000) described a procedure for setting and evaluating performance standards for writing assessments. Their work is not directly applied to multiple measures in the typical sense, but it generalizes directly and may be very valuable. Their procedure is applied to a writing performance assessment scored on four domains of effective writing using a 4-point rating scale for each domain. In the generalization of this procedure, the four domain scores can be viewed as if they were separate measures. Scores from each domain are added together to form a composite. The composite reflects a compensatory strategy because a score of 10, for example, could be obtained from a variety of scores on each of the four domains.

The authors constructed packets of compositions such that each packet had the same total score while the profile of domain scores for each composition in the packet varied. Standard-setting judges were given careful directions and essentially were asked to classify each packet as *pass* or *fail*. *Pass* and *fail* were defined in terms of whether the packet reflected writing that merited a high school diploma. The Rasch (1980) measurement model was used to analyze the data and calibrate the judges' ratings (*fail* = 0, *pass* = 1) onto ". . . a judgmental scale of writing competence." A three-facet model was used to calibrate the data, with the facets being scoring round, packet, and judges. The procedure defined a measurement scale on which the standard, packets, and judges could be located. The standard was a specific value on the scale; packets scoring above that value were a pass and below it a fail.

The application of this procedure to multiple measures seems quite promising. In such an approach, standardized scores from multiple assessments would replace the four writing domains. The packets would be comprised of students' work from various assessments that had earned the same total score when summed across the assessments. The total score, however, could be achieved through different combinations of performance on the various measures. Judges would rate each packet by assigning it to a performance level category.

USING DISCRIMINANT ANALYSIS
AND GEOMETRIC DISTANCES

Carlson (1996), Jaeger (1995), and to some extent Engelhard and Gordon (2000) described procedures for classifying students based on multiple measures that focus on profiles of students' achievement. The actual mechanisms of these procedures vary, but the importance of looking at achievement as a whole reflected in a set of measures is made clear in these approaches. This section examines two procedures for classifying students that focus on students' achievement profiles but also incorporate performance standards set on each individual measure. These procedures involve the application of discriminant analysis and the use of geometric distances (Johnson & Wichern, 1998; Stevens, 1996). The procedures are explained and compared by applying them to a set of test data. The particulars of the testing situation and the construction of criterion groups are described, followed by the discriminant analysis and application of geometric distances.

Student Sample and Measurement Instruments

In the study, 10th-grade students were tested on the mathematics portion of a statewide assessment program. Data for 31,565 students were available, from which a random sample of 4,518 students (15%) was selected for analysis. Forty-seven percent of the students were female, 53% were male, and 79% were White.

Students took a multiple-choice (MC) mathematics test and responded to an open-ended (OE) mathematics task. The 60-item multiple-choice test covered calculation and estimation, measurement, statistics and probability, and geometry. Four equated versions of the test were administered. KR-20s for the tests were .92 or .93. The multiple-choice portion used an IRT item bank approach to calibrate items, place them on a common scale, and construct equivalent forms. The scale for the bank was set to have an origin of 200 and a standard deviation of 10. Student performance was reported on this scale.

The mathematics open-ended tasks are designed to assess three dimensions of mathematics: communication, conceptual understanding, and

TABLE 12.1
Descriptive Statistics and Correlations for the Achievement Measures

Measure	Mean	Standard Deviation	Correlation Coefficients		
			MC	OE1	OE2
MC	234.00	10.2	1.00		
OE1	4.73	2.7	0.63	1.00	
OE2	7.29	3.8	0.64	0.91	1.00

processes and strategies. Students' work is scored on the remaining three dimensions by two raters using a 6-point scoring rubric. For the purpose of exploring the procedures in this study, the open-ended data were used to simulate two different and correlated open-ended measures. A measure that is referred to as OE1 was constructed by adding together the communication and conceptual understanding ratings of Rater 1. A measure called OE2 was constructed by adding together the communication, conceptual understanding, and processes and strategies ratings of Rater 2. These two constructed OE measures provided simulated measures necessary to explore the discriminant analysis and geometric distance approaches.

In actual application, it would be important to know the reliability of the multiple-choice tests and the generalizability of the open-ended measures. The typical reliabilities of the 10th-grade tests used in the assessment program were above .90. Generalizability measures for the open-ended assessments were not available. Student performance on these measures and the correlations among the measures are shown in Table 12.1.

Setting Standards, Defining Criterion Groups, and Developing Criterion Group Profiles

The profile-matching approaches begin by setting standards separately for each assessment. The actual state standards for the multiple-choice test expressed in scale scores were used in this study. The standards for the open-ended assessments were constructed for this example. The standards were applied to the data with a conjunctive strategy to identify students who defined criterion groups for the advanced, proficient, and novice performance levels. Students in the advanced criterion group reach the advanced level on each measure, students in the proficient criterion group are at the proficient level on each measure, and students in the novice criterion group are identified as those who attain novice-level achievement on each measure. The achievement classification of students in these criterion groups is unambiguous in the sense that the overall classification is consistent with the classification on each measure. The noncriterion group was defined as those students not in one of the criterion groups.

Performance standards for defining the three levels of achievement on the three measures are shown in Table 12.2 along with the means and standard deviations of the criterion groups and the noncriterion group.

The means of the achievement measures show the expected pattern across the criterion groups: The advanced group outperformed the proficient group and the proficient group outperformed the novice group. The means of the noncriterion group students fell at or just above the means of the proficient group. The variability within the noncriterion group was quite high compared with the variability of the more homogeneously assembled criterion groups.

A classification profile code can be developed for each student by first defining the advanced, proficient, and novice levels on each measure as 1, 2, and 3 respectively. Each student has a code of 1, 2, or 3 on each measure, and a three-digit code is constructed by concatenating these three numbers. There are 27 possible combinations of three performance levels across three measures, and thus there are 27 possible classification profile codes (e.g., 111, 112, 113, 121, 122, 123, ... , 331, 332, and 333). Only 3 of these 27 profile classification codes provide unambiguous overall classifications. These are 111, 222, and 333 codes for the advanced, proficient, and novice criterion groups. The process results in 24 classification profiles that yield ambiguous overall classifications for students. For example, what overall single classification should be assigned to students with classification profiles of 322, 232, and 223? Should all students with the same

TABLE 12.2
Performance Standards and Group Means and Standard Deviations
for Advanced, Proficient, Novice, and Noncriterion Groups

Performance Levels		Score Ranges, Means, and Standard Deviations		
		MC	OE1	OE2
1	Advanced score range	249–280	8–12	11–18
Advanced	Group mean	255	9.06	13.29
$n = 261$	SD	5.4	1.03	1.49
2	Proficient score range	239–248	5–7	7–10
Proficient	Group mean	242	5.76	8.46
$n = 262$	SD	3.2	.80	1.21
3	Novice score range	000–238	0–4	0–6
Novice	Group mean	226	2.22	3.70
$n = 1,843$	SD	5.8	1.11	1.67
Noncriterion group	Group mean	236	6.21	9.47
$n = 2,152$	SD	8.3	2.11	2.77

classification profile, for example 121, be assigned to the same overall classification group?

The next step in the profile-matching approaches involves constructing an achievement profile for each of the three criterion groups (advanced = 111, proficient = 222, and novice = 333) in terms of the original measures. This is accomplished by calculating the mean on each measure for the respective criterion groups (the median also could be calculated). The basic task of the profile-matching approaches is to take the achievement profile for students who are not in one of the criterion groups and find the criterion group achievement profile to which it most closely matches. Two procedures are applied to this task. These are the use of discriminant analysis and geometric distance measures.

THE DISCRIMINANT ANALYSIS APPROACH

Discriminant analysis is a multivariate procedure designed to investigate problems involved in classifying students or any other type of research units. Discriminant analysis is routinely used to estimate the probability that a given student belongs in a particular group out of a set of possible groups to which the student might be assigned. The probabilities for group membership are estimated based on that student's scores on a set of independent variables (multiple measures).

There are several steps involved in applying discriminant analysis to the data examined in this chapter. First, three groups of students were identified from among the 4,518 students studied. The process began by identifying all students who were in the conjunctively defined advanced, proficient, or novice groups. There were 2,366 such students with group classification codes of 111, 222, or 333. A random sample of two thirds (1,585) of these students was used as the baseline criterion group to develop the discriminant functions. The other one third (781) of the students was used as a cross-validation sample. There were 2,152 students who had ambiguous group classifications (e.g., 121, 213, 332, etc.). These students constitute the test group and were those whose classification categories were assigned by means of the discriminant analysis.

In the second step, the discriminant analysis is performed on the baseline criterion group alone. This results in a set of discriminant functions and weights that, when applied to the three measures in the study, maximize the differences among the advanced, proficient, and novice groups. The weights are called *discriminant coefficients* and are applied to form weighted linear combinations of the measures called *discriminant functions*. The discriminant functions are used to estimate the probabilities of group membership. The results of applying the procedure are shown in Table

TABLE 12.3
Mean and Standard Deviation of the Probabilities
for Assigned Classifications for the Criterion Group,
Cross-Validation, and Test Groups

Actual or Assigned Classification	N	Assigned Classification					
		Advanced		Proficient		Novice	
		Mean	SD	Mean	SD	Mean	SD
Advanced							
Criterion group	182	.974	.048	.026	.048	.000	.000
Cross-validation	79	.979	.051	.021	.051	.000	.000
Test group	413	.836	.158	.164	.158	.000	.000
Proficient							
Criterion group	194	.008	.017	.965	.104	.026	.104
Cross-validation	68	.007	.015	.948	.123	.044	.131
Test group	1,354	.067	.115	.893	.136	.050	.104
Novice							
Criterion group	1,209	.000	.000	.020	.063	.980	.063
Cross-validation	634	.000	.000	.015	.050	.985	.050
Test group	385	.000	.000	.147	.151	.853	.151

12.3. The procedure works quite effectively for the baseline criterion group as seen by the average classification probabilities. The average probabilities of students being assigned to the group in which they are known to belong were .96 or greater. These results are not especially surprising because the probabilities are based on the discriminant functions that are applied to the data on which they were derived. The analysis results in each student being assigned to a group that can be compared to the student's known group membership. The overall percentage of consistent classifications is 99.4%. All students had a match between their actual and assigned classifications, except for nine students, who had a profile code of novice (333) and were classified as proficient (2) based on the discriminant analysis.

Next, the discriminant functions derived from the baseline criterion group were applied to the cross-validation sample. The results of this cross-validation analysis are also shown in Table 12.3. Students in the cross-validation sample show very high average probabilities of being assigned to the group in which they are known to belong. The overall percent of consistent classifications is 98.8%. All students had a match between their actual and assigned classifications except 11 students, who had profile codes of novice (333) but who were classified as proficient (222) based on the discriminant analysis. The high degree of cross-validation suggests that the baseline and cross-validation criterion groups can be combined in the final discriminant analysis used to classify students who are not in the conjunctively defined criterion groups.

The last step is to apply discriminant analysis to the test group. The average probability for the assignment of students in the test group to each classification group is also shown in Table 12.3. On average, it was very clear how students should be classified. There were 413 students in the test group assigned to the advanced group. The average probability for these students being in the advanced group was .836. The average probability of these students being in the proficient group was only .164. There were 1,354 students from the test group assigned to the proficient group. The average probabilities of these students being in the advanced, proficient, and novice groups were .067, .893, and .050, respectively. Last, there were 385 students from the test group assigned to the novice category. The average probability of these students being in the novice group as .853 while the average probability of their being in the proficient group was only .147.

The number of students assigned to each classification category based on the discriminant analysis is shown in Table 12.4. There are six profile codes in Table 12.4 with frequencies of 0 because no student had these profiles. In each of these cases, there is both a 1 and a 3 in the profile code, indicating a striking difference in the level of performance on two of the three measures.

Twenty students with profile codes of 333 were placed in the novice category by the performance standards, but were assigned to the proficient category in the discriminant analysis. These students had emerged in the earlier analyses of the criterion groups. In practice, they would most likely have to retain the profile code and classification they earned by the conjunctive application of the performance standards. It is informative to examine the scores of these 20 students on the three measures and compare them to the scores needed to be placed in the proficient group. These data are shown in Table 12.5. The 20 novices assigned to the proficient category in the discriminant analysis had mean scores so close to the scores needed to be in the proficient category that the discriminant function would assign them to that group.

The power of the discriminant analysis to differentiate students with the same observed profile code can be seen by examining the 34 students with the 121 profile code. Eighteen of these students are assigned to the advanced category and 16 are assigned to the proficient category. The descriptive statistics for these 121 students are reported in Table 12.6 along with the standards for being in the advanced group. The differences between the achievement of these two subgroups were quite small, but the 121 students assigned to the advanced group outperformed the 121 students assigned to the proficient group on each of the three measures.

TABLE 12.4
Frequency for Profile Codes Crossed With Assigned Classification

Profile Code	Total	Assigned Classification		
		1	2	3
111	261	261	0	0
112	26	21	5	0
113	0	0	0	0
121	34	18	16	0
122	53	2	51	0
123	5	0	5	0
131	0	0	0	0
132	7	0	7	0
133	14	0	11	3
211	380	308	72	0
212	50	1	49	0
213	0	0	0	0
221	82	1	81	0
222	262	0	262	0
223	19	0	19	0
231	0	0	0	0
232	63	0	59	4
233	136	0	53	83
311	224	62	162	0
312	70	0	70	0
313	0	0	0	0
321	87	0	86	1
322	542	0	499	43
323	75	0	37	38
331	0	0	0	0
332	285	0	72	213
333	1,843	0	20	1,823

GEOMETRIC DISTANCE APPROACH

A second approach to matching students to the achievement profiles of various criterion groups involves the use of geometric distances. In this approach, the means for a particular criterion group are identified as they were when discriminant analysis was applied (Table 12.2). For example, the means of the advanced criterion group for MC, OE1, and OE2 are 255, 9.06, and 13.29, respectively. A student with a profile of 266, 8.1, and 9.0 has a geometric distance from this criterion profile called the *Euclidean distance*. The procedure for calculating the Euclidean distance is illustrated in Table 12.7. For each measure, the difference between the student's score and the advanced group's mean score is calculated, the difference is squared, the squared differences for all measures are added together, and

TABLE 12.5
Scores Needed to Reach Proficient and Mean Scores
for Novice Students Assigned to the Proficient Category

	Measure		
Variable	MC	OE1	OE2
Score needed to reach proficient classification	239	5.0	7.0
Mean scores of novices reclassified as proficient	237	4.0	5.7

TABLE 12.6
Criteria for Advanced Category and Descriptive Statistics
for Students With the 121 Profile Code

			MC Advanced = 249		OE1 Advanced = 8		OE2 Advanced = 11	
Profile Code	Assigned Classification	N	Mean	SD	Mean	SD	Mean	SD
121	1	18	254	4.4	6.8	.38	12.0	.34
121	2	16	252	2.2	6.4	.51	11.4	.50

TABLE 12.7
Illustration of the Procedure for Calculating the Euclidean Distance

	Measures			Sum of the
Type of Data	MC	OE1	OE2	Squared Differences
Criterion Group Profile	255	9.06	13.29	
Student Profile	265	8.06	10.29	
Profile Differences	+10	−1	−3	
Differences Squared	100	1	9	110

the square root of the sum of the squared distances is calculated. The student's distance from the advanced criterion group in this example is 10.5 (square root of 110). The same student has distances of 23.2 and 31.3 from the proficient and novice criterion groups, respectively. Students are assigned to the group to which they are closest, and therefore this student is assigned to the advanced group.

Standardized Distances

The preceding discussion describes the *raw* Euclidean distance, so called because it is based on unstandardized scores. The Euclidean distances for unstandardized data can be misleading because the magnitude of the distance varies due to the scale ranges of the individual assessment instruments. In this study, the mathematics multiple-choice data were on a much broader scale than the scales used for the open-ended assessments. This difference in scales would result in the MC test data having more influence on the Euclidean distances than the open-ended assessments, and therefore more influence on how students are classified.

Standardizing the data can control the influence of scale variation on the distance measures and classifications that are based on these distances. Any standardization that results in all measures having the same variance is appropriate. The T-score standardization was applied to the data in this study so that the mean of the measures was 50 and the standard deviation was 10. The distance is calculated on the standardized data in the same way as on the raw data.

Mahalanobis Distances

A final refinement of the distance measure that could be explored is the Mahalanobis (1963) distance. This distance index removes the influence of differences in scale variation and also removes the redundancy in the estimation of the distance that occurs because of intercorrelations among the variables. If the measures employed are correlated, and especially if they are highly correlated, the Euclidean distance is inflated. The use of the Mahalanobis distance is analogous to estimating the pooled variance for two correlated groups with a term that removes the shared covariance. The use of the Mahalanobis distance treats the data from the measures as if the measures are completely independent of each other. The application of the Mahalanobis creates a statistical independence among the measures that does not reflect the actually data and that may defeat the purpose of using multiple measures to assess the same construct. The Mahalanobis distance defines a location for the criterion groups that are the centroids used in the discriminant analysis and yields the same classifications of students as the discriminant analysis procedure.

COMPARING CLASSIFICATIONS BASED ON DIFFERENT APPROACHES

Students were classified into the advanced, proficient, and novice groups based on discriminant analysis, geometric distances applied to raw data, and geometric distances applied to standardized data. Consistencies among these classifications were examined by the following cross-tabulation comparisons: (a) standardized and raw distances, (b) raw distances and discriminant analysis, and (c) standardized distances and discriminant analysis.

Classifications Based on Raw and Standardized Distances

The consistency between the classifications based on these procedures is shown in the cross-tabulation in Table 12.8. The 2,152 students in the test group were cross-classified, and 1,332 students had the same classifications based on the two methods. This is an agreement rate of only 62%.

Classifications Based on Raw Distances and Discriminant Analysis

The cross-tabulation with students classified based on raw distances and discriminant analysis is shown in Table 12.9; 1,162 students had the same classification for an agreement rate of 54%.

Classifications Based on Standardized Distances and Discriminant Analysis

The cross-tabulation of students classified according to standardized distances and discriminant analysis is shown in Table 12.10; 1,968 students had the same classification for an agreement rate of 92%. Using the classification based on the discriminant analysis as an arbitrary origin for

TABLE 12.8
Cross-Tabulation of Student Classifications Based
on Raw and Standardized Distances

Classification Based on Standardized Data	Classification Based on Raw Data		
	Advanced	Proficient	Novice
Advanced	85	250	0
Proficient	49	917	436
Novice	0	85	330

TABLE 12.9
Cross-Tabulation of Student Classifications Based
on Raw Distances and Discriminant Analysis

Classification Based on Raw Distances	Classification Based on Discriminant Analysis		
	Advanced	Proficient	Novice
Advanced	74	60	0
Proficient	333	811	108
Novice	6	483	277

TABLE 12.10
Cross-Tabulation of Student Classifications Based
on Standardized Distances and Discriminant Analysis

Classification Based on Standardized Distances	Classification Based on Discriminant Analysis		
	Advanced	Proficient	Novice
Advanced	320	15	0
Proficient	93	1,286	23
Novice	0	53	362

purposes of description, the standardized distance approach moves 93 students down from advanced to proficient, 53 students down from proficient to novice, while moving 15 students up from proficient to advanced, and 23 students up from novice to proficient.

Discussion of Classification Comparisons

These analyses reveal a very high rate of agreement in classifications based on the standardized distance and discriminant analysis classifications. The classifications based on raw distance measures seem at odds with classifications from the other two methods. The inconsistency in classifications based on the raw data reflects the differences in scale for the measurement instruments as compared with their standardized representation.

To further examine the relationships between the standardized distances and discriminant analysis classifications, the mean scores and standard deviations for students from the criterion group for each performance level are presented in Table 12.11. The same information is provided for students in the test group as classified by the discriminant analysis and standardized distance methods. An inspection of the means in Table 12.11 reveals very small differences between the means of the criterion group and the means of students assigned to each criterion group by the two profile-matching methods. These similarities in the achievement profiles and the very high agreement rate (92%) for the two profile-matching procedures suggest that the choice of one method over the other cannot be based on purely empirical considerations.

SUMMARY FOR DISCRIMINANT ANALYSIS AND GEOMETRIC DISTANCES

The profile-matching strategies share in common the identification of achievement profiles for criterion groups to which students who do not fit neatly in a conjunctively defined criterion group are matched. Discrimi-

TABLE 12.11
Descriptive Statistics for Criterion Groups and Test Students Assigned to
Standardized Distance and Discriminant Analysis Methods

Group by Classification Levels	Group Size	Achievement Measure					
		MC		OE1		OE2	
		Mean	SD	Mean	SD	Mean	SD
Advanced							
Criterion Group	261	255	5.4	9.06	1.03	13.29	1.49
Test Group							
Standardized distance	335	246	5.3	8.78	1.18	13.01	1.66
Discriminant	413	244	5.6	8.80	1.03	12.97	1.57
Proficient							
Criterion Group	262	242	3.2	5.76	0.80	8.46	1.21
Test Group							
Standardized distance	1,402	237	6.7	6.30	1.61	9.50	2.14
Discriminant	1,354	236	7.3	6.19	1.45	9.27	2.00
Novice							
Criterion Group	1,843	226	5.8	2.22	1.11	3.70	1.67
Test Group							
Standardized distance	415	229	7.6	3.79	1.46	6.52	1.77
Discriminant	385	230	8.2	3.46	1.32	6.37	1.78

nant analysis functions like a regression procedure; it predicts the probability of group membership and produces classifications that reflect the
consistency in individual measures. Rescaling and standardizing the measures do not change the results of the discriminant analysis. Such transformations are simply linear changes of scale and do not change the relationships among the measures. The discriminant analysis is also unchanged by
assigning weights to the data from the various measures. The actual
discriminant coefficients could be changed or weighted to reflect beliefs
about the importance of different measures. Such weightings, however,
would no longer result in accurate estimation of the probability of group
membership.

The use of geometric distances to match students to criterion group
achievement profiles has several variations. The use of standardized distances produces results different from the results based on raw score distances. The standardized distances remove the influence of differences in
the scales for the various measures. While using standardized distances,
differential weights could be assigned to the difference between students'
scores and the criterion groups' means for a particular variable. These
weights could make a student's distance from a variable larger or smaller
to reflect opinions about the importance of the content reflected by that
measure. Furthermore, the weights could be assigned not just for a partic-

ular measure, but also for a specific criterion group. For example, the contribution of the multiple-choice test could be increased or decreased in calculating a student's distance from just the advanced criterion group but not the distance from the proficient and novice groups.

CONCLUSIONS AND RECOMMENDATIONS

This chapter examined conceptual and technical issues involved in setting standards for using multiple measures, reviewed strategies and procedures that have been used to combine multiple measures, and illustrated the use of discriminant analysis and geometric distances for classifying students. The analysis of all the information leads to the following conclusions.

The quality of individual measures is the key to fair and meaningful assessment in a multiple-measurement setting. The use of several measures cannot compensate for the consequences of using a measure or measures that are only tangentially related to the content standards. The use of data from such measures, because the data are easy to collect or happen to be available, may introduce invalidity into the measurement and thereby into the classification of students. Data from a single carefully developed or judiciously selected standards-based measure is likely to be more appropriate. The use of multiple measures does not perform magic.

The instructional and curricular value of performance standards is directly related to the degree to which performance standards reflect the curriculum. The performance-curriculum link is closest when judges in standard-setting procedures examine the actual instruments used and data obtained from them. The performance–curriculum link becomes more remote when judges in standard-setting procedures reflect on composite data or weighted composite data that combine results from several assessment instruments.

The discriminant analysis and geometric distance procedures described in this chapter reflect both conjunctive and compensatory strategies. In both procedures, the criterion groups are conjunctively defined. All other students, however, are classified in a compensatory fashion that allows relatively high performance on one or more measures to balance relatively low performance on others.

The classifications of students based on the discriminant analysis and standardized distances are very similar. The similarity in these results needs to be confirmed with the application of the procedures to other data. In addition, it is important to investigate the achievement and characteristics of students with inconsistent classifications from the two procedures. Such empirical investigations provide information useful in deciding which procedure to recommend. It seems unlikely, however, that additional empirical research will yield results that compellingly support the use of one procedure over the other.

At this time, the use of standardized geometric distances seems especially promising. The procedure has the following features:

1. Performance standards can be set on the original raw score scale of the instruments;
2. The standardized scores have a one-to-one correspondence to the raw scores, so the raw-score performance standards have a unique standardized score equivalent;
3. The procedures use the achievement profiles of conjunctively defined criterion groups;
4. Students are classified based on closest match, which embodies a compensatory element; and
5. Weights can be assigned to distances for particular measures for one or all criterion groups to reflect judgments about relative importance.

The procedure is also relatively easy to explain and is already somewhat familiar to educators. High standards can be set on individual measures using procedures with which many educators are already familiar and that may already have been applied. These standards are maintained by using conjunctively defined criterion groups. Students are classified based on the criterion group profile to which they have the closest match. This process can be explained in words like, "Dale is in the advanced group because Dale's scores are more like the students' in that group than in any other." The process of matching achievement to a standard is roughly analogous in its general structure to matching students' constructed responses to benchmark or exemplar papers. This is a matching process with which many educators are familiar. Many educators are interested in weighing data from different measures to reflect opinions about the relative importance of each measure. Not to endorse such an approach, but such weighings can be incorporated into the standardized distance procedure quite easily. Last, it seems useful to mention that the geometric distance approach can be implemented using any standard spreadsheet or database software.

REFERENCES

American Educational Research Association. (1999). Position statement of the American Educational Research Association concerning high-stakes testing in preK-12 education. *Educational Researcher, 17*(8), 24–25.

American Educational Research Association, American Psychological Association, National Council on Measurement Education. (1999). *Standards for educational and psychological testing*. Washington, DC: American Educational Research Association.

Angoff, W. H. (1971). Scales, norms, and equivalent scores. In R. L. Thorndike (Ed), *Educational measurement* (2nd ed., pp. 508–600). Washington, DC: American Council of Education.

Carlson, D. (1996, October). *Adequate yearly progress in Title I of the Improving America's School Act of 1994: Issues and strategies*. Study Group on Adequate Yearly Progress, Council of Chief State School Officers.

Cizek, G. J. (Ed.). (2001). *Setting performance standards: Concepts, methods, and Perspectives*. Mahwah, NJ: Lawrence Erlbaum Associates.

Engelhard, G., & Gordon, B. (2000). Setting and evaluating performance standards for high stakes writing assessment. In M. Wilson & G. Engelhard (Eds.), *Objective measurement: Theory into practice* (Vol. 5, pp. 3–15). Stamford, CT: Ablex.

Gulliksen, H. (1950). *Theory of mental tests*. New York: Wiley.

Haladyna, T. M., & Hess, R. K. (1999). Conjunctive and compensatory standard-setting models in high stakes testing. *Educational assessment, 6*(2), 129–153.

Impara, J. C., & Plake, B. S. (Eds.). (1995). Standard setting for complex performance tasks (Special Issue). *Applied Measurement in Education, 8*(1).

Jaeger, R. M. (1982). An iterative structured judgment process for establishing standards on competency tests: Theory and application. *Education Evaluation and Policy Analysis, 4*, 461–476.

Jaeger, R. M. (1995). Setting standard for complex performance: An iterative, judgmental policy-capturing strategy. *Educational Measurement: Issues and Practices, 14*, 16–20.

Johnson, R. A., & Wichern, D. W. (1998). *Applied multivariate statistics* (4th ed.). Upper Saddle River, NJ: Prentice-Hall.

Mahalanobis, P. C. (1963). On the generalized distance in statistics. *Proceedings of the National Institute of Science, 12*, 49–55.

Mehrens, W. A. (1990). Combining evaluation data form multiple sources. In J. Millman & L. Darling-Hammond (Eds.), *The new handbook of teacher evaluation: Assessing elementary and secondary schoolteachers* (pp. 322–334). Newbury Park, CA: Sage.

Messick, S. (1995a). Validity of psychological assessments: Validation of inferences from person's responses and performance as scientific inquiry into score meaning. *American Psychologist, 50*, 741–749.

Messick, S. (1995b, Winter). Standards of validity and the validity of standards in performance assessment. *Educational Measurement: Issues and Practice*, pp. 5–8.

Nedelsky, L. (1954). Absolute grading standards for objective tests. *Educational and Psychological Measurement, 14*, 3–19.

Nunnally, J. C. (1967). *Psychometric theory*. New York: McGraw-Hill.

Plake, B. S. (1995). The performance domain and structure of the decision space. *Applied Measurement in Education, 8*(1), 3–14.

Plake, B. S. (1998). Setting performance standards for professional licensure and certification. *Applied Measurement in Education, 11*(1), 65–80.

Rasch, G. (1980). *Probabilistic models for some intelligence and attainment tests*. Chicago: University of Chicago Press.

Stevens, J. (1996). *Applied multivariate statistics*. Mahwah, NJ: Lawrence Erlbaum Associates.

Wang, T. (1998). Weights that maximize reliability under congeneric models. *Applied Psychological Measurement, 22*(2), 179–187.

Chapter 13

Linking Bilingual Mathematics Assessments: A Monolingual IRT Approach

Seung W. Choi
Marty McCall
Oregon Department of Education

The need to include more and different populations in state assessment has spurred innovative psychometric thinking. Other chapters in this book discuss ways to assess more special education students by expanding the range of measurement. This chapter is about using translated mathematics tests to extend the assessment system to more English-language learners (ELLs). It addresses the technical problem of putting different language versions of a test on the same scale. The use of translated tests is not unique to education. Multilingual tests are widely used in technical certification and for armed forces and civil services exams in countries with more than one official language. Many recent advances in cross language testing have arisen from the globalization of business and technology. Nevertheless, problems of creating equivalent tests on a common scale are not, as yet, entirely solved. This chapter discusses some of these issues and reports Oregon's efforts to grapple with them.

Chapter 14 describes the development of Oregon's side-by-side bilingual test format to address the needs of students who may have partial literacy in both languages. For example, a native Spanish speaker who has received math instruction in English may not know the Spanish word for *diagonal* or *quotient*. A student may lack the level of English syntax needed to understand a complex problem. Presenting the problem in both languages gives the student the best chance to provide answers based on math proficiency without language interference. In response to similar concerns, the National Assessment of Educational Progress (NAEP) field tested items with English and Spanish versions on facing pages in 1995 with promising results (Anderson, Jenkins, & Miller, 1996).

These tests are considered standard versions of the statewide math tests. Scores earned on the side-by-side test are included in group statistics and are considered evidence of meeting (or failing to meet) state performance standards. In the following discussion, items and tests in English are compared to Spanish/English side-by-side tests and items, not to Spanish-only tests and items. The terms *Spanish test* and *Spanish item* refer to the side-by-side Spanish–English format.

THE EQUATING PROBLEM

Doran and Holland (2000) defined *equating* as "statistical and psychometric methods used to adjust scores obtained on different tests measuring the same construct so that they are comparable" (p. 281). In the Rasch context, a test can be linked to an established scale if it contains a set of items with known difficulties or if it is administered to a set of examinees with known abilities. Two or more tests can be linked to one another if they contain a set of common items or if they are administered to a common set of examinees. In this case, the English language version of the test is linked to the logit scale using common items. Item difficulties and person abilities on the English version are regarded as known values. Our task is to link the Spanish test to the English test. How can this be done?

The Common Examinee Design

Some researchers use a common examinee design by administering both versions to a group of people who are fluent in both languages (Berberoglu, Sireci, & Hambleton, 1997; Boldt, 1969; Sireci & Berberoglu, 1997). The bilingual group design has been criticized because fluent bilinguals are not likely to be a representative sample of either language population (Sireci, 1997). True bilinguals equally proficient in both languages are rare and may represent a narrow span of the proficiency spectrum. Furthermore, bilinguals are probably immune to the differences in language and culture that might affect the performance of their monolingual cohorts. In Oregon, fluent bilingualism is not typical of the student population, so the common person design is not advisable.

Nor are there truly common items. Translation is rarely completely transparent, although test designers make every effort to prevent translation errors. Double translation, back translation, and field trials are conducted to see that differences are not due to errors or ambiguity in translation. (See Gierl & Khalif, 2000; Gierl, Rogers, & Klinger, 1999, for a study of types of translation error; see Hambleton, 1993, for a discussion of acceptable translations procedures; see chap. 15 for a description of the translation process Oregon used.) Nevertheless, translation may still introduce error into the equating process. The side-by-side format may also introduce error. Students are given unlimited time to take Oregon's tests, but the extra reading time required of a student using dual-language versions may cause items to function differently.

An alternative approach to the bilingual group design is a method using separate monolingual examinees to link different language versions of a test to a common scale (Woodcock & Muñoz-Sandoval, 1993). The source language test is translated into the target language, and each language version is separately administered to the corresponding language group. Items are calibrated separately and linked through linguistically transparent items. IRT-based methods for evaluating differential item functioning (DIF) are typically used to determine item equivalence across languages (Berberoglu, Sireci, & Hambleton, 1997; Sireci, Foster, Olsen, & Robin, 1997). Items that show DIF across the tests are considered unique to the separate language versions. Items with low DIF values are used in common item equating to link the translated test to another test or to a common scale. This monolingual design is more appropriate for Oregon's population. This study investigates the application of an IRT common item equating procedure to link a translated Spanish mathematics test to a score scale established in English.

OVERVIEW OF THE STUDY

Wainer (2000) said that researchers who want to equate translated tests must make one of two untenable assumptions: (a) Both language populations have the same ability distribution, or (b) item difficulties are the same in both languages. We have chosen to adopt the second of these assumptions, proceeding cautiously and recognizing that the assumption is weak. The first part of the study evaluates the entire data set for the presence of DIF. The object of this part of the study is to see how much group difference remains when size and ability density differences are taken into account. The second part compares the results of using different types of anchor items in equating. Much of the study involves the search for a defensible set of linking items. The third part of the study investigates the effect of the equating designs on student scores and on judgments about student proficiency. The three parts are outlined as follows:

1. Evaluate the degree to which DIF is present in the data
   a. Administer Spanish and English tests to separate populations

   b. See whether there is DIF in the data set
      • Compute likelihood ratios for DIF and non-DIF conditions
      • Calculate root mean squared error between item estimates
2. Conduct equating using three different linking schemes
      • Use items with low DIF as anchors
      • Use items chosen by experts as anchors
      • Assume English calibrations are accurate
3. Evaluate the impact of different linking types on student outcomes
      • See whether the choice of equating type has an effect on achieve-
        ment category

METHOD

Subjects

In 1998, ELLs had the opportunity to participate in the Spanish side-by-
side version of the Oregon statewide mathematics multiple-choice assessments. Decisions about whether to participate were made by teachers
and/or instructional teams who knew the individual students. The tests
were administered at four grade levels (3rd, 5th, 8th, and 10th). However,
only third and fifth grades had a large enough sample of Spanish participants, hence third- and fifth-grade tests are the focus of the present study.
Altogether, 314 third graders and 308 fifth graders took Form A of the
mathematics multiple-choice test. (Note: Only one of the four equivalent
forms was translated and available in the Spanish–English format.) The
English version was taken by 8,895 third-grade students and 8,762 fifth-
grade students.

*Part 1. Evaluating Differential Item Functioning (DIF) in the Data
Set.* The purpose of this part of the study is to see whether items actually
function differently in the two versions of the test. An item exhibits DIF if
the probability of a correct response is affected by group membership.
Lord (1980) wrote, "If an item has a different item response function for
one group than for another, it is clear that the item is biased" (p. 212).
Millsap and Everson (1993) defined DIF as "differences in the functioning
of a test or item among groups that are matched on the attribute measured by the test or item" (p. 298). Budgell, Raju, and Quartetti (1995) gave
a modified definition of DIF for translated tests: "For translated assessment instruments tests are said to exhibit measurement equivalence when
individuals who are equal in the trait measured by the test but who come
from different cultural and linguistic groups have the same observed
score" (p. 309). To detect DIF, the researcher compares the response

function for two or more groups matched on ability. This is difficult in the cross-language context. If we had a way to match examinees on ability, we would not have an equating problem.

What we can do is compare the likelihood that DIF does not exist in the data set to the likelihood that it does. The IRT likelihood ratio (LR) procedure (Thissen, Steinberg, & Wainer, 1988, 1993) for detecting DIF was used to evaluate the equivalence of the items across languages. Forty items in third grade and 60 items in fifth grade were calibrated according to the one-parameter logistic model (Rasch, 1960) using the computer program BILOG-MG (Zimowski, Muraki, Mislevy, & Bock, 1996). Likelihood ratio chi-square tests were conducted to provide a statistical test of translation DIF (Sireci, Foster, Olsen, & Robin, 1997).

BILOG-MG handles DIF analysis in a manner similar to nonequivalent groups equating: The group proficiency levels are assumed to be different, and the relative differences in item difficulties between groups are examined under the constraint that the mean item difficulties of the groups are equal. The LR chi-square statistic compares the fit to the data between two nested models as:

$$G^2(d.f.) = 2\log\frac{Likelihood[Augmented]}{Likelihood[Compact]}, \tag{1}$$

where *d.f.* is the difference between the number of item parameters in the augmented (general) number and the compact (constrained) model for two groups. As a first step, all responses were calibrated according to the one-parameter Rasch model in a single group—as if they came from the same population. This model (the NO DIF condition) treats the data as if no item exhibits group differences. Next, the data in two groups were analyzed separately using the augmented (All DIF) model, which assumes that all items may exhibit DIF. Then the difference between the maximum marginal likelihoods of the item parameters of the two models was compared as shown in Eq. (1). Essentially, we are asking: "How well do the data fit if we assume no DIF?" "How well do they fit if we assume DIF is present?" "Does the DIF model fit significantly better than the NO DIF model?"

Under the null hypothesis (NO DIF effects for item difficulties), the difference between the log likelihoods of the augmented and compact models is distributed in large samples as chi-square with $[(n - 1)(m - 1)]$ degrees of freedom, where n is the number of items and m is the number of groups. A significant chi-square indicates that the model containing group item effects (ALL DIF) fits the data significantly better than the model that contains no such effects (NO DIF). The null hypothesis of NO DIF under the Rasch model is defined as finding no significant or reliable difference between the item difficulty parameter for all items across language groups. If the constrained (NO DIF) model does not fit the data, this is considered evidence that differential item effects are present.

The current alternative hypothesis (ALL DIF) tests all items on the tests and is therefore highly constrained. A series of LR less constrained tests can be performed in addition to the comparison of two extreme models (Berberoglu, Sireci, & Hambleton, 1997). These tests can pinpoint items or groups of items contributing most to the overall difference. Based on the results of an initial linking study, the constraint of equality across groups can be removed for the items that show noticeable difference in their difficulty estimates. The resulting less constrained model can be tested against the ALL DIF model (Sireci et al., 1997; Thissen, Steinberg, & Wainer, 1993).

Sampling Conditions

The Spanish sample was smaller than the English sample, and patterns of raw scores were different. As a group, Spanish speakers scored lower than English speakers. (This was somewhat expected because most Spanish speakers have had interrupted educations in both the United States and their native countries.) To control for sample size and ability distribution, the LR test was replicated under two conditions. Both conditions used the entire Spanish sample and 10 random samples of English examinees. Sample sizes for the two language groups were matched to prevent the likelihood statistics from being unduly weighted by the English respondents. In the first condition (full population), the 10 English samples were drawn from the overall sample of students who took the English-only test. In the second condition (matched population), the proficiency distribution of the groups taking the English and Spanish side-by-side versions was matched. To accomplish this, the Spanish side-by-side examinees were ranked according to overall raw score and divided into deciles. Ten random samples from the English group were drawn to reflect the density of the Spanish side-by-side population within the score groups formed by Spanish decile groupings. The resulting matched random samples from the English population had distributions that are similar to the Spanish sample. A SAS macroprogram was written for the random sampling of matched ability groups.

In addition to the LR test, the root mean squared error (RMSE) of item-difficulty estimates was computed as another measure of DIF in the data set. Item-difficulty estimates calibrated on the entire English population served as known parameters. The item-difficulty estimates from the Spanish and 10 English samples under both full and matched population conditions were equated to the English metric using the test characteristic curve equating procedure (Stocking & Lord, 1983) implemented in the

EQUATE program (Baker, 1995). The RMSE for the item parameter estimates was computed as:

$$RMSE = \sqrt{\frac{\sum_{i=1}^{k}(b_i - \hat{b}_i)^2}{k}}, \tag{2}$$

where b_i is the known item difficulty for Item i estimated based on the entire English population and $\hat{b}_i$ is the equated difficulty estimate from the Spanish or English samples.

Part 2. Looking for Links.   When English and Spanish side-by-side items are calibrated separately, item-difficulty estimates are not necessarily on a common metric. However, relative difficulties of Spanish side-by-side and English-only items can be examined without any equating procedures. To the extent that a strong linear relationship exists between difficulty estimates for Spanish side-by-side and English-only items, a common item equating procedure can adequately remove the differences in the centering and dispersion of item-difficulty estimates. One of the assumptions underlying the use of common item equating in cross-lingual assessments is that the translation of items into another language does not make the items uniformly more difficult or easier than the source language items. However, if difficulty estimates are offset by factors other than group ability differences, arbitrarily aligning them can, in fact, induce a bias into the comparison of scores across languages. This study seeks to minimize error by finding the least biased set of items.

Multiple-group IRT analyses can be used to identify individual items showing DIF. The BILOG-MG computer program compares item-difficulty estimates for two groups under the assumption that the mean difficulty of the translated items is equal to that of original items. The procedure is analogous to the mean/sigma equating procedure (Marco, 1977) using all items as anchor items. This study uses Stocking and Lord's (1983) test characteristic curve equating method instead of the Marco method to place difficulty estimates on a common metric. The test characteristic curve equating procedure was expected to provide linking constants that are less susceptible to outlying items with a significant level of DIF. Assuming asymptotic normality of difficulty item estimate, $\hat{b}_i$ for item i, the null hypothesis, H_0: $b_{Ei} = b_{Si}$, can be evaluated in a simple asymptotic significance test (Lord, 1980) as shown in Eq. (2) by referring d_i to the standard normal distribution table:

$$d_i = \frac{\hat{b}_{Ei} - \hat{b}_{Si}}{\sqrt{Var\,\hat{b}_{Ei} + Var\,\hat{b}_{Si}}},$$

where $\hat{b}_{Ei}$ is the English difficulty estimate for Item i, $\hat{b}_{Si}$ is the Spanish side-by-side difficulty estimate, and $Var\ \hat{b}_{Ei}$ and $Var\ \hat{b}_{Si}$ are the squared standard errors associated with item-difficulty estimates for English and Spanish, respectively. Muraki and Engelhard (1989) proposed a criterion of about 2 in absolute value to judge an item to exhibit DIF. All items showing $|d_i|$ of 1.96 or larger were identified as DIF items.

In addition to the multiple-group IRT analyses, the English and Spanish-bilingual data were calibrated separately using the BILOG-MG computer program. The English item-difficulty estimates in logits were then equated to the existing bank (RIT) scale using the common-item equating procedure. This transformation affected only the mean and standard deviation of the distribution of English item-difficulty estimates. The RIT (Rasch Unit) scale has a mean of approximately 200 and a standard deviation of 10 at 3rd grade and is vertically linked to higher grades with common anchor items.

Difficulty estimates for the Spanish side-by-side items were then equated to the English metric using the test characteristic curve equating procedure (Stocking & Lord, 1983), presuming a common-item non-equivalent group equating design. Three different sets of common items were identified and used in subsequent equating procedures. In the first condition, all 40 items in third grade and all 60 items in fifth grade were used as anchor items to equate Spanish item-difficulty estimates to the English metric. The second condition uses items with low DIF ($|d_i| < 1.96$) as anchor items. In the third condition, a set of anchor items was identified by expert bilingual content specialists. To identify the third set of linking items, a bilingual mathematics content specialist and a bilingual mathematics teacher were asked to choose a set of items most amenable to clear translation and least dependent on language and culture across the two language groups. These three sets of items were used as anchor item blocks in a common item linking study to set the bilingual Spanish scale onto the common metric. Items excluded from the linking blocks were treated as unique items.

Part 3. Comparison of Scaled Scores—Impact. We wanted to know whether different equating methods would yield very different student scores or affect the percentage of students meeting state proficiency standards. After the series of common-item linking studies were run, tests were rescored under the three equating conditions. The resulting item-difficulty estimates were used to estimate three separate scaled scores for students who took the Spanish side-by-side version. The similarity between these separately scaled scores and the impact on meeting the standard were compared.

RESULTS

Part 1: DIF Analysis

Significant DIF was found under both full- and matched-population conditions, but LR chi-square statistics were substantially smaller under the matched-population condition. The matched condition reduces differences in item-difficulty estimates obtained based on the Spanish sample and 10 random samples of English students.

Table 13.1 summarizes the results of the translation DIF analyses. Under both conditions, the LR chi-square statistics (G^2) were significant ($p < .001$) across all 10 replications, indicating that the completely unconstrained model (ALL DIF) fits the data significantly better than the completely constrained model (NO DIF). Thus, the null hypothesis that there is no significant or reliable difference between the item parameters for the English and Spanish groups was rejected, indicating that one or more items function differently due to translation error and/or group membership.

TABLE 13.1
Summary of Translation DIF—Likelihood Ratio (LR) Analyses

Grade	Sample	Full Population			Matched Population		
		G^2	df	p	G^2	df	p
3	1	298.45	40	<.001	137.10	40	<.001
	2	256.47	40	<.001	140.52	40	<.001
	3	321.88	40	<.001	101.11	40	<.001
	4	281.85	40	<.001	109.63	40	<.001
	5	268.67	40	<.001	161.62	40	<.001
	6	259.20	40	<.001	120.13	40	<.001
	7	329.08	40	<.001	110.22	40	<.001
	8	295.39	40	<.001	146.08	40	<.001
	9	280.43	40	<.001	128.43	40	<.001
	10	315.92	40	<.001	146.49	40	<.001
	Mean	264.30			118.30		
5	1	525.95	60	<.001	263.01	60	<.001
	2	538.15	60	<.001	231.97	60	<.001
	3	531.11	60	<.001	250.44	60	<.001
	4	519.75	60	<.001	247.28	60	<.001
	5	541.35	60	<.001	315.30	60	<.001
	6	554.02	60	<.001	246.36	60	<.001
	7	510.58	60	<.001	272.54	60	<.001
	8	487.41	60	<.001	268.99	60	<.001
	9	468.38	60	<.001	284.44	60	<.001
	10	535.81	60	<.001	248.45	60	<.001
	Mean	521.25			262.88		

When differences in population ability were controlled (matched population) in LR analyses, DIF effects became smaller, but were still significant. The average LR chi-square statistic ($G^2_{(40)}$) was 264.3 for third grade under the full-population condition, whereas average $G^2_{(40)}$ dropped to 118.3 for the matched-population condition. A similar result was found for fifth grade—the average $G^2_{(60)}$ was 521.25 for the full-population condition compared with 262.88 for the matched-population condition.

Table 13.2 shows the RMSE of Spanish side-by-side item calibrations and the RMSE of the 10 English-only samples. The RMSE for Spanish calibrations for third grade was 0.283 in logit unit, compared with the average RMSE of 0.120 for English samples under full population condition. However, when English samples were drawn from the population matched to the Spanish distribution, the average RMSE increased to 0.217, which is more comparable to that of the Spanish group. A similar trend was found in fifth grade—the average RMSE for the matched-English samples (0.257) was closer to the RMSE for the Spanish group (0.387) and larger than the average RMSE for the full-English samples (0.140). However, it is worth noting that the difference in RMSEs for the Spanish group and matched-English samples was larger for 5th grade (0.130) compared with 3rd grade (0.066). The matched population condition is a more accurate representation of the effect of translation error. It shows how much error the Spanish sample exhibits beyond that of an English sample of similar range and density.

Figure 13.1 graphically displays the RMSEs presented in Table 13.1. The RMSEs for the item-difficulty estimates for both full- and matched-

TABLE 13.2
RMSE of Item-Difficulty Estimates

	Grade 3		Grade 5	
Language	Full Population	Matched Population	Full Population	Matched Population
Spanish	0.283		0.387	
English 1	0.112	0.204	0.128	0.269
English 2	0.122	0.213	0.115	0.277
English 3	0.121	0.227	0.143	0.242
English 4	0.132	0.227	0.154	0.245
English 5	0.099	0.218	0.148	0.267
English 6	0.099	0.225	0.135	0.251
English 7	0.138	0.195	0.138	0.274
English 8	0.132	0.230	0.148	0.231
English 9	0.119	0.203	0.149	0.246
English 10	0.124	0.227	0.141	0.269
English Mean	0.120	0.217	0.140	0.257
English SD	0.013	0.013	0.011	0.016

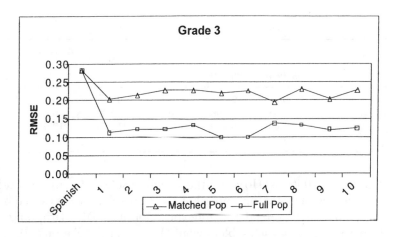

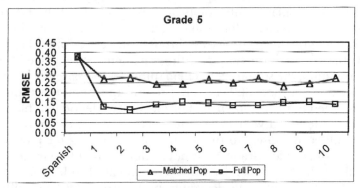

FIG. 13.1. RMSE for Spanish and 10 English replications for both full-and matched-population conditions

population conditions across 10 replications are plotted, as well as the RMSE for the Spanish item difficulty estimates.

Part 2: Common Item-Linking Analyses

Table 13.3 shows the number of items included in each common anchor-item block and descriptive statistics including correlation coefficients between the English and Spanish item-difficulty estimates after the initial linking study. The correlation coefficients ranged from 0.86 to 0.98. The correlation was 0.93 for all 40 items in Grade 3 and 0.90 for all 60 items in Grade 5. The 28 third-grade items and 39 fifth-grade items selected based on the differential item functioning statistic (d_i) had higher correlation coefficients: 0.98 for Grade 3 and 0.97 for Grade 5. The 17 items selected by expert judges in Grade 3 had a correlation of 0.95, which is slightly higher

TABLE 13.3
Descriptive Statistics of Linking Items

Variable	Grade 3			Grade 5		
	All Items	NO-DIF	Expert	All Items	NO-DIF	Expert
Number of items	40	28	17	60	39	16
Correlation	0.93	0.98	0.95	0.90	0.97	0.86
Mean	196.05	195.79	193.13	212.24	212.95	212.03
SD	7.71	8.38	7.29	8.54	8.50	7.57

than that for all 40 items. However, the 16 judge-selected items in Grade 5 had a correlation of 0.86. This somewhat lower correlation was caused by an outlying item, which showed a significant amount of DIF. Dropping that item from the common anchor block would boost the correlation to 0.94.

Figure 13.2 displays scatter plots of third-grade English and Spanish item-difficulty estimates before equating and for all three equating conditions. The identity line is projected through the scatter plots. Figure 13.3 displays the same information for fifth-grade items. As expected from the high correlation, the scatter plot of item difficulty estimates was quite tight for Grade 3. No distinct outliers were present. In Conditions 2 and 3, the items included in the common anchor block were denoted as black triangles. Items identified with Lord's chi-square showed the most compact pattern, adhering closely to the identity line. The scatter plot of item-difficulty estimates for Grade 5 was not as tight as that for Grade 3, as expected from the lower correlation. There appeared to be a few items in Grade 5 that are significantly deviant from the order of relative difficulties between languages.

To estimate how much of the observed difference in item difficulties is due to translation and group membership rather than sampling fluctuation, item-difficulty estimates obtained from the Spanish and 10 random samples of English examinees are plotted against the final English item-difficulty estimates derived from the entire English sample (Figs. 13.4 and 13.5).

The equated item-difficulty estimates obtained from the 10 random samples formed a tighter inner band in Figs. 13.4 and 13.5 than the cloud formed by Spanish item-difficulty estimates equated to the English metric. From a visual inspection, several items appeared to be located outside of the inner band; these were all Spanish items. The Spanish items identified as outliers based on a visual inspection tend to agree with the items excluded by the criterion set based on a differential item functioning statistic (d_i). The inner band formed by the equated item-difficulty estimates for 10 random samples provides an intuitive visual check that is analogous to an empirical standard error for item-difficulty estimates.

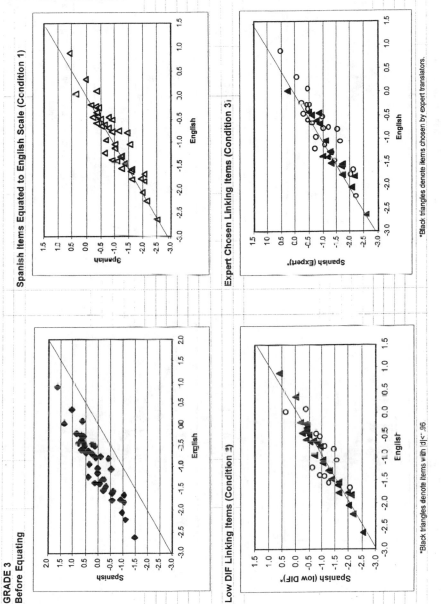

GRADE 3
Before Equating

Spanish Items Equated to English Scale (Condition 1)

Low DIF Linking Items (Condition 2)

*Black triangles denote items with |d|<.96

Expert Chosen Linking Items (Condition 3)

*Black triangles denote items chosen by expert translators.

FIG. 13.2. English item-difficulty estimates plotted against Spanish item-difficulty estimates under different equating conditions (Grade 3).

329

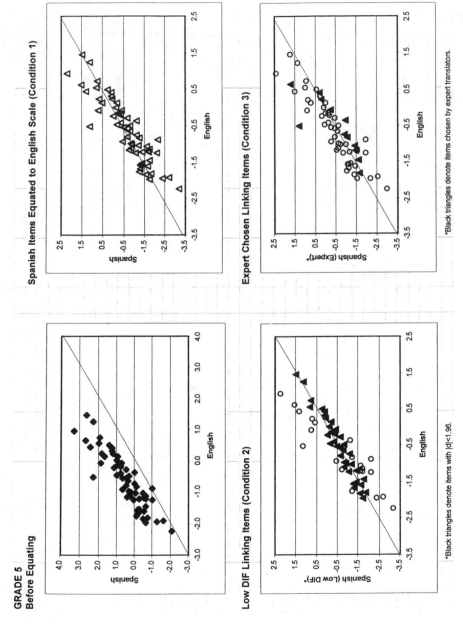

FIG. 13.3. English item-difficulty estimates plotted against Spanish item-difficulty estimates under different equating conditions (Grade 5).

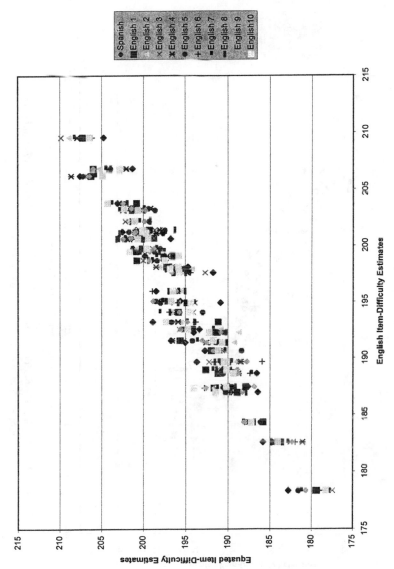

FIG. 13.4. English item-difficulty estimates plotted against equated item-difficulty estimates from the Spanish and 10 English samples (Grade 3).

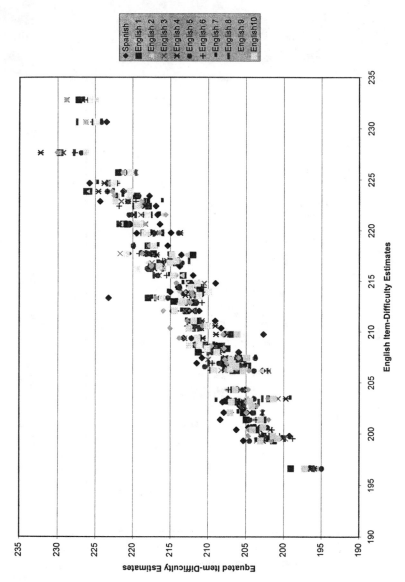

FIG. 13.5. English item-difficulty estimates plotted against equated item-difficulty estimates from the Spanish and 10 English samples (Grade 5).

Part 3: Comparison of Scaled Scores

Raw number correct scores were transformed into the RIT (Rasch unit) scores. Four raw to RIT score conversions were run for Spanish raw scores based on different sets of linked item-difficulty estimates. Tables 13.4 and 13.5 summarize the results of the estimated proficiency measures for the English group and the Spanish group linked through various sets of common anchor items. The mean proficiency measures for the third-grade English group was 206.61, compared with the mean of 195.34 for the Spanish group based on the English calibrations. The mean RIT scores for the fifth-grade English and Spanish groups were 218.43 and 208.82, respectively.

Tables 13.4 and 13.5 also include the mean proficiency estimates obtained from three different sets of linked item-difficulty estimates. These mean proficiency measures ranged from 194.38 to 195.34 for Grade 3. The difference between the lowest and highest mean proficiency estimates in Grade 3 was approximately 1 RIT or 0.1 logit, indicating practically no variation in mean proficiency measures across various linking procedures. In Grade 5, the mean proficiency measures for Spanish students ranged from 208.54 for the condition where all 60 items were used as common anchor items to 210.34 for the expert chosen linking items.

To meet the mathematics proficiency standard in third grade, students must have a RIT score greater than or equal to 202. Fifth graders need a score of 215 or above to meet the standard. As presented in Tables 13.4 and 13.5, the percentage of students meeting the standard was evaluated under all linking conditions. Condition 1 resulted in the same percents meeting criteria when linked scores were compared to scores based on English-only calibration in both third and fifth grades. Seven third-grade students met the standard when the English calibrations were used, but failed to meet the standard under Conditions 2 and 3. In fifth grade, the

TABLE 13.4
Comparison of Scaled Scores (Grade 3)

Variable	English Group	Spanish Group English Calibration	Equated Spanish Group All Items	NO DIF	Expert
N	8,895	314	314	314	314
Mean raw score	27.02	19.34	19.34	19.34	19.34
Mean scaled score	206.61	195.34	195.35	195.04	194.38
SD of scaled scores	12.32	10.21	10.16	10.16	10.16
% Meeting standard	65.7	24.52	24.52	22.29	22.29
% Not meeting standard	34.3	75.48	75.48	77.71	77.71

TABLE 13.5
Comparison of Scaled Scores (Grade 5)

Variable	English Group	Spanish Group English Calibration	Equated Spanish Group		
			All Items	NO DIF	Expert
N	8,762	308	308	308	308
Mean raw score	36.74	25.80	25.80	25.80	25.80
Mean scaled score	218.43	208.82	208.54	208.60	210.34
SD of scaled scores	10.44	7.25	7.75	7.75	7.75
% Meeting standard	60.8	16.56	16.56	16.56	21.75
% Not meeting standard	39.2	83.44	83.44	83.44	78.25

equating based on expert chosen anchor items yielded somewhat different results compared with the English calibration and other equating procedures. About 16.56% fifth graders met the standard under English calibration, equatings based on all items, and on a DIF statistic (d_i), whereas 21.75% would meet the standard on the basis of the equating with expert chosen anchor items. Sixteen fifth-grade students who did not meet the standard based on the English calibration did meet it when the items identified by experts were used in equating. However, two fifth-grade items chosen by experts were outliers. This makes the set of items exhibit less dependability than the third-grade set.

DISCUSSION

The results of this study indicate that the English and Spanish–English side-by-side versions of the third- and fifth-grade mathematics multiple-choice tests are very similar. In reviewing the performance of students, the order of difficulty for both the English and Spanish–English were predominantly the same. It was determined that some items functioned differently between the two groups of examinees. When tests were equated under a number of common item linking designs, there was little difference in the impact on overall score or judgment of mastery for the Spanish group.

A series of LR chi-square tests comparing ALL DIF and NO DIF models indicated that one or more translated items perform differently. DIF was substantially reduced when item difficulties were estimated from samples with matched ability levels. However, the extent of differential item functioning that remained when populations were matched was still statistically significant.

After evaluating DIF, the next step was to determine whether equating the Spanish and English tests has an impact on the use and interpretation of scores in the school setting. IRT common item linking procedures were used under the assumption that translation and/or adaptation does not affect the overall level of item difficulties. Translated tests were equated to the common metric and criterion of the source language tests using three types of anchor items: all English items, items identified by experts as being free from translation errors, and items that exhibited little DIF under Lord's chi-square test. No substantive difference was found between the English calibration and the Spanish calibrations linked through the various sets of common anchor items. The detectable differences between items on the two tests did not result in substantial impact on decisions about individuals in a school setting.

POLICY IMPLICATIONS

Dual-language assessments provide a way for more English language learners to participate meaningfully in large-scale assessment. Construction of these tests requires a fusion of substantive knowledge and measurement expertise. For this reason, it is wise to assemble a team of subject matter experts (SMEs), bilingual translators and item reviewers, teachers who deal with English-language learners in a K to 12 setting, and measurement experts. Care in test construction is essential including, but not limited to (a) selection of items amenable to translation, (b) translation by professionals, and (c) review of translated items by a literate bilingual group looking for clarity of meaning and for the presence of cultural assumptions that could cause confusion. Dual-language tests must be administered as power tests, allowing students as much time as they want to complete the assessment. For students, the work of referring information back and forth in the languages causes the test to take more time than a comparable monolingual test.

No matter how carefully experts construct tests, there is no guarantee of score comparability without the use of psychometric methods for scaling and equating. Conversely, statistical methods alone cannot tell us whether it is advisable to proceed with linking procedures. Professional judgment is needed to ensure comparable meaning of translated items, demonstrate that items address subject content, and attend to linguistic and cultural elements that can introduce construct-irrelevant variance. Much of this chapter deals with mechanisms for ensuring statistical equivalence. The methods used suggest that equating dual-language tests is feasible and yields comparable scores. Yet without the professional judgment used in translation and test construction, statistics would not be sufficient to ensure validity.

DIF persists in the data despite efforts to control language and cultural factors. Again, DIF is a statistical concept that augments or extends, but does not replace, substantive judgment. Detection of DIF can reveal patterns of functional group differences that are not apparent from looking at the text of items or at total student scores. As such, it provides a framework for fruitful discussion. We cannot assume that all DIF comes from translation error or item presentation. One of the difficulties in using tests with populations from different language and cultural groups is determining which sources of difference are part of the construct and which are not. There is broad consensus that language differences are not part of the math construct. Indeed, the side-by-side format was devised so that test scores for Spanish-speaking students would indicate knowledge of math rather than knowledge of English. However, there is no statistical test to determine whether differences for groups matched on ability are relevant to the latent trait. For example, many of the Spanish-speaking students in the United States learned math in Mexico or Central America. They may not have had exposure to the logic and problem-solving techniques mandated by new curricula even if their computational skills are good. This is a genuine group difference that would contribute to statistical DIF. Is it part of the construct? Is it a cultural component?

DIF studies are often undertaken to identify models of low-DIF items for item writers and translators (Gierl, Khalif, & Klingen, 1999; Gierl & Khalif, 2000). Yet DIF studies can also have instructional implications. Two of the items identified by experts as likely to have few translation errors are outliers (see Fig. 13.5, Condition 3). Examination of the items showed that both are almost pure computation questions with very little language. Both items present a problem with fractions. It turns out that the sequence of presentation for fractions in the math curriculum differs between Oregon and Mexico, where most of the students have been educated. Many students seem to have missed basic instruction in fractions in both countries. Consequently, these items end up with higher calibrations in Spanish than in English. Fractions are clearly part of the mathematics construct, so we did not conclude that these items should be eliminated or changed. We did conclude that there was a need to make sure that students arriving in the United States in mid- or late elementary grades get instruction in the concepts and notation of fractions.

We cannot answer these questions statistically, but we can determine whether DIF has an affect on judgments of mastery. The study of impact reveals that differences in items made no detectable differences in overall decisions about student mastery.

IMPLICATIONS FOR FURTHER STUDY

This study showed that the side-by-side format is a statistically viable method for assessing math. Because mathematics tests are known to be more amenable to translation than academic subjects with heavier verbal components, the encouraging results of this study do not necessarily generalize to other subject areas or types of assessments. Further investigation in other subject matters is warranted. It would also be interesting to extend the present study to other IRT models (e.g., the two- and three-parameter logistic models) and/or other equating procedures.

Statistical detection of differential item functioning indicates areas of interest for SMEs. It would be valuable to have a panel of math curriculum experts and expert translators compare items that exhibit high DIF under Lord's chi-square to those showing low DIF. The content of the items may give insight into the source of the difference. If a pattern of cultural difference, problem type, or cognitive style emerges, this would give future item writers guidance in creating items that have higher fidelity to the latent trait.

Students responding to dual-language tests may use a variety of mental techniques in solving problems. They also may have learned math in a different context so that their cognitive processes differ from those of students schooled monolingually in the United States. For these reasons, it would be advisable to conduct a study of dimensionality to see whether the dual-language test has the same structural characteristics as the English test. It would also be interesting to conduct think-aloud studies to see how students exploit the features of the side-by-side presentation.

REFERENCES

Anderson, N. E., Jenkins, F. F., & Miller, K. E. (1996). *NAEP inclusion criteria and testing accommodations. Findings from the 1995 field test in mathematics.* Washington, DC: Educational Testing Service.

Baker, F. B. (1995). *EQUATE Computer Program, version 2.1.* Madison, WI: Department of Educational Psychology, University of Wisconsin.

Berberoglu, G., Sireci, S. G., & Hambleton, R. K. (1997, March). *Comparing translated items using bilingual and monolingual examinees.* Paper presented at the annual meeting of the National Council on Measurement in Education, Chicago, IL.

Boldt, R. F. (1969). *Concurrent validity of the PAA and SAT for bilingual Dade School County high school volunteers* (College Entrance Examination Board Research and Development Report 68-69, No. 3). Princeton, NJ: Educational Testing Service.

Budgell, G. R., Raju, N. S., & Quartetti, P. A. (1995). Analysis of differential item functioning in translated assessments instruments. *Applied Psychological Measurement, 19*(4), 309–321.

Doran, N. J., & Holland, P. W. (2000). Population invariance and the equatability of tests: Basic theory and the linear case. *Journal of Educational Measurement, 37,* 281–306.

Gierl, M., & Khalif, S. (2000, April). *Identifying sources of differential item functioning on translated achievement tests: A confirmatory analysis.* Paper presented at annual meeting of the National Council on Measurement in Education, New Orleans.

Gierl, M., Rogers, W., & Klinger, D. (1999, April). *Using statistical and judgmental reviews to identify and interpret translation DIF.* Paper presented at annual meeting of the National Council on Measurement in Education, Montreal.

Hambleton, R. K. (1993). *Translating achievement tests for use in cross-national studies* (ERIC Document 358-128). New York: International Association for the Evaluation of Educational Achievement.

Lord, F. M. (1980). *Application of item response theory to practical testing problems*. Hillsdale, NJ: Lawrence Erlbaum Associates.

Marco, G. L. (1977). Item characteristic curve solutions to three intractable testing problems. *Journal of Educational Measurement, 14*, 139–160.

Millsap, R. E., & Everson, H. T. (1993). Methodology review: Statistical approaches for assessing measurement bias. *Applied Psychological Measurement, 17*, 297–333.

Muraki, E., & Engelhard, G. (1989, April). *Examining differential item functioning with BIMAIN*. Paper presented at the annual meeting of the American Educational Research Association, San Francisco.

Rasch, G. (1960). *Probabilistic models for some intelligence and attainment tests*. Copenhagen: Danmarks Paedogogiske Institut. (Reprint, 1980, with Foreword and Afterword by Benjamin D. Wright, Chicago: University of Chicago Press.)

Sireci, S. G. (1997). Problems and issues in linking assessments across language. *Educational Measurement: Issues and Practice, 1*, 12–29.

Sireci, S. G., Foster, D. F., Olsen, J., & Robin, F. (1997, March). *Comparing dual-language versions of an international Certification Exam*. Paper presented at the annual meeting of the National Council on Measurement in Education as part of the symposium "Large-Scale Test Adaptation Projects: Designs, Results, and Suggestions for Improving Practice," Chicago.

Sireci, S. G., & Berberoglu, G. (1997, March). *Evaluating translation DIF using bilinguals*. Paper presented at the annual meeting of the American Educational Research Association, Chicago, IL.

Stocking, M. L., & Lord, F. M. (1983). Developing a common metric in item response theory. *Applied Psychological Measurement, 7*, 201–210.

Thissen, D., Steinberg, L., & Wainer, H. (1988). Use of item response theory in the study of group differences in trace lines. In H. Wainer & H. Braun (Eds.), *Test validity* (pp. 147–169). Hillsdale, NJ: Lawrence Erlbaum Associates.

Thissen, D., Steinberg, L., & Wainer, H. (1993). Detection of differential item functioning using the parameters of item response models. In P. Holland & H. Wainer (Eds.), *Differential item functioning* (pp. 67–113). Hillsdale, NJ: Lawrence Erlbaum Associates.

Wainer, H. (2000). Comparing the incomparable: An essay on the importance of big assumptions and scant evidence. *Educational Measurement: Issues and Practice, 18*(4), 11–16.

Woodcock, R. W., & Muñoz-Sandoval, A. F. (1993). An IRT approach to cross-language test equating. *European Journal of Educational Assessment, 9*(3), 233–241.

Zimowski, M. F., Muraki, E., Mislevy, R. J., & Bock, R. D. (1996). *BILOG-MG: Multiple-group IRT analysis and test maintenance for binary items*. Chicago, IL: Scientific Software.

IMPLEMENTATION ISSUES

Chapter 14

Participation in Large-Scale State Assessment and Accountability Systems

Patricia J. Almond
Oregon Department of Education

Camilla Lehr
Martha L. Thurlow
Rachel Quenemoen
National Center on Educational Outcomes,
University of Minnesota

We are beginning a new century committed to the principles of standards-based educational reform in the United States. We have established national and state assessment systems developed around high academic standards, and we use these assessment systems to measure student progress toward the standards. The public is accustomed to learning frequently and routinely about the academic achievement of students in schools at the local, state, national, and international levels. Reports on student performance are standard fare in newspapers, on the evening news, and in political campaigns. Across the nation, citizens want information about educational results; they expect public education to be held accountable for all students, and they demand evidence of improvement where needed. This avid attention to the results of schooling accompanies a comprehensive, nationwide push to improve education, the standards-based reform movement. The last two decades of the 20th century have also seen a major change in the demographic makeup of society. Our public schools are serving an increasingly diverse population of students—students with varied cultural backgrounds, of wide-ranging socioeconomic status (SES), and with many more significant disabilities. For this more diversified student body to benefit from school reform efforts, all students must participate in the large-scale assessment programs designed as part of the accountability system in standards-based reform. What does it mean to participate in a large-scale assessment? In this chapter, we take a straightforward approach. Participation in large-scale assessment means students take national, state, or district tests; have their tests scored; and have the scores reported as part of the data used to measure student and school performance against standards, hold schools accountable, and identify school improvement strategies.

Research indicates that, in the past, many students have been excluded from state assessment programs (Erickson, Thurlow, & Ysseldyke, 1996). The National Assessment of Educational Progress (NAEP) determined that half of all special needs students were excluded from NAEP in 1992 and 1994 (Mazzeo, Carlson, Voelkl, & Lutkus, 2000). This finding raised two important concerns about NAEP. First, could some excluded students have been meaningfully tested? Second, were exclusion practices introducing bias into results? The observations made about NAEP were also expressed about state and district large-scale assessments. It became clear that many students, especially those with special needs, were routinely being excluded from testing.

Teachers, testing professionals, school district administrators, and others provide a variety of explanations. For example, in some cases, it is said that the student did not *fit* the test according to test publishers' norming specifications. In other cases, students who were in different categorical programs (e.g., special education, resource rooms, mental health treatment programs, programs for students with limited English proficiency) were not included. Sometimes groups of students were sent on field trips on testing day. Still other explanations are offered. For example, the student read Braille and the test was only available in print, or the student was in an ungraded program and the test was considered inappropriate. These reasons are difficult to reconcile with concerns about students who are arbitrarily exempted, concerns about representativeness and interpretation of results based on testing a limited sample of students, and concerns about practices that appear to purposefully excuse low-performing students to raise results reported for groups. These concerns were addressed in federal legislation specifying requirements to include, assess, and report results for *all* students (Elementary & Secondary Education Act, 1994; Individuals With Disabilities Education Act [IDEA], 1997).

With renewed emphasis on accountability in the schooling of *all* of our children, there is momentum to include children in testing who may have been left out previously. This chapter identifies critical issues in the participation of all students in large-scale assessment, reviews the relevant research, describes current studies related to participation, and makes recommendations to improve our ability to successfully include *all* students.

CRITICAL ISSUES

In the last half of the 20th century, nearly every state across the nation established educational content and performance standards for all students in an attempt to improve academic achievement. Student progress toward these standards began being measured using large-scale assessments (Olson, Bond, & Andrews, 1999; Thurlow, Ysseldyke, Gutman, & Geenan, 1998). Federal legislation passed in the 1990s demanded equity in opportunity and access; looked for participation of all students, including special needs students, in accountability systems; and asked for the standards for students in special education to be consistent, to the extent possible, with the standards applied to students in general education. In addition, all students, including students with disabilities, must participate in state- and district-wide assessments with appropriate accommodations when necessary. States responding to reform, legislation, and their citizenry established accountability systems and began to report on their public schools. What follows is a brief description of several factors influencing full participation and standards-based educational reform.

National Education Reform Movement

The movement toward standards-based learning and accountability has gathered momentum and is now a reality in many states. In nearly all cases, states developed such tests as part of the national standards-based reform movement. Two events propelled the movement nationally: the New Standards Project and the National Education Goals. The New Standards Project appeared at the same time that the public in this country began seeing U.S. students compared academically to Japanese, German, and other students around the globe. In the early 1900s, the New Standards Project, a joint effort of the Learning Research and Development Center (LRDC) at the University of Pittsburgh and the National Center on Education and the Economy, explored a national examination system based on performance assessments. In September 1989, then-President George Bush and all 50 state governors held an Education Summit in Charlottesville, Virginia. The outcome was the creation of a framework for action called the National Education Goals, which were adopted in 1990. This summit set education improvement as a top priority. States have since developed tests to measure the progress of schools toward state or locally defined standards for all students.

Three Federal Directives Call for Full Participation

Three specific directives at the federal level support full participation. Reauthorization of the Title 1 legislation in 1994 and the reauthorization of legislation concerning special education in 1997 are the most recent. Both call for improved achievement of students covered by the legislation through challenging standards and assessment. The newest versions of these two landmark education acts share a solid foundation with corresponding civil rights legislation that has been maturing over three decades. A brief summary of each follows.

Elementary and Secondary Education Act. In 1994, Congress reauthorized the Elementary and Secondary Education Act (ESEA). After 1994, states began to address the Improving America's School Act (IASA) Title I requirements in conjunction with other state and federal legislation. The Title I provisions of the act required that expectations and outcomes for students served by Title I be the same as for all other children. This reauthorization, called the Improving America's Schools Act (IASA) of 1994, required that states set challenging standards for student achievement and develop and administer assessments to measure student progress toward those standards. *All* students in schools receiving Title I funds were to be held to these standards, and progress of *all* students was to be measured by these assessments and the results reported to the public. Based on the assessment reports reflecting the progress of *all* students toward high standards, schools would make the instructional and structural changes needed to ensure that *all* of their students would meet the standards.

Title I requirements reflect the expectation that all students can master challenging standards in the core curriculum. The law requires that standards be set and assessments be designed for mathematics and language arts/reading as well as for other areas if the state has chosen to assess in those areas. Results of these assessments and other indicators are used to determine whether schools are meeting adequate yearly progress requirements, leading to continuous assessment and improvement of student achievement on core curriculum content standards for the system. In response to these requirements, assessment systems have been designed more as systems checks for school improvement purposes than as tools for assessment of individual student performance.

The National Research Council (1999) studied the assumptions of the IASA reform requirements and used the phrase *theory of action* to describe the intent of the legislation. Overall, the intended outcome of standards-based reform as portrayed by the theory of action is increased levels of learning and achievement for *all* students in our nation's schools. The theory of action assumes that all students are included in all components of the reform agenda—standards, assessments, flexibility, and strict accountability. It assumes that all students benefit from this inclusion:

> Generally, the idea of standards-based reform states that, if states set high standards for student performance, develop assessments that measure student performance against the standards, give schools the flexibility they need to change curriculum, instruction, and school organization to enable their students to meet the standards, and hold schools strictly accountable

for meeting performance standards, then student achievement will rise. (p. 15)

Individuals With Disabilities Education Act. Students with disabilities were specifically included in the definition of all students in IASA 1994, but the amendments to the Individuals with Disabilities Education Act (IDEA) of 1997 further clarified congressional expectations. Specifically, in IDEA 1997 states were required to include children with disabilities in "general State and district-wide assessment programs, with appropriate accommodations, where necessary." Where students with disabilities could not participate even with accommodations, states were required to conduct alternate assessments and develop guidelines for the participation of students in these alternate assessments. Under this reauthorization, decisions remained with the IEP team. When the student with a disability would not participate in testing, the team was required to explain why the assessment was not appropriate and how the child would be assessed. IDEA focused state and district attention on the challenges of full participation of students with disabilities in assessment systems and, linked with the IASA legislation, on the challenges of understanding and developing inclusive accountability systems that will improve outcomes for all students (Thurlow, House, Boys, Scott, & Ysseldyke, 2000).

Civil Rights. Federal legislation of the past decade closely linked education reform to national concerns over equity. In the last three decades of the 20th century, Congress enacted a number of civil rights statutes prohibiting discrimination in educational programs and activities receiving federal financial assistance, thus ensuring equal access to a quality education for many targeted student populations, such as students of color, economically disadvantaged students, students with disabilities, students with limited English proficiency, and females as a group. These statutes were: Title VI of the Civil Rights Act of 1964 (prohibiting race, color, and national origin discrimination); Title IX of the Education Amendments of 1972 (prohibiting sex discrimination); Section 504 of the Rehabilitation Act of 1973 (prohibiting disability discrimination); Title II of the Americans With Disabilities Act of 1990 (prohibiting disability discrimination by public entities); and the Age Discrimination Act of 1975 (prohibiting age discrimination). The civil rights laws represent a national commitment to end discrimination in education and mandate bringing the formerly excluded into the mainstream of American education. As these were being implemented, discussions were characterized by continual tension between equity and excellence, equality and quality.

Recent work linking educational reform practice with legal issues, specifically civil rights issues, addresses that tension. Legal focus in the 1990s was on the right of all students to have both opportunity and success in educational settings. Based on a review of case law, Arthur L. Coleman, then-Deputy Assistant Secretary for Civil Rights, U.S. Department of Education, concluded, "The goals of guaranteeing excellence through the promotion of high academic standards and ensuring that all students have fair opportunities to achieve success in public education are inseparable, mutually dependent goals" (Coleman, 1998, p. 85). Coleman made it clear that the legal expectation is *not* that results will be equal. Instead, each child should have an equal *opportunity* to achieve high academic standards as measured by appropriate assessment processes. In that context, students must be given a fair opportunity to succeed on any high-stakes assessment process, but not a guarantee they will succeed. Unequal test scores do not necessarily point to inequities. Integrity of the test or decision process becomes the proof of fairness, indicated by careful alignment of standards, curriculum and instruction, assessment, and opportunity for intervention as the student works toward successfully taking the high-stakes assessment.

Multiple Purposes and Full Participation

One critical issue for full participation in large-scale assessment is the complexity of implementation at the state level. State education agencies must respond to their citizens and the local education agencies as well as to national reform movements, federal legislation, and state legislatures. No two constituents raise the same set of concerns. Schools want little to do with assessments for systems accountability unless the results will inform instruction (i.e., the systems must answer practical questions such as, Are the students strong or weak in algebraic concepts?). Taxpayers and therefore legislatures want to know that the money they spend translates into student learning. At the national level, we all want to know that our nation's students are globally competitive while governors and congressional representatives want assurance that students in their states are competitive compared with students in other states. Parents want to know that their sons and daughters are learning what they need to know to be successful in college and in life and may consider this the main purpose of testing. To earn their keep, state assessment systems attempt to do it all, often by asking the same assessment to fulfill several of these purposes.

   Understanding the issues surrounding multiple purposes of assessment systems is critical to understanding the issues that arise in implementing full participation (Almond, Quenemoen, Olsen, & Thurlow, 2000). Tests should be valid for the purpose that they are intended to serve and also for the population they measure. William Mehrens (see chap. 7, this volume) distinguishes between the purposes and stakes of state assessment programs and reminds us that assessments used for one purpose may look quite different from those used for another purpose. As Bob Linn (see chap. 2, this volume) indicates, recent state assessment and accountability systems attempt to support a variety of interpretations and serve a variety of purposes. Both Mehrens and Linn call for alignment of test use with test validity and emphasize the need for future studies on the validity of assessments to serve multiple purposes. Linn also addresses specific issues related to testing students with disabilities—in particular, validity in the context of test accommodations or modifications. He considers questions about the adequacy of removing the effect of the disability as ". . . fundamentally questions of validity of interpretations and uses of tests for individuals with disabilities."

What are the purposes that can be applied to large-scale assessments? The Committee on Appropriate Test Use identified seven distinct purposes for standardized student assessment at federal, state, and local levels (Heubert & Hauser, 1999). These purposes include: aiding in instructional decisions about individual students, providing information about the status of the education system, motivating change, evaluating programs, holding schools accountable for student performance, encouraging change in classroom instruction, and certifying individual student achievement or mastery. Each state has its own combination of purposes and its own collection of assessments to meet those purposes.

The theory of action discussed earlier provides a framework to organize the standards-based reform movement and provides a context for the multiple purposes of large-scale assessment. States have the mission of improved student achievement. The formula to achieve that mission includes standards and assessment for all students.

How have states woven together accountability for improved student achievement with full participation and other purposes? Many states instituted their own accountability mandates. Some states enhanced or redesigned existing large-scale assessments to meet federal systems' accountability requirements, demanding higher rates of participation and providing more accommodations. Some developed new systems in response to federal legislation. In some cases, districts, schools, teachers, and students became collectively or individually accountable for achievement. In many states, there continues to be an overlap in the function of the tests among purposes of accountability, school improvement, and measurement of individual student or group performance (Olson et al., 1999).

Emphasis on accountability spurred the participation requirements of recent federal legislation. When it comes to public schooling, public institutions are asked to assure taxpayers and their elected officials that, in fact, education is delivering a quality product with the funds expended. If improved student achievement is the target and equity is intended, then *all* students must participate in all aspects of the theory of action, including standards, assessment, and flexibility in addition to accountability. Students must be assessed on the standards, and schools must be held accountable for improved student achievement, not for some students or those traditionally assessed but for *every* student.

Accountability by itself does not inspire unanimous support from parents, teachers, and schools at the local level. Many believe testing strictly for purposes of accountability consumes too much valuable instructional time and interferes with local control of the education program. To be taken seriously, state mandates need to promote student achievement in ways that inform instruction and document improvement. As seen from the local level, state systems must benefit students and teachers directly.

This chapter focuses primarily on participation in large-scale assessments at the national, state, and local levels for the purposes of instructional improvement and system accountability. Yet the additional multiple purposes surrounding assessment systems are part of the fabric of assessment and education reform. All of the purposes become entangled with full participation. Although accountability for public education inevitably addresses every single student, an assessment system that includes all students and responds to all of its purposes must resolve a myriad of substantive technical issues. It appears that we are building toward assessment systems that can inform instruction and certify mastery for every individual student while simultaneously assuring the community, the legislature, and the Congress that public education is delivering its product—improved student achievement for all students. McDonnell (1994) concluded, "consequently, one criterion policymakers are likely to use in judging the feasibility of different assessment strategies is the extent to which multiple expectations can be met by the same system" (p. 11).

Intended and Unintended Consequences of Large-Scale Assessment

Clearly, there is legal impetus for including all students in assessment and accountability systems, but, we are compelled to ask, will these reforms affect special needs students positively and will the benefits outweigh the risks?

Despite the intended positive outcomes of higher student achievement, the potential for unintended negative consequences also exists. Preliminary data about the intended and unintended consequences of school reform for students with disabilities suggest the reform movement has influenced the implementation of additional policies and procedures, which must be examined for students in different groups. These secondary policies and practices are also intended to improve student learning and achievement. For example, states have begun to implement policies to end social promotion. The overall intent of these policies is to ensure that students have mastered grade-level material before being promoted. However, among the unintended effects of this policy may be an increase in the number of students retained and in the number of students who drop out; again, different groups of students may be affected differently (Quenemoen, Lehr, Thurlow, Thompson, & Bolt, 2000). As we implement standards-based reform and include all students in assessment and accountability systems, addressing positive and negative consequences of the reform for all students is essential. Understanding the complexities of varied and sometimes conflicting purposes and mandates for assessment is a primary challenge and another critical issue in addressing participation of all students in large-scale assessment.

The NAEP study on the inclusion of students with disabilities and limited English proficient (LEP) students raised an issue about the capacity to provide comparisons over time (Mazzeo et al., 2000). As the report pointed out, "accurately reporting changes requires keeping assessment procedures and instrumentation comparable." Although it is desirable to expand the number of LEP students and students with disabilities included in NAEP, making procedural modifications to the administration of NAEP can have an unintended consequence of clouding "the interpretation of changes in achievement over time" (Mazzeo et al., 2000, p. 14).

Another technical issue raised by the same NAEP study is the issue of the validity of results from nonstandard administrations and the comparability to results obtained under standard conditions. Data from the nonstandard administrations ". . . may not be able to be summarized and reported according to the same NAEP scale used for results obtained under standard conditions" (Mazzeo et al., 2000, p. 14). That is, do scale score results obtained under nonstandard conditions convey the same information about educational achievement as corresponding results obtained under standard conditions?

A final area of concern comes from the high-stakes nature of assessment results. There are two types of high stakes—those for individual students and those for schools, districts, and administrators. The draw of rewards can provide an inducement for students and/or schools to work harder to reach for the *brass ring*. For students or schools well below the standard, rewards or sanctions can provide a disincentive if achieving standards seems too far out of reach. There has been resistance among state education, school, and district personnel who are unaccustomed to including special needs students in assessments and reporting. For them the potential of having group results decline with the inclusion of special needs populations is a risk. In some communities, declines in scores bring sanctions. As one school principal commented after learning about the additional emphasis on including special needs students, "I just want to know how you are going to use the information against me." Responses such as this may be accompanied by less than enthusiastic implementation in the thrust for inclusion.

REVIEW OF RELEVANT RESEARCH AND CURRENT STUDIES ON PARTICIPATION

Common sense tells us that students excluded from large-scale state and district assessments are less likely to receive instruction in the curriculum content associated with those tests than are their tested classmates. Students with disabilities, students from disadvantaged backgrounds, and students who do not speak English as a first language have struggled to overcome low educational expectations for some time. Federal laws such as IASA and IDEA can be seen as legislated attempts to raise the bar. Indeed, studies have shown that expectations can be raised for many students. For example, *appropriate* assessment of English-language learners with tests that are nonbiased and more inclusive (e.g., language simplification) increase participation rates and validity of test results (Kopriva, 2000; Liu, Thurlow, Erickson, & Spicuzza, 1997), and many students with disabilities can participate in large-scale assessments without using accommodations (U.S. Department of Education, 2000). Inclusive school reform approaches begin with the assumption that all students can be included in the accountability system and all students have the opportunity to participate in the assessment and succeed.

There is evidence to suggest that benefits of reform efforts are tied to students who are a part of the movement, and it is reasonable to infer that those who are not included in the accountability system may not benefit from results of the reform effort (August & Hakuta, 1997; Thurlow, Elliott, & Ysseldyke, 1998). If students with disabilities, disadvantaged students, or students for whom English is a second language do not participate, there is less incentive to enhance their educational programs and improve their performance. An old adage suggests we "measure what we treasure." All of the students in our nation's schools are valuable, and we must include all of them in the measurement system to ensure they are afforded the opportunity to equally benefit from the reform movement.

It has become clear that when students are not included in large-scale assessments, we get an inaccurate understanding of student results and progress. If participation rates are not based on all students, comparing test results across schools, districts, and states is not valid (Zlatos, 1994). Even within the same school district, results can differ from school to school based on varying rates for including all students in testing. For example, School A may show a 90% passing rate on the state exam, whereas School B shows an 80% passing rate. It would appear that School A is out-performing School B unless participation rates are also reported for each school. When results and rates are reported together, it is found that School A only tested 70% of their students, whereas School B included 98% of their student enrollment. This scenario routinely plays out in schools and districts throughout the country. Furthermore, when high stakes are attached to large-scale assessments and special education students are allowed to be excluded from testing, students may be over-identified for special education (Allington & McGill-Franzen, 1992). This trend in identification of students as disabled results in both inaccurate representation of students who are truly disabled and an incomplete picture for system accountability.

Current Status of Large-Scale Assessment and Participation Nationwide

Large-scale assessment has steadily moved toward more inclusive practices over the past 10 years, especially since the reauthorization of IASA in 1994 and IDEA in 1997. It is no longer a question of *whether* students will participate, but *how* students will participate (IDEA, 1997). The Council of Chief State School Officers summarized the status of state student assessment programs (1997–1998) in its 1999 summary report (Olson et al., 1999). At that time, 48 of the 50 states had statewide assessment programs; the most commonly assessed grade levels were 4, 8, and 11, and the subject areas assessed most often were math and language arts/reading. Types of assessment included norm-referenced tests, criterion-referenced tests, writing assessments, performance assessments, and portfolios. The authors noted that, although nearly every state has a large-scale assessment program in place, the only constant in state assessment is change. In addition to changes in standards, test content, assessment approaches, and philosophies, many states use a combination of assessment types and formats to meet the purposes that their assessments are expected to address. Many of these changes are resulting in more inclusive assessment systems.

Participation rates of students with disabilities vary tremendously. A survey of state directors of special education conducted by NCEO indicated that more students with disabilities are participating in statewide testing, but only 23 states provided actual participation data (Thompson & Thurlow, 2000). Rates of participation for students with disabilities in these states ranged from 15% to 100%. Findings from the Council of Chief State School Officers' survey of state assessment directors indicate 40 states continued to allow some students with disabilities to be exempted from all state assessments in 1998. Thirty-six states reported allowing exemptions for English-language learners on all state assessments. Although more students with disabilities and students with limited English proficiency are participating in statewide testing, rates continue to vary widely across districts and states. In addition, accuracy of the participation rates is questionable, and the information continues to be difficult to collect (Olson et al., 1999). More precise information about the assessment of all students, including students with disabilities, must be gathered and reported to accurately reflect what is occurring for these students.

One example of a purposeful effort to increase the participation of all students in assessments is the National Assessment of Educational Progress (NAEP). At least half of all special needs students were excluded from NAEP assessments in 1992 and 1994 (U.S. Department of Education, 2000). Due primarily to concerns about excluding students who could be meaningfully assessed and concerns about bias produced by differences in participation rates across regions, NAEP conducted a study of two ways to possibly increase participation of all students. First, NAEP revised the criteria for including students in the assessment. The goal was to make the criteria clearer, more inclusive, and more likely to be applied consistently. Second, testing accommodations were offered to students with disabilities (whose IEP specified accommodations for testing) and LEP students (who required accommodations to take the test in English). Findings from this study show that "the inclusion of data from nonstandard administrations had no discernible effect on aggregate NAEP scaling results in mathematics and science at any of the three grades" (4, 8, and 12), and that "there were no significant differences in the overall means or in the means for significant subgroups at any of the three grades" (Mazzeo et al., 2000, p. xv). This effort to make the nation's measure of educational progress more inclusive sends a powerful message about the importance of including all students in reforms aimed at improving education. More important, it suggests that doing so will not suppress reported results.

Decision Making and Participation

Currently there are four generally agreed on ways that students may participate in large-scale assessments. These include participation (a) without accommodations, (b) with standard accommodations, (c) with nonstandard accommodations, and (d) in the alternate assessment. A fifth alternative has been to exempt some students from assessments altogether. However, the decision-making process for determining how a student participates is not always clear. The criteria used to increase participation rates of students with disabilities and English-language learners indicates the ambiguity of making decisions about which students are to be included in large-scale assessments and how they will participate. Recommendations for making participation decisions highlight the need for a clear decision-making process and clear documentation of these decisions on the IEPs of students with disabilities (Ysseldyke, Thurlow, McGrew, & Shriner 1994). However, in 1996, few states required participation decisions to be documented in the IEP (Erickson et al., 1996). English-language learners (ELL) also need clear decision making and documentation regarding participation and, as a group, lack the focal point provided for students with disabilities by the IEP.

Decisions about test participation continue to be made in an unsystematic manner and vary widely within states, districts, and schools. In an examination of decision making about participation in statewide assessments, DeStefano and Shriner (2000) found that participation tended to be an all-or-none phenomenon. Students either participated or they did not, and fewer than 10% of the sample took part of the state assessment, although this was encouraged. Teachers received training to help them make decisions about how students should participate in the state assessment. The authors argued that the training produced a more consistent, coherent, and legally defensible basis for making participation and accommodation decisions. This points to the need for improved clarity in criteria used for decision making across districts and states. It also points to the need for continued and additional staff development that enables educators to make informed decisions about the participation of all students, especially those with disabilities and ELLs.

Although guidelines for decision making about testing emphasize basing decisions on the individual needs of each student, other factors may inadvertently sway decisions made in schools. Oregon produced a bilingual Spanish–English side-by-side version of a mathematics assessment available to Hispanic students learning English as a second language. After equating studies were completed, the side-by-side assessment was administered as a standard administration to students who requested it. The group results from the first year of implementation showed a dramatic increase in participation for schools with large numbers of Hispanic students. Results also showed a drop in achievement when group results were reported in the press. Such effects of increased participation could ultimately affect future decisions about including all students in statewide assessments.

Increasing Participation With Accommodations

Few studies to date clearly demonstrate the effects of the availability of accommodations on rates of participation. The most notable findings come from the NAEP 1996 assessment. Participation rates for students with disabilities and LEP students increased in Grades 4 and 8 when accommodations were provided on the mathematics assessment (U.S. Department of Education, 2000). Primarily based on these findings, states expect participation rates to increase when accommodations are provided. Schools with increased participation rates may find that they have lowered group results when compared with prior years. Future studies may need to explore the rates of participation related to both standard and nonstandard accommodations.

Although federal law states that "children with disabilities must be included in state and district wide assessments with appropriate accommodations where necessary" (IDEA, 1997), the law does not explain which accommodations are acceptable, which may compromise the validity of the test results, or which students should receive accommodations. Educators, parents, and students must shoulder the responsibility for making good decisions about the use of accommodations. Most states have tried to grapple with the situation, and most have written guidelines to indicate which accommodations are considered standard and which are considered nonstandard (Thurlow, House, Boys, Scott, & Ysseldyke, 2000). Test publishers have also grappled with this question and have developed guidelines about accommodations that can be aggregated with other test results and those that cannot (CTB McGraw-Hill, 2000). Parents, teachers, and students have struggled to determine which accommodations are necessary based on the student's instructional program, needs, and accommodations used in the classroom. Finding common ground among policymakers, test publishers, practitioners, and parents can be a challenge.

Defining Accommodations: Implications for Participation. Accommodations are typically described as "changes in testing materials or procedures that enable the student with disabilities to participate in an assessment in a way that allows abilities to be assessed rather than disabilities" (Thurlow, Elliott, & Ysseldyke, 1998, p. 28). Accommodations are typically categorized according to whether they are changes in presentation (items read aloud), response (mark answers in the booklet), setting (use of a study carrel), or timing/scheduling (frequent breaks). For students with disabilities, the purpose of providing accommodations is to level the playing field so students can show what they know without interference from their disabilities. Some researchers reserve the term *accommodations* for changes in the way tests are administered or taken that do not result in changes to the construct being measured (Tindal, 1998). Tindal and Fuchs (1999) completed the most comprehensive synthesis to date of research on test accommodations. They suggest that a test change is considered an accommodation if it does not alter the construct being measured, is based on individual need, and is effective for students who need the change and not effective for others.

Changes in the way tests are administered or taken that may or do change the construct being measured are commonly referred to as *modifications, adaptations, alterations*, and *nonstandard, nonallowable*, or *nonapproved accommodations* (Thurlow & Wiener, 2000). The terminology can be confusing, and it is important to recognize that terms may have different meanings in various contexts. For example, Title I differentiates *accommodations* from *adaptations*. IDEA uses both *accommodation* and *modification*, but does not distinguish between the two. Some states use the term *modification* to indicate a testing change that alters the validity or comparability of the test score. Other states use terms like *nonallowed accommodation* or *nonapproved accommodation*. In most cases, accommodations (we call them *nonallowable*) that result in a change in the content or performance standards of what is being assessed yield results that cannot be aggregated with those results from the original standardized test.

The use of accommodations should be determined according to individual need on each portion of the assessment. It is important to understand the implications of selecting nonallowable accommodations because the resulting score may not be included in the accountability system. Any test change that is not allowed or not counted requires careful consideration. If it is determined that a student needs a nonallowable accommodation, it is important to understand and specify the implications of using that accommodation.

State Policies on Accommodations.   Nearly all states have policies on accommodations, and an examination of state policies on accommodations shows that these policies change frequently (Thurlow, House et al., 2000). In addition, there is little consistency across policies. For example, reading the test aloud is one of the most widely allowed *and* one of the most widely prohibited accommodations. Other controversial accommodations include the use of calculators, spell checkers, and extended time. The most commonly offered accommodations are large print and Braille; however, these are not the most frequently used. Most students who use accommodations use more than one at a time. This has implications for research tied to examining the effects of accommodations. Variation in accommodations policies for ELLs also exists. In 1998, English-language learners were allowed to use accommodations for all assessments in 29 states and were not allowed to use them for any assessments in 7 states.

The percentage of students using accommodations also varies widely across states (Thompson & Thurlow, 1999). Information collected from a survey of state directors of education yielded data from 12 states on the number of students with disabilities who used accommodations. The data show tremendous variability, and the percentage of students with disabilities who used accommodations ranged from less than 10% to over 80%.

States have made great strides in addressing the need for accommodations to enhance participation of all students. However, their efforts have also resulted in extreme variability, which reflects opinions and the status of research in the area of accommodations. Few states have a clear system of (a) tracking and documenting the decision-making process or the accommodations that students receive on tests, (b) recording the type of accommodation on the test protocol, and (c) compiling the data for state records. Furthermore, even if states have a system in place, results across states (districts or schools) may not be comparable due to inconsistencies in defining accommodations and terminology.

Accommodations Research. Clearly, there are many types of accommodations; unfortunately, we know very little about their uses and effects. The synthesis on test accommodations research compiled by Tindal and Fuchs (1999) addressed only 21 of the 65 accommodations listed, and many of the findings were contradictory or inconclusive. Many accommodations are listed for use without adequate supporting data. As a result, most policies and decisions about accommodations are based on opinion and expert judgment. Fortunately, the need for more methodologically sound research on the effects of test changes for diverse student populations is being recognized (National Association of State Directors of Special Education [NASDSE], 1999).

Some recent studies are helping us make better decisions about accommodations for students with disabilities—for example, studies investigating the utility of data-based assessment processes (e.g., curriculum-based measurement) to supplement teacher judgments about test accommodations suggest teachers may have a tendency to overaward accommodations not differentially effective for students with learning disabilities (Fuchs, Fuchs, Eaton, Hamlett, & Karns, 2000). Attention is being given to the importance of conducting carefully controlled experimental studies, and investigations of specific accommodations such as marking responses in test booklets and reading the test aloud have been conducted (Tindal, Heath, Hollenbeck, Almond, & Harniss, 1998). Research is also being conducted using large extant databases to analyze differential item functioning resulting from accommodations used by students with and without disabilities (Bielinski & Ysseldyke, 2000; Koretz, 1996). Each of these research approaches has an associated set of strengths and areas of weakness. In all cases, the need for researchers and practitioners to collaborate is paramount. Continued research is critical if we are to provide students with disabilities access to tests and maintain validity of test results.

Many of the issues associated with determining accommodations for students with disabilities and large-scale assessment are similar for students with limited English proficiency. A recent document entitled *Ensuring Accuracy in Testing for English Language Learners* (Kopriva, 2000) included information that can be used to increase the rate of participation in large-scale assessments for this population of students. Much of the empirical work on improving participation in large-scale assessments for LEP students focuses on test accommodations. Special emphasis is currently being given to reducing bias in testing (e.g., how items are developed and chosen for inclusion in the assessment) and constructing tests that support equity as they are being developed. Examples of studies focused on specific accommodations include investigations of oral and written administration of math tests in English and Spanish (Kopriva, 1994); use of extended time (Hafner, 1999); responding in written form or in native language (Abedi, Lord, Hofstetter, & Baker, 2000); and use of dictionaries (Albus, Bielinski, Thurlow, & Liu, 2001). A movement toward making tests more accessible to all students may decrease the need for accommodations. For example, to allow greater access, many test companies have incorporated larger print, decreasing the need for accommodations for some children with visual disabilities. Allowing tests to be untimed and reducing the verbal load on nonreading tests are other ways that tests may be constructed to decrease the need for accommodations. Attention to test development and increasing accessibility for all students without affecting the construct being measured will result in more inclusive participation.

Use of Alternate Assessments to Promote Participation

A small percentage of students will not be able to take regular tests even with accommodations. If all students are to participate, these students must be assessed using alternate assessments. Estimates suggest the percentage of students who will take alternate assessment is between 1% and 2% of the total student population (Notice of Proposed Rule Making, 1997). Students who take alternate assessments are generally those who are unable to show what they know on regular paper-and-pencil tests. The eligibility of students to participate in alternate assessments is typically determined by the IEP team and based on comprehensive historical or longitudinal data (Warlick & Olsen, 1998). The 1997 amendments to IDEA required states to have alternate assessment systems in place by July 1, 2000. Again, IDEA does not specify the form that alternate assessments should take, provide information about scoring, or clarify the type or number of students who should take alternate assessments. Frontline policymakers—administrators and educators in states and districts—are launching their first efforts to develop, implement, and administer quality alternate assessments as this chapter is being written.

Alternate Assessments: Development and Implementation. Information collected from an online survey designed to gather information about the status and development of alternate assessments shows that few states were actually implementing their alternate assessments, but most states were close to being ready to do so (Thompson, Erickson, Thurlow, Ysseldyke, & Callender, 1999). Nearly all states were developing alternate assessments using the expertise of assessment personnel from both special and general education. Involvement of both special and regular educators in the development of alternate assessments reflects the important role they can play in moving toward a more inclusive educational system. Stakeholders involved in the development of alternate assessments note a "renewed sense of professional pride, an increased awareness of the vocation, and an increased appreciation of the dedication and commitment to the success of all students" (Burgess & Kennedy, 1998, p. 11).

Most states are designing their alternate assessments based on general education standards (Thompson et al., 1999). Some states and/or districts have chosen not to base alternate assessments on state standards, but on separate skill sets not linked to general education standards or assessments. This may result in unintended consequences (like prohibiting student access to standards) and further separation of education programs (e.g., Title I, Bilingual Education, Special Education) each with their own curriculum. Approaches to developing alternate assessments are linked with philosophies toward participation and inclusive assessment. For example, Oregon clarified its plan to develop an approach that would include all students in a single comprehensive assessment system (Oregon Department of Education, 1999):

> We are attempting to have all students included in a single comprehensive assessment system and to avoid having an assessment that is the "alternate." The term "alternate" assessment suggests an undesirable contrast between the "real" assessment and the "alternate" assessment. Oregon's implementation of the alternate assessment requirement will be a lower end measure of the Career Related Learning (CRL) standards adopted by the State Board for the Certificate of Advanced Mastery. This CRL assessment design, intentionally does not exclude a student from academic achievement measures. Students assessed on career related learning measures might also be working toward academic standards in reading, math, science, or social science and vice versa. The two are intended to be mutually inclusive whenever possible, not mutually exclusive. (p. 1)

States are indeed moving forward with the development and implementation of their alternate assessments. The most prevalent alternate assessment approach is the collection of a body of evidence that assesses functional indicators of progress toward state standards using a variety of performance-based strategies. Two states—Oregon and Colorado—are launching novel performance measures that focus on standardized stimulus events and emphasize comparability in reporting. Other alternate assessments commonly take the form of checklists or rating scales of functional skills or an IEP analysis. Information collected by NCEO suggests the greatest needs are in developing scoring procedures and determining how data are reported. At this time, measures of proficiency vary across states more than do alternate assessment approaches. Extreme variability in the labels assigned to the measures of proficiency and also in what is measured by the alternate assessment will make it difficult to compare the performance of students taking alternate assessments across states. States are also wrestling with questions about who will score alternate assessments as well as procedures for scoring. Reliability and validity of alternate assessment scores must be addressed, and, again, the need for research and training is an issue that comes to the forefront. Beyond implementation and scoring of alternate assessments is a related important issue to consider as more and more students participate in large-scale assessments: How will the results of the alternate assessment be used? As alternate assessments are being developed and implemented nationwide, it is critical to identify practical uses of results early in the implementation.

Reporting Issues and Use of Data

The use of data from assessments in which all students have participated is a key issue to consider as we move to include all students in large-scale assessment systems. The standards reform movement emphasizes well-defined outcomes, assessment, and public reporting of scores as the basic accountability strategy. However, it is important to recognize that the work is not finished when the scores are reported. Participation of all students in large-scale assessments yields data that are used to make important decisions. It is imperative to limit decisions to those directly aligned with the purpose for which the test was developed and validated. Decisions made on the basis of a single test score from a large-scale assessment should be questioned—especially those that have high stakes attached and those that are tied to individual students (Heubert & Hauser, 1999). Most states use the data from large-scale assessments to guide statewide policy decisions (81%). Seventy-nine percent of the states indicate they use test results to guide curricular instructional decisions, 74% use them to guide decisions to reform schools, and 63% use test results to guide decisions about individual students (Thompson & Thurlow, 1999).

Developing accurate reporting practices and programs that include students with disabilities has proved difficult. Despite IDEA requirements for public reporting of assessment participation and performance data from students with disabilities, only 14 states included participation data, and only 17 states included performance data for students with disabilities in an analysis of 1999 public state reports (Thurlow, Nelson, Teelucksingh, & Ysseldyke, 2000). Major reasons for reporting difficulties include missing data or lack of data and the misalignment of data-collection efforts and data-management responsibilities (Erickson et al., 1996). Although calculating participation rates seems relatively straightforward, basic information about who participates in the assessment is still not consistently collected. IDEA and IASA require states to report the number of students tested, but reporting in the form of numbers yields limited information. Use of a denominator indicating the number of students enrolled on the day of the test is recommended so that participation rates can be calculated. Although there have been increases in the reporting of participation and performance data for various student groups, there are still significant challenges to be overcome in providing complete and accurate results from large-scale assessment.

Reporting the data is not sufficient to meet the letter or intent of IDEA or Title I statutes. A document from the U.S. Department of Education (2000b) highlighting questions and answers about state- and district-wide assessments noted:

> Participation of students with disabilities in State and district-wide assessments is not participation just for the sake of participation. Participation in these assessments should lead to improved teaching and learning. Furthermore, under IDEA, States must use information about the performance of children with disabilities in State and district-wide programs to revise their State Improvement Plans as needed to improve their performance. Under Title I, States and LEAs also use the results to review the performance of LEAs and schools, respectively, and to identify LEAs and schools in need of improvement. (p. 1)

The 1994 Title I requirements address the expectation that high standards must be set for all students. In addition, Title I law requires that states monitor adequate yearly progress toward achieving the goal of all students meeting high standards. The National Research Council (1999) suggested, "the concept [of adequate yearly progress] is central to accountability" (p. 85). Recognizing the challenges of defining and implementing the concept, they provided three strategies to ensure that schools will improve based on data:

- Measures of adequate yearly progress should include a range of indicators, including indicators of instructional quality as well as student outcomes.

- Measures of adequate yearly progress should include disaggregated results by race, gender, economic status, and other characteristics of the student population.
- The criterion for adequate yearly progress should be based on evidence from the highest-performing schools with significant proportions of disadvantaged students. (NRC, 1999, p. 88)

These three strategies should be considered in the light of efforts to ensure full participation in the assessment and accountability systems. Each state has unique adequate yearly progress definitions and processes, and all students should be included in these definitions and processes. The intended benefit of adequate yearly progress is improved teaching and learning, with improvement plans based on data. Clearly, if all students are to benefit from the data-based decision making that drives improvement, results for all students must be reported, and the results must count as part of the adequate yearly progress measures. When all students participate in statewide assessments, we can have a better picture of how well the schools in our nation are educating our students.

RECOMMENDATIONS

Including all students in large-scale assessments is not only critical for improving the achievement of all of our nation's students, but is now required by federal mandate. For all students to benefit from standards-based reform, all students must participate in the accountability systems designed to measure the degree to which our schools and students are meeting expectations. It appears that decisions about participation in assessments vary in response to several circumstances, including alignment between the assessment and the instruction, teacher knowledge, test validity, and the effect of reported results on educators. For example, special needs students are more likely to be excluded from participating in large-scale assessments if high stakes for schools or districts are attached to the test results. Special needs students are more likely to be excluded if the assessments or their purposes are of questionable validity for special populations. Also, students are more likely to be excluded if they have not been exposed to the curriculum or content being assessed or if teachers, parents, and/or students think the tests are irrelevant. In addition, there is anecdotal evidence that low-performing students may at times be excluded from testing to prevent their scores from suppressing group results. For the purpose of this chapter, we developed two sets of recommendations. The first set addresses needed research in the development, implementation, and analysis of inclusive large-scale assessment. The second set consists of practical recommendations intended to help guard against inappropriate test use while the nation continues to promote full participation and more research is being conducted. Underlying both sets of recommendations is the need to anchor policy in research. Tindal and Fuchs (1999) proposed that, "Somehow, researchers and practitioners need to collaborate more effectively and conduct broader research . . . on more diverse student populations, different tests, and with different decisions" (Tindal & Fuchs, 1999, p. 97). We support their appeal, and our strongest recommendation is for an alliance among those responsible for the technical, practical, and policy aspects of large-scale inclusive assessment.

More Validity Research

States and districts must document the technical adequacy of their assessments for the purposes that their assessments are expected to address. To do this, they begin by citing available research and methodologies that support the uses of their assessments, but more is needed. Given documented technical issues in the validity of assessment results for some purposes and some students, the question becomes not whether all students are included in the accountability system, but *how* they will be legitimately included. The use of multiple measures to ensure high-quality data for all students, with clear linkages of the body of evidence to the accountability index, is essential. Fairness in the use of results comes, in part, from the validity of the data and, in part, from equal participation. Only through these two aspects can test data be used for improvement. This chapter highlights areas of needed research that seem to flow from the move to full participation of all students in state and district assessments. We call for six areas of research that we believe will improve the ability of large-scale assessment systems to confidently draw conclusions from their assessments for all students, including special needs students.

Establish Validity for Diverse Populations. Our first recommendation is to establish the validity of existing assessments for students not originally included in the standardization sample and students for whom the interpretations of results have not been previously substantiated. Particularly in standardized norm-referenced assessments, the original standardization sample may provide limited ability to use the results of these assessments for different populations. We need both methodologies that extend assessments to new populations and guidelines for developing assessments with diverse standardization populations. We are at a crossroads, one in which policy is clearly ahead of documented technical adequacy. Future studies on assessment validity should include in their initial design diverse and representative populations of the students to be tested.

Establish Validity for Multiple Purposes.   Our second recommendation is to research the validity of using the same test to inform multiple purposes such as instructional planning, determine achievement against the standards, and certify individual student performance. Clearly more research is needed here. As states implement fully inclusive systems for multiple purposes, they need to validate the interpretations made from the results of these assessments. States should insist on additional research before encouraging some interpretations from their assessment systems. Without such research, caution is called for in using the results of large-scale assessments for individual student instructional planning, using a single test score to make decisions about an individual when the assessment was designed primarily to measure system performance, using particular assessments for multiple purposes that affect both groups and individuals, and determining the impact of accommodations on test validity. State assessment systems must, out of necessity, find ways to focus on accountability while also addressing student achievement in ways that both inform instruction and document improvement if they are to obtain cooperation and willing participation from students and local school districts.

Determine Validity for Nonstandard Accommodations.   We encourage the continuation of research on nonstandard test accommodations and the establishment of valid approaches for analyzing, reporting, and interpreting results for students tested with nonstandard accommodations. One essential need in the area of assessment and reporting is articulated in the NCEO Policy Direction on nonstandard accommodations (Thurlow & Wiener, 2000). Students in most states who take their assessments with modifications or nonstandard accommodations are not included in summary reports, and interpretations on meeting standards are not available for assessments taken under nonstandard accommodation conditions. We face the incongruity of needing to conduct assessments under nonstandard conditions and to report these results to comply with federal requirements and being unable to do so within existing technical guidelines. How to report these data and what to make of them is an essential next step in inclusive assessment and definitely an area that requires a partnership.

Establish the Reliability and Validity of Alternate Assessments.   Particularly in relation to established state content and performance standards, new alternate assessment systems, recently employed to address the IDEA '97 requirement for assessing all students, must be shown to be technically adequate. These measures are typically performance based with scoring systems whose reliability rests on a limited research base. Additionally, the content of the alternate assessments has been crafted with the intent to align them to specified content and performance standards. Initial work on this alignment was accomplished under considerable time constraints and again produced limited documentation about the success of the alignment. The technical adequacy of these measures needs to be documented and raised to the same quality level as that of traditional academic achievement measures.

Focus on Both Achievement and Progress. We recommend applying learning theory to the use of large-scale assessments and employing methodology around measuring and reporting on progress in achievement— not just performance against standards, but movement toward standards. At this time, it seems that the focus of large-scale assessment mostly centers on students taking the tests and then systems reporting their scores. If the accountability system embedded in standards-based reform is to be meaningful, educators, policymakers, and researchers must shift the focus to how outcome data are to be used. The intent is to improve the education system for all students, and special emphasis must be given to analyzing progress and performance gains and accurately interpreting results for all students. Results must translate into findings and information that can be used to produce improved learning for kids.

Continue Research Funding on the Affects of Participation Issues. We have barely scratched the surface in the area of research on participation in large-scale assessment. A multitude of questions must be rigorously studied so that our decisions about achievement are not based on biased judgments and opinions. Continued investigation is needed in these areas of research so that we can better understand the use of large-scale assessment with diverse populations, the effects of various accommodations on test validity for those populations, and the relationship between alternate assessments and the original content and performance standards established for *all* students. Some of these questions are beginning to be addressed, but timeliness is critical because special needs students across the nation increasingly participate in state and district large-scale assessments and have their scores reported to the public.

What to Do in the Meantime

State and district large-scale assessments are an integral part of public schooling in the United States. The nation did not wait until all of the research on validity was in before beginning to use assessments and their results to evaluate students, schools, and the performance of our public education systems. Decisions based on test results are being made now and will continue, so we must consider what educators should do in the meantime. In this section, we suggest several actions to take while we await definitive research on inclusive large-scale assessment.

Recognize and Understand the Federal Requirements Pertaining to Participation. It is clear there is similar intent and consistency in the requirements of federal legislation such as IASA, IDEA, and civil rights laws. Each sends a strong message about students' participation in large-scale assessment. The Office of Civil Rights (2000) summarized this common intent stating that, "In fact, the promotion of challenging learning standards for all students—coupled with assessment systems that monitor progress and hold schools accountable—has been the centerpiece of the education policy agenda of the federal government as well as many states" (p. ii).

It is essential that policymakers, educators, parents, researchers, and test publishers remain up to date on federal legislation. In addition to the primary language of the legislation, policymakers, practitioners, and test publishers need to be fully aware of the array of federal guidance and policy memos that inform implementation. For example, the Office of Special Education Programs (2000) provided a question-and-answer memorandum to clarify policy and practice related to Title I and IDEA legislation on inclusive assessment and accountability (Heumann & Warlick, 2000). Additional Title I guidance is available from several other sources as well. These guidance documents, specifically address the inclusion of students who are English-language learners and students with disabilities (U.S. Department of Education, Office of Elementary and Secondary Education, personal communication, September 7, 2000; *Peer reviewer guidance for evaluating evidence of final assessments under Title 1 of the Elementary and Secondary Education Act,* 1999).

Consider Implications of Multiple Purposes of Assessments. It is important to understand that tests are used for different purposes, and one test may not meet all needs. For example, a test that is designed for system accountability may not provide sufficient information to help design a student's instructional program. However, assessment systems are required to allow all students to participate in large-scale assessments, either as is, with accommodations, or in an alternate assessment. A state test given in Grade 8 may be extremely difficult for a student in Grade 8 who is reading at a fourth-grade level. However, this is not an appropriate reason to exclude the student from assessments used to measure performance of the school system in the district or state. In this case, multiple pieces of data may need to be collected for the student to meet all of the purposes for which the student is being assessed. In addition, it may be necessary to consider accommodations to allow tests to be more accessible for students or work toward making the assessment system broader in its ability to measure a wider range of student achievement.

The technical adequacy of existing large-scale assessments may not currently meet the challenges of multiple purposes and populations. The challenge is to improve our assessment options, not to exclude students based on that technical inadequacy. Yet states, districts, schools, parents, and the media should use caution and request additional research before encouraging some interpretations from their assessment systems. These include: relying on the results of large-scale annual assessments for individual student instructional planning, using a single test score to make decisions about an individual when the assessment was designed primarily to measure system performance, inappropriately using particular assessments for multiple purposes that affect both groups and individuals, and deciding the impact of accommodations on test validity without sufficient technical documentation.

Increase Communication Between Key Stakeholders. To promote full participation, it is critical that communication among researchers, policymakers, test publishers, parents, and practitioners takes place. This has not always occurred. For example, policymakers have established accommodation guidelines for their states that indicate which accommodations are allowable, but these may not match those specified by the publisher of the state's test. Furthermore, parents and practitioners may believe an accommodation is necessary based on a student's instructional program, but the accommodation may not be listed as an allowable accommodation on either the state or publisher list. In the meantime, researchers are focused on identifying which accommodations affect the validity of test scores using experimental designs that are difficult to generalize to real-world situations occurring in the classroom. Key stakeholders must make time for opportunities to exchange information and create networks that facilitate conversations among themselves about a variety of issues.

Continue to Improve Participation Policies and Practice. States have made clear progress in establishing policies on the participation of students in large-scale assessments. In 1993, only 28 states had policies on the participation of students in assessment; currently 48 states have these policies (Thurlow et al., 2000). However, there is variability in these policies reflected in length, specificity, and content. In the past, the National Center on Educational Outcomes provided suggestions about information that is essential to include in these policies (Elliott, Thurlow, & Ysseldyke, 1996). An updated set of recommendations suggests that policies must address the following in relation to participation: purpose and rationale for including all students in state and district assessments, explanations of who designed the guidelines, how students will be included and how decisions are made and documented, a clear process for compiling data, and a plan for dissemination and training, about how data are reported and used, and for evaluating and improving the assessment system.

Provide Training for Those Making Participation Decisions. The rapid pace of implementing inclusive large-scale assessments has not allowed sufficient opportunities for training. In many cases, parents, educators, and administrators are making decisions about participation or accommodations without clear procedures in place or an understanding of the effects of their decisions. Often educators are faced with conflicting information or they are given information that is misleading. Misinformation can promote misunderstandings that result in anxiety and feelings of helplessness or anger. Even before procedures can be put into place, training must explain the rationale for implementing large-scale assessment so that educators see the usefulness and benefits of having all students participate. Once there is a clear understanding, issues such as documentation of participation decisions, implications of accommodations use, or best practice in reporting can be addressed. Although taking time for training is a challenge, not implementing a comprehensive training package is likely to lead to confusion and perhaps even irreparable damage.

In conclusion, research to establish and improve the validity for inclusive large-scale assessment is strongly recommended within a partnership that includes measurement professionals, practitioners, researchers, and policymakers. Our recommendations recognize the lag between practice and technical adequacy for inclusive assessments and extend beyond the proposal of a research agenda to include recommendations for actions to be taken in the short term. There is a chasm between our awareness about the right thing to do—that is, be accountable for the achievement for all of the students in our public schools, and our technical knowledge about how to do this fairly within the context of our current large-scale assessment systems.

REFERENCES

Abedi, J., Lord, C., Hofstetter, C., & Baker, E. (2000). Impact of accommodation strategies on English language learners test performance. *Educational Measurement: Issues and Practice, 19*(3), 16–26.

Albus, D., Bielinski, J., Thurlow, M., & Liu, K. (2001). *The effect of a simplified English language dictionary on a reading test.* Manuscript submitted for publication, University of Minnesota.

Allington, R. L., & McGill-Franzen, A. (1992). Unintended effects of educational reform in New York. *Educational Policy, 6,* 397–414.

Almond, P., Quenemoen, R., Olsen, K., & Thurlow, M. (2000). *Gray areas of assessment systems* (Synthesis Report 32). Minneapolis: University of Minnesota, National Center on Educational Outcomes.

August, D., & Hakuta, K. (Eds.). (1997). *Improving schooling for language minority students.* Washington, DC: National Academy of Science.

Bielinski, J., & Ysseldyke, J. (2000, June). *The impact of testing accommodations on test score reliability and validity.* Paper presented at the annual conference of the Council of Chief State School Officers, Snowbird, UT.

Burgess, P., & Kennedy, S. (1998). *What gets tested gets taught, who gets tested gets taught: Curriculum framework development process.* Lexington, KY: University of Kentucky, Mid-South Regional Resource Center.

Coleman, A. L. (1998). Excellence and equity in education: High standards for high-stakes tests. *Virginia Journal of Social Policy and the Law, 6*(1), 81–113.

CTB McGraw-Hill. (2000). *Guidelines for using the results of standardized tests administered under nonstandard conditions.* Monterey, CA: Author.

DeStefano, L., & Shriner, J. (2000, June). *Strategies for improving teachers' decisions about participation and accommodation of students with disabilities in large-scale assessment.* Paper presented at the annual conference on large-scale assessment by the Council of Chief State School Officers, Snowbird, UT.

Elementary & Secondary Education Act as Amended by the Improving America's Schools Act of 1994, Pub. L. No. 103-382.

Elliott, J., Thurlow, M., & Ysseldyke, J. (1996). *Assessment guidelines that maximize the participation of students with disabilities in large-scale assessments: Characteristics and considerations* (Synthesis Report 25). Minneapolis, MN: University of Minnesota, National Center on Educational Outcomes.

Erickson, R., Thurlow, M., & Ysseldyke, J. (1996). *Neglected numerators, drifting denominators, and fractured fractions: Determining participation rates for students with disabilities in statewide assessment programs* (Synthesis Report 23). Minneapolis, MN: University of Minnesota, National Center on Educational Outcomes.

Fuchs, L. S., Fuchs, D., Eaton, S. B, Hamlett, C. L., & Karns, K. M. (2000). Supplementing teacher judgments of mathematics test accommodations with objective data sources. *School Psychology Review, 29*(1), 65–85.

Hafner, A. (1999, June). *Assessment accommodations that provide valid inferences for LEP students.* Paper presented at the annual conference of the Council of Chief State School Officers, Salt Lake City, UT.

Heubert, J. P., & Hauser, R. M. (1999). *High stakes testing for tracking, promotion, and graduation.* Washington, DC: National Academy Press.

Heumann, J. E., & Warlick, K. R. (2000). Questions and answers about provisions in the Individuals with Disabilities Education Act Amendments of 1997 related to students with disabilities and state and district-wide assessments (*Office of Special Education Programs Memorandum 00-24*). Washington, DC: U.S. Department of Education, Office of Special Education Programs.

Individuals with Disabilities Education Act Amendments of 1997, 20 U.S.C. Sec. 1400 *et seq.*

Kopriva, R. (1994). *Validity issues in performance assessment for low, mid and high achieving ESL and English only elementary students* (Technical Report). Sacramento, CA: California Department of Education.

Kopriva, R. (2000). *Ensuring accuracy in testing for English language learners.* Washington, DC: Council of Chief State School Officers.

Koretz, D. (1996). *The assessment of students with disabilities in Kentucky* (SCE Technical Report No. 431). Los Angeles, CA: CRESST.

Liu, K., Thurlow, M., Erickson, R., & Spicuzza, R. (1997). *A review of the literature on students with limited English proficiency and assessment* (Minnesota Report 11). Minnesota Assessment Project, University of Minnesota.

Mazzeo, J., Carlson, J. E., Voelkl, K., & Lutkus, A. D. (2000). *Increasing the participation of special needs students in NAEP* (NCES Publication No. 2000-473). Washington, DC: National Center for Educational Statistics.

McDonnell, L. M. (1994). *Policymakers' views of student assessment* (CSE Technical Report 378). Los Angeles, CA: CRESST.

National Association of State Directors of Special Education. (1999). *Test changes: An empirical basis for defining accommodations*. Washington, DC: Author.

National Research Council. (1999). *Testing, teaching, and learning: A guide for states and school districts*. Washington, DC: Author.

Notice of Proposed Rule Making. (1997). Assistance to States for the Education of Children with Disabilities, Preschool Grants for Children with Disabilities, and Early Intervention Program for Infants and toddlers with Disabilities; Proposed Rule 62 Fed. Reg. 55026-55135, Wednesday, October 22, 1997.

Office of Civil Rights. (2000). *The use of tests when making high-stakes decisions for students: A resource guide for educators and policymakers*. Washington, DC: Author.

Olson, J. F., Bond, L., & Andrews, C. (1999). *State student assessment programs: Data from the annual survey*. Washington, DC: Council of Chief State School Officers.

Oregon Department of Education. (1999, June). *A case for comprehensive*. Concept paper presented at the Alternate Assessment Forum preconference to the Large Scale Assessment conference, Snowbird, UT.

Quenemoen, R., Lehr, C., Thurlow, M., Thompson, S., & Bolt, S. (2000). *Social promotion and students with disabilities: Issues and challenges in developing state policies* (Synthesis Report 34). Minneapolis: University of Minnesota, National Center on Educational Outcomes.

Thompson, S., Erickson, R., Thurlow, M., Ysseldyke, J., & Callender, S. (1999). *Status of the states in the development of alternate assessments* (Synthesis Report 31). Minneapolis, MN: University of Minnesota, National Center on Educational Outcomes.

Thompson, S., & Thurlow, M. (1999). *1999 state special education outcomes*. Minneapolis, MN: National Center on Educational Outcomes.

Thompson, S., & Thurlow, M. (2000). *State alternate assessments: Status of IDEA alternate assessment requirements take effect* (Synthesis Report 35). Minneapolis, MN: University of Minnesota, National Center on Educational Outcomes.

Thurlow, M. L., Elliott, J., & Ysseldyke, J. (1998). *Testing students with disabilities: Practical strategies for complying with district and state requirements*. Thousand Oaks, CA: Corwin.

Thurlow, M. L., House, A. L., Boys, C., Scott, D. L., & Ysseldyke, J. E. (2000). *Assessment participation and accommodation policies for students with disabilities in 1999*. Minneapolis, MN: University of Minnesota, National Center on Educational Outcomes.

Thurlow, M. L., Nelson, J., Teelucksingh, E., & Ysseldyke, J. (2000). *Where's Waldo? A third search for students with disabilities in state accountability reports*. Minneapolis, MN: University of Minnesota, National Center on Educational Outcomes.

Thurlow, M. L., & Wiener, D. (2000). *Non-approved accommodations: Recommendations for use and reporting* (Policy Directions No. 11). Minneapolis, MN: University of Minnesota, National Center on Educational Outcomes.

Thurlow, M., Ysseldyke, J., Gutman S., & Geenan, K. (1998). *An analysis of inclusion of students with disabilities in state standards documents* (Technical Report 19). Minneapolis, MN: University of Minnesota, National Center on Educational Outcomes.

Tindal, G. (1998). *Models for understanding the task comparability in accommodated testing*. Washington, DC: Council of Chief State School Officers.

Tindal, G., & Fuchs, L. S. (1999). *A summary of research on test changes: An empirical basis for defining accommodations*. Lexington, KY: University of Kentucky, Mid-South Regional Resource Center.

Tindal, G., Heath, B., Hollenbeck, K., Almond, P., & Harniss, M (1998). Accommodating students with disabilities on large-scale tests: An empirical study of student response and test administration demands. *Exceptional Children, 64*(4), 439–450.

U.S. Department Education. (1999). *Peer reviewer guidance for evaluating evidence of final assessments under Title 1 of the Elementary and Secondary Education Act*. Washington, DC: Office of Elementary and Secondary Education.

U.S. Department of Education. (2000). *Increasing the participation of special needs students in NAEP: A report on 1996 NAEP research activities* (National Center for Education Statistics 2000-473). Washington, DC: NCES.

Warlick, K., & Olsen, K. (1998). *How to conduct alternate assessments: Practices in nine states.* Lexington, KY: University of Kentucky, Mid-South Regional Resource Center.

Ysseldyke, J. E., Thurlow, M. L., McGrew, K. S., & Shriner, J. G. (1994). *Recommendations for making decisions about the participation of students with disabilities in statewide assessment programs* (Synthesis Report 15). Minneapolis, MN: University of Minnesota, National Center on Educational Outcomes.

Zlatos, B. (1994). Don't test, don't tell: Is "academic red-shirting" skewing the way we rank our schools? *The American School Board Journal, 181*(11), 24–28.

Chapter 15

Assessment of English-Language Learners in the Oregon Statewide Assessment System: National and State Perspectives

Richard P. Durán
University of California–Santa Barbara

Catherine Brown
Oregon State Department of Education

Marty McCall
Oregon State Department of Education

Oregon's response to the assessment of English-language learners[1] (ELLs) can inform progress on national assessment issues as well as issues unique to Oregon. Like other states, Oregon is deeply involved in responding to national- and state-level calls for education reform, including calls for the use of assessments as tools to inform accountability and the use of assessment in making increasingly high-stakes decisions about students' educational progress and certification. In this chapter, we examine Oregon's strategies and outcomes for ELL assessment introduced since passage of 1991 legislation creating the Oregon Statewide Assessment System.[2] We begin with mention of national policy issues and related assessment concerns in the area of ELL assessment and the dovetailing of these concerns with fundamental validity issues in assessment.

Implementation of standards-based education reform and related assessments for ELL students has proved to be problematic for states (Na-

---

[1]We here define *English-language learners* (ELLs) as persons from a non-English background who are identified as limited English proficient based on state or testing agency procedures. Alternatively in the field such persons are identified as *limited English proficient*.

[2]Related discussions of assessment policy issues, legal issues, and test development and administration issues faced in maximizing participation of ELLs and special education students are discussed in other chapters in this volume. See the chapters by Phillips and Hollenbeck, and Choi in particular.

tional Research Council, 1997). Federal statutes and education legislation place a premium on maximizing participation of students in assessments of value to improving educational outcomes for students while emphasizing fair and equitable assessment and instruction of all students.[3] The situation is complex because assessment remedies prescribed or recommended by court decisions and education laws may only be partially implemented, and accompanying validity research to back up use on existing or new assessments, likewise, is only partially implemented.

For example, Title I of the 1994 Improving America's Schools Act (IASA) made important stipulations regarding steps that states should take to maximize participation of ELL students in assessments set against state education standards as a requirement for states' receipt of Title I funding. According to Title I, by the 1997 to 1998 school year, states were expected to have challenging standards in place for reading, mathematics, and possibly other subjects for *all* students. By the beginning of the 2000 to 2001 school year, states were to have put in place high-quality yearly assessments, at least in reading and mathematics, to gauge students' progress against standards. Third, within 5 years from enactment of the law, corresponding to 2000 to 2001, states were expected to define and operationalize adequate yearly progress of students toward attaining standards based on state assessments and other measures. Guidelines developed by the U.S. Department of Education (1996) for implementing Title I offer specific advice regarding ELL students. This advice regarding assessment states (as cited in American Institutes for Research [AIR], 1999):

> Inclusion of LEP students, who shall be assessed, to the extent practicable, in the language and form most likely to yield accurate and reliable information on what they know and can do to determine their mastery of skills in subjects other than English. (To meet this requirement, the State shall make every effort to use or develop linguistically accessible assessment measures, and may request assistance from the Secretary if those measures are needed.) (p. 7)

Regarding instruction, the guidelines state as follows (cited in American Institutes for Research, 1999):

---

[3]Valuable documents summarizing and addressing these concerns include but are not restricted to the Office of Civil Rights' report, *The Use of Tests When Making High Stakes Decisions for Students"* (U.S. Department of Education, 2000), the National Research Council (1999a) report to Congress *High Stakes: Testing for Tracking, Promotion, and Graduation*, the National Research Council (2000) report *Testing English-Language Learners in U.S. Schools*, the American Educational Research Association, American Psychological Association, National Council on Measurement in Education (1999) *Standards for Educational and Psychological Testing*, the National Research Council (1997) report *Improving the Schooling for Language-Minority Children*, and the CCSSO (Kopriva, 2000) report *Ensuring Accuracy in Testing for English Language Learners*.

All students, including economically disadvantaged students, limited-English proficient students (LEP) students and students with diverse learning needs, are expected to learn the same general high-quality content, rather than a separate curriculum for certain students, although a wide range of instructional methods and strategies could be used. (p. 7)

Title VII of the 1994 Improving America's Schools Act has complementary provisions affecting assessment of LEP students that must be met for states to qualify for funding. These include the provision that, as part of their Biennial Evaluation Reports on the educational status of LEP students, states must provide:

- information regarding the validity and reliability of assessment instruments,
- information about how students are achieving the challenging state content and performance standards, and
- data comparing LEP students with non-LEP students with regards to achievement in academic content areas, school retention, English proficiency, and native language proficiency where applicable. (American Institutes for Research, 1999, p. 9)

There is considerable consensus in the field of measurement and educational policy formulation that assessment of ELLs, in light of such stipulations, raises major challenges. The *Standards for Educational and Psychological Testing* (American Educational Research Association, American Psychological Association, National Council on Measurement in Education, 1985, 1999) holds that every assessment is, in part, also a language assessment in that language is always involved in administering and responding to test items. Clearly, when tests are administered in English, ELLs' performances are affected by their proficiency in English as well as their knowledge of the content and skills reflected in assessment items. Standard 9.1 of the 1999 Standards states, "Testing practice should be designed to reduce threats to the reliability and validity of test score inferences that may arise from language" (p. 97) in assessment contexts where language skills are not the primary or intended construct being assessed.

An initial question faced by states and other agencies administering large-scale assessments is whether ELLs are capable of being assessed in English *at all* using standard assessment instruments and administration procedures. If not, then ELLs must be excluded altogether or other instruments and assessment procedures must be used to assess these students in the intended construct areas.

The following four areas of understanding are pivotal to addressing these questions and deserve elaboration: (a) understanding of ELLs' critical background and educational characteristics and their relevance to students' prior and current educational experiences, (b) design and implementation of procedures to determine whether students from non-English backgrounds can participate in available and relevant assessments, (c) determination of how students participate in assessments, and (d) analysis of assessment results and provision of opportunities for ELL students to learn the content and skills targeted by policy and assessments.

BACKGROUND AND EDUCATIONAL CHARACTERISTICS

The schooling and assessment of English learners need to be interpreted in the context of sound knowledge about the the sociocultural and educational background of these students. Students' school achievement has been found to be related to family socioeconomic and educational attainment, home language practices, and family mobility. Other important factors include length of residence in a predominantly English environment in the United States, prior formal schooling patterns, English language proficiency, and, particularly, academic proficiency in English (Butler & Stevens, 1997). As shown later, not all of the foregoing necessarily weigh in a decision about whether and how English learners participate in assessments. However, in the end, these factors have important implications for developing strategies to match assessments with students' opportunity to learn the skills and knowledge targeted by states and federal educational policies.

For students to participate meaningfully in assessment, there also needs to be confidence that assessments are meaningful for students given any prior opportunities they may have had to learn the skills and content being assessed. Although extremely low test scores may result if students have had little or no exposure to skills and content under assessment, assessments of ELL students' achievement may yield statistically less reliable information about what students actually know and can do in the content and performance domains under assessment in comparison with English background students (Abedi, Lord, Hofstetter, & Baker, 2000). Further, the administration of an assessment under these circumstances may also prove to be frustrating and senseless to students.

Participation: Exclusion Versus Inclusion

Maximizing participation of ELLs in statewide assessments is a critical federal policy and state-level goal. If states and local education agencies (LEAs) are accountable for the achievement of all their students, then failure to include English learners in assessments in significant numbers invalidates the analyses of school needs and services, misses information regarding the progress of such students, and distorts evidence of the overall achievement levels and progress of students in a state. The rapid rates of growth in the English-learner populations and federal and state policy requirements cited earlier have had a dramatic impact on states. However, it is difficult to obtain definitive data on what is occurring because of the rapid policy changes among states and the use of differing standards among states to interpret and implement policies.

Next we rely on data compiled by Rivera, Stansfield, Scialdone, and Sharky (2000) in a content analysis of official 1998 to 1999 state documents regarding inclusion and accommodation policies and implementation. The study in question was sponsored by the Office of Bilingual Education and Language Minority Affairs. It is important to note that the results of this study, although suggestive of important trends, cannot be assumed to reflect accurate accounts of current state policies and practices due to the dynamic changes occurring from year to year in these policies and practices. There is variation among states in identifying critical variables that define the population of limited English proficient students (termed ELLs here) and the meaning and scope of testing accommodations intended to increase participation of ELLs in assessments. This variation adds to the difficulty of identifying commonalities and differences in policies and practices among states.

According to Rivera et al. (2000), by the 1998 to 1999 school year, 48 states had implemented formal policies for the inclusion or exclusion of ELL students in state assessments, with much of this impetus traceable to attempts to fulfill the provisions of the Improving America's School Act (IASA) and Title I in particular.

With regard to identification of ELLs, Rivera et al. (2000) reported that 41 of 49 states with statewide assessments in 1998 to 1999 utilized definitions of *limited English proficiency* in their assessment programs. Fifteen of these states used the definition provided by the IASA Act of 1994.[4] Another 26 states utilized alternative definitions of LEP status.

---

[4] The federal definition of *limited English proficiency* is found in Section 1 of the Bilingual Education Act, Title VII of the Elementary and Secondary Education Act, as amended in the Improving America's Schools Act of 1994 and states: PART E—GENERAL PROVISIONS.

SEC. 7501. DEFINITIONS; REGULATIONS.

Except as otherwise provided, for purposes of this title—

(8) Limited English proficiency and limited English proficient.—The terms "limited English proficiency" and "limited English proficient," when used with reference to an individual, mean an individual—

(A) who—

(i) was not born in the United States or whose native language is a language other than English and comes from an environment where a language other than English is dominant; or

The following four classes of inclusion/exclusion criteria were common: (a) [English-proficiency] language criteria, (b) time-related criteria, (c) academic criteria, and (d) other judgment-related criteria. In 1998 to 1999, nearly half of all states used formal and informal assessment of English language proficiency as one criterion for making inclusion decisions. States, to a lesser extent, also relied on information about the language services currently provided to students and information about students' native language proficiencies.

With regard to time criteria for inclusion/exclusion decisions, 1998 to 1999 state document data indicate that 35 states had provisions for excluding or including students in English-language assessments based on the number of years they had exposure to English-language schooling. Twenty-one states allowed LEP students to be excluded from assessments for up to 3 years, 11 other states allowed exemption up to 2 years, and 2 for more than 3 years. One state had no time limit (Rivera, Stansfield, & Sharkey, 2000).

How ELLs Participate in Assessments

The participation of ELLs in a state assessment is desirable only if this participation yields valid information regarding students' proficiency in the content and skill domains targeted for assessment. States' efforts to follow professional testing and assessment standards for ELLs is being advanced by their strategies and ongoing programs of research and development, which are addressing how the performance of ELLs on assessments meets professional and technical assessment standards for reliability, validity, and assessment fairness.

As Kopriva (2000) pointed out, the underlying issues about how best to include ELLs in assessment are deeply intertwined in and permeate the processes of assessment design, development, administration, scoring, and reporting of assessment results. Each of these issues is implicated when considering how states include ELLs in assessments. As we show in this chapter, Oregon has made considerable strides in these areas. However, for synoptic purposes, the basic strategies for ELL students' participation in state assessments are fairly circumscribed.

(ii) is a Native American or Alaska Native or who is a native resident of the outlying areas and comes from an environment where a language other than English has had a significant impact on such individual's level of English language proficiency; or

(iii) is migratory and whose native language is other than English and comes from an environment where a language other than English is dominant; and

(B) who has sufficient difficulty speaking, reading, writing, or understanding the English language and whose difficulties may deny such individual the opportunity to learn successfully in classrooms where the language of instruction is English or to participate fully in our society.

First, ELL students participating in state assessments can be administered the same English-language assessments given to other students using identical administration procedures. Second, they can be given these assessments using other administration procedures. Third, ELL students might be administered assessments other than normal state assessments, but targeted at the same constructs as the state assessments. Just as there is variation in defining limited English proficiency status, there is also variation in the terminology that states use to describe those strategies to maximize participation of ELL students in assessments. The term *assessment accommodation* is widely used nationally to refer to changes in assessments that permit ELL students to take essentially the same assessments (questions and exercises) administered other students.

In Oregon, the term *accommodation* has a different meaning. It means changes in test administration or test presentation that are judged not to affect the validity of test results. Scores from tests taken with accommodations are treated the same as scores based on nonaccommodated administrations of tests in terms of measurement scale properties, reporting, and decision making. Changes in test administration or presentation that are judged to lead to invalid scores are called *modifications*. Scores from assessments administered in undermodified conditions in Oregon cannot be used as evidence of students meeting state assessment standards. Such scores are not included in reports regarding students' performances in the aggregate or by reporting subgroup categories, nor are they used in evaluating schools' performance.

In understanding Oregon's contribution nationally, it is helpful to review the notion of accommodation in its more common usage in most states. Nationally, accommodations in assessment are most commonly implemented in the administration procedures for assessments, the format and presentation of assessment questions and exercises, and the response formats permitted examinees (Kopriva, 2000).

States show considerable variation in the particular accommodations used. The summary of this variation and the usage patterns that follow are taken from Rivera, Stansfield, and Sharkey (2000). Nearly half of all states allowing accommodations for ELL students permit accommodations in the administration of assessment questions and in the presentation or response formats for test questions and exercises.

Adjusting the setting for an assessment (such as administering an assessment in a small group, individualized administration of an assessment, or administering an assessment in an isolated space) was available as an accommodation by all 37 states that indicated they allowed accommodations for ELL students in 1998 to 1999.

Varying the timing conditions for administering an assessment was also widely available as an accommodation option. Allowing extra time during assessments and time breaks during an assessment were the most common timing accommodations given to ELL students, although this is not an issue in a state such as Oregon. Extra time to complete oral reading of questions in English was possible in 24 states for some portions of an assessment. This was the most popular time accommodation of all.

Use of a bilingual word list or bilingual dictionary was the most frequent presentation accommodation. Eleven states in 1998 to 1999 permitted this accommodation on all tests while another 10 states allowed it only on some components of the state tests. Although use of a bilingual word list or dictionary was permissible in 22 states, only 4 (Colorado, Massachusetts, Oregon, and Wyoming) allowed use of bilingual tests where instructions and test items were available in two languages simultaneously. Of these states, only Wyoming had allowed bilingual test presentation for all its state tests. Use of translated tests (from English to another target language) of English in place of English-language assessments (or bilingual version tests) was available in 11 states. Although Spanish was the most predominant non-English language associated with translated tests, other target languages included Chinese, Haitian Creole, Hmong, Korean, Vietnamese, and Russian.

Assessments and Opportunity to Learn

At present, we lack a comprehensive and current analysis of states' strategies for using assessment information to guide provision of educational services leading to ELL students' attainment of state content and performance standards under provisions of federal regulations such as Title I and Title VII. The current period of assessment reform has placed intense demands on states both to implement and align assessments with state standards. This is often in a context where both assessments systems and state standards have required step-by-step planning, development, implementation, and vetting among concerned stake holders and constituencies. As a result, the capacity of states to align teacher preparation programs and in-service staff development programs to align instruction, and opportunity to learn, with state standards and assessment has lagged in implementation. By mid-2000, only 13 states (Oregon included) had submitted evidence to the U.S. Department of Education for evaluation of their state assessment systems for compliance with Title I provisions (U.S. Department of Education, 2000). Given the evidence available, Oregon has been "conditionally approved." Two conditions to be addressed are the ability to disaggregate by "free and reduced lunch" and establishing a process for including students testing under modified conditions (or being exempted from testing) in the school report card.

As noted in the following section, Oregon's implementation of its assessment system is highly integrated with its standards and accountability system, and it also includes development of strategies for involving teachers and teacher trainers as assessors of students.

THE OREGON CONTEXT

Oregon has been experiencing continuous growth in its minority population. In 1995, the number of students of Hispanic origin attending Oregon schools amounted to 8% of the state's student population. During the 1999 to 2000 school year, the number of Hispanic students had risen to 9.5% of the total student population. Students of Russian origin comprised the second largest language minority student population in Oregon, approaching the percentage rates for students of Hispanic origin.

Requirements for a Certificate of Initial Mastery and Standards

The Oregon Education Act for the 21st Century, enacted into law in 1991, sets forth an assessment program leading to a Certificate of Initial Mastery (CIM). Students participate in statewide testing designed to assess the state-adopted content standards benchmarked at Grades 3, 5, 8, and 10. The state tests are not gatekeepers; students may advance to the next grade regardless of their scores. However, schools are required to communicate to parents the student status in relation to the benchmark standard.

To obtain a CIM, students must demonstrate criterion levels of performance in (English—reading, writing, and speaking—mathematics, science, social science, the arts, and second language). These performances are to be measured using combinations of (a) state multiple-choice tests, (b) state on-demand assessments, and (c) collections of student work aligned to the benchmark expectations for the content standards.

Professional testing standards are central to executing this charge. Oregon Education Code states: "The Department of Education shall implement statewide a valid and reliable assessment system for all students that meets technical adequacy standards" (ORS 329.485). This concern for establishing technical adequacy first requires a shared public understanding of the meaning of standards. Next we illustrate how content and performance standards are elaborated in state code.

The following is an example of a content standard (one of six within mathematics) for statistics and probability. The standard states: "Carry out and describe experiments using measures of central tendency and variability." Under this content standard, the Grade 8 benchmark for statistics specifies:

- Plan and conduct experiments and simulations using data to make predictions or support arguments.
- Collect and analyze data using measures of central tendency and variability.
- Make inferences and convincing arguments.
- Compute a variety of statistics.

An example of a performance standard in writing is: At Grade 10, students must:

Take the state on-demand writing assessment (over three sessions).

Score a composite total of 40 points or higher from the two raters using a 6-point scale (Ideas and Content, Organization, Sentence Fluency, & Writing Conventions)—with conventions doubled—as well as having no score from either rater lower than a 3.

Produce classroom work samples.

Write three papers showing expository and persuasive and either narrative or imaginative writing, which may include a research paper with citations, or a business, technical, or vocational paper—scoring at the four level or higher in each of the same required traits as the state writing assessment.

In Oregon, communication and dissemination of content and performance standards such as the foregoing have taken into account the language background of students and their families. For example, the adopted content and performance standards cited were translated directly into Spanish and published in a side-by-side format available to students, families, and the general public. This step of making information on standards available to Oregon's major non-English-language communities contributes toward the goal of ensuring that the public understands that the same content and performance standards are expected of all students.

Oregon's Development of Spanish–English Assessments

In accordance with federal guidelines such as those mentioned earlier in this chapter, Oregon Education policy states,

The State Board [of Oregon] believes that immigrant, national origin, and limited English proficient students can perform to the same high standards as all students when provided with comprehensible instruction. The Board believes that it is the legal and ethical responsibility of the school to provide comparable educational programs [including assessments] designed for children and youth whose home language is other then English. For students whose home language is other than English, the Board believes that equitable educational opportunity includes comprehensible instruction in the core curriculum to prevent students from falling behind as they learn English, *and* English as a second language classes which provide an articulated transition between the student's native language foundation and the development of the cognitive/academic levels of English proficiency that are used in English-language classroom instruction."[5]

The prior statutes require all Oregon public school students to participate in statewide assessment and data-collection systems, comparisons to be made between performance levels of minority and nonminority children, and school improvement plans to address the needs of minority children and additional services be made available if, at any point, a student is not making adequate progress.

The Evolution of Oregon's Spanish/English Assessments in Writing, Multiple-Choice Mathematics, and Mathematics Problem Solving

In April, 1995, the State Board approved the development of Spanish-language versions of the Oregon Statewide Assessment. The direction given to the Department was for the Spanish–English assessments to be considered modified assessments until research had been completed revealing the relationship between the Spanish–English versions of the assessments and those produced only in English.

With the assistance of a grant from the U.S. Department of Education, Office of Educational Research and Improvement (OERI), the Oregon Department of Education investigated the reliability and validity of assessments for those students who were not yet fully literate in English.

As the writing scoring guide (rubric) was translated into Spanish, some additions were required—such as, for example, the diacritical marks appropriate to Spanish orthography being considered in conventions. The writing prompts are presented to the students in a side-by-side Spanish–English format. Students can respond using either language. Native Spanish speakers (and readers) score the student responses.

In addition to writing, the department field tested and then fully implemented a side-by-side Spanish–English and Russian–English format for multiple-choice mathematics and mathematics problem-solving assess-

[5]Oregon State Board of Education Policy (3820.5)
Ref.: Civil Rights Act, 1964; IASA, 1995; ORS 329.025, 329.035, 329.465, and 336.082; ORS 336.074 and 336.079; ORS 317.013 and OAR 581-23-100; IASA, ORS 329.105, ORS 329.115, ORS 329.485, ORS 329.900, and ORS 342.443

ments. The mathematics problem-solving scoring guide was translated into both Spanish and Russian.

With both the mathematics problem-solving and writing assessments, raters are trained in exactly the same manner as the raters scoring papers completed in English. All raters use the same training materials (the writing training materials are supplemented by papers in Spanish). All raters participate in the same qualifying process, use the same refresher papers, and follow the same procedures for scoring.

The writing and mathematics side-by-side bilingual assessments use a strategy of translating items from English into a Spanish or Russian equivalent as opposed to developing new and/or different items in each language and then developing English equivalents. Through the OERI grant, members of the Office of Assessment and Evaluation as well as the Office of Student Services met with the Technical Design Team (TDT) in September 1997 to facilitate this process and ensure quality. The TDT (an advisory group of nationally renowned experts)[6] was charged with overseeing the technical adequacy of the Oregon Statewide Assessment Program. As a part of their assignment, the group reviewed the process and results of the bilingual (Spanish–English) assessments and was informed of plans and progress on developing English–Russian assessment as well as about the feasibility of developing additional dual-language assessments.

Given that assumptions about the equivalence of item difficulties across language populations are required (see Choi & McCall, chap. 13, this volume), the TDT advised that the department had established reasonable evidence under the circumstances to confirm that the English assessments and the bilingual language assessments in mathematics and writing provided the same information about student achievement. Their advice for cleaning up small steps in the process (i.e., include a final review of the format prior to printing) was implemented.

In December 1997, the State Board approved reclassifying the bilingual assessments from modified administration status to standard administration status. Then in 1998, the State Board adjusted the decision. This means that student responses to the writing prompt in any language other than English are considered a modified administration and cannot be

---

[6]Members of the technical design team:
Thomas Haladyna, Arizona State University (Chairman); Barbara Dodd, University of Texas at Austin; Russell Gersten, University of Oregon; Robert Hess, Arizona State University; Ronald Houser, Portland Public Schools; Robert Linn, University of Colorado; Martha Thurlow, University of Minnesota; Gerald Tindal, University of Oregon; Cecilia Navarrete, New Mexico Highlands University; Richard Durán, University of California at S.B.; William Koch, University of Texas at Austin; Joan Herman, National Center for Research on Evaluation, Standards & Student Testing.

considered as evidence of progress toward meeting the CIM standard. Students using the Spanish–English or Russian–English formats of the mathematics problem solving are considered a standard administration—regardless of the language of response—so that their work can be considered as evidence of progress toward meeting the CIM standard. Students using the Spanish–English format of the mathematics multiple-choice tests are also considered standard administration (after the equating work completed by Seung Choi). The last exception is that students using the Russian–English format of the mathematics multiple-choice tests are still considered modified because the number of students is still too small to run the data analysis necessary to ask the State Board to consider this a standard administration.

Who Takes the Bilingual Assessments?

Work continues in the development of clear guidelines to schools for deciding which students should be administered the side-by-side Spanish–English bilingual or Russian–English bilingual assessments. The guidelines attempt to establish a balance between a zero exclusion policy and exempting those students who cannot reasonably and fairly be excluded because of language differences.

Oregon's Guidelines for Participation of LEP Students in Assessments

As mentioned in the introduction to this chapter, federal law, including the Civil Rights Act of 1964 and ensuing case law, and the Improving America's Schools Act require that non-English-proficient students be given equal opportunity to participate in and benefit from any program or activity customarily granted to all students. Regulations from Oregon's Educational Act for the 21st Century and from the federal Improving America's Schools Act require that any statewide assessment program be available to all students.

Therefore, all ELLs are considered eligible to participate in the Oregon Statewide Assessment Program, and their Oregon Statewide Assessment scores are to be included in the collections of data and information used by local schools and districts for school improvement planning.

In Oregon, a teacher and instructional team who know an individual student are asked to make one of three decisions about administering an assessment of that student. This decision should be made on a test-by-test basis in consultation with the student's parent or guardian and/or the student. The first option is to have the student participate in the standard administration of the assessment. This essentially means that the student takes the test in a manner consistent with the test administration manual and certain allowable accommodations. Either the English or bilingual (side-by-side Spanish–English or Russian–English) format of the writing, mathematics multiple-choice, or mathematics problem-solving test may be used. Under the guidelines, the assessment formatted only in English should be used as a standard administration for those students scoring a 4 or above on the English reading and writing subtests of the Woodcock–Muñoz Language Survey or a 4 in English on the Language Assessment Scales–Reading and Writing (LAS-RW) (reading and writing).

ESL and/or bilingual Spanish students who score above a 1 on the Spanish or Russian version of the reading and writing subtests of the Woodcock–Muñoz Language Survey or a 2 or above on the LAS-RW tests (or attain a comparable score on a similar test) will participate in the Oregon Statewide Assessment Program using the side-by-side versions. (Note: LAS-O is not an acceptable measurement of reading or writing.)

A second option is to modify the test administration conditions so that they are appropriate for students with disabilities or ELLs. Possible modifications are typically identified in the classroom during instruction. They are selected specifically to give the student access to the test. Individuals who participate in any of the assessments for the Oregon Statewide Assessment Program under modified testing conditions will have their tests scored, compared to the standards, and returned, but these scores will not be included in the school, district, or state averages, nor will they be included in evaluations for Title 1-A.

The third option is to exempt the student from test participation on the basis of inadequate literacy in the language of assessment. Students who are preliterate or who score 1 on the reading and writing subtests of the Woodcock–Muñoz Language Survey (in the English–Spanish or English–Russian versions) or LAS-RW, or who receive a similar score on a comparable language proficiency test, may be exempted from testing.

One obstacle to consistent implementation of these guidelines has been local control for guideline implementation that allows teachers to use any of a number of tools to determine the literacy skills required for students to participate in assessments. The guidelines refer to the Woodcock–Muñoz Language Survey, the LAS-RW, and/or a comparable assessment tool, which is to be used to diagnose literacy levels. However under state code, the version of acceptable literacy assessment tools cannot be specified by the state so local schools implement different criteria for establishing students' literacy readiness for assessments. Finding the point where the same information is obtained about the student is frequently a matter of opinion instead of an equitable decision-making model.

How Were the Spanish–English Assessments Designed?

The assessment design procedure for language learners used in Oregon begins with establishment of a "Bilingual Review Panel." Educators from around the state representing the various benchmark levels (3rd, 5th, 8th, and 10th grades) and coming from a variety of cultures, including Spanish and Russian speaking countries, make up the panel.

The Bilingual Review Panel Undertakes a Number of Activities

The panel members begin by reviewing the English versions of the tests. The first decision is which test items will be able to be translated into Spanish and Russian and still make sense (from a context point of view). If the test format is multiple choice, the panel then reviews the answer choices to determine if they will be able to be translated into Spanish and Russian without changing the intention of the test items.

If either of the first two reviews identifies words and/or contexts that will not translate, the panel suggests a comparable setting or choice of words. These new choices are then used on both the English and Spanish–Russian sides of the side-by-side assessment. Next, a professional translator takes the approved items (and answer selections) and translates the materials into Spanish or Russian producing documents in the same electronic format as the final assessments.

The review panel next reviews the printed version of the translations identifying words for which there are discrepancies in translation or spelling. It is the work of the panel to come to agreement on words and spellings appropriate for all Spanish or Russian student readers in Oregon and at the same level as the English. The tests are then put into a side-by-side format with Spanish–Russian in one column and English in the next. The review panel then reviews the final version of the assessments prior to large-scale reproduction. Subsequently, districts order the appropriate numbers of testing materials for their students expected to participate in the side-by-side format of the assessments.

A small sample from one of the assessments appears next illustrating the format and appearance of bilingual multiple-choice items in the context of the Grade 5 mathematics assessment.

10	10
Which of the choices is the BEST estimate of the size of the angle below?	¿Cuál de las siguientes opciones es el MEJOR cálculo de la medida del ángulo que aquí aparece?

 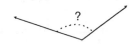

A. 60°   B. 120°   C. 165°   D. 210°   A. 60°   B. 120°   C. 165°   D. 210°

11
What is the greatest common factor of the
following numbers?
                6, 12, 24
        A. 3   B. 6   C. 12   D. 24

11
¿Cuál es el máximo factor común de los
siguientes números?
                6, 12, 24
        A. 3   B. 6   C. 12   D. 24

First Results of Spanish–English Assessments in Writing, Multiple-Choice Mathematics, and Problem Solving

The results of students completing the Oregon Statewide Writing Assessment in Spanish have been very similar to those of students completing the assessment in English. The performance of students completing the Oregon Statewide Mathematics Problem Solving or multiple-choice Mathematics Assessment in Spanish have NOT been very similar to those of students completing the assessments in English. Here again, the chart shows the difference in the number (N) of students participating for the two groups:

1996–1997 Mathematics Problem-Solving Assessment

Grade	English "N"	Spn/Eng "N"
05	38,621	154
08	38,252	133
10	32,766	93

For mathematics problem solving, the score on the 6-point scale that is required to meet standard is a "4" or better in each dimension. During 1996 to 1997, students from all backgrounds had a long way to go to meet standard. Students participating in the test using the Spanish–English format were farther away from the standard than those students using the English format.

English—Spanish–English Problem Solving

1997		CU	PS	C	V	COR
5	S/E	2.4	2.3	2.3	3.0	17%
	Eng	2.9	2.8	2.9	2.8	44%
8	S/E	2.2	2.0	2.2	2.6	8%
	Eng	2.9	2.7	2.9	2.7	47%
10	S/E	1.7	1.6	1.7	2.3	13%
	Eng	2.6	2.5	2.7	2.4	36%

For mathematics problem solving, the table shows average scores for students using the bilingual format (Spanish–English) and the English formats of the assessment. Students are scored in four dimensions:

CU—conceptual understanding

PS—processes and strategies

C—communication

V—verification

COR—percent of students arriving at a correct solution

Several years of observing classrooms around Oregon have shown that students whose first language is not English are often being provided access to only a portion of the mathematics content, although the state assessments measure student ability across the entire range of mathematics content described in the content standards.

The following chart indicates the average scores for students at each of the grade levels tested and the comparison to the performance level identified as meeting the standard on the multiple-choice mathematics assessments.

	1996–1997			1999–2000 % Meeting Standard		
Average Scores		English Spanish–English	The Standard	English	Spanish–English	Russian–English
Grade 3	201	190	202	75%	34%	36%
Grade 5	215	202	215	70%	24%	14%
Grade 8	230	218	231	56%	4%	12%
Grade 10	234	218	239	40%	1%	4%

A Description of the Scoring Procedure

For the performance assessments required of *all* students as evidence for the Certificate of Initial Mastery, official Oregon Department of Education scoring guides are used. In writing, the analytical trait scoring guide has been evolving statewide over the previous 18 years. Thousands of teachers around the state are comfortable with using the scoring guide and have proved to be reliable raters, making consistent decisions about student work. The transition into using a scoring guide in Spanish has been extremely efficient. During the training and scoring sessions, all information (except the printed papers used by all sites) is shared in Spanish only, allowing the raters to focus.

Each piece of student work is scored on a scale from 1 to 6 in each of the six traits: Ideas/Content, Organization, Voice, Word Choice, Sentence Fluency, and Conventions. The descriptors used for each of the levels of the scoring guide provide the students with specific information as to their strengths and areas on which to work. If a paper is blank or written on an unrelated topic, it is given a *no score*.

In making a decision related to the Certificate of Initial Mastery, not all traits are used—only Ideas/Content, Organization, Sentence Fluency, and Conventions.

In mathematics problem solving, the analytical trait scoring guide has been evolving over the previous 7 years, but used statewide for only the last 4 years. Hundreds of teachers around the state are becoming comfortable with using the scoring guide and have proved to be reliable. Each piece of student work is scored on a scale from 1 to 6 in each of the four dimensions in addition to receiving a score for the accuracy of the solution. The dimensions are: Conceptual Understanding, Processes and Strategies, Verification, and Communication. Again, the descriptors used for each of the levels of the scoring guide provide the students with specific information as to their strengths and areas on which to work.

During the training and scoring sessions for the bilingual assessments, most information among scorers is shared only in English. Many of the student responses are in a combination of Spanish–English or Russian–English, requiring the raters to focus on both languages at the same time. In multiple-choice mathematics, the same items (and therefore answer selections) are used in English as are translated into Spanish and Russian. The scoring procedure relies on the same scanner program as the rest of the multiple-choice mathematics (for details about the scaling, see chap. 13 by Choi & McCall).

How Did the Rater Reliability on Performance Assessments Compare?

In the process of scoring any of the performance assessments in Oregon, the same procedures are followed. The raters (educators from around Oregon) are provided an overview of the scoring guide with some scored anchor papers to use as references. Next the raters are trained in the specifics of the tasks/prompts they will be seeing. The raters must then qualify (by scoring a set of papers within 90% accuracy) prior to beginning scoring.

During the actual scoring, the percentage of time an individual rater matches (either adjacent or exact) the second rater is frequently checked, and that information serves as feedback to the raters (interrater reliability). Additionally, student work from a set of refresher papers is scored after each long break. The scores are compared to the expert key and across all sites.

When the scoring is completed, final interrater reliability percentages summarize the reliability of scoring. With 2 years of experience, the rater reliability for scoring the Spanish–English writing assessments was:

3rd grade   97%
5th grade   97%

8th grade 99%
10th grade 97%

1997 was the first year for raters to score the Spanish mathematics problem solving. The rater reliability was:

5th grade 90%
8th grade 94%
10th grade 97%

In 2000, the reliability was relatively identical across all writing sites and across all mathematics problem-solving score sites.

Disseminating Information About Spanish–English Assessments in Writing, Multiple-Choice Mathematics, and Mathematics Problem Solving

During the first 2 years (1995–1996, 1996–1997) in which bilingual assessments were administered, official notices from the Deputy Superintendent of Education were sent to every public school, district office, educational service district, and Title VII coordinator in the state to describe the progress of the Spanish–English assessments and invite participation in the pilot tests. In addition, annual presentations were made at the Oregon Association of Compensatory Educators' Conference. Here samples of the standards and assessments were shared with teachers, parents, and administrators working with English-language learners (ELLs). Also the information was shared with groups of teachers of Spanish for Spanish Speakers at the annual Oregon Summer Bilingual Institute, and more generally outside of professional meeting contexts with English as a Second Language teachers, bilingual teachers, parents, teaching assistants, and administrators and school counselors.

The Oregon State Board of Education was kept informed about the development of the side-by-side Spanish–English assessments. This progress has been reported in newspapers around the state. Now it is hoped that these will be a part of a district's normal material order sent to the assessment distribution center.

What Assessment Support Materials Are Provided to Teachers?

The mathematics problem-solving support packet consists of English, Spanish, and Russian versions of many of the assessment components. In Oregon, most mathematics teachers working with ELLs are not Spanish readers, requiring that the materials be available in both languages. The packet consists of background in the use of the scoring guide, the scoring guide, samples of student work accompanied by scores and commentaries explaining the scores, a collection of tasks (in a side-by-side format), and a student language version of the scoring guide.

The sample tests created for mathematics provide a practice version of the state assessments. The pages are provided in Spanish, Russian, and English. The multiple-choice tests are half the length of the state assessment, but represent the same range of items and content expectations of the state assessment. These tests are presented in a side-by-side format. The sample tests for Grades 3, 5, 8, and 10 include an introduction to state testing policy and programs, test-taking tips, a practice bubble sheet, identification of the score reporting categories, and a table to convert the raw score to the RIT scale.

Building Toward Opportunities to Learn

Districts and schools need to combine the data provided from the modified tests with data from the standard administration and local data on exempt students when planning for school improvement. The 2000 Oregon Statewide Assessment Administration Manual provides a helpful orientation. It states:

> Students whose home language is Spanish or Russian may be most confident of the "context" of the assessments in their home language, but the "content" in English. The side-by-side format of the state assessment addresses this issue in a way students have found to be most meaningful. The model developed in Oregon is being looked at with great interest by other states.

As mentioned earlier in this chapter, there is a need to understand the teaching and learning opportunities arising from participation or exclusion in state assessments. For the 1997 to 1998 assessments, the department provided a survey instrument with the Spanish–English assessments to discover who was participating in this format of the assessment. A small sample of questions from the survey appears next.

1. Marca donde fuiste a la escuela en cada grado.
Complete the bubble indicating where you attended school for each appropriate grade:

	K	1	2	3	4	5	6	7	8	9	10	11	12
USA - USA	O	O	O	O	O	O	O	O	O	O	O	O	O
México - Mexico	O	O	O	O	O	O	O	O	O	O	O	O	O
Otro - Other	O	O	O	O	O	O	O	O	O	O	O	O	O
Otro - Other	O	O	O	O	O	O	O	O	O	O	O	O	O

3. ¿Qué idioma hablas en la casa?
What language do you speak at home?

O Español	O Inglés	O Más español	O Más inglés	O Los dos igual
O Spanish	O English	O Mostly Spanish	O Mostly English	O Both the same

A report entitled, "Will the National Education Goals Improve the Progress of English Language Learners?"[7] provides a rationale for the survey:

> We cannot help all students meet the Goals unless we know who they are, including understanding their linguistic and cultural backgrounds. . . . Demographic trends should affect program design and instruction. It is imperative that systems be put in place to collect adequate information about students' language backgrounds and educational histories, including languages in which they have been taught and the curricula of those courses. . . . The same standards must guide the instruction of all students, including ELLs. Studies have documented important instructional features that can help ensure the educational success of ELLs. Whatever program model is chosen, challenging academic programs need to be made available to ELLs at all levels.

NEW DIRECTIONS

Oregon has made much progress over the past decade in assessment of ELLs as part of its state assessment attuned to national and state efforts to implement educational reform serving all students. Yet much remains to be done. The following steps for augmenting state assessments in reading, mathematics, and science are examples of new challenges undertaken by Oregon in this area. Each of the efforts described next for development of new items and assessments follows the same basic quality control for assessments and validation process that all Oregon assessments must follow. The efforts described represent proactive strategies to improve existing assessments. They also exemplify how states can maintain an active program of assessment development and assessment validation that is an integral part of the planning and implementation process of a mature state assessment system in the era of educational reform.

In the area of reading assessment, active work is underway in Oregon to enhance the item pools capable of assessing the lowest achieving students at the three benchmark grades (3, 5, and 8) and at the 10th-grade CIM

---

[7]From the Evaluation Assistance Center-East, the George Washington University, October 1993.

level. Attention is being given to the development of plain-English read-ing items, with lower item difficulty levels than for existing items and that cover the intended skills referenced by benchmark standards. The new plain-English items would minimize language-processing demands that are unrelated to the English reading standard targeted for assessment by an item. Psychometric research will be undertaken to ensure that this new, extended pool of reading items will yield scores on the same scale as other items, and that the scale within and across benchmark levels as a whole will become a more sensitive measure of growth in reading proficiency as stu-dents progress across grades. This new direction in the reading assess-ment will improve assessment of students across a greater range of ability levels against the standards set at each benchmark level and for the CIM. Yet the improvement will be especially helpful for ELL students and other students who are in need of the greatest development of skills. At present, it is not possible to assess the lowest performing students with great accu-racy because of the paucity of items that can capture their existing compe-tencies in reading and that over years can show progress toward meeting benchmark and CIM standards.

In the mathematics assessment, work is underway to develop a plain-English mathematics assessment at each benchmark level and for the CIM that would be an additional regular assessment joining the existing assess-ment in English and the Spanish-English or Russian-English side-by-side assessments. As with these other assessments, the new mathematics assess-ment would address the same intended mathematics content standards at each level, but would minimize the use of English skills unrelated to the mathematical knowledge and skills under assessment. The new assess-ment would include items that cover the same range of difficulty levels as on the other mathematics, and would yield scores on the same scales as these assessments. The new plain-English mathematics assessment would be attractive for use with ELLs in place of or as an alternative to the exist-ing assessments, especially given that these students are more likely to be receiving their mathematics instruction solely in English as they progress through the grades. There is also the possibility that the effort to develop plain-English mathematics items might impact the item development process for the existing English mathematics (and bilingual) assessment. For example, if the new plain-English mathematics assessment were able to show greater psychometric reliability than the existing English mathe-matics assessment, while covering the same range of ability levels against standards, it would suggest that the two assessments become just one as-sessment relying on plain-English strategies for item development.

This approach brings up concerns about the nature of learning and the nature of the subject matter. How much of science and mathematics is in-trinsically linguistic? Item writers already strive to write clearly and simply.

Can we fully assess these subjects in plain English because many of the concepts are complex and much of the vocabulary is academic? How much linguistic mediation occurs mentally when students solve mathematics problems or analyze scientific data? These and other problems will continue to surface in the course of test development and field testing. The concept is young at this point and is likely to change character as it develops.

A plain-English item development strategy is also underway for the Oregon science assessments at each benchmark level and the CIM level that would follow the same logic as for the plain-English mathematics assessments. The new assessment would measure students against the same standards and yield scores on the same metric as existing science assessments. Again, as with the mathematics assessment, items on the new assessment would be designed to reduce the impact of English skills that are unrelated to the standards targeted for assessment by an item.

In addition, work is underway toward developing side-by-side dual-language science assessments paralleling the previous work on the mathematics assessment. As was the case with the mathematics assessment, Spanish-English assessments are being targeted in the initial assessment development work, with work on Russian-English side-by-side assessments conceivable in future work.

Yet additional possibilities for enhancing assessment of ELLs are under active consideration. One of these is the possibility of making Spanish-language writing assessments an acceptable accommodated assessment for writing assessment at the three benchmark levels preceding the CIM should psychometric validation work support this decision. Another possible assessment enhancement under consideration is the use of bilingual glossaries in science assessments at all three benchmark levels as part of an accommodated science assessment.

Efforts such as foregoing put Oregon among the leaders in state assessment systems responsive to changes that must be made to bring the benefits of education reform to all students, including ELLs. However, the challenges faced in improving state assessments of ELLs are immense and do not always reflect educational policy constraints under the immediate control of a state assessment system as an institution within a state. In the case of Oregon, the lack of a state-level tracking system for student data is a fundamental constraint in making assessment serve the needs of ELLs. Implementation of such a student tracking system would permit better, individualized monitoring of ELL students, especially in light of their greater mobility in comparison to other students and the subsequent need to diagnose their immediate learning needs. Development of a student tracking system will make a dramatic improvement in the utility of the state assessment system to track students' progress toward meeting Oregon's goals for educational reform and will improve the quality of information to education planners and policymakers implementing reform efforts.

REFERENCES

Abedi, J., Lord, C., Hofstetter, C., & Baker, E. (2000). Impact of accommodation strategies on English language learners' test performance. *Educational Measurement: Issues and Practice, 19*(3), 16–26.

American Educational Research Association, American Psychological Association, National Council on Measurement in Education. (1985). *Standards for educational and psychological testing.* Washington, DC: American Educational Research Association.

American Educational Research Association, American Psychological Association, National Council on Measurement in Education. (1999). *Standards for educational and psychological testing.* Washington, DC: American Educational Research Association.

American Institutes for Research. (1999). *Background paper reviewing laws and regulations, current practice, and research relevant to inclusion and accommodations for students with limited English proficiency.* Unpublished paper prepared for the National Assessment Governing Board, Palo Alto, CA.

Butler, F., & Stevens, R. (1997). *Accommodation strategies for English language learners on large scale assessments: Student characteristics and other considerations* (CSE Technical Report 448). Los Angeles: Center for Evaluation, National Center for Research on Evaluation, Standards, and Student Testing.

Kopriva, R. (2000). *Ensuring accuracy in testing for English language learners.* Washington, DC: Council of Chief State School Officers.

National Research Council. (1997). Improving schooling for language minority children: A research agenda. In D. August & K. Hakuta (Eds.), *Committee on developing a research agenda on the education of limited-English proficient and bilingual students, Board on Children, Youth, and Families, National Research Council.* Washington, DC: National Academy Press.

National Research Council. (1999). High stakes: Testing for tracking, promotion, and graduation. In J. P. Heubert & R. M. Hauser (Eds.), *Committee on appropriate test use, Board on Testing and Assessment, National Research Council.* Washington, DC: National Academy Press.

National Research Council. (2000). Testing English-language learners in U.S. schools. Report and Workshop Summary. In K. Hakuta & A. Beatty (Eds.), *Committee on educational excellence and testing equity, Board on Testing and Assessment, National Research Council.* Washington, DC: National Academy Press.

Rivera, C., Stansfield, C. L., & Sharkey, M. (2000). *An analysis of state policies for the inclusion and accommodation of English language learners in state assessment program during 1998–1999.* Arlington, VA: The George Washington University Center for Equity and Excellence in Education.

U.S. Department of Education. (1996, April). *Title I, Part A Policy Guidance: Improving Basic Programs Operated by Local educational Agencies, Guidance on Standards, Assessment, and Accountability.* Washington, DC: Office of Elementary and Secondary Education.

U.S. Department of Education. (2000). *The use of tests when making high-stakes decisions for students: A resource guide for educators and policymakers.* Washington, DC: Office of Civil Rights.

Chapter 16

Determining When Test Alterations Are Valid Accommodations or Modifications for Large-Scale Assessment

Keith Hollenbeck
University of Oregon

The 1997 amendments to the Individuals with Disabilities Education Act (IDEA '97) contain powerful declarations pertaining to the participation of students with disabilities in large-scale testing. The reauthorized legislation mandated that "Children with disabilities are included in general state and district-wide assessment programs with appropriate accommodations where necessary" (IDEA, Section 612 (a)(17)(A). Although IDEA '97 requires participation, the "IDEA legislation and regulations provide little guidance on the particulars of assessment accommodations for students with disabilities" (Henry, 1999, p. 32). Henry concluded that "the IDEA legislation and regulations contain a key word when referencing accommodation and modification: *appropriate*. But language defining just what is or is not appropriate is absent and we are left to use professional judgment as to what constitutes good practice" (p. 99). Besides IDEA '97, multiple legal mandates exist that decree participation of students with disabilities in standards-based curriculum, instruction, and assessment with appropriate accommodations and modifications. For an elegant discussion of those legal mandates, see Phillips' chapter (chap. 6) in this volume.

DEFINING ACCOMMODATIONS AND MODIFICATIONS

Before districts and schools can implement any of the legally mandated test alterations, they must first understand how accommodations and modifications differ. Bruininks et al. (1994), Thurlow, Ysseldyke, and

Silverstein (1993), and Thurlow, Hurley, Spicuzza, and El Sawaf (1996) concluded that the terms *accommodation* and *modification* are used inter-changeably and lack a "formal consensus" (p. 1) of meaning. In an attempt to clarify the relationship of the two concepts, Tindal, Hollenbeck, Heath, and Almond (1997) placed accommodations and modifications at oppo-site ends of a continuum and characterized them as follows.

Modifications

A test alteration that changes the construct being assessed or "works across the board for all students with equal effect" (Tindal et al., 1997, p. 2) is de-fined as a modification. Modifications result in a change in the test (how it is given, how it is completed, or what construct is being assessed) and work equally well for all students. For example, if the standard administration of a statewide multiple-choice reading comprehension test called for stu-dents to read test items themselves, then altering the assessment so that the passages and questions were read aloud would change the construct from silent-reading comprehension to listening comprehension and would move the alteration toward a modification. In a second example, if a test were speeded (timed) and the alteration called for extended time limits, such a change most likely would compromise the assessment's stan-dardization procedures and any judgments based on those norms. Thus, altering the speeded test's time limits reasonably would constitute a modi-fication. Consequentially, a modified score would not be interpreted in the same way as a score obtained under standard conditions. Because some students cannot participate meaningfully in large-scale assessment without modifications, methods for modifying assessment systems become necessary. Helwig's chapter (chap. 17, this volume) explicates such meth-ods. He notes that, for some students, altering the construct being as-sessed might be the only recourse to exempting them altogether. Echoing Burns' (1998) notion, Helwig suggests that accommodations will not amend test content nor rectify its deficiencies.

Accommodations

Psychometrically, accommodations should remove construct-irrelevant va-riance in scores by providing unique and differential access so that "certain students or groups of students may complete the test and tasks without other confounding influences of test format, administration, or respond-ing" (Tindal et al., 1997, p. 1). An accommodation can be "thought of as a corrective lens for such potential score distortions" (Chiu & Pearson, 1999, p. 4). Accommodations are commonly defined by three attributes. First, an accommodation must alter the test's presentation or response method so that it provides students with better access to demonstrate what they know. Second, it must not change the assessment construct(s) of interest (Tindal et al., 1997). Finally, an accommodation must provide differentiated access (Fuchs, 1999; Fuchs & Fuchs, 1999; Fuchs, Fuchs, Eaton, Hamlett, & Karns, 1999). Fuchs (1999) clarified differential access by noting that an accommodation is justified when students with disabilities perform at least one standard deviation higher because of the test alteration as students without disabilities receiving the same alteration.

In a similar attempt to determine whether an assessment alteration was an accommodation or modification, Phillips (chap. 6, this volume) adapted earlier questions she has posed before (Phillips, 1993, 1994): (a) How do scores compare between the proposed alteration and its standard administration? (b) What is the relationship between the skill(s) or knowledge being assessed and the proposed alteration? (c) What score benefit might examinees without disabilities gain if allowed the same alteration? (d) What are the reliability and validity of procedures used for determining who gets the alteration? and (e) What is the capability of the examinee moving toward standard administration conditions?

Clarifying Accommodations

To summarize this array of definitions, Hollenbeck, Rozek-Tedesco, and Finzel (2000) specified four attributes that must be present for a test alteration to be considered an accommodation: (a) *unchanged constructs*—test alterations must not alter the construct(s) being measured; (b) *individual need*—the test alterations must be based on individual need and, thus, are not chosen haphazardly; (c) *differential effects*—test alterations must be differential in effect by student or group; and (d) *samenesses of inference*—test alterations must generate similar inferences between accommodated and standard scores. The degree to which these four attributes are present determines the degree to which the test alteration moves along the continuum between accommodation and modification. Their presence signifies an accommodation, whereas their absence signifies a modification. Furthermore, as it moves closer to being a modification, the validity of inferences and decisions becomes more suspect. The next section further defines the four attributes.

Unchanged Constructs. As stated earlier, an accommodation must not alter the construct(s) of interest. For example, on math assessments, an accommodation for a poor reader might be to have question stems and stem choices read aloud (assuming that reading was not an integral ingredient of the math construct being assessed). Cox and Poe (1991) maintained that "mathematical achievement of children correlates highly with their ability to read mathematics" (p. 108). Although the read-aloud accommodation for math tests does not eliminate a student's need to solve written math problems (a change in construct of interest), it does eliminate the confounding factor of reading ability. Limiting the confound of reading is important because, as Tack (1995) noted, mathematics tests that largely reflect written mathematics in its verbal context (as opposed to symbolic) are in part measuring reading ability rather than pure mathematical ability. Results from a study conducted by Newman (1977) determined that at least 35% of errors on math achievement tests might be reading-related problems. This research illustrated that a significant percentage of the variance observed on math tests is determined by reading skill. Therefore, it is imperative that tests and testing conditions be constructed so that low readers are free to demonstrate their math problem-solving capabilities and are not constrained by their reading disabilities.

Individual Need. Emphasis must be placed on the necessity for test alterations, not merely the potential benefit from such alterations. Need minimizes the effects of the student's disability by eliminating irrelevant access skills (see Phillips, chap. 6, for a discussion on need vs. want). Oppositely, benefit provides the potential for an unfair advantage over students taking the test under standard conditions. The question becomes, what does the student need to access the test conditions, not what are the optimal conditions for understanding what the student can do in some absolute sense. The fact that a student may be expected to achieve a higher score with test alterations is not an appropriate sole criterion for providing test changes. More important, accommodations must not be confused with optimal performance. Although test alterations may improve a student's performance by eliminating irrelevant skills, test alterations do not guarantee that a student's score will increase. An appropriate test alteration (an accommodation) only guarantees that the decisions based on the scores will be valid.

Differential Effects. Although accommodations do not change the construct being tested, they should "differentially affect a student's or group's performance in comparison to a peer group" (Tindal et al., 1997, p. 1). If the test alteration works for all or fails to work at all, then this change is group defined not individually defined. The focus is on an interaction between the type of student (the student's need) and the type of test alteration. Agreeing with the differential performance perspective, Fuchs (1999) and Phillips (1994, chap. 6) suggest that, for an accommodation to be considered legitimate, the resulting increase in performance for students with disabilities must exceed the increase attained by students in general education.

Samenesses of Inference. Viable accommodations, as defined in this chapter, must ensure the integrity of the decision-making process as well as validate score decisions (Messick, 1982). Because of differential outcomes, "accommodations should work for those who need it and should be neutral for students who do not need it" (Tindal, Helwig, & Hollenbeck, 2000, p.5). Furthermore, validity dictates that any score inference from an accommodated test should be the same as for standard administration scores. Stakeholders must have confidence regarding their inferences about student performance based on test scores (Lenz & Mellard, 1990), especially regarding high-stakes decisions. The goal is to be sure that accommodated results reflect the examinee's true capabilities and are not a function of the perceptions or biases of another person or score inflation or deflation.

The What and When Questions for Accommodations

To meet the intent of IDEA '97, teachers within school districts must utilize accommodation research that has been conducted around large-scale assessments to answer the *what* question: What accommodation(s) is/are valid for our specific large-scale testing program? Indeed, most states have some document that specifies *what* accommodations are legal to use within their assessment system. However, IDEA '97 and state documentation fail to provide the *when* of accommodations: When should certain accommodations be used on large-scale assessments? Instead, the *when* questions are left to the IEP team. Thus, federal and state offices of special education assume that the IEP team can answer the *when* questions. However, that assumption about IEP team knowledge of accommodations might be considered suspect as described next.

TEACHERS AS MEASUREMENT EXPERTS

Implicit in the appropriate identification of accommodations and modifications is teacher knowledge. Knowledge of what constitutes accommodations or modifications is important because IDEA '97 portrays members of the IEP team as measurement-competent decision makers. Although teachers are expected to be measurement-competent educators, significant deficits in teachers' knowledge concerning testing have been found. Most teachers' knowledge about testing and measurement comes from "trial-and-error learning in the classroom" (Wise, Lukin, & Roos, 1991, p. 39). Although the trial-and-error method causes inconsistent learning across teachers, those knowledge deficits are not specific to general education teachers. Shepard's (1983) research determined that neither school psychologists nor teachers of the learning disabled were likely to be competent in their knowledge and application of assessment. Corroborating Shepard's conclusions, Siskind (1993) found that special educators were not well informed about assessment and assessment procedures. Consequently, classroom teachers who lack collegiate training in assessment may not be able to utilize their school resource personnel (because of similar collegiate training deficits) as expert sources for assistance on accommodation issues. Educators need assessment knowledge to determine appropriate accommodations that control for extraneous interference that might result in mismeasurement of achievement, such as "attributes of the students, the assessment process and/or the assessment environment that is unrelated to student achievement but influences test results" (Stiggins, 1991, p. 9). Assessment knowledge is also requisite for valid score reporting, referencing, and interpretation as called for in IDEA '97.

One way the lack of assessment knowledge manifests itself is in variations in test administration conditions (e.g., allowing accommodations or not allowing accommodations). Langenfeld, Thurlow, and Scott's (1997) review of research showed that "accommodations for students in the academically-oriented classes varied from district to district . . . [and] children who failed in one district might have succeeded in another district that was more willing to meet their needs" (p. 26). Hollenbeck, Tindal, and Almond's (1998) research on teachers' knowledge of accommodations mirrored the Langenfeld et al. findings. Hollenbeck et al. found inconsistent application of appropriate and allowable statewide assessment accommodations. Their findings showed that, on average, 54.8% of teachers correctly identified whether specific alterations (as listed in the statewide testing manual) would require the statewide assessment protocol to be marked modified. When broken down by general education teachers and special education teachers, the percentage changed very little. General education teachers averaged 51.6% correct, whereas the special education teachers averaged 57.4% correct. Furthermore, their survey showed that the group as a whole used few of the allowable testing accommodations. Overall, respondents reported using 44.7% of the listed accommodations for students on IEPs. Like earlier results, the general education teachers' percentages and special education teachers' percentages differed only slightly. General education teachers reported using an average of 48% of the testing accommodations, whereas the special education teachers used an average of 41.8% of the accommodations. The authors concluded that the IEP teams' (or the individual teachers') inconsistent application of accommodations contributed to differential exclusion of students throughout the state and depressed the validity of interpretations.

While acknowledging that IDEA amendments require school personnel to make judgments about accommodations for students with disabilities,

Fuchs and Fuchs (1999) urged "caution when relying on teacher judgments about test accommodations" (pp. 26–27). Their recent studies found a lack of connection among teacher decisions, students' needs, test accommodations, and derived benefits. From their research, they concluded that "teachers awarded accommodations to large numbers of students who benefited from the accommodation no more than students without a disability" (p. 27) and "many educators have relatively little understanding of the purpose of test accommodations . . . [and] have little experience in observing the actual effects of accommodations for students with and without disabilities" (p. 29).

Although the *when* questions have been left to the IEP team by federal and state mandates, research has shown that this notion is questionable at best. IEP teams are left to their own professional judgment with little clear guidance about how to proceed. They need a decision-making process grounded in accommodation and large-scale assessment research. Remember it is neither the test nor its accommodation that are validated—it is the consequences of those decisions that are validated (Messick, 1988, 1994). For more detail, see Linn's (chap. 2) in-depth validity discussion where he describes the requisite evidential and consequential basis necessary for supporting a particular use or interpretation of an assessment.

ACCOMMODATIONS AS A VALIDITY ISSUE

Considering that high-stakes, consequential testing is "primarily intended to serve the decision making needs of the user institution" (Messick, 1982, p. 9), validity issues at the individual level are often overlooked with regard to various test accommodations. The degree to which validity judgments change because of accommodation usage fluctuates from inconsequential to significant. However, validity of statewide assessments is really a misnomer. Validity is not a singular characteristic; rather, it relates to the judgments formulated from the results that required validation (Messick, 1988, 1994; Willingham, 1988). Cronbach (1988) described validity as an attempt to "locate the boundaries within which it [the validity generalizations] holds" (p. 14). Furthermore, singular validity evidence does not determine the validity of an inference. The various forms of validity by themselves are no more than "strands within a cable of validity arguments" (Cronbach, 1988, p. 4).

Paradoxically, although accommodations are utilized to reduce measurement error, they may interject additional sources of error into the assessment model that had not yet been calibrated. The presence of extraneous factors—those that are not part of the test and are irrelevant to the construct of interest—may spuriously decrease or increase scores within subgroups so that any valid interpretation of that subgroup's score will be suspect (Hollenbeck, Rozek-Tedesco, Tindal, & Glasgow, 2000a). The amount of error (variance) found in a score contradicts any advantageous qualities of reliability and validity (Howell, Fox, & Morehead, 1993). Hence, the total error variance, including the inconsistent use of accommodated tests by teachers, negatively correlates to its reliability.

Because statewide tests are used for high-stakes decision making at the local, state, and federal levels, we must ensure that assessments administered to people with handicaps "reflect their aptitude or achievement levels rather than their impairments" (Benderson, 1988, p. 3). Not only must all teachers function as classroom measurement experts, but they must also understand that their choices about the use or nonuse of accommodations affects the validity of decisions at all levels resulting from the students' scores.

Of course, a wide variety of accommodations are presently in use, including Braille, audiotapes, large print, oral responses, extended time, and interpretation of directions (Yell & Shriner, 1996). However, the amount of experimental research conducted on accommodations is minimal (Koretz & Hamilton, 1999; Thurlow, Ysseldyke, & Silverstein, 1995; Tindal & Fuchs, 1999). This lack of research limits the number of "strands within the cable of validity arguments." The goal should be to employ only those accommodations that allow participation in statewide testing in a way that represents students' abilities not their disabilities.

RESEARCH ON ACCOMMODATIONS

Some of the more extensive studies of test accommodations have been carried out by Educational Testing Service (ETS) on its Graduate Record Examination (GRE) and the Scholastic Aptitude Test (SAT; Willingham et al., 1988). ETS researchers have documented evidence of comparability between standard and nonstandard administrations for most test-takers on the SAT and GRE for (a) reliability (Bennett, Rock, & Jirele, 1986; Bennett, Rock, & Kaplan, 1985, 1987), (b) factor structures (Rock, Bennett, & Kaplan, 1987), (c) item difficulty (Bennett, Rock, & Kaplan, 1985, 1987), and (d) test performance. Not all results were supportive, however. For example, ETS researchers found that the SAT underpredicted college grades (Braun, Ragosta, & Kaplan, 1986) and extended time overpredicted college performance (Willingham et al., 1998) for certain groups of students with disabilities.

The ETS studies investigated the technical quality, utility, and fairness of various test alterations. Thus ETS can document the validity of certain score interpretations for diverse populations based on empirical evidence. More important, ETS showed that (a) not all test alterations are comparable, and (b) test alterations must be empirically verified for equivalence.

REVIEW OF RESEARCH

The test alteration research reviewed next is derived from a list of four general groups of test alterations: (a) setting factors, (b) presentation factors, (c) response factors, and (d) statewide rater factors. Each factor is examined in detail.

SETTING TEST ALTERATIONS

Setting refers to the physical location or physical environment where the assessment is administered. Figure 16.1 presents questions that help clarify whether setting test alterations should be considered an accommodation or a modification based on individual student needs. These questions are followed by a summary of setting research as it relates to accommodations.

Setting Question 1 asks about a student's ability to work independently. Some students may need assessment time distributed over a longer time frame. Most statewide tests take 45 minutes or longer to complete. If the student is unaccustomed to performing independently for an extended amount of time, then suggesting that the student receive more time would not be an appropriate choice. However, if the student is highly distractible, breaking the testing sessions into smaller units might be a powerful accommodation assuming that the assessment was not speeded, but rather a power test. The same can be said for unmotivated students. Burns (1998) suggested that distractible or unmotivated students may become disinterested after finishing only a portion of the items, so that "doubling the testing time [extending rather than reducing time] may do little more than compound the disinterest" (p. 191).

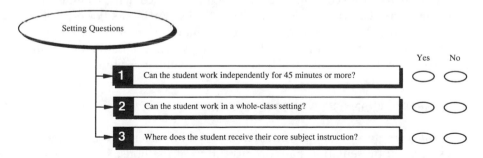

FIG. 16.1.   Setting questions.

Question 2 asks about the student's ability to function in whole-class settings. If the student is easily distracted, requires constant refocusing, or requires teacher-controlled pacing, then testing the student in smaller groups might be an appropriate accommodation. Many statewide tests allow for considerable variation when discussing the physical setting of the testing environment.

Question 3 asks about the student's familiarity with the testing environment or test proctor. If the testing environment and/or proctor are new and unfamiliar to the student, then the student may not do as well. Although familiarity is an important concept that needs to be addressed, any decision regarding familiarity of environment or proctor must be empirically validated. Answers to these three questions help establish an assessment environment in which the student can concentrate and remain on task.

Research on Test Alterations

Three main studies have been completed around physical environment. Abikoff, Courtney, Szeibel, and Koplewicz (1996) manipulated the physical environment using three auditory stimulation conditions for elementary school-aged boys labeled with and without attention deficit hyperactivity disorder (ADHD). They found positive results for a background condition for ADHD students, but no such benefits for non-ADHD students.

Derr-Minneci (1990) studied another aspect of setting—tester familiarity—and found that students performed better when assessed by their regular classroom teacher than when they were assessed by an unfamiliar adult (the school psychologist). Results show that not only did students make more errors when tested in an office outside the classroom than when tested at the teacher's desk, but they also read more words correctly at the teacher's desk compared with the office. In contrast to Derr-Minneci's research, Stoneman and Gibson (1978) found that small children with developmental delays performed better when tested in an assessment office rather than in their own classroom. Tester familiarity research has also been completed by the Fuchs (Fuchs & Fuchs, 1989; Fuchs, Featherstone, Garwick, & Fuchs, 1984; Fuchs, Fuchs, & Power, 1987; Fuchs, Fuchs, Garwick, & Featherstone, 1983), where they reported positive significant effects for performance in the presence of familiar examiners (typically the student's teacher) versus unfamiliar examiners.

PRESENTATION TEST ALTERATIONS

Presentation refers to how the assessment was administered to the student. Research on presentation has covered different methods, such as large type, read-aloud, computers, pacing issues, and syntax/language simpli-

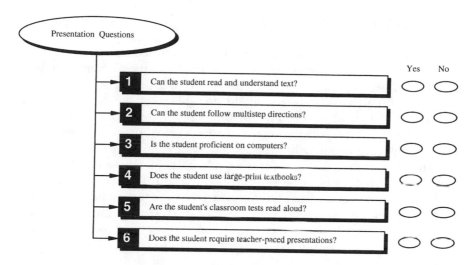

FIG. 16.2.   Presentation questions.

fication. The questions in Fig. 16.2 help clarify whether presentation test alterations should be considered an accommodation or a modification based
on individual students needs and are followed by a summary of presentation research.

For Presentation Question 1, if a student cannot read and/or understand text at or near grade level, it may be impossible for him or her to
complete the standard statewide assessment. Reading is not only an enabling skill for the language arts assessment, but it is also an enabling skill
that allows access to math or any other subject matter. For students with severe reading disabilities, test alterations predicated on more time will probably be inappropriate and ineffective because no amount of time can be a
proxy for the lack of reading access skills necessary to complete the task.

Question 2 asks about the student's ability to carry out multistep directions. Many statewide tests have multistep directions and require students
to remember those directions over subsequent problems. Rereading the
directions or presenting the directions in simplified language may be an
appropriate accommodation for certain students.

Question 3 asks about possible alternative testing formats. Although
most statewide tests are paper and pencil, some states are exploring computers as a way to deliver alternative assessments. However, if the student
is not proficient with the computer as a learning tool, asking the student to
take a test on the computer would be inappropriate. Knowledge and use
of presentation tools are important components of the validation process.

Question 4 asks about text print issues. If the student requires large-
print textbooks to function in the classroom, then an appropriate test alteration would be large-print tests. Although large print may not meet the

accommodation standard of differential effects, it is a necessary physical accommodation.

Question 5 asks about classroom assessment presentation. Again, if the student requires that classroom tests be read aloud, then it may be appropriate for the statewide test to be read aloud. As a caveat, teachers should make sure that reading the test aloud does not alter the construct being measured (e.g., reading aloud the reading test) or compromise their statewide test rules and regulations. If the construct being measured is altered or the test rules are violated, then the test alteration would be a modification.

Finally, Question 6 asks about the student's need for pacing. If the student cannot pace him or herself through the test, then the teacher may need to refocus the student's attention or break the testing time into more manageable units. Again, a quick check of the test rules and regulations could determine whether refocusing and/or shorter time, multiple-testing sessions might be considered an accommodation on that test.

Presentation Research

Large Type. Increasing the type size of a test is usually associated with visual impairments. Perez (1980) found that for secondary-level students on the Florida statewide test, the large-print version resulted in higher scores. Likewise, Beattie, Griese, and Algozzine (1983) observed that third-grade students with visual disabilities taking the Florida statewide large-print reading assessment approximated the scores of their general education peers taking the standard-sized print. At the postsecondary level, Bennett, Rock, and Jirele (1987) and Bennett, Rock, and Kaplan (1987) looked at the large-print and standard-print versions of the GRE and SAT, respectively. Bennett's research found no differential item functioning between the two versions. Although this research did not show a differential impact for students with visual disabilities and their general education peers, large-print accommodations are needed for students with visual disabilities.

Read-Aloud. Although the read-aloud research is mixed, its success as an accommodation appears related to the student's ability to solve complex math problems. Helwig, Rozek-Tedesco, Tindal, Heath, and Almond (1999) found that a video read aloud benefited the elementary-age low reader–high math group. Likewise, Tindal, Heath, Hollenbeck, Almond, and Harniss (1998) found that fourth-grade students with IEPs performed significantly better on the read-aloud version. Overall, the performance of general education students was not affected by the mode of item presentation, whereas the special education students significantly improved in their performance when the test questions and choices were read aloud.

Weston (1999) also detected significantly large effects for fourth-grade students with disabilities on the math read-aloud.

Conversely, Tindal, Glasgow, Helwig, Hollenbeck, and Heath (1998), Tindal, Almond, Heath, and Tedesco (1998), and Hollenbeck, Rozek-Tedesco, Tindal, and Glasgow (2000b) found no benefit for math tests read-alouds. Specifically, Tindal, Glasgow, et al. (1998) found that for fourth, fifth, seventh, and eighth graders, no significant group gains were present. Likewise, the Tindal, Almond, et al. (1998) fourth-grade single-subject math research found that performance was not enhanced with a read-aloud accommodation. Finally, Hollenbeck et al. (2000b) found that the computer read-aloud did not result in significantly higher scores for fourth graders.

Pacing. In the only study found involving pacing of large-scale testing, Hollenbeck et al. (2000a) examined whether a teacher-paced (video presentation) accommodation or a student-paced (computer presentation) accommodation produced better scores for middle school students with disabilities or general education students on a large-scale math test. Their results show a statistically significant main effect for students' status. General education students outperformed students with disabilities on both the student-paced (computerized) and teacher-paced (video) math tests. When teacher paced versus student-paced scores were analyzed by status, it was found that pacing significantly influenced the mean scores. In other words, the mean scores for students with disabilities and the lowest general education students were raised when the accommodation was student-paced (the computer version) versus when the teacher paced the accommodation (the video).

Computer Presentation. Although research is mixed on computer versus paper-and-pencil presentation, few research findings favor computer test presentation over its paper-and-pencil counterpart. Early research (Curtis & Kropp, 1961) revealed higher scores for the computer presentation of standardized tests versus the same test in booklet form. Likewise, Burke's (1998) results show that for older high school students computerized versions of tests (ranging from GED to ARC transition tests) produced significantly better scores for students with learning disabilities, but not for their peers with developmental delays or in general education.

In contrast to those findings, Hollenbeck et al. (2000a, 2000b) found no differences between paper-and-pencil and computerized statewide multiple-choice math assessments for middle school students and for elementary school students. Moreover, Horton and Lovitt (1994) found that middle and high school students performed slightly better on the paper-and-pencil version on interpretive comprehension questions, but marginally better on the computerized version for factual comprehension questions. Keene and Davey (1987) detected no differences for high school students, and Swain (1997) uncovered no differences for third graders on the computerized versus paper-and-pencil KeyMath-R test.

Language Simplification. In one of the few studies found, Miller's (1998) research with middle schoolers analyzed simplified language on math multiple-choice problems similar to those on the Oregon statewide math assessment. Miller found no significant difference for the simplified language test. In a further analysis of the Miller data, Tindal, Anderson, Helwig, Miller, and Glasgow (1999) also found no treatment effects for either students with learning disabilities or those in general education.

RESPONSE TEST ALTERATIONS

Response refers to the method by which the student responds to the assessment. Research on response has covered different methods, such as writing in the test booklet versus on the answer sheet, use of a scribe, or use of word processors instead of handwriting. The questions in Fig. 16.3 clarify whether response test alterations should be considered an accommodation or a modification based on individual students needs. The response questions listed in Fig. 16.3 are followed by a summary of response research. Again, the response research is specific to accommodations.

Response Question 1 asks about the student's ability to adequately use the allotted testing time. Most large-scale assessments have stringent rules regarding the amount of time allowed for each test or subtests (Burns,

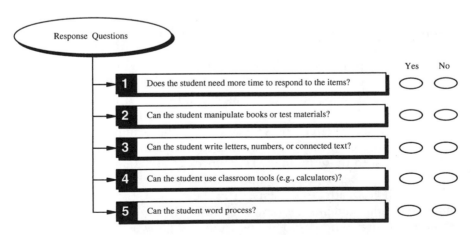

FIG. 16.3. Response questions.

1998). This places the focus on providing a suitable quantity of time to validly assess the construct in question.

Question 2 asks about the student's ability to manipulate testing materials. If the student has trouble tracking from the test booklet to the answer sheet or has trouble organizing multiple pieces of paper, then having the student mark in the test booklet may be an appropriate accommodation.

Question 3 asks about the student's ability to answer test questions. Most statewide tests ask for fill-in-the-bubble, single-word, short-answer, or complete extended responses. A skill deficit in this area may prevent students from validly answering test questions—showing what they know and can do. Although a student with this disability may benefit from using a word processor, it must meet the criteria established in the Presentation and Response Questions. Again, being facile with the required tool is an important skill to show what you know.

Question 4 asks about the student's ability to use common classroom tools, ranging from calculators to computer keyboards. As stated earlier, before any tool can be used as an accommodation, the student must be able to use it with facility and understand when and where to best use it.

Question 5 asks about the student's ability to use a word processor. Before a word processor can be used as a valid response accommodation, the student's (a) ability to keyboard, (b) use word-processing tools (like spell checkers and grammar checkers), and (c) familiarity with test taking on computers must be known. Further, permissibility of using this accommodation (state guidelines) must be clarified.

Response Research

Timing Research. Researchers have reported high positive correlations between extra time allowed and score. As early as 1931, Baxter reported high correlations for college students on timed tests such as the Otis Self-Administering Test, the Army Alpha Revised Form Five, and the College Aptitude Test. Baxter's findings were replicated by Lord (1956) and Mollenkopf (1960). Both researchers found that added time significantly and positively changed the percentile rankings achieved by high school or older test takers.

In a unique investigation, Hollenbeck and Tindal (2001) investigated not the addition of time, but the reduction of time for Oregon's statewide writing test. Oregon administration rules require students to write over a 3-day period. Students with learning disabilities (LD) usually employ less conventional methods of composing, such as "question and answer task" (Sexton, Harris, & Graham, 1998, p. 295), "knowledge-telling strategy" (Englert & Raphael, 1988, p. 514), or a "retrieve-and-write process" (DeLaPaz & Graham, 1997, p. 167). These types of processes greatly shorten the time required to generate a complete essay. Using composite trait scores of students who wrote for 2 days versus students who wrote for 3 days, Hollenbeck and Tindal (2001) found that the mean average of students who wrote for 2 days was significantly higher than those students who wrote for 3 days. These differences favoring the 2-day group held for both the students with disabilities, although their scores were not significantly different, and for general education students. In similar research, Crawford (2000) found that, for third and fifth graders, a 30-minute writing performance in the fall predicted (correlated strongly) the winter performance on student's 3-day Oregon statewide writing test in the winter. Furthermore, the student's 30-minute winter writing performance resulted in moderate to strong correlations with the winter statewide test for students in general and special education at both grade levels.

In areas other than writing, Educational Testing Service (ETS) has conducted extensive research on time accommodations for their tests. On the Preliminary Scholastic Aptitude Test (PSAT), Harris (1992) found no significant score differences for high school juniors taking a regular-timed and extended-time test. Oppositely, Centra's (1986) research showed an average gain of 30 to 38 points for high school students with disabilities taking the Scholastic Aptitude Test (SAT) under an extended-time condition. Time accommodation research on other large-scale tests—like the Iowa Test of Basic Skills (ITBS) and the Metropolitan Achievement Test (MAT)—has also shown differential outcomes. On the Comprehensive Test of Basic Skills (CTBS), Perlman, Borger, Collins, Elenbogen, and Wood (1996) reported positive outcomes for middle school students with disabilities. However, Munger and Lloyd (1991) found no differences for students with and without disabilities. On the MAT 6 mathematics subtest, Gallina's (1989) research revealed that elementary students with disabilities scored in the average range when taking the modified time version versus scoring in the poor range when taking the standard version. Finally, Watkins' (1996) research revealed that for the student without a disability, extended time does not significantly improve test performance if the test was well designed for the standard administration time.

It should be noted that the majority of all time-related research has been conducted with college-age students. Further, much of this research utilized college admission tests or college entrance examinations. Researchers like Alster (1997), Bennett, Rock, and Jirele (1986), Centra (1986), Power and Fowles (1996), and Rock, Bennett, and Jirele (1988) all used students of college age in their studies. This is important because research limited to college admission testing represents a restricted group of tests for students with disabilities (e.g., college-bound secondary students). The number of students with disabilities who participate in such tests is very small (proportionately) and may not be representative of the larger group of such individuals (within any disability group or even in the general population). Thus, the results of college admission testing research, although informative, may not be generalizable to accommodation studies for large-scale statewide assessment.

Marking in Booklets Versus on Answer Sheets. Four studies examined the differences between marking answers on a separate answer sheet versus marking answers directly in the test booklet. The assumption by many is that students have difficulty moving between the test booklet and the test answer sheet, and that difficulty translates into lower scores because of construct-irrelevant factors. At best, research results are mixed on this test alteration. Wise, Duncan, and Plake (1985) found third-grade students using separate answer sheets without practice scored significantly lower than their peers who answered in the test booklet on the Iowa Test of Basic Skills (ITBS). However, Wise, Plake, Eastman, and Novak (1987) could not replicate the previous finding. Wise et al. found no response mode effect and no evidence of a treatment by ability interaction for third, fourth, or fifth graders on the California Achievement Test (CAT). In a third study, Mick (1989), ascertained that older teenage students with learning disabilities or mental handicaps performed better using the answer sheet rather than marking in the test booklets. Finally, Tindal et al. (1998) detected no significant differences for fourth graders on the Oregon statewide math multiple-choice test. They found that student performances were not higher when students were allowed to mark in the test booklet directly versus on the bubble answer sheet.

Dictating to a Scribe. For students with motor impairments or dysgraphia, using a scribe is a possible accommodation. MacArthur and Graham's (1987) research showed that for elementary-age students with learning disabilities, dictation produced longer and better compositions that were significantly longer and higher in quality. Koretz' (1997) post hoc research on the Kentucky statewide assessment for 4th, 8th, and 11th graders found that the dictation accommodation had the strongest effect across all tested subject areas and grade levels. In corroborating research, Trimble's (1998) reanalysis of the Koretz data supported the assertion that dictation was an effective accommodation, although not to the degree that Koretz found.

Computer Response. A majority of computer response research is in the area of written language. Many teachers and administrators presuppose that word processing enables students to attend to more complex tasks within the writing process because the computer performs the simpler, time-consuming secretarial tasks. However, Cochran-Smith's (1991) meta-analysis identified problems in interpreting computer word-processing research. They noted that it is difficult to "separate out effects of word-processing from the effects of other interrelated variables" (p. 142). Much of the research has proved inconclusive. Nichols' (1996) research with sixth graders showed no differences between word-processed and paper-and-pencil essays. Supporting this position, Langone's line of research (Langone et al., 1995; Langone et al., 1996) found no differences between word-processed and paper-and-pencil tests.

In research supporting the use of word processing, Bangert-Downs' (1993) meta-analysis found that approximately two thirds of the studies concluded that word processing improved the quality of students' writing. Similar to Bangert-Downs' findings, Owston, Murphy, and Wideman's (1992) research with sixth, seventh, and eighth graders determined that stories created on a word processor were rated significantly higher than those created using paper and pencil even when accounting for length and appearance. In another line of research, MacArthur (1998, 1999) explored the use of word processors with speech synthesis and found that correctly spelled words increased dramatically for some students but not others. MacArthur's follow-up analysis hypothesized that the depressed scores were caused by the difficulty of learning to use the word-processor software.

However, not all research supports the use of word processing. Using students who were college enrollees, Powers, Fowles, Farnum, and Ramsey (1994) found that when the original handwritten essays were rescored as word-processed essays, the average score decreased significantly. In contrast, when the original computer-produced essays were rescored as handwritten, the mean score increased slightly. Like Powers et al., Arnold et al. (1990) found that word-processed papers received significantly lower scores than handwritten papers. This was also true of handwritten papers converted to word-processed essays. Osborne's (1999) research with students with disabilities summarized these prior findings by stating that a majority of students were still disadvantaged in written examinations although they were utilizing word processors. Similar results for middle schoolers were found by Hollenbeck, Tindal, Harniss, and Almond (2001) and for high schoolers by Hollenbeck, Linder, and Almond (2001) on the Oregon statewide writing assessment. Hollenbeck, Tindal, et al. (2001) found that when the original handwritten compositions were transcribed into a word-processed format and then rated by state judges, the original handwritten compositions were rated significantly higher than the word-processed composition. Hollenbeck, Linder and Almond's (2001) findings corroborated the Hollenbeck, Tindal et al. (2001) results. Both studies found that essays scored in handwritten form were rated significantly higher than the same essay rated in word-processed form for total composite trait score. Furthermore, the Helwig et al. (2000) factor analysis of middle school Oregon statewide writing assessments detected a unidimensionality of writing within mode (either handwritten or word processed) and across traits. When handwritten or word-processed writing samples were analyzed by themselves, a single factor was found for each, but two factors were found when handwritten and word-processed essays were evaluated simultaneously.

Research on Accommodations Linked to the Statewide Raters

Accommodation results must not only be reliable to be considered valid, but the results must be reproducible. Reproducibility involves the statewide raters—raters across the state must not only score the product the same, but fairly. If assessments suffer from rater-by-accommodation interactions, then the validity of inferences is rendered suspect. The rater questions listed in Fig. 16.4 help clarify whether raters influence the validity of inferences.

Rater Question 1 asks the IEP team to explore factors at the assessment-rating level. If the test protocol is machine-scored, one could assume that rater bias would not be present. However, if the test is subjectively scored, then rater bias is a much greater possibility. For example, research has shown that statewide raters were more punitive in their rating of essays that were typed. Thus, a word processor as test alteration would be considered a modification because the scores of examinees tested under standard conditions have different meanings from scores from examinees tested with the requested test alteration.

Question 2 asks about the stability of rater judgment. If rater judgment is not stable across testing sessions or from one year to the next, then decisions and judgments regarding student competency are not stable and valid across time. The lack of stability influences not only judgments regarding individual progress, but also program evaluations. Instability of rater judgment can be considered a confound, calling into question any long-term accommodation research by introducing extraneous factors that are not part of the statewide test and are irrelevant to the construct of interest.

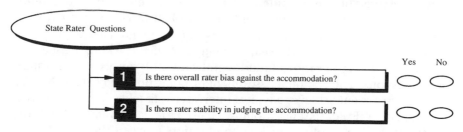

FIG. 16.4. Rater questions.

Rater Research

Hollenbeck, Tindal, and Almond's (1999) results indicate that state raters graded word-processed essays more harshly than handwritten essays. Results show that the statewide scoring rubric lacked scale stability when applied to identical essays presented in different response modes. Instead of providing better access that reveals student competence in the writing process, the word-processing response mode appeared to punish students for using it. These rater confounds negatively influenced the essay scores so that students using word processors were not accurately and fairly evaluated. If scores vary depending on the vehicle (response mode) used to create them, then it is not likely that scores can be interpreted meaningfully (Dietel, Herman, & Knuth, 1991). Most important, these findings suggest that word-processed essays are not an appropriate accommodation for statewide writing tasks (usually handwritten) because the results violate Tindal's (1998) task comparability requirement, Phillips' (1993, 1994) requirement that standard administration scores have the same meaning as the accommodated condition, and Hollenbeck, Rozek-Tedesco, and Finzel's (2000) samenesses of inference requirement.

The Hollenbeck et al. (1999) findings indicate that the state raters have not achieved the consistency necessary for high-stakes decisions because "judgment is the crucial link in the chain of reasoning from performance to inference about students" (Mislevy, 1994, p. 34). High-stakes assessment is of little value if the stability of results from one judge to another cannot be relied on over time. Because the statewide writing test has high-stakes consequences, valid generalizations from it are suspect. Hollenbeck et al. (1999) determined that exact match statistics were low enough to undermine the validity of the scores for comparing groups of students, schools, or districts across the state.

A final issue related to accommodations linked to the statewide raters is scale stability (i.e., the consistency of application of the scoring criteria across rating sessions or from one year to the next). The maintenance of scale stability across various rating occasions and across various raters ensures a greater fidelity of judgment accuracy—a reliability and validity concern. "Standards of fairness and methodological rigor mandate that criteria apply uniformly across . . . sets of papers" (Quellmalz, 1981, p. 13) within the year and across the years. Quellmalz, when tracking the stability of rating scale application, found significant differences within raters across sessions. The National Assessment of Educational Progress (NAEP) writing assessment achieves a typical interrater reliability of .91 to .95 per rating session (Frederiksen & Collins, 1989). However, Wainer (1993) reported that stability of rating scale application between the NAEP 1984 writing assessment and the 1988 NAEP writing assessment was so poor that mere statistical adjustments could not detect student change. Instead, the necessary comparisons required a massive rescoring of combined 1984 and 1988 NAEP essays. The NAEP's lack of stability across scoring sessions may still exist today. In a secondary analysis of the Hollenbeck et al. (2001) data, Hollenbeck (2001) found significant differences between the two state-wide scoring sessions of the same writing assessment. Although this finding may be confounded by input mode (handwritten vs. typed), Hollenbeck, Linder, and Almond (2001) also reported finding writing score differences across time where input mode was not a confound. Not only is rater reliability important within sessions, it is imperative to have reliability across sessions so that decisions and judgments regarding student competency are stable and valid across time (Quellmalz, 1981).

RESEARCH CONCLUSIONS

Clearly, the most significant problem in assessment accommodations is the lack of a consistent decision-making model for including students in statewide assessment programs with appropriate accommodations across all states. IDEA legislation and regulations distinctly assigned responsibility for determining assessment accommodations with the IEP team as part of the IEP process. Without such a model, school IEP teams make decisions idiosyncratically and unsystematically. The quality of the professional judgments rendered by IEP teams is a direct function of their professional skills and knowledge. Thus, creating a decision-making model is one of the most critical components for ensuring appropriate test alterations. The next section describes a system that integrates the decision making for participation of students with disabilities and ensures systematic and valid accommodation decisions. Rather than having the IEP teams base their decisions for participation in testing and use of accommodations on anecdotal information collected in unsystematic ways, teachers would use the decision matrix information in conversations with their IEP teams to compare student performance with grade-level peers or expected performance levels. In this approach, judgments about appropriate accommodations are grounded on reliable information regarding student performance.

DEVELOPING A DECISION-MAKING MODEL

Figure 16.5 displays a decision-making model that utilizes hypothesis generation that will assist in structuring an inquiry into the proposed test alterations. This decision-making model suggests the use of action research projects (single-subject research) for two important reasons. First, the action research can be used to empirically validate the proposed test alter-

Decision-making Flowchart

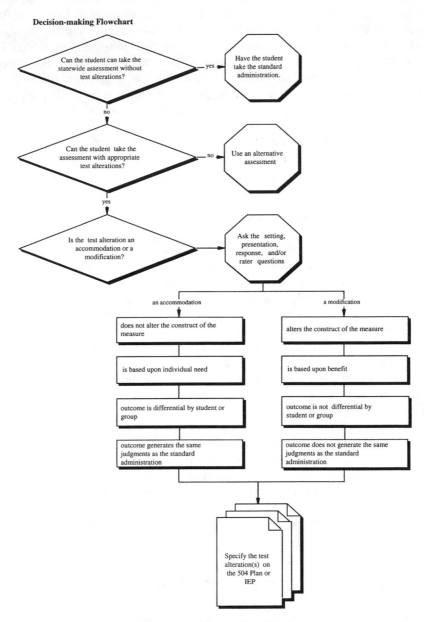

FIG. 16.5.   Decision-making flowchart.

ations. Second, action research can establish an empirical basis for determining whether the proposed test alterations are accommodations or modifications. To assist in that determination, the last part of the model outlines the important attributes of both an accommodation and a modification.

CONCLUSION

The ultimate goal of every large-scale test accommodation is "not to subvert existing educational standards" (Burns, 1998, p. 61), but to diminish the effects of the disability while upholding valid assessment interpretations. Test alterations that have "no impact on better measuring the student's ability rather than disability is not a valid accommodation" (Burns, 1998, p. 59). Unfortunately, this chapter's review of research revealed that choosing most accommodations is at worst ineffective for group decisions and at best effective only for individual students. Although most accommodations appear to be ineffectual, some research suggests that certain test alterations can occur without invalidating interpretations of the score. For example, research cited in this chapter has shown that teachers can administer certain large-scale math tests by reading them aloud, presenting the test via videotape or computer, or using simplified language without fear that a student's score would be unfairly inflated. Nonetheless, not all test alterations can be categorized into this grouping. Thus, more large-scale research is needed to document whether specific test alterations should always be thought of as accommodations or modifications. However, although more accommodation research may be an admirable agenda, it does not provide the immediate answer for the decision-making teams.

Team Member Qualifications. Before any decision-making team considers a particular large-scale accommodation, two functional requisites must be in place. First, not only must the group be intimately familiar with its state's list of acceptable accommodations and modifications, it must be knowledgeable of the state's policies regarding the use of statewide assessment accommodations and modifications. Team members must understand the permissibility of using any proposed alteration. Second, the group must understand what constructs the statewide test proposes to measure because those constructs define the alterations that are extraneous to the measured skill(s) and knowledge (an accommodation) and those that modify the skill(s) or knowledge being assessed (a modification).

Alterations Usually Considered Accommodations. If those two foundations listed earlier are in place, then the following alterations can be considered because, in all probability, they do not alter the skill(s) and knowledge being assessed:

- *Manipulating the physical environment*—The physical environment of the assessment room could be altered by using small groups, study carrels, and so on, which allows the student to attend better to the task at hand.
- *Tester familiarity*—The person administering the test should be familiar with the students so that the tester can attend to their special assessment needs.
- *Marking in the test booklet*—Students with visual tracking problems could mark in the test booklet to alleviate errors attributable to movement across pages.
- *Pacing*—Prompting students or verbally refocusing students toward task completion can increase completion rates.

Alterations That May or May Not Be Considered Accommodations. The next set of test alterations may or may not be judged as an accommodation because of state policy, assessment guidelines, constructs being assessed, and/or research specific to your state's statewide test.

- *Read-alouds*—It is important to recall that (a) read-alouds benefited many elementary students with disabilities but not older students, and (b) reading may be thought of as an attribute of the construct being assessed.
- *Computer-assisted testing*—Although research is varied, most computer-presented tests did not benefit students by providing differential outcomes versus the paper-and-pencil counterpart.
- *Time (extended or reduced)*—In most cases, alterations in timing are only appropriate if the test is a power test, not a speeded test, and even then extra time may give specific students unfair advantages because it misconstrues performance relative to the normative reference group by inflating scores.

Cautions About Accommodation Decisions. Most test alterations are being implemented in the absence of empirical data (Hollenbeck et al., 1999; Hollenbeck, Rozek-Tedesco, & Finzel, 2000; Shriner, Gilman, Thurlow, & Ysseldyke, 1995) and are commingled (e.g., task and content are codependent; Hollenbeck et al., 2000a). Moreover, many teachers have little basis for claiming that certain test alterations are actually an accommodation because they know little about the interaction of their students' characteristics and specific test demands. Regrettably, educators cannot simply rely on research findings to assist in this decision making. Instead, educators must structure their inquiry process and change their findings into conclusions. Specifically, attention to the consequences of changing the assessment is necessary. Educators must address the validity of decisions as a result of the proposed test alteration.

Adding to this lack of consistency is the disparity across statewide tests—statewide testing systems are very idiosyncratic. Some states rely on standardized, norm-referenced tests while others have developed their own assessments. Because the various statewide tests have specific task demands unique to themselves, the generalizability of accommodations findings are circumscribed (Linn, 1993; M. D. Miller, 1996; Ruiz-Primo, Baxter, & Shavelson, 1993). Consequently, the various statewide tests are more or less robust in their capacity to be validly altered.

This chapter calls for (a) a more informed educator/tester; (b) a decision-making model, such as the one presented in Fig. 16.5, for recommending test alterations for students; and (c) a prescriptive and empirical approach for choosing appropriate test alterations. Furthermore, state and local education agency administrators must play proactive roles by specifying a statewide process that clarifies the distinction between testing alterations that are appropriate (accommodations) and those that alter the content and performance level of what is tested (modifications).

Finally, appropriate decisions about test alterations require measurement-competent educators (O'Sullivan & Chalnick, 1991). Teachers and IEP team members need to recognize the difference between test alterations that work for a particular student and those that do not while still generating the same outcome judgments. This obligates educators to use more than simple checklists. Rather, it requires specific information about the student's performance generated by single-subject or action-research projects.

Utilizing single-subject or action research as a point of departure, educators must engage in these projects with each child suspected of needing test alterations. This research must clearly identify the appropriate independent variables that isolate specific test alterations. Test alterations must be investigated in isolation rather than in combination so that threats to valid conclusions are systematically reduced. Not isolating the specific test alterations makes it impossible to definitely predict the effect of any specific test alterations for an individual student.

REFERENCES

Abikoff, H., Courtney, M. E., Szeibel, P. J., & Koplewicz, H. S. (1996). The effects of auditory stimulation on the arithmetic performance of children with ADHD and non-disabled children. *Journal of Learning Disabilities, 29,* 238–246.

Alster, E. H. (1997). The effects of extended time on algebra test scores for college students with and without learning disabilities. *Journal of Learning Disabilities, 30,* 222–227.

Arnold, V., Legas, J., Obler, S., Pacheco, M. A., Russell, C., & Umbdenstock, L. (1990). *Do students get higher scores on their word-processed papers? A study of bias in scoring hand-written vs.*

word-processed papers. Whittier, CA: Rio Hondo College (ERIC Document Reproduction Service No. ED 345 818).

Bangert-Downs, R. L. (1993). The word-processor as an instructional tool: A meta-analysis of word-processing in writing instruction. *Review of Educational Research, 63*(1), 69–93.

Baxter, B. (1931). An experimental analysis of the contributions of speed and level in an intelligence test. *The Journal of Educational Psychology, 22*, 285–296.

Beattie, S., Griese, P., & Algozzine, B. (1993). Effects of test modifications on the minimum competency performance of learning disabled students. *Learning Disability Quarterly, 6*, 75–77.

Benderson, A. (1988). *Testing, equality, and handicapped people*. Princeton, NJ: Educational Testing Service (ERIC Document Reproduction Service No. ED 303 944).

Bennett, R. E., Rock, D. A., & Jirele, T. (1986, February). *The psychometric characteristics of the GRE General Test for three handicapped groups* (ETS Research Report RR–86–6). Princeton, NJ: Educational Testing Service.

Bennett, R. E., Rock, D. A., & Kaplan, B. A. (1985, November). *The psychometric characteristics of the SAT for nine handicapped groups* (ETS Research Report RR–85–49). Princeton, NJ: Educational Testing Service.

Bennett, R. E., Rock, D. A., & Kaplan, B. A. (1987). SAT differential item performance for nine handicapped groups. *Journal of Educational Measurement, 24*(1), 44–55.

Braun, H., Ragosta, M., & Kaplan, B. (1986, October). *The predictive validity of the Scholastic Aptitude Test for disabled students* (ETS Research Report RR-86-38). Princeton, NJ: Educational Testing Service.

Bruininks, R. H., Gilman, C. J., McGrew, K. S., Scott, D. L., Shriner, J. G., Spande, G., Thurlow, M. L., & Ysseldyke, J. E. (1994). *Testing accommodations for students with disabilities: A review of the literature* (Synthesis Report 4). Minneapolis, MN: University of Minnesota, National Center on Educational Outcomes.

Burke, M. (1998, October). *Computerized test accommodations: A new approach for inclusion and success for students with disabilities*. Paper presented at Office of Special Education Program Cross Project Meeting, Technology and the Education of Children with Disabilities: Steppingstones to the 21st Century.

Burns, E. (1998). *Test accommodations for students with disabilities*. Springfield, IL: CC Thomas Publishers.

Centra, J. A. (1986). Handicapped student performance on the scholastic aptitude test. *Journal of Learning Disabilities, 19*, 324–327.

Chiu, C. W. T., & Pearson, P. D. (1999). *Synthesizing the effects of test accommodations for special education and limited English proficient students*. Paper presented at the 1999 National conference on Large Scale Assessment, Snowbird, UT.

Cochran-Smith, M. (1991). Word-processing and writing in elementary classroom: A critical review of the literature. *Review of Educational Research, 61*, 107–155.

Cox, J. M., & Poe, V. L. (1991). The math-reading connection: A graded word list to estimate mathematics ability. *Reading Improvement, 28*(2), 108–112.

Crawford, L. (2000). *The effects of time and discourse type on a writing performance assessment*. Unpublished doctoral dissertation, University of Oregon, Eugene.

Cronbach, L. J. (1988). Five perspectives on the validity argument. In H. Wainer & H. I. Braun (Eds.), *Test validity* (pp. 3–17). Hillsdale, NJ: Lawrence Erlbaum Associates.

Curtis, H. A., & Kropp, R. P. (1961). A comparison of scores obtained by administering a test normally and visually. *Journal of Experimental Education, 29*, 249–260.

DeLaPaz, S., & Graham, S. (1997). Strategy instruction in planning. Effects on the writing performance and behavior of students with learning difficulties. *Exceptional Children, 63*, 167–181.

Derr-Minneci, T. F. (1990). A behavioral evaluation of curriculum-based assessment for reading: Tester, setting, and task demand effects on high- level vs. low-level readers (doctoral dissertation, Lehigh University). *Dissertation Abstracts International, 51*, 0105.

Dietel, R. J., Herman, J. L., & Knuth, R. A. (1991). *What does research say about assessment?* [Online]. Available: http://www.ncre.org/sdrs/areas/stw_egys/4assess.htm.

Englert, C. S., & Raphael, T. E. (1988). Constructing with formal prose: Process, structure, and metacognitive knowledge. *Exceptional Children, 54*, 513–520.

Frederiksen, J. R., & Collins, A. (1989). A systems approach to educational testing. *Educational Researcher, 18*(9), 27–32.

Fuchs, D., Featherstone, N. L., Garwick, D. R., & Fuchs, L. S. (1984). Effects of examiner familiarity and task characteristics on speech-and-language impaired children's performance. *Measurement and Evaluation in Guidance, 16*, 198–204.

Fuchs, D., & Fuchs, L. S. (1989). Effects of examiner familiarity on Black, Caucasian, and Hispanic children: A meta-analysis. *Exceptional Children, 55*, 303–308.

Fuchs, D., Fuchs, L. S., Garwick, E. R., & Featherstone, N. (1983). Test performance of language-handicapped children with familiar and unfamiliar examiners. *The Journal of Psychology, 114*, 37–46.

Fuchs, D., Fuchs, L. S., & Power, M. H. (1987). Effects of examiner familiarity on LD and MR students' language performance. *Remedial and Special Education, 8*(4), 47–62.

Fuchs, L. S. (April 1999). *Curriculum-based measurement: Updates on its application in standards-based assessment systems.* Charlotte, NC: Council of Exceptional Children.

Fuchs, L. S., & Fuchs, D. (1999). Fair and unfair testing accommodations. *School Administrator, 56*(10), 24–27.

Fuchs, L. S., Fuchs, D., Eaton, S. B., Hamlett, C., & Karns, K. (1999). *Mathematics test accommodations for students with learning disabilities: Supplementing teacher judgments with the dynamic assessment of test accommodations.* Unpublished manuscript, Peabody College of Vanderbilt University.

Gallina, N. B. (1989). *Tourettes's syndrome: Significant achievement and social behavior variables* (doctoral dissertation, City University of New York). *Dissertation Abstracts International, 50*, 46.

Harris, C. S. (1992). *Assessing problem-solving skills on selected questions from the scholastic aptitude test* (unpublished doctoral dissertation). New Brunswick, NJ: Rutgers.

Helwig, R., Rozek-Tedesco, M. A., Tindal, G., Heath, B., & Almond, P. (1999). Reading as an access to mathematics problem solving on multiple choice tests for sixth–grade students. *Journal of Educational Research, 93*, 113–125.

Helwig, R., Stieber, S., Tindal, G., Hollenbeck, K., Heath, B., & Almond, P. (2000). *A comparison of factor analyses of handwritten and word-processed writing of middle school students.* Manuscript submitted for publication.

Henry, S. (1999). Accommodating practices. *School Administrator, 56*(10), 32–34, 36–38.

Hollenbeck, K. (2001). *The stability of statewide writing score across scoring sites.* Unpublished manuscript, University of Oregon.

Hollenbeck, K., Linder, C., & Almond, P. (2001). *Statewide writing score comparability of various brailling tools used by students with visual impairments.* Unpublished manuscript, University of Oregon.

Hollenbeck, K., Rozek-Tedesco, M., & Finzel, A. (2000, April). *Defining valid accommodations as a function of setting, task, and response.* Presentation at the meeting of the Council of Exceptional Children, Vancouver, BC, Canada.

Hollenbeck, K., Rozek-Tedesco, M., Tindal, G., & Glasgow, A. (2000a). An exploratory study of student-paced versus teacher-paced accommodations for large-scale math tests. *Journal of Special Education Technology, 15*(2), 29–38.

Hollenbeck, K., Rozek-Tedesco, M., Tindal, G., & Glasgow, A. (2000b). *Computation as a predictor of large-scale test scores.* Unpublished manuscript, University of Oregon.

Hollenbeck, K., & Tindal, G. (2001). *Accommodating students on large-scale writing tests: Consideration of time in the writing process.* Manuscript submitted for publication.

Hollenbeck, K., Tindal, G., & Almond, P. (1998).Teachers' knowledge of accommodations as a validity issue in high-stakes testing. *Journal of Special Education, 32,* 175–183.

Hollenbeck, K., Tindal, G., & Almond, P. (1999). Reliability and decision consistency: An analysis of writing mode at two times on a statewide test. *Educational Assessment, 6*(1), 23–40.

Hollenbeck, K., Tindal, G., Harniss, M., & Almond, P. (2001). *Handwritten versus word-processed statewide compositions: Do judges rate them differently?* Manuscript submitted for publication.

Horton, S. V., & Lovitt, T. C. (1994). A comparison of two methods of administering group reading inventories to diverse learners. *Remedial and Special Education, 15,* 378–390.

Howell, K. W., Fox, S. L., & Morehead, M. K. (1993). *Curriculum-based assessment: Teaching and decision making* (2nd ed.). Pacific Grove, CA: Brooks/Cole.

Keene, S., & Davey, B. (1987). Effects of computer-presented text on LD adolescents' reading behaviors. *Learning Disability Quarterly, 10,* 283–290.

Koretz, D. (1997). *The assessment of students with disabilities in Kentucky* (CSE Technical Report 431). Los Angeles: UCLA, CRESST.

Koretz, D., & Hamilton, L. (1999). *Assessing students with disabilities in Kentucky: The effects of accommodations, format, and subject* (CSE Technical Report 498). Los Angeles: UCLA, CRESST.

Langenfeld, K., Thurlow, M., & Scott, D. (1997. *High stakes testing for students: Unanswered questions and implications for students with disabilities* (Synthesis Report No. 26). Minneapolis, MN: University of Minnesota National Center on Educational Outcomes.

Langone, J., Levine, B., Clees, T., Malone, M., & Koorland, M. (1996). The differential effects of a typing tutor and microcomputer-based word-processing on the writing samples of elementary students with behavior disorders. *Journal of Research on Computing in Education, 29*(2), 141–158.

Langone, J., Willis, C., Malone, M., Clees, T., & Koorland, M. (1995). Effects of computer-based word-processing versus paper/pencil activities on the paragraph construction of elementary students with learning disabilities. *Journal of Research on Computing in Education, 27*(2), 171–183.

Lenz, B. K., & Mellard, D. (1990). Content area skill assessment. In R. A. Gable & J. M. Hendrickson (Eds.), *Assessing students with special needs* (pp. 117–145). New York: Longman.

Linn, R. L. (1993). Educational assessment: Expanded expectations and challenges. *Educational Evaluation and Policy Analysis, 15*(1), 1–6.

Lord, F. M. (1956). A study of speed factors in tests and academic grades. *Psychometrika, 21,* 31–50.

MacArthur, C. A. (1998). Word-processing with speech synthesis and word prediction: Effects on the dialogue journal writing of students with learning disabilities. *Learning Disability Quarterly, 21,* 151–166.

MacArthur, C. A. (1999). Word prediction for students with severe spelling problems. *Learning Disability Quarterly, 22,* 158–172.

MacArthur, C. A., & Graham, S. (1987). Learning disabled students' composing under three methods of test production: Handwriting, word processing, and dictation. *Journal of Special Education, 21*(3), 22–42.

Messick, S. (1982). The values of ability testing: Implications of multiple perspectives about criteria and standards. *Educational Measurement: Issues and Practice, 1*(3), 9–12, 20, 26.

Messick, S. (1988). The once and future issues of validity: Assessing the meaning and consequences of measurement. In H. Wainer & H. I. Braun (Eds.), *Test validity* (pp. 89–103). Hillsdale, NJ: Lawrence Erlbaum Associates.

Messick, S. (1994). The interplay of evidence and consequences in the validity of performance assessments. *Educational Researcher, 23*(2), 13–23.

Mick, L. B. (1989). Measurement effects of modifications in minimum competency test formats for exceptional students. *Measurement and Evaluation in Counseling and Development, 22*, 31–36.

Miller, M. D. (1996). *Generalizability in Connecticut.* Unpublished manuscript written for Council of Chief State School Officers.

Miller, S. (1998). *The relationship between language simplification of math word problems and performance for students with disabilities.* Unpublished master's project, University of Oregon, Eugene, OR.

Mislevy, R. J. (1994). *Test theory reconceived* (CSE Technical Report 376). Los Angeles: UCLA, CRESST.

Mollenkopf, W. G. (1960). Time limits and the behavior of test takers. *Educational and Psychological Measurement, 20*, 223–230.

Munger, G. F., & Lloyd, B. H. (1991). Effect of speededness on test performance of handicapped and nonhandicapped examinees. *Journal of Educational Research, 85*, 53–57.

Newman, M. A. (1977). An analysis of sixth-grade pupils' errors on written mathematical tasks. In M. A. Clements & J. Foyster (Eds.), *Research in mathematics education in Australia* (Vol. 1, pp. 239–258). Melbourne: Swineburne Press.

Nichols, L. M. (1996). Pencil and paper versus word-processing: A comparative study of creative writing in the elementary school. *Journal of Research on Computing in Education, 29*(2), 159–166.

Osborne, P. (1999). Pilot study to investigate the performance of dyslexic students in written assessments. *Innovations in Education and Training International, 36*, 155–160.

O'Sullivan, R. G., & Chalnick, M. K. (1991). Measurement-related course work requirements for teacher certification and recertification. *Educational Measurement: Issues and Practice, 10*(1), 17–19, 23.

Owston, R. D., Murphy, S., & Wideman, H. H. (1992). The effects of word-processing on students' writing quality and revision strategies. *Research in the Teaching of English, 26*, 249–273.

Perez, J. V. (1980). Procedural adaptations and format modification in minimum competency testing of learning disabled students: A clinical investigation (doctoral dissertation, University of South Florida). *Dissertation Abstracts International, 41*, 0206.

Perlman, C. L., Borger, J., Collins, C. B., Elenbogen, J. C., & Wood, J. (1996). *The effects of extended time limits on learning disabled students' scores on standardized reading tests.* Paper presented at the annual meeting of the National Council on Measurement in Education, New York, NY.

Phillips, S. E. (1993). Testing accommodations for disabled students. *Education Law Reporter, 80*, 9–32.

Phillips, S. F. (1994). High stakes testing accommodations: validity versus disabled rights. *Applied Measurement in Education, 7*(2), 93–120.

Powers, D. E., & Fowles, M. E. (1996). Effects of applying different time limits to a proposed GRE writing test. *Journal of Educational Measurement, 33*, 433–452.

Powers, D. E., Fowles, M. E., Farnum, M., & Ramsey, P. (1994). Will they think less of my handwritten essay if others word-process theirs? Effects on essay scores of intermingling handwritten and word-processed essays. *Journal of Educational Measurement, 31*, 220–233.

Quellmalz, E. (1981). *Problems in stabilizing the judgment process.* Los Angeles, CA: UCLA Center for the Study of Evaluation of Instructional Programs. (ERIC Document Reproduction Service No. ED 212 650)

Rock, D. A., Bennett, R. E., & Jirele, T. (1988). Factor structure of the Graduate Record Examinations General Test in handicapped and nonhandicapped groups. *Journal of Applied Psychology, 73*, 383–392.

Rock, D. A., Bennett, R. E., & Kaplan, B. A. (1987). Internal construct validity of a college admissions test across handicapped and nonhandicapped groups. *Educational and Psychological Measurement, 47*, 193–205.

Ruiz-Primo, M. A., Baxter, G. P., & Shavelson, R. J. (1993). On the stability of performance assessments. *Journal of Educational Measurement, 30*, 41–54.

Sexton, M., Harris, K. R., & Graham, S. (1998). Self-regulated strategy development and the writing process: Effects on essay writing and attributions. *Exceptional Children, 64*, 295–311.

Shepard, L. (1983). The role of measurement in educational policy: Lessons from the identification of learning disabled. *Educational Measurement: Issues and Practice, 2*(3), 4–8.

Shriner, J. G., Gilman, C. J., Thurlow, M. L., & Ysseldyke, J. E. (1995). Trends in state assessment of educational outcomes. *Diagnostique, 20*(1–4), 101–119.

Siskind, T. G. (1993). Teachers' knowledge about tests modifications for students with disabilities. *Diagnostique, 18*, 145–157.

Stiggins, R. J. (1991). Relevant classroom assessment training for teachers. *Educational Measurement: Issues and Practice, 10*(1), 7–12.

Stoneman, Z., & Gibson, S. (1978). Situational influences on assessment performance. *Exceptional Children, 44*, 166–169.

Swain, C. R. (1997). A comparison of a computer-administered test and a paper and pencil test using normally achieving and mathematically disabled young children (doctoral dissertation, University of North Texas). *Dissertation Abstracts International, 58*, 58.

Tack, K. D. (1995). *The influence of reading skills on the Ohio ninth grade proficiency test of mathematics.* Bowling Green, OH: Bowling Green State University. (ERIC Document Reproduction Service No. ED 386 703)

Thurlow, M., Hurley, C., Spicuzza, R., & El Sawaf, H. (1996). *A review of the literature on testing accommodations for students with disabilities* (Synthesis Report No. 9). Minneapolis, MN: University of Minnesota National Center on Educational Outcomes.

Thurlow, M. L., Ysseldyke, J. E., & Silverstein, B. (1993). *Testing accommodations for students with disabilities: A review of the literature* (Synthesis Report 4). Minneapolis, MN: National Center on Educational Outcomes.

Thurlow, M. L., Ysseldyke, J. E., & Silverstein, B. (1995). Testing accommodations for students with disabilities. *Remedial and Special Education, 16*, 260–270.

Tindal, G. (1998). *Models for understanding task comparability in accommodated testing.* A publication for the Council of Chief State School Officers, Washington, DC.

Tindal, G., Almond, P., Heath, B., & Tedesco, M. (1998). *Single subject research using audio cassette read-aloud in math.* Unpublished manuscript, University of Oregon.

Tindal, G., Anderson, L., Helwig, R., Miller, S., & Glasgow, A. (1999). *Accommodating students with learning disabilities on math tests using language simplification.* Unpublished Manuscript, University of Oregon.

Tindal, G., & Fuchs, L. (1999). *A summary of research on test changes: An empirical basis for defining accommodations.* Lexington, KY: University of Kentucky, Mid-South Regional Resource Center.

Tindal, G., Glasgow, A., Helwig, B., Hollenbeck, K., & Heath, B. (1998). *Accommodations in large-scale tests for students with disabilities: An investigation of reading math tests using video technology.* Unpublished manuscript for Council of Chief State School Officers, Washington, DC.

Tindal, G., Heath, B., Hollenbeck, K., Almond, P., & Harniss, M. (1998). Accommodating students with disabilities on large-scale tests: An experimental study. *Exceptional Children, 64*, 439–450.

Tindal, G., Helwig, R., & Hollenbeck, K. (2000). An update on test accommodations: Perspectives of practice to policy. *Journal of Special Education Leadership, 12*(2), 11–20.

Tindal, G., Hollenbeck, K., Heath, W., & Almond, P. (1997). *The effect of using computers as an accommodation in a statewide writing test* (Technical Research Report). Eugene, OR: University of Oregon, Behavioral Research and Teaching.

Trimble, S. (1998). *Performance trends and use of accommodations on a statewide assessment* (Maryland/Kentucky State Assessment Series Report No. 3). Minneapolis, MN: National Center on Educational Outcomes.

Wainer, H. (1993). Measurement problems. *Journal of Educational Measurement, 30*(1), 1–21.

Watkins, R. (1996). Extended time for tests is a reasonable accommodation. http://www.emory.edu/EMORY_REPORT/erarchive/1996/February/Effeb.19.

Weston, T. (1999, April). *The validity of oral presentation in testing*. Montreal, Canada: American Educational Research Association.

Willingham, W. W. (1988). Testing handicapped people: The validity issue. In H. Wainer & H. I. Braun (Eds.), *Test validity* (pp. 89–103). Hillsdale, NJ: Lawrence Erlbaum Associates.

Willingham, W. W., Ragosta, M., Bennett, R. E., Braun, D. A., Rock, D. A., & Powers, D. E. (1988). *Testing handicapped people*. Boston: Allyn & Bacon.

Wise, S. L., Duncan, A. L., & Plake, B. S. (1985). The effect of introducing third graders to the use of separate answer sheets on the ITBS. *Journal of Educational Research, 78*, 306–309.

Wise, S. L., Lukin, L. E., & Roos, L. L. (1991). Teacher beliefs about training in testing and measurement. *Journal of Teacher Education, 42*(1), 37–42.

Wise, S. L., Plake, B. S., Eastman, L. A., & Novak, C. D. (1987). Introduction and training of students to use separate answer sheets: Effects on standardized test scores. *Psychology in the Schools, 24*, 285–288.

Yell, M. L., & Shriner, J. G. (1996). Inclusive education: Legal and policy implication. *Preventing School Failure, 40*, 101–108.

Chapter 17

A Methodology for Creating
an Alternative Assessment System
Using Modified Measures

Robert Helwig
University of Oregon

The significance of statewide assessments has increased dramatically over the past three decades. This is partly the result of state legislatures, departments of education, and the public's call for increased educational accountability. The yardstick of educational success, while formerly centered on inputs such as per-pupil expenditures, class size, or new construction, now focuses on outputs including graduation rates, college admittance, and, most important, standardized test scores (Bowers, 1991; Erickson, Ysseldyke, Thurlow, & Elliott, 1998). However, the high standards accompanying this accountability have proved problematic for significant numbers of students with learning disabilities (LD). Issues of item difficulty, format, and cognitive demands in both traditional standardized tests and performance tasks present significant challenges to these students. In many cases, the challenges result in low test performance and give school personnel little useful information about these students' achievement and/or progress.

Historically, because of low test performance, many LD students have been excluded from statewide testing (Fuchs et al., 2000). This unquestionably changed as a result of the 1997 reauthorization of the Individuals with Disabilities Education Act (IDEA). Two major requirements of IDEA are that *all* students (a) take part in statewide assessment, and (b) are provided access to the general education curriculum that requires attention to present levels of performance and progress monitoring. The purpose of the present chapter is to illustrate one methodology for developing and field testing a modified assessment system through which LD students can be included in large-scale testing programs. Our work is also relevant to many low-achieving students without LD. Thus, we often use the term *low achiever* when referring to either group. Most of this chapter describes a several month process undertaken at the University of Oregon to create a series of measures in reading and mathematics to be used as alternatives to a standard statewide test. The procedures we describe are generally applicable not only to situations with a similar purpose, but also to the development of modified testing systems on a smaller scale, such as within a school district. Although this chapter focuses on LD students, the methodology is appropriate for use in developing systems for other populations, such as students with severe cognitive impairments.

Two general categories describe the alteration of standard testing procedures of large-scale assessments: *accommodations* and *modifications*. Because these terms are used inconsistently and sometimes interchangeably throughout the research literature, we present a working definition for each. We refer to an accommodation as a change in standardized testing conditions, including content, that does not change the construct under investigation (Fuchs et al., 2000; Hollenbeck, chap. 16, this volume; Phillips, chap. 6, this volume). Some common types of test accommodations include the use of Braille, testing in small groups, increasing the size of answer bubbles, and providing a scribe for a student with cerebral palsy (Elliott, Thurlow, Ysseldyke, & Erickson, 1997). Accommodations are only effective when test takers can take advantage of the change in testing conditions. For example, one method of accommodating poor readers on mathematics problem-solving tasks is to read the problem aloud to these students. Because the construct under consideration is problem solving within the domain of mathematics, reading problems to students does not change the construct. Those who do not have the mathematical skill to solve the problem will gain nothing from the problem-presentation accommodation. Yet poor readers with more advanced math skills will be able to compete on equal terms with proficient readers (Helwig, Rosek-Tedesco, Heath, Tindal, & Almond, 1999). A detailed discussion concerning accommodations can be found in Hollenbeck (chap. 16, this volume) and Phillips (chap. 6, this volume).

For the population we targeted, test accommodations by themselves were generally not sufficient due to low-proficiency levels in basic skills. Therefore, test modifications were employed. A test modification is a change in testing procedures, including content, that results in the measurement of a different construct than measured using standard procedures (Tindal & Fuchs, 1999). For example, providing a student with a starter sentence for an essay when administration directions call for all work to be done by the student is a test modification. Reading text passages aloud to students on a test of reading comprehension is another test modification, as is substituting passages with a lower readability level. Test modifications render the results incompatible with scores obtained under standard testing conditions and are thus disaggregated. The rest of this chapter focuses exclusively on test modifications rather than accommodations.

The defining property of a test modification is a change in the construct being assessed. A *construct* is a psychological characteristic usually comprised of multiple systematically related elements that can be inferred but not directly observed (Haynes & O'Brien, 2000). Constructs should be imbedded within a conceptual framework. This framework "specifies the meaning of the construct, distinguishes it from other constructs, and indicates how measures of the construct should relate to other variables" (American Educational Research Association, American Psychological Association, & National Council on Measurement in Education, 1995, p. xx).

Test modifications result in the testing of a different psychological characteristic than that for which the test was originally designed. The goal of validating a modified assessment system, however, is to focus on a closely related characteristic so that meaningful comparisons can take place among results from students within both systems. For example, a typical state reading curriculum goal might concern reading comprehension. Reading comprehension is a construct. It cannot be directly observed, but rather must be inferred from a variety of student behaviors. One common method of measuring reading comprehension is to have students read text passages and answer multiple-choice questions about their content. A modification of this process would be to have students read a list of vocabulary words and choose a correct definition for each. Although both methods measure some portion of text comprehension, it is clear that there are important differences in how these results can be interpreted. Depending on the passages, tests using the first method might measure such skills as synthesizing, analyzing, summarizing, or inferring information from written text, as well as a knowledge of word meanings. Tests of vocabulary would undoubtedly put much more emphasis on the last skill and, therefore, measure a different, although related, construct.

Another method of measuring reading comprehension is to tally the number of words students can read from a passage in a set period of time. Although it may appear that this type of task measures reading speed rather than comprehension, the two are closely related. (We discuss this fact in a later section.) Consequently, a test of reading fluency can be used as a measure of reading comprehension. It is clear, however, that the precise skills measured by a multiple-choice comprehension task, a test of fluency, and vocabulary items are different. In other words, these tests measure different constructs. It is for this reason that we consider the latter two assessments to be modified.

The following portion of this chapter concerns the difficulties many LD students encounter with large-scale tests as they are commonly administered. Following this discussion, we use a three-step process to describe our methodology for creating a modified assessment system. The first step describes how to identify a target population and how to select a sample of subjects. The second step describes how to identify the domains within which the test occurs and how the tests can be developed. In the third step, we report the results of our own field testing. Throughout this three-step process, we make a case for developing a body of evidence in support of construct validity as is commonly done in the validation of standardized large-scale assessment systems. The final section of the chapter describes how certain modified assessment tasks can help provide LD students access to the general education curriculum by monitoring student progress toward benchmark goals throughout the school year.

HIGH STANDARDS AND STUDENTS
WITH LEARNING DISABILITIES

School accountability in the current educational reform movement translates into high-stakes testing conducted in thousands of buildings across the nation. As the stakes have risen, so, too, have the standards, as evidenced by legislation such as Goals 2000, which calls for "world class standards," "challenging subject matter," and students who are "first in the world in math and science." A major goal of the reform movement is "higher academic standards and more demanding and uniform expectations for all students' performance" (Gronna, Jenkins, & Chin-Chance, 1998, p. 484). School districts are likely to pay close attention to these standards, with promises of additional funding, regulatory waivers, and public praise or at least anonymity for the winners, and threats of funding loss, nonaccreditation status, or even takeover or dissolution for the losers (Erickson et al., 1998).

The benchmarks for success are higher than they were even a decade ago. In 1968, only 13 states used test results to measure student progress in academic subjects (Dyer & Rosenthal, 1971). In addition, these results were released predominately to educational personnel on a limited basis to individual parents and/or students, but never to the public. The primary purpose of these programs was to aid teachers in their efforts to help individual students (Bettinghaus & Miller, 1973). By the mid-1970s, most states had passed some type of accountability legislation mandating the measurement of student performance (Bowers, 1991). By 1985, statewide tests to measure student performance levels were in place in 34 states (Goertz, 1986). By the late 1990s, only Iowa failed to mandate that all students in at least one grade level participate in some form of statewide achievement test. Today, the publication by the local press of district and/or school level test results, including information on the number of students who meet state requirements, is commonplace.

As tests have become more rigorous, it is not unusual to find significant numbers or even the majority of test takers fail to meet established state standards. For example, approximately one fourth of the students in Grades 3 through 8 taking the 1997–1998 North Carolina statewide tests in reading and mathematics did not meet minimum state competency levels (North Carolina Department of Education, 1998). In Oregon, 48% and 64% of 10th-grade students taking the 1999 statewide tests in reading and math did not meet performance standards (Oregon Department of Education, 1999). In 1998, 56% and 62% of Louisiana students did not meet National Assessment of Educational Progress (NAEP) basic competency requirements in reading and mathematics, respectively. The prior numbers are conservative estimates of achievement levels of students within these states because many students with disabilities do not participate in standardized testing programs (Tindal & Fuchs, 1999).

For a variety of reasons, LD students are especially unlikely to be able to demonstrate achievement on many statewide assessments. In reading, many LD students have language deficits in areas such as semantics and syntax that cause difficulties with deriving meaning from text (Smith, 1991). Also, low-fluency reading, common in this population requires that students spend cognitive energies on decoding at the expense of comprehension (Samuels, 1987). Short-term memory deficits compound this problem (Dockrell & McShane, 1993).

Many difficulties in reading carry over into mathematics as states increasingly move away from tests of computation to problem solving, in which significant amounts of text are used to provide information and context. When this is done, the constructs of math problem solving and reading comprehension become difficult to separate (Tack, 1995). Apart from difficulties associated with poor reading, significant numbers of LD students are also plagued with difficulties in solving problems involving numbers, computation, and analytic reasoning. This is due, in part, to deficiencies in several areas of mathematics, such as (a) the inaccurate (Geary, 1990) and/or slow retrieval (Goldman, Pelligrino, & Mertz, 1988) of math facts, (b) a lack of awareness of appropriate solution strategies (Pelligrino & Goldman, 1987), (c) a failure to use the most appropriate computaional strategy (Geary, Windaman, Little, & Cormier, 1987), (d) determining the appropriate operation to use when solving word problems (Montague & Bos, 1990), and (e) identifying extraneous information (Cawley, Miller, & School, 1987).

In writing, many LD students lack self-regulatory and general control operations necessary for coordinating cognitive processes such as perception, memory, and language (Meltzer, 1991). In addition, students suffering from attention deficit disorder (ADD) may experience (a) uneven recall of writing conventions, (b) difficulty remaining focused throughout the essay writing process, and (c) difficulty attending to multiple simultaneous details such as spelling, punctuation, legibility, grammar, and coherence (Levine, 1987). Similar to automaticity in reading, students who spend too much energy on spelling and handwriting cannot devote sufficient resources to the cognitive processes necessary for composing (Berninger & Stage, 1996).

Increasingly, students are being asked to demonstrate their academic proficiency through the use of performance tasks (Elliott, 1998). It is hoped that these types of assessments will benefit special students in many of the same ways that they have been touted as beneficial for students in the general education curriculum (Mehrens, 1992). However, several authors have voiced serious concerns that these assessments may, in fact, prove problematic for students with disabilities. For example, Choate and Evans (1992) question whether LD students can demonstate the planning and independence needed for extended-duration projects. Poteet, Choate, and Stewart (1993) raised concerns about special students' struggles with the complex language and abstract content of most performance assessments. In addition, many of the cognitive requirements of performance tasks may be difficult for LD students, including ignoring irrelevant information, planning and monitoring performance, and generalizing from one context to another (Dalton, Tivnan, Riley, Rawson, & Dias, 1995). Students with LD also exhibit difficulties refocusing their attention and developing solution strategies (Swanson, 1987). In addition, most performance tasks call for students to communicate in writing, which is an area of well-documented difficulty for many LD students (Graham & MacArthur, 1988).

It seems clear, then, that higher, more demanding standards serve as an additional challenge for low achievers. As described previously, in many cases accommodations do not address the underlying factors of the disability. Because of low proficiency in the construct in question, those students who are unable to solve problems created to measure high standards of academic achievement are unlikely to benefit from accommodations such as more time, the use of private carrels, or having the problem read to them. To the contrary, the most likely method of eliciting from these students a meaningful response for evaluative interpretation is to modify the original problem.

METHODOLOGY FOR CREATING
A MODIFIED ASSESSMENT SYSTEM

Given the difficulties many LD students encounter with standardized statewide testing, it is critical that methods for modifying current assessment systems are developed and field tested. Next we describe one attempt to meet this challenge by discussing (a) population selection, (b) testing domain identification, and (c) field test results. Our goal is for our methods to be generalizable to others working in a variety of assessment systems and student populations. According to the *Standards for Educational and Psychological Testing* (American Educational Research Association, American Psychological Association, & National Council on Measurement in Education, 1995), "Validity is the most important consideration in test evaluation" (p. 9). All tests, not just traditional large-scale assessments, must be held to this standard (Mehrens, 1992). Therefore, a central theme of our discussion is the validity of the modified measures we developed. Throughout the description of our methods, we make reference to a modification of the six aspects of construct validity described by Messick (1995): content, substantive, structural, generalizability, external, and consequential.

Content validity (in regard to statewide testing) refers to the match between curriculum goals and test coverage. Substantive validity adds to content validity by verifying not only the congruence of domains, but also the match between assumed and actual cognitive processes. Structural fidelity refers to the consistency of scoring models and the internal structure of the construct in question. The generalizability of a test is the extent to which interpretations of test results are valid across tasks, populations, and settings. The external aspects of construct validity refer to the degree to which test results reflect external evidence of the construct in question, such as related tests, observations, or reports. This is often referred to as *criterion validity*. Consequential validity includes an evaluation of the consequences, both intended and unintended, of test score interpretation, particularly those associated with bias and fairness. For an in-depth discussion of validity and statewide assessment systems, see Linn (chap. 2, this volume). In our discussion, we subsume substantive validity within content validity (Benson, 1998) and postpone references to consequential validity until a later section. We make this latter decision not because the consequences of assessment are unimportant, but because of the current debate concerning the appropriateness of including this aspect in a unified concept of validity (Linn, 1997; Mehrens, 1997; Moss, 1995; Shepard, 1997).

Population Selection

Before attempting to design any type of assessment system, it is necessary to identify a target population (i.e., the group of students for which the assessment program is intended). This step is crucial because it defines the types of tasks that will be created as well as constrains the sampling plan that will be used to include students in field testing. At the same time, however, it raises concerns over generalizability. Limiting field testing of potential new measures to a specific population increases the likelihood that result interpretations will be applicable to that particular group alone (Salvia & Ysseldyke, 1988). This issue is addressed in a later section.

We identified LD students as our target population, although our methods are applicable to other groups as well. For example, most students with low-incidence disabilities, such as moderate to severe cognitive impairments, are likely to be in need of testing modifications. With minor alterations, the general procedures we describe can be used with this or other populations. We focused on LD students for two reasons. First, LD is a high-incidence disability, through which our work could have an effect on large numbers of students. Second, because previous work in this area has been limited, a logical initial step is to design an assessment system closely aligned with an already existing one. As described later, the use of LD students makes this task less difficult. In this section, we describe how both school districts and individual students were identified for participation in our project.

In selecting subjects for our research, we chose to include approximately equal numbers of students with and without learning disabilities. This served two primary goals. First, including large numbers of LD students (our target population) was necessary to generate sufficient data for statistical analyses. Second, including general education students provided evidence for the generalizability of the measures by generating data from a diverse population (Cook & Campbell, 1979). For many LD students, current large-scale testing practices are adequate to measure their status in relation to statewide achievement standards. For others, current systems work only marginally well or not at all. When a representative sample of general education students is added to this mix of LD students, a wide range of academic abilities can be applied to each modified assessment. In the section on field testing, we describe how this process aids in defining the constructs under consideration, as well as helps to ensure that the new modified measures fit comfortably within the existing assessment system. It is also critical that the study population be diverse in terms of other variables that may affect generalizability, such as gender, ethnicity, socioeconomic status (SES), and geographic location.

Although including students in both general and special education aids in clarifying the construct being tested, there are important differences in the generalizability of statewide tests and modified assessments. The former are designed to generalize to as large a sample as possible. Modified tasks, such as the ones we developed, are designed for a specific population. Therefore, the accuracy of the inferences made from modified-measures test scores apply to a highly restricted range of achievement levels. The primary purpose of including a diverse group of students in field testing is to link the modified measures to the original construct.

Test Domain Identification

A logical starting point in the creation of modified assessments is an examination of the existing assessment system. The statewide assessment of reading we attempted to modify was typical of many reading comprehension tests. Students read a series of passages and answered corresponding multiple-choice questions. The passages usually vary in content and format from fiction examples, such as prose and poetry, to nonfiction examples, such as biographies, recipes, and tables of contents. Most tests of this type cover a variety of domains such as: (a) literal, inferential, and evaluative comprehension; (b) understanding word meanings; (c) recognizing literary forms; and (d) analyzing the use of literary elements and devices. The mathematics problem-solving test was also typical of many other large-scale tests. Students are presented with a problem statement and a multiple-choice set of answers. Many items contain graphics, such as pictures, tables, or charts. The word count of individual items varies from less than 10 to several dozen. Some items require the memorization of facts, such as recognizing the names of geometric figures. Other items require the application of algorithms, such as finding the average of a set of numbers. Many items call for either a conceptual knowledge of some mathematical principal or the use of higher order thinking skills beyond that which is required to carry out the individual procedures necessary to solve the problem. Many items require both of these skills. Typically, these tests cover such domains as geometry, probability and statistics, estimation, measurement, and number theory.

Identification Methodology. Before determining what types of alternative measures to create, it is necessary to identify the areas within the existing assessment system that need modification. This will depend on the purpose of the change and can be seen as a three-step process. The first is to identify aspects of the current assessment that prove particularly problematic for the target population (in our case, low achievers). Second, potential modified measures are identified through a review of research. The distinguishing feature of these instruments is their criterion validity with measures of the original construct. Finally, field testing is initiated to determine whether criterion validity is maintained when testing is conducted using the specific population under consideration. This last requirement is critical because it captures the entire purpose of the test modification (i.e., because the target population cannot be accurately assessed within the existing system of evaluation, a new system is necessary so that this can take place).

Reading Example. Although it is clear that the prior criteria are subjective, an example from our experience illustrates how they can be put into practice. In reading, the standard test requirement of having students read extended text passages clearly proved to be an insurmountable hurdle for many within our target group (Step 1). Many LD students have language deficits in areas such as semantics and syntax that cause difficulties with deriving meaning from text (Smith, 1991). As detailed later in this section, we identified several test modifications for field testing. We use one of those modifications here to illustrate the application of Steps 2 and 3. We determined that a simple test of vocabulary would be a possible candidate for a modified measure. Vocabulary tests appear to meet the requirement of Step 2 because they have been shown to correlate relatively highly with large-scale tests of reading comprehension (Step 2). Admittedly, vocabulary tests do not measure comprehension in the same way that can be accomplished by having students read a passage and respond to multiple-choice questions. This issue of content/substantive validity is addressed in more detail later, but we repeat ourselves here by stating that the measures we are pursuing are considered modified because they differ in some important way from the original assessment task. Clearly, there is significant content addressed in a general reading comprehension measure that is not addressed in a vocabulary test. This is referred to as *construct underrepresentation* (Messick, 1989). Step 3 requires that a vocabulary test can be used within the target population to measure the new construct. Evidence that this is the case is presented next in the section on field testing.

We identified five different types of reading measures to utilize in our field testing. These included an oral reading fluency (ORF), a maze task, and tests of vocabulary, word identification, and spelling. All of these measures possess two characteristics we believe are critical to our research. The first is that each measure had been shown in previous research to be predictive of achievement on tests of reading comprehension (Espin & Deno, 1994; Espin & Foegen, 1996; Marston, 1989; Juel, Griffith, & Gough, 1986). This is an example of the external aspect of construct validity, where the criterion validity of a task is evaluated based on the degree to which it correlates with some recognized measure of the construct in question (Tindal & Marston, 1990). Strong correlations provide evidence that Step 2 is satisfied. In our case, the correlations indicate that all five tasks measure a construct related to the standardized reading comprehension task we wished to modify. Thus, vocabulary and comprehension possess moderately high correlations with each other. Students with strong vocabularies tend to read with high comprehension, whereas weak vocabularies indicate poor comprehension. Similar statements can be made concerning the other measures. The importance of this criterion validity cannot be overemphasized in establishing the link between two instruments that are expected to measure related constructs. Some early work in test theory defined validity wholly in terms of correlations with external measures (see e.g., Gulliksen, 1950).

In addition to the strong criterion validity of our five tasks, previous studies have shown that each measure was effective over a range of ability levels. For example, the comprehension of moderate and moderately high-fluency readers can be differentiated, as can the comprehension of low- and very low-fluency readers (Espin & Deno, 1993). Because of this latter relationship, we believed it was likely that field tests would provide evidence to satisfy the requirements of Step 3.

This is not to say that the same ORF, maze task, or spelling test can be equally predictive of how both high and low achievers will perform on a test of reading comprehension. For example, a spelling test designed for middle achievers in a given grade level may not be sensitive enough to distinguish differences in students at the extremes. In other words, very low achievers may not be able to spell any of the words correctly, whereas very high achievers might have no misspellings. For this reason, we created four versions of each modified measure—one corresponding to Grades 1, 3, 5, and 8. Within each grade level we tested (3, 5, and 8), each student took each task at his or her own grade level plus one (Grades 3 and 5) or two (Grade 8) levels below. Thus, each eighth-grade student, both those with and without LD, took an eighth-grade maze task, a fifth-grade maze task, and a third-grade maze task. By following this procedure, each student was able to correctly respond to enough items on at least one of the levels so that meaningful data could be gathered.

As with performance assessments, a major concern with many modified measures, including our own, is content/substantive validity. An ideal alternative task covers the same curriculum goals and content as the appropriate statewide test attempts to cover. Typical state content standards cover information and concepts, as well as skills (Linn, 1988). Taken individually, our tasks offer insufficient coverage of the subject matter domain of reading comprehension. As mentioned earlier, typical reading comprehension tests might reward students who are familiar with a wide variety of types of reading matter, such as tables of content, poetry, recipes, prose, biographies, written directions, newspaper articles, and so on. It is likely that there are significant numbers of students who are skilled in one or more of the areas of vocabulary, reading fluency, spelling, or maze completion, but have little or no experience with genres such as poetry or have never read or seen a recipe. Clearly the construct being measured by a reading comprehension test will be different than that of any of the modified tasks. Although some students may spell accurately but know little or nothing about a table of contents, it is certain that significantly fewer students will be skilled in all five of the modified measures tasks and still score low on reading comprehension tests. By evaluating students' reading comprehension based on their performance on all of the modified measures, rather than examining each individually, a more accurate picture of their skills emerges. In other words, students who are skilled in all five areas are more likely to have high reading comprehension than are students who are skilled in only one or a few of these areas. Some of this increase in correlation may be due to common correlates such as intelligence (Daneman, 1982), but a significant amount is likely due to a greater congruence of constructs.

Math Example.   We followed a similar three-step process in mathematics. First (Step 1), we identified factors within the statewide mathematics multiple-choice test that rendered the test beyond the capabilities of the very low achievers in whom we were interested. In this case, we felt that a combination of (a) high reading demands, (b) items that combined a variety of skills, and (c) reliance on the memorization of algorithms combined to form an insurmountable barrier to many within our target group. Next, we identified tasks that would measure a similar construct (mathematics problem solving) as the statewide test (Step 2) and would differentiate the achievement of low as well as high achievers (Step 3).

Based on previous research we had conducted on various mathematics tests used for a variety of purposes in diverse settings and grade levels (Helwig et al., 1999), we identified a series of individual test items. Collectively, the items addressed Step 1 by (a) using relatively few words, (b) addressing only one major concept per item, and (c) relying on conceptual understanding rather than on knowledge of solution strategies or algorithms. Step 2 was satisfied by the fact that our previous work had indicated that each item had a relatively strong correlation with general mathematics achievement. We included items from a variety of achievement levels (identified by grade level as we did in measuring reading achievement). Again, each student responded to items at and below their grade level. As in reading, this feature helped us gain evidence during field testing to satisfy Step 3.

Content/substantive validity consists not only of subject matter coverage, but also the intellectual processes required to complete various tasks designed to define the construct in question. If test makers assume that all students will attempt problem solutions using specific cognitive processes when, in fact, a variety of strategies are used, the validity of test interpretations can be questioned (American Educational Research Association, American Psychological Association, & National Council on Measurement in Education, 1999). For example, consider a problem that asks students to find the area of a rhombus. Some students may have memorized the area formula for this shape. Other students may divide the figure into right triangles and combine the area of each of these figures. Some students may block the rhombus into unit squares. Each of these strategies defines a different construct of mathematics problem solving. Although differences exist between each method, the most dissimilar is probably the first strategy in which a formula was used because relatively little conceptual knowledge is needed to generate a correct solution. For this reason, we chose to concentrate on conceptual understanding in our modified measure of mathematics. Problem solving is grounded in the understanding of basic concepts rather than algorithms. We felt that, although the content of our measure was somewhat different than that tested by the state, there was a relatively strong congruence among the conceptual knowledge, skills, and proficiencies assessed by the two measures.

It should be evident at this point that the measures we chose to investigate, in both mathematics and reading, differ significantly from the options taken by several states. Many are still developing measures for students unable to participate in their regular assessment system. Several states allow IEP teams to create alternative assessments, whereas others use performance assessments or portfolios (Landau, Vohs, & Ramano, 1998). It is difficult to imagine locally created assessments meeting minimum standards of validity. At the same time, although "performance assessments may have face validity, such validity pertains only to what the test appears superficially to measure, and is not sufficient for accountability purposes" (Burger & Burger, 1994, p. 9). Specifically, various authors have questioned the reliability, generalizability, and content validity (construct underrepresentation) of these types of measures (Linn, Baker, & Dunbar, 1991; Mehrens, 1992; Shavelson, Baxter, & Gao, 1993). Portfolios suffer from these same deficiencies (Koretz, Stecher, Klein, & McCaffrey, 1994; Moss et al., 1992). In addition, research has found unacceptably low correlations between both types of assessments and established standards of achievement (criterion-concurrent validity) such as large-scale multiple-choice tests (Gentile, 1992; Koretz et al., 1994). For a more complete discussion of the status of performance assessments in the large-scale testing system, see Tindal (chap. 1, this volume).

Alternative Methods. Before we conclude this section, we make three points of clarification. First, the measures we chose to investigate do not form a comprehensive list, even if we restrict the target population to low achievers with LD. Other measures also warrant investigation. For example, in reading, one promising strategy might be to keep the same format as the state test with the exception of severely restricting the length of text passages. This would serve to mitigate some of the language deficits of low achievers (Rothkopf & Billington, 1983; Spyridakis & Standal, 1987; Surber, 1992). These modified tasks would clearly meet the requirements of Step 2. If research can be found that indicated this task can differentiate between various performance levels of low achievers, Step 3 would also be satisfied. A wide variety of other measures offer possibilities as well. We restricted our investigation to the measures described earlier primarily because of limitations of how many different tasks we could realistically ask students to perform in a field test. Each of these measures could easily be administered by classroom teachers to monitor progress throughout the year. We discuss this last point in greater detail later.

The second point of clarification is that if the existing system is not effective at measuring the achievement of some target group because of a mismatch between the achievement level of the group and the achievement level the test attempts to measure, the most straightforward and effective method of modifying the test is simply to alter the level of the test while retaining the format. For example, suppose it is believed that some target group cannot perform effectively on our multiple-choice reading comprehension test—not because students had difficulty processing long text passages, but because they could not understand the vocabulary used. In this case, the first attempt at test modification should be to lower the readability level of the passages. Granted, this renders the results of the two versions incompatible. However, the constructs being measured will undoubtedly be more closely related than would be the case if completely new measures were employed. The content of the modified task could remain relatively constant. Many of the cognitive processes would remain unchanged as well. However, because the same test content elicits different solution strategies from different grade levels, the constructs tested will not be identical (Tindal & Marston, 1990). The process will also likely be much less complicated. The how-to directions we offer in this chapter, however, are aimed at cases where there are fundamental flaws in the measurement system when applied to a specific population that simple difficulty level modifications will not eliminate.

Our third point of clarification is that the general methodology we used applies to the development of systems of modified measures for other populations as well. For example, most statewide systems of measuring achievement cannot be used with students with low-incidence disabilities such as moderate to severe cognitive impairments. Therefore, the development of a modified assessment program using global curriculum goals is warranted. An identical three-step process to the one outlined before can be used. The focus of each step is different, but the strategy remains the same. For example, reading comprehension is an important goal of students with this disability, as it is with almost all students. However, whereas our focus was on alleviating problems resulting from student difficulties with extended text passages, a system designed for lower achievers might focus on simple key word recognition such as MEN, WOMEN, STOP, WALK, DANGER, or PHONE. In mathematics, problem solving may still be the focus, but counting, shape recognition, or computation might be the target skills. In both these examples from reading and mathematics, all aspects of validity are likely to be affected and in many cases suffer. For example, even more so than with our measures, there would be critical differences in the content of a standard reading comprehension test and interpreting individual words such as MEN or STOP. In addition, there probably exists a relatively small domain of important words such as those listed earlier, thereby severely restricting the amount of material students could be expected to learn. "A narrowing of instruction to the sample, rather than the general domain it is intended to represent, destroys the validity of inferences about the larger domain" (Linn, 1988, p. 8). Yet if a curriculum goal is to have students demonstrate literal, inferential, or evaluative comprehension, there may be less difference because at least some portion of these skills is imbedded in recognizing key words. Much of the loss of validity is unavoidable due to the differences in the populations for which each of the tasks is designed. The primary difference in developing test modifications for this population is the relative lack of research to guide task creation. In this case, Steps 2 and 3 undergo their primary test during field testing.

In summary, the methodology for developing alternative measures is straightforward and involves three steps. First, a careful examination of the existing assessment system is undertaken to identify what characteristic(s) of the existing assessment prove the most difficult for the target population to overcome. This defines the target area for test modification. Next, potential alternative measures are identified through literature reviews or personal experience. These are scrutinized to see that they measure a similar construct as the original assessment (Step 2) and are sensitive measures for the target population (Step 3). In some cases, there may be little direct research linking the new measures to the old, particularly when test modifications are being made for a group very dissimilar to the target population of the original assessment. Extrapolation, judgment, and professional experience play important roles at this point. Regardless of how much research is available, the crucial information concerning the validity of the new measures will come through field testing.

Field Testing

Field testing involves administering the modified measures to a sample population of students to gain information concerning the external (or criterion) and structural validity of the tasks. We have identified four major components of this process. The following section includes a description of how each was addressed within our project.

Establishing a Measurement Standard.   The first major component involves establishing a measure to serve as the standard. The criterion validity of a measure is commonly evaluated by comparing students' performance on the task to some accepted measure with established reliability and validity (Benson, 1998). If the achievement standard is defined by a department of education, as in our case, the obvious standard would be the statewide test of achievement in the appropriate area. For example, to determine whether a test of oral retell is a good measure of the type of reading comprehension measured by a statewide reading test, the two measures should be given to a group a students and the results compared. If the ranking of student results for both tests is the same, it is a good indication that the tests measure the same thing. For our purposes, however, this strategy is problematic. We could not give the standard statewide test to our target population because, as we have stated a priori, it is not effective in measuring many of these students' achievement. This is likely the case in most instances when an existing system is being modified.

The alternative is to use a replacement assessment that measures a construct similar to the original instrument. For example, we might have chosen a different reading comprehension test or used lower grade level versions of the statewide tests we were attempting to modify. Either of these alternatives would have been acceptable if we were able to establish a strong relationship between the two tests based on previous validity studies. In our case, we used two existing computer-adaptive tests (CAT) created specifically to generate scores directly comparable to student scores earned on the statewide tests in reading and mathematics. The primary difference in the scaling of the two tests is the fact that the CAT, because of its ability to adapt to each student's individual responses and target a specific ability level, is able to accurately measure much lower levels of achievement than the standard statewide test. Thus, we had measures that had been validated with the statewide test (Hauser, 1998; Kingsbury, 1999) to assess a closely related construct and were accessible to our low-achieving students. This point is crucial. If we had used the Stanford Achievement Test (SAT), for example, as our standard for reading comprehension or math problem solving, we probably could have established a high correlation between these and the statewide tests. However, because the formats of the two tests are very similar, many of our low achievers probably would not have been able to generate meaningful scores on the SAT any better than they could on the original test.

Establishing Concurrent Validity.   The second major component of field testing involves establishing the concurrent validity between the modified measure(s) and the standard by which the construct in question is being measured. As described before, previous research by others had indicated that each of our five modified reading measures had been shown to be moderately to highly correlated with some measure of reading achievement. Our field testing confirmed this. We found correlations between the various versions of the five reading tasks and the CAT to range from .52 to .75, with a mean of .67. In addition, the correlations were consistent across both grade levels and task. In other words, each modified measure correlated with the CAT to approximately the same magnitude, while this magnitude did not change from grade level to grade level. This concurrent validity indicates that some portion of the reading comprehension construct measured by the CAT (and, therefore, the statewide test) is embedded within each of the measures. It is possible to have high correlations between sets of events that have little in common. However, because our tasks all involve reading of some type, we conclude that we were measuring a common factor. The correlations, within each grade level, between the modified mathematics measures and the CAT were approximately .09 higher than those within reading, providing evidence that similar constructs were being tested in this domain as well.

Establishing Structural Validity. The third component of field testing is to examine the structural validity of the modified measures. This provides evidence of the internal consistency of the measures (Benson, 1998). In our particular case, we viewed the five reading tasks as an integrated assessment rather than as five separate measures. Therefore, one of the methods by which we chose to examine their structure was to calculate the intercorrelations among all tasks. We found these correlations to range from moderate to high. If we had not found such strong relationships, we would have had to reevaluate our conclusions. Two tasks that measure related constructs should have at least a moderate correlation with one another (Tindal & Marston, 1990). If all the modified tasks correlated well with the CAT, but one or more had a low correlation with the others, a closer examination would be warranted. For example, suppose an investigator was interested in reading fluency and found relatively high correlations between a test of fluency and each of the following: letter recognition, phonemic segmentation, rhyming, and spelling. Suppose, further, that each of these latter measures was highly intercorrelated with the exception of spelling. We might conclude that, although spelling and reading fluency have some strong association with each other (based on their strong correlation), they may not share a construct closely related to reading speed. Additional testing would probably be called for before spelling could be put forth as a valid modified measure of reading fluency. There are several other procedures besides correlation analysis that address structural validity. Some of these are discussed in a later section.

In mathematics, we field tested only one modified measure. As a result, we could not perform an analysis similar to the one we used for reading.

Using several measures can provide more information than using a single instrument because the convergence of data from several sources adds greatly to one's confidence that different tasks measure related constructs. For this reason, we are more confident that the five reading tasks we tested are valid alternative measures than we are of the single modified math task we created despite the higher correlations present between the CAT and the latter.

Establishing Generalizability Across Groups.   The fourth component of field testing is to verify the criterion validity of the modified measures across a diverse sample of students. Although we were interested in an assessment system for low achievers, using only these students in our sample would limit the generalizability of results. Even if we had found universally high correlations among all measures, it could be argued that the construct being measured for low achievers on all instruments was significantly different from what is measured for other populations. Using students from a wide range of ability levels helps eliminate this argument. As described, we used approximately equal sample sizes of students with and without LD. After examining the correlations for the total population, we split the analysis by educational classification. When comparing students enrolled in special and general education, we found no significant differences in the correlations between the modified measures and the CAT in an overwhelming majority of cases. In other words, ORFs, mazes, or tests of vocabulary, word identification, or spelling can effectively predict the concurrent reading comprehension levels of high-achieving students. They can also do this for students of middle and low achievement. A similar result was found within mathematics. The fact that the tests appear to function the same across different ability levels is another piece of evidence that, in large part, the same constructs were being measured within each ability group.

As a final test of validity, we examined, within each grade level and in both reading and mathematics, the correlations between each level of each modified measure and the CAT. We split this analysis by educational classification. As expected, correlations were generally higher for LD students when the analyses involved below grade-level measures and were higher for students in general education when the analyses used grade-level measures. For example, all fifth-grade students took both a fifth-grade vocabulary test and a third-grade vocabulary test. For students in special education, the third-grade test was a better predictor of how they performed on the CAT. For the general education students, the better predictor was the fifth-grade version. A similar pattern held over the remaining tasks and grade levels. As a result, we are inclined to conclude that an appropriate level of each modified measure can be found for each student in our target population so that it can be an effective indicator of reading comprehension.

As was the case with the previous sections, this description of our own field testing is presented as a general guide for others with similar goals. In most cases, it is through field testing that the majority of evidence concerning the validity of the modified measures becomes available. Because of the narrow focus of investigations such as these, it is unlikely that field testing will duplicate previous research. In our case, we knew from our literature review and our own work that the modified measures we had chosen were related to general math and reading achievement. Until we had verified this relationship with the appropriate target standard, however, we lacked critical evidence that our chosen tasks reflected the specific constructs in question.

Summary

"A 'strong' program of construct validation requires an explicit conceptual framework, testable hypotheses deduced form it, and multiple lines of relevant evidence to test the hypotheses" (Burger & Burger, 1994, p. 6). We have attempted, within the confines of one chapter, to offer a view of our work in validating a series of modified measures for possible use with a statewide assessment system. "One does not validate a test per se, but what is validated is the interpretation of the scores derived from the test" (Benson, 1998, p. 10). Thus, the precise methods we describe are specific to our purpose. An identical process used for a different purpose (e.g., to validate measures for students with severe cognitive impairment or gifted students) would have a very different interpretation. However, the general process that we followed are generalizable to other populations and purposes.

We divided our methodology into three steps (population selection, testing domain identification, and field testing). These, in turn, were broken down into further divisions. This was done primarily as a presentation tool and not because of any presumption that a formula exists by which assessment systems can be developed and validated. Each piece of evidence we collected, indicating that scores from the measures we created could be used to describe the targeted constructs, adds to their validity. Test validation is an ongoing process that ends not for theoretical reasons but for practical ones. Due to space limitations, we have not described our process in its entirety. Also, we could have collected different or additional evidence. In fact, this is our intent.

For example, a clearer perspective of the external validity of our measures might be gained through an experimental design. One group could be given an intervention designed to improve the construct of reading comprehension. A control group would see no treatment. Improvement in both reading comprehension scores as well as scores on the modified reading measures within the experimental group, coupled with stagnate scores in the control group, would provide evidence of a common factor within both assessment systems. To add to the structural validity of a test, Benson (1998) proposed the use of confirmatory factor analysis to link test items to the structure of the theoretical domain in question, followed by generalizability theory to examine domain coverage. Numerous other methods of providing evidence have been used, and many are applicable to our situation.

Only recently have alternative measurement systems designed for LD students begun to undergo the rigorous validation processes given traditional standardized tests. The intent of this section was to facilitate that process. In the next section, we look at one of the consequences of using our system of modified measures.

Progress Monitoring

IDEA 1997 requires school districts to provide statements concerning how students with disabilities, including LD, will be involved in and progress in the general curriculum. Part of this requirement can be met by holding all students to the same curriculum goals and periodically sampling student behaviors from within this domain. Although statewide test scores can provide useful information for accountability purposes or program evaluations, the potential for statewide assessments to serve as benchmarks for individual student progress monitoring is often overlooked. In most cases, large-scale tests are of little use in monitoring progress because they are given relatively infrequently. Many states only test every other year or less. Testing more often than once per year is impractical because of the time commitment. For this reason, students and school staff often have little foresight as to which individuals are in danger of failing to meet minimum state criteria. This problem is not addressed if modified measures follow a similar format as standard tests.

As Tindal (chap. 1, this volume) points out, teaching and learning are the often forgotten component of assessment. This appears to be the case despite efforts to the contrary. One of Messick's (1989) key components of test validity is the "functional worth of scores in terms of social consequences of their use" (p. 5). According to Principle 1 of the National Forum on Assessment (1995), "Assessment systems, including classrooms and large-scale assessments, are organized around the primary purpose of improving student learning" (p. 6). The document went on to state that, "by documenting and evaluating student work over time, teachers obtain information for understanding student progress in ways that can guide future instruction" (p. 6). Yet a typical article on test validity may contain no information that links test scores with teaching or learning. In the previous section, we detailed the procedures we used for field testing to help build a body of evidence in favor or against the validity of the scores derived from the modified measures we created. In this section, we make a case for our choice of these measures based on the consequences of their use.

The vast majority of students for whom our modified measures are designed do not meet minimum state standards in the targeted area. Nevertheless, it is critical that local educational staff have information concerning these students' progress. It is for this reason that we purposefully limited our choice of potential modified measures to those types that could be used by classroom teachers throughout the year to monitor the progress of individual students. To be used for this purpose, these measures had to meet three criteria. First, each measure had to be able to be administered in a relatively short period of time (in most cases, less than 15 minutes). Second, the measures had to lend themselves to the creation of alternate forms. Finally, the scoring of each task had to be relatively quick and straightforward so that teachers could see results and chart student progress in a timely fashion.

To effectively monitor progress, students' present level of performance must be checked several times during the school year. This will not take place if tasks take an unacceptable amount of valuable instruction time away from students. Tasks given at least monthly can serve to inform all parties not only which students are performing at acceptable levels, but also what kind of progress each student is making in relation to state standards. It is unrealistic to expect teachers to devote an hour or more per month for each goal. Tasks that are quick to administer (our individually administered ORFs took only 1 minute per student, whereas our group reading and math tasks took from 5–15 minutes each) are much more likely to be used.

It is necessary to have a quantity of alternate forms of each modified task because of their frequent administration. In many cases, these tasks are created locally, often by classroom teachers, rather than test publishers. In many cases, then, it is desirable to choose tasks that do not require specialized knowledge or procedures to create alternate forms. In our case, we chose measures that represented a range of expertise. Creating comparable reading passages to be used for weekly or monthly ORFs or mazes can probably be accomplished by classroom teachers selecting passages from basal readers of the appropriate level. Creating comparable vocabulary or spelling tests would probably require some field testing to complete a database of words to be randomly selected for each administration.

Not all tasks lend themselves to alternate forms especially if created locally. For example, in previous investigations of math items, we found that some geometry problems were good indicators of math achievement. One of the best discriminators of elementary school achievement, as measured by the statewide mathematics test, was an item that asked students to identify a sphere from a picture. An alternative test form should include an item that tests a similar construct within mathematics. Finding such an item is problematic due to the relatively small domain of geometric figures students are exposed to in elementary school. Identifying squares, cubes, circles, or lines would likely measure different skills. This fact contributed to our decision to omit this item in our modified mathematics task. Instead, we included items such as ordering a string of numbers or shading in some fractional part of a figure. The difficulty of these items is much less controlled by the numbers selected than by the overriding concept.

The prior example illustrates a trade-off that often exists between construct congruence and the feasibility of alternate form creation. As noted in a previous section, a reading comprehension task that used short text passages would likely measure a similar construct as that measured by a task with a similar format but using extended passages. In the absence of sophisticated scaling techniques, however, it would be extremely difficult to create equivalent alternate forms. To intuitively select two passages of equal readability, ask questions of equal difficulty while addressing the same construct is unlikely. A series of assessments centered on short passages might be highly correlated to a standard extended passage assessment and may test a closely related construct. However, because of the unpredictable difficulty level of each of the alternate tasks, they would have limited usefulness in monitoring progress.

The final criterion requires that tasks can be scored quickly and easily. Tasks that require outside scoring are likely to be used infrequently. Sending out answer sheets and waiting for their return defeats part of the purpose of monitoring progress. When feedback is immediate, critical decisions such as instructional changes, interventions, and placement decisions can be made more appropriately. If word counts are marked on the administrator's copy of an ORF, each reading fluency score can be recorded almost instantaneously. Several of the other modified measures we field tested were multiple-choice tasks of 12 to 15 items. For these, a classroom could be scored in a short period of time. We also used only raw scores in all of our fieldwork. This eliminates the need for teachers to perform score conversions or use tables, thus adding to the system's overall efficiency.

It should be emphasized that the progress-monitoring tasks we have discussed are not identical to the ones used to replace an existing assessment system. Official modified measures would, of course, be secured documents. However, teachers within a state using ORFs as an alternative reading comprehension measure for low achievers could, with little difficulty, create text passages for their own use. The achievement measured with these passages would undoubtedly closely mimic that measured by the ORF given by the state. It is unlikely that local personnel could mirror this level of comparability if they attempted to create their own standard assessments.

CONCLUSIONS

In recent years, national and state standards of academic achievement have risen significantly. Many of the reasons for this change are political, and much of the implementation has been ill conceived (Marzano & Kendal, 1997; Popham, 1997). Nevertheless, the standards movement seems to enjoy strong public support and is unlikely to fade quickly. Often excluded in the past from large-scale testing, students enrolled in special education, including those with learning disabilities, are now mandated to participate. Several factors combine to make typical standardized test inappropriate for these students. Coupled with the standards movement is a renewed interest in alternative systems of assessment, such as portfolios and performance assessments. These bring a new set of skills and proficiencies that make them no more appropriate assessment instruments for certain populations than are standardized tests.

The majority of alternative assessment systems created for low-performing students are implemented without attention to the same standards that typically accompany large-scale tests. We have described a methodology that attempts to put test validity at the forefront of test development. At the same time, we have looked beyond testing solely for accountability purposes and envisioned an assessment system in which the test can be used to help inform instruction. Although this has long been touted as one of the goals of testing, too often statewide assessments are seen as dictating the curriculum rather than aiding teachers. It is our hope that this chapter can serve as an inspiration (rather than a strict template) for others to develop assessment systems in which assessment and instruction are partners.

REFERENCES

American Educational Research Association, American Psychological Association, & National Council on Measurement in Education. (1995). *Standards for educational and psychological testing*. Washington, DC: American Educational Research Association.

American Educational Research Association, American Psychological Association, & National Council on Measurement in Education. (1999). *Standards for educational and psychological testing*. Washington, DC: American Educational Research Association.

Benson, J. (1998). Developing a strong program of construct validation: A test anxiety example. *Measurement: Issues and Practice, 17*(1), 10–17, 22.

Bettinghaus, E. P., & Miller, G. R. (1973). *A dissemination system for state accountability programs-Part 1: Reactions to state accountability programs*. Denver, CO: State Department of Education Cooperative Accountability Project (ERIC Document Reproduction Service No. ED 111 841).

Berninger, V. W., & Stage, S. A. (1996). Assessment and intervention for writing problems of students with learning disabilities or behavioral disabilities. *B.C. Journal of Special Education, 20*(2), 5–23.

Bowers, J. J. (1991). Evaluating testing programs at the state and local levels. *Theory Into Practice, 30*(1), 52–60.

Burger, S. E., & Burger, D. L. (1994). Determining the validity of performance-based assessment. *Measurement: Issues and Practice, 13*(1), 9–15.

Cawley, J. F., Miller, J. H., & School, B. A. (1987). A brief inquiry of arithmetic word-problem-solving among learning disabled secondary students. *Learning Disability Focus, 2,* 87–93.

Choate, J. S., & Evans, S. S. (1992). Authentic assessment of special learners: Problem or promise? *Preventing School Failure, 37*(1), 6–9.

Cook, T. D., & Campbell, D. T. (1979). *Quasi-experimentation. Design and analysis for field settings*. Chicago: Rand McNally.

Dalton, B., Tivnan, T., Riley, M. K., Rawson, P., & Dias, D. (1995). Revealing competence: Fourth-grade students with and without disabilities show what they know on paper-and-pencil and hands-on performance assessments. *Learning Disabilities Research & Practice, 10,* 198–214.

Daneman, M. (1982). The measurement of reading comprehension: How not to trade construct validity for predictive power. *Intelligence, 6,* 331–345.

Dockrell, J., & McShane, J. (1993). *Children's learning difficulties: A cognitive approach*. Oxford: Blackwell.

Dyer, H. S., & Rosenthal, E. (1971). *State educational assessment programs*. Princeton, NJ: Educational Testing Service (ERIC Document Reproduction Service No. ED 056 102).

Elliott, J., Thurlow, M., Ysseldyke, J., & Erickson, R. (1997). *Providing assessment accommodations for students with disabilities in state and district assessments*. NCEO Policy Directions (Eric Document Reproduction Service No. ED 416 628).

Elliott, S. N. (1998). Performance assessment of students' achievement: Research and practice. *Learning Disabilities Research and Practice, 13,* 233–241.

Erickson, R., Ysseldyke, J., Thurlow, M., & Elliott, J. (1998). Inclusive assessments and accountability systems. *Teaching Exceptional Children, 31*(2), 4–9.

Espin, C. A., & Deno, S. L. (1993). Performance in reading from content area text as an indicator of achievement. *Remedial and Special Education, 14*(6), 47–59.

Espin, C. A., & Deno, S. L. (1994). Curriculum-based measures for secondary students: Utility and task specificity of text-based reading and vocabulary measures for predicting performance on content-area tasks. *Diagnostique, 20*(1–4), 121–142.

Espin, C. A., & Foegen, A. (1996). Curriculum-based measures at the secondary level: Validity of three general outcome measures for predicting performance on content-area tasks. *Exceptional Children, 62,* 497–514.

Fuchs, L. S., Fuchs, D., Eaton, S. B., Hamlett, C., Binkley, E., & Crouch R. (2000). Using objective data sources to enhance teacher judgments about test accommodations. *Exceptional Children, 67,* 67–81.

Geary, D. C. (1990). A componential analysis of early learning deficits in mathematics. *Journal of Experimental Child Psychology, 49,* 363–383.

Geary, D. C., Windaman, K. F., Little, T. D., & Cormier, P. (1987). Cognitive addition: Comparison of learning disabled and academically normal elementary school children. *Cognitive Development, 2,* 249–269.

Gentile, C. (1992). *Exploring new methods for collecting students' school-based writing: NAEP's 1990 portfolio study*. Washington, DC: National Center for Educational Statistics.

Goertz, M. E. (1986). *State educational standards: A 50-state survey*. Princeton, NJ: Educational Testing Service (ERIC Document Reproduction Service No. ED 275 762).

Goldman, S. R., Pelligrino, J. W., & Mertz, D. L. (1988). Extended practice of basic addition facts: Strategy changes in learning-disabled children. *Cognition and Instruction, 5*, 223–265.

Graham, S., & MacArthur, C. (1988). Written language of the handicapped. In C. Reynolds & L. Mann (Eds.), *Encyclopedia of special education* (pp. 1178–1181). New York: Wiley.

Gronna, S. S., Jenkins, A. A., & Chin-Chance, S. A. (1998). The performance of students with disabilities in a norm-referenced, statewide standardized testing program. *Journal of Learning Disabilities, 31*, 482–493.

Gulliksen, H. (1950). *Theory of mental tests*. New York: Wiley.

Hauser, C. (1998, December). *Linking state and district measurement scales using item response theory: Toward informing local policy and standard setting*. Paper presented at the meeting of the 14th annual Washington State Assessment Conference, SeaTac, WA.

Haynes, S. N., & O'Brien, W. H. (2000). *Principles and practice of behavioral assessment*. New York: Kluwer Academic/Plenum.

Helwig, R., Rozek-Tedesco, M. A., Tindal, G., Heath, B., & Almond, P. J. (1999). Reading as an access to mathematics problem solving on multiple-choice tests for sixth-grade students. *Journal of Educational Research, 93*, 113–125.

Juel, C., Griffith, P. L., & Gough, P. B. (1986). Acquisition of literacy: A longitudinal study of children in first and second grade. *Journal of Educational Psychology, 78*, 243–255.

Kingsbury, G. G. (1999). *A comparison of test scores from the Iowa Test of Basic Skills and the Meridian Checkpoint Assessment levels tests*. Unpublished manuscript, Northwest Evaluation Association, Tigard, OR.

Koretz, D., Stecher, B., Klein, S., & McCaffrey, D. (1994). Vermont portfolio assessment program: Findings and implications. *Measurement: Issues and Practice, 13*(3), 3–16.

Landau, J. K., Vohs, J. R., & Ramano, C. A. (1998). *All kids count: Including students with disabilities in statewide assessment programs*. Boston: Federation for Children with Special Needs. (ERIC Document Reproduction Service No. ED 419 324).

Levine, M. D. (1987). *Developmental variation and learning disorders*. Cambridge, MA: Educators Publication Service.

Linn, R. L. (1988). State-by-state comparisons of achievement: Suggestions for enhancing validity. *Educational Researcher, 17*(3), 6–9.

Linn, R. L. (1997). Evaluating the validity of assessments: The consequences of use. *Educational Measurement: Issues and Practice, 16*(2), 14–16.

Linn, R. L., Baker, E. L., & Dunbar, S. B. (1991). Complex, performance-based assessment: Expectations and validation criteria. *Educational Researcher, 20*(8), 15–21.

Marston, D. B. (1989). A curriculum-based measurement approach to assessment: What it is and why do it. In M. R. Shinn (Ed.), *Curriculum-based measurement: Assessing special children* (pp. 18–78). New York: Guilford.

Marzano, R. J., & Kendall, J. S. (1997). National and state standards: The problems and the promise. *NASSP Bulletin, 81*(590), 26–41.

Mehrens, W. A. (1992). Using performance assessment for accountability purposes. *Measurement: Issues and Practice, 11*(1), 5–9, 20.

Mehrens, W. A. (1997). The consequences of consequential validity. *Educational Measurement: Issues and Practice, 16*(2), 16–18.

Meltzer, L. J. (1991). Problem-solving strategies and academic performance in learning-disabled students: Do subtypes exist? In L. V. Feagans, E. J. Short, & L. J. Meltzer (Eds.), *Subtypes of learning disabilities: Theoretical perspectives and research* (pp. 163–188). Hillsdale, NJ: Lawrence Erlbaum Associates.

Messick, S. (1989). Validity. In R. L. Linn (Ed.), *Educational measurement* (3rd ed., pp. 13–103). New York: Macmillan.

Messick, S. (1995). Standards of validity and the validity of standards in performance assessment. *Educational Measurement: Issues and Practice, 14*(4), 5–8.

Montague, M., & Bos, C. S. (1990). Cognitive and metacognitive characteristics of eighth grade student's mathematical problem solving. *Learning and Individual Differences, 2,* 109–127.

Moss, P. A. (1995). Themes and variations in validity theory. *Educational Measurement: Issues and Practices, 14*(2), 3–13.

Moss, P. A., Beck, J. S., Ebbs, C., Matson, B., Muchmore, J., Steele, D., & Taylor, C. (1992). Portfolios, accountability, and an interpretive approach to validity. *Educational Measurement: Issues and Practice, 11*(3), 12–21.

National Forum on Assessment. (1995). *Principles and indicators for student assessment systems.* Cambridge, MA: Author.

North Carolina Department of Education. (1998). *The North Carolina preliminary state testing results 1997–98 multiple-choice end-of-grade and end-of-course tests.* Author Raleigh: North Carolina State Department of Public Instruction. (ERIC Document Reproduction Service No. ED 425 182).

Oregon Department of Education. (1999). *Oregon statewide assessment results: Percent of students meeting performance standards in reading/literature and mathematics.* Salem, OR: Author.

Pelligrino, J. M., & Goldman, S. R. (1987). Information processing and elementary mathematics. *Journal of Learning Disabilities, 20,* 23–32.

Popham, W. J. (1997). The standards movement and the emperor's new clothes. *NASSP Bulletin, 81*(590), 21–25.

Poteet, J. A., Choate, J. S., & Stewart, S. C. (1993). Performance assessments and special education: Practice and prospects. *Focus on Exceptional Children, 26*(1), 1–20.

Rothkopf, E. Z., & Billington, M. J. (1983). Passage length and recall with test size held constant: Effects of modality, pacing, and learning set. *Journal of Verbal Learning and Verbal Behavior, 22,* 667–681.

Salvia, J. A., & Ysseldyke, J. E. (1988). *Assessment in special and remedial education* (4th edition). Boston: Houghton-Mifflin.

Samuels, S. J. (1987). Factors that influence listening and reading comprehension. In R. Horowitz & S. J. Samuels (Eds.), *Comprehending oral and written language* (pp. 295–325). San Diego, CA: Academic Press.

Shavelson, R. J., Baxter, G. P., & Gao, X. (1993). Sampling variability of performance assessments. *Journal of Educational Measurement, 30,* 215–232.

Shepard, L. A. (1997). The centrality of test use and consequences for test validity. *Educational Measurement: Issues and Practice, 16*(2), 5–8, 13.

Smith, C. R. (1991). *Learning disabilities: The interaction of learner, task, and setting.* Boston: Allyn & Bacon.

Spyridakis, J. H., & Standal, T. C. (1987). Signals in expository prose: Effects on reading comprehension. *Reading Research Quarterly, 22,* 285–298.

Surber, J. R. (1992). The effect of test expectation, subject matter, and passage length on study tactics and retention. *Reading Research and Instruction, 31,* 32–40.

Swanson, H. L. (1987). Information processing theory and learning disabilities: A commentary and future perspective. *Journal of Learning Disabilities, 20,* 3–7.

Tack, K. D. (1995). *The influence of reading skills on the Ohio Ninth Grade Proficiency Test of Mathematics* (ERIC Document Reproduction Service No. ED 386 703).

Tindal, G., & Fuchs, L. (1999). *A Summary of Research on Test Changes: An Empirical Basis for Defining Accommodations.* Lexington: University of Kentucky, Mid-South Regional Resource Center.

Tindal, G. A., & Marston, D. B. (1990). *Classroom-based assessment: Evaluating instructional outcomes.* Columbus, OH: Merrill.

Chapter 18

Out-of-Level Testing Revisited: New Concerns in the Era of Standards-Based Reform

Martha L. Thurlow
John Bielinski
Jane Minnema
James Scott
University of Minnesota

As with most educational practices, out-of-level testing has gone in and out of favor over the years. Testing a student at a level above or below his or her grade level is referred to variously as out-of-level testing, off-level testing, functional-level testing, and instructional-level testing. Variations of the practice emerge in tailored testing and adaptive testing.

With the recent swell in the use of large-scale assessments across the United States, there is now renewed interest in using out-of-level testing (Thurlow, Elliott, & Ysseldyke, 1999). As before, proponents and opponents argue over the value of using this approach. But now, because of the current emphasis on standards-based assessments, the number of those arguments has increased. Standards-based assessments, which are generally used for educational accountability systems, are designed to measure what a student knows and can do in relation to what society considers important for students to know and do. One of the arguments concerns the use of out-of-level testing as a way to include students with disabilities in assessment systems—a use for which out-of-level testing was not originally intended.

Is it possible to accurately measure standards achievement if a student is tested at a grade other than that for which the standards were defined? Can an accurate measure of student performance be obtained if the student cannot respond to most of the items because they are too difficult? If so, does this apply to students with disabilities in the same way as it might to other low-performing students? Does the use of out-of-level testing have any broader implications, such as effects on expectations and instruction, especially in relation to students with disabilities?

We explore these and related issues in this chapter first by reviewing the (a) history of out-of-level testing and how it has been used in the past, (b) the psychometric reasons that support out-of-level testing, and (c) the assumptions underlying the psychometric arguments for out-of-level testing. With this as a basis, we explain why assessment developers have additional work to do before they can implement standards-based, out-of-level testing and why additional research on this approach to testing is needed.

We do not address tailored and adaptive testing here because they are not typical approaches in current standards-based assessments (Olson, Bond, & Andrews, 1999). Indeed, such approaches may be the wave of the future in that they are better able to address the needs of students who read below grade level or who are at achievement levels significantly below their grade-level peers.

HISTORY OF OUT-OF-LEVEL TESTING

Out-of-level testing seems to have first emerged in the mid-1960s, when educators in Philadelphia complained about the invalidity of using nationally standardized instruments to test poor readers (Ayrer & McNamara, 1973). A decision by the Philadelphia school system to implement a policy of out-of-level testing was based on findings from the 1961 doctoral research of J. A. Fisher, who investigated the performance of high- and low-ability students when tested either 2 years above or 2 years below their assigned grades. Fisher's research indicated that those students tested out-of-level (high-ability students tested 2 years above grade level and low-ability students tested 2 years below grade level) earned scores that better discriminated among the ability levels of the students. In addition, the students indicated that the out-of-level tests were better suited to their abilities.

The enactment of the Elementary and Secondary Education Act (ESEA) in 1965 pushed forward the popularity of out-of-level testing. ESEA, which provided significant Title I federal funds to districts, required that the funds be accounted for by showing the extent to which positive outcomes were attained by students participating in funded activities. Title I generally was provided to students needing remediation (usually in reading) who were in schools with significant numbers of children living in poverty. Need for services typically was determined by performance on standardized measures. Usually these measures were norm referenced and administered in the fall and spring to provide a pre- and postmeasure of performance. In this way, test scores were used to both measure student growth (in terms of gains or losses; Howes, 1985) and determine continued eligibility for services.

As happened in Philadelphia, teachers in Rhode Island became concerned about how accurate grade-level test results were, especially if they were being used for accountability purposes (Long, Schaffran, & Kellogg, 1977). The Department of Education in Rhode Island decided that local educators could determine what approach to take with individual students—whether to test them at grade or instructional level.

These and other factors probably led test publishers to begin developing norms for tests so that the norms extended above and below the grade level at which a test was intended to be taken (Smith & Johns, 1984). This collection of normative data for students in other than the designated test grades provided support for the use of out-of-level testing in Title I programs. Test publishers emphasized that if out-of-level testing were used, the obtained scores had to be converted to grade-level scores, and specific guidelines for doing so were provided. Whether this recommendation was followed or even monitored is not addressed in the literature. What is known is that there is no record of what states used or did not use or even which states allowed the use of out-of-level testing. Furthermore, although there might have been justification about better discrimination among students when out-of-level testing was endorsed by publishers, the reason teachers and other school personnel used out-of-level testing tended to go back to concerns about how appropriate it is to test students with tests that are too difficult for them.

PSYCHOMETRIC SUPPORT
FOR OUT-OF-LEVEL TESTING

Psychometric support for out-of-level testing rests on the argument that scores based on one set of items can be translated into scores based on another set of items, and that increasing reliability will also result in increasing validity. It is argued that out-of-level scores are more accurate than grade-level scores for students who would score low on in-level tests. Students' scores are considered to be low when fewer than a third of the items are answered correctly. This level corresponds to the chance level, where the score is one that could be obtained through random guessing on a multiple-choice item. Having fewer scores below the chance level is deemed desirable because the scores obtained are considered to be better quality scores.

From the prior scenario, it is assumed that low scores represent random guessing. This is an important assumption because so much emphasis is placed on chance-level scoring in the out-of-level testing literature. However, there are many other assumptions—regarding accuracy, precision of scores, and vertical equating procedures—that underlie the use of out-of-level testing. Each of these assumptions needs to be examined further. Since out-of-level testing first emerged for norm-referenced tests, our discussion begins there. Later we address the transition to standards-based, criterion-referenced testing.

Norm-Referenced Test Development

When norm-referenced tests are developed, one goal is to select items that produce precise test scores for the majority of test takers. Test developers do this by selecting items that are moderately difficult for those students taking the test at the targeted grade level. For elementary students, test developers select items that about 70% of the normative sample pass (a p value of .70); for high school students, they select items that 50% of the normative sample pass (a p value of .50). These levels are selected because the tests then produce scores that are very precise for most students— those scoring between 40% and 80% correct overall. Trying to extend traditional tests so that they produce precise scores across a broader range would require the tests to include many more items, which is unreasonable because the tests would become too long and costly.

To produce more reliable scores for those students who do not fall within the 40% to 80% correct range, test publishers design tests so that adjacent levels overlap substantially in content and skills. Adjacent levels are linked statistically so that scores from students taking different items can be reported on a common scale. Using a procedure of vertical scaling enables test developers to mitigate floor and ceiling effects, yet obtain scores for students that are reliable and accurately reflect ability in a given domain. Using out-of-level testing for norm-referenced tests capitalizes on these designs, as long as there is an appropriate match between the content and skills measured by the test and the instruction that the student receives in the classroom.

Analyzing Precision and Accuracy

In psychometric theory, *precision* refers to the consistency of a measurement—the reproducibility of test scores. It is influenced by random error. Test scores vary across occasions; the greater the random error, the more variable the test scores and the lower the precision. *Accuracy* refers to the validity of a measurement. Accuracy is influenced by systematic error. A measure can be precise (i.e., give about the same score each time), yet not be accurate (see Fig. 18.1).

Improved test score accuracy of scores should be the primary reason for using out-of-level testing, yet most empirical studies of how out-of-level testing affects test scores have emphasized two criteria: reliability and per-

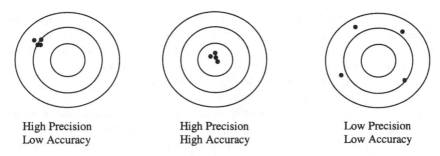

| High Precision | High Precision | Low Precision |
| Low Accuracy | High Accuracy | Low Accuracy |

FIG. 18.1.   Possible relationships between precision and accuracy.

centage of scores at or above the chance level. Both of these are proxies for measurement precision, not measurement accuracy. Although reliability can provide information about measurement precision for a group of test scores, it does not provide information about the precision of an individual score.

There are several reasons that measurement of reliability is not a good measure of the accuracy of an individual's score. First, reliability is probably an inappropriate criterion when extreme test scores are estimated even if it provides a relatively reasonable estimate for scores at or near the mean. One reason for this is that students with the same score do not have the same pattern of responses to individual items. Another reason is that reliability is related to the characteristics of the sample of students from which it was calculated. A change in the sample results in a change in the reliability. Using reliability as a measure of accuracy implies that precision is constant across ability levels, but this is not true. If it were, there would be no need for out-of-level testing.

A series of mathematical models, collectively referred to as *item response theory* (IRT), provides further insight into how out-of-level testing affects precision. IRT states that the probability of a person responding correctly to an item depends on the difficulty of the item. Across many individuals with different ability levels, the probabilities form a curve called an *item-characteristic curve*. The curve is vaguely s-shaped, indicating that it is relatively flat at the lower and upper extremes, but essentially vertical in the middle range. The areas at the top and bottom, where the curve is relatively flat, are where the item does not differentiate well among individuals of different ability. Along the vertical in the middle range, the differentiation is great. Thus, the item is said to provide more information in this area. As noted by Bielinski, Thurlow, Minnema, and Scott (2000), in the flat areas, "a substantial change in ability corresponds to only a very small change in the probability of getting the item correct" (p. 12).

Item information functions are generated to denote the degree of differentation provided by individual items at various levels of ability (see

Fig. 18.2, for example). In addition, item information functions can be added together to generate a function for an entire test. A test is most informative across the ability levels that correspond to the difficulty levels in which most items lie. This is in the middle of the test, but the range may vary depending on the ability levels covered by test items.

Similar information can be gleaned by talking about the standard error of measurement. When plotted, the standard error of measurement forms a U-shaped curve, indicating higher error for either very low or very high scores (see Fig. 18.3). When error is higher, there is less confidence that the score a student obtained is the student's true score. Most norm-referenced tests are developed to maximize test information for the majority of test takers. With the assumption of a normal curve distribution of examinee ability, this means that items are selected to form a normal distribution. In other words, these tests are most informative for test takers with ability levels falling between ± 1. Test scores for examinees at either extreme contain large amounts of measurement error. To produce more precise scores for poor performers, there would need to be many more easy items on the test.

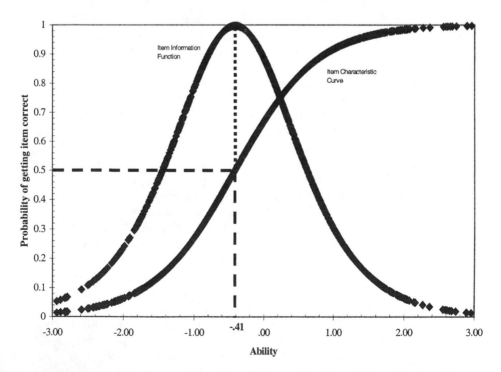

FIG. 18.2.   Item characteristic curve and the associated item information function for an item with a difficulty equal to –.41.

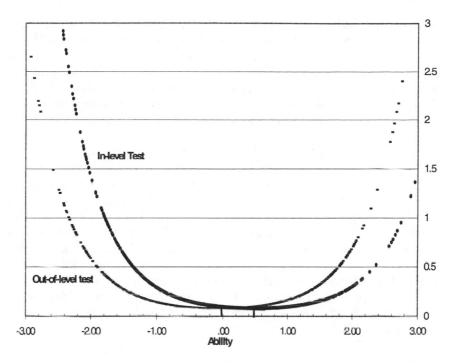

FIG. 18.3. Standard error of measurement for two hypothetical tests that differ in their average difficulty level.

Instead of including additional easy items, it is simpler to give the student an easier version of the test. The student is then more likely to earn a score that is near the middle of the score distribution where the scores are more precise. Having scores that are more precise, however, does not ensure that they are more accurate measures of the student's performance. When student scores come from different tests, with different scales, they have to be transposed onto the same scale.

Vertical Scaling.   Placing scores on the same scale involves vertical equating, with the end result being a single scale that spans all levels of a test. However, vertical equating introduces measurement error (Kim & Cohen, 1998). For example, two tests (or two levels of a test) must measure the same ability for vertical equating to be appropriate. Although test publishers select items that overlap in content and skills at the adjacent levels of a test, they still may not satisfy the assumption that each measures the same ability (Yen, 1985).

For vertical scaling to be appropriate, there must also be a common set of examinees that takes both tests (single-group design) or a common set of items appearing on both tests (anchor test design; Hambleton & Swaminathan, 1995). The latter approach is the one now used most often (Vale, 1986). The anchor test procedure is used with pairs of adjacent level tests. Equating constants are calculated and entered into a formula developed to estimate equating error. If all item-difficulty estimates fall on a line, the equating error is zero. In practice, there are many items that do not fall on the line, indicating that the equating procedure is introducing error. This introduction of error reduces the precision of measurement of a student's score.

There are other ways in which error is introduced when different levels of a test are used (such as simultaneous calibration of item parameters). Although this error should be about the same as that from other procedures, Kim and Cohen (1998) concluded that the accuracy of linking can only be accomplished through simulation studies. Demonstrating that the assumptions of their equating models are met, or showing the amount of equating error, is now required by the *Standards for Educational and Psychological Testing* (American Psychological Association, American Educational Research Association, National Council on Measurement in Education, 1999). Yet publishers of the most frequently norm-referenced tests (e.g., CTBS5, SAT9, etc.) do not provide this information (Bielinski, Scott, Minnema, & Thurlow, 2000).

Test Score Accuracy. Arguments for out-of-level testing usually involve mention of the increased accuracy that results from reduced guessing and the elimination of floor effects. Guessing and floor effects are both sources of bias that may produce scores that are higher than is actually the case. Arguments against out-of-level testing usually involve mention of the nonalignment of test content and instructional content and sometimes, too, the bias introduced by test score equating procedures.

Guessing is a source of systematic error. It is often implied in the out-of-level testing literature that low-performing students guess more than other students. If this is the case, then the scores of low-performing students are more contaminated by error than the scores of other students, and the earned scores might actually underestimate their true scores. Reducing the number of chance-level scores is said to demonstrate the effectiveness of out-of-level testing (Ayrer & McNamara, 1973; Cleland & Idstein, 1980; Crowder & Gallas, 1978; Easton & Washington, 1982; Howes, 1985; Jones, Barnette, & Callahan, 1983; Powers & Gallas, 1978; Slaughter & Gallas, 1978; Yoshida, 1976). However, no study has actually demonstrated that chance-level scores are obtained solely by guessing (Bielinski et al., 2000). Similarly, there are no studies showing that scores at or below the chance level are contaminated more by guessing than are other scores. In fact, there is evidence that low-performing students tend to omit more items; their performance, uncorrected for guessing, will be underestimated (Lord, 1975).

The importance of curriculum–test overlap also seems to be ignored in statistical treatments of out-of-level testing. It has been suggested that, indeed, the validity of out-of-level test scores depends, in part, on the purpose for administering the test. When tests are used simply to measure growth, out-of-level testing may be appropriate. Yet when the purpose of the test score is to determine proficiency relative to specific content standards that are linked to grade level, then out-of-level testing may be inappropriate. Out-of-level test items typically tap different content and measure different skills than those measured by in-grade-level test items. Predictions cannot be made beyond the skills measured by the test that is taken. This means, for example, that reporting how a student does on algebra items based on the student's performance on computation items is inappropriate. When the level to which one descends in selecting an out-of-level test for a student is minimal (e.g., one level), the effects of curriculum alignment may be minimal as well. However, some studies have indicated that students may have to be tested more than one level below the in-grade testing level to see a substantial decrease in the number of chance scores (Cleland & Idstein, 1980; Jones et al., 1983; Slaughter & Gallas, 1978). It is likely that the overall alignment in content tested is less and less when the student is moved more than one level below grade level.

Unresolved Issues Surrounding Out-of-Level Testing

Most of the literature that addresses out-of-level testing consists of position papers and scholarly writings that contain discussion of the psychometric properties of testing students out of level and recommendations for implementing out-of-level testing. The amount of research on the topic is minimal. Furthermore, the research that has been conducted has concentrated almost exclusively on students at the lower end of the scoring continuum, not on students earning average scores. Scores for these students may also decrease if they take a lower level of the test. This latter omission in our knowledge about out-of-level testing raises concerns about the use of out-of-level testing in state and district assessment programs.

There seems to be some confirmation in the literature that scores of high-performing examinees decrease when an out-of-level test is used. For example, Slaughter and Gallas (1978) divided students into three groups based on their performance on an in-level test. The three groups included those scoring (a) near the floor, (b) between floor and ceiling, and (c) at or above the ceiling. All students took the in-level test and then the group was divided into two—half took the adjacent lower level, and the other half took the test two levels below.

Using a common metric, Slaughter found that the difference scores between the grade level and the adjacent lower level were, on average, of the same magnitude across groups and that the scores dropped for all groups (although none was significant). However, when the out-of-level test was two levels below the in-level test, there were differences in the effects for different groups. The floor group showed a statistically significant drop, whereas the other two groups showed drops of about the same magnitude as in the first comparison. These data verify that the scores drop regardless of performance level. Thus, by giving only the low-performing students the out-of-level test, the gap between them and higher performing students is being artificially increased.

With the current requirements that students with disabilities be included in state and district assessments, and that their performance be reported, there are many concerns expressed about students who are unable to take tests at their own grade levels. Although out-of-level testing has been subjected to some research, only a few studies have specifically included students with disabilities (Cleland & Idelstein, 1980; Jones et al., 1983; Yoshida, 1976), and none of these studies was conducted in relation to standards-based assessments. All used norm-referenced tests. Yet overall, the studies were mixed in their results and do not directly dissuade the seemingly widespread perception that out-of-level testing is suitable assessment practice for testing students with disabilities. For example, Yoshida examined the test-item statistics for students who were tested out of level, based on teacher-selected levels, compared them to the statistics for the standardization samples, and found the statistics to be comparable. However, teacher selection of test level resulted in some students being tested as many as 10 grades below their assigned grades—a practice not currently recommended by test companies as appropriate practice.

Cleland and Idelstein (1980) looked at students who were scoring at the floor level. They found that the percentage of students at this level did not change for in-level and out-of-level testing when students were assigned to levels using scores from a locator test. Overall, the scores of students tested out of level were lower when the scores were converted back to the in-level norms, compared with what the scores were when tested on the in-level test.

Jones et al. (1983) found that testing students with mild disabilities (e.g., learning disabilities, emotional/behavioral disabilities, mild mental retardation) at a lower level did not substantially reduce the amount of measurement error. Item validities did not improve significantly for the out-of-level tests. As a result, Jones et al. (1983) stated that when making a decision about out-of-level testing, it is probably more important to consider the congruence between the content of the test level and the instructional program, suggesting that the instructional program and test alignment may be more important than reliability or validity considerations.

Beyond the lack of recent standards-based research on out-of-level testing for students with disabilities, several other pieces of information are missing (Minnema, Thurlow, Bielinski, & Scott, 2000). For example, research on out-of-level testing has not provided a good estimate of the extent to which out-of-level testing is used, either currently or in the past. Research in the 1990s did not indicate the prevalence of the use of out-of-level testing at the school level. To better inform policymaking, there is a need for descriptive information on the prevalence of out-of-level testing across the United States, both for students in general and for students with disabilities.

There are clear concerns about specific psychometric issues surrounding out-of-level testing. These seem to have either been ignored or to have been so mired in assumptions that they were taken for granted. Hence, we do not have the psychometric research that we need to really understand the effects of out-of-level testing on poor performing students, much less students with disabilities. Further research related to precision and accuracy is needed. It will be necessary to consider whether the gain in precision attributed to out-of-level testing outweighs the loss in precision that occurs when converting out-of-level test scores back to in-level test scores. Furthermore, there is a significant need to better examine the guessing patterns of students, including those who are low performing and those who are high performing, as well as the guessing patterns of students with disabilities.

When examining the extent to which out-of-level testing is employed, it is also important to determine the extent to which use of out-of-level testing adheres to test publisher recommendations. For example, there is a need for someone to determine the appropriate testing level if a student is to be tested out of level. Yet there is little available to help in this decision. At a minimum, it would require that test publishers provide conversion tables.

Much of the literature on out-of-level testing refers to the effects of student frustration and emotional trauma on test scores (Minnema et al., 2000). Still there is no literature on these effects. We know nothing about how often such effects are noted nor whether they are related in any way to other characteristics, such as the student's level of academic functioning, the support of parents, or a variety of other such variables.

The context of testing out of level clearly has changed over the years. Its original use for Title I evaluations in the 1970s changed to the point where it is now recommended for use by some governmental agencies even for standards-based assessments rather than the traditional criterion-referenced assessments. Yet we have no data on the consequences of using out-of-level testing, either in terms of the expectations that are held for students or the quality of education provided to students. Studies on the intended and unintended consequences of out-of-level testing are critical.

ACKNOWLEDGMENT

Preparation of this chapter was supported, in part, by a grant (# H324D990058) from the U.S. Department of Education, Office of Special Education Programs. Points of view expressed in this chapter are those of the authors and not the Department or offices within it.

REFERENCES

American Psychological Association, American Educational Research Association, & National Council of Measurement in Education. (1999). *Standards for educational and psychological testing*. Washington, DC: American Psychological Association.

Ayrer, J. E., & McNamara, T. C. (1973). Survey testing on an out-of-level basis. *Journal of Educational Measurement, 10*(2), 79–84.

Bielinski, J., Scott, J., Minnema, J., & Thurlow, M. (2000). *Test publishers' views on out-of-level testing* (Out-of-Level Testing Report 3). Minneapolis, MN: University of Minnesota, National Center on Educational Outcomes.

Bielinski, J., Thurlow, M., Minnema, J., & Scott, J. (2000). *How out-of-level testing affects the psychometric quality of test scores* (Out-of-Level Testing Report 2). Minneapolis, MN: University of Minnesota, National Center on Educational Outcomes.

Cleland, W. E., & Idstein, P. M. (1980, April). *In-level versus out-of-level testing of sixth grade special education students*. Paper presented at the annual meeting of the National Council on Measurement in Education, Boston, MA.

Crowder, C. R., & Gallas, E. J. (1978, March). *Relation of out-of-level testing to ceiling and floor effects on third and fifth grade students*. Paper presented at the annual meeting of the American Educational Research Association, Toronto, Ontario, Canada.

Easton, J. A., & Washington, E. D. (1982, March). *The effects of functional level testing on five new standardized reading achievement tests*. Paper presented at the annual meeting of the American Educational Research Association, New York, NY.

Hambleton, R. K., & Swaminathan, H. (1995). *Item response theory: Principles and applications*. Boston, MA: Kluwer Nijhoff.

Howes, A. C. (1985, April). *Evaluating the validity of Chapter 1 data: Taking a closer look*. Paper presented at the annual meeting of the American Educational Research Association, Chicago, IL.

Jones, E. D., Barnette, J. J., & Callahan, C. M. (1983, April). *Out-of-level testing for special education students with mild learning handicaps*. Paper presented at the annual meeting of the American Educational Research Association, Montreal, Quebec, Canada.

Kim, S H., & Cohen, A. S. (1988). A comparison of linking and concurrent calibration under item response theory. *Applied Psychological Measurement, 22*(2), 131–143.

Long, J. V., Schaffran, J. A., & Kellogg, T. M. (1977). Effects of out-of-level survey testing on reading achievement scores of Title I ESEA students. *Journal of Educational Measurement, 14*(3), 203–213.

Lord, F. M. (1975). Formula scoring and number-right scoring. *Journal of Educational Measurement, 12*(1), 7–11.

Minnema, J., Thurlow, M., Bielinski, J., & Scott, J. (2000). *Past and present understandings of out-of-level testing: A research synthesis* (Out-of-Level Testing Report 1). Minneapolis, MN: University of Minnesota, National Center on Educational Outcomes.

Olson, J. F., Bond, L., & Andrews, C. (1999). *Data from the annual survey: State student assessment programs.* Washington, DC: Council of Chief State School Officers.

Powers, S., & Gallas, E. J. (1978, March). *Will out-of-level norm-referenced testing improve the selection of program participants and the diagnosis of reading comprehension in ESEA Title I programs?* Paper presented at the annual meeting of the American Educational Research Association, Toronto, Ontario, Canada.

Slaughter, H. B., & Gallas, E. J. (1978, March). *Will out-of-level norm-referenced testing improve the selection of program participants and the diagnosis of reading comprehension in ESEA Title I programs?* Paper presented at the annual meeting of the American Educational Research Association, Toronto, Ontario, Canada.

Smith, L. L., & Johns, J. L. (1984). A study of the effects of out-of-level testing with poor readers in the intermediate grades. *Reading Psychology: An International Quarterly, 5,* 139–143.

Thurlow, M. L., Elliott, J. L., & Ysseldyke, J. E. (1999). *Out-of-level testing for students with disabilities* (NCEO Policy Directions 9). Minneapolis, MN: University of Minnesota, National Center on Educational Outcomes.

Vale, C. D. (1986). Linking item parameters onto a common scale. *Applied Psychological Measurement, 10*(4), 333–344.

Yen, W. M. (1985). Increasing item complexity: A possible cause of scale shrinkage for unidimensional item response theory. *Psychometrika, 50*(4), 399–410.

Yoshida, R. K. (1976). Out-of-level testing of special education students with a standardized achievement batter. *Journal of Educational Measurement, 13*(3), 215–221.

Chapter 19

Reporting Results of Student Performance on Large-Scale Assessments

Jim Ysseldyke
J. Ruth Nelson
University of Minnesota

Inclusive accountability systems and public reporting of the results of education for all students are important tools to help schools and students meet high educational standards. Many states have designed accountability systems that provide information to those inside and outside the educational system on the extent to which school districts, individual schools, and students are achieving desired results. The 1997 reauthorization of the Individuals with Disabilities Education Act (PL 105-17) requires state education agencies to report, with the same frequency they do for nondisabled students, the numbers of students participating in regular and alternate assessments. In addition, performance data for students with disabilities must be disaggregated and reported in the reporting of student results.

The most common way to document students and school district progress has been through publication of state accountability reports. These documents provide demographic data on school districts, teachers, and students; data on student performance; and school finance information (Bond & Roeber, 1996). Each year representatives of the Council of Chief State School Officers (CCSSO) and representatives of the North Central Education Laboratory publish information on state assessment practices based on the results of an annual survey of state assessment directors. In those reports Bond and Roeber (1995, 1996) indicated that states use their assessment and accountability systems for six purposes: improving instruction, program evaluation, school performance reporting, student diagnosis or placement, high school graduation, and school accreditation.

Personnel at the National Center on Educational outcomes at the University of Minnesota have been engaged for a number of years in systematic review of the reports that state education agencies issue on the performance of students. Three studies have been completed from reports gathered between 1995 and 1999 (Thurlow, Langenfeld, Nelson, Shin, & Coleman, 1998; Thurlow, Nelson, Teelucksingh, & Ysseldyke, 2000; Ysseldyke et al., 1998b). Every state now produces some type of assessment and/or accountability report, and some produce several reports. Different agencies produce reports on student performance on different tests (e.g., norm-referenced, standards-based), and the reports are produced for different audiences (e.g., legislatures, parents). Thurlow et al. (1998) noted that the reports are highly varied and contain little information on the performance of students with disabilities; this remains true today even with the federal changes of IDEA 1997. Later in this chapter, we give more detailed information about the data available on students with disabilities in these educational accountability reports.

First we consider what state and district reports should look like with specific consideration to issues of content. Then we describe ways in which they should be formatted and review the research on what the reports actually look like. We include a brief section on the actual results that states are reporting on the performance and progress of students, and conclude with a list of important considerations.

WHAT SHOULD STATE AND DISTRICT ASSESSMENT REPORTS LOOK LIKE?

Together with our colleagues, we have worked with personnel in many state departments of education. Consistently, these individuals have expressed concerns about the kinds of information that should be included in reports on the performance and progress of students. SEA personnel ask questions such as, "Should we sort out students with disabilities from others when we report?" "When we do so, how do we maintain confidentiality for individual student scores?" They also, of course, express concerns about the impact of including students with disabilities on overall state scores.

Because personnel in so many states express concern about reporting results, members of the CCSSO State Collaborative on Assessment and Student Standards (SCASS), a group focusing on assessment of special education students, met to devise a set of desired criteria for state and school district educational accountability reports. Members of the group included state assessment directors, state special education directors, and university personnel. Participants brainstormed about the characteristics of good reports that would go to audiences of parents, policymakers, or the general public. Table 19.1 lists the criteria identified by the participants. These are discussed next.

TABLE 19.1
Checklist of Guidelines for State and District
Educational Accountability Reports

Variable	Content
Clear	• Clear statement of intended audience
	• Clear statement of intended purpose
	• Clear statement of states' conceptual model for its accountability system (including inputs, processes, and results)
	• Clear statement of state standards (or goals) or mission/vision
	• Clear statement of assumptions
	• Clear statement of who was included in the population of students being reported on
Comprehensive	• Comprehensive, yet concise set of inputs, processes, and results
	• Data on all students, including students with disabilities and limited English proficient students (students with disabilities and limited English proficient students' results are disaggregated)
Comparative	Includes enough information to enable people to make fair:
	• comparisons among schools, districts, states, regions, and standards
	• judgments about changes over time for schools, districts, and states
Concise	• Includes no more information than is necessary to convey a message to an intended audience . . . brief
Cautions	• Provides cautions against: scapegoating, unintended consequences, and negatives
Confidentiality	• Maintains confidentiality of low-frequency student populations

	Format
Readable	• Appropriate for the intended audience
Responsive to needs of intended audiences	• Answers audience questions and provides accurate profile
Layout	• Not cluttered or complex
	• Organized and easy to find information (e.g., reader's guide, table of contents, index, glossary)
	• Interesting (e.g., includes catchy titles, pictures, or other devices to get and hold audience interest)
Links	• Statement of how and where to get additional copies
	• Statement of how to get more detailed information
Executive summary	• Bulleted summary of report for a "quick read"

Important Overall Questions

Is the report readable? • Yes • No
Is the report fair? • Yes • No
Is the report concise? • Yes • No
Is the report visually attractive? • Yes • No
Is the report accurate? • Yes • No

Clear Reports

Clarity is the most important characteristic of a good report. If a report is not clear, it does not matter whether it is concise or comprehensive. There are several aspects of clarity. Reports should include a clear statement of the intended audience. Reports that are written for various audiences necessarily differ. Specification of the intended audience helps readers figure out quickly whether they are among those who should read the report.

Reports should also include a clear statement of purpose. Sometimes reports are developed and disseminated to inform the general public of how schools in one state are doing compared with another. In other instances, the reports convey performance relative to a set of state standards.

State reports should include a description of the overall conceptual framework used in the state's accountability system. An example of a conceptual framework is the one developed by Ysseldyke, Krentz, Elliott, Thurlow, Erickson, and Moore (1998a) and shown in Fig. 19.1. Ysseldyke

FIG. 19.1.   Framework for educational accountability with domeans, indicators, and sources of information.

et al. (1998a) specified a model that included inputs/resources, educational processes, and educational results. States and school districts should devise outcomes frameworks and include in their reports a description of the overall conceptual framework they use. When listing indicators, brevity is critical. LaPointe (1996) suggested that the key is to select a small, manageable number of indicators and provide evidence of these indicators for each school, system, or state, and then demand that readers take these indicators into account when making decisions.

State personnel should also be clear about their mission or vision in the introductions to reports of student performance. It is helpful if audiences know the goals or standards toward which students are working. *Accountability* is defined as a process of informing those inside and outside a school about the extent to which the school is achieving desired goals or standards (Braucn, O'Reilly, & Moore, 1992). Specification of state standards or objectives lets readers know intended targets.

Certain fundamental assumptions underlie accountability systems. For example, some states assume that their accountability and assessment systems are for all students. Some assume that certain kinds of students should be excluded from assessments. Others assume that the accommodations they give to students with disabilities do not change the nature of the assessment. Any and all assumptions should be explicitly stated.

States must include in their reports very clear information about the nature of the population included in the assessment and the population reported on. Although one might expect that these would be the same group, this is not always the case. When students with disabilities or limited English proficiency are excluded, there should be a very clear statement indicating this. Failure to describe the population of students on whom a state is reporting contributes to bogus or faulty comparisons.

Comprehensive Reports

Reports on the performance and progress of schools, systems, or states should include information on educational inputs, educational processes, and results. There are reciprocal relationships among these three factors, as illustrated in Fig. 19.1. Policymakers need to be thinking about how they can allocate resources differently or change educational processes to achieve better results.

State and district reports must include information on the performance and progress of all students, including students with disabilities and limited English proficiency. Data on the performance of these students should be disaggregated. We have included in Table 19.2 an example of the ways in which data might be reported in a state using the same proficiency standards for both the general and alternate tests. Table 19.3 is an illustration

TABLE 19.2
Percentages of Students Performing at Various Levels on the State Test

Variable	Students Who Took the Test Without Accommodations	Students Who Took the Test With Accommodations	Students Who Took the Alternate Test
Advanced	11%	4%	6%
Proficient	22%	7%	2%
Apprentice	47%	36%	19%
Novice	20%	53%	73%

TABLE 19.3
Performance of Students With Disabilities on the Alternate Test

Variable	%
Proficient	16
Emerging	51
Beginner	31

of a separate table used when the proficiency levels for the alternate assessment differ from those of the standard assessment. When data are reported in this manner, it is clear who is being reported on. The two tables indicate different ways to report disaggregated data. When students with disabilities are excluded from accountability systems and reports, this can impact their education. Students who have been left out of assessments and out of accountability reports tend not to be considered when reform efforts are being implemented (Leone, McLaughlin, & Meisels, 1992). Often "what gets measured gets taught." More important, "Who gets measured gets taught." Removal of students with disabilities and limited English proficiency from the accountability track can result in their removal or elimination from the curriculum track, and this will limit their educational opportunities (Koehler, 1992).

Comparative Reports

Reports should include enough information to enable people to make fair comparisons among schools, districts, states, and regions. They should contain enough information to enable readers to make decisions about changes in performance over time. It is necessary for those who prepare reports to indicate whether a standards-based or norm-referenced perspective is being used. When norm-referenced comparisons are made, it is critical to indicate the nature of the group to whom students are being compared and the extent to which students in the district or state are like those to whom they are being compared. The critical issue here is one of acculturation rather than gender, race, or ethnicity. Readers need to be told the extent to which the students included in the report have had backgrounds, experiences, and opportunities similar to those students in the comparison group.

When standards-referenced comparisons are made, it is important to state the standards and indicate whether students with disabilities and those without disabilities are working toward the same or different standards. It is also critical to include thorough descriptions of the students on whom you are reporting. Comparisons are limited when it is difficult or impossible for readers to figure out who is the subject of a report.

Concise Reports

Brevity is a desired characteristic of reports. They should include no more information than that necessary to convey their message to the intended audience.

Cautionary Statements

School personnel indicate that they worry about people misinterpreting the data included in their reports. Some of this worry can be alleviated by including in the report direct statements about how data should and should not be used. Much of this can be accomplished with a clear statement of purpose and intended audience. Yet it is probably also important to anticipate unintended consequences and include statements that avert these. Those who report could indicate, for example, that "the data in this report should not be used to make judgments about teacher performance because individual teachers' classes often include very different kinds of students," or, "Student mobility should be considered in making decisions about student performance. The Roosevelt district includes large numbers of students ($N = 123$) who have been in the district less than 6 months."

Confidentiality Statements

In some instances, there are very small numbers of specific types of students in a school or district. For example, it may be the case that the Cody, Wyoming schools have only two students who are blind. Provision of information on the performance of blind students by the district would give out information too easily identified as indicative of the performance of these two students. The general rule of thumb used when reporting data is that there should be at least 10 students in the group.

HOW SHOULD STATE REPORTS BE FORMATTED?

In the preceding section, we addressed primarily the kinds of content that should be included in state reports. There are also important format considerations. Some of these are described next.

Readable

Reports should be written in language suitable for the intended audience. Parents and legislators, for example, do not easily understand the kinds of educational jargon understood by teachers.

Responsive to Audience Needs

Those who read reports on the performance and progress of students have differing kinds of needs. They ask different kinds of questions about student progress. They understand different kinds of information. Reports should be written in ways that answer the specific questions that different groups may have.

Organized

Personnel at the National Center on Educational Outcomes reviewed a large number of state reports. Some of the reports were so cluttered and complex that it was virtually impossible to decipher the information included. Others were organized in ways that made it easy to find information. Features that enhance readability include tables of contents, indexes, reader's guides, and glossaries.

It is not necessary to include extensive information in state reports. In our review of some reports, we found ourselves saying, "This report includes more information than I could ever possibly want to know." Reports should include information on how additional information can be obtained by people who need it.

Reports should include executive summaries. Most readers of state reports have a limited amount of time to devote to reading the reports. It is helpful to include a brief summary of a report's highlights or, better yet, a bulleted list of findings.

WHAT DO STATE ASSESSMENT REPORTS LOOK LIKE?

Current state practices of reporting students' performance and progress are a function of the things people say or think should be reported, tradition, or what other states are doing. According to Thurlow et al. (1998), states vary greatly in their reporting practices. State accountability reports vary in format, length, level of information given, kinds of information given, focus, and stated purposes (Thurlow et al., 1998). Some states produce two- or three-page reports, whereas others produce five or six 500-page volumes annually. Many states use tables, spreadsheets, and the Internet to communicate their educational results. A few states give only state-level data; others give specific information about schools, district, and state performance.

Thurlow et al. (1998) found that few states included information about the performance of students with disabilities in reports they published between Fall 1995 and Spring 1997. In their 1998 report, Thurlow et al. indicated that only 12 states included such information in their reports. In their second examination of state reporting practices, Ysseldyke et al. (1998b) found no major changes in either the number of states reporting on students with disabilities or the nature of the data reported. At that time, only 13 states included test-based outcomes data on the participation of students with disabilities in assessments. Once again, a larger number of states ($N = 38$) included information about the nature of the educational program for students with disabilities. These data were required for federal reporting prior to IDEA '97 and included information on factors like graduation and exit, enrollment, dropout rates, and time spent in various settings.

In 1998, we found that 50% to 80% of students with disabilities were reported to be participating in statewide assessments. Performance data indicated generally lower performance of students with disabilities compared with other students. For example, 30% to 50% fewer students with disabilities were meeting standards than were students without disabilities. Thompson and Thurlow (1999) found that 23 states were able to provide information on the participation of students with disabilities. Yet all states except five (four of which did not respond to the item) indicated that they disaggregated data on students with disabilities. The one state that indicated it did not disaggregate data was a state that had no statewide assessment.

In the most recent evaluation of state reports (Thurlow, Nelson, Teelucksingh, & Ysseldyke, 2000), we found that 14 states included information on the numbers of students with disabilities who had participated in their assessment system (Connecticut, Delaware, Maine, Minnesota, Nebraska, New Hampshire, New Jersey, New York, North Carolina, South Carolina, Texas, Vermont, Virginia, West Virginia). In this most recent analysis of state public documents, issued between March 1998 and March 1999, the authors reviewed 171 reports looking specifically for information on educational results and process indicators for all students, but particularly focusing on disaggregated data for students with disabilities. Thurlow et al. (2000) coded the kinds of information reported using as a template the Framework for Educational Accountability developed by the National Center on Educational Outcomes (Ysseldyke, Krentz, Elliott,

Thurlow, Erickson, & Moore, 1998) and shown earlier in this chapter. Seventeen states disaggregated performance data for students with disabilities as specified in IDEA '97. Although IDEA '97 requires states to report performance data for students with disabilities as often as they do for regular education students, of 74 reports that did not include data on students with disabilities, over 50 included performance data on regular education students. Although 20 states reported graduation exam results for regular education, only 35% ($N = 7$ states) reported these results for students with disabilities. Of those states that did provide disaggregated performance data, the differences in proficiency rates between all students and students with disabilities on eighth-grade state assessments ranged from 23% to 47% in reading, 19% to 42% in math, and 25% to 44% in writing (Thurlow et al., 2000).

The vast majority of the data states collect and report on concern educational results and educational processes. Very few states (Kansas, New York, and Vermont) reported on students with disabilities in other domains (Thurlow et al., 2000). Kansas continued to report data in the domain of Personal and Social Well-Being (the number of violent acts toward staff and students committed by students with disabilities). New York and Vermont reported data in the domain of Satisfaction (e.g., satisfaction with vocational services and special education services).

Examining the educational process data, researchers found that the majority of states (38) reported on the enrollment of students with disabilities—data that have been required to be collected for several years. Of the 14 states that did provide participation data, the participation rates of students with disabilities ranged widely from 33% to 97%. A handful of states did provide dropout data, data on use of accommodations on assessments, absentee rates the day of testing, and in-grade retention rates.

Use of Reports

States usually do not include clear statements of purpose in their reports. The reports are used for a variety of purposes. For example, some states use the reports for accreditation, whereas others use them for technical assistance to districts, provision of diplomas, or to provide local, district, and national comparisons. State reports are only as good as the data on which they are based. Thurlow et al. (1998) reported that state reports include little information on middle schools. There is an absence of information, for example, on how performance in middle school classes affects academic choices in high school. There is also little information in state reports on how students fare once they leave school. Although students have many options following graduation (e.g., employment, enrollment in technical schools, colleges, or universities), there is little information in state reports on the options that they use.

How Are Students With Disabilities Performing?

It is difficult to aggregate and analyze achievement data provided by states. States use different tests (multiple published norm-referenced tests, custom-made norm-referenced and standards-based measures), in different content areas, at different grade levels, and at different times of year. One state may assess students in Grades 3, 5, 7, and 9 while another assesses students at every grade level. Comparisons are also confused by the use of different scoring rubrics, kinds of accommodations permitted, participation criteria, and the fact that tests differ in their degree of difficulty. Take, for example, data from Maryland, where differences in the percentages of students with disabilities and students without disabilities meeting standards range from 5% to 87%.

Changes in Reporting Practices Over Time

Several changes have occurred over the 4 years that NCEO personnel have examined state accountability reports. First, there has been a significant increase in the number of accountability reports published from 113 reports to 171 reports. More and more reports are being put on the World Wide Web. Although IDEA '97 required states to report on the participation and performance of students with disabilities in large-scale assessments, the number of states that include these data in public reports has not increased significantly.

There was an increase in two states (from 12 to 14) providing disaggregated participation data and an increase in 6 states (from 11 to 17) providing disaggregated performance data. Interestingly, the range in the percentage of students participating in assessments increased. In 1997, the range was from 50% to 80%. In 1999, the range was from 33% to 97%. Percentages increased in some states, and they actually decreased in others.

When performance data are examined, there is always a gap between the percentage of students with disabilities. In the earlier NCEO investigations, the gap in percentage of all students and students with disabilities meeting the standards ranged from 30% to 50%. In a later investigation, the gap at eighth grade ranged from 20% to 50%.

How Are Data Reported

There are three major ways in which states report data on the performance and progress of students with disabilities. It is critical to know which method is being used. The following approaches are listed in order of their frequency of use.

Descriptive Reports for a Year: Most often states simply report the numbers of students meeting standards by grade within a given year.

Annual Comparisons: States sometimes show the numbers of students with and without disabilities passing or meeting standards across years within the same grade.

Grade Comparisons: States sometimes show the numbers of students with and without disabilities passing or meeting standards across grades within a given year.

Cautions in Interpreting Trends

Ysseldyke and Bielinski (1999, 2000) reported on factors that lead to misinterpretation of trends in performance of students with and without disabilities. In their 1999 report, they showed that relatively large numbers of students are reclassified from general to special education and vice versa each year. They show that the students who move from general to special education are among the lowest functioning students in general education. They also showed that the converse was true—that the highest functioning students with disabilities are moved from special to general education classification each year. This transition increases the gap in performance of students in general and special education. One must track the same students from year to year to get an accurate picture of trends.

In their 2000 paper, Ysseldyke and Bielinski showed that there are more than 20 factors that affect trends. These factors are listed in Table 19.4. They are grouped by student factors, factors related to the test, and state policy matters that affect trends.

SUMMARY

In this chapter, we identified the commonly agreed on characteristics of good state assessment and accountability reports. The reports should be clear, comprehensive, comparative, concise, and include confidentiality statements and cautionary statements. They should also be readable, responsive to audience needs, and well organized. We discussed the kinds of reports that states are issuing and reported what the data look like on participation and performance of students with disabilities. We concluded by raising a number of cautions about factors that lead to misinterpretation of data on trends in gaps between the performance of students with and without disabilities.

Over the next 10 years, state assessment and accountability will increase. Growing numbers of students with disabilities will participate in

TABLE 19.4
Factors Affecting Interpretation of Trends in the
Performance of Students With Disabilities

Factors	Description
Student	Transition of students between general and special education
	Differential dropout between groups
	Students excluded or exempted from participation in testing
	Changes in participation rates over time
	Mobility of students in and out of district or state
	Retention of students at grade level
	Reliability of classification decisions
Test	What tests are used in states being compared
	Change from year to year in the test used
	Whether tests are given each year
	Fidelity of accommodations
	Differential validity
State Policies and Practices	The state's rules about accommodations that are permitted
	State standards-setting policies and practices
	Stakes assigned to student performance
	Use and manner of reporting out-of-level testing
	How students who do not receive a score are reported
	Students who attend charter schools, schools of choice, and so on
	School consolidations, grade reconfigurations, or changes in feeder patterns

state assessment systems, and states will increasingly report on how the students perform. We also expect that states will report on trends in student performance across grades and time. We sincerely hope the information provided in this chapter will lead to improved reporting, improved accuracy in interpretation, and ultimately improved results for students with disabilities.

REFERENCES

Bond, L., & Roeber, E. (1995). *State education accountability reports and indicator reports: Status of reports across the states 1995.* Washington, DC: Council of Chief State School Officers.

Bond, L., & Roeber, E. (1996). *State education accountability reports and indicator reports: Status of reports across the states 1996.* Washington, DC: Council of Chief State School Officers.

Brauen, M., O'Reilly, F., & Moore, M. (1994). *Issues and options in outcomes-based accountability for students with disabilities.* Rockville, MD: Westat.

Koehler, P. (1992). *The assessment of special needs students in Arizona.* Unpublished manuscript.

LaPointe, A. (1996). *An inventory of the most widely used measurement practices.* Washington, DC: American Institutes for Research.

Leone, P., McLaughlin, M., & Meisels, S. (1992). *Holding schools accountable for disabled students' outcomes.* College Park, MD: University of Maryland, Westat, Inc., Mathematica Policy Research, Inc.

Thompson, S., & Thurlow, M. (1999). *1999 state special education outcomes: A report on state activities at the end of the century.* Minneapolis, MN: University of Minnesota, National Center on Educational Outcomes.

Thurlow, M., Langenfeld, K., Nelson, J., Shin, H., & Coleman (1998). *State accountability reports: What are states saying about students with disabilities?* Minneapolis, MN: University of Minnesota, National Center on Educational Outcomes.

Thurlow, M., Nelson, J., Teelucksingh, E., & Ysseldyke, J. (2000). *Where's Waldo: A third search for students with disabilities in state accountability reports.* Minneapolis, MN: University of Minnesota, National Center on Educational Outcomes.

Ysseldyke, J., & Bielinski, J. (1999). *Effects of failure to consider student reclassification on the interpretation of trends in the test performance of students with disabilities.* Paper presented at the annual meeting of the American Educational Research Association, New Orleans, LA.

Ysseldyke, J., & Bielinski, J. (2000). *Critical questions to ask when interpreting or reporting trends in the large-scale test performance of students with disabilities.* Washington, DC: Council of Chief State School Officers.

Ysseldyke, J., Krentz, J., Elliott, J., Thurlow, M., Erickson, R., & Moore, M. (1998). *NCEO framework for educational accountability.* Minneapolis, MN: University of Minnesota, National Center on Educational Outcomes.

Ysseldyke, J., Thurlow, M., Langenfeld, K., Nelson, J., Teelucksingh, E., & Seyfarth, A. (1998). *Educational results for students with disabilities: What do the data tell us?* Minneapolis, MN: University of Minnesota, National Center on Educational Outcomes.

Part **IV**

EPILOGUE

Chapter 20

Research to Improve Large-Scale Testing

Thomas M. Haladyna
Arizona State University West

The first large-scale achievement test, the *Stanford Achievement Test*, was introduced in 1923. Since then, we have witnessed a steady stream of theory and research affecting educational achievement testing. Although we have a better technology for testing as a result of this research, many problems remain to be solved that will improve our testing technology.

This book addresses some important problems facing those of us involved in large-scale achievement testing. It is the product of a diverse array of educators working on a variety of problems that reflect long-term programmatic effort. Their cumulative contribution and the contributions of others lend ample support to the notion that large-scale student achievement testing is a long, slow developmental process. The chapters in this volume speak eloquently to recent progress with many of the problems we face. With respect to the future of large-scale achievement testing, what lies ahead? It is the object of this chapter to answer that question.

First, it provides important contexts that permeate every aspect of achievement testing today. These contexts are systemic reform, cognitive psychology, and the evolving concept of validity. Second, it discusses some major problems and topics for future theory and research. These problems principally draw from chapters found in this book, but also extend to other problems and topics not addressed here. Third, it reaffirms the need to dedicate resources and personnel to validity research and research on problems that continue to challenge us.

THREE FACTORS INFLUENCING LARGE-SCALE
TESTING OF STUDENT ACHIEVEMENT

Three factors powerfully influence current large-scale testing. Any consideration of a research agenda for current student achievement testing has to acknowledge these factors as they identify problems, seek resources to study the problem, and complete research. They are as follows.

Systemic Reform in Education

Educational reform is a continuous process of change driven by the public's need to improve education to meet the changing needs in our society. Although the reason for a particular reform may vary from time to time, the public is generally dissatisfied with the current level of achievement of our students. *Achievement* is usually defined as performance on a large-scale achievement test.

An important aspect of the current systemic reform is accountability. Traditionally, accountability involved the loose exchange of information from researchers to policymakers so that their decisions regarding programs and resources would be well thought out. A newer form of accountability holds the teacher responsible for student learning. In a truer sense, this is responsibility not accountability. In a retrospective essay, Linn (2000) argued that in this current form of high-stakes accountability that the bad outweighs the good.

In their new book, *Implementing Change: Patterns, Principles, and Potholes*, Hall and Lord (2001) presented and discussed 12 change principles that apply to educational reform and involve large-scale testing. These 12 principles form a good basis for evaluating any reform effort and getting a perspective on how the reform is working. Evaluation of educational reform involves research on the effects of testing on students and student learning. To understand what students should be learning and how we are testing students, we need to know more about the current educational reform movement and its bases.

THE EMERGENCE OF COGNITIVE LEARNING
THEORY AS A PARADIGM FOR DEFINING
STUDENT LEARNING AND HOW IT WILL
BE MEASURED

The current cycle of reform seems to derive from several sources. One source is cognitive psychology, which emphasizes the learning and testing of construct-centered abilities, such as reading comprehension, writing, mathematical and scientific problem solving, and critical thinking. At the same time, behavioral learning theory with its emphasis on teaching basic knowledge and skills and criterion-referenced and competency-based testing is giving way to performance testing. This is an awkward time for learning theories as they apply to teaching and testing. This period of transition affects students, teachers, and other educators, particularly those involved in achievement testing (Shepard, 1991).

A seminal chapter by Snow and Lohman (1989) may have been one of the catalysts for promoting these cognitive and social-constructivist learning theories because each involves testing. We learn to teach and test complex abilities that are construct-referenced (Messick, 1984). Thus, the focus may be shifting away from testing just knowledge and skills to testing more complex chains of behavior that involve the use of knowledge and skills. Performance testing seems to offer the highest fidelity in relation to the ideal abilities they intend to measure, and this new emphasis opens up interesting problems for test makers.

THE EVOLVING CONCEPT OF VALIDITY FOR STUDYING INTERPRETATIONS AND USES OF TEST SCORES IN LARGE-SCALE TESTING PROGRAMS

The third influence is this evolving concept of construct validity. As Linn (chap. 2, this volume) points out, Cronbach and Meehl (1955) provided a seminal statement about construct validity. Cronbach's (1971) chapter in *Educational Measurement* is another major milestone in the development of construct validity as the *whole of validity*. In its early days, construct validity was often viewed by practitioners as something for theoreticians. It was vague about what we do in the practical side of designing tests and interpreting and using test scores. Messick's (1975, 1984) influential essays culminating in his chapter "Validity" in the third edition of *Educational Measurement* (Messick, 1989) and essays by Cronbach (1988), Kane (1992), and Shepard (1993), to mention a few, brought construct validity into the mainstream of thinking about testing. Evidence of validity development is found in the recently published *Standards for Educational and Psychological Testing* (American Educational Research Association, American Psychological Association, & National Council on Measurement in Education, 1999).

The chapters in this volume speak to the importance of validity and its evolution. Linn provides a good background and place for validity in this age of accountability. Gersten pays tribute to the work of Messick and underscores the importance of his work in today's assessment. Haladyna shows how validity evidence can be used to provide documentation to support the interpretation and use of test scores. Mehrens expands the recent idea of consequences as related to validity. His research and documentation show that some conclusions about assessments may be premature, but there is growing evidence of the good and bad of some types of large-scale testing. Phillips discusses legal aspects of testing for special populations, pointing out that these legal considerations are inextricably linked to validity and consequences for all students.

PROMISING AREAS FOR RESEARCH IN LARGE-SCALE TESTING

In this second section of this chapter, we view some promising areas for future research affecting large-scale achievement testing programs. These areas draw heavily from the chapters in this book, but also extend beyond what its covers.

Validity

As stated in the previous section, the unified concept of validity championed in the 1990s is becoming more generally accepted. As a field of study, validity is rapidly evolving. The rebirth of construct validity as the main validity paradigm has made it richer and deeper in meaning, especially for practitioners. The new *Standards* (American Educational Research Association, American Psychological Association, & National Council on Measurement in Education, 1999) provide an incredible array of issues requiring validity evidence. Test developers need to understand validity and document validity evidence to shape an argument about the validity of each test score interpretation and use in their testing programs. We should expect to continue to see the growth of validity as a central paradigm in achievement testing. This idea will be more inclusive and incorporate ideas about educational reform, learning theory, and better methods to solve many problems described in this and other chapters in this volume. The heart of validity is validity evidence, which comes from the documentation of processes and research studies.

We should note a subtle distinction between two types of research on testing. The first is a routine, seemingly mundane type that is part of most large-scale testing programs. Haladyna provides an exhaustive list of this type of validity research. Reliability studies are a major type of validity evidence. Equating studies ensure comparability of scores across diverse test forms. Item analysis gives us information about the performance of test items. A second type of test research usually involves new theories or problems in testing. This type of research is published in journals or reported at conferences. This research attempts to improve testing practices. We need both types of research, but the first type is clearly intended to provide validity evidence, whereas the second type is clearly intended to solve problems we face in designing and developing testing programs and validating test score interpretations and uses. The thrust of this chapter is clearly in the direction of this second type of research.

Dimensionality

Dimensionality (structure of data) is important from several validity standpoints. First, the intended interpretation strongly depends on the structure of the data. As Tate points out, dimensionality pervades test design, test development, scoring, and interpretation. The use of subscores critically depends on validity evidence supporting the interpretation and use of subscores as meaningful subunits of a total test score. Test sponsors seldom make the case that subscores are different from the global measure from which they were derived. Studies of dimensionality importantly address this concern.

We can describe the field of large-scale assessment as having different types of research. The first seeks an ideal way to analyze data. Tate provides a good review of different methods of analysis, including factor analysis, item response theory (IRT), and correlations in the framework of multitrait and multimethods. The second type is any routine validity study of the structure of data for each achievement test. This study is done to satisfy the need to provide a basis for interpreting data to policymakers, media, and parents. The third type of research is any exploratory study of student achievement to learn about the influences of curriculum and instruction on learning. Does curricular emphasis or instructional emphasis change the construct under development?

Computer Technology

Computer technology has made significant changes in our lives, and it is not surprising that it would be a vital part of the future of large-scale testing. What are the most promising of the technological advances? What problems are solved? What is the role of research in the implementation of these technologies?

Computerized-Testing (CT) of Knowledge and Skills. Paper-and-pencil testing may be nearing its end. Online web testing is coming of age. CT using computer workstations to administer and score fixed-length tests may become more routine. The states of Georgia and Oregon are ready to initiate CT for their students. Other states should fall into line. As we become more technologically capable, nearly all testing can be administered online. Ironically, there is very little published research about the equivalence of CT and comparable paper-and-pencil tests. Thus, we have leaped into CT without adequate validity research to ensure equivalence. The essential question is: Is a student disadvantaged by taking either CT or the equivalent paper-and-pencil version of a test?

Computerized Adaptive Testing (CAT). The theory for computerized adaptive testing is well established, and its principles are well utilized in CAT testing programs in the United States. Although published research on the equivalence of CAT and paper-and-pencil testing is not extensive, some of this may be in-house, unpublished, and intended to justify the use of CAT over paper and pencil. As we become more sophisticated at technical documentation of validity evidence, test sponsors using CAT should be more willing to share their findings with the public. In doing so, we may be more inclined to accept CAT more widely than we do.

Computerized Performance Testing Featuring High-Fidelity Simulations. At the same time that computers and the Internet are being used to administer and score tests, we have some exceptional research going on that enters the world of high-fidelity computer simulation of complex cognitive behaviors. One example is the Dental Interactive Simulation Corporation (http://home.netscape.com/DISC). A partnership between a confederation of dental agencies involved in testing and the Educational Testing Service (ETS) has produced a series of simulations and a scoring method for patient problems in dentistry and dental hygiene. Plans have been made to produce scorable simulations for education and evaluation. Another example is for licensure. The Architect Registration Examination, sponsored by the National Council of Architectural Registration Boards (http://www.nearb.org/general/about.html), in partnership with ETS has developed impressive simulations and a computerized scoring system. The theoretical work of Mislevy (1993, 1996a, 1996b) and Behar (1993) and their colleagues led to this promising emergent technology. It provides a glimpse into the new world of testing, in which computer simulations provide the bases for testing, and complex scoring algorithms provide test scores without the need for human scoring. Cognitive learning theory figures strongly in this kind of research. The time is approaching when such simulations and their scoring engines will drive large-scale testing. This work is theory driven, and the developmental costs are currently an impediment. As we improve our understanding of the theories driving these developments and as technologies improve for designing simulations and the scoring engine, this innovation in the testing of cognitive abilities will be more widespread.

Computerized Essay Scoring. The onset of large-scale performance testing has created a burgeoning industry for scoring performance tests using trained evaluators who use rubrics (descriptive rating scales). With continued interest in the teaching and measuring of writing ability, it should not be surprising that theories of computerized scoring of essays have led researchers to develop methods for scoring essays that virtually eliminate human judgment. However, the costs of scoring student writing and other student performance, such as mathematical problem solving, are soaring. Estimates for scoring range from $4 per student to over $20 per student. Although the public and elected officials support performance testing, there are limits to this support.

In response to this problem, ETS researchers have developed *e-rater*—a sophisticated prototype computer program that, in conjunction with human scorers, scores test takers' essays (http://www.ets.org/textonly/aboutets/escoredx.html). Computational linguistics provides the means to identify and measure variables that correlate with human-judged test scores. These variables may include length of essay, word choice, syntactic variety, and structure of discourse.

Pennsylvania is in the middle of a 3-year pilot program with Vantage Learning to grade the essay portion of the Pennsylvania's state assessment (http://www.intellimetric.com). A computer program, IntelliMetric™, identifies the features associated with each grade point from a set of pregraded responses. Like the ETS software, this method analyzes content and structural features of essays. The company has already programmed 90 commonly used essay questions so that a scoring service can be offered without the need for human calibration.

In both of these methods, human judgment is used to provide a target for the computer program. Then a weighted scoring system is based on the variables found to predict the human ratings. Because most of the essay scoring can be long and tedious, computer scoring increases efficiency and reduces cost, and rater consistency is higher when a computer is involved. Unlike human scorers, computers do not suffer from fatigue or other rater maladies. As with many computer technologies, validity evidence and basic research seem to be underappreciated. Published research does not yield clear benefits of computerized scoring of essays. This is not to say that these emerging technologies are suspect, but merely that research should verify the claims about scoring consistency and reliability. As we shift to using computerized scoring, we need evidence that documents the validity of this kind of scoring.

Choosing Item Formats

Item formats exist in great variety (Bennett, 1993; Haladyna, 1997, 1999; Martinez, 1999; Snow, 1993). Rodriguez provides some good evidence about the equivalence of MC and performance measures when the construct being measured is knowledge and mental skills. Martinez expands the idea about the cognitive complexity of item formats and their capabilities. Haladyna (submitted for publication) argued that trade-offs exist in choosing item formats when the objective involves some abstract, higher order construct such as writing ability. These recent articles give us hope that the scientific basis for item writing is being more firmly established to be supported by the incredible growth of statistical theories of test scores. The issue of which item format to use for any assessment is a complex issue that requires better theories and better measurement practices. Research provides an important key about the equivalency or differences in student performance as a function of the item format. Ryan and DeMark delve into gender-by-format interaction and provide some interesting and important findings. They show us a taxonomy of constructs that interweave writing ability in different ways into the construct being measured. This kind of research sets out a path for future research on item formats, but other paths exist that also require our attention.

Writing Test Items

The most essential and important building block of any test is the test item. The history of developing test items is checkered. Ebel (1951) wrote that item writing is more art than science, yet Ebel has contributed mightily to improving item writing in his long career. Still critics in various epochs have persistently told us that item writing is the Cinderella of testing (Cronbach, 1970; Haladyna, 1999; Nitko, 1985; Roid & Haladyna, 1982).

The science of multiple-choice item writing is still in its infancy, but the science of writing performance items is even less advanced—still in the womb, so to speak. The scientific basis for performance testing needs considerable attention if this format continues to be used. There should be no doubt that performance formats are necessary. Complex cognitive behavior is best suited to performance formats, but technical problems continue to abound with these formats (Linn, 1994; Linn, Baker, & Dunbar, 1991).

With increased emphasis on teaching and testing the application of knowledge and skills, item writing technology needs to be more concerned about the issue of cognitive demand elicited by the item. This new research will take the lead from cognitive psychologists, who value what kind of thinking contributes to the choice of various multiple-choice options or the underlying cognitive process used to read with comprehension, write coherently, or solve complex mathematical or scientific problems. This new research will probably involve interviewing students as they work on tests.

CONSTRUCT-IRRELEVANT VARIANCE

Construct-irrelevant variance is a term first used by Messick (1989) to designate a type of systematic error that threatens the validity of interpretations and uses of standardized achievement test scores. We are just beginning to understand the scope of this threat to validity.

Rodriguez informs us about the format issue as a potential problem in achievement testing. Engelhard addresses the problem of rater effects as another source of construct-irrelevant variance. Ryan and DeMark also tackle the gender-by-format interaction issue, another source of construct-irrelevant variance. Haladyna (in press) identifies and documents other sources of construct-irrelevant variance, including inappropriate test preparation, instructional emphasis that may narrow the curriculum, inappropriate test administration, cheating, excessive or inappropriate motivation or exhortation of students to perform well, anxiety, fatigue, not considering the special problems of students with disabilities, second-language learners, and students living in poverty when reporting group test results, scoring errors or foulups, failure to verify the key, and testing norm errors among others. Clearly, construct-irrelevant variance is a very large field, which is seldom systematically studied. Differential item functioning and person fit analyses provide some promising tools for studying construct-irrelevant variance, and this field should expand as we develop new investigative tools and delve more deeply into the various sources of construct-irrelevant variance.

Construct Underrepresentation

A companion idea to construct-irrelevant variance is construct underrepresentation. Again, Messick (1989) described instances where the construct to be measured is explicated by a test or test battery that only partially fulfills the description of the construct. A good example comes from traditional large-scale testing that measures only knowledge and skills but seldom tests the application of knowledge and skills in systematic ways. Performance testing is one way to capture the complexity of advanced cognitive abilities like reading, writing, mathematical and scientific problem solving, and critical thinking in social studies. However, any performance test typically involves one or two items that do not adequately represent the construct. It is easy to see why we underrepresent a construct because performance testing has so many limitations (Kane, Crooks, & Cohen, 1999; Linn, 1994; Linn, Baker, & Dunbar, 1991). Messick (1995b) was particularly sensitive to this issue. Defining a universe of problems and sampling from this universe seems to be a much-needed part of performance testing. We might argue that most tests of cognitive abilities underrepresent the construct so a great deal of theoretical work and validating research is required.

Taylor captures the nature of this problem and one tangible solution: work samples. Yet this approach, while appropriate, has many pitfalls to consider before we can utilize work samples in any large-scale testing. The most important feature of this work is that using classroom-based performance testing in a large-scale assessment gives hope that the construct being measured (e.g., writing) is being better representing by the inclusion of a variety of performance assessments instead of a single writing prompt one time per year.

In most instances, the most fundamental step in construct validation—construct definition—is needed. We have not yet mastered the craft of defining constructs, which would simplify its measurement. Theoretical work is needed to identify the dimensions of reading comprehension based on different types of reading passages, the domain of writing prompts by writing modes, or the domain of mathematical problems neatly arranged in a taxonomy also neatly connected to requisite knowledge and skills.

Vertical Scaling to Measure Growth of Cognitive Abilities

As more tests use a performance format that requires the professional judgment of trained raters using scoring guides (rubrics), we are faced with the problem of vertical scaling that we faced decades ago with multiple-choice items. As many states go to high-stakes test score use, it would be helpful to develop vertical scales that transcend grades. Students could then use test scores in early grades to chart their progress toward mastery of writing to the point that they pass the state test. This kind of vertical scale is needed in writing because that is the most common performance format in current assessments. However, in the future, we will probably need such a scale for mathematical problem solving as well.

Standard Setting

In this volume, Ryan discusses ways to profile multiple sources of student achievement to aid in making more consistent pass–fail decisions. One of American Educational Research Association's (2000) guidelines for large-scale assessments is the use of multiple sources of data when making a high-stakes decision. Ryan reviews some recent developments and demonstrates several methods of combining diverse measures to influence a pass–fail decision. Although standard setting has a well-established technology for multiple-choice tests (Cizek, 2001), we are beginning to address the more complex issues of standard setting and comparability with performance tests where rating scales are used to develop student test scores. Even more vexing is standard setting when a test consists of multiple-choice and performance formats.

Added to this problem of setting a standard, Glass (1978) has given us many valid criticisms of standard setting using the traditional multiple-choice item format. His criticisms seem to apply to performance testing as well. Standard setting is still a neonatal science. As testing specialists have stated, standard setting is really evaluation, not measurement. Yet because the evaluation is applied to test scales, testing specialists continue to be interested in the myriad of problems presented in standard setting. Thus, theory and research on standard setting will continue to evolve jointly in response to the urgent need for better standard setting.

Inclusion/Accommodations/Modifications

This volume contains chapters addressing many problems of testing students from special populations. We have had a history of neglecting students with disabilities or language difficulties when it comes to testing. Federal laws and heightened concerns have raised national awareness of the problems of testing special populations. Eight chapters in this book address a variety of problems dealing with these special populations. These chapters provide ample evidence that research on accommodations and modifications is very new and will continue to stretch our thinking and resources. Although the special populations may collectively include less than 30% of all students, these students are persistently low achieving and require careful measurement of their achievement and programs that match their needs. The following are some of the most urgent or interesting areas of research in this large category.

Simplified Language.   Duran addresses problems of English-language learners (ELLs) and the need for accommodated assessments that help students make the transition from a non-English native language to English. He cites the interesting and important work of Jamal Abedi and his colleagues at the University of California at Los Angeles with simplified language. Attention to making the vocabulary and syntax of test items appropriate to the majority of students taking the test removes reading as a construct-irrelevant variance. In assessments requiring writing that do *not* directly measure writing, writing ability can also be a source of construct-irrelevant variance.

Side-by-Side Testing.   Continuing this theme that ELLs are not tested very adequately in large-scale assessment, some interesting research has been conducted on methods for helping students make the transition from their native language to English. Choi and McCall report their study on side-by-side testing and overcoming the obstacles to getting a valid interpretation of a student's reading or mathematics ability.

ACCOMMODATIONS AND MODIFICATIONS
FOR STUDENTS WITH DISABILITIES

Motivated by federal law and funding, large-scale testing programs are becoming more attentive to the needs of students with disabilities. Two chapters in this book give ample testimony to the influence of research on issues of how tests and testing conditions can be changed to compensate for disabilities and obtain better measures of student achievement (Helwig, Hollenbeck). Phillips discusses the legal aspects of this problem. We have ample evidence that students with disabilities are most likely to achieve well below national averages, but the determination that they have learning deficits is somewhat muddied by the administration of tests where a disability is a source of construct-irrelevant variance. Research that sorts out construct-irrelevant variance can contribute greatly to advancing the measurement of disabled students' achievement.

CONSEQUENCES OF LARGE-SCALE TESTING

Mehrens makes clear that we lack sufficient research on the consequences of large-scale testing on student achievement and other factors. Considering the importance of this idea of consequences, it should not be surprising to see considerable research attention paid to the idea that systemic reform and high-stakes testing will have a profound effect on students and their parents, teachers, and the public. The argument will not be won with political rhetoric or in the court of opinion. Research should inform us as to the good and bad of large-scale testing. We have some hints from Linn (2000) and Mehrens that these consequences may not be very positive, but we need more extensive research on consequences.

What are some promising lines of inquiry? The new AERA guidelines for high-stakes achievement testing provide some hints about what we might be studying. Standard 1 states that students must be provided with multiple opportunities. Does a high standard coupled with multiple opportunities to exceed a passing point really stimulate student learning? Standard 2 addresses adequate resources and opportunities to learn. We need research that shows the extent to which content standards are being implemented and the extent to which each student has an opportunity to learn, considering the various disabilities that many students bear. Standard 5 calls for alignment between the test and curriculum. We need to know whether these alignments exist. Standard 7 calls for meaningful opportunities for remediation. Failing students need diagnoses and remedial instruction with more time to learn. Standard 8 calls for appropriate attention to language differences among examinees. Standard 9 calls for appropriate attention to students with disabilities. We need research that looks into what we are doing for these populations where achievement is usually below our expectations. Standard 12 explicitly calls for ongoing evaluation of intended and unintended effects of high-stakes testing.

From these standards and from Mehrens, we can see that research on consequences should be a major aspect of future testing research. This emerging body of research on consequences should provide enough information to inform policymakers about the future of improved large-scale testing.

SUMMARY

The second part of this chapter briefly touched on areas within large-scale testing that will occupy test specialists for years to come. There are many more problems to study than there are personnel and resources to study them, so progress on many fronts will probably be slow. The scientific bases for testing practices continues to develop due to theory development and research. The focus on construct validity in school reform helps us better understand the role that future research will play on large-scale testing of student achievement. School reform will continue in wave after wave because that seems to be the motivating force behind this continued quest for increasing student learning. Large-scale testing will continue to be a dominant aspect of reform.

IN CLOSING

Because the public values large-scale testing of student learning and because accountability will persist, large-scale testing will continue to figure prominently in our schools, school districts, states, and even at the national and international levels. Research and development activities continue to drive improvements in large-scale testing. The sponsor of this research is necessarily the federal government, but state agencies and school districts should continue to play important roles. Test companies can ill afford not to be active participants in this enterprise because each company must maintain a competitive edge. Finally, universities support research through their missions, and our professional journals give ample testimony to the value of this research to testing. These are exciting times in testing. The chapters in this book document the latest accomplishments and also provide glimpses of some of the problems we face and where we might go to find solutions.

REFERENCES

American Educational Research Association. (2000). Position statement of the American Educational Research Association concerning high-stakes testing in preK–12 education. *Educational Researcher, 29,* 24–25.

American Educational Research Association, American Psychological Association, & National Council on Measurement in Education. (1974). *Standards for educational and psychological tests.* Washington, DC: American Psychological Association.

American Educational Research Association, American Psychological Association, & National Council on Measurement in Education. (1999). *Standards for educational and psychological testing.* Washington, DC: American Educational Research Association.

Bejar, I. (1993). A generative approach to psychological and educational measurement. In N. Frederiksen, R. J. Mislevy, & I. Bejar (Eds.), *Test theory for a new generation of tests* (pp. 297–323). Hillsdale, NJ: Lawrence Erlbaum Associates.

Bennett, R. E. (1993). On the meaning of constructed response. In R. E. Bennett & W. C. Ward (Eds.), *Construction versus choice in cognitive measurement: Issues in constructed response, performance testing, and portfolio assessment* (pp. 1–27). Hillsdale, NJ: Lawrence Erlbaum Associates.

Cizek, G. J. (Ed.). (2001). *Setting performance standards: Concepts, methods, and perspectives.* Mahwah, NJ: Lawrence Erlbaum Associates.

Cronbach, L. J. (1970). Review of *On the theory of achievement test items. Psychometrika, 35,* 509–511.

Cronbach, L. J. (1971). Test validation. In R. L. Thorndike (Ed.), *Educational measurement* (2nd ed., pp. 443–507). Washington, DC: American Council on Education.

Cronbach, L. J. (1988). Five perspectives on validation argument. In H. Wainer & H. Braun (Eds.), *Test validity* (pp. 3–17). Hillsdale, NJ: Lawrence Erlbaum Associates.

Cronbach, L. J., & Meehl, P. E. (1955). Construct validity in psychological tests. *Psychological Bulletin, 52,* 281–302.

Ebel, R. L. (1951). Writing the test item. In E. F. Lindquist (Ed.), *Educational Measurement* (1st ed., pp. 185–249). Washington, DC: American Council on Education.

Glass, G. V. (1978). Standards and criteria. *Journal of Educational Measurement, 15,* 237–261.

Haladyna, T. M. (1997). *Writing test items to evaluate higher-order thinking.* Boston: Allyn & Bacon.

Haladyna, T. M. (1999). *Developing and validating multiple-choice test items* (2nd ed.). Mahwah, NJ: Lawrence Erlbaum Associates.

Haladyna, T. M. (2000). *Essentials of standardized achievement: Validity and accountability.* Needham Heights, MA: Allyn & Bacon.

Haladyna, T. M. (submitted for publication). *The role of fidelity and proximity in choosing a test item format.* Phoenix, AZ: Arizona State University West.

Hall, G. E., & Hord, S. M. (2001). *Implementing change: Patterns, principles, and potholes.* Boston: Allyn & Bacon.

Kane, M. T. (1992). An argument-based approach to validity. *Psychological Bulletin, 112,* 527–535.

Kane, M., Crooks, T., & Cohen, A. (1999). Validating measures of performance. *Educational Measurement: Issues and Practice, 18*(2), 5–17.

Linn, R. L. (2000). Assessment and accountability. *Educational Researcher, 29*(2), 4–16.
Linn, R. L. (1994). Performance assessment: Policy promises and technical measurement standards. *Educational Researcher, 23*(9), 4–14.
Linn, R. L., Baker, E. L., & Dunbar, S. B. (1991). Complex, performance-based assessment: Expectations and validation criteria. *Educational Researcher, 20*(8), 15–21.
Martinez, M. E. (1999). Cognition and the question of test item format. *Educational Psychologist, 34*(4), 207–218.
Messick, S. (1975). The standard problem: Meaning and value in measurement and evaluation. *American Psychologist, 30*, 955–966.
Messick, S. (1984). The psychology of educational measurement. *Journal of Educational Measurement, 21*, 215–237.
Messick, S. (1989). Validity. In R. L. Linn (Ed.), *Educational measurement* (3rd ed., pp. 13–104). New York: American Council on Education and Macmillan.
Messick, S. (1995a). Validity of psychological assessment: Validation of inferences from persons' responses and performances as scientific inquiry into score meaning. *American Psychologist, 50*, 741–749.
Messick, S. (1995b). Standards of validity and the validity of standards in performance assessment. *Educational Measurement: Issues and Practice, 14*(4), 5–8.
Moss, P. A. (1992). Shifting conceptions of validity in educational measurement: Implications for performance assessment. *Review of Educational Research, 62*, 229–258.
Mislevy, R. J. (1993). Foundations of a new test theory. In N. Frederiksen, R. J. Mislevy, & I. Bejar (Eds.), *Test theory for a new generation of tests* (pp. 19–39). Hillsdale, NJ: Lawrence Erlbaum Associates.
Mislevy, R. J. (1996a). *Some recent developments in assessing student learning.* Princeton, NJ: Center for Performance Assessment at the Educational Testing Service.
Mislevy, R. J. (1996b). Test theory reconceived. *Journal of Educational Measurement, 33*, 379–417.
Nitko, A. J. (1985). Review of Roid and Haladyna's "A technology for test item writing." *Journal of Educational Measurement, 21*, 201–204.
Roid, G. H., & Haladyna, T. M. (1982). *Toward a technology of test-item writing.* New York: Academic Press.
Shepard, L. A. (1991). Psychometrician's beliefs about learning. *Educational Researcher, 20*, 2–9.
Shepard, L. A. (1993). Evaluating test validity, *Review of Research in Education, 19*, 405–450.
Snow, R. E. (1993). Construct validity and constructed-response tests. In R. E. Bennett & W. C. Ward (Eds.), *Construction versus choice in cognitive measurement: Issues in constructed response, performance testing, and portfolio assessment* (pp. 45–60). Hillsdale, NJ: Lawrence Erlbaum Associates.
Snow, R. E., & Lohman, D. F. (1989). Implications of cognitive psychology for educational measurement. In R. L. Linn (Ed.), *Educational measurement* (3rd ed., pp. 263–332). New York: American Council on Education and Macmillan.

Author Index

Subject Index